PRINCETON THEOLOGICAL SEMINARY

AN OCCASIONAL PUBLICATION OF

STUDIES IN REFORMED THEOLOGY AND HISTORY

David Willis, Editor

ARDENS ET VIVENS

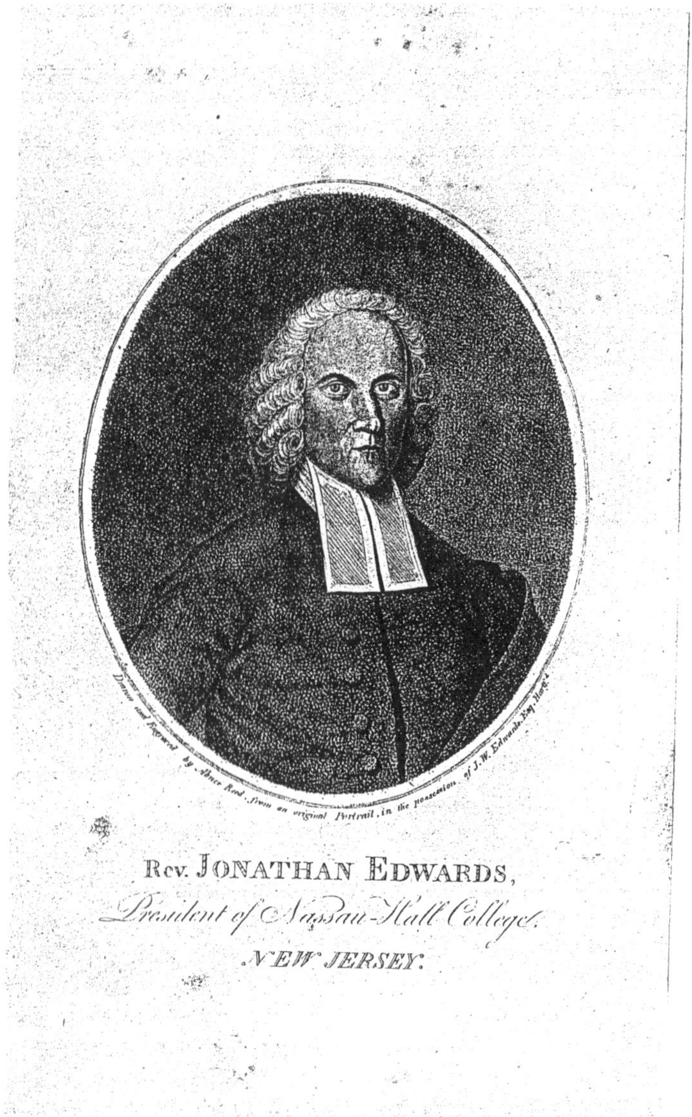

Frontispiece, *The Works of President Edwards* (1808), the first American collected edition.
Permission of the Massachusetts Historical Society.

The

Printed Writings

of

Jonathan Edwards

1703-1758

A BIBLIOGRAPHY

BY

Thomas H. Johnson

REVISED EDITION

BY

M. X. Lesser

Professor Emeritus
Northeastern University

PRINCETON THEOLOGICAL SEMINARY
2003

Wipf and Stock Publishers
199 W 8th Ave, Suite 3
Eugene, OR 97401

The Printed Writings of
Jonathan Edwards, 1703–1758
A Bibliography
By Johnson, Thomas H. and
Lesser, M. X.

ISBN 13: 978-1-60608-318-5
Publication date 1/1/2009
Previously published by
Princeton Theological Seminary,
2003

Distributed and managed by
Wipf and Stock Publishers.
For all orders and inquiries
please contact us at:
http://www.wipfandstock.com
info@wipfandstock.com
orders@wipfandstock.com

Library of Congress Cataloging-in-Publication Data

Johnson, Thomas Herbert.
The printed writings of Jonathan Edwards, 1703-1758 : a bibliography / by Thomas H. Johnson. – Rev. ed. / by M.X. Lesser. – Princeton, N.J. : Princeton Theological Seminary, 2003.
p. cm.
"An occasional publication of Studies in Reformed theology and history / David Willis, editor"—P.
Includes bibliographical references and index.
ISBN 0-1-889980-18-8
1. Edwards, Jonathan, 1703-1758—Bibliography. I. Lesser, M. X. II. Title.
Z8255.5.J69 2003

Printed by Cadmus Professional Communications

CONTENTS

Illustrations iii
Preface v
Foreword ix
The Society of Colonial Wars in the State of New Jersey xiii
God Glorified in the Work of Redemption 1
A Divine and Spiritual Light 1
A Faithful Narrative of the Surprising Work of God 2
Letters 18
Discourses on Various Important Subjects 22
The Distinguishing Marks of a Work of the Spirit of God 22
The Resort and Remedy of Those That Are Bereaved by the Death of an Eminent Minister 30
Sinners in the Hands of an Angry God 30
Some Thoughts Concerning the Present Revival of Religion in New England 42
The Great Concern of a Watchman for Souls 46
The True Excellency of a Minister of the Gospel 47
The Church's Marriage to Her Sons and to Her God 47
A Treatise Concerning Religious Affections 47
True Saints, When Absent from the Body, are Present with the Lord 64
An Humble Attempt to Promote God's People in Extraordinary Prayer 64
A Strong Rod Broken and Withered 68
An Account of the Life of the Late Reverend Mr. David Brainerd 68
An Humble Inquiry into the Rules of God Concerning the Qualifications 89
Christ the Great Example of Gospel Ministers 92
Prefaces 92
A Farewell Sermon 94
Misrepresentations Corrected and Truth Vindicated 96
True Grace Distinguished from the Experience of Devils 96
A Careful and Strict Inquiry into the Modern Prevailing Notions of that Freedom of Will 98
The Great Christian Doctrine of Original Sin Defended 108
Remarks on the Essays 115
The Life and Character of the Late Reverend Mr. Jonathan Edwards 115
Ruth's Resolution 119
Sermons on Various Important Subjects 119
Two Dissertations 122
The Justice of God in the Damnation of Sinners 124
A History of the Work of Redemption 126
An Essay on the Nature of True Virtue 140
An Account of the Conversion of the Late Reverend and Learned Mr. Jonathan Edwards 140
The Excellency of Christ 143
Sermons on the Following Subjects 144

A Dissertation on God's Last End in the Creation of the World 145
The Eternity of Hell Torments 147
Practical Sermons Never Before Published 148
Twenty Sermons on Various Subjects 148
The Wisdom of God Displayed in the Way of Salvation 150
Miscellaneous Observations on Important Theological Subjects 150
Remarks on Important Theological Controversies 151
Advice to Young Converts 151
Resolutions 153
On Fulfilling Engagements and Paying Debts 158
Account of Abigail Hutchinson 159
Theological Questions 161
Justification by Faith Alone 162
Jesus Christ Gloriously Exalted Above All Evil 162
The Importance and Advantage of a Thorough Knowledge of Divine Truth 163
Great Guilt No Obstacle to the Pardon of the Returning Sinner 163
Pardon for the Greatest Sinners 164
The Manner in which the Salvation of the Soul Is to Be Sought 164
The Way to Heaven 165
Lost Convictions 165
Charity and Its Fruits 165
Jonathan Edwards's Last Will 168
Observations Concerning the Scripture Oeconomy of the Trinity 168
The Flying Spider 169
An Unpublished Essay of Edwards on the Trinity 169
The Perpetuity and Change of the Sabbath 170
Wicked Men Useful in Their Destruction Only 170
The Sin and Folly of Procrastination 170
Sinners in Zion Tenderly Warned 171
The Peace which Christ Gives His True Followers 171
The True Christian's Life a Journey 171
Fleeing out of Sodom 171
Hypocrites Deficient in the Duty of Prayer 172
The Vain Self-Flatteries of the Sinner 172
Beauty of the World 172
Christian Charity, or the Duty of Charity to the Poor 172
The Most High, a Prayer-Hearing God 173
Selections 173
Collected Editions 188
Index of Titles 233
Index of Translations 241
Printers and Publishers 243
Libraries 249

ILLUSTRATIONS

Frontispiece	Frontispiece, *The Works of President Edwards* (1808)
Page	
xvi	Title page, *God Glorified* (1731)
3	Title page, *The Duty and Interest of a People* (1736)
31	Title page, *Sinners in the Hands of an Angry God* (1741)
63	Title page, *True Saints* (1747)
83	Title page, *Das Leben von David Brainerd* (1856)
90	Title page, *Humble Inquiry* (1749)
95	Title page, *A Farewell Sermon* (1751)
120	Title page, *Ruth's Resolution* (1764)
123	Title page, *Two Dissertations* (1765)
127	Title page, *A History of the Work of Redemption* (1774)

PREFACE

BY LATE 1931, James Thayer Gerould, then head of Princeton University Library, had been working "for some months, at odd moments, on a detailed bibliography" of Jonathan Edwards. He had been to "a large number of libraries in New England, New York, and Philadelphia," and was planning to visit the Library of Congress "before long." He had also prepared a seven-page, double-columned checklist of titles, editions, and dates and had sent it off to "thirty or more" libraries, among them the Case in Hartford, the Crozer in Rochester, the Grosvenor in Buffalo, and the Peabody in Baltimore; the University of Chicago, Indiana, Michigan, and Minnesota; Bowdoin College, Colgate, Dartmouth, and Trinity. Still, he was unable to locate a dozen or so items at the time, and sought out Charles Evans in hopes that his work on early American imprints might yield some clues. Evans offered a few as marginalia to his letter, pleading time and memory, and closed with, "Your researches show how far and wide the good influences of Jonathan Edwards have extended." Such were the beginnings of Edwards's academic recovery.[1]

Writing five years later to the Presbyterian Board of Publication about a copy of *Sinners in the Hands of an Angry God*, Gerould remarked that he was "on the point of publishing" his work, and days later, in a note to the Newberry Library on the Leeds collected edition, added that the bibliography was "going through the press." Within months he had galley proofs, within a year he had left the reading of them because of illness. Malcolm O. Young, reference librarian at Princeton, took over the task and continued the pursuit of texts, making more than twenty inquiries, receiving a reply to one of the last of them in early 1940. When *The Printed Writings of Jonathan Edwards* appeared later that year, it bore the imprint of Princeton University Press, a dedication to Gerould, and an introduction by Thomas H. Johnson.[2]

Johnson had written about Edwards before, in two journal articles and in his Harvard dissertation, and as co-editor with Clarence H. Faust of an Edwards anthology.[3] Precisely when he became active in the preparation of the bibliography remains a mystery, for there is no mention of him in the archival materials and only hints of his presence elsewhere, in signed book notes at the Congregational Library and Oberlin College, both undated; his introduction to the text bears little resemblance to the original typescript and the galley proofs of it. Again at some unspecified time,

---

[1]The letter, dated December 10, 1931, is among the Gerould papers in the archives at Princeton University; for the academic recovery, see M. X. Lesser, *Jonathan Edwards: A Reference Guide* (Boston, 1980), pp. xxviii-xxxi and pp. 150-176.

[2]The letters are dated December 3, 1936, December 14, 1936, and January 9, 1940; Johnson's introduction is dated May 18, 1940. Gerould retired in 1937; he died in 1951.

[3]"Jonathan Edwards' Background of Reading," *Publications of the Colonial Society of Massachusetts* 28 (December 1931):193-222; "Jonathan Edwards and the 'Young Folks' Bible,'" *New England Quarterly* 5 (January 1932):37-54; "Jonathan Edwards as a Man of Letters" (Harvard dissertation, 1934); and *Jonathan Edwards: Representative Selections* (New York: American Book Co., 1935). Gerould reviewed *Representative Selections*, finding Johnson's bibliography particularly useful: *Modern Philology* 34 (August 1936):102-103.

Gerould made "all correspondence, and manuscript notes" available to him, and it was from these that the final draft of *The Printed Writings* emerged.[1]

The current work not only extends the reach of the original almost seventy years—Johnson's latest entry is a 1935 imprint, *Representative Selections*—and adds substantially to its list—eighty or so before 1940, about half again as many since then, or from 346 numbered entries to 536—it also alters markedly the appearance of the text. Except for transliterations, the title page of each item attempts a quasi-facsimile transcription, such that each line reproduces the style, though not the size, of the type of the title (roman, italics, black letter, and small caps); terminates each line with a vertical; inserts bracketed descriptives for rules, borders, ornaments, and publishers' devices; and remarks typographical errors—*Abigial, Edward's, Estter, Issac, Princetown*, for example—but not variant forms—*dependance, vertue, Cornhil, Newengland, Newhaven, Newjersey, Pensylvania.* Each entry offers an account of the contents of the text and notes publication anomalies, but the revision has abandoned the finding lists of the original. Although several copies of a text may have been examined for the revision, only one is recorded, so that the measurements (and collation and pagination) refer to that copy, not, as in the original, to "the largest composite" measurements of some reported, and therefore unexamined, copies held at several libraries. At the close of each entry are resources for such finding lists in the National Union Catalog (NUC) and the Online Computer Library Center (OCLC); for microtexts of eighteenth-century and early nineteenth-century items, in Early American Imprints (EAI), first and second series, and of eighteenth-century ones in the English Short Title Catalog (ESTC); for reference to Johnson (THJ); and for recently published texts, the International Standard Book Number (ISBN). Added to an index of titles by entry number, as in Johnson, is an index of translations, as well as a list of printers and publishers and another of libraries cited. The major depositories of early Edwards items remain very much as they were in the 1930s—American Antiquarian Society, American Tract Society, Beinecke Library, Boston Public Library, Congregational Library, Drew University, Firestone Library, Harvard Divinity School, Houghton Library, John Carter Brown Library, Library of Congress, Massachusetts Historical Society, New York Public Library, Princeton Theological Seminary, and Yale Divinity School; theological seminaries, such as, Asbury, Gordon-Conwell, and Southern Baptist, hold more recent items. The revision preserves the general order of the original, arranging titles and categories by date of first publication, and chronologically within each, and retains its valuable introduction to the whole, its extended commentary on the Leeds collected edition, and several briefer notes on individual texts.

Like James Thayer Gerould before me, I have called upon librarians in New England, New York and New Jersey, Philadelphia and Washington, none more often than Yves Hyacinthe, Monica Slayton, and Kathleen Walsh, of the Interlibrary Loan Office at Northeastern University, who through it all brought goodwill, wit, and countless titles to my desk. Away from it, I have tried the patience of many other librarians, among them, Freeman Barton, Gordon-Conwell Theological Seminary;

[1]Johnson joined the faculty of the Lawrenceville School in 1937, edited *The Puritans* (New York: American Book Co.) with Perry Miller in 1938, and edited *The Poetical Works of Edward Taylor* (New York: Rockland Editions) in 1939. In time he would write the Edwards entry in the *Literary History of the United States* (New York: Macmillan, 1948)—and compile its reader's bibliography—and edit *The Complete Poems of Emily Dickinson* (Boston: Little, Brown and Co., 1957). Johnson retired in 1967; he died in 1985.

Nancy Birkrem, Mount Holyoke College; John A. Collins, Lamont Library, Harvard; Joan Duffy, Yale Divinity School; William T. Faucon, Boston Public Library; Elise Bernier-Feeley, Forbes Library; Stephen Ferguson, Firestone Library, Princeton; Nicholas Graham, Massachusetts Historical Society; Susan Halpert, Houghton Library, Harvard; William O. Harris, Princeton Theological Seminary; Seth Kasten, Union Theological Seminary; Meredith M. Kline, Gordon-Conwell Theological Seminary; Karl Krueger, Lutheran Theological Seminary; Karen V. Kukil, Smith College; Marie E. Lamoureux, American Antiquarian Society; Phil Lapsansky, Library Company of Philadelphia; Donna M. Maguire, Harvard Divinity School; Lucy K. Marks, Drew University; Larry Martins, Mudd Library, Yale; Martha-Jane Moreland, Salem State College; Dawn Piscitello, Boston University; Richard R. Ring, John Carter Brown Library; Linda Roberts, Congregational Library; Kenneth J. Ross, Presbyterian Historical Society; David Smith, New York Public Library; Gerald R. Wager, Library of Congress; Laura K. Whitney, Harvard Divinity School; Harold Field Worthley, Congregational Library; Diana Yount, Andover Newton Theological School; and R. Eugene Zepp, Boston Public Library. And I have written to scores of others, among them, Henry Boostra, Calvin College; Elizabeth Dunn, Duke University; Elizabeth Freebairn, Newberry Library; Elizabeth James, British Library; Anita Johnson, Pittsburgh Theological Seminary; Hannah Kirsch, Asbury Theological Seminary; Urs B. Leu, Zentralbibliothek Zürich; Desmond McTernan, British Library; Kristen Mitrisin, American Tract Society; Charles Parry, National Library of Wales; Michael Pullin, Southwestern Baptist Theological Seminary; Ed Vermue, Oberlin College; and Stephen R. Tabor, Huntington Library. From Min Kyung Hyun, Harry H. Kuoshu, and Safaa Shaheen, Northeastern University, and Sang Hyun Lee, Princeton Theological Seminary, I have borrowed transliterations; from Walter H. Lippincott, Director, Princeton University Press, permission to use material from *The Printed Writings*; and from Blaise Bisaillon, Director, Forbes Library, and William M. Fowler, Jr., Director, Massachusetts Historical Society, permission to include photocopies from their holdings.

To Denis B. Woodfield, Governor Emeritus, Society of Colonial Wars in the State of New Jersey, and Stephen D. Crocco, James Lenox Librarian, Princeton Theological Seminary, who used their good offices to bring this project to print, I tender a writer's gratitude—to the Society for its generous grant and to the Seminary for its valued imprint.

To all of these, I owe the very nature of the work. To others, I owe the welfare of its compiler: to Wilson H. Kimnach, *The Works of Jonathan Edwards*, for his early and continued support; to Jon Lanham, Lamont Library, Harvard, for his thoughtful words; to Rosemary Woodfield, Princeton, for her gracious hospitality; to Harvey and Judy Glaser, Islamorada, for their gift of friendship; and to Lee, yet again, for the pleasures of her company.

M. X. L.

Swampscott, Massachusetts
July 6, 2003

FOREWORD

A BIBLIOGRAPHY of the printed writings of Jonathan Edwards may be fairly offered without apology. During his lifetime he achieved considerable rank, both here and abroad, among Protestant dialecticians. Wherever the doctrines of Calvin found adherents, his writings, widely printed, were seized upon to buttress a crumbling orthodoxy that still has significant historic importance. That much of his intellectual vigor and acumen spent itself in defense of issues long since dead is beside the point. As the first, and certainly the greatest, American Calvinist, and as the leading philosopher here before William James, his place in American cultural history is permanently secure.

During the eighteenth century Edwards was possibly better known abroad than at home. His reputation throughout Protestant Europe is attested by the great number of editions of his works published in London, Glasgow, and Edinburgh, and the frequent translation of his works into Dutch, French, and German.[1] Though of course Boston publishers constantly met the local demand for his writings, Edwards was not considered here what might be termed a "leading light." Samuel Willard and Increase and Cotton Mather were dead before Edwards's career was really begun. The influential ministers in Boston and Cambridge were advocating a more liberal theology than Edwards was willing to support. To be sure, Thomas Prince, Thomas Foxcroft, Joseph Sewall, and William Cooper endorsed Edwards's *Faithful Narrative*, when it appeared in 1737, as a true attestation of a religious revival in New England.[2] But how far the account would have circulated unless it had been sponsored by Benjamin Colman, at that time Boston's most vigorous leader of the liberal wing of the clergy, there is no way of telling. Edwards's interest in revivals, and his support of the evangelist Whitefield drew down upon him the outspoken condemnation of Charles Chauncy, who violently opposed such "New Lightism," and answered Edwards's *Some Thoughts on Revivals*, in 1742, with his testy *Seasonable Thoughts*. With none of these urban gentlemen was Edwards ever upon intimate terms.

Since the only professor of divinity in New England, during the second quarter of the century, was Edward Wigglesworth, occupant of the newly created chair at Harvard, a potent determiner of polity in the New England churches, and a bitter opponent of Whitefield, it is scarcely strange that Edwards was never invited to deliver an "Election Sermon," the most important public address of the day, annually presented before the Magistrate and the General Court. Even in England and Scotland

---

[1]Although ten texts were translated into Dutch during the eighteenth century, only one was translated into German, *Faithful Narrative* in 1738; the earliest French translation was of *Humble Attempt* in 1823.

[2]An eighteen-page abridgment of Edwards's letter to Benjamin Colman about the Northampton revival was appended to William Williams's *Duty and Interest of a People*, published in Boston in 1736. The complete text of *Faithful Narrative* was first published in London in 1737 with a preface, dated October 12, 1737, by Isaac Watts and John Guyse, and was reissued unchanged in Edinburgh (and Glasgow) later that year. The first American, or third, edition was published in Boston the following year with a preface, dated November 4, 1738, by Joseph Sewall, Thomas Prince, John Webb, and William Cooper, and a letter of attestation to Colman, dated October 11, 1738, by six Hampshire County (Massachusetts) ministers, William Williams, Ebenezer Devotion, Stephen Williams, Peter Reynolds, Nehemiah Bull, and Samuel Hopkins; another edition the same year added the Watts and Guyse preface. Thomas Foxcroft first appears in an Edwards text as one of five signatories to a preface to *Humble Attempt*, dated January 12, 1747/8.

it was not among the more fashionable clergy that Edwards was recognized as a powerful thinker. His *Faithful Narrative* was recommended in London, as the title page indicates, by the more humble nonconformists, Isaac Watts and John Guyse. Edwards's *Life of Brainerd*, one of the most popular missionary biographies of all times, was extracted, edited, and recommended by a vigorous exhorter, John Wesley, and not by the established London clergymen. Among Edwards's correspondents there are no prominent figures of church or state. Instead there are found almost exclusively lesser known Scotch Presbyterian ministers, who looked upon him as the ablest Calvinistic spokesman they knew, one who could effectively battle against Arminianism and the dangerous heterodoxies in an age of deistic compromise. Even among the lists of subscribers, often attached to the eighteenth century editions of his treatises, the names of leading divines are strikingly absent.

Edwards's first published work, *God Glorified*, was a sermon preached when he was twenty-seven years old "on the Publick Lecture in Boston," on July 8, 1731. It was published "at the Desire of several Ministers and Others, in Boston, who heard it," as the preface recalls. It was one of the few sermons that Edwards ever preached on the lecture platform. During his lifetime twenty-four separate items were published. *The Great Christian Doctrine* had been completed before his death, but was issued posthumously. Edwards wrote voluminously, and, in all, roughly sixty items have been separately printed. Exclusive of reprints, his most frequently published works have been *Life of Brainerd*, *Religious Affections*, *Faithful Narrative*, and *History of Redemption*, all of which appeared in approximately thirty editions. *Sinners in the Hands of an Angry God*, one of his most persistently remembered sermons, has gone through but twenty-three editions, though two of them appeared in the first quarter of the twentieth century. The treatise on which his reputation was most securely founded, *A Careful and Strict Inquiry*, has gone through twenty editions. Those next in demand seem to have been *The Great Christian Doctrine* and *Some Thoughts on Revivals*, works which were issued in thirteen and twelve editions respectively.

All of Edwards's works published during his life were initially brought out in this country, the first twenty-two by Boston publishers. *True Grace* (1758) was the earliest of his works to be first published in New York. In the same year, *Remarks on the Essays* appeared in Edinburgh, the earliest of his works to be published first abroad.[1]

Edwards's published writings may conveniently be classified. Of his sermons, exclusive of those first gathered from manuscript in the collected editions, twenty are of a philosophical and theological nature. The four ordination and three funeral sermons were never republished as separate items, and were doubtless printed, as was customary, by the desire and at the expense of the subject's family or town. His most important writings were the treatises, and of the fourteen that were published—all, in fact, that he wrote—seven were posthumously issued. He compiled but one biography, *Life of Brainerd.* It is in the style and manner of other contemporary biographies, in that it is a spiritual history rather than a narrative account, but it is notable as the most frequently reprinted of all Edwards's works—as recently issued, indeed, as 1925—and it has usually been looked upon as a model for missionary histories. It is furthermore the first biography written in America that achieved wide notice abroad as well as at home.

---

[1]As noted above, the complete text of *Faithful Narrative* was first published in London. *True Grace* was published in New York in 1753, *Remarks on the Essays* in Edinburgh in 1758; the first volume of the collected works was published in Leeds in 1806, that of the American edition two years later.

The *Faithful Narrative* and the *Conversion of Edwards* may properly be termed narrative essays. Extracts from both have been frequently made, and they have been widely circulated and distributed as tracts. For the rest, there remain only his letters, some published during his lifetime, but most of them later; and the single preface which he wrote for Joseph Bellamy's *True Religion,* published in 1750.

It is significant of Edwards's power as a theologian and essayist that five of his works have been separately issued since 1900. Besides *Sinners in the Hands*, *Life of Brainerd*, and *Careful and Strict Inquiry*, there have appeared editions of *Religious Affections* and *Humble Attempt*. Ten of his works have been translated, most frequently into Dutch and Welsh, but also into French, German, Arabic, and Gaelic.[1] *Sinners in the Hands* was translated during the nineteenth century into Choctaw. Though American libraries have been canvassed for translations with some thoroughness, European libraries have of necessity been less carefully searched.

It may be useful to draw attention to certain problems that are involved in establishing an Edwards bibliography. No attempt is made to include data relating to Edwards, or to list manuscripts. Even with such limits in mind, however, discrimination has been necessary. All anthology selections from Edwards's writings have been excluded. The well known apostrophe in praise of Sarah Pierrepont, first printed in Dwight's *Life of President Edwards* (1829), pp. 114-115, was never issued as a separate item except in anthologies, and therefore is not listed herein. When Edwards's collected works first appeared in 1806, several sermons, never before published, were first issued. In subsequent editions of the collected works, further sermon material was added. Titles of all such sermons, with identifying data, will be found in the index. It will be seen that reprints of the later collected editions were very numerous during the nineteenth century. All such reprints that have been seen are described.

The bibliographical description of items attempts: (1) To reproduce the title page exactly in line, punctuation, spelling, and capitalization of initial letters. (2) To describe the format when evidence is present. It is very rare indeed that laid paper was used by publishers after 1800, and consequently when wove paper is used, only linear measurements, in centimeters, is given. Linear measurements, given for all items examined, may not correspond exactly to any single item. They represent the largest composite measurements which have been found. Uncut items are so designated.[2] (4) To collate the item by signature and pagination. (5) To supply finding lists. (6) To add any further bibliographical data that may be pertinent or useful.

For convenience in identification, each item is arbitrarily numbered, and reference to items is therefore by number rather than by page. The order in which items appear is chronological according to the first issue of the first edition of each item.

A word may be useful about the various tract societies which, during the nineteenth century, often printed and distributed certain treatises of Edwards, or extracts from them, in enormous numbers. The Religious Tract Society (of London) was founded in 1799 as an interdenominational

---

[1]Edwards was also translated into Swedish before the publication of *The Printed Writings* and into Afrikaans, Chinese, Italian, Korean, and Spanish, as well as German and French, after it; see M. X. Lesser, "'An Honor Too Great': Jonathan Edwards in Print Abroad," *Jonathan Edwards in Historical Memory*, David Kling and Douglas A. Sweeney, eds. (Columbia: University of South Carolina Press, 2003), pp. 297-319.

[2]The enumeration lacks (3).

organization, and brought out six Edwards items under its imprint. The American Tract Society published fifteen Edwards items between 1827 and 1845, and reprinted them innumerable times. The Society must have distributed approximately a million Edwards items before it ceased, in 1892, to list them among its publications. Founded in 1825, as a national society with headquarters in New York City, it was organized, through mutual agreement, from a combination of the New York Religious Tract Society (organized 1812) and the New England Tract Society (organized 1814). New York became the headquarters of the national society, while the New England group (whose name had been changed in 1823 to American Tract Society) became a branch, located in Boston. The Boston organization withdrew in 1859, and remained independent until 1897, when it was again united as a branch.

The Presbyterian Board of Publication, of Philadelphia, began to include Edwards items in its catalogue in 1841. From that year until 1903, it brought out six items. It was the custom of the Board to include in the imprint of its first edition the date and the name of the publishing agent. The item was then stereotyped, and printed again and again. The reprints omit the date from the imprint.[1]

The compiler of this bibliography wishes first of all to acknowledge his great debt to the work of Dr. James Thayer Gerould, formerly Librarian of Princeton University. It was he who first conceived and undertook the task, before illness compelled its postponement. It was his generosity that made available all correspondence and manuscript notes, relative to an Edwards bibliography, which he had gathered. The general arrangement of the material continues to follow, therefore, the plan which he established.

As all who stray into the field of colonial Americana must do, the compiler turned for advice to Lawrence C. Wroth, Esq., whose aid was generous and wise.

The information presented regarding the American Tract Society publications has been secured from the offices of the Society. The data concerning the Presbyterian Board's method of publication, together with further details accompanying the items, have been most helpfully supplied by Dr. Thomas C. Pears, Jr., Manager of the Department of History of the Presbyterian Historical Society.

Were it not for the cooperation of the librarians and staffs of the many score of institutions from which information has been sought, and whose assistance has always been graciously extended, the task could never have been accomplished.

It is with special pleasure that the compiler acknowledges the unceasing help and encouragement of every sort which he has received from Princeton University; from Mr. Lawrence Heyl, Associate Librarian; from Mr. Lawrence Thompson, Curator of Special Collections; and most of all from Mr. Malcolm O. Young, Reference Librarian, who from first to last has been infinitely resourceful and sagacious.

T. H. J.

Lawrenceville, New Jersey
18 May 1940

---

[1]Abbreviations used in the finding lists follow.

THE SOCIETY OF COLONIAL WARS IN THE STATE OF NEW JERSEY

FOR MORE than a hundred years, The Society of Colonial Wars in the State of New Jersey has focused on promoting awareness of the history and achievements of our colonial ancestors through prizes, endowments, fellowships, awards, grants— and publishing books like this. *The Printed Writings of Jonathan Edwards* not only meets our period of interest—from the settlement of Jamestown to the Battle of Lexington—it also celebrates the work of a man who profoundly affected the course of American religious history, and the Society is very pleased to fund its publication.

The Society of Colonial Wars in the State of New Jersey was organized on May 1, 1894, received its Charter from the General Society (formed in 1893) on May 8, 1894, and was incorporated under the laws of the State of New Jersey on July 26, 1894. Our mission as a Society has always been to perpetuate the names, memory, or deeds of those brave and courageous men, who, in the military or civil service, by their acts or counsel, assisted in the establishment and continuance of the American Colonies; to collect and secure for preservation and publication the manuscripts, rolls, records, and other documents relating to the period; to inspire among the members and their descendants the fraternal and patriotic spirit of their forefathers; to promote in the community respect and reverence for American institutions and their history and for the principles and acts of those indomitable men which make these institutions possible; and to instill and foster patriotism, service, and devotion to the nation.

The New Jersey Society holds an Annual Court in the spring, to which ladies are invited, and a Semi-Annual General Court in fall. Our Council—Society Officers and Board Members—meets four times each year, twice in conjunction with the General Courts and separately in February and September. Our General Courts have been held in different locations over the years, most recently at The Nassau Club in Princeton. Council Meetings are usually held there.

Some of our more recent activities include grants to help restore the Proprietary House in Perth Amboy, the home of the Province of East Jersey's last Royal Governor; the 1761 Brearley House in Lawrenceville (John Brearley was one of five members of the New Jersey delegation to sign the Declaration of Independence); and historic Saint Michael's Episcopal Church in Trenton (Colonel Rall, the Hessian Commander at the first Battle of Trenton, died on its steps).

For a number of years the Society has also made an annual award to the William Trent House in Trenton. Built in 1719, it was occupied by three Governors of the Colony and the State of New Jersey—Lewis Morris (1742-1746), Philemon Dickerson (1835-1838), and Rodman McCamley

Price (1854-1859). Last year, we helped fund a special climate-controlled environmental system for the 237-year-old Huntington-Lawrence-Jessup House in Woodbury, New Jersey. We also provided the Mount Vernon Ladies Associationxiv—the owners of our first President's Virginia home—with a grant that allowed "A George Washington Biography Lesson" to be placed in every primary school throughout the State of New Jersey.

The Great Seal of the Society of Colonial Wars in the State of New Jersey is a copy of the ancient Coat of Arms of the Colonial Province of New Jersey with the motto *Fortier Pro Patria* in base surmounted by a British Royal Crown.

The New Jersey Society has 145 members at present. Any gentleman of good moral character and reputation above 18 years of age of lineal descent in the male or female line from an ancestor who served in the Army, Navy, or Militia under authority of one of the Colonies that formed the United States from the settlement of Jamestown, May 13, 1607, to the Battle of Lexington, April 19, 1775, or who held office in the Colonies as a member of a legislative body, is eligible. We also have a junior membership category for any age from birth to 18.

Would you like to become part of our cause, conserving the memory and artifacts of our nation's great Colonial past and "keeping the flame alive" for future generations? You can reach us at P.O. Box 9, Hopewell, N. J. 08525-0009, or visit us at www.colonialwarsnj.org.

The

Printed Writings

of

Jonathan Edwards

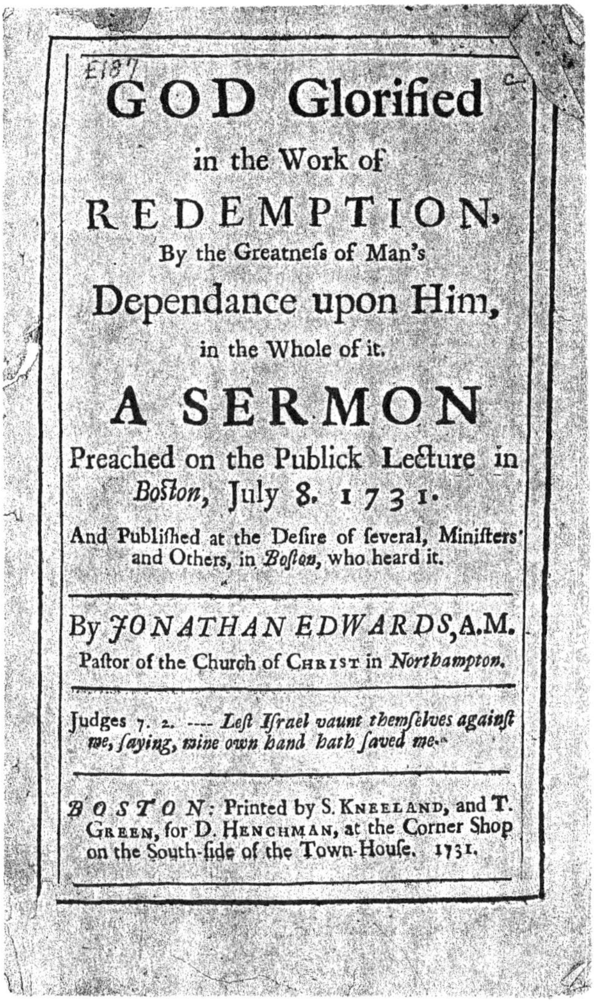

GOD Glorified
in the Work of
REDEMPTION,
By the Greatneſs of Man's
Dependance upon Him,
in the Whole of it.

A SERMON
Preached on the Publick Lecture in
Boſton, July 8. 1731.

And Publiſhed at the Deſire of ſeveral, Miniſters and Others, in *Boſton*, who heard it.

By *JONATHAN EDWARDS*, A.M.
Paſtor of the Church of CHRIST in *Northampton*.

Judges 7. 2. ---- *Leſt Iſrael vaunt themſelves againſt me, ſaying, mine own hand hath ſaved me.*

BOSTON: Printed by S. KNEELAND, and T. GREEN, for D. HENCHMAN, at the Corner Shop on the South-ſide of the Town-Houſe. 1731.

Title page, *God Glorified* (1731). Permission of the Massachusetts Historical Society.

GOD GLORIFIED IN THE WORK OF REDEMPTION

1 • [within double rules] GOD Glorified | in the Work of | REDEMPTION, | By the Greatneſs of Man's | Dependance upon Him, | in the Whole of it. | A SERMON | Preached on the Publick Lecture in | *Boston*, July 8. 1731. | And Publiſhed at the Deſire of ſeveral, Miniſters | and Others, in *Boſton*, who heard it. | [rule] | By *JONATHAN EDWARDS*, A.M. | Paſtor of the Church of CHRIST in *Northampton.* | [rule] | Judges 7. 2.---- *Leſt Iſrael vaunt themſelves againſt | me, ſaying, mine own hand hath ſaved me.* | [rule] | *BOSTON:* Printed by S. KNEELAND, and T. | GREEN, for D. HENCHMAN, at the Corner Shop | on the South-ſide of the Town-Houſe. 1731.

8vo.; 17.5 x 10.5 cm.; [A]^4, B-D^4; [4], ii, 25, [1] p.

Contents: prp. [1]: [decorative rule] | Mr. *Edwards*'s | SERMON | AT THE | Publick Lecture in *Boſton*, | *July* 8. 1731. | [decorative rule] (verso blank); prp. [3]: title (verso blank); p. i: [decorative rule] | TO THE | READER. [signed] Boſton, Auguſt | 17. 1731. | T. Prince, | W. Cooper.; p. [1]: [decorative rule] | GOD Glorified in Man's | Dependance. | [decorative rule]; p. [26]: blank.

THJ 1 EAI 1:3415 NUC NE0046598 OCLC 43664434
Massachusetts Historical Society

2 • [decorative rule] | God Glorified in | Man's Dependence | [decorative rule] | By Jonathan Edwards | [decorative rule] | FROM THE INHERITANCE OF OUR FATHERS | – Series XXVI No. 2 | [decorative rule]

13 x 9 cm.; 35 p.

Notes: published c. 1986, one of a dozen Edwards sermons issued separately by The Inheritance Publishers.

Contents: front cover, p. [1]: title; p. [2]: JONATHAN EDWARDS | [biography]; p. 3: GOD GLORIFIED IN MAN'S DEPENDENCE; p. 35: [publisher's note] | [1 line]; back cover, p. [36]: [advertisement] | [decorative rule] | THE INHERITANCE PUBLISHERS | P. O. Box 1334 | Grand Rapids, Michigan 49501.

OCLC 47870478
Gordon-Conwell Theological Seminary

3 • God Glorified | in Man's Dependence | By | Jonathan Edwards

21.6 x 13.5 cm.; 17, [3] p.

Contents: front cover: God Glorified | in Man's Dependence | by | Jonathan Edwards | Messages from God's servants | in former days | [6 lines] | [ornament] | [in 2 cols., col. 1]: The Teleios Ministry of | Camelback Bible Church | 3900 East Stanford Drive | Paradise Valley, AZ 85253 | 955-6370 | [col. 2]: April, 1998; front cover (verso): Teleios Sermon # 31 | [35 lines]; p. [1]: title; p. [18]: *Notes and Personal Application*; pp. [19-20]: blank; back cover (recto): [advertisement].

OCLC 48540861
Gordon-Conwell Theological Seminary

A DIVINE AND SUPERNATURAL LIGHT

4 • A | Divine and Supernatural | LIGHT, | Immediately imparted to the Soul by the | *SPIRIT* of *GOD*, | Shown to be both a | *Scriptural*, and *Rational* DOCTRINE; | In a SERMON | Preach'd at *Northampton*, | And Publiſhed at the Deſire of ſome of the Hearers. | [rule] | By *Jonathan Edwards*, A. M. | Paſtor

of the Church there. | [rule] | Job 28. 20.—*Whence then cometh wiſdom? and where is | the place of underſtanding?* | Prov. 2. 6. *The LORD giveth wiſdom.* | Iſa. 42. 18. *Look ye blind that ye may ſee.* | 2 Pet. 1. 19.—*Until the day dawn and the day-ſtar ariſe | in your hearts.* | [double rule] | *BOSTON*: | Printed by S. KNEELAND and T. GREEN. | [short rule in two parts] | M,DCC,XXXIV.

8vo.; 18.6 x 11.3 cm.; [A]^4, B-D^4, E^3; [6], 31, [1] p.

Contents: prp. [1]: Mr. *Edwards*'s | SERMON | ON THE | Reality of Spiritual Light (verso blank); prp. [3]: title (verso blank); prp. [5]: *The* PREFACE [signed] *J. E.*; p. 1: THE | *Reality of Spiritual Light*.; p. [32]: [Taken from the Excellent Dr. *Watts*'s HYMNS.] | *The Humble enlightened, and Carnal Reaſon | humbled*: Or, *The Sovereignty of Grace*, | Luke 10. 21, 22 | [24 lines].

THJ 2 EAI 1:3768 NUC NE0046530 OCLC 5994865

Boston Public Library

5 • *A Divine and Supernatural Light, im- | mediately imparted to the Soul by the Spirit | of God, ſhown to be both a Scriptural and | Rational Doctrine.* | [short tapered rule] | A | SERMON, | PREACHED AT NORTHAMPTON, | AND PUBLISHED | AT THE DESIRE OF SOME OF THE HEARERS, | IN THE YEAR 1734. | [short decorative rule] | BY JONATHAN EDWARDS, A. M. | Late Preſident of New-Jerſey College. | [short decorative rule] | [thick-thin rule] | *BOSTON:* | PRINTED AND SOLD BY MANNING & LORING, | NO. 2, CORNHILL. | [Price 4 dols. per hundred, 75 cts. per dozen, 8 cts. ſingle.]

12mo.; 20.3 x 11.7 cm. (uncut); [A]-B^6; 24 p.

Notes: in some copies, [Published for Charitable Distribution.] substituted for the price; in some copies, bound with AN | ACCOUNT | OF THE | Revival of Religion in Boston, | IN THE YEARS 1740-1-2-3. | [short line of stops] | BY THOMAS PRINCE, | *One of the then Pastors of the Old South Church.* | [short line of stops] | "We have heard with our ears, O God! our fathers have told us, what work thou | didst in their days, in the times of old.— Psalm xliv, 1." | "Thus saith the Lord, stand ye in the ways, and see, and ask for the old paths, | where is the good way and walk therein, and ye shall find rest for your souls.— | Jeremiah vi, 16." | [short thick-thin rule] | BOSTON: | REPUBLISHED BY SAMUEL T. ARMSTRONG, 50, CORNHILL. | *Crocker & Brewster, Printers.* | 1823.

Contents: p. [1]: title (verso blank); p. [3]: The Reality of Spiritual Light.; p. 21: OF THE ANNIHILATION OF THE WICKED. | *The following concluſive obſervations are extracted | from a Sermon of Preſident Edwards, on the Eternity | of Hell Torments.*

THJ 3 EAI 2:4135 NUC NE0046520 OCLC 3098729

Massachusetts Historical Society

6 • [decorative rule] | Spiritual Light | [decorative rule] | By Jonathan Edwards | [decorative rule] | FROM THE INHERITANCE OF OUR FATHERS | – Series XXVII, No. 12 | [decorative rule]

12.7 x 8.5 cm.; 29, [1] p.

Notes: published c. 1989.

Contents: front cover, p. [1]: title; p. [2]: JONATHAN EDWARDS | [biography]; p. 3: SPIRITUAL LIGHT; p. [30]: blank; back cover (recto): blank; back cover (verso): [1 line] | [publisher's note] | [decorative rule] | THE INHERITANCE PUBLISHERS | P.O. Box 1334 | GRAND RAPIDS, MICHIGAN 49501.

OCLC 47885676

Gordon-Conwell Theological Seminary

A FAITHFUL NARRATIVE OF THE SURPRISING WORK OF GOD

7 • THE | DUTY and INTEREST of a *People*, | AMONG WHOM | RELIGION has been planted, | TO

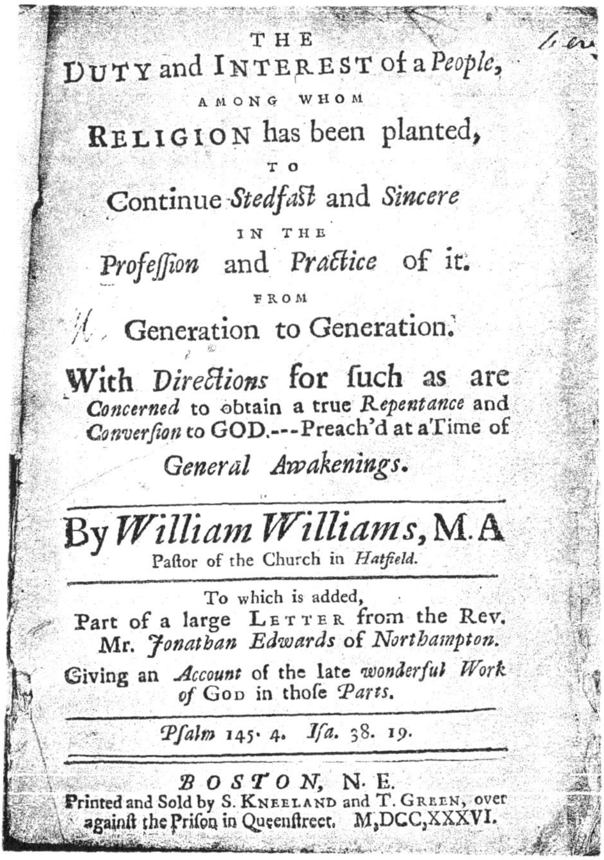

THE
DUTY and INTEREST of a *People*,
AMONG WHOM
RELIGION has been planted,
TO
Continue *Stedfast* and *Sincere*
IN THE
Profession and *Practice* of it.
FROM
Generation to Generation.

With *Directions* for such as are *Concerned* to obtain a true *Repentance* and *Conversion* to GOD.---Preach'd at a Time of *General Awakenings*.

By *William Williams*, M.A
Pastor of the Church in *Hatfield*.

To which is added,
Part of a large LETTER from the Rev. Mr. *Jonathan Edwards* of *Northampton*.
Giving an *Account* of the late *wonderful Work of* GOD in those *Parts*.

Psalm 145. 4. *Isa.* 38. 19.

BOSTON, N. E.
Printed and Sold by S. KNEELAND and T. GREEN, over against the Prison in Queenstreet. M,DCC,XXXVI.

Title page, William Williams, *Duty and Interest of a People* (1736). Permission of the Massachusetts Historical Society.

| Continue *Stedfast* and *Sincere* | IN THE | *Profeſſion* and *Practice* of it. | FROM | Generation to Generation. | With *Directions* for ſuch as are | *Concerned* to obtain a true *Repentance* and | *Converſion* to GOD.---Preach'd at a Time of | *General Awakenings.* | [rule] | By *William Williams*, M. A | Paſtor of the Church in *Hatfield.* | [rule] | To which is added, | Part of a large LETTER from the Rev. | Mr. *Jonathan Edwards* of *Northampton.* | Giving an *Account* of the late *wonderful Work* | *of* GOD in thoſe *Parts.* | [rule] | *Pſalm* 145. 4. *Iſa.* 38. 19. | [double rule] | *BOSTON*, N. E. | Printed and Sold by S. KNEELAND and T. GREEN, over | againſt the Priſon in Queenſtreet. M,DCC,XXXVI. *stet* M. A

8vo.; 15.1 x 9.6 cm.; π[1], A[4], B-H[8], I[4], [K]-L[8], M-O[4], P[2]; [2], viii, 120, [2], 38, 19, [1] p.

Notes: running title: *The late wonderful Work of GOD in the County of* Hampſhire; mounted on the verso of the title page: This *Book* belongs to | *The* New-England-*Library*, | Begun to be collected by *Thomas Prince*, | upon his entering *Harvard-College*, July 6. | 1703; and was given by ſaid *Prince*, to | remain therein for ever.

Contents: prp. [1]: title (verso blank); p. i: THE | PREFACE. [signed] Hatfield, May 6. 1736. | W. Williams.; p. 1: The Duty and Intereſt | of a Chriſtian People.; prp. [1]: DIRECTIONS | To ſuch as are Concern'd | To obtain a true | *CONVERSION* | unto GOD, | With the *Scripture Characters* of it. | In a DISCOURSE on *Jer.* 4. 1. | Preach'd at a Time of *Extraordinary Awakenings.* | [rule] | By William Williams, M. A. | Paſtor of the Church in *Hatfield.* | [rule] | 2 Cor. 5. 17. *If any Man be in Chriſt, he is a new Crea-* | *ture.* | 2 Pet. 1. 10.--- *Brethren, give diligence to make your Cal-* | *ling and Election ſure.* | [rule] | *BOSTON:* Printed & Sold by S. KNEELAND | and T. GREEN in Queen-ſtreet. 1736. (verso blank); p. 1: Directions to ſuch as are | Concern'd to obtain a | true Converſion unto | GOD.; p. 1: APPENDIX.; p. 2: The LETTER follows, | Northampton, Novem. 6. 1736. [signed] *Jonathan Edwards*.; p. 19: ADVERTISEMENT. | IF *the Taſte here given of Mr.* Edwards his Ex- | cellent Letter *excite in Perſons of Piety a* | *Deſire to have the* whole of it publiſh'd; *it is* | *hereby notified that* Subſcriptions *for that End will* | *be taken by Meſſi* Kneeland *and* Green, *at their* | Printing houſe *in* Queen-ſtreet, Boſton; *The whole* | *will be contained in* five Sheets. (verso blank).

THJ 4 EAI 1:4103 NUC NW0332736 OCLC 22580079
Boston Public Library

8 • A Faithful | NARRATIVE | OF THE | Surprizing Work of GOD | IN THE | CONVERSION | OF | Many HUNDRED SOULS in *Northampton*, | and the Neighbouring Towns and | Villages of *New-Hampſhire* in *New-* | *England.* | In a LETTER to the Rev[d]. Dr. BENJAMIN | COLMAN of *Boſton.* | Written by the Rev[d]. Mr. EDWARDS, Miniſter of | *Northampton*, on *Nov.* 6. 1736. | And Publiſhed, | With a Large PREFACE, | By Dr. WATTS and Dr. GUYSE. | [double rule] | *LONDON*; | Printed for JOHN OSWALD, at the *Roſe and Crown*, in | the *Poultry*, near *Stocks-Market*. M.DCC.XXXVII. | Price ſtitch'd 1 *s*. Bound in Calf-Leather, 1 *s*. 6 *d*.

12mo.; 16.7 x 9.9 cm.; A[6], a[2], B-F[12], G[6]; xvi, 132 p.

Notes: in Edwards's hand on the flyleaf of his presentation copy: It must be noted that the Rev. publishers of the ensuing narrative by much abridging of it, and altering the phrase and manner of expression, and not strictly observing the words of the original, have through mistake, published some things diverse from fact, which is the reason some words are crossed out: and besides there are some mistakes in the preface, which are noted in the margins.

Contents: p. [I]: title (verso blank); p. [iii]: THE | PREFACE. [signed] *London, Oct.* 12. 1737. | ISAAC WATTS. | JOHN GUYSE.; p. [1]: A Faithful | NARRATIVE | OF | The Surprizing Work of GOD in the | Converſion of many Hundred Souls in | *Northampton*, of *New-England, &c.* | In a LETTER to the Rev[d]. DR. COLMAN | of *Boſton, &c.*; p. 132: ADVERTISEMENT.

THJ 5 ESTC T78816 NUC NE0046582 OCLC 3165314
Beinecke Library

9 • A Faithful | NARRATIVE | OF THE | Surpriſing Work of GOD | IN THE | CONVERSION | OF | Many HUNDRED SOULS in *Northampton*, | and the Neighbouring Towns and Vil- | lages of *New-*

Hampſhire in *New- Eng-* | *land.* | In a LETTER to the Reverend Dr. BEN- | JAMIN COLMAN of *Boſton.* | Written by the Reverend Mr. EDWARDS, Mi- | niſter of *Northampton*, on *Nov*. 6. 1736. | And Publiſhed, | With a Large PREFACE, | By Dr. WATTS and Dr. GUYSE. | [rule] | *EDINBURGH,* | Reprinted for *J. Oſwald* Book-ſeller in *London*; and ſold | by Meſſieurs *J. Paton, J. Davidſon, J. Traill, G. Ha-* | *milton, A. Duning*, Book-ſellers in *Edinburgh*; and by | *T. Lumiſden* and *J. Robertſon* Printers in the *Fiſh-mar-* | *ket* there: Alſo at *Glaſgow* by *J. Barrie* Book-ſeller | there. MD.CC.XXXVII. Price ſtitch'd 1 *ſh.*

8vo.; 16.5 x 9.7 cm.; [A]^4, B-S^4, T^2; xvi, 132 p.

Notes: in some copies, Price ſtitch'd 8*d*. substituted for Price ſtitch'd 1 *ſh*.

Contents: p. [i]: title (verso blank); p. [iii]: THE | PREFACE. [signed] *London, Oct*. 12. 1737. | ISAAC WATTS. | JOHN GUYSE.; p. [1]: A Faithful | NARRATIVE | OF | The Surpriſing Work of GOD in the | Converſion of many Hundred Souls | in *Northampton*, of *New-England*, | &c. | In a LETTER to the Reverend DR. COL- | MAN of *Boſton, &c.*; p. 132: ADVERTISEMENT.

THJ 6 ESTC N9610 NUC NE0046563
Forbes Library

10 • A Faithful | NARRATIVE | OF THE | Surprizing Work of GOD | IN THE | CONVERSION | OF | Many HUNDRED SOULS in *Northampton*, | and the Neighbouring Towns and | Vil- | lages of *New-Hampſhire* in *New-England.* | In a LETTER to the Rev^d Dr. BENJAMIN | COLMAN of *Boſton.* | Written by the Reverend Mr. EDWARDS, Miniſter | of *Northampton*, on *Nov*. 6. 1736. | And publiſhed, | With a Large PREFACE, | *By Dr.* WATTS *and Dr.* GUYSE. | [rule] | *The* SECOND EDITION. | [rule] | *LONDON:* | Printed for JOHN OSWALD, at the *Roſe* and *Crown*, in | the *Poultry*, near *Stocks-Market*. M DCC XXXVIII. | Price ſtitch'd 1 *s*. bound 1 *s*. 6 *d*.

12mo.; 16.2 x 9.3 cm.; [A]^6, B-M^6; xvi, 126, [2] p.

Contents: p. [i]: title (verso blank); p. [iii]: THE | PREFACE. [signed] ISAAC WATTS. | *London, Oct*. 12. 1737. | JOHN GUYSE.; p. [1]: A Faithful | NARRATIVE | OF | The Surprizing Work of GOD in the | Converſion of many Hundred Souls in | *Northampton*, of *New-England, &c.* | In a LETTER to the Reverend | Dr. COLMAN of *Boſton, &c.*; p. [127]: ADVERTISEMENT.

THJ 8 ESTC T59375 NUC NE0046571 OCLC 11141532
Houghton Library

11 • A Faithful | NARRATIVE | OF THE | Surpriſing Work of GOD | IN THE | CONVERSION | OF | Many HUNDRED SOULS in *Northampton*, and | the Neighbouring Towns and Villages of | *New-Hampſhire* in *New-England.* | In a LETTER to the Reverend Dr. BEN- | JAMIN COLMAN of *Boſton.* | Written by the Reverend Mr. EDWARDS, Miniſter | of *Northampton*, on *Nov*. 6. 1736. | And Publiſhed, | With a Large PREFACE, | By Dr. WATTS and Dr. GUYSE. | [rule] | *EDINBURGH.* | Printed by THOMAS LUMISDEN and JOHN | ROBERTSON, and ſold at their Printing-houſe | in the *Fiſh-market.* | M. DCC. XXXVIII.

8vo.; 16.5 x 10 cm. (uncut); [A]^4, B-N^4, [O]^2; xii, 93, [3] p.

Contents: p. [i]:title (verso blank); p. iii: THE | PREFACE. [signed] *London, Oct*. 12. 1737. | ISAAC WATTS. | JOHN GUYSE.; p. 1: A Faithful | NARRATIVE | OF | The Surpriſing Work of GOD in the Con- | verſion of many Hundred Souls in *North-* | *ampton*, of *New-England, &c.* | In a LETTER to the Reverend Dr. COLMAN of | *Boſton, &c.*; pp. [94-96]: [advertisement].

THJ 9 NUC NE0046565
Forbes Library

12 • A Faithful | NARRATIVE | OF THE | Surprifing Work of GOD | IN THE | CONVERSION | OF | Many HUNDRED SOULS in *Northampton*, and | the Neighbouring Towns and Villages of | the County of *Hampfhire*, in the Province | of the *Maffachufetts-Bay* in *New-England.* | In a LETTER to the Reverend | Dr. BENJAMIN COLMAN, of *Bofton.* | [rule] | Written by the Rev[d]. Mr. EDWARDS, Minifter of | *Northampton, Nov.* 6. 1736. | [rule] | With a PREFACE by Several | MINISTERS. | [rule] | The THIRD EDITION. | [rule] | *BOSTON: N. E.* Printed & Sold by S. KNEELAND | and T. GREEN, and D HENCHMAN, inCorn-Hill. 1738. *stet* inCorn-Hill

8vo.; 15.1 x 9.1 cm.; [A]^4, B-L^4; [2], v, [1], 79, [1] p.

Notes: of the three issues of the first American, or third, edition, this one lacks the Watts-Guyse preface, reflecting, perhaps, Edwards's displeasure with it (see 8).

Contents: prp. [1]: title (verso blank); p. [i]: The PREFACE. [signed] [in 2 cols., col. 1] Bofton, Novemb. | 4th. 1738. | [col. 2] Jofeph Sewall | Thomas Prince | John Webb | William Cooper.; p. [vi]: TO the REVEREND | *Benjamin Colman*, D. D. | Paftor of a Church in *Bofton.* | *Weftfield*, Octob. 11 1738. [signed] *William Williams*, Paftor of *Hatfield.* | *Ebenezer Devotion* ------ of *Suffield.* | *Stephen Williams* -------- of *Long Meadow.* | *Peter Reynolds* -------- of *Enfield.* | *Nehemiah Bull* -------- of *Westfield.* | *Samuel Hopkins* ------- of *W. Springfield.*; p. v: *P.S.* Since the writing this Preface, One of us has receiv'd a | Letter from a Reverend and very worthy Minifter in | *Glafgow*, in which is the following *Passage*; | "The Friends of ferious Religion here were much re- | frefhed with a printed Account of the extraordinary Suc- | cefs of the Gofpel, of late, in fome Parts of *New England.* | If you can favour me with more particular Accounts of | thofe joyful Events, when you have Opportunity of writing | to me, it will much oblige me." p. [1]: A Faithful | NARRATIVE | OF | The Surprizing Work of GOD in the | Conversion of many Hundred Souls in | *Northampton*, of *New-England, &c.* | In a LETTER to the Rev[d]. Dr. COLMAN | of Bofton, *&c.* [signed] *Northampton,* | *Nov.* 6. 1736. | *Jonathan Edwards.*; p. [80]: blank.

THJ 7
Princeton University

12A • A Faithful | NARRATIVE | OF THE | Surprifing Work of GOD | IN THE | CONVERSION | OF | Many HUNDRED SOULS in *Northampton*, and | the Neighbouring Towns and Villages of | the County of *Hampfhire*, in the Province | of the *Maffachufetts-Bay* in *New-England.* | In a LETTER to the Reverend | Dr. BENJAMIN COLMAN, of *Bofton.* | [rule] | Written by the Rev[d]. Mr. EDWARDS, Minifter of | *Northampton, Nov.* 6. 1736. | [rule] | Publifhed with a Large PREFACE by the Rev. | Dr. WATTS and Dr. GUYSE of *London:* | To which a Shorter is added by Some of the | Reverend Minifters of *BOSTON.* | Together with an ATTESTATION from Some of the | Reverend *Minifters* of *Hampfhire.* | [rule] | The THIRD EDITION. | [rule] | *BOSTON: N. E.* Printed & Sold by S. KNEELAND | T. GREEN, over againft the Prifon in Queen-ftreet. 1738.

12mo.; 15.8 x 9 cm.; [A]^4, a^1, A^3, B-L^4; [2], viii, v, [1], 79, [1] p.

Notes: pp. [i]-v repeated.

Contents: prp. [1]: title (verso blank); p. [i]: THE | PREFACE [signed] *London, October* | 12. 1737. | *ISAAC WATTS.* | *JOHN GUYSE.*; p. [i]: PREFACE. [signed] [in 2 cols., col 1.] Bofton, Novemb. | 4th. 1738. | [col. 2] Jofeph Sewall | Thomas Prince | John Webb | William Cooper. | *P.S.* Since the writing this Preface, One of us has receiv'd a | Letter from a Reverend and very worthy Minifter in | *Glafgow*, in which is the following *Passage*; | "The Friends of ferious Religion here were much re- | frefhed with a printed Account of the extraordinary Suc- | cefs of the Gofpel, of late, in fome Parts of *New England.* | If you can favour me with more particular Accounts of | thofe joyful Events, when you have Opportunity of writing | to me, it will much oblige me."; p. [vi]: TO the REVEREND | *Benjamin Colman*, D. D. | Paftor of a Church in *Bofton.* | *Weftfield*, Octob. 11 1738. [signed] *William Williams*, Paftor of *Hatfield.* | *Ebenezer Devotion* ------ of *Suffield.* | *Stephen Williams* ------ of *Long Meadow.* | *Peter Reynolds* ------ of *Enfield.* | *Nehemiah Bull* ------ of *Westfield.* | *Samuel Hopkins* ------ of *W. Springfield.*; p. [1]: A Faithful | NARRATIVE | OF | The Surprizing Work of GOD in the | Conversion of many Hundred Souls in | *Northampton*, of *New-England, &c.* | In a LETTER to the Rev[d]. Dr. COLMAN |

of Boſton, &c. [signed] *Northampton,* | *Nov.* 6. 1736. | *Jonathan Edwards*.; p. [80]: blank.
THJ 7A EAI 1:4240 NUC NE0046567 OCLC 16769647
Massachusetts Historical Society

12B • The THIRD EDITION. | [rule] | *BOSTON*: *N. E.* Printed by S. KNEELAND and | T. GREEN, for D. HENCHMAN, in Corn-Hill. 1738.
Notes: identical with the above except for the imprint.
THJ 7B NUC NE0046569
Harvard Divinity School

13 • Glaubwüridge Nachricht | von dem herrlichen | Werck GOttes, | Welches ſich | In Bekehrung vieler hundert | Seelen zu Northampton und an | andern Orten in Neu=Engeland | geäuſſert hat, | Wieſolche | von einem Lehrer, vermittelſt | eines an Herrn D. Colmann in Boſton erlaſſenen | Briefes, mitgetheilet, und von Herrn D. Watts | und D. Guyſen voriges Jahr zu Londen in | Engliſcher Sprache herausgegeben | worden, | Nummehro mit einer kurtzen Einlei= | tung in die Geſchichte der Chriſtlichen Ge= | meinden in obgedachten Americaniſchen | Landen, und einigen Anmer= | ckungen verſehen, | von | Johann Adam Steinmetz, | Kön. Preuſſ. Conſiſtorial-Rath, General-Superint. im Hertzog= | thum Magdeburg, und Abt zu Berga. | [rule] | Magdeburg, gedruckt bey Chriſt. Leberecht Fabern, | Königl. Preuſſ. privil. Buchdr. 1738. *stet* GOttes *stet* Colmann
8vo.; 17.4 x 10.3 cm.; [x]^8, xx^8, xxx^8, A-K^8; [48], 160 p.
Notes: a German translation of *Faithful Narrative*, the only work of Edwards published in Germany; p. 32 misnumbered 23, p. 155 misnumbered 127 (pp. 19-31, 23, 33-154, 127, 156-160).
Contents: prp. [1]: title (verso blank); prp. [3]: In Chriſto, dem allgemeinen | Heilande geliebteſter | Leſer. [signed] Joh. A. Steinmetz; p. [1]: Die Vorrede Hn. D. Watts | und D. Guysens. [signed] Londen, | den 12. Octobr. | 1737. | Iſaac Watts, | John Guyſe.; p. 19: Glaubwüridge Nachricht | von dem herrlichen | Werck GOttes, | Welches ſich | In Bekehrung vieler hundert Seelen | zu Northampton und an andern | Orten in Neu=Engeland | geäuſſert hat, | mitgetheilet in einem Schreiben | an den | Herrn Doctor Colmann | in Boſton.
THJ 10 NUC NE0046596
Houghton Library

13A • [in red ink] Glaubwüridge Nachricht | von dem herrlichen | [in red ink] Werck GOttes, | Welches ſich | [in red ink] In Bekehrung vieler hundert | Seelen zu Northampton und an | andern Orten in Neu=Engeland | geäuſſert hat, | Wie ſolche | [in red ink] von einem daſelbſtigen Lehrer, vermittelſt | eines an Herrn D. Colmann in Boſton erlaſſenen | Briefes, mitgetheilet, und von Herrn D. Watts | und D. Guyſen voriges Jahr zu Londen in | Engliſcher Sprache herausgegeben | worden, | [in red ink] Nummehro mit einer kurtzen Einlei= | tung in die Geſchichte der Chriſtlichen Ge= | meinden in obgedachten Americaniſchen | Landen, und einigen Anmer= | ckungen verſehen, | von | [in red ink] Johann Adam Steinmetz, | Kön. Preuſſ. Conſiſtorial-Rath, General-Superint. im Hertzog= | thum Magdeburg, und Abt zu Berga. | [rule] | Magdeburg und Leipzig, | In Verlegung ſel. Chriſtoph Seidels Wittwe, und | G. E. Scheidhaures, 1738.
Notes: identical with the above except for the imprint and the lines on the title page in red ink; the errors in pagination have been corrected.
NUC NE0046597 OCLC 41879522
John Carter Brown Library

14 • GELOOFWAARDIG HISTORISCH | [in red ink] BERICHT, | Van 't Heerlyke Werk Godts, geopenbaart | in de *Bekeeringe van veele Honderden van* | *Zielen*, in *Northampton*, en op andere |

Plaatſen in *Nieuw-Engelandt:* | [in red ink] BRIEFSGEWYSE GESCHREVEN, | Door den Eerw. HEERE | [in red ink] JONATHAN EDWARDS, | Aan Dr. *Colman* te *Boſton*; uytgegeeven door | de Drs. *Iſaac Watts* en *Joh. Guiſe* te *London:* | Met | Een *korte Inleydinge*, van den *Oorſprong der Chriſte-* | *lyke Gemeentens* in die Geweſten van *America*, | en eenige *Aanmerkingen*, | Door | [in red ink] JOHAN ADAM STEINMETZ, | Conſiſtorie-Raadt van den Koning van *Pruyſſen*, Ge- | neraal Superintendent van 't Hertogdom *Maag-* | *denburg*, enz. uyt het *Engelſch* en *Hoog-* | *duytſch* vertaalt, | Door | [in red ink] ISAAC LE LONG. | [ornament] | t'AMSTERDAM. | [in red ink] By HENDRIK VAN BOS, Boekverkoper, op de | hoek van de Voorburgwal en Molſteeg. 1740.

8vo.; 15.2 x 9.8 cm.; $*^7$, A-O^8, P^7; [14], 237, [1] p.

Notes: a Dutch translation of *Faithful Narrative*, the first of ten in the eighteenth century.

Contents: prp. [1]: title; prp. [2]: PSALM CXX. Vers. 1. | *De Werken des Heeren zyn* | *grot; zy worden ge1ocht van* | *alle die der luſt in hebben*; prp. [3]: VOORBERICHT, | VOOR DEN | NEDERDUYTSCHEN | LESER [signed] Iſaac Le Long; p. 1: KORTE | INLEYDINGE, | Van den *Oorsprong* der *Christelyke Ge-* | *meentens* in eenige Geweſten van | *America*, van JOHAN ADAM | STEINMETZ [signed] JOH. ADAM STEINMETZ, In 't Klooſter *Berga*, | den 18 *April* 1738.; p. 45: VOORREDEN | VAN DE | DRS. ISAAC WATTS | en JOH. GUISE [signed] ISAAC WATTS | JOH. GUISE, *London*, den 12 *October*, | 1737.; pp. [63]-237: text; p. [238]: blank.

THJ 11 NUC NE0046689

Library of Congress

14A • TWEEDE DRUK. | t'AMSTERDAM. | By HENDRIK VAN BOS, Boekverkoper, op de | hoek van de Voorburgwal en Molſteeg. 1742.

Notes: identical with the above except for the imprint.

THJ 11A NUC NE0046591 OCLC 42451560

New York Public Library

15 • *Part of a Letter ſent to the Reverend Mr.* Whitefield, *from the Reverend* | *Mr.* Edwards *of* Northampton *in* New-England, December 14, 1740.

Notes: The *WEEKLY HISTORY:* | OR, | An Account of the moſt Remarkable Parti- | culars relating to the preſent Progreſs of | the Goſpel. | [rule] | *London*: Printed by *J. Lewis* in *Bartholomew-Cloſe*, near *Weſt-Smithfield.* | [Price One Penny.], was issued in eighty-four numbers in London from April 11, 1741, to November 13, 1742; other than this extract, there is a brief mention of Edwards in a letter from Benjamin Colman to George Whitefield, no. 17 (August 1, 1741):2, and an advertisement for *Distinguishing Marks*—earnestly recommended by the Rev. Dr. | *Watts*, and the Rev. Mr. *Whitefield* to the ſerious Peruſal of all Chriſtians, | and to Miniſters of every Denomination in particular—no. 53 (April 10, 1742):4; for the complete text of the letter, see *Letters and Personal Writings*, ed. George S. Claghorn, *The Works of Jonathan Edwards*, vol. 16 (New Haven: Yale University Press, 1998), p. 87.

Contents: caption title; *The Weekly History*, no. 9 (June 6, 1741):[1]-2.

Beinecke Library

16 • *Extract from Mr.* Edward'*s Narrative of the ſurpriſing* | *Work of God in the Converſion of many hundred Souls* | *in* Northampton, &c. in New England, *of which the* | *third Edition is atteſted by ſix other Miniſters beſides* | *Mr.* Edwards. *stet* Edward'*s*

Notes: *The Glasgow-Weekly-History* was edited by William McCulloch and issued weekly from December 1, 1741, in fifty-two numbers.

Contents: caption title; THE | *Glaſgow-Weekly-History* | Relating to the | LATE PROGRESS | OF THE | GOSPEL | At HOME and ABROAD; | BEING | A Collection of Letters, partly reprin- | ted from the *London-Weekly-History*, | and partly printed firſt here at *Glaſ-* | *gow*. | For the YEAR 1742. | [double rule] | GLASGOW: | Printed by William Duncan, 1743., no. 21 (1742):7-8 and no. 22 (1742):1-3.

THJ 12
Massachusetts Historical Society

17 • [*Revival* of *Religion* at NORTHAMPTON.]

Notes: THE | Chriftian Hiftory, | CONTAINING | *ACCOUNTS* | OF THE | Revival *and* Propagation | OF | *RELIGION* | IN | GREAT-BRITAIN & AMERICA. | *For the* YEAR | 1743 | [decorative rule] | [ornament] | [decorative rule] | *BOSTON, N. E.* | Printed by S. KNEELAND and T. GREEN, | for T. PRINCE, junr. 1744. was issued weekly in Boston from March 5, 1743 to February 23, 1745 in 104 numbers; the excerpt appears under the general heading *Some* INSTANCES *of the tranfient* REVIVAL *of it* | *in the prefent Day*; the entry proper begins the following week and concludes the week after under the caption [Mr. EDWARDS'S *Account finifhed.*].

Contents: caption title; *The Christian History*, no. 14 (June 4, 1743):112; no. 15 (June 11, 1743):115-120; and no. 16 (June 18, 1743):121-128.

THJ 13 EAI 1:5154 OCLC 26541026
Congregational Library

18 • A | NARRATIVE | OF THE | Late Work of GOD, | AT and NEAR | *NORTHAMPTON*, | IN | *NEW-ENGLAND.* | EXTRACTED from | Mr. *EDWARDS*'S LETTER | TO | Dr. *COLEMAN*, | By JOHN WESLEY, M. A. | Fellow of *Lincoln* College, OXFORD. | [decorative rule] | *Briftol:* Printed by *Felix Farley.* | And fold by him at his Houfe in *Caftle-Green*; at the | *School-Room* in the *Horfe-Fair*, and by *J. Wilfon* in | *Wine-ftreet:* In LONDON, by *T. Trye*, near *Grey's-* | *Inn-Gate, Holborn*; *Henry Butler*, at the Corner of | *Bow Church-Yard*, and at the *Foundry* near *Moorfields:* | In *Exeter* by *B. Thorne*, and *E. Score:* As alfo at the | feveral Societies in *England.*

12mo.; 16.7 x 9.8 cm.; $[A]^6$, B-D^6; 48 p.

Notes: John Wesley abridged five Edwards works: *Faithful Narrative* (c. 1744), *Distinguishing Marks* (1744), *Some Thoughts* (1745), *Life of Brainerd* (1758), and *Religious Affections* (1801). *Distinguishing Marks* and *Religious Affections* were reissued as *The Work of the Holy Spirit in the Human Heart* (1841); all were frequently reprinted.

Contents: p. [1]: title (verso blank); p. [3]: A | NARRATIVE | OF | The late WORK of GOD, | At and Near | *Northampton*, in NEW-ENGLAND.; p. 48: *ERRATUM.*

THJ 14 ESTC T78831 NUC NE0046734 OCLC 18525084
Houghton Library

19 • [*Revival of Religion at* Northampton.]

Notes: reprinted from *The Christian History*, concluding with Edwards's December 12, 1743, letter to Thomas Prince (see 48). THE | *Christian Monthly History:* | OR, AN | ACCOUNT | OF THE | REVIVAL and PROGRESS | OF | RELIGION, | *Abroad*, and at *Home.* | [rule] | To be Publifhed Monthly | [rule] | ACTS XV. 3. *And they paffed through----* | *declaring the Conversion of the Gentiles: And* | *they caufed great Joy unto all the Brethren.* | [rule] | *EDINBURGH:* | Printed by R. FLEMING and A. ALISON, and Sold | by the Bookfellers in Town and Country. | [short rule] | M.DCC.XLIII. was edited by James Robe, of Kilsyth, and issued monthly from November 1743 to December 1745.

Contents: caption title; *The Christian Monthly History*, no. 3 (June 1745):87-92 and no. 4 (July 1745):[93]-114.

THJ 15 OCLC 8704380
Congregational Library

20 • Van den Eerwaardigen Heere J. ED- | WARDS, uyt *Northampton*, in | *New-Engelandt*, den 14. *December* | 1740. aan eenenanderen *Leeraar.* | *Eerwaarde en Geliefde Heere!*

Notes: first published in the [London] *Weekly-History*, no. 9 (June 6, 1741):[1]-2, one of many revival accounts in a Dutch compilation; THJ cites the book but not the very limited Edwards selection in it.

Contents: caption title; pp. 123-124 in NADERE GELOOFWAARDIGE | BERICHTEN | Van het Heerlyke Werk Godts, | geopenbaart in de | OPWEKKINGE | EN | BEKEERINGE | Van veele duyfenden van Zielen, op veele | Plaatfen in | NIEUW-ENGELANDT, | Begrepen in een groot getal eigenhandige | Brieven van Predikanten en andere Ge- |

loofwaardige Perfoonen daar te lande. | Meerendeels in 't Engelfch uitgegeven door den Wel- | Eerwaardigen en Godvruchtigen Heere | ISAAK WATTS, | *Doctor in de Heilige Godgeleerdheid en Bedienaar des* | *H. Euangeliums te Londen,* | Vervolgens in 't Hoogduytfch overgebragt en met | een Voorreden en eenige Aanmerkingen verrykt, | door den Eerwaardigen Heere | JOHAN ADAM STEINMETZ, | *Confiftorie-Raadt van den Koning van Pruiffen en Generaal* | *Superintendent van 't Hertogdom Maagdenburg, enz.* | En thans in 't Nederduitfch vertaalt door | ISAAK LE LONG. | [ornament] | *TE LEEUWARDEN,* | By R. J. NOORDBEEK, Boekverkooper, 1750.

8vo.; 16.5 x 10.5 cm. (uncut); [†]^{8}, ††^{8}, A-L^{8}; [32], 176 p.
THJ 16 NUC NE0046731
John Carter Brown Library

21 • [From PRINCE'S Chriftian Hiftory, N° 15,16.]

Contents: caption title; pp. 35-44 in HISTORICAL COLLECTIONS | RELATING TO | REMARKABLE PERIODS | OF | THE SUCCESS | OF | THE GOSPEL, | AND | EMINENT INSTRUMENTS | EMPLOYED IN PROMOTING IT. | IN TWO VOLUMES. | MATTH. XXVIII. 19, 20. GO AND TEACH ALL NATIONS:—AND LO, | I AM WITH YOU ALWAY, EVEN TO THE END OF THE WORLD. | COMPILED BY | JOHN GILLIES, | ONE OF THE MINISTERS OF GLASGOW. | *IN MAGNIS VOLUISSE.* | VOL. II. | GLASGOW, | PRINTED BY ROBERT AND ANDREW FOULIS | MDCCLIV.

8vo.; 20.5 x 12.4 cm.; [a]-b^{4}, A-Z^{4}, Aa-Zz^{4}, Aaa-Mmm^{4}, Nnn^{2}; 468 p.
THJ 17 NUC NE0046560 OCLC 4800892
Harvard Divinity School

22 • A | NARRATIVE | OF THE LATE | WORK of GOD | AT and NEAR | *Northampton* in *New-England.* | Extracted from | Mr. *Edward*'s Letter to Dr. *Coleman.* | [rule] | By *JOHN WESLEY*, M. A. | Late Fellow of *Lincoln College, Oxon.* | [rule] | The SECOND EDITION. | [rule] | [ornament] | [double rule] | LONDON: | Printed by HENRY COCK; | And fold at the Foundery, near Upper Moor-fields, | by T. TRYE, at Gray's-Inn-Gate; and by R. | AKENHEAD, on Tine Bridge, Newcaftle. MDCCLV. | [Price Four-Pence.] *stet Edward*'s

12mo.; 16.6 x 9.9 cm.; [A]^{6}, B-D^{6}; 48 p.
Contents: p. [1]: title (verso blank); p. [3]: A | NARRATIVE | OF | The late WORK of GOD, *&c.*
THJ 18 ESTC N9955 NUC NE0046735 OCLC 10346259
Houghton Library

23 • A FAITHFUL | NARRATIVE | OF THE | SURPRISING WORK OF GOD | IN THE | CONVERSION | OF | Many HUNDRED SOULS in *Northampton*, and the | Neighbouring Towns and Villages of *New-* | *Hampfhire* and *New-England.* | In a LETTER to the Rev. Dr. *Benjamin Colman* of *Bofton.* | By the Rev. Mr. *Edwards*, Minifter of *Northampton.* | AND PUBLISHED | WITH A LARGE PREFACE, | *By Dr.* WATTS *and Dr.* GUYSE. | [rule] | A NEW AMERICAN EDITION. | [rule] | *ELIZABETH-TOWN:* | PRINTED BY SHEPARD KOLLOCK. | M,DCC,XC.

12mo.; 16.4 x 10.4 cm.; [A]^{6}, B-K^{6}, L^{4}; xiii, [14]-125, [3] p.
Notes: some copies lack blank L_4.
Contents: p. [i]: title (verso blank); p. [iii]: THE | PREFACE [signed] ISAAC WATTS. | JOHN GUYSE. | LONDON, *October* 12, 1737.; p. [14]: A FAITHFUL | NARRATIVE | OF | The Surprifing Work of GOD in the Conver- | fion of many HUNDRED SOULS in *Northamp-* | *ton*, of *New-England, &c.* | In a LETTER to the Rev. Dr. *Colman* of *Bofton, &c.*; pp. [126-128]: blank.
THJ 19 EAI 1:45867 OCLC 9495028
Smith College

24 • A FAITHFUL | NARRATIVE | OF THE | SURPRISING WORK OF GOD | IN THE |

CONVERSION | OF | Many HUNDRED SOULS in *Northampton*, and the | Neighbouring Towns and Villages of *New-* | *Hampſhire* and *New-England.* | In a LETTER to the Rev. Dr. *Benjamin Colman* of *Boſton.* | By the Rev. Mr. *Edwards*, Miniſter of *Northampton.* | AND PUBLISHED | WITH A LARGE PREFACE, | *By Dr.* WATTS *and Dr.* GUYSE. | TO WHICH IS ADDED, | TRUE GRACE, | DISTINGUISHED FROM THE | EXPERIENCE OF DEVILS; | IN A SERMON, | Preached before the Synod of New-York. | [rule] | A NEW AMERICAN EDITION. | [rule] | *ELIZABETH-TOWN:* | PRINTED BY SHEPARD KOLLOCK. | M,DCC,XC.

12mo.; 16.4 x 9.8 cm.; [A]^{6}, B-K^{6}, L^{4}, A-C^{6}, D^{4}; xiii, [14]-125, [3], 43, [1] p.

Notes: The date 1790 on the title page of this printing of *A Faithful Narrative* is evidently an error, for Kollock first advertised this second printing on September 21, 1791. (See his *New Jersey Journal* of that date.) The 1791 date in imprints of *True Grace* is therefore more likely to be correct.—THJ. It was issued separately in that year; see 259.

Contents: p. [i]: title (verso blank); p. [iii]: THE | PREFACE. [signed] ISAAC WATTS. | JOHN GUYSE. | LONDON, *October* 12, 1737.; p. [14]: A FAITHFUL | NARRATIVE | OF | The Surpriſing Work of GOD in the Conver- | ſion of many HUNDRED SOULS in *Northamp-* | *ton*, of *New-England, &c.* | In a LETTER to the Rev. Dr. *Colman* of *Boſton, &c.*; pp. [126-28]: blank; p. [1]: TRUE GRACE, | DISTINGUISHED FROM THE | EXPERIENCE OF DEVILS; | IN A | SERMON, | PREACHED BEFORE THE | *SYNOD* OF *NEW-YORK*, | CONVENED AT | *NEWARK* IN *NEW-JERSEY*, | On SEPTEMBER 28, N.S. 1752. | [short tapered rule] | [PRINTED BY THE DESIRE OF THE SYNOD.] | [short tapered rule] | BY JONATHAN EDWARDS, A. M. | Paſtor of the Church of Chriſt in Stockbridge in New-England. | [short tapered rule] | 2 CORINTHIANS xi. 3. | *I fear, leſt by any means, as the Serpent beguiled Eve through* | *his ſubtilty, ſo your minds ſhould be corrupted from the ſim-* | *plicity that is in Chriſt.* | Verſe 14.–*For Satan himſelf, is transformed into an angel of* | *light.* | [tapered rule] | *ELIZABETHTOWN:* | PRINTED BY SHEPARD KOLLOCK. | [short rule] | M.DCC.XCI.; p. [2]: *At a Meeting of the* SYNOD *of* NEW-YORK, *at* | NEWARK, September 28, 1752. | The SYNOD agree, to deſire the Reverend | Mr. EDWARDS, to publish his Sermon, preach- | ed before them. | *A true Copy*, | RICHARD TREAT, *Syn. Clerk.*; p. [3]: TRUE GRACE, | DISTINGUISHED FROM THE | EXPERIENCE OF DEVILS.; p. [44]: blank.

THJ 20 EAI 1:22477 NUC NE0046573 OCLC 9495028

John Carter Brown Library

25 • SOME REMARKABLE | NARRATIVES | OF THE | Succeſs of the Goſpel, | IN AMERICA, | In the Beginning of this Century. | [short tapered rule] | WRITTEN BY THE LATE | Rev. JONATHAN EDWARDS, A. M. | Miniſter at Northampton, in New-England, and | afterwards Preſident of the College | of New-Jerſey; | And by other Miniſters in America. | [short tapered rule] | *To which is added,* | AN ACCOUNT OF THE CHARACTER | OF | THE REV. DAVID BRAINERD, | Miſſionary to the Indians. | [short tapered rule] | *He hath made his wonderful works to be remembered.* | Pſal. cxi. 4. | [short tapered rule] | HUDDERSFIELD: | PRINTED AND SOLD BY J. BROOK; | SOLD ALSO BY SCATCHERD AND WHITAKER, | LONDON, 1791.

12mo.; 14 x 8.8 cm.; [A]^{6}, B-G^{6}; xiv, [15]-84 p.

Contents: p. [i]: title (verso blank); p. [iii]: INTRODUCTION.; p. [15]: Mr. Edwards's Narrative &c; p. 34: A NARRATIVE | OF THE | REVIVAL of RELIGION, | AT | New-London-Derry, in Pennſylvania [by Samuel Blair]; p. 57: A NARRATIVE | OF THE | REVIVAL of RELIGION, | AT | Wrentham, in the Maſſachuſetts. [by Henry Messenger and Elias Haven]; p. 73: AN | ACCOUNT OF THE CHARACTER | OF | THE REV. DAVID BRAINERD, | Miſſionary to the Indians. | [Extracted from Mr. Edwards's Sermon at his | Funeral.].

THJ 21 ESTC T78839 NUC NE0046807 OCLC 27083557

Forbes Library

26 • A | NARRATIVE | OF THE LATE | WORK OF GOD | AT AND NEAR | *NORTHAMPTON IN NEW-ENGLAND.* | EXTRACTED FROM | The Rev. JONATHAN EDWARDS's | LETTER, | *To Dr. COLEMAN.* | [short wavy rule] | BY *JOHN WESLEY*, M. A. | Late Fellow of Lincoln-College, Oxford.

| [short wavy rule] | [short wavy rule] | *THE THIRD EDITION.* | [short wavy rule] | [short wavy rule] | *LONDON:* | Printed for G. WHITFIELD, City-Road, and ſold at the | Methodiſt Preaching-Houſes in Town and Country. | 1798. | [short rule] | [PRICE FOUR-PENCE.]

12mo.; 17.6 x 10.6 cm.; [A]^{6}, B-C^{6}, D^{8}; 49, [3] p.

Contents: p. [1]: title (verso blank); p. 3: A | NARRATIVE | OF THE LATE | WORK OF GOD, &c.; pp. [50-51]: [advertisement]; p. [52]: blank.

ESTC T173613 OCLC 41533794

Redwood Library and Athenaeum

27 • A FAITHFUL | NARRATIVE | OF THE | *SURPRISING WORK OF GOD,* | IN THE | CONVERSION OF MANY HUNDRED SOULS, | *IN NORTHAMPTON,* | AND THE NEIGHBOURING TOWNS AND VILLAGES OF NEW | HAMPSHIRE, IN NEW ENGLAND; | IN A | *LETTER TO THE REV. DR. COLMAN, OF BOSTON,* | WRITTEN BY | THE REV. MR. EDWARDS, | MINISTER OF NORTHAMPTON, ON NOV. 6, 1737. | And published, with a large Preface, | *BY DR. WATTS AND DR. GUYSE.* | [thick-thin rule] | London: | PRINTED BY C. WHITTINGHAM, | *Dean Street, Fetter Lane,* | FOR W. BUTTON, PATERNOSTER-ROW. | [short tapered rule] | *Price stitched* 1*s.* *Bound* 1*s.* 6*d.*

12mo.; 18.4 x 11.1 cm.; [A]^{6}, B-H^{6}, I^{2}; xii, 84 [i.e., 87], [1] p.

Notes: published c. 1800; pp. 85-87 misnumbered 145-147 (pp. [1]-84, 145-147).

Contents: p. [i]: title (verso blank); p. [iii]: *THE PREFACE.* [signed] ISAAC WATTS, | LONDON, | *Oct.* 12, 1737. | JOHN GUYSE.; p. [1]: A FAITHFUL | NARRATIVE, | *&c. &c.*; p. 147: Printed by C. WHITTINGHAM, Dean-street, Fetter-lane, London; p. [88]: [advertisement].

THJ 22 ESTC T186357 NUC NE0046575 OCLC 19640105

Boston Public Library

28 • A | *FAITHFUL NARRATIVE* | OF THE | SURPRISING WORK OF GOD, | IN THE | CONVERSION | OF MANY HUNDRED SOULS IN NORTHAMPTON, AND THE | NEIGHBORING TOWNS AND VILLAGES OF NEW- | HAMPSHIRE AND NEW-ENGLAND. | In a Letter to Dr. BENJAMIN COLMAN, of Boston. | BY JONATHAN EDWARDS, | Minister of Northampton. | *FROM THE LONDON EDITION, OF* 1737. | [thick-thin rule] | PRINTED BY HENRY RANLET, EXETER, N. H. | [short line of stops] | 1805.

12mo.; 19.7 x 11.4 cm. (uncut); [A]^{6}, B-F^{6}, G^{4}; [2], [3]-75, [5] p.

Notes: p. 65 misnumbered p. 37 (pp. [3]-64, 37, 66-75).

Contents: p. [1]: title (verso blank); p. [3]: A | FAITHFUL NARRATIVE | OF THE | *Surprising Work of God, &c.* | In a Letter to Dr. BENJAMIN COLMAN, of Boston.; p. [76]: blank; pp. [77-80]: [advertisement].

THJ 23 EAI 2:8377 NUC NE0046576 OCLC 12227847

Congregational Library

29 • A FAITHFUL | NARRATIVE | OF THE | SURPRISING WORK OF GOD, | IN THE | CONVERSION | OF | MANY HUNDRED SOULS | *In Northampton, and the neighbouring Towns and Villages* | *of New-Hampshire, in New-England,* | IN A LETTER | TO THE | REV. DR. BENJAMIN COLMAN, OF BOSTON. | Written by the Rev. Mr. EDWARDS, Minister of | Northampton, on Nov. 6, 1736. | PUBLISHED | WITH A | *LARGE PREFACE* | BY DR. WATTS AND DR. GUYSE. | AND RE-PUBLISHED | WITH A | RECOMMENDATORY ADVERTISEMENT, | BY THE REV. J. FAWCETT, A. M. AND THE REV. | W. STEADMAN. | [short decorative rule] | HALIFAX: | Printed and Sold by HOLDEN and DOWSON, Hall-End; Sold alſo by | BUTTON,

Paternoster Row, and CROSBY and Co. | Stationer's Court, LONDON. | [short rule] |1808.

12mo.; 17.7 x 10.3 cm.; $[A]^6$, B-L^6, M^2; xviii, 117, [1] p.

Contents: p. [i]: title (verso blank); p. [iii]: ADVERTISEMENT. [signed] J. FAWCETT, | W. STEADMAN.; p. [v]: THE | PREFACE. [signed] ISAAC WATTS. | JOHN GUYSE. | *London, Oct.* 12, 1737.; pp. [1]-117: text; p. 117: Holden and Dowson, Printers, Halifax. [Yorkshire]; p. [118]: blank.

THJ 24 NUC NE0046577 OCLC 13137613
Princeton University

30 • REMARKABLE | NARRATIVES | OF THE | Success of the Gospel, | IN AMERICA, | IN THE BEGINNING OF THE LAST CENTURY. | [short decorative rule] | WRITTEN BY THE LATE | REV. JONATHAN EDWARDS, A. M. | MINISTER AT NORTHAMPTON, IN NEW-ENGLAND, | *And afterwards President of the College of New-Jersey*; | AND BY OTHER MINISTERS. | [short thick-thin rule] | To which is added, an Account of the Character of the | REV. DAVID BRAINERD, | MISSIONARY TO THE INDIANS. | [short decorative rule] | He hath made his wonderful works to be remembered.----*Pſal.* cxi. 4. | [short thick-thin rule] | Huddersfield: | PRINTED BY J. BROOK, MARKET-PLACE. | [short rule] | 1810.

12mo.; 14 x 8.2 cm.; $[A]^6$, B-G^6; xiv, [15]-84 p.

Notes: in some copies, the spacing and type of the title page vary.

Contents: p. [i]: title (verso blank); p. [iii]: INTRODUCTION.; p. [15]: Mr. Edwards's Narrative, &c.; p. 34: A NARRATIVE | OF THE | REVIVAL of RELIGION, | AT | New-London-Derry, in Penſylvania.; p. 57: A NARRATIVE | OF THE | REVIVAL of RELIGION, | AT | Wrentham, in the Maſſachuſetts.; p. 73: AN | ACCOUNT OF THE CHARACTER | OF | THE REV. DAVID BRAINERD, | Miſſionary to the Indians. | [Extracted from Mr. Edwards's Sermon a his | Funeral.]

NSE 0006146 OCLC 42263918
Princeton University

31 • A | FAITHFUL NARRATIVE | OF | THE SURPRISING WORK OF GOD, | IN | *THE CONVERSION OF MANY HUNDRED SOULS*, | IN NORTHAMPTON, | AND THE NEIGHBOURING TOWNS AND VILLAGES OF | NEW HAMPSHIRE, IN NEW ENGLAND; | IN A | LETTER TO THE REV. DR. COLMAN, OF BOSTON. | [short rule] | BY THE REV. MR. EDWARDS, | MINISTER OF NORTHAMPTON, ON NOV. 6, 1737. | [short rule] | AND PUBLISHED WITH | *A LARGE PREFACF, BY DR. WATTS AND DR. GUYSE.* | [short thick-thin rule] | *BUNGAY:* | PRINTED AND PUBLISHED BY J. M. MORRIS. | [short rule] | 1823. *stet PREFACF*

22 x 12.8 cm.; $[a]^4$, b^2, B-L^4, M^2; xi, [1], [13]-95, [1] p.

Contents: p. [i]: title (verso blank); p. [iii]: PREFACE. [signed] *London,* | *Oct.* 12, 1737. | ISSAC [*sic*] WATTS. | JOHN GUYSE.; p. [12]: blank; p. [13]: A | FAITHFUL NARRATIVE, | *&c. &c.*; p. 95: *J. M. Morris, Printer, Bungay.*; p. [96]: blank.

THJ 25 NUC NE0046578 OCLC 13763920
Southern Baptist Theological Seminary

32 • A | NARRATIVE | OF THE | LATE WORK OF GOD, | AT AND NEAR | NORTHAMPTON, IN NEW-ENGLAND. | EXTRACTED FROM | *Mr. EDWARDS's LETTER to Dr. COLEMAN,* | BY JOHN WESLEY, M. A. | *Late Fellow of Lincoln-College, Oxford.*

Contents: pp. [89]-137 in A | CHRISTIAN LIBRARY: | CONSISTING OF | EXTRACTS FROM AND ABRIDGMENTS OF | THE | CHOICEST PIECES | OF | Practical Divinity | WHICH HAVE BEEN PUBLISHED IN THE ENGLISH TONGUE. | [short decorative rule] | IN THIRTY VOLUMES: | FIRST PUBLISHED IN 1750, IN FIFTY VOLUMES, DUODECIMO | [short rule] | BY THE REV. JOHN WESLEY, A. M., | SOMETIME FELLOW OF

LINCOLN COLLEGE, OXFORD. | [short rule] | Vol. XXX. | [short thick-thin rule] | *LONDON:* PUBLISHED AND SOLD BY J. KERSHAW. | 14, *City-Road, and* 66, *Paternoster-Row.* | [short rule] | 1827.

21.1 x 12.8 cm.; 481 p.

THJ 26 NUC NE0046736 OCLC 6969185

Boston University

33 • A | NARRATIVE | OF THE | REVIVAL OF RELIGION | IN | NEW ENGLAND; | WITH | THOUGHTS OF THAT REVIVAL. | BY | JONATHAN EDWARDS, A. M. | [short rule] | WITH | AN INTRODUCTORY ESSAY, | BY | JOHN PYE SMITH, D. D. | HOMERTON. | [short tapered rule] | GLASGOW: | PRINTED FOR WILLIAM COLLINS; | WILLIAM WHYTE & CO. AND WILLIAM OLIPHANT, EDINBURGH; | W. F. WAKEMAN; AND WM. CURRY, JUN. & CO. DUBLIN; | WHITTAKER, TREACHER, & ARNOT; HAMILTON, ADAMS, & CO. | SIMPKIN AND MARSHALL; BALDWIN & CRADOCK; | AND HURST, CHANCE, & CO. LONDON | [short rule] | MDCCCXXIX.

18 x 10.4 cm.; $[A]^{12}$, $B\text{-}X^{12}$, Y^{1}; xlviii, [49]-506 p.

Notes: in some copies, three leaves of advertisement added.

Contents: p. [i]: SELECT | CHRISTIAN AUTHORS, | WITH | INTRODUCTORY ESSAYS. | N$^{o.}$ 48 (verso blank); frontispiece: [engraving] | REV^{D}. JONATHAN EDWARDS | PUBLISHED BY WILLIAM COLLINS GLASGOW | Eng^{d}. on Steel by W. H. Lizars Edin^{r}.; p. [iii]: title; p. [iv]: Printed by W. Collins & Co. | Glasgow.; p. [v]: INTRODUCTORY ESSAY. [signed] J.P.S. | HOMERTON, *April*, 1829.; p. [xlvii]: CONTENTS.; p. [49]: PREFACE. [signed] ISAAC WATTS. | JOHN GUYSE. | LONDON, *Oct.* 12, 1737.; p. [57]: NARRATIVE. | [short tapered rule] | IN A LETTER TO THE REV. DR. COLMAN | OF BOSTON.; p. [156]: blank; p. [157]: THOUGHTS | ON THE | REVIVAL OF RELIGION | IN | NEW ENGLAND, | AND | THE WAY IN WHICH IT OUGHT TO BE ACKNOWLEDGED | AND PROMOTED. | [short rule] | FIRST PUBLISHED IN MDCCXLII. (verso blank); p. [159]: PREFACE.; p. [161]: THOUGHTS | ON THE | REVIVAL OF RELIGION.; p. 506: Printed by Collins & Co. | Glasgow.

THJ 27 NUC NE0046737 OCLC 16394911

Princeton Theological Seminary

34 • A | FAITHFUL NARRATIVE | OF THE | SURPRISING WORK OF GOD | IN THE | CONVERSION | OF | MANY HUNDRED SOULS | IN NORTHAMPTON, | AND THE NEIGHBOURING TOWNS AND VILLAGES | OF NEW-HAMPSHIRE, IN NEW-ENGLAND: | *In a Letter to the Rev. Dr. Colman,* | At that time Pastor of Brattle Street Church, Boston. | [short rule] | BY PRESIDENT EDWARDS. | [short rule] | WITH PREFACES, | BY THE REV. DR. WATTS AND DR. GUYSE OF LONDON, AND BY | THE BOSTON MINSTERS. | [short rule] | Revised from the Boston Edition of 1738. | [short rule] | JAMES LORING, | SABBATH SCHOOL BOOK-STORE, WASHINGTON-ST. BOSTON. | [short rule] | 1831.

14.2 x 7.7 cm.; $[1]^{8}$, $2\text{-}10^{6}$, 11^{8}, 12^{2}; xv, [1], [13]-140 p.

Contents: p. [i]: title; p. [ii]: BOSTON EDITION OF 1831. | [short rule] | [advertisement] | [dated] BOSTON, AUGUST, 1831.; p. [iii]: PREFACE, | BY DR. WATTS AND DR. GUYSE. [signed] ISAAC WATTS. | JOHN GUYSE.; p. [xi]: PREFACE, | BY THE BOSTON MINISTERS. [signed] Boston, November 4th, 1738. | JOSEPH SEWALL. | Minister of the Old South Church. | THOMAS PRINCE. | Minister of Old South Church. | JOHN WEBB. | Minister of New North Church. | WILLIAM COOPER. | Minister of Brattle Street Church; p. [xvi]: TO THE | REV. BENJAMIN COLMAN, D. D. | PASTOR OF A CHURCH IN BOSTON. [signed] WILLIAM WILLIAMS, Pastor of Hatfield. | EBENEZER DEVOTION, " of Suffield. | STEPHEN WILLIAMS, " of Longmeadow. | PETER REYNOLDS, " of Enfield. | NEHEMIAH BULL, " of Westfield. | SAMUEL HOPKINS, " of West Springfield.; p. [13]: A | FAITHFUL NARRATIVE.; p. [117]: CONVERSION | OF | PRESIDENT EDWARDS. | FROM AN ACCOUNT WRITTEN BY HIMSELF.; p. [138]: TESTIMONY | OF THE | REV. MR. COOPER, IN FAVOUR OF REVIVALS.

THJ 28 NUC NE00465801 OCLC 13583689

Boston Public Library

35 • A | NARRATIVE | OF | MANY SURPRISING CONVERSIONS IN NORTHAMPTON | AND VICINITY. | WRITTEN IN 1736. | TOGETHER WITH SOME THOUGHTS ON THE REVIVAL | IN NEW ENGLAND. | WRITTEN IN 1740. | TO WHICH IS ADDED AN ACCOUNT OF THE CONVERSION OF | THE AUTHOR. | [short rule] | BY JONATHAN EDWARDS, | *Minister at Northampton, and afterwards President of* | *Nassau Hall College, N. J.* | [short rule] | WORCESTER: | PUBLISHED BY MOSES W. GROUT. | [2 short lines of stops] | 1832.

17.4 x 10.5 cm.; π^2, 1-23^8, 24^6; 382, [2] p.

Contents: frontispiece: [engraving] | J. H. Hills Sc. | REV. JONA. EDWARDS.; p. [1]: title; p. [2]: WORCESTER: | MOSES W. GROUT, PRINTER.; p. [3]: CONTENTS. (verso blank); p. [5]: NARRATIVE. | [short rule] | TO THE REV. DR. COLMAN.; p. [80]: blank; p. [81]: THOUGHTS | ON THE | REVIVAL OF RELIGION | IN | NEW ENGLAND. (verso blank); p. [83]: THE AUTHOR'S PREFACE.; p. [85]: ADVERTISEMENT.; p. [87]: REVIVAL OF RELIGION.; p. [362]: blank; p. [363]: CONVERSION | OF | PRESIDENT EDWARDS. | WRITTEN BY HIMSELF. (verso blank); p. [365]: CONVERSION.; p. 381: *Extract from his Resolutions*.; pp. [383-384]: blank.

THJ 29 NUC NE0046732 OCLC 11720325

Forbes Library

36 • EDWARDS ON REVIVALS: | CONTAINING | A FAITHFUL NARRATIVE | OF THE | SURPRISING WORK OF GOD IN THE CONVERSION OF | MANY HUNDRED SOULS IN NORTHAMPTON, | MASSACHUSETTS, A. D. 1735. | ALSO, | THOUGHTS | ON THE | REVIVAL OF RELIGION IN NEW ENGLAND, 1742, | AND THE WAY IN WHICH IT OUGHT TO BE ACKNOW- | LEDGED AND PROMOTED. | BY JONATHAN EDWARDS, A. M., | PASTOR OF THE CHURCH OF CHRIST IN NORTHAMPTON; AFTERWARDS PRESIDENT OF | NASSAU HALL COLLEGE, PRINCETON, N. J. | WITH | INTRODUCTORY REMARKS, AND A FULL GENERAL INDEX, | PREPARED BY THE PRESENT EDITOR. | NEW YORK: DUNNING & SPALDING. | 1832.

21 x 13.2 c m.; [1]^4, 2-53^4; xxix, [1], [31]-424 p.

Notes: p. 247 misnumbered 147 (pp. [31]-246, 147, 248-424).

Contents: frontispiece: [engraving] | Smith, Sc. | REV. JONA. EDWARDS.; p. [i]: title; p. [ii]: "Entered, according to act of congress, in the year 1832, by Charles Spaulding, in the | clerk's office of the southern district of New York." | [short rule] | SLEIGHT AND ROBINSON, PRINTERS; p. [iii]: CONTENTS.; p. [v]: RECOMMENDATIONS.; p. [ix]: INTRODUCTORY REMARKS. [signed] THE EDITOR. | *New York, March*, 1832.; p. [xvii]: A FAITHFUL NARRATIVE | OF THE | SURPRISING WORK OF GOD, | IN THE | CONVERSION OF MANY HUNDRED SOULS | IN NORTHAMPTON, | AND THE NEIGHBORING TOWNS AND VILLAGES OF NEW HAMPSHIRE, | IN NEW ENGLAND: | *In A Letter to the Rev. Doctor Colman*, | At that time Pastor of Brattle street Church, Boston. | [short rule] | BY PRESIDENT EDWARDS. | [short rule] | WITH PREFACES, | By the Rev. Dr. Watts and Dr. Guyse of London, and by the Boston Ministers. (verso blank); p. [xix]: PREFACE, | BY DR. WATTS AND DR. GUYSE. [signed] ISAAC WATTS. | JOHN GUYSE. | *London, October* 12, 1737.; p. [xxvi]: PREFACE, | BY THE BOSTON MINISTERS. [signed] *Boston, November 4th*, 1738. | JOSEPH SEWALL, | Minister of Old South Church. | THOMAS PRINCE, | Minister of Old South Church. | JOHN WEBB, | Minister of New North Church. | WILLIAM COOPER, | Minister of Brattle street Church.; p. [xxx]: TO THE | REV. BENJAMIN COLMAN, D. D. | PASTOR OF A CHURCH IN BOSTON. | [short rule] | *Westfield, October* 11, 1738. [signed] WILLIAM WILLIAMS, Pastor of Hatfield. | EBENEZER DEVOTION, " of Suffield. | STEPHEN WILLIAMS, " of Longmeadow. | PETER REYNOLDS, " of Enfield. | NEHEMIAH BULL, " of Westfield. | SAMUEL HOPKINS, " of West Springfield.; p. [31]: A FAITHFUL NARRATIVE.; p. [112]: blank; p. [113]: THOUGHTS | ON | THE REVIVAL OF RELIGION | IN NEW ENGLAND, | AND | THE WAY IN WHICH IT OUGHT TO BE ACKNOWLEDGED | AND PROMOTED. | IN FIVE PARTS. | [short rule] | BY JONATHAN EDWARDS, A. M. | PASTOR OF THE CHURCH OF CHRIST, AT NORTHAMPTON | [short rule] | Prepare ye the way of the Lord, make straight in the desert a highway for | our God......ISAIAH xl. 3. (verso blank); p. [115]: PREFACE.; p. [117]: THOUGHTS ON THE REVIVAL, &c.; p. [412]: blank; p. [413]: INDEX.; p. [423]: A TABLE OF SCRIPTURE TEXTS, | CITED OR ILLUSTRATED IN THIS VOLUME.

THJ 30 NUC NE0046544 OCLC 39491370
Harvard Divinity School

37 • EDWARDS ON REVIVALS: | CONTAINING | A FAITHFUL NARRATIVE | OF THE | SURPRISING WORK OF GOD IN THE CONVERSION OF | MANY HUNDRED SOULS IN NORTHAMPTON, | MASSACHUSETTS, A.D. 1735. | ALSO, | THOUGHTS | ON THE | REVIVAL OF RELIGION IN NEW ENGLAND, 1742, | AND THE WAY IN WHICH IT OUGHT TO BE ACKNOWLEDGED | AND IMPROVED. | BY JONATHAN EDWARDS, A.M., | PASTOR OF THE CHURCH OF CHRIST IN NORTHAMPTON; AFTERWARDS PRESIDENT OF | NASSAU HALL COLLEGE, PRINCETON, N. J. | WITH | INTRODUCTORY PREFACE | BY REV. JOHN ANGEL JAMES. | AND | CAREFULLY REVISED, WITH NOTES AND INTRODUCTION, | BY REV. WILLIAM PATTON, D.D., | NEW YORK, U.S., N.A. | LONDON: | PUBLISHED BY JOHN SNOW, 35, PATERNOSTER ROW. | 1839.

23.7 x 14.9 cm.; π^1, a-b^4, B-P^4, Q^2; xvii, [1], 116 p.

Notes: in two columns; paper covers repeat the title within decorative rules, adding *Price Two Shillings*.

Contents: p. [i]: title; p. [ii]: LONDON: | Printed by A. SIMPSON, Warwick Lane, | Paternoster Row.; p. [iii]: INTRODUCTORY PREFACE. [signed] J. A. JAMES | *Edgbaston, June* 19, 1839; p. [v]: INTRODUCTORY PREFACE. [signed] W. PATTON | *London, July*, 1839; p. [xiii]: PREFACE. [signed] ISAAC WATTS. | JOHN GUYSE. | *London, October* 12*th*, 1737; p. [xvi]: PREFACE. [signed] JOSEPH SEWALL, | Minister of Old South Church. | THOMAS PRINCE, | Minister of Old South Church. | JOHN WEBB, | Minister of New North Church. | WILLIAM COOPER, | Minister of Brattle-street Church.; p. xvii: TO THE | REV. BENJAMIN COLMAN, D. D. | PASTOR OF A CHURCH IN BOSTON [signed] WILLIAM WILLIAMS, Pastor of Hatfield. | EBENEZER DEVOTION, Pastor of Suffield. | STEPHEN WILLIAMS, Pastor of Long Meadow. | PETER REYNOLDS, Pastor of Enfield. | NEHEMIAH BULL, Pastor of Westfield. | SAMUEL HOPKINS, Pastor of West Springfield.; p. [xviii]: CONTENTS.; p. [1]: A FAITHFUL NARRATIVE.; p. [25]: THOUGHTS ON THE REVIVAL OF RELIGION | IN NEW ENGLAND | AND THE WAY IN WHICH IT OUGHT TO BE ACKNOWLEDGED AND PROMOTED. | In Five Parts. | [short rule] | BY JONATHAN EDWARDS, A.M., | PASTOR OF THE CHURCH OF CHRIST, NORTHAMPTON. | [short rule] | Prepare ye the way of the Lord, make straight in the desert a highway for our God–ISAIAH xl. 3.

THJ 31 NUC NE0046545 OCLC 14714556
Princeton University

38 • REVIVALS OF RELIGION: | THEIR | NATURE, DEFENCE, AND MANAGEMENT. | BY THE REV. JONATHAN EDWARDS, M.A., | PASTOR OF THE CHURCH OF CHRIST AT NORTHAMPTON, | IN CONNECTICUT. | ABRIDGED BY THE REV. JOHN WESLEY, A.M., | LATE FELLOW OF LINCOLN COLLEGE, OXFORD. | LONDON: | PUBLISHED BY JOHN MASON, | AT THE WESLEYAN CONFERENCE, | 14, CITY-ROAD; | AN SOLD AT 66, PATERNOSTER-ROW. | [short rule] | 1842.

14.7 x 9.1 cm.; [A]^2, B-Z^6, AA^6, BB^4; [4], 282, [1], 1 p.

Contents: prp. [1]: A NARRATIVE | OF | THE LATE WORK OF GOD, | AT AND NEAR | NORTHAMPTON, IN NEW-ENGLAND. | EXTRACTED FROM MR. EDWARDS'S LETTER TO | DR. COLEMAN. (verso blank); prp. [3]: title; prp. [4]: LONDON: | PRINTED BY JAMES NICHOLS, | HOXTON-SQUARE.; p. [1]: NARRATIVE | OF | THE LATE WORK OF GOD, | AT AND NEAR | NORTHAMPTON, IN NEW-ENGLAND.; p. [81]: THOUGHTS | CONCERNING THE | PRESENT REVIVAL OF RELIGION | IN | NEW-ENGLAND. | Prepare ye the way of the Lord, make straight in the desert a high- | way for our God.–Isaiah xl. 3. (verso blank); pp. [83]-282: text; pp. [1]-2: [advertisement].

NSE 0006148 OCLC 7845927
Asbury Theological Seminary

39 • [Extracts.]

Notes: no caption title; part of Success of the Gospel in America, extracted from *The Christian History*, nos. 15 and 16 (see 17).

Contents: pp. 288-292 in HISTORICAL COLLECTIONS | RELATING TO | REMARKABLE PERIODS | OF THE | SUCCESS OF THE GOSPEL. | COMPILED BY | THE REV. JOHN GILLIES, D.D. | [short rule] | PUBLISHED ORIGINALLY IN 1754, AND NOW REPRINTED WITH A PREFACE AND | CONTINUATION TO THE PRESENT TIME; | BY | THE REV. HORATIUS BONAR, | KELSO. | [short rule] | KELSO: | JOHN RUTHERFURD, MARKET PLACE. | EDINBURGH: | JOHN JOHNSTONE; W. P. KENNEDY; CHARLES ZIEGLER; | WILLIAM OLIPHANT & SONS; AND ROBERT OGLE. | CARLISLE: J. F. WHITRIDGE. | LONDON: JAMES NISBET & CO.; R. GROOMBRIDGE. | [short rule] | MDCCCXLV.

23.5 x 15.5 cm.; π^8, $[A]^4$, $B\text{-}Z^4$, $2A\text{-}2Z^4$, $3A\text{-}3Z^4$, $4A\text{-}4C^4$, $4D^3$; xvi, viii, [9]-582 p.

THJ 32 OCLC 6561010

Princeton Theological Seminary

39A • [Extracts.]

Notes: facsimile reprint; title page (verso): *First Banner of Truth Trust edition* 1981.

Gordon-Conwell Theological Seminary

40 • [Extracts.]

Notes: no caption title; title page (verso): Entered according to Act of Congress, in the year 1859, by the American | Tract Society, in the Clerk's Office of the District Court for the Southern | District of New York.

Contents: pp. 71-75 in REVIVAL | SKETCHES AND MANUAL. | IN TWO PARTS. | BY REV. HEMAN HUMPHREY, D. D., | PITTSFIELD, MASS. | [short rule] | PUBLISHED BY THE | AMERICAN TRACT SOCIETY, | 150 NASSAU-STREET, NEW YORK.

18.8 x 11.2 cm.; $[1]^{12}$, $2\text{-}19^{12}$, 20^{11}; 476, [2] p.

THJ 33 OCLC 2783484

Princeton Theological Seminary

40A • [Extracts.]

Notes: title page (verso): SPRINKLE PUBLICATIONS | P. O. Box 1094 | Harrisonburg, Virginia 22801 | [ornament] | First published by the American Tract Society | 150 Nassau-Street, New York | [ornament] | Entered according to Act of Congress, in the year 1859, by the | American Tract Society, in the Clerk's Office of the District | Court for the Southern District of New York. | [ornament] | Typesetting by Strait Gate Publications, Salem, Virginia. | Editing and Indexes compiled for this reprint | by G. Wm. Fowler, Jr. | [ornament] | This reprint by Sprinkle Publications 1999.

21.2 x 13.5 cm.; xxiv, 396 p.

OCLC 42936766

Pensacola Christian College

41 • Jonathan Edwards | *The Narrative* | Being a faithful narrative of the surprising work | of God in the conversion of souls in Northampton | and neighboring towns and villages in New Eng- | land, in a letter to the Rev. Doctor Colman of | Boston, on November 6, 1736. | Abridged | *With Preface, Biographical Sketch,* | *Notes and Comments* | by | James A. Stewart | *Author - Missionary* | Author of | *Heaven's Throne Gift,* | *Evangelism,* | *The Lordship of Christ,* | *etc., etc.* | KREGEL PUBLICATIONS | Grand Rapids 6, Michigan | 1957

21 x 13 cm.; 82 p.

Contents: p. [1]: *Jonathan Edwards:* | *The Narrative*; p. [2]: [quotation] [signed] JONATHAN EDWARDS; p. [3]: title; p. [4]: Copyright 1957 by | James A. Stewart | [2 lines]; p. [5]: [dedication] (verso blank); p. [7]: Contents (verso blank); p. 9: Preface; p. [14]: blank; p. 15: Biographical Sketch; pp. 19-82: text.

OCLC 382754

Harvard Divinity School

42 • JONATHAN EDWARDS | A NARRATIVE OF | SURPRISING | CONVERSIONS | SOVEREIGN GRACE PUBLISHERS | Wilmington, Delaware 19808 | 1972

21.7 x 13.8 cm.; 109, [3] p.

Contents: p. [1]: JONATHAN EDWARDS | A NARRATIVE OF | SURPRISING | CONVERSIONS (verso blank); p. [3]: title (verso blank); p. [5]: CONTENTS; p. 7: A NARRATIVE OF SURPRISING CONVERSIONS; p. 52: THE | DISTINGUISHING MARKS | OF A | WORK OF THE SPIRIT OF GOD; p. 101: AN ACCOUNT OF THE | REVIVAL OF RELIGION IN NORTHAMPTON | IN 1740-1742, AS COMMUNICATED IN A LETTER | TO A MINISTER OF BOSTON; pp. [110-112]: [advertisement].

OCLC 4456770

Towson University

43 • A FAITHFUL | NARRATIVE | OF THE | SURPRISING | WORK OF GOD | JONATHAN EDWARDS | BAKER BOOK HOUSE | Grand Rapids, Michigan

17.4 x 13 cm.; 101, [1] p.

Contents: p. [1]: p. A FAITHFUL | NARRATIVE | OF THE | SURPRISING | WORK OF GOD (verso blank); p. [3]: title; p. [4]: Reprinted 1979 by Baker Book House | Formerly published in | *Thoughts on the Revival of Religion in New England* | issued by the American Tract Society | [4 lines]; p. [5]: CONTENTS (verso blank); p. [7]: NARRATIVE | OF THE | SURPRISING WORK OF GOD. | 1735.; p. [102]: blank.

ISBN 0801033543 OCLC 6387494

Manchester College

44 • THE | SURPRISING | WORK OF | GOD | JONATHAN | EDWARDS | [publisher's device] *Whitaker House*

20.5 x 13.2 cm.; 122 p.

Contents: p. [1]: THE | SURPRISING | WORK OF | GOD (verso blank); p. [3]: title; p. [4]: [5 lines] | © 1997 by Whitaker House | Whitaker House | 30 Hunt Valley Circle | New Kensington, PA 15068 | [16 lines]; p. [5]: What follows is Jonathan Edwards' personal, | eyewitness account of the awesome move of | the Holy Spirit throughout New England | during the Great Awakening, 1734-35. (verso blank); p. [7]: Contents (verso blank); pp. 9-122: text.

ISBN 0883682370 OCLC 37451804

Harvard Divinity School

45 • Nollaun hoesim iyagi | Yonjok taegaksong pogoso | Jonathan Edwards | Chung Boohong Jung | [publisher's device] | Kidokkyo Munso Son'gyohoe

21 x 13.5 cm.; 161, [3] p.

Notes: a Korean translation of *Faithful Narrative*.

Contents: p. [1]: title; p. [2]: *A Faithful Narrative of* | *the Surprising Work of God* | in the Conversion of Many Hundred Souls, | in Northampton, and the Neighbouring Towns | and Villages of New Hampshire in New England; | in A Letter to the Rev. Dr. Colman of Boston. | *By* | Jonathan Edwards | *Translated by* | Boohong Jung | Korean edition | Copyright © 1997 by Christian Literature Crusade | Seoul, Korea; p. [3]: [recommendation]; p. [6]: [translator's introduction]; p. [8]: [editor's introduction]; p. [21]: [contents]; (facing p. 22: photocopy of the first page of the letter to Colman [in Korean]); pp. [25]-144: text; p. [145]: [Sinners in the Hands of an Angry God]; p. [158]: blank; p. [159]: [Edwards's postscript]; pp. [162-163]:[publication data]; p. [164]: blank.

ISBN 8934105836 OCLC 50534467

Gordon-Conwell Theological Seminary

LETTERS

46 • A | LETTER | TO THE | AUTHOR | OF THE | PAMPHLET | Called | An Answeer to the |

Hampſhire Narrative. | [rule] | Prov. XXX. xxxii. *If thou haſt done fooliſhly in lifting* | *up thy ſelf, if thou haſt thought evil, lay thine Hand* | *upon thy Mouth.* | [rule] | [ornament] | [rule] | *BOSTON:* Printed in the Year 1737. *stet* ANSWEER

8vo.; 18.3 x 11.5 cm. (uncut); [A]^4, B-L^4; [4], 84 p.

Notes: unsigned; in some copies, *ERRATA.* slip mounted on p. 84.

Contents: prp. [1]: A | Letter to the Author | of the ANSWER to the | *Hampſhire Narrative.* (verso blank); prp. [3]: title; prp. [4]: The PREFACE.; p. 1: A | LETTER, *&c*.; slip inserted following p. 84: *ERRATA.*

THJ 34 EAI 1:4152 NUC NE0046706 OCLC 7579249

Massachusetts Historical Society

47 • *From* ſeven *Rev.* Paſtors *in the* County *of* | Hampſhire.

Notes: signed by Stephen Williams, *Pastor of a Church in* Springfield. | Peter Reynolds, *Pastor of the Church in* Enfield. | Jonathan Edwards, *Pastor of the Church in* Northampton. | Samuel Allis, *Pastor of the Church in* Somers. | John Woodbridge, *Pastor in the ſecond Church in* Hadley. | David Parsons, jun. *Pastor of the third Church in* Hadley. | Edward Billing, *Pastor of the Church in* Cold Spring. | County of *Hampſhire,* | *June* 30. 1743.; reprinted (slightly altered) in *The Christian Monthly History*, no. 3 (January 1744):32-34; see *Works* (Yale), 16:111-112; Rev. Timothy Woodbridge, of Hatfield, and Rev. Chester Williams, of Hadley, sign another, shorter attestation following the first (p. 180).

Contents: caption title; *The Christian History*, no. 23 (August 6, 1743):178-180.

THJ 35 OCLC 4045567

Congregational Library

48 • NEW-ENGLAND. | Continuation *of the State of Religion at* NORTHAMP- | TON *in the County of* HAMPSHIRE *about a hundred* | *Miles* weſtward *of* BOSTON; *By the Rev. Mr.* ED- | WARDS, *in a letter to the Rev. Mr.* PRINCE, *dated* | Dec. 12. 1743.

Notes: see *Works* (Yale), 16:115-127.

Contents: caption title; *The Christian History*, no. 46 (January 14, 1743):367-368; no. 47 (January 21, 1743):369-376; no. 48 (January 28, 1743):377-381.

OCLC 4045567

Congregational Library

49 • Copies of the | TWO LETTERS | Cited by | The Rev. Mr. CLAP, Rector of the College | at NEW-HAVEN, | In his late printed Letter to a Friend in *Boſton*, con- | cerning what he has reported, as from Mr. | EDWARDS of *Northampton*, concerning the Rev. | Mr. WHITEFIELD. | Communicated in | *A Letter to a Friend.* | With ſome Reflections on the Affair thoſe | Letters relate to, and Rector CLAP'S Manage- | ment therein. | [rule] | By *JONATHAN EDWARDS,* A. M. | Miniſter of the Goſpel at *Northampton*, and Writer of | thoſe Letters. | [rule] | *BOSTON:* | Printed and Sold by *S. Kneeland* and *T. Green* in | Queen-Street. 1745.

8vo.; 15.6 x 11.3 cm. (uncut); [A]-B^4; 16 p.

Contents: p. [1]: title; p. 2: *A Copy of the firſt Letter cited by the Rev. Mr.* | Clap. [signed] *Jonathan Edwards.* | *Northampton Oct.* 18. 1744.; p. 5: *A Copy of the ſecond Letter cited by Mr.* Clap. [signed] *Northampton, Feb.* | 4th 1744, 5. | *Jonathan Edwards.*

THJ 36 EAI 1:5581 NUC NE0046506 OCLC 13364877

Congregational Library

50 • AN | Expoſtulatory Letter | From the Rev. | Mr. *Edwards* of *Northampton,* | TO THE | Rev. Mr. *Clap,* | Rector of *Yale College* in *New-Haven,* | In Reply to his late printed Letter to him, relat- | ing to what he reported concerning the Rev. Mr. | WHITEFIELD, at *Boſton* and *Cambridge* and | elſewhere,

as from Mr. *Edwards*; making the | Falſity of that Report yet much more manifeſt. | [rule] | Job. 34. 4. *Let us chuſe to ourſelves Judgment; let us | know among ourſelves what is good.* | [rule] | *BOSTON:* Printed and Sold by *Kneeland* and | *Green* in *Queenſtreet*. 1745.

8vo.; 15.8 x 10.8 cm. (uncut); [A]-B^4; 16 p.

Contents: p. [1]: title (verso blank); p. 3: *A Letter*, &c. [signed] *Jonathan Edwards* | *Northampton*, | May 20. 1745.

THJ 37 NUC NE0046558 OCLC 39311696

Harvard Divinity School

51 • *To the Rev. Mr.* James Robe *Miniſter of the Goſpel* | *at* Kilſyth *in* Scotland.

Notes: dated *Northampton, May* 12, 1743 and signed JONATHAN EDWARDS.; see *Works* (Yale), 16:107-110.

Contents: caption title; *The Christian Monthly History*, no. 5 (August 1745):127-130.

THJ 38 OCLC 8704380

Congregational Library

52 • *Mr.* Edwards's *Letter* to his Scots *Correspondent.*

Notes: dated Northamptoun [*sic*], Nov. 20, 1745, and signed JONATHAN EDWARDS., the letter was probably to Rev. John MacLaurin, Glasgow; see *Works* (Yale), 16:179-197.

Contents: caption title; *The Christian Monthly History*, no. 8 (November 1745):234-254.

THJ 39 OCLC 8704380

Congregational Library

53 • *Extract of a Part of the Reverend Mr.* Jonathan | Edwards'*s Letter, concerning Mr.* Whitefield'*s Pro- | greſs, Reception, and Succeſs in* New-England.

Notes: probably after September 16, 1745, to friends in Scotland; see *Works* (Yale), 16:174-179.

Contents: caption title; *The Christian Monthly History*, no. 9 (December 1745):259-263.

THJ 40 OCLC 8704380

Congregational Library

54 • A LETTER FROM REV. JONATHAN EDWARDS, TO HON. | THOMAS HUBBARD, ESQ. OF BOSTON, RELATING TO | THE INDIAN SCHOOL AT STOCKBRIDGE. | STOCKBRIDGE, AUG. 31, 1751.

Notes: see *Works* (Yale), 16:[394]-405.

Contents: caption title; *Collections of the Massachusetts Historical Society*, 10 (1809):142-153.

THJ 41 OCLC 1756821

Massachusetts Historical Society

55 • *Letter from President Edwards.*

Notes: dated *Northampton, May* 18, 1742, to MY DEAR FRIEND; probably a letter dated May 10, 1742, to Deacon Moses Lyman, Goshen. Reprinted in *Bibliotheca Sacra*, 28 (January 1871):95-97; see *Works* (Yale), 16:101-103.

Contents: running title; *The Spirit of the Pilgrims*, 6 (September 1833):545-546.

THJ 42 OCLC 6052803

Gordon-Conwell Theological Seminary

56 • ORIGINAL LETTER FROM PRESIDENT EDWARDS.

Notes: dated Northampton, June 15, 1750, to Joseph Bellamy, the letter is followed by "an account of the doings of the council that sat here last week," which was published in Boston, apparently by Edwards, later that year as The RESULT | Of a COUNCIL of Nine Churches | Met at Northampton, *June* 22. 1750. | WITH | A PROTEST againſt the ſame, | By a Number of the ſaid Council; it closes with a plea for prayers–"we are now thrown upon the ocean of the wide world"–a sentiment echoed in Edwards's letter to John Erskine twenty days later–"I am now as it were thrown upon the wide ocean of the world." No manuscript has been found for the Bellamy letter; for the Erskine letter, see *Works* (Yale), 16: 347-356.

Contents: caption title; *Evangelical and Literary Magazine* 5 (July 1822):366.

OCLC 5879138

Gordon-Conwell Theological Seminary

57 • ARTICLE VI. | ORIGINAL LETTER OF PRESIDENT EDWARDS.

Notes: dated Stockbridge, Nov. 18, 1757 [i.e., 1754] to Maj. Joseph Hawley; see *Works* (Yale), 16:645-654.

Contents: caption title; *Bibliotheca Sacra*, 1 (August 1844):579-591.

THJ 43 OCLC 6288728

Gordon-Conwell Theological Seminary

58 • *The Rev.* Mr EDWARDS *of Stockbridge to the Rev.* Mr ERS- | KINE *of Culross, April* 12, 1757.

Notes: see *Works* (Yale), 16:702-705.

Contents: caption title; pp. 522-523 in HISTORICAL COLLECTIONS | RELATING TO | REMARKABLE PERIODS | OF THE | SUCCESS OF THE GOSPEL. | COMPILED BY | THE REV. JOHN GILLIES, D.D. | [short wavy rule] | PUBLISHED ORIGINALLY IN 1754, AND NOW REPRINTED WITH A PREFACE AND | CONTINUATION TO THE PRESENT TIME; | BY | THE REV. HORATIUS BONAR, | KELSO: | [short wavy rule] | KELSO: | JOHN RUTHERFURD, MARKET PLACE. | EDINBURGH: | JOHN JOHNSTONE; W. P. KENNEDY; CHARLES ZIEGLER; | WILLIAM OLIPHANT & SONS; AND ROBERT OGLE. | CARLISLE: J. F. WHITRIDGE. | LONDON: JAMES NISBET & CO.; R. GROOMBRIDGE. | [short rule] | MDCCCXLV.

8vo.; 23.5 x 15.5 cm.; π^8, $[A]^4$, $B\text{-}Z^4$, $2A\text{-}2Z^4$, $3A\text{-}3Z^4$, $4A\text{-}4C^4$, $4D^3$; xvi, viii, [9]-582 p.

THJ 44 OCLC 6561010

Princeton Theological Seminary

58A • *The Rev.* Mr EDWARDS *of Stockbridge to the Rev.* Mr ERS- | KINE *of Culross, April* 12, 1757.

Notes: facsimile reprint; title page (verso): *First Banner of Truth Trust edition* 1981.

ISBN 0851513255 OCLC 7870401

Gordon-Conwell Theological Seminary

59 • VII. | LETTERS WRITTEN BY THE CELEBRATED PRESIDENT | EDWARDS, AND THE VENERABLE CORNELIUS WINTER | COMMUNICATED BY SIR JOHN DICKERTON WILLIAMS, FROM ORIGINALS IN | HIS POSSESSION: NOT BEFORE PRINTED. | PRESIDENT EDWARDS addressed the following letter to the | 'Rev. Thomas Prince, in Boston.' Mr. Prince has endorsed | upon it—'On the death of my dear daughter Deborah.'

Notes: dated Northampton, July 27, 1744; see *Works* (Yale), 16:146-147.

Contents: caption title; *The Biblical Review and Congregational Magazine*, 1 (1846):223-224.

THJ 45 OCLC 1776520

Harvard Divinity School

60 • LETTER OF JONATHAN EDWARDS.

Notes: dated Northampton, May 22, 1744, to Benjamin Colman; see *Works* (Yale), 16:144-45.

Contents: caption title; *Proceedings of the Massachusetts Historical Society*, 2d ser., 10 (January 1896):429.

THJ 46 OCLC 16955300

Massachusetts Historical Society

61 • *The Manuscripts of Jonathan Edwards.*

Notes: parts of two letters, one dated March 25, 1743, to Sarah Pierpont Edwards, the other dated January 15, 1746/7, to Joseph Bellamy; see *Works* (Yale), 16:104-105 and 216-218.

Contents: caption title; *Proceedings of the Massachusetts Historical Society*, 2d ser., 15 (March 1901):8-9, 12-14.

THJ 47 OCLC 16955300
Massachusetts Historical Society

62 • *Jonathan Edwards at Portsmouth, New Hampshire.*
Notes: dated July 28, 1749, to Mary Edwards; see *Works* (Yale), 16:288-290.
Contents: caption title; *Proceedings of the Massachusetts Historical Society*, 2d ser., 15 (March 1901):19-20.
OCLC 16955300
Massachusetts Historical Society

63 • SIX LETTERS OF JONATHAN EDWARDS TO | JOSEPH BELLAMY.
Notes: dated Northampton, October 3, 1746; Northampton, January 15, 1746/7; Northampton, June 11, 1747; Northampton, April 4, 1748; Northampton, December 6, 1749; and Stockbridge, [June 1756]; see *Works* (Yale), 16:211, 216-218, 223, 245-246, 308-310, and 688-689.
Contents: caption title; *The New England Quarterly*, 1 (April 1928):226-242.
THJ 48 OCLC 1759778
Massachusetts Historical Society

64 • AN UNPUBLISHED LETTER BY JONATHAN EDWARDS.
Notes: dated May 7, 1750, to Peter Clark, Salem Village; see *Works* (Yale), 16:341-347.
Contents: caption title; *The New England Quarterly* 29 (June 1956):228-233.
OCLC 1759778
Massachusetts Historical Society

DISCOURSES ON VARIOUS IMPORTANT SUBJECTS

65 • DISCOURSES | on Various | *Important Subjects*, | Nearly concerning the great Affair of the Soul's | Eternal Salvation, | Viz. | I. Juſtification by Faith alone. | II. Preſſing into the Kingdom of GOD. | III. *Ruth*'s Reſolution. | IV. The Juſtice of GOD in the Damnation | of Sinners. | V. The Excellency of JESUS CHRIST. | Delivered at *Northampton*, chiefly at the Time of the | late wonderful pouring out of the Spirit of GOD | there. | [rule] | By *Jonathan Edwards*, A.M. | Paſtor of the Church of CHRIST in *Northampton* | [rule] | Deut. iv. 8.—*Take heed to thy ſelf, and keep thy Soul dili- | gently, leaſt thou forget the Things which thine Eyes have ſeen, | and leaſt they depart from thy Heart all the Days of thy Life*. | [rule] | *BOSTON*: Printed and Sold by S. KNEELAND and | T. GREEN, in Queen-ſtreet over againſt the Priſon. | MDCCXXXVIII.
8vo.; 17.3 x 10.7 cm.; [A]^4, B-D^8, E-Z^4, Aa-Ll^4; [2], vi, 286, [2] p.
Notes: p. 26 misnumbered 30; p. 30 misnumbered 26; p. 160 misnumbered 15 (pp. 1-25, 30, 27-29, 26, 31-159, 15, 161-286); in some copies, the numbering is corrected; the text on the title page is usually cited as Deut. 4:9.
Contents: prp. [1]: title (verso blank); p. [i]: PREFACE.; p. vi: *ERRATA*.; p. 1: JUSTIFICATION | BY | *Faith* alone.; p. 131: Preſſing into the Kingdom | of GOD.; p. 173: *Ruth*'s Reſolution.; p. 192: The Juſtice of GOD in the | Damnation of Sinners.; p. 244: The Excellency of | *CHRIST*.; pp. [287-288]: blank.
THJ 49 EAI 1:4239 NUC NE0046509 OCLC 3695344
American Antiquarian Society

THE DISTINGUISHING MARKS OF A WORK OF THE SPIRIT OF GOD

66 • THE | Diſtinguiſhing Marks | Of a Work of the | SPIRIT of GOD. | Applied to that uncommon

Operation that has | lately appeared on the Minds of many of the | People of this Land: | With a particular Confideration of the extraor- | dinary Circumftances with which this Work | is attended. | A DISCOURSE | Delivered at *New-Haven, September* 10th 1741. | Being the Day after the Commencement; | And now Publifhed at the earneft Defire of many | Minifters and other Gentlemen that heard it; with | great Enlargements. | [rule] | By *Jonathan Edwards*, A. M. | Paftor of the Church of CHRIST at *Northampton.* | [rule] | With a Preface by the Rev. Mr. COOPER of *Bofton.* | [rule] | Joh 10. 4, 5. *And the Sheep follow him, for they know his* | *Voice; and a Stranger will they not follow, but will flee* | *from him, for they know not the Voice of Strangers.* | [rule] | *BOSTON*: Printed and Sold by S. KNEELAND and | T. GREEN, in Queenftreet, over againft the Prifon. 1741. *stet* Joh

8vo.; 16 x 10.5 cm. (uncut); [a]^4, aa^4, aaa^2, B-P^4; [2], xviii, 110, [2] p.

Contents: prp. [1]: title (verso blank); p. i: TO THE | READER. [signed] Bofton, Nov. 20. | 1741. | W. Cooper.; p. 1: The Marks of a Work of | the true SPIRIT.; p. 110: *ERRATA*.; pp. [111-112]: blank.

THJ 50 EAI 1:4711 NUC NE0046514 OCLC 3253047

Massachusetts Historical Society

67 • THE | DISTINGUISHING MARKS | Of a WORK of the | SPIRIT of GOD. | Applied to that UNCOMMON OPERATION that | has lately appeared on the Minds of many of | the People of this Land: | With a particular Confideration of the extraordinary | Circumftances with which this Work is attended. | A DISCOURSE | Delivered at *New-Haven, September* 10th, 1741. | Being the Day after the Commencement; | And now publifhed at the earneft Defire of many | Minifters and other Gentlemen that heard it; with | great Enlargements. | [rule] | By *Jonathan Edwards*, A. M. | Paftor of the Church of CHRIST at *Northampton.* | [rule] | With a Preface by the Rev. Mr. COOPER of *Bofton.* | [rule] | JOHN 10. 4, 5. *And the Sheep follow him, for they know his Voice; and a* | *Stranger will they not follow, but will flee from him, for they know not* | *the Voice of Strangers.* | [rule] | BOSTON, *Printed:* | PHILADELPHIA, *Re-printed and Sold by* BENJAMIN | FRANKLIN, *in Market-Street*, 1742.

8vo.; 15.7 x 9.8; [A]^4, B-M^4, N^2; xvi, 84 p.

Contents: p. [i]: title (verso blank); p. [iii]: TO THE | READER [signed] Bofton, Nov. 20. | 1741. | W. COOPER.; p. 1: THE | MARKS of a WORK | OF THE | TRUE SPIRIT.; p. 84: *ERRATA*.

THJ 51 EAI 1:4937 NUC NE0046517

Historical Society of Pennsylvania

68 • THE | DISTINGUISHING MARKS | OF A | WORK | OF THE | SPIRIT of GOD, | Applied to that uncommon OPERATION that has | lately appeared on the Minds of many of the | People in *New-England*: | WITH A | Particular CONSIDERATION of the extraordinary CIRCUM- | STANCES with which this WORK is attended. | [rule] | By JONATHAN EDWARDS, *A M.* | Paftor of the Church of CHRIST at *Northampton*, and | Author of the *New-England* NARRATIVE, which was | lately reprinted at *London*, and recommended by the | Rev. Dr. *I. Watts*, and Dr. *Guyfe*. | [rule] | With a Preface by the Rev. Mr. COOPER of *Bofton*, | and Letters from the Rev. Dr. COLMAN, giving | fome Account of the prefent Work of GOD in | thofe Parts. | [rule] | *BOSTON:* Printed 1741. | *LONDON:* Reprinted by S. MASON Book- | feller in *Wood-Street*. MDCCXLII. *stet A M.*

8vo.; 21.2 x 13.2 cm.; π^1, [A]^4, B-H^4, I^2, [a]^2, K^2; [2], xii, [13]-76 p.

Contents: prp. [1]: THE | DISTINGUISHING MARKS | OF A | WORK | OF THE | SPIRIT of GOD.; prp. [2]: [advertisement] | *ERRATA*.; p. [i]: title (verso blank); p. [iii]: TO THE | READER. [signed] | Bofton, Nov. 20. | 1741. | W. COOPER.; p. [13]: THE | MARKS of a WORK | OF THE | TRUE SPIRIT.; p. [69]: LETTERS | FROM | *NEW-ENGLAND*,

| Confirming the Truth of a great and confpi- | cuous Work of God on the Souls of Men | there.

THJ 52 ESTC N2948 NUC NE0046516 OCLC 14756353

Harvard Divinity School

69 • THE | DISTINGUISHING MARKS | OF A | WORK | OF THE | SPIRIT of GOD, | Applied to that uncommon OPERATION that | has lately appeared on the Minds of many | of the People in *New-England:* | WITH A | Particular CONSIDERATION of the extraordinary | CIRCUMSTANCES with which this WORK is | attended. | [rule] | By *JONATHAN EDWARDS*, A. M. | Paftor of the Church of CHRIST at *Northampton*, and AU- | THOR of the *New-England* NARRATIVE. | [rule] | With a PREFACE by the Rev. Mr. COOPER of *Bofton*, | and LETTERS from the Rev. Dr. COLMAN, giving | fome ACCOUNT of the prefent WORK of *GOD* in | thofe Parts. | [rule] | To which is prefix'd, an Epiftle to the *Scots* Reader, by the | Rev. Mr. *John Willifon*, Minifter of the Gofpel at *Dundee*. | [rule] | *GLASGOW* | Printed for R. SMITH, at the *Gilt-Bible*, oppofite | to *Gibfon's Land, Salt-Mercat*. MDCCXLII.

8vo.; 15.9 x 9.3 cm.; π^4, A-K^4, L^2; [8], iii-xiv, 15-86 [i.e., 84] p.

Notes: lacks pp. i-ii; prp. [2]: T*HE Rev. Mr.* GEORGE WHITEFIELD | (*befides his frequent Commendations of* | *this* Pamphlet *in his* Sermons *to his Audience*) | *gives the following Character of it, in a Letter to* | *the Rev. Mr.* WILLIAM M'CULLOCH, *Mini-* | *fter at* Cambuflang. | "THERE is a *Sermon* lately publifhed by | "Mr. EDWARDS of *Northampton* in *New-Eng-* | "*land*, and printed in *London*, which I defire | "you and your Friends would have, and | "recommend most earnestly. 'Tis the beft | "Thing of its Kind I ever faw. You would | "think the *Author* had been at *Cambuflang*." | See the *Weekly History*, No. 25.

Contents: prp. [1]: title; prp. [2]: *Advertifement*.; prp. [3]: PREFACE | TO THE | *SCOTS* READER. [signed] *Dundee, June* 23*d*. | 1742. | JO. WILLISON.; prp. [8]: blank; p. iii: TO THE | READER. [signed] *BOSTON*, | Novem. 20. 1741. | [brace] | W. COOPER.; p. 15: THE | MARKS of a WORK | OF THE | TRUE SPIRIT.; p. 81: LETTERS | FROM | *NEW-ENGLAND*, | Confirming the Truth of a great and con- | fpicuous Work of God on the Souls of | Men there.

THJ 53 ESTC 181993 NUC NE0046522 OCLC 38911664

Yale Divinity School

70 • THE | DISTINGUISHING MARKS | OF A | WORK | OF THE | SPIRIT of GOD, | APPLIED TO | That uncommon OPERATION that has lately | appear'd on the Minds of many of the People | in *New--England:* | WITH A | Particular CONSIDERATION of the extraordinary CIR- | CUMSTANCES with which this WORK is attended. | [rule] | By JONATHAN EDWARDS, *A. M.* | Paftor of the Church of CHRIST at *Northampton*, and Author | of the *New-England* NARRATIVE, which was lately reprin- | ted at *Edinburgh*, and recommended by the Rev. Dr. *I. Watts* | and Dr. *Guyfe*. | [rule] | With a Preface by the Rev. Mr. COOPER of *Bofton*, and Let- | ters from the Rev. Dr. COLMAN, giving fome Account of the | prefent Work of GOD in thofe Parts. | [rule] | To which is prefix'd, an Epiftle to the *Scots* Reader, by the Rev. | Mr. JOHN WILLISON Minifter of the Gofpel at *Dundee*. | [rule] | *EDINBURGH*, | Printed by T. LUMISDEN and J. ROBERTSON, and fold at their | Printing-houfe in the *Fifh-market*, and by J. TRAILL Book- | feller in the *Parliament-clofs*. M.DCC.XLII. *stet clofs*

8vo.; 17.7 x 10.8 cm.; $[A]^4$, B-K^4; xvi, 17-80 p.

Notes: sig. D_2 mislettered B_2.

Contents: p. [i]: title (verso blank); p. iii: PREFACE | TO THE | *SCOTS* READER. [signed] *Dundee, June* 23. | 1742. | JO. WILLISON.; p. vii: TO THE | READER. [signed] Bofton, Nov. 20. | 1741. | W. COOPER.; p. 17: THE | MARKS of a WORK | OF THE | TRUE SPIRIT; p. 76: LETTERS | FROM | *NEW-ENGLAND*, | Confirming the Truth of a great and conspicu- | ous Work of God on the Souls of Men there.

THJ 54 ESTC N2947 NUC NE0046519 OCLC 15137991

John Carter Brown Library

71 • THE | DISTINGUISHING MARKS | OF A | WORK | OF THE | Spirit of GOD. | Extracted from Mr. EDWARDS. | Minifter of *Northampton*, in *New-England.* | [rule] | By *JOHN WESLEY*, M. A. | Fellow of *Lincoln-College, Oxford.* | [rule] | [ornament] | [double rule] | *LONDON:* | Printed by W. STRAHAN; and fold by T. TRYE, | near *Gray's-Inn Gate, Holbourn*; and at the *Foun- | dery*, near *Upper Moorfields*. MDCCXLIV. | [Price Fourpence.]

12mo.; 16.8 x 9.8 cm.; $[A]^6$, $B\text{-}D^6$; 48 p.

Contents: p. [1]: title (verso blank); p. 3: THE | Diftinguifhing Marks, *&c.*

THJ 55 ESTC N2950 NUC NE0046523 OCLC 4662980

Houghton Library

72 • THE | DISTINGUISHING MARKS | OF A | WORK | OF THE | Spirit of GOD. | Extracted from Mr. EDWARDS, | Minifter of *Northampton* in *New-England.* | [rule] | By *JOHN WESLEY*, M. A. | Late Fellow of *Lincoln-College, Oxon.* | [rule] | The SECOND EDITION. | [rule] | [ornament] | [double rule] | LONDON: | Printed by HENRY COCK; | And fold at the Foundery, near Upper Moor-fields, | by T. TRYE, at Gray's-Inn-Gate; and by R. | AKENHEAD, on Tine Bridge, Newcaftle. | MDCCLV. | [Price Four-Pence.]

12mo.; 16.3 x 8.4 cm.; $[A]^6$, $B\text{-}D^6$; 48 p.

Contents: p. [1]: title; p. 2: THE | Diftinguifhing Marks, &c.

THJ 56 ESTC T34703 NUC NE0046524 OCLC 18525068

Forbes Library

73 • THE | Diftinguifhing Marks | OF A | WORK | OF THE | *SPIRIT of GOD.* | EXTRACTED FROM MR. EDWARDS, | Minifter of Northampton, in New-England. | [rule] | By JOHN WESLEY, M. A. | Late Fellow of Lincoln College, OXON. | [rule] | *PRICE EIGHT PENCE.* | PHILADELPHIA: | PRINTED BY *PARRY HALL*, NO. 149. CHESTNUT STREET; | AND SOLD BY *JOHN DICKINS*, NO. 182. RACE | STREET, NEAR SIXTH STREET. | [short rule] | M.DCC.XCII.

12mo.; 16.4 x 10.5 cm.; $[A]^6$, $B\text{-}D^6$, 45, [3] p.

Contents: frontispiece: [engraving] | THE REV^{D}. JOHN WESLEY M.A. | AGED 88; p. [1]: title (verso blank); p. [3]: THE | Diftinguifhing Marks, &c.; p. [46]: blank; pp. [47-48]: [advertisement].

EAI 1:46436 NUC NE0046525 OCLC 30552266

Drew University

74 • THE | Diftinguifhing Marks | OF A | WORK | OF THE | *SPIRIT* of *GOD.* | Extracted from Mr. EDWARDS, | Minifter of Northampton, in New-England. | [rule] | By *JOHN WESLEY*, M. A. | Late Fellow of Lincoln-College, Oxon. | [rule] | The THIRD EDITION. | [thin-thick rule] | *LONDON:* | Printed by G. PARAMORE, North-Green, Worfhip-Street. | Sold by G. WHITFIELD, at the Chapel, City-Road; and at the | Methodift Preaching-Houfes in Town and Country. 1795. | [Price FOUR-PENCE.]

12mo.; 18.5 x 11.5 cm.; $[A]^6$, $B\text{-}C^6$, E^4; 43, [1] p.

Notes: sig. D mislettered E.

Contents: p. [1]: title; p. [2]: THE | Diftinguifhing Marks, &c.; p. [44]: blank.

ESTC N2949 OCLC 40509408

Drew University

75 • THE | Diftinguifhing Marks | OF A | WORK | OF THE | *SPIRIT* of *GOD.* | Extracted from Mr. EDWARDS, | Minifter of Northampton, in New-England. | [rule] | By JOHN WESLEY, M.A. | Late

Fellow of Lincoln College, Oxon. | [rule] | The THIRD EDITION. | [double rule] | *LONDON:* | Printed by J. PARAMORE, at the Foundery, near | Upper Moorfields; and fold at the New Chapel, | in the City Road. [Price Four-Pence.]

12mo.; 17 x 10 cm.; [A]^6, B-D^6; 48 p.
Notes: published c. 1795.
Contents: p. [1]: title; p. [2]: THE | Diftinguifhing Marks, &c.
THJ 57 ESTC T226538 NUC NE0046526 OCLC 15123189
Drew University

76 • THE | Diftinguifhing Marks | OF A | WORK | OF THE | *SPIRIT* of *GOD.* | Extracted from Mr. EDWARDS, | Minifter of Northampton, in New-England. | [rule] | By JOHN WESLEY, M. A. | Late Fellow of Lincoln College, Oxon. | [rule] | The FOURTH EDITION. | [double rule] | *DUBLIN:* | For B. DUGDALE, No. 150, CAPEL-STREET. | [short rule] | M,DCC,XC.

12mo.; 16.4 x 9.6 cm.; [A]^6, B-D^6; 48 p.
Notes: issued as the fourth edition and dated 1790, or five years before the third edition, it appears to be a reprint of the undated London issue (above).
Contents: p. [1]: title; p. [2]: THE | Diftinguifhing Marks, &c.
ESTC N8900 OCLC 40509407
Duke University

77 • THE | DISTINGUISHING MARKS | OF A | WORK | OF THE | SPIRIT OF GOD. | EXTRACTED FROM MR. EDWARDS, | Minifter of Northampton, in New-England. | [short decorative rule] | *By JOHN WESLEY, M. A.* | Late Fellow of Lincoln-College, Oxford. | [short decorative rule] | The FOURTH EDITION. | [short wavy rule] | [short decorative rule] | LONDON: | Printed at the Conference-Office, North-Green, Finsbury- | Square, G. STORY, Agent. Sold by G. WHITFIELD, | New-Chapel, City-Road: and at the | Methodift Preaching-Houfes in | Town and Country. | 1803. | Price Four-Pence.

12mo.; 18.2 x 11.1 cm.; A-C^6, D^4; 41, [3] p.
Contents: p. [1]: title (verso blank); p. [3]: THE | Diftinguifhing Marks, &c.; p. 41: Conference Office Norrth-Green [sic], Finsbury Square: GEO. STORY Agent; p. [42]: blank; pp. [43-44]: [advertisement].
OCLC 30520216
Drew University

78 • THE | MARKS OF A WORK | OF THE | *TRUE SPIRIT,* | A SERMON, | PREACHED IN THE TIME OF A GREAT AWAKENING | AND ATTENTION TO RELIGION, A.D. 1741-2. | [short decorative rule] | BY THE LATE JONATHAN EDWARDS, A. M. | Then Paftor of the firft Church in Northampton, afterwards | Prefident of the College of New-Jerfey. | [short decorative rule] | TO WHICH IS PREFIXED, | SOME BRIEF REMARKS RESPECTING | THE PRESENT | *REVIVAL OF RELIGION* | IN THE WESTERN COUNTRY. | [double rule] | PRINTED AT BOSTON, 1742— | REPRINTED AT PITTSBURGH BY JOHN ISRAEL, 1803.

12mo.; 19.3 x 11.8 cm. (uncut); [A]^6, B-H^6; xxi, [1], [23]-96 p.
Contents: [i]: title (verso blank); p. iii: *PREFACE.* [signed] J. HUGHS. | *Weft-Liberty, February 5th*, 1803.; p. ix: TO THE | READER. [signed] Bofton, Nov. 20. | 1741 | *W. Cooper.*; p. [xxii]: blank; p. [23]: THE | MARKS OF A WORK | OF THE | *TRUE SPIRIT.*
THJ 58 EAI 2:4136 NUC NE0046720 OCLC 15435828
Presbyterian Historical Society

79 • THE | DISTINGUISHING MARKS | OF | A WORK | OF THE | SPIRIT OF GOD. | *Extracted from Mr. EDWARDS,* | MINISTER OF NORTHAMPTON, IN NEW-ENGLAND. | BY JOHN WESLEY, M. A. | *Late Fellow of Lincoln-College, Oxford.*

Contents: p. [259]: title (verso blank); pp. [261]-305 in A | CHRISTIAN LIBRARY: | CONSISTING OF | EXTRACTS FROM AND ABRIDGMENTS OF | THE | CHOICEST PIECES | OF | Practical Divinity | WHICH HAVE BEEN PUBLISHED IN THE ENGLISH TONGUE. | [short decorative rule] | IN THIRTY VOLUMES: | FIRST PUBLISHED IN 1750, IN FIFTY VOLUMES, DUODECIMO | [short rule] | BY THE REV. JOHN WESLEY, A. M., | SOMETIME FELLOW OF LINCOLN COLLEGE, OXFORD. | [short rule] | Vol. XXX. | [short thick-thin rule] | *LONDON:* PUBLISHED AND SOLD BY J. KERSHAW. | 14, *City-Road, and* 66, *Paternoster-Row.* | [short rule] | 1827.

21.1 x 12.8 cm.; 481 p.

THJ 59 NUC NE0046521 OCLC 6969185

Boston University

80 • THE | WORK OF THE HOLY SPIRIT | IN | THE HUMAN HEART. | BY | REV. JONATHAN EDWARDS, M. A., | Pastor of the Church of Christ at Northampton, | in Connecticut. | BEING TWO TRACTS ON THAT SUBJECT, | ABRIDGED BY REV. JOHN WESLEY, A.M. | New-York: | PUBLISHED BY LANE & SCOTT, | 200 Mulberry-street. | JOSEPH LONGKING, PRINTER. | 1849.

15.3 x 10.4 cm.; $[1]^8$, $2\text{-}13^8$; 202, [6] p.

Notes: in some copies, collation and pagination differ: $[1]^8$, $2\text{-}12^8$, 13^6; 202, [2] p.

Contents: p. [1]: title (verso blank); p. [3]: ADVERTISEMENT. [signed] J. M'CLINTOCK | *March* 1, 1849.; p. [6]: blank; p. [7]: THE | DISTINGUISHING MARKS | OF A | WORK OF THE SPIRIT OF GOD. (verso blank); p. [9]:THE DISTINGUISHING MARKS | OF A | WORK OF THE SPIRIT OF GOD.; p. [84]: blank; p. [85]: A TREATISE | ON | RELIGIOUS AFFECTIONS: | IN THREE PARTS. | ABRIDGED BY REV. JOHN WESLEY. | PART I.–Containing the Nature of the Affections, and their | Importance in Religion. | PART II.–Showing what are no certain Signs that Religious | Affections are gracious, or that they are not. | PART III.– Showing what are Distinguishing Signs of truly | gracious and holy Affections. (verso blank); p. [87]: TO THE READER. [signed] JOHN WESLEY | BRISTOL, *September* 1, 1773; p. [89]: A TREATISE | ON | RELIGIOUS AFFECTIONS.; pp. [203-208]: blank.

NUC NE0046890 OCLC 17459517

Drew University

80A • New-York: | PUBLISHED BY CARLTON & PHILLIPS, | 200 MULBERRY-STREET. | 1853.

14.6 x 9.4 cm.; $[1]^8$, $2\text{-}13^8$; 202, [6] p.

Notes: identical with the above except for the imprint and three leaves of advertisement following p. 202.

THJ 60 NUC NE0046891 OCLC 2527722

Brown University

80B • Cincinnati: | PUBLISHED BY SWORMSTEDT & POE, | FOR THE METHODIST EPISCOPAL CHURCH, AT THE WESTERN BOOK | CONCERN, CORNER OF MAIN AND EIGHTH STREETS. | [short rule] | R. P. THOMPSON, PRINTER. | 1854.

14.9 x 9.5 cm.; $[1]^8$, $2\text{-}12^8$, 13^6; 202, [2] p.

Notes: identical with the above except for the imprint; lacks advertisement.

OCLC 24893390

Cincinnati Bible College and Seminary

80C • New-York: | PUBLISHED BY CARLTON & PHILLIPS, | 200 MULBERRY-STREET. | 1855.

14.6 x 9.3 cm.; $[1]^8$, $2\text{-}13^8$; 202, [6] p.

Notes: identical with the above except for the imprint and three leaves of advertisement following p. 202.

OCLC 18161027

Nazarene Theological Seminary

81 • THE | WORK OF THE HOLY SPIRIT | IN | THE HUMAN HEART. | BY | THE REV. JONATHAN EDWARDS, M.A., | PASTOR OF THE CHURCH OF CHRIST AT NORTHAMPTON, IN CONNECTICUT. | BEING TWO TRACTS ON THAT SUBJECT. | ABRIDGED BY THE REV. JOHN WESLEY, A.M. | REVISED BY T. O. SUMMERS, D.D. | [short decorative rule] | Nashville, Tenn.: | PUBLISHED BY E. STEVENSON & F. A. OWEN, AGENTS, | FOR THE METHODIST EPISCOPAL CHURCH, SOUTH. | 1857.

14.7 x 9.8 cm.; $[1]^{16}$, $2\text{-}6^{16}$, 7^{6}; v, [1], 7-199, [5] p.

Contents: p. [i]: title; p. [ii]: STEREOTYPED AND PRINTED BY A. A. STITT, | SOUTHERN METHODIST PUBLISHING HOUSE, NASHVILLE, TENN; p. iii: Introductory Note. [signed] The Editor. | NASHVILLE, TENN., Jan. 1, 1857; p. v: THE | DISTINGUISHING MARKS | OF A | WORK OF THE SPIRIT OF GOD. (verso blank); p. 7: THE | DISTINGUISHING MARKS | OF A | WORK OF THE SPIRIT OF GOD.; p. [82]: blank; p. 83: A TREATISE | ON | RELIGIOUS AFFECTIONS: | IN THREE PARTS. | ABRIDGED BY REV. JOHN WESLEY. | PART I.–Concerning the Nature of the Affections, and their Im- | portance in | Religion. | PART II.–Showing what are no certain Signs that Religious Affec- | tions are gracious, or that they are not. | PART III.– Showing what are Distinguishing Signs of truly gra- | cious and holy Affections. (verso blank); p. 85: To the Reader. [signed] JOHN WESLEY | BRISTOL, Sept. 1, 1773; p. 87: A TREATISE | ON | RELIGIOUS AFFECTIONS.; p. [200]: blank.; pp. [201-204]: [advertisement].

OCLC 9859407

Centenary College of Louisiana

81A • NASHVILLE, TENN.: | PUBLISHING HOUSE OF THE M. E. CHURCH, SOUTH. | J. D. BARBEE, AGENT, | 1889

14.7 x 9.8 cm.; $[1]^{16}$, $2\text{-}6^{16}$, 7^{4}; v, [1], 7-199, [1] p.

Notes: identical with the above except for the imprint and lack of advertisement.

NUC NE0046892 OCLC 27806870

Southern Methodist University

81B • NASHVILLE, TENN.: | PUBLISHING HOUSE OF THE M. E. CHURCH, SOUTH. | BARBEE & SMITH, AGENTS, | 1890.

15 x 9.8 cm.; $[1]^{16}$, $2\text{-}6^{16}$, 7^{4}; v, [1], 7-199, [1] p.

Notes: identical with the above except for the imprint.

OCLC 7988570

University of Mississippi

81C • NASHVILLE, TENN.; DALLAS, TEX.: | PUBLISHING HOUSE, M. E. CHURCH, SOUTH. | BINGHAM & SMITH, AGENTS, | 1903.

14.3 x 8.5 cm.; $[1]^{16}$, $2\text{-}6^{16}$, 7^{4}; v, [1], 7-199, [1] p.

Notes: identical with the above except for the imprint.

OCLC 16729639

North American Baptist Seminary

82 • Une œuvre du Saint-Esprit: | ses vrais signes | Jonathan Edwards | EUROPRESSE | [publisher's device]

13.5 x 21.5 cm.; 126 p.

Notes: a French translation of *Distinguishing Marks*.

Contents: p. [1]: title; p. [2]: Editions EUROPRESSE | B.P. 505 | 71322 Chalon-sur-Saône cédex | France | [6 lines] | © Préface et traduction française: Europresse s.a.r.l. 1996 | *Première impression en française 1996* | [5 lines]; p. [3]: Table des matières (verso blank); p. [5]: Préface [signed] *Les Editeurs*; pp. [21]-126: text.

ISBN 2906287776

Bibliotheque Nationale

83 • THE WORK | OF THE | HOLY SPIRIT | IN THE | HUMAN HEART | by | THE REV. JONATHAN EDWARDS, M.A. | Pastor of the Church of Christ at Northampton, in Connecticut | BEING TWO TRACTS ON THAT SUBJECT | abridged by | THE REV. JOHN WESLEY, A.M. | edited by | T.O. SUMMERS, D.D. | [publisher's device] | SCHMUL PUBLISHING CO. | SCHMUL'S WESLEYAN BOOK CLUB SALEM, OHIO

21.3 x 14.2 cm.; 122 p.

Contents: p. [1]: title; p. [2]: Copyright © 1998 by Schmul Publishing Co. | [12 lines]; p. [3]: CONTENTS; p. [4]: PUBLISHER'S PREFACE; p. [5]: INTRODUCTORY NOTE; p. [7]: THE DISTINGUISHING MARKS OF A WORK OF THE SPIRIT OF GOD; p. [49]: A TREATISE ON RELIGIOUS AFFECTIONS; p. [108]: *For related reading.*

ISBN 0880193808 OCLC 39722502

Point Loma Nazarene University

84 • SEGNI CARATTERISTICI DI UN'OPERA | DELLO SPIRITO DI DEO | * * * | Jonathan Edwards | Sentieri Antichi | "*...domandate dei sentieri antichi...*" (Gerermia 6:16)

20.4 x 12.50 cm.; xx, 67, [1] p.

Notes: an Italian translation of *Distinguishing Marks*.

Contents: p. [i]: half title (verso blank); p. [iii]: title; p. [iv]: Titolo originale: | Distinguishing Marks of a Work of the Spirit of God, *Works of* | *Jonathan Edwards*, volume 2, pp. 260-277, prima edizione della | Banner of Truth di Edimburgo 1974. | [publisher's device] DUTCH REFORMED TRACT SOCIETY | [2 lines] | © Sentieri Antichi, 1998. | [8 lines] | VIA A. ROSSATO 14 | 00123 LA STORTA | ROMA | [1 line]; p. [v]: [photocopy portrait of Edwards]; p. [vi]: blank; p. [vii]: INDICE; p. [viii]: blank; p. ix: INTRODUZIONE ALL 'EDIZIONE ITALIANA [signed] Gli Editori; p. 1: SEGNI CRATTERISTICI DI UN'OPERA | DELLO SPIRITO DI DEO | *"Carissimi, non crediate a ogni spirito, ma provate | gli spiriti per sapere se sone da Dio; perché molti fal- | si profeti sono sorti nel mondo."* | (I Giovanni 4:1); p. [68]: blank.

ISBN 8887420092

Biblioteca Nazionale Centrale

85 • THE | SPIRIT | OF | REVIVAL | [rule] | DISCOVERING THE WISDOM | OF JONATHAN EDWARDS | [rule] | ARCHIE PARRISH | AND | R. C. SPROUL | With the Complete, Modernized Text of | *The Distinguishing Marks of a Work of the Spirit of God* | [rule] | CROSSWAY BOOKS • WHEATON, ILLINOIS | A DIVISION OF GOOD NEWS PUBLISHERS

22.7 x 14.9 cm.; 223, [1] p.

Contents: p. [1]: THE SPIRIT OF REVIVAL (verso blank); p. [3]: title; p. [4]: *The Spirit of Revival* | Copyright © 2000 by Archie Parrish | [43 lines]; p. [5]: CONTENTS; p. [8]: blank; p. [9]: [acknowledgments] (verso blank); p. [11]: FOREWORD | by *Archie Parrish*; p. [16]: blank; p. [17]: INTRODUCTION | *by R. C. Sproul*; p. [40]: blank; p. [41]: PREFACE | *by William Cooper* | [short rule] | THE DISTINGUISHING MARKS | OF A WORK OF THE SPIRIT OF GOD | *by Jonathan Edwards* (verso blank); p. [43]: PREFACE | *by William Cooper*; p. [52]: blank; p. [53]: THE DISTINGUISHING MARKS | OF A WORK OF THE SPIRIT OF GOD | *By Jonathan Edwards*; p. [151]: EPILOGUE | [short rule] | APPENDIX | [short rule] | DISCUSSION GUIDE | [short rule] | SESSION AGENDAS (verso blank); p. [153]: EPILOGUE; p. [159]: APPENDIX; p. [177]: DISCUSSION GUIDE; p. [186]: blank; pp. [187-214]: [session agendas]; p. [215]: SCRIPTURE INDEX; p. [219]: GENERAL INDEX; p. [224]: blank.

ISBN 1581341377 OCLC 42682949

Harvard Divinity School

86 • CARACTERISTICAS DE UN | AUTENTICO AVIVAMIENTO | PRESENTANDO A JONATHAN EDWARDS | AL CONTEXTO LATINO | Introductión y Comentarios | Por Ernie Klassen

21.7 x 14.3 cm.; xliii, [1], 176 p.

Notes: a Spanish translation of *Distinguishing Marks*.

Contents: p. [i]: title; p. [ii]: [4 lines] | © Octubre del 2002 | [4 lines] | GRAFITEC Y CIA S.R.L. R.U.C 20138078508 | Lima Perú; p. [iii]: *DEDICACIÓN* (verso blank); p. [v]: *ARADECIMIENTO*; p. [vi]: ORACIONES POR EL AVIVAMIENTO | PERSONAL DEL SALMO 119; p. vii: INDICE; p. x: blank; p. xi: LAS CARACTERISTÍSTICAS

DE UN AUTENTICO AVIVAMIENTO | Prólogo | Rev. Javier Cortázar; p. xii: LAS CARACTERISTÍSTICAS DE UN AUTENTICO AVIVAMIENTO | Prólogo | Dr. Humberto Lay; p. xiv: LAS CARACTERISTÍSTICAS DE UN AUTENTICO AVIVAMIENTO | Prólogo | Dr. Alfredo Smith; p. xvi: "Las marcas Distintivas del Espíritu de Dios" | ("Señales que Distinguen") | Obra Escrita por Jonathan Edwards | Prólogo | Dr. R. C. Sproul; p. xvii: LAS CARACTERISTÍSTICAS DE UN AUTENTICO AVIVAMIENTO | Prólogo | Dr. Douglas Sweeney; p. xix: INTRODUCCION | | Las Características de un Auténtico Avivamiento | Jonathan Edwards | sobre el avivamiento en el mundo latino; p. xx: blank; p. xxi: Abstracto | "Las Características de un Auténtico Avivamiento; p. xxiii: Reseña Biográfica | de | Jonathan Edwards | Pastor, Evangelista, Teólogo, Avivador, Filósofo, Ecuador | pur Ernie Klassen; p. xxxiii: Prefacio a la obra para el lector latino; p. [xliv]: blank; p. 1: Prefacio original a la obra de Edwards | pur William Cooper (1741); p. 18: blank; p. 19: text; p. 137: Bibliografía de Material en Español; p. 141: Páginas Web en Español; p. 147: Bibliografía en Inglés; p. 159: blank; p. 151: Apéndice #1 | "NARRATIVA PERSONAL"; p. 161: Apéndice #2 | Las 70 Resoluciones de Edwards; p. 171: Apéndice #3 | Cómo Tener un Avivamiento Personal; p. 175: Apéndice #4 | Doce preguntas para rendir cuentas a un amigo.

OCLC 51451647

Asbury Theological Seminary

THE RESORT AND REMEDY OF THOSE THAT ARE BEREAVED BY THE DEATH OF AN EMINENT MINISTER

87 • [within mourning borders] *The* Refort *and* Remedy *of thofe | that are bereaved by the Death | of an eminent Minifter.* | [mourning rule] | A | SERMON | Preached at *Hatfield*, Sept. 2. 1741. | Being the Day of Interment of the Reverend | Mr. *William Williams*, | the aged and venerable *Paftor* of that Church. | And publifhed at the united Requeft of thofe Reve- | rend and Honoured Gentlemen, the *Sons* of the | Deceafed. | As alfo by the Defire and at the Expence of the *Town.* | [mourning rule] | By *Jonathan Edwards*, M.A. | Paftor of the Church of CHRIST at *Northampton.* | [mourning rule] | James 1. 17.----*The Father of Lights, with whom | is no Variablenefs, neither Shadow of Turning.* | [mourning rule] | *BOSTON*, Printed by G. ROGERS, for J. | EDWARDS in Cornhil. 1741.

8vo.; 18.3 x 11.3 cm.; [A]^4, B-C^4; 22, [2] p.

Notes: also reprinted (in collected editions) as *The Sorrows of the Bereaved Spread before Jesus.*

Contents: p. [1]: Mr. *Edwards*'s | SERMON | On The Death of the Aged | Mr. WILLIAMS. | (verso blank); p. [3]: title (verso blank); p. [5]: The Sorrows of the Bereaved | fpread before JESUS.

THJ 61 EAI 1:4712 NUC NE0046758 OCLC 16520476

Massachusetts Historical Society

SINNERS IN THE HANDS OF AN ANGRY GOD

88 • SINNERS | In The Hands of an | Angry GOD. | A SERMON | Preached at *Enfield*, *July* 8th 1741. | At a Time of great Awakenings; and attended with | remarkable Impreffions on many of the Hearers. | [rule] | By *Jonathan Edwards*, A.M. | Paftor of the Church of CHRIST in *Northampton.* | [rule] | Amos ix. 2, 3. *Though they dig into Hell, thence fhall mine Hand | take them*; *though they climb up to Heaven, thence will I bring | them down. And though they hide themfelves in the Top of | Carmel, I will fearch and take them out thence*; *and though | they be hid from my Sight in the Bottom of the Sea, thence I will | command the Serpent, and he fhall bite them.* | [rule] | *BOSTON:* Printed and Sold by S. KNEELAND | and T. GREEN, in Queen-Street over againft the | Prifon. 1741.

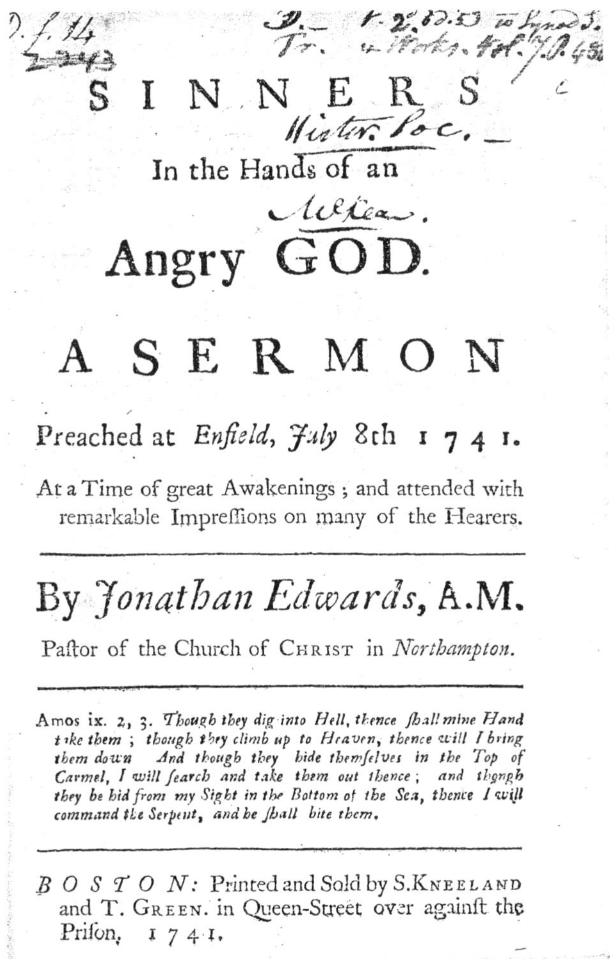

SINNERS

In the Hands of an

Angry GOD.

A SERMON

Preached at *Enfield*, *July* 8th 1741.

At a Time of great Awakenings; and attended with remarkable Impressions on many of the Hearers.

By *Jonathan Edwards*, A.M.

Pastor of the Church of CHRIST in *Northampton*.

Amos ix. 2, 3. *Though they dig into Hell, thence shall mine Hand take them; though they climb up to Heaven, thence will I bring them down. And though they hide themselves in the Top of Carmel, I will search and take them out thence; and though they be hid from my Sight in the Bottom of the Sea, thence I will command the Serpent, and he shall bite them.*

BOSTON: Printed and Sold by S. KNEELAND and T. GREEN. in Queen-Street over against the Prison, 1741.

Title page, *Sinners in the Hands of an Angry God* (1741). Permission of the Massachusetts Historical Society.

8vo.; 18.4 x 12 cm.; [A]^4, B-C^4, D^2; [2], 25, [1] p.

Contents: prp. [1]: Mr. *Edwards*'s | SERMON | On the Danger of the | UNCONVERTED. (verso blank); p. [1]: title (verso blank); p. 3: Sinners in the Hands of an | angry GOD.; p. [26]: blank.

THJ 62 EAI 1:4713 NUC NE0046782 OCLC 36881250

Congregational Library

89 • SINNERS | In The Hands of an | Angry GOD. | A SERMON | Preached at *Enfield*, *July* 8th 1741. | At a Time of greatAwakenings; and attended with | remarkable Impreſſions on many of the Hearers. | [rule] | By *Jonathan Edwards*, A.M. | Paſtor of the Church of CHRIST in *Northampton*. | [rule] | Amos ix. 2, 3. *Though they dig into Hell, thence ſhall | mine Hand take them*; *though they climb up to Heaven, | thence will I bring them down. And though they hide | themſelves in the Top of Carmel, I will ſearch and take | them out thence*; *and though they be hid from my Sight | in the Bottom of the Sea, thence I will command the | Serpent, and he ſhall bite them.* | [rule] | The Second Edition. | [rule] | *BOSTON:* Printed and Sold by S. KNEELAND | and T. GREEN, in Queen-Street over againſt the | Priſon. 1742. *stet* greatAwakenings

8vo.; 17.5 x 10.5 cm. (uncut); [A]^4, B-C^4; 20 [i.e., 24] p.

Notes: pp. 7-8, 19-20 repeated (pp. [1]-[4], 5-8, 7-8, 9-19, 19-20).

Contents: p. [1]: Mr. *Edwards*'s | SERMON | On the Danger of the | UNCONVERTED. (verso blank); p. [3]: title (verso blank); p. 5: Sinners in the Hands of an | angry GOD.

THJ 63 EAI 1:4938 NUC NE0046783 OCLC 36868733

Beinecke Library

90 • SINNERS | In The Hands of an | *Angry GOD.* | [rule] | A | SERMON | Preached at *Enfield*, *July* 8th 1741. | At a Time of great Awakenings; and attended with remark- | able Impreſſions on many of the Hearers. | [rule] | By *Jonathan Edwards*, A. M. | Paſtor of the Church of CHRIST in *Northampton*. | [rule] | With a Preface by the Reverend Mr. JOHN WILLISON Miniſter of | the Goſpel at *Dundee*. | [rule] | Amos ix. 2, 3. *Though they dig into Hell, thence ſhall mine Hand | take them; though they climb up to Heaven, thence will I bring | them down. And though they hide themſelves in the Top of* Car- | mel, *I will ſearch and take them out thence; and though they be | hid from my Sight in the Bottom of the Sea, thence I will com- | mand the Serpent, and he ſhall bite them.* | [rule] | *BOSTON*, Printed: | *EDINBURGH*, Reprinted by T. LUMISDEN and J. ROBERT- | SON, and ſold at their Printing-houſe in the *Fiſh-market*. 1745.

8vo.; 17.9 x 11.2 cm.; [A]^4, B-C^4; vi, 7-24 p.

Contents: p. [i]: title (verso blank); p. iii: PREFACE. [signed] *J. W.*; p. 7: Sinners in the Hands of an Angry GOD.

THJ 64 ESTC T78837 NUC NE0046784

John Carter Brown Library

91 • SINNERS | IN THE HANDS OF AN | ANGRY GOD. | A | SERMON | Preached at ENFIELD, July 8th, 1741. | At a Time of great Awakenings; and attended with | remarkable Impreſſions on many of the Hearers. | [rule] | By JONATHAN EDWARDS, *A. M.* | Paſtor of the Church of CHRIST in NORTHAMPTON. | [rule] | Amos ix. 2, 3. *Though they dig into Hell, thence ſhall mine | Hand take them; though they climb up to Heaven, thence | will I bring them down. And though they hide themſelves in | the Top of Carmel, I will ſearch and take them out thence; | and though they be hid from my Sight in the Bottom of the | Sea, thence I will command the Serpent, and he ſhall bite them.* | [rule] | Re-printed by particular Deſire. | [rule] | BOSTON, Printed: | NEW-YORK, Re-printed, and Sold by JOHN

HOLT, | at the EXCHANGE, 1769.

8vo.; 18.2 x 11.3 cm.; [A]^4, B-C^4; 23, [1] p.

Contents: p. [1] title (verso blank); p. [3]: *Sinners in the Hands of an angry GOD.*; p. [24]: blank.

THJ 65 EAI 1:11244 NUC NE0046787 OCLC 17167303

Library of Congress

92 • *SINNERS in the HANDS of an* | *angry GOD.* | A | SERMON | PREACHED at ENFIELD, July 8th, 1741. | At a Time of great Awakenings; and at- | tended with remarkable Impreſſions on | many of the Hearers. | [rule] | *By* JONATHAN EDWARDS, *A. M.* | Paſtor of the Church of Chriſt in Northampton. | [rule] | Amos ix. 2, 3. *Though they dig into Hell, thence ſhall* | *mine hand take them; though they climb up to Heaven,* | *thence will I bring them down. And though they hide* | *themſelves in the top of Carmel, I will ſearch and take* | *them out thence; and though they be hid from my ſight* | *in the bottom of the ſea, thence I will command the Ser-* | *pent, and he ſhall bite them.* | *BOSTON:* | Printed for KNIGHT SEXTON | at *Hartford.* | M DCC LXX.

8vo.; 16.5 x 9.9 cm. (uncut); [A]^4, B-D^4, E^2; 36 p.

Contents: p. [1]: title; p. [2]: *Sinners in the Hands of an angry GOD.*

THJ 66 EAI 1:11640 NUC NE0046788

Beinecke Library

93 • SINNERS | In the Hands of an | Angry GOD. | A | SERMON | Preached at *Enfield, July* 8$^{th.}$ 1741. | At a Time of great Awakenings; and attended with | remarkable Impreſſions on many of the Hearers. | [rule] | By *Jonathan Edwards*, A. M. | Paſtor of the Church of CHRIST in *Northampton.* | [rule] | THE THIRD EDITION. | [rule] | Amos ix. 2, 3. "Though they dig into Hell, thence ſhall mine | "Hand take them; though they climb up to Heaven, thence | "will I bring them down. And though they hide themſelves | "in the Top of Carmel, I will ſearch and take them out thence; | "and though they be hid from my Sight in the Bottom of the | "Sea, thence I will command the Serpent, and he ſhall bite | "them." | [double rule] | *BOSTON:* Re-printed and Sold by S. KNEELAND, next | to the Treaſure's Office in Milk-Street. MDCCLXXII.

4to.; 19.5 x 12.2 cm.; [A]^4, B-C^4, D^2; 27, [1] p.

Contents: p. [1]: [decorative rule] | Mr. *Edwards*'s | SERMON | On the Danger of the | UNCONVERTED. | [decorative rule] | (verso blank); p. [3]: title (verso blank); p. [5]: [decorative rule] | Sinners in the Hands of an | angry GOD. | [decorative rule]; p. 28: blank.

THJ 67 EAI 1:42339 OCLC 36868444

Forbes Library

94 • SINNERS | IN THE HANDS OF AN | ANGRY GOD. | A | SERMON | PREACHED AT ENFIELD, JULY 8, 1741. | AT A TIME of GREAT AWAKENINGS; and attended with | REMARKABLE IMPRESSIONS on many of the Hearers. | BY JONATHAN EDWARDS, A. M. | Paſtor of the Church of CHRIST in *Northampton.* | The FOURTH EDITION. | Amos ix. 2, 3. "Though they dig into Hell, thence ſhall mine | "hand take them; though they climb up to Heaven, thence | "will I bring them down. And though they hide themſelves | "in the top of Carmel, I will ſearch and take them out | "thence; and though they be hid from my Sight in the Bot- | "tom of the Sea, thence I will command the Serpent, and he | "ſhall bite them." | [short tapered rule] | SALEM, (*Commonwealth of* MASSACHUSETTS) Re-Printed | and Sold by G. ROULSTONE, in PAVED-STREET. | M.DCC.LXXXVI.

8vo.; 18 x 11.9 cm.; [A]^4, B-D^4; 32 p.

Contents: p. [1]: [decorative rule] | MR. EDWARDS'S | SERMON | On the Danger of the | UNCONVERTED. | [decorative rule] (verso blank); p. [3]: title (verso blank); p. [5]: Sinners in the Hands of an Angry GOD.

THJ 68 EAI 1:19618 NUC NE0046791 OCLC 21264012

Beinecke Library

95 • *Sinners in the Hands of an angry God.* | [thick-thin rule] | A | SERMON, | Preached at ENFIELD, *July* 8th, 1741, | AT A TIME OF | GREAT AWAKENINGS; | AND ATTENDED WITH | REMARKABLE IMPRESSIONS | ON MANY OF THE HEARERS. | [short thick-thin rule] | *By the late Reverend Mr.* JONATHAN EDWARDS, | *Prefident of the College of* New-Jerfey. | [short thin-thick rule] | *NEW-YORK:* | Printed by JAMES ORAM, for CORNELIUS DAVIS, | Bookfeller, No. 212 Water-Street, | M,DCC,XCVI.

12mo.; 16.3 x 10.5 cm. (uncut); [A]-B^6; 22, [2] p.

Contents: p. [1]: title (verso blank); p. [3]: *Sinners in the Hands of an angry God.*; p. [23]: *The* DEATH *of the* SAINT *and the* SINNER | *contrafted.*; p. [24]: [advertisement].

THJ 69 EAI 1:30382 NUC NE0046792 OCLC 43639540

Forbes Library

96 • *Sinners in the Hands of an angry God.* | [double rule] | A | SERMON, | *Preached at Enfield, July* 8, 1741, | AT A TIME OF | GREAT AWAKENINGS; | AND ATTENDED WITH | REMARKABLE IMPRESSIONS | ON MANY OF THE HEARERS. | [short double rule] | *By the late Reverend Mr.* JONATHAN EDWARDS, | *Prefident of the College of New-Jerfey.* | [short double rule] | NEW-YORK: | *Printed by* G. FORMAN, *oppofite the Poft-Office, for* | C. DAVIS, *No.* 94, *Water-ftreet.* | 1797.

12mo.; 14.3 x 8.7 cm.; [A]^{12}, B^6; 33, [3] p.

Contents: p. [1]: title (verso blank); p. [3]: *Sinners in the Hands of an angry GOD.*; p. [34]: *The* DEATH *of the* SAINT *and the* SINNER *con- | trafted.*; p. [35]: [advertisement] (verso blank).

THJ 70 EAI 1:32072 NUC NE0046793 OCLC 7641790

American Antiquarian Society

97 • *SINNERS* | IN THE | HANDS OF AN ANGRY GOD. | A | SERMON, | PREACHED AT *ENFIELD, July* 8th, 1741. | AT A TIME OF GREAT AWAKENINGS; AND ATTENDED | WITH REMARKABLE IMPRESSIONS ON | MANY OF THE HEARERS. | [short thick-thin rule] | By *JONATHAN EDWARDS,* A. M. | Paftor of the Church of CHRIST in *NORTHAMPTON.* | [short double rule] | FOURTH EDITION. | [short double rule] | Amos ix. 2, 3. "Though they dig into Hell, thence fhall mine | Hand take them; though they climb up to Heaven, thence will I | bring them down. And though they hide themfelves in the top | of Carmel, I will fearch and take them out thence; and though | they be hid from my fight in the bottom of the Sea, thence I will | command the Serpent, and he fhall bite them." | [short thick-thin rule] | Charleftown: | PRINTED AND SOLD BY SAMUEL ETHERIDGE, | *who keeps conftantly for fale, an affortment of cheap RELIGIOUS | TRACTS, for charitable diftribution. Orders (for ready money) | executed from any part of the United States.* | [short tapered rule] | 1802.

4to.; 18.7 x 10.4 cm.; [A]^4, B^2, C^4; 20 p.

Contents: p. [1]: title (verso blank); p. [3]: SINNERS | IN THE | HANDS OF AN ANGRY GOD.

THJ 71 EAI 2:2174 NUC NE0046796 OCLC 29080541

Forbes Library

98 • SINNERS IN THE HANDS OF AN ANGRY GOD.

Contents: caption title; pp. [367]-383 in THE | SALVATION OF ALL MEN | STRICTLY EXAMINED; | AND THE | *ENDLESS PUNISHMENT* | OF THOSE WHO DIE IMPENITENT, | *ARGUED AND DEFENDED AGAINST THE OBJECTIONS* | *AND REASONINGS OF THE LATE* | REV. DOCTOR CHAUNCY, OF BOSTON, | IN HIS BOOK ENTITLED | "*THE SALVATION OF ALL MEN*," &c. | [short decorative rule] | BY JONATHAN EDWARDS, D. D. | PASTOR OF A CHURCH IN NEW HAVEN. | [thick-thin rule] | Come now, and let us reaſon together, ſaith the LORD—Iſai. I. 18. | Is not my way equal? Are not your ways unequal?—Ezek. xviii. 25. | [thin-thick rule] | GLASGOW: | PRINTED BY *STEPHEN YOUNG*, PRINCE'S STREET | FOR *ADAM FERGUSON*, THE PUBLISHER. | RUTHERGLEN BRIDGE. | [short thick-thin rule] | 1802.

19.2 x 11.2 cm.; [3], 4-283, [1] p.
OCLC 137266623
Gordon-Conwell Theological Seminary

99 • SINNERS | IN THE | HANDS OF AN ANGRY GOD. | [short thick-thin rule] | A | SERMON, | PREACHED AT ENFIELD, JULY 8, 1741, AT A TIME OF | GREAT AWAKENINGS; AND ATTENDED WITH | REMARKABLE IMPRESSIONS ON MANY | OF THE HEARERS. | [short double rule] | BY JONATHAN EDWARDS, | *Former President of Princeton College.* | [short double rule] | SCHENECTADY: | PRINTED BY RIGGS & STEVENS. | [short line of stops] | 1815.

18 x 10.4 cm. (uncut); [1]-2⁶; 24 p.
Contents: p. [1]: title (verso blank); p. [3]: A SERMON.
THJ 72 EAI 2:34626 NUC NE0046798 OCLC 17201558
Beinecke Library

100 • A | SERMON, | PREACHED AT ENFIELD, JULY 8, 1741. | [short double rule] | BY JONATHAN EDWARDS, A. M. | Pastor of the Church of Christ at Northampton, Mass. | [short double rule] | UTICA, | RE-PRINTED BY ARIEL WORKS, | LIBERTY-STREET. | [short line of stops] | 1826.

20.5 x 12.3 cm.; 15, [1] p.
Contents: p. [1]: title; p. [2]: B. B. DRAKE, PRINTER.; p. [3]: A SERMON. | [short decorative rule] | SINNERS IN THE HANDS OF AN ANGRY GOD. | [short decorative rule]; p. [16]:blank.
THJ 73 NUC NE0046799 OCLC 47107444
Utica Public Library

101 • *Sinners in the hands of an angry God.* | [short rule] | A | SERMON, | BY THE VENERATED | PRESIDENT EDWARDS, | RE-WRITTEN, SO AS TO RETAIN HIS | THOUGHTS | IN A MODERN STYLE. | [short decorative rule] | BY DANIEL A. CLARK. | [short decorative rule] | Amherst: | PRINTED AND PUBLISHED BY CARTER & ADAMS. | [short rule] | 1826.

24.4 x 14.7 cm. (uncut); [1]-2⁴, 3²; 20 p.
Notes: p. [2]: IT is the opinion and the grief of many, that the excellent ser- | mons, and other writings, of President Edwards, are too much | neglected by the churches of the present day, and that the prin- | cipal cause of that neglect is to be attributed to the style in | which his pungency of thought is communicated. Hence the | attempt to put this sermon in other language as an experiment. | The difficulty of the task none will doubt, who shall undertake a | single page. If the attempt should fail, still nothing is lost, and | much may be gained, if it should induce some other person to do, | *more successfully*, what the author conceives practicable and im- | portant.
Contents: p. [1]: title; p. [2]: [editorial note]; p. [3]: SERMON.
THJ 74 OCLC 1407881
Amherst College

102 • SELECT SERMONS. (No. 25. | [rule] | SINNERS IN THE HANDS OF AN | ANGRY GOD. | [short rule] | BY JONATHAN EDWARDS. | [short rule] | DEUT. xxxii. 35. | *Their foot shall slide in*

due time.

17 x 10 cm.; 24 p.

Notes: published c. 1830.

Contents: caption title; pp. [1]-17: text; p. 18: CHRIST'S INVITATION TO THE LABOUR- | ING AND HEAVY-LADEN. | [short rule] | ABRIDGED FROM THOMAS BOSTON. | [short rule] | MATT. XI. 28 *Come unto me, all ye that labour, and are | heavy laden, and I will give you rest.*; p. 24: London: Printed for the Religious Tract Society; 56. Paternoster Row, | by H. Fisher, Son, & P. Jackson. | Price Twopence, or Sixteen Shillings per Hundred.

THJ 75 NUC NE0046780 OCLC 50008549

Duke University

103 • SINNERS | IN THE | HANDS OF AN ANGRY GOD. | BY THE | REV. PRESIDENT EDWARDS. | PHILADELPHIA: | PRESBYTERIAN BOARD OF PUBLICATION. | A2 5

19.4 x 11.7 cm.; [A]-B^4; 16 p.

Notes: first published in 1841; numbered at head, pp. [1]-16, and foot, pp. [5]-20; in some copies, front cover: [within thick-thin rules] No. XXIV. | SINNERS | IN THE | HANDS OF AN ANGRY GOD. | BY THE | REV. PRESIDENT EDWARDS. | PHILADELPHIA: | PRESBYTERIAN BOARD OF PUBLICATION. | PAUL T. JONES, PUBLISHING AGENT.; in some copies, the back cover (verso) is blank; in some copies, address: 821 or 1934; in some copies, p. 16: Printed by | WM. S. MARTIN. | [short rule] | Stereotyped by | S. DOUGLAS WYETH | No. 7 Pear St. Philadelphia.

Contents: front cover: [within decorative rules] No. 24. | SINNERS | IN THE | HANDS OF AN ANGRY GOD. | BY THE | REV. PRESIDENT EDWARDS. | [short line of stops] | PHILADELPHIA: | PRESBYTERIAN BOARD OF PUBLICATION, | No. 265 CHESTNUT STREET. (verso blank); p. [1]: title; p. [2]: SINNERS | IN THE | HANDS OF AN ANGRY GOD.; back cover (verso): [within decorative rules] no. 24 | "WILT THOU NOT REVIVE US AGAIN?" | [60 lines] | PRESBYTERIAN BOARD OF PUBLICATION.

THJ 76 NUC NE0046795 OCLC 13393416

Boston Public Library

103A • SINNERS | IN THE | HANDS OF AN ANGRY GOD. | BY THE | REV. PRESIDENT EDWARDS. | PHILADELPHIA: | PRESBYTERIAN BOARD OF PUBLICATION.

Contents: pp. [1]-16 (also paged [5]-20) in A SERIES | OF | TRACTS | ON THE | DOCTRINES, ORDER, AND POLITY | OF THE | PRESBYTERIAN CHURCH | IN THE | UNITED STATES OF AMERICA. | EMBRACING | SEVERAL ON PRACTICAL SUBJECTS. | VOL. III. | PHILADELPHIA: | PRESBYTERIAN BOARD OF PUBLICATION.

18.9 x 11.2 cm.; [2], 394, [2] p.

THJ 76A NUC NE0046781 OCLC 28088277

Presbyterian Historical Society

104 • HATAK YOSHUBA | UHLEHA HUT | CHIHOWA ANUKHOBELA YA IBBAK FOYUKA. | [short double rule] | SINNERS IN THE HANDS | OF AN | ANGRY GOD. | A Sermon by the Rev. President Edwards. | [short double rule] | PARK HILL, CHEROKEE NATION: | MISSION PRESS: JOHN CANDY AND JOHN F. WHEELER, PRINTERS. | [2 short lines of stops] | 1845.

17.8 x 10.7 cm.; [A]-B^6, C^2; 28 p.

Notes: a Choctaw translation of *Sinners in the Hands of an Angry God*, by Alfred Wright.

Contents: p. [1]: title; pp. 2-28: text.

THJ 77 NUC NE0046614 OCLC 24102020

Boston Athenaeum

105 • PEACAICH | ANN AN | LAMHAIBH DHE 'N A FHEIRG: | SEARMOIN | LEIS AN | URRAMACH IONATAN EDWARDS. | GLASGOW: | DUNCAN MACVEAN. | 1848.

12.6 x 8.4 cm.; 32 p.
Notes: a Gaelic translation of *Sinners in the Hands of an Angry God.*
Contents: p. [1]: title (verso blank); pp. [3]-32: text; p. 32: BELL AND BAIN, PRINTERS, ST. ENOCH SQUARE.
THJ 78 NUC NE0046745
National Library of Scotland

106 • [within decorative rules] Maw'izah | fi ghadab Allah ala alkhutah
24 x 16.5 cm.; 35 p.
Notes: an Arabic translation of *Sinners in the Hands of an Angry God*, published in Beirut, 1849.
Contents: prp. [1]: title (verso blank); p. [1]: Maw'izah | fi ghadab Allah ala alkhutah; p. 35: [publication data].
OCLC 23485971
University of Michigan

107 • SINNERS IN THE HANDS OF AN ANGRY GOD.
Contents: caption title; pp. 395-408 in HISTORY AND REPOSITORY | OF | PULPIT ELOQUENCE, | (DECEASED DIVINES,) | CONTAINING | THE MASTERPIECES | OF | BOSSUET, BOURDALOUE, MASSILLON, FLECHIER, ABRADIE, TAYLOR, BARROW, | HALL, WATSON, M'LAURIN, CHALMERS, EVANS, EDWARDS, DAVIES, | JOHN M. MASON, ETC., ETC., | WITH DISCOURSES | FROM | CHRYOSTOM, BASIL, GREGORY NAZIANZEN, AUGUSTINE, ATHANASIUS, AND OTHERS | AMONG THE "FATHERS," AND FROM WICKLIFFE, LUTHER, CALVIN, MELANCTHON, | KNOX, LATIMER, ETC., OF THE "REFORMERS." | ALSO, | SIXTY OTHER CELEBRATED SERMONS, | FROM AS MANY EMINENT DIVINES IN THE GREEK AND LATIN, ENGLISH, GERMAN, IRISH, FRENCH, | SCOTTISH, AMERICAN, AND WELSH CHURCHES; A LARGE NUMBER OF WHICH HAVE NOW, FOR | THE FIRST TIME, BEEN TRANSLATED. THE WHOLE ARRANGED IN THEIR | PROPER ORDER, AND ACCOMPANIED WITH | HISTORICAL SKETCHES OF PREACHING | IN THE DIFFERENT COUNTRIES REPRESENTED, AND | BIOGRAPHICAL AND CRITICAL NOTICES | OF THE SEVERAL PREACHERS AND THEIR DISCOURSES. | BY | REV. HENRY C. FISH, | AUTHOR OF PREMIUM ESSAY, "PRIMITIVE PIETY REVIVED." | [short rule] | IN TWO VOLUMES. | VOL. II. | [short rule] | NEW YORK: | PUBLISHED BY M. W. DODD, | BRICK CHURCH CHAPEL, CITY HALL SQUARE. | [short rule] | 1856.
22.8 x 12.3 cm.; 622 p.
THJ 79 OCLC 8037818
Amherst College

108 • <u>Sinners in the Hands of an Angry God</u>. | PEACAICH | ANN AN | LAMHAIBH DHE 'NA FHERIG. | [short rule] | SEARMOIN | LEIS AN | URRAMACH IONATAN EDUARDS. | [short rule] | EDINBURGH: | MACLACHLAN & STEWART, 64 SOUTH BRIDGE. | [short rule] | 1863.
13.4 x 8.4 cm.; 32 p.
Contents: p. [1]: title (verso blank); pp. [3]-32: text; p. 32: D. R. COLLIE & SON, PRINTERS, EDINBURGH.
National Library of Scotland

108A • <u>Sinners in the Hands of an Angry God</u>. | PEACAICH | ANN AN | LAMHAIBH DHE 'NA FHERIG. | [short rule] | SEARMOIN | LEIS AN | URRAMACH IONATAN EDUARDS. | [short rule] | EDINBURGH: | MACLACHLAN & STEWART, 64 SOUTH BRIDGE. | [short rule] | 1876.
14.7 x 9.6 cm.; 32, [4] p.
Contents: p. [1]: title (verso blank); pp. [3]-32: text; p. 32: H. & J. PILLANS, PRINTERS, EDINBURGH.; pp. [33-36]: [advertisement].
THJ 80
National Library of Scotland

108B • <u>Sinners in the Hands of an Angry God</u>. | PEACAICH | ANN AN | LAMHAIBH DHE 'NA

FHERIG. | [short rule] | SEARMOIN | LEIS AN | URRAMACH IONATAN EDUARDS. | [short rule] | EDINBURGH: | MACLACHLAN & STEWART, 64 SOUTH BRIDGE. | [short rule] | 1889.

14 x 8.4 cm.; 32 p.
Contents: p. [1]: title (verso blank); pp. [3]-32: text; p. 32: H. & J. PILLANS, PRINTERS, EDINBURGH.
OCLC 30854696
National Library of Scotland

109 • SINNERS IN THE HANDS OF AN ANGRY GOD.

Notes: *The Highland Pulpit* was published monthly under the direction of the Board of Deacons of The Highland Baptist Church, Louisville, Ky.; front cover: [with decorative borders] OCTOBER, 1894. | HIGHLAND | [short rule] | [ornament] FIFTY CENTS PER YEAR. [ornament] | [short rule] | [photocopy: engraving of the church] | [short rule] | [ornament] SINGLE COPIES, TEN CENTS. [ornament] | [short rule] | [ornament] PULPIT. [ornament] | [short double rule] | *OFFICE AT PASTOR'S STUDY, 1203 Morton Avenue,* | *LOUISVILLE, KY.*
Contents: caption title; *The Highland Pulpit*, 1 (October 1894):[83]-100.
THJ 81 NUC NE0046801 OCLC 39475827
Asbury Theological Seminary

109A • [Sinners In The | Hands Of An Angry God. | By The | Rev. President Edwards. | Published By Highland Pulpit, | Louisville, Ky.]

18.1 x 12 cm.; no signature; 16 p.
Notes: Reprinted shortly after (presumably).—THJ. No copy has been located.
THJ 81A

109B • [within decorative rules] Sinners | in the | Hands | of an | Angry God. | [ornament] | By JONATHAN EDWARDS. | [ornament] | Published by | THE BAPTIST BOOK CONCERN, INC., | Louisville, Ky. | 5 cents each; $2.50 per hundred.

19.9 x 12.4 cm.; 16 p.
Notes: According to *The American Catalogue*, this item was issued by the Baptist Book Concern in 1901. No copy has been definitely located. It seems probable, however, that the item may be that located in the New York Public Library, measuring 19.6 x 11 cm., with t.p. (pp. 1-2) missing. The text in this copy begins on p. [3]. Pages following p. 14 are missing; it is to be supposed that a final leaf (pp. 15-16) is gone.—THJ. The New York Public Library handwritten catalogue card reads: Louisville, Ky.: Baptist Book Concern, [18--] | 16 pp. 12°; the copy at Congregational Library is authentic and complete.
Contents: p. [1]: title (verso blank); p. [3]: SINNERS IN THE HANDS OF AN ANGRY GOD.
THJ 81B NUC NE0046794
Congregational Library

110 • Sinners in the Hands | of | An Angry God | [short rule] | SERMON BY | Jonathan Edwards | [ornament] | [double rule] | PENTECOSTAL PUBLISHING COMPANY | LOUISVILLE, KENTUCKY

17.8 x 13 cm.; [32] p.
Notes: published c. 1921; unpaged.
Contents: p. [1]: title (verso blank); p. [3]: SINNERS IN THE HANDS OF AN | ANGRY GOD.
NUC NE0046802 OCLC 7884844
Southern Baptist Theological Seminary

111 • [within decorative rules] SHORT SKETCHES OF THE LIFE | AND SERVICE | OF | JONATHAN EDWARDS | INCLUDING HIS GREAT SERMON | SINNERS IN THE HANDS | OF AN ANGRY GOD | PREACHED FROM THE TEXT: | "THEIR FOOT SHALL SLIDE IN DUE TIME" | DEUT. 32:35 |

CONTAINING ALSO THE INSPIRING POEM | SOME THINGS WE KNOW | [short rule] | WRITTEN BY A. J. EDWARDS | [short rule] | PRICE, POST PAID, 15 CENTS | [short rule] | ADDRESS A. J. EDWARDS | P.O. BOX 1805, FORT WORTH, TEXAS | OR | BIBLE LESSONS AND LECTURES COMPANY | FORT WORTH, TEXAS | COPYRIGHTED, 1922, BY A. J. EDWARDS | [below decorative rule] C. C. PAXTON CO., PRINTERS, FT. WORTH

20 x 12.6 cm.; 16 p.

Contents: front cover (recto): title; front cover (verso): BRIEF HISTORY OF THE SERMON; p. [1]: FOREWORD [signed] A. J. EDWARDS.; pp. 4-16: text; back cover (recto): SOME THINGS WE KNOW | [short rule] | (Copyrighted 1922, by A. J. Edwards.); back cover (verso): [advertisement].

THJ 82   NUC NE0046778   OCLC 13363461

Emmanuel School of Religion

112 • [within decorative rules] SINNERS | In The Hands of an | ANGRY GOD | By JONATHAN EDWARDS | [ornament] | PRICE 10 CENTS A COPY | 4 for 25c; 10 for 50c; 25 for $1.00; 100 for $3.00 | (Postage Included) | [thick-thin rule] | Published By | BAPTIST TABERNACLE | Paducah, Kentucky | Distributed By | I. W. ROGERS | Phone 2175-W 2704 Tenn. St. Paducah, Ky.

19.6 x 13.9 cm.; 16 p.

Notes: published c. 1930.

Contents: p. [1]: title; p. [2]: *Brief History of The Sermon*; p. [3]: Sinners In The Hands of An Angry God.

OCLC 19770597

Wheaton College

113 • [within decorative rules] *Sinners In The Hands* | *Of An Angry God* | BY JONATHAN EDWARDS | Preached July 8, 1741 | [ornament] | Single copy [line of stops] 20 cents | 6 copies for [line of stops] $1.00 | 25 copies for [line of stops] $3.75 | 50 copies for [line of stops] $6.50 | 100 copies for [line of stops] $10.00 | (75 or more copies at the 100 rate.) | (Write for prices on 500 or more.) | Above prices include postage. | *THE FAITH PUBLISHERS* | I. W. Rogers, Mgr. | Hickory, Ky.

20.2 x 12.9 cm.; 15 p.

Notes: published c. 1930.

Contents: p. [1]: title; p. [2]: THE PREACHER | [25 lines] | [short rule] | THE SERMON | [14 lines] | *THE PUBLISHERS*; p. [3]: Sinners In The Hands Of An Angry God.

OCLC 11845161

Cincinnati Bible College and Seminary

114 • [within an unfurled banner] Sinners in | the Hands of | an Angry God | Sermon by | Jonathan Edwards

20.2 x 9.4 cm.; 37, [3] p.

Notes: published c. 1940.

Contents: frontispiece: [photocopy: drawing] | JONATHAN EDWARDS; p. [1]: title; p. [2]: Published by The | Metropolitan Church Assn. | Waukesha, Wisconsin; pp. [3]-37: text; pp. [38-40]: [advertisement].

OCLC 27552160

Taylor University

115 • SINNERS | IN THE HANDS | OF AN ANGRY | GOD | Sermon by Jonathan Edwards | Preached July 8, 1741 | "Their feet shall slide in due time" | Deut. 32:35

15.2 x 9.3 cm.; 30 p.

Notes: published c. 1950.

Contents: front cover, p. [1]: title (verso blank); pp. 3-30: text; p. [31]: blank; back cover, p. [32]: [publisher's

device] | Reiner Publications | SWENGEL, PA. 17880
OCLC 10234253
Gordon College

116 • [Abstract from a celebrated sermon preached by Jonathan Edwards after a whole night of prayer by the members of his congregation, resulting in many conversions.]
13 cm.; 1 folded sheet, [3] p.
Notes: an extract of *Sinners in the Hands of an Angry God* (St. Louis: Faith Words Publishing House, c. 1960); the only holder cannot locate it.
OCLC 30830900

117 • Die Sünder | in den Händen | eines | zornigen Gottes | Von Jonathan Edwards
21 x 14.7 cm.; 15, [1] p.
Notes: a German translation of *Sinners in the Hands of an Angry God*, published c. 1960.
Contents: p. [1]: title; p. [2]: Übersetzung von Ernst Rüegger | [rule] | VORTWORT [signed] *A.L.* [Albert Lüscher, editor] | Eigentum der Übersetzung: Pflug-Verlag, Langenthal; p. 3: *"Zu seiner Zeit soll ihr Fuſs gleiten" (5. Mose 32, 35)*; p. [16]: [advertisement].
Schweizerische Landesbibliothek

118 • [decorative rule] | Sinners in the Hands of an | Angry God | [decorative rule] | by Rev. Jonathan Edwards | [decorative rule] | FROM THE INHERITANCE OF OUR FATHERS | – Series XXII No. 3 | [decorative rule]
13.6 x 8.8 cm.; 34 p.
Notes: published c. 1977; no copy of an earlier issue, Series I, No. 2, has been located.
Contents: front cover, p. [1]: title; p. [2]: [biography]; p. 3: Sinners in the Hands of an | Angry God; back cover (recto): [advertisement] | [publisher's note] | [1 line]; back cover (verso): [decorative rule] | [advertisement] | [decorative rule] | THE INHERITANCE PUBLISHERS | *P. O. Box 1334* | *Grand Rapids, Michigan 49501* | [decorative rule].
OCLC 47870477
Gordon-Conwell Theological Seminary

119 • Sinners | in the | Hands | of an | Angry | God | [short rule] | JONATHAN EDWARDS | [short rule]
19.7 x 13.2 cm.; 22 p.
Notes: published c. 1985.
Contents: front cover, p. [1]: title; p. [2]: Published By | Sword of the Lord Publishers | [1 line] | [advertisement]; p. [3]: [photocopy] | Jonathan Edwards | 1703-1758 | THE MOST FAMOUS SERMON EVER | PREACHED IN AMERICA; p. [4]: About Jonathan Edwards. . .; p. [5]: *Sinners in the Hands of an* | *Angry God*; p. [23]: [advertisement]; back cover, p. [24]: [advertisement] | SWORD of the LORD | [short rule] | PUBLISHERS | P.O. BOX 1099, MURFREESBORO, TN 37133 | 50¢/810-8.
ISBN 0873988108 OCLC 20142721
Gordon-Conwell Theological Seminary

120 • Jonathan Edwards
Notes: pp. [111]-138: Sermons in stone | *by Allan I. Ludwig* | *with a text by Jonathan Edwards* [photographs of early American tombstones interleaved with text]; p. 130: *The following is excerpted from the "Applications" section of Jonathan Edwards's sermon,* Sinners in the Hands of an Angry God, *delivered on 8 July 1741 at Enfield, Connecticut.*
Contents: caption title; *FMR* 1, no. 6 (November 1984):130-131, 138.
OCLC 10764669
Mary Washington College

121 • Sinners | in the Hands | of an | Angry God | [short rule] | *by* | Jonathan Edwards | P&R |

PUBLISHING | P.O. BOX 817 • PHILLIPSBURG • NEW JERSEY 08865-0817

21 x 13.8 cm.; 32 p.

Contents: p. [1]: title; p. [2]: Foreword | copyrighted 1992 | by John D. Currid | Printed by | P&R Publishers | Phillipsburg, New Jersey | 1992 | [10 lines]; p. 3: Foreword [signed] John D. Currid, Ph.D. | Associate Professor of Religion | Grove City College | Reformation Day, 1991; p. [8]: blank; p. [9]: Sinners | in the Hands | of an | Angry God | [short rule] | Jonathan Edwards; p. [10]: blank; p. 11: Enfield, Connecticut | July 8, 1741.

ISBN 0875522335 OCLC 25009372

Gordon-Conwell Theological Seminary

122 • SINNERS | IN THE HANDS | OF AN | ANGRY GOD | *by* | JONATHAN EDWARDS | [short rule] | MADE EASIER TO READ | *by* | JOHN JEFFERY FANELLA | P&R | PUBLISHING | P.O. BOX 817 • PHILLIPSBURG • NEW JERSEY 08865-0817

21.5 x 13.5 cm.; 32 p.

Contents: p. [1]: title; p. [2]: © 1996 by John Jeffery Fanella | [22 lines]; p. 3: Foreword [signed] JOHN F. MACARTHUR, JR.; p. [6]: blank; p. 7: Enfield, Connecticut | July 8, 1741 | *Deuteronomy 32:35* | *—"Their foot shall slip in due time."—*; p. 29: Publisher's Postscript: | The Way of Life.

ISBN 0875522130 OCLC 34943213

Harvard Divinity School

123 • SINNERS IN THE HANDS | OF AN ANGRY GOD | Jonathan Edwards

21.6 x 17.5 cm.; 28 p.

Notes: published c. 1996.

Contents: front cover: title; p. 1: SINNERS IN THE HANDS OF AN ANGRY GOD | Jonathan Edwards, July 1741, Enfield, Connecticut; back cover: [23 lines] | [publisher's device] | CANDLESTICK PUBLISHING | Books on Faith and Freedom | P.O. BOX 39241, San Antonio, Texas 78218-1241 | [1 line] | [publisher's device].

ISBN 0962742341 OCLC 48421655

Gordon-Conwell Theological Seminary

124 • Sinners in the Hands of | an Angry God | *by* | Jonathan Edwards | Messages from God's servants | in former days | [6 lines] | [ornament] | [in 2 cols., col. 1]: The Teleios Ministry of | Camelback Bible Church | 3900 East Stanford Drive | Paradise Valley, AZ 85253 | 955-6370 | [col. 2]: September, 1996

21.6 x 13.5 cm.; 19, [3] p.

Contents: front cover: title; front cover (verso): Teleios Sermon # 12 | [32 lines]; p. [1]: title; p. [20]: *Notes and Personal Application*; pp. [21-22]: blank; back cover (recto): [advertisement].

OCLC 49537960

Gordon-Conwell Theological Seminary

125 • SINNERS | in the | HANDS | of an | ANGRY | GOD | JONATHAN EDWARDS | [publisher's device] *Whitaker House*

17.5 x 10.3 cm.; 64 p.

Contents: p. [1]: SINNERS | in the | HANDS | of an | ANGRY | GOD (verso blank); p. [3]: title; p. [4]: [2 lines] | SINNERS | IN THE | HANDS | OF AN | ANGRY | GOD | [2 lines] | Copyright © 1997 by Whitaker House | Whitaker House | 30 Hunt Valley Circle | New Kensington, PA 15068 | [6 lines]; p. [5]: Contents (verso blank); p. 7: Introduction; pp. 13-64: text.

ISBN 0883684152 OCLC 37914981

Gordon-Conwell Theological Seminary

126 • [series notation] | Chinnohan Hananim ui son e | puttullin choeindul | Jonathan Edwards | Ahn Bo Hun | [illustration] | [on the right vertically] [illustration] | 6 | [imprecation] | Sinners | in the Hands

| of an Angry | God | [Word of Life Press]

18.2 x 12.9cm.; 86, [2] p.

Notes: a Korean translation of *Sinners in the Hands of an Angry God.*

Contents: pp. [1-2]: blank; p. [3]: title; p. [4]: SINNERS IN THE HANDS OF AN ANGRY GOD | by Jonathan Edwards | 1998 / Korean by Word of Life Press, | Seoul, Korea. | Printed in Korea; p. 5: [Sinners in the Hands of an Angry God]; p. 6: *Sinners in the Hands of an Angry God*; p. 7: [Sinners in the Hands of an Angry God | [quotation] [Deut. 32:35]; p. [44]: blank; p. 45: [The Future Punishment of the Wicked Unavoidable and Intolerable]; p.46: *The Future Punishment of the Wicked | Unavoidable and Intolerable*; p. 47: [The Future Punishment of the Wicked Unavoidable and Intolerable] | [quotation] [Ezek. 22:14]; p. [87]: blank; p. [88]: [publication data].

ISBN 8904180538 OCLC 48063326

Gordon-Conwell Theological Seminary

127 • *Taller de Escudos Norteamericanos* | JONATHAN EDWARDS | PECADORES EN MANOS | DE UN DIOS AIRADO (1741) | (Texto bilingüe) | Introducción y notas de | José Antonio Gurpegui | Traducción de | Julio César Santoyo | Universidad de Léon

21 x 10.8 cm.; 107, [1] p.

Notes: a Spanish translation of *Sinners in the Hands of an Angry God*, no. 57 in the series *Taller de Escudos Norteamericanos*, published in 2000.

Contents: p. 1: title; p. 2: [14 lines] | © UNIVERSIDAD DE LEON | Secretarido de Publicaciones | ISBN: 84-7719-883-7 | Depósito Legal: —34798-2000 | Printed in Spain – Impresso en Españo; p. 3: [editorial board]; p. 4: Taller de Escudos Norteamericanos [signed] Juan Jóse Coy; p. 5: INTRODUCCIÓN; p. 21: FILOSOFÍA DE EDWARDS; p. 31: EL GREAT AWAKENING (EL GRAN DESPERTAR); p. 40: LOS SERMONES DE EDWARDS; p. 54: PECADORES EN MANOS DE UN DIOS AIRADO; p. 69: BIBLIOGRAFÍA CITADA; p. [73]: JONATHAN EDWARDS: | SINNERS IN THE HANDS | OF AN ANGRY GOD | PECADORES EN MANOS | DE UN DIOS AIRADO (1741); p. [108]: blank.

ISBN 8477198837 OCLC 45246949

University of Léon

128 • Sondaars | in die Hand | van 'n | TOORNIGE | God | Amerika se beroemdste preek! | [within publisher's device] WOORDVERSPREIDING UITGEWERS

21 x 14.7 cm.; 36 p.

Notes: an Afrikaans translation of *Sinners in the Hands of an Angry God.*

Contents: front cover: Sondaars | in die Hand | van 'n | TOORNIGE | God | Amerika se beroemdste preek! | *Jonathan Edwards* (verso blank); p. [3]: title; p. 4: Uitgegee deur | WOORDVERSPREIDING | p/a Sonlandpark Apteek | [2 lines] | [barcode] | Eerste uitgawe, eerste druk 2001 | [3 lines] | Redakteur: Josef Coetzee | Omslagontwerp: John-Wesley Franklin | [4 lines]; p. 5: [publisher's device] | *UNITGEWERS MET 'N MISSIE* (verso blank); p. 7: INLEIDING; pp. 11-35: text; p. 36: [advertisement]; back cover: [advertisement].

ISBN 0958422079 OCLC 48569797

State Library of South Africa

SOME THOUGHTS CONCERNING THE PRESENT REVIVAL OF RELIGION IN NEW ENGLAND

129 • Some Thoughts | Concerning the prefent | *Revival of Religion* | IN | NEW-ENGLAND, | And the Way in which it ought to be | acknowledged and promoted, | Humbly offered to the Publick, in a | TREATISE on that Subject. | In Five PARTS; | [in 2 cols., col. 1] PART I. Shewing that | the Work that has of | late been going on in | this Land, is a glori- | ous Work of GOD. | PART II. Shewing the | Obligations that all are | under, to acknowlege, | rejoice in and promote | this Work, and the | great Danger of the | contrary. | PART III. Shewing in | many Inftances, where- | [short vertical rule, col. 2]

in the Subjects, or zea- | lous Promoters, of this | Work have been inju- | rioufly blamed. | PART IV. Shewing what | Things are to be cor- | rected or avoided, in | promoting this Work, | or in our Behaviour | under it. | PART V. Shewing pofi- | tively what ought to | be done to promote | this Work. | [rule] | By *JONATHAN EDWARDS*, A. M. | Paftor of the Church of CHRIST at *Northampton.* | [rule] | Ifai. 40. 3. *Prepare ye the Way of the Lord, make ftrait* | *in the Defart a high-Way for our God.* | [rule] | *BOSTON:* Printed and Sold by *S. Kneeland* | and *T. Green* in *Queen-Street*, 1742. *stet* acknowlege *stet* *Defart*

12mo.; 14.6 x 8.8 cm.; [A]^6, B-Z,^{6} Aa-Ii^6; [2], iv, 378 p.

Notes: p. 106 misnumbered 206 (pp. 1-105, 206, 107-378).

Contents: prp. [1]: title (verso blank); p. i: THE | PREFACE.; pp. 1-378: text; p. 378: ERRATA.

THJ 83 EAI 1:4939 NUC NE0046808 OCLC 8434261

Massachusetts Historical Society

130 • SOME | THOUGHTS | Concerning the prefent | REVIVAL of RELIGION | IN | *NEW-ENGLAND*, | AND | The Way in which it ought to be acknow- | ledged and promoted; | Humbly offer'd to the Publick, in a | TREATISE on that Subject, | In Five PARTS. | [in 2 cols., col. 1] PART I. Shewing that the Work | that has of late been going on | in that Land, is a glorious | Work of God. | PART II. Shewing the Obliga- | tions that all are under, to | acknowledge, rejoice in and | promote this Work; and | the great Danger of the con- | trary. | PART III. Shewing, in many | [short vertical rule, col. 2] Inftances, wherein the Sub- | jects, or zealous Promoters, | of this Work have been inju- | rioufly blamed. | PART IV. Shewing what Things | are to be corrected or avoided | in promoting this Work, or | in our Behaviour under it. | PART V. Shewing pofitively | what ought to be done to pro- | mote this Work. | [rule] | By JONATHAN EDWARDS, *A. M.* | Paftor of the Church of Chrift at *Northampton.* | [rule] | Ifa. xl. 3. *Prepare ye the Way of the Lord, make ftraight in the* | *Defert a High-way for our God.* | [rule] | *BOSTON*, Printed: | *EDINBURGH*, Reprinted by T. LUMISDEN and J. RO- | BERTSON, and fold at their Printing-houfe in the *Fifh-market.* | M.DCC.XLIII.

8vo.; 17.2 x 10.7 cm.; [A]^2, B-Z^4, Aa-Dd^4, Ee^5; iv, 221 [i.e., 217], [1] p.

Notes: p. 41 misnumbered 33; lacks pp. 125-128 (pp. 1-40, 33, 42-124, 129-221).

Contents: p. [i]: title (verso blank); p. iii: THE | PREFACE.; pp. 1-221: text; p. [222]: blank.

THJ 84 ESTC T78841 NUC NE0046810 OCLC 12981917

Houghton Library

131 • THOUGHTS | Concerning the | PRESENT REVIVAL | OF | RELIGION | IN | *NEW-ENGLAND.* | [rule] | By *JONATHAN EDWARDS*, A. M. | Paftor of the Church of Chrift at *Northampton.* | [rule] | Abridg'd by JOHN WESLEY, *A. M.* | Fellow of *Lincoln-College, Oxford.* | [rule] | *Prepare ye the Way of the Lord, make ftraight in the* | *Defert a High-Way for our God.* ISA. xl. 3. | [double rule] | *LONDON:* | Printed by W. STRAHAN; and fold by T. TRYE, | near *Gray's-Inn Gate, Holborn*; HENRY BUTLER, | in *Bow Church-Yard*; and at the *Foundery* near | *Upper-Moor-Fields.* MDCCXLV. | [Price 8 *d.* unbound.]

12mo.; 17.6 x 10.7 cm.; [A]^6, B-K^6, L^2; 124 p.

Contents: p. [1]: title (verso blank); p. [3]: THOUGHTS | Concerning the | PRESENT REVIVAL | OF | RELIGION | IN | *NEW-ENGLAND.*

THJ 85 ESTC T78842 NUC NE0046817 OCLC 9843266

Massachusetts Historical Society

132 • THOUGHTS | CONCERNING THE | REVIVAL | OF | RELIGION | IN | NEW-ENGLAND. | [short wavy rule] | BY *JONATHAN EDWARDS*, A. M. | Paſtor of the Church of CHRIST at NORTHAMPTON. | [short wavy rule] | ABRIDGED | BY *JOHN WESLEY*, M. A. | LATE FELLOW OF LINCOLN COLLEGE, OXFORD. | "Prepare ye the Way of the LORD, make ſtraight in | the deſert a high-way for our GOD." Iſa. xl. 3. | [short wavy rule] | *LONDON:* | PRINTED FOR G. WHITFIELD, CITY-ROAD; AND | SOLD AT THE METHODIST PREACHING-HOUSES | IN TOWN AND COUNTRY. 1798. | [short wavy rule] | [PRICE EIGHT-PENCE.]

12mo.; 17.1 x 10.1 cm.; $[A]^6$, $B-K^6$; 117, [3] p.

Contents: p. [1]: title (verso blank); p. [3]: THOUGHTS | CONCERNING THE REVIVAL OF | RELIGION IN | New-England.; pp. [118-120]: [advertisement].

THJ 86 ESTC T174512 NUC NE0046812
Presbyterian Historical Society

133 • SOME THOUGHTS | CONCERNING THE PRESENT | *Revival of Religion* | IN | NEW-ENGLAND, | AND THE WAY IN WHICH IT OUGHT TO BE ACKNOW- | LEDGED AND PROMOTED, | *HUMBLY OFFERED TO THE PUBLIC IN A* | TREATISE ON THAT SUBJECT. | IN FIVE PARTS. | [in 2 cols., col. 1] PART I. *Shewing that the work* | *that has of late been going on in* | *this land, is a glorious work of* | *God.* | PART II. *Shewing the obligations* | *that all are under to acknow-* | *ledge, rejoice in and promote this* | *work, and the great danger of* | *the contrary.* | PART III. *Shewing in many in-* | *ſtances, wherein the ſubjects,* | [short wavy vertical rule, col. 2.] *or zealous promoters of this* | *work, have been injuriouſly* | *blamed.* | PART IV. *Shewing what things* | *are to be corrected or avoided,* | *in promoting this work, or in* | *our behaviour under it.* | PART V. *Shewing poſitively what* | *ought to be done to promote this* | *work.* | [short decorative rule] | BY JONATHAN EDWARDS, A. M. | Paſtor of the Church of CHRIST at *Northampton.* | [short decorative rule] | Iſai. 40. 3. *Prepare ye the Way of the Lord, make straight* | *in the desert a high-way for our God.* | [wavy rule] | *LEXINGTON*, (K.) | RE-PRINTED BY JOSEPH CHARLESS, FROM A BOS- | TON EDITION PRINTED IN THE YEAR 1742. | [short tapered rule] | 1803.

18mo.; 15.2 x 9.3 cm.; $[A]^{18}$, $B-L^{18}$, M^8; iv, [5]-412 p.

Contents: p. [i]: title (verso blank); p. [iii]: THE PREFACE.; pp. [5]-390: text; p. [391]: *Subscribers' Names.*; p. 412: [advertisement].

THJ 87 EAI 2:4137 NUC NE0046813 OCLC 13898358
Yale Divinity School

134 • *THOUGHTS* | ON THE | REVIVAL OF RELIGION | IN | NEWENGLAND, | ABOUT THE YEAR | ONE THOUSAND SEVEN HUNDRED AND FORTY, | IN A | TREATISE, | OFFERED TO THE PUBLIC ON THAT SUBJECT. | [short decorative rule] | BY JONATHAN EDWARDS, A. M. | [short decorative rule] | PREPARE YE THE WAY OF THE LORD, MAKE STRAIGHT IN THE DES- | ERT A HIGHWAY FOR OUR GOD.—*Isaiah* xl. 3. | [short decorative rule] | PUBLISHED AT WORCESTER, | BY ISAIAH THOMAS, JUN. | *MARCH*—1808. | [short decorative rule] | ISAAC STURTEVANT, PRINTER.

20.3 x 12.4 cm.; $[A]^4$, $B-W-Z^4$, $2A-2I^4$; vi, [2], [9]-263 [i.e., 271], [1] p.

Notes: p. 199 misnumbered 109; pp. 209-216 repeated (pp. [9]-198, 109, 200-216, 209-263).

Contents: p. [i]: title (verso blank); p. [iii]: [advertisement]; p. [v]: AUTHOR's PREFACE.; p. [vii]: CONTENTS. (verso blank); p. [9]: REVIVAL OF RELIGION | IN | NEWENGLAND.; p. [264]: blank.

THJ 88 EAI 2:14923 NUC NE0046822 OCLC 8125524
Harvard Divinity School

135 • THOUGHTS | ON THE | REVIVAL OF RELIGION | IN | NEW-ENGLAND, | and | THE WAY IN WHICH IT OUGHT TO BE ACKNOWLEDGED | AND PROMOTED. | In five parts; | I. Shewing that the work that has of late been go- | ing on in this land, is a glorious work of God. | II. Shewing the obligations that all are under, | to acknowledge, rejoice in, and promote this | work, and the great danger of the contrary. | III. Shewing in many instances, wherein the sub- | jects, or zealous promoters of this work, have | been injuriously blamed. | IV. Shewing what things are to be corrected or | avoided, in promoting this work, or in our be- | haviour under it. | V. Shewing positively what ought to be done to | promote this work. | [short tapered rule] | BY JONATHAN EDWARDS, A. M. | Pastor of the Church of Christ at Northampton. | [short tapered rule] | Prepare ye the way of the Lord, make strait in the desert a high | way for our God....*Isaiah* xl. 3. | [short thick-thin rule] | *NORTHAMPTON:* | PUBLISHED BY SIMEON BUTLER. | *J. Metcalf....Printer.* | 1819.

14.3 x 8.5 cm.; $[1]^6$, $2\text{-}30^6$; 360 p.

Contents: p. [1]: title (verso blank); p. [3]: *PREFACE.*; p. [7]: REVIVAL OF RELIGION.

THJ 89 EAI 2:47883 NUC NE0046823 OCLC 5850061

Forbes Library

136 • THOUGHTS | CONCERNING | THE PRESENT REVIVAL OF RELIGION | IN | New-England. | [short rule] | BY JONATHAN EDWARDS, A. M. | *Pastor of the Church of Christ, at Northampton.* | [short rule] | ABRIDGED BY JOHN WESLEY, A. M. | Late Fellow of Lincoln College, Oxford. | [short thick-thin rule] | *Prepare ye the way of the Lord, make straight in the desert a high-way | for our God.*—Isa. xl. 3.

Contents: p. [139]: title; p. [140]: JAMES NICHOLS, PRINTER, | No. 2, Warwick Square, Newgate Street; pp. [141]-258 in A | CHRISTIAN LIBRARY: | CONSISTING OF | EXTRACTS FROM AND ABRIDGMENTS OF | THE | CHOICEST PIECES | OF | Practical Divinity | WHICH HAVE BEEN PUBLISHED IN THE ENGLISH TONGUE. | [short decorative rule] | IN THIRTY VOLUMES: | FIRST PUBLISHED IN 1750, IN FIFTY VOLUMES, DUODECIMO | [short rule] | BY THE REV. JOHN WESLEY, A. M., | SOMETIME FELLOW OF LINCOLN COLLEGE, OXFORD. | [short rule] | Vol. XXX. | [short thick-thin rule] | *LONDON:* PUBLISHED AND SOLD BY J. KERSHAW. | 14, *City-Road, and* 66, *Paternoster-Row.* | [short rule] | 1827.

21.1 x 12.8 cm.; 481 p.

THJ 90 OCLC 6969185

Boston University

137 • No. 278. | MEANS OF A REVIVAL. | [BY PRESIDENT EDWARDS.]

17.2 x 10.7 cm.; 8 p.

Notes: First published in 1833, 171,000 copies of this tract were distributed by 1875. This is a very attenuated summary of the conclusions to "Some Thoughts."—THJ; it was reprinted, pp. [1]-8 (also paged [265]-272), in TRACTS | OF THE | AMERICAN TRACT SOCIETY. | General Series. | [engraving] | Vol. VIII. | PRINTED BY THE | AMERICAN TRACT SOCIETY, | 150 NASSAU-STREET, NEW YORK.

Contents: caption title; p. 8: PUBLISHED BY THE AMERICAN TRACT SOCIETY.

THJ 91 OCLC 36112613

American Tract Society

138 • THOUGHTS | ON THE | REVIVAL OF RELIGION | IN | NEW ENGLAND, 1740. | TO WHICH IS PREFIXED | A NARRATIVE | OF THE | SURPRISING WORK OF GOD | IN | NORTHAMPTON, MASS., 1735. | [short wavy rule] | BY JONATHAN EDWARDS, A. M. | PASTOR OF THE CHURCH OF CHRIST IN NORTHAMPTON, AND AFTERWARDS | PRESIDENT OF NASSAU HALL COLLEGE, PRINCETON, N. J. | [short wavy rule] | PUBLISHED

BY | THE AMERICAN TRACT SOCIETY. | 150 NASSAU-STREET, NEW-YORK. | [short rule] | D Fanshaw, Printer.

18.8 x 10.8 cm.; [1]^{12}, 2-18^{12}, 19^{7}; 446 p.

Notes: By 1875, 16,413 copies had been distributed.—THJ; it was first published in 1845; in some copies, frontispiece portrait (no engraver); minor variants in title page; p. [2]: This edition is reprinted from the Worcester edition of Presi- | dent Edwards' works, with some corrections of inaccuracies of | style, and the omission, in three or four instances, of denomina- | tional terms which might be considered reproachful of some evan- | gelical Christians. The several parts of the work have also been | subdivided with appropriate heads, and a new table of contents | prepared.

Contents: p. [1]: title; p. [2]: [publisher's note]; p. [3]: CONTENTS.; p. [7]: NARRATIVE | OF THE | SURPRISING WORK OF GOD. | 1735.; p. [102]: blank; p. [103]: THOUGHTS | ON THE | REVIVAL OF RELIGION, | IN | NEW ENGLAND | A.D. 1740, | AND | THE WAY IN WHICH IT OUGHT TO BE | ACKNOWLEDGED | AND PROMOTED. | [short wavy rule] | "Prepare ye the way of the Lord, make straight in the desert a highway | for our God." Isaiah 40:3. | [short wavy rule] | PUBLISHED BY | THE AMERICAN TRACT SOCIETY, | 150 NASSAU-STREET, NEW-YORK. | [short rule] | D. Fanshaw, Printer.; p. [104]: ADVERTISEMENT.; p. [105]: THE AUTHOR'S PREFACE.; p. [107]: REVIVAL OF RELIGION | IN | NEW ENGLAND.

THJ 92 NUC NE0046819 OCLC 4872872

Gordon-Conwell Theological Seminary

139 • SPIRITUAL PRIDE, | ITS DECEITFUL NATURE AND EVIL FRUITS; | WITH WARNING AGAINST ITS CORRUPT INFLUENCE IN | THE PROFESSING CHURCH, AS THE ROOT OF DISSENSION, | FALSE PRINCIPLES, AND MANY PRACTICAL | ERRORS; | AND AN EXHORTATION TO MINISTERS AND PEOPLE. | BY | PRESIDENT EDWARDS. | (ABRIDGED.) | FIRST PRINTED IN 1742. | "One is your Master, even Christ, and all ye are brethren."–Matt. xxiii. 8. | "ONLY by PRIDE cometh contention."–Prov. xiii. 10. | "The fear of the Lord is to hate evil, PRIDE, and arrogancy, and the evil way | and the froward mouth."–Prov. viii. 13. | "We wrestle not against flesh and blood, but against spiritual wicked- | ness in high places" [marg., against wicked spirits in heavenly places]– | Eph. vi. 12. | LONDON: | WARD & CO., 27, PATERNOSTER ROW. | [short rule] | *Sixpence*.

14 x 9 cm.; π^{1}, [A]^{6}, B-F^{6}, G^{4}; xii, [2], [13]-80 p.

Notes: p. iv: The following treatise is taken from "Thoughts on the | Revival of Religion in New England," which has been | often reprinted. The copy used is a Scotch edition of | 1743, and the more valued as having been the venerable | John Newton's, whose autograph and, most likely, his marks it bears.

Contents: p. [i]: title; p. [ii]: Published for the benefit of the "Aged Pilgrim's Friend | Society," instituted in 1807, for granting Annual Life | Pensions of Ten and Five Guineas to the Aged Christian | Poor, of both sexes, and of *every religious denomination*, | who are over sixty years of age, and who give Scriptural | evidence that they are of the "Household of Faith." | [ornament] About 340 Pensioners are now upon the Society.; p. [iii]: PREFACE. [signed] E. H. | *Bermondsey*, | *May* 28, 1853.; p. [xi]: BIOGRAPHICAL SKETCH OF THE AUTHOR.; prp. [1-2]: INDEX.; p. [13]: SPIRITUAL PRIDE.; p. 80: [short rule] | [8 lines] | [signed] J. BERRIDGE. | [short rule] | W. H. Collingridge, City Press, Long Lane.

THJ 93

National Library of Scotland

THE GREAT CONCERN OF A WATCHMAN FOR SOULS

140 • *The great Concern of* A WATCHMAN FOR SOULS, | *appearing in the* DUTY *he has to do, and the* | ACCOUNT *he has to give, repreſented & improved*, | IN A | SERMON | Preach'd at the | ORDINATION | Of the REVEREND | Mr. *Jonathan Judd*, | To the Paſtoral Office over the Church of

CHRIST, | in the New Precinct at *Northampton*, | *June* 8. 1743. | [decorative rule] | By *Jonathan Edwards*, M.A. | Paſtor of the firſt Church of CHRIST in *Northampton*. | [decorative rule] | Ezra 8. 29. *Watch ye, and keep them, until ye weigh* | *them before the Chief of the Prieſts, and the Levites,* | *and Chief of the Fathers of* Iſrael, *at* Jeruſalem, *in* | *the Chambers of the Houſe of the* LORD. | [decorative rule] | BOSTON, Printed by *Green*, *Buſhell*, and *Allen*, for | *N. Procter*, at the *Bible* and *Dove* in *Ann-Street*, | near the *Draw-Bridge*. MDCCXLIII.

8vo.; 15.8 x 10.2 cm. (uncut); [A]^4, B-F^4, G^1; 50 p.

Contents: p. [1]: Mr. *Edwards*'s | SERMON | AT THE | ORDINATION | Of the REVEREND | Mr. *Jonathan Judd*. (verso blank); p. [3]: title (verso blank); p. [5]: The Watchman's | *Duty* and *Account*.; p. 41: THE | *CHARGE* | Given by the Rev. Mr. *Hopkins* | of *Springfield*.

THJ 94 EAI 1:5172 NUC NE0046610 OCLC 41879527

Princeton University

THE TRUE EXCELLENCY OF A MINISTER OF THE GOSPEL

141 • The true Excellency of a MINISTER of the GOSPEL. | [rule] | A | SERMON | Preach'd at *Pelham*, Aug. 30. 1744. Being the Day of the | ORDINATION | OF THE | Rev^d Mr. *Robert Abercrombie* | TO THE | Work of the Goſpel Miniſtry | In that Place. | [rule] | By *Jonathan Edwards*, A.M. | Paſtor of the firſt Church in *Northampton*. | [rule] | [ornament] | [rule] | Deut. xxxiii. 8. *And of* Levi *he ſaid, Let thy* Thumim *and thy* Urim *be with* | *thy Holy One*. | [rule] | *BOSTON*: Printed by ROGERS and FOWLE; for W. MC ALPINE | in Union-Street. 1744.

4to.; 19.9 x 14.7 cm.; [A]^4, B-C^4; 22, [2] p.

Contents: p. [1]: title (verso blank); p. [3]: THE | True Excellency of a Goſpel Miniſter.; pp. [23-24]: blank.

THJ 95 EAI 1:5385 NUC NE0046871 OCLC 31356800

Massachusetts Historical Society

THE CHURCH'S MARRIAGE TO HER SONS AND TO HER GOD

142 • *The Church's Marriage to her Sons, and* | *to her GOD:* | A | SERMON | Preached at the INSTALMENT of the | Rev. Mr. *Samuel Buel* | As Paſtor of the Church and Congregation at | *Eaſt-Hampton* on *Long-Iſland*, | September 19. 1746. | [rule] | *By* JONATHAN EDWARDS, *A. M.* | Paſtor of the firſt Church in *Northampton* in *New-England*. | [rule] | *BOSTON:* | Printed and Sold by *S. Kneeland* and *T. Green* in | Queen-Street. 1746.

8vo.; 18.8 x 12.3 cm.; A-E^4, F^2; 43, [1] p.

Contents: p. [1]: Mr. *Edwards*'s | SERMON | At the *Inſtalment* of the Reverend | Mr. *Samuel Buel*. (verso blank); p. [3]: title (verso blank); pp. 5-43: text; p. [44]: blank.

THJ 96 EAI 1:5766 NUC NE0046494 OCLC 6130647

Harvard Divinity School

A TREATISE CONCERNING RELIGIOUS AFFECTIONS

143 • A | *TREATISE* | Concerning | Religious Affections, | In Three PARTS; | PART I. Concerning the

Nature of the *Affections*, | and their Importance in *Religion.* | PART II. Shewing what are *no certain Signs* that *re- | ligious Affections* are *gracious*, or that they are *not.* | PART III. Shewing what are *diſtinguiſhing Signs* of | truly gracious and *holy Affections.* | [rule] | By *Jonathan Edwards*, A.M. | And Paſtor of the *firſt* Church in *Northampton.* | [rule] | Levit. ix. ult. and x. 1, 2. *And there came a Fire out from before the | Lord,-----upon the Altar; -----which when all the People ſaw, they | ſhouted and fell on their Faces. And* Nadab *and* Abihu ----- *offered | ſtrange Fire before the Lord, which he commanded them not: And there | went out a Fire from the Lord, and devoured them, and they died before | the Lord.* | Cant. ii. 12, 13. *The Flowers appear on the Earth, the Time of the | Singing of Birds is come, and the Voice of the Turtle is heard in our | Land; the Fig-tree putteth forth her green Figs, and the Vines with the | tender Grape, give a good Smell.* Ver. 15. *Take us the Foxes, the | little Foxes, which ſpoil the Vines; for our Vines have tender Grapes.* | [rule] | *BOSTON:* | Printed for S. KNEELAND and T. GREEN in *Queen- | ſtreet*, over againſt the Priſon. 1746.

4to.; 19.2 x 13.2 cm.; [A]^4, B-Y^8, Z^4, §*§^{4}; [2], vi, 343, [9] p.

Notes: p. 215 misnumbered 115 (pp. [1]-214, 115, 216-343).

Contents: prp. [1]: title (verso blank); p. [i]: THE | *PREFACE.*; pp. [1]-343: text; p. [344]: *ERRORS to be corrected.*; p. [345]: A TABLE of the Contents | of the foregoing Treatiſe.; p. [352]: [advertisement].

THJ 97 EAI 1:5767 NUC NE0046835 OCLC 6194142

Massachusetts Historical Society

144 • A | TREATISE | CONCERNING | RELIGIOUS AFFECTIONS: | In THREE PARTS. | PART I. Concerning the Nature of the *Af- | fections*, and their Importance in *Religion.* | PART II. Shewing what are no certain Signs | that *religious Affections* are gracious, or that | they are *not.* | PART III. Shewing what are *diſtinguiſhing Signs* | of truly *gracious* and *holy Affections.* | [rule] | By the late Rev. JONATHAN EDWARDS, *A. M.* | and Preſident of the College of *New Jerſey.* | [rule] | ABRIDGED by WILLIAM GORDON. | [rule] | Levit. ix. ult. and x. 1, 2. *And there came a Fire out from | before the Lord—upon the Altar;—which when all the | People ſaw, they | ſhouted, and fell on their Faces. And* Na- | dab *and Abihu—offered ſtrange Fire before the Lord, which | he commanded them not: and there | went out a Fire from | the Lord, and devoured them, and they died before the Lord.* | Cant. ii. 12, 13. *The Flowers appear on the Earth; the | Time of the Singing of Birds is come, and the Voice of the | Turtle is heard in our Land; the Fig-tree putteth forth her | green Figs, and the Vines with the tender Grape, give a good | Smell.* Ver. 15. *Take us the Foxes, the little Foxes, which | ſpoil the Vines; for our Vines have tender Grapes.* | [rule] | LONDON: | Printed for T. FIELD, at the Wheat-ſheaf the Corner of | Pater-noſter Row, Cheapſide. 1762.

12mo.; 16.4 x 10.1 cm.; [A]^6, B-M^{12}, N^6; xii, 263, [13] p.

Contents: p. [i]: title (verso blank); p. [iii]: THE | AUTHOR'S PREFACE.; p. [ix]: THE | PREFACE | OF THE | COMPILER of this ABRIDGMENT.; p. xii: ERRATA.; pp. [1]-263: text; p. [264]: blank; p. [265]: A TABLE of the CONTENTS | of the foregoing Treatiſe.

THJ 98 ESTC T78848 NUC NE0046838

John Carter Brown Library

149 • A | TREATISE | Concerning | Religious Affections, | In Three PARTS; | PART I. Concerning the Nature of the *Affections*, | and their Importance in *Religion.* | PART II. Shewing what are *no certain Signs* that *reli- | gious Affections* are *gracious*, or that they are *not.* | PART III. Shewing what are *diſtinguiſhing Signs* of | truly gracious and *holy Affections.* | [rule] | By *Jonathan Edwards*, A. M. | And Paſtor of the *firſt* Church in *Northampton.* | [rule] | Levit. ix. ult. and x. 1, 2. *And there came a Fire*

out from before the | Lord,-----upon the Altar;-----which when all the People ſaw, they | ſhouted and fell on their Faces. And Nadab *and* Abihu-----*offered | ſtrange Fire before the Lord, which he commanded them not: And | there went out a Fire from the Lord, and devoured them, and they | died before the Lord.* | Cant. ii. 12, 13. *The Flowers appear on the Earth, the Time of the | Singing of Birds is come, and the Voice of the Turtle is heard in our | Land; the Fig-tree putteth forth her green Figs, and the Vines with | the tender Grape, give a good Smell.* Ver. 15. *Take us the Foxes, | the little Foxes, which ſpoil the Vines; for our Vines have tender | Grapes.* | [rule] | The SECOND EDITION. | [rule] | *BOSTON* PRINTED: | NEW-YORK; Re-printed by J. PARKER, for GARRAT NOEL, | near the Merchant's Coffee-Houſe. 1768.

8vo.; 20.3 x 14.2 cm. (uncut); [A]^8, B-Z^8, Aa-Gg^8, Hh^4; [2], vi, 470, [10] p.

Notes: p. 57 misnumbered 56; p. 323 misnumbered 223 (pp. [1]-56, 56, 58-322, 223, 324-470).

Contents: prp. [1]: title (verso blank); p. [i]: THE | *PREFACE.*; pp. [1]-470: text; p. [471]: A TABLE of the Contents | of the foregoing Treatiſe.; p. [480]: blank.

THJ 99 EAI 1:10890 NUC NE0046839 OCLC 3658712

Houghton Library

150 • A | TREATISE | CONCERNING | RELIGIOUS AFFECTIONS. | IN THREE PARTS. | PART I. Concerning the Nature of the *Affec- | tions*, and their Importance in *Religion.* | PART II. Shewing what are *no certain Signs* that | *religious Affections* are *gracious*, or that they | are *not.* | PART III. Shewing what are *diſtinguiſhing Signs* | of truly gracious and *holy Affections.* | By JONATHAN EDWARDS, A. M. | And Paſtor of the firſt Church in Northampton | Lev. ix. ult. and x. 1. 2. And there came a fire out from before the Lord,---- | upon the altar;---which when all the people ſaw, they ſhouted and fell on | their faces. And Nadab and Abihu----offered ſtrange fire before the Lord, | which he commanded them not: and there went out fire from the Lord, | and devoured them, and they died before the Lord. | Cant. ii. 12. 13. The flowers appear on the earth, the time of the ſinging of | birds is come, and the voice of the turtle is heard in our land. The fig-tree | putteth forth her green figs, and the vines with the tender grape give a | good ſmell. Ver. 15. Take us the foxes, the little foxes which ſpoil the | vines: for our vines have tender grapes. | EDINBURGH: | Printed by JOHN GRAY, | For E. & C. DILLY, in the Poultry, London; and J. WOOD, | Edinburgh. MDCCLXXII.

8vo.; 20.6 x 12.6 cm.; [A]^4, B-Z^4, Aa-Zz^4, Aaa^4; viii, 356, [12] p.

Contents: p. [i]: title (verso blank); p. [iii]: THE | PREFACE.; pp. [1]-356: text; p. [357]: A TABLE of the Contents of the foregoing | Treatiſe.; p. [368]: blank.

THJ 100 ESTC T78845 NUC NE0046840 OCLC 4269634

John Carter Brown Library

151 • A | TREATISE | CONCERNING | RELIGIOUS AFFECTIONS, | IN THREE PARTS. | PART I. Concerning the Nature of the *Affec- | tions*, and their Importance in *Religion.* | PART II. Shewing what are *no certain Signs* that | *religious Affections* are *gracious*, or that they | are *not.* | PART III. Shewing what are *diſtinguiſhing Signs* | of truly gracious and *holy Affections.* | By JONATHAN EDWARDS, A. M. | Preſident of the College of New Jerſey. | [rule] | The FOURTH EDITION. | [rule] | Lev. ix. ult. and x. 1, 2. And there came a fire out from before the | Lord,--upon the altar;--which when all the people ſaw, they | ſhouted and fell on their faces. And Nadab and Abihu--offered | ſtrange fire before the Lord, which he commanded them not: | And there went out a fire from the Lord, and devoured them, | and they died before the Lord. | Cant. ii. 12, 13. The flowers appear on the earth, the time of | the ſinging

of birds is come, and the voice of the turtle is | heard in our land. The fig-tree putteth forth her green figs, | and the vines with the tender grape give a good ſmell. Ver. | 15. Take us the foxes, the little foxes, which ſpoil the vines: | for our vines have tender grapes. | [rule] | Printed for GEORGE KEITH, in *Gracechurch-Street.* | MDCCLXXIV.

8vo.; 19 x 11.4 cm.; $[A]^8$, $B\text{-}Z^8$, $Aa\text{-}Gg^8$, Hh^4; [2], vi, 470, [10] p.

Notes: p. 57 misnumbered 56; p. 323 misnumbered 223 (pp. [1]-56, 56, 58-322, 223, 324-470); although called the fourth edition, no third has been found; perhaps, the first Edinburgh (1772) was considered a third edition since it fell between the New York second (1762) and the London fourth (1774).

Contents: prp. [1]: title (verso blank); p. [i]: THE | *PREFACE.*; pp. [1]-470: text; p. [471]: A TABLE of the Contents | of the foregoing Treatiſe.; p. [480]: blank.

THJ 101 ESTC T176400 NUC NE0046841 OCLC 36814471

John Carter Brown Library

152 • VERHANDELING | OVER DE | GODSDIENSTIGE | HARTSTOGTEN, | DOOR | *JONATHAN EDWARDS,* | *Profesſor en Predikant, te* Northampton, | *in* Nieuw-Engeland. | [rule] | UIT HET ENGELSCH VERTAALD | DOOR | MARINUS VAN WERKHOVEN. | [thick-thin rule] | *Te UTRECHT,* | Bij de Wed. J. J. VAN POOLSUM. | Stads-Drukkeres. | M. DCC. LXXIX.

8vo.; 22.2 x 13.3 cm.; π^1, $*^8$, $**^7$, $***^4$, $***^8$, $****^4$, $A\text{-}Z^8$, $Aa\text{-}Pp^8$, Qq^4; [64], 614 p.

Notes: a Dutch translation of *Religious Affections*.

Contents: prp. [1]: title; prp. [2]: attestation [signed] Uit naam en last der Faculteit, | ÆGIDIUS GILLISSEN | *SS. Theol. Doct. & Prof. h. t.* | *Fac. Decanus.* | LEIDEN | *den 23 October* 1779.; prp. [3]: BERICHT | VAN DEN | UITGEEVER. [dated] *Den 13*[den] *van Wijnmaand,* | 1779.; prp. [41]: VOORREDE des SCHRIJVERS.; prp. [57]: INHOUD.; p. [1]: VERHANDELING | OVER DE | GODSDIENSTIGE | HARTSTOGTEN.

THJ 102 NUC NE0046888 OCLC 45231287

Harvard Divinity School

153 • A | TREATISE | CONCERNING | RELIGIOUS AFFECTIONS. | IN THREE PARTS. | PART I. Concerning the Nature of the AFFECTIONS, and | their Importance in RELIGION. | PART II. Shewing what are NO CERTAIN SIGNS that RE- | LIGIOUS AFFECTIONS are GRACIOUS, or that they | are NOT. | PART III. Shewing what ARE DISTINGUISHING SIGNS | of truly gracious and HOLY AFFECTIONS. | [rule] | *By* JONATHAN EDWARDS, A. M. | And Paſtor of the firſt Church at Northampton. | [rule] | Lev. ix. ult. and x. 1, 2. *And there came a fire out from before the* | *Lord,—upon the altar;—which when all the people ſaw, they ſhouted,* | *and fell on their faces. And Nadab and Abihu—offered ſtrange fire* | *before the Lord, which he commanded them not: and there went out fire* | *from the Lord, and devoured them, and they died before the Lord.* | Cant. ii. 12, 13. *The flowers appear on the earth, the time of the ſinging* | *of birds is come, and the voice of the turtle is heard in our land. The* | *fig-tree putteth forth her green figs, and the vines with the tender grape* | *give a good ſmell.* Verſ. 15. *Take us the foxes, the little foxes, which* | *ſpoil the vines: for our vines have tender grapes.* | [double rule] | ELIZABETH-TOWN: | Printed by SHEPARD KOLLOCK, for ROBERT HODGE, | No. 237, *Queen-Street,* NEW-YORK. | [short rule] | M,DCC,LXXXVII.

8vo.; 19.8 x 12.2 cm.; π^8, $D\text{-}Z^4$, $Aa\text{-}Zz^4$, $Aaa\text{-}Rrr^4$, Sss^2; viii, [8], [25]-499, [9] p.

Notes: p. 164 misnumbered 264 ([25]-163, 264, 165-499); in some copies, pp. [3-4] bound before [1-2], [7-8] before [5-6]; in other copies, these errors have been corrected.

Contents: p. [i]: title (verso blank); p. [iii]: THE | PREFACE.; p. [9]: SUBSCRIBERS NAMES.; p. [25]: THE | LIFE | Of the Reverend | MR. JONATHAN EDWARDS.; p. 107: APPENDIX, No. I. | *Containing a brief* ACCOUNT *of Mrs.* ESTHER | BURR, *and ſome Extracts of* LETTERS *wrote by her*.; p. 111: APPENDIX, No. II. | *Containing a ſhort Sketch of Mrs.* EDWARDS'S LIFE *and* | CHARACTER.; pp. [117-118]: blank; p. [119]: A | TREATISE | CONCERNING |

RELIGIOUS AFFECTIONS. | IN THREE PARTS.; p. [500]: blank; p. [501]: A TABLE *of the* CONTENTS *of the* | *foregoing* TREATISE.
THJ 103 EAI 1:20339 NUC NE0046842 OCLC 5851482
Forbes Library

154 • A | TREATISE | CONCERNING | RELIGIOUS AFFECTIONS, | IN THREE PARTS. | *PART FIRST.* | CONCERNING THE NATURE OF THE AFFECTIONS, AND | THEIR IMPORTANCE IN RELIGION. | *PART SECOND.* | SHEWING WHAT ARE NO CERTAIN SIGNS THAT RELI- | GIOUS AFFECTIONS ARE GRACIOUS, OR THAT THEY | ARE NOT. | *PART THIRD.* | SHEWING WHAT ARE DISTINGUISHING SIGNS OF TRULY | GRACIOUS AND HOLY AFFECTIONS. | [rule] | BY JONATHAN EDWARDS, A. M. | And Paſtor of the firſt Church in *Northampton.* | [rule] | [short tapered rule] | EDINBURGH: | PRINTED FOR W. LAING, HEAD OF CANONGATE; | AND J. MATTHEWS, No. 18. STRAND, LONDON. | 1789.
12mo.; 17.6 x 10.1 cm.; π^1, A-Z^6, Aa-Qq^6; [2], viii, [9]-472 p.
Notes: in some copies, sig. B^6 (repeated) follows sig. Rr^2 (pp. [9]-472, [473-484]: [advertisement]).
Contents: prp. [1]: title (verso blank); p. [i]: *INTRODUCTION.*; pp. [9]-472: text.
THJ 104 ESTC T78849 NUC NE0046843 OCLC 30651486
Forbes Library

155 • A | TREATISE | CONCERNING | RELIGIOUS AFFECTIONS, | IN THREE PARTS. | [short decorative rule] | *PART FIRST.* | CONCERNING THE NATURE OF THE AFFECTIONS, AND | THEIR IMPORTANCE IN RELIGION. | [short decorative rule] | *PART SECOND.* | SHEWING WHAT ARE NO CERTAIN SIGNS THAT | RELIGIOUS AFFECTIONS ARE GRACIOUS, OR THAT | THEY ARE NOT. | [short decorative rule] | *PART THIRD.* | SHEWING WHAT ARE DISTINGUISHING SIGNS OF TRULY | GRACIOUS AND HOLY AFFECTIONS. | [rule] | BY JONATHAN EDWARDS, A. M. | And Paſtor of the firſt Church in NORTHAMPTON. | [rule] | [short decorative rule] | *BOSTON:* | PRINTED FOR B. LARKIN, J. WHITE, THOMAS | AND ANDREWS, D. WEST, E. LARKIN, jun. | J. WEST, AND THE PROPRIETOR OF THE | BOSTON BOOK-STORE. | [short double rule] | 1794.
12mo.; 16.7 x 10.3 cm.; $[A]^6$, B-W-Z^6, Aa-Kk^6; viii, [9]-406, [2] p.
Contents: p. [i]: title (verso blank); p. [iii]: INTRODUCTION.; pp. [9]-406: text; pp. [407-408]: blank.
THJ 105 EAI 1:26932 NUC NE0046844 OCLC 5866915
Massachusetts Historical Society

156 • A | TREATISE | CONCERNING | RELIGIOUS AFFECTIONS, | IN THREE PARTS. | *PART FIRST.* | CONCERNING THE NATURE OF THE AFFECTIONS, AND | THEIR IMPORTANCE IN RELIGION. | *PART SECOND.* | SHEWING WHAT ARE NO CERTAIN SIGNS THAT RELIGIOUS | AFFECTIONS ARE GRACIOUS, OR THAT THEY ARE NOT. | *PART THIRD.* | SHEWING WHAT ARE DISTINGUISHING SIGNS OF TRULY | GRACIOUS AND HOLY AFFECTIONS. | [double rule] | BY JONATHAN EDWARDS, A. M. | And Paſtor of the Firſt Church in *Northampton.* | [short tapered rule] | *PHILADELPHIA:* | PRINTED FOR MATHEW CAREY, | NO. 118, MARKET-STREET. | [short tapered rule] | OCT. 22, 1794.
8vo.; 17.6 x 11.2 cm.; π^1, B-Z^4, Aa-Yy^4; [2], vi, [7]-351, [1] p.
Notes: p. 309 misnumbered 306 (pp. [7]-308, 306, 310-351, [352]).
Contents: prp. [1]: title (verso blank); p. [i]: INTRODUCTION.; pp. [7]-351: text; p. [352]: blank.

THJ 106 EAI 1:26933 NUC NE0046845 OCLC 6477147
Houghton Library

157 • A | TREATISE | CONCERNING | RELIGIOUS AFFECTIONS. | IN THREE PARTS. | PART I. Concerning the nature of the AFFECTIONS, and | their Importance in RELIGION. | PART II. Shewing what are NO CERTAIN SIGNS that | RELIGIOUS AFFECTIONS are GRACIOUS or that | they are not. | PART III. Shewing what are DISTINGUISHING SIGNS | of truly gracious and HOLY AFFECTIONS. | BY JONATHAN EDWARDS, A. M. | And Paftor of the firft Church in Northampton. | Lev. ix. ult. and x. 1. 2. And there came a fire out from before the Lord, | — upon the altar;—which when all the people faw, they fhouted and | fell on their faces. And Nadab and Abihu—offered ftrange fire before | the Lord, which he commanded them not: and there went out a fire | from the Lord, and devoured them, and they died before the Lord. | Cant. ii. 12. 13. The flowers appear on the earth, the time of the finging | of birds is come, and the voice of the turtle is heard in our land. The | fig-tree putteth forth her green figs, and the vines with the tender | grapes give a good fmell. Ver. 15. Take us the little foxes, the little | foxes which fpoil the vines; for our vines have tender grapes. | [short tapered rule] | *LONDON:* | PRINTED for the BOOKSELLERS | [short thick-thin rule] | M,DCC,XCVI. *stet* the little foxes, the little | foxes

12mo.; 17.8 x 10.4 cm.; π^5, A-Z^6, Aa-Nn^6, Oo^4; x, 439, [1] p.

Contents: p. [i]: title (verso blank); p. [iii]: THE | PREFACE.; pp. [1]-439: text; p. [440]: blank.

THJ 107 ESTC T78847 NUC NE0046846 OCLC 3067084
John Carter Brown Library

158 • A | TREATISE | ON | RELIGIOUS AFFECTIONS: | IN THREE PARTS. | [short wavy rule] | PART I. Containing the Nature of the AFFECTIONS, | and their Importance in RELIGION. | PART II. Shewing what are no certain Signs that | RELIGIOUS AFFECTIONS are gracious, or that they | are NOT. | PART III. Shewing what are DISTINGUISHING SIGNS | of truly GRACIOUS and HOLY AFFECTIONS. | [short wavy rule] | By the Rev. JONATHAN EDWARDS, A. M. | Prefident of the College of New-Jerfey. | [short wavy rule] | Abridged by the Rev. JOHN WESLEY. | [short line of asterisks] | *LONDON*: | Printed at the Conference-Office, North-Green, Finsbury-Square. | G. STORY, Agent. Sold by G. WHITFIELD, New-Chapel, | City-Road, and at the Methodift Preaching-Houfes in | Town and Country. 1801.

12mo.; 15.6 x 9.5 cm.; $[A]^6$, B-F^6; 69, [3] p.

Notes: p. 3: 1. THE defign of Mr. EDWARDS in the Treatife, | from which the following Extract is made, | feems to have been (chiefly, if not altogether) to ferve | his hypothefis. In three preceding tracts, he had given | an account of a glorious work in New-England; of | abundance of finners of every fort and degree, who | were in a fhort time converted to God. But in a few | years, a confiderable part of thefe "turned back as a | dog to vomit." What was the plain inference to | be drawn from this? Why, that a true believer may | "make fhipwreck of the Faith." How then could | he evade the force of this? Truly by eating his own | words, and proving, (as well as the nature of the thing | would bear,) that they were no believers at all! | 2. In order to this, he heaps together fo many | curious, fubtle, metaphyfical diftinctions, as are fuf- | ficient to puzzle the brain, and confound the intellects, | of all the plain men and women in the univerfe; and | to make them doubt of, if not wholly deny, all the | work which God had wrought in their souls. | 3. Out of this dangerous heap, wherein much | wholefome food is mixt with much deadly poifon, I have | felected many remarks and admonitions, which may be | of great ufe to the children of God. May God write | them in the hearts of all that defire to walk as Chrift | alfo walked!

Contents: p. [1]: title (verso blank); p. 3: TO THE READER [signed] JOHN WESLEY. | *Briftol, Sept.* 1, 1773.; p. 4: ON | RELIGIOUS AFFECTIONS.; p. 69: Printed by G. STORY, North-Green, Finsbury-Square.; pp. [70-72]: [advertisement].

THJ 108 NUC NE0046850 OCLC 18930621
Princeton Theological Seminary

159 • A | TREATISE | CONCERNING | RELIGIOUS AFFECTIONS, | IN THREE PARTS. | [in 2 cols., col. 1] I. NATURE OF THE AFFEC- | TIONS, AND THEIR IMPORT- | ANCE IN RELIGION. | II. SHEWING WHAT ARE NO | CERTAIN SIGNS THAT RE- | LIGIOUS AFFECTIONS ARE | [short double vertical rule, col. 2] GRACIOUS, OR THAT THEY | ARE NOT. | III. SHEWING WHAT ARE | DISTINGUISHING SIGNS OF | TRULY GRACIOUS AND HO- | LY AFFECTIONS. | [short decorative rule] | BY THE LATE REVEREND | JONATHAN EDWARDS, A. M. | PRESIDENT OF THE COLLEGE OF NEWJERSEY. | [short decorative rule] | [thick-thin rule] | PUBLISHED AT WORCESTER, | BY ISAIAH THOMAS, JUN. | [short decorative rule] | *ISAAC STURTEVANT, PRINTER.* | [short line of stops] | 1808.

20.4 x 12.7 cm.; [A]^4, B-W-Z^4, 2A-2W-2Z^4, 3A-3D^4; viii, [9]-416 p.

Contents: p. [i]: title (verso blank); p. [iii]: INTRODUCTION.; p. [9]: RELIGIOUS AFFECTIONS.

THJ 109 EAI 2:14924 NUC NE0046834 OCLC 3067074
Harvard Divinity School

160 • CYFARWYDDIADAU | AC | Annogaethau I Gredinwyr, | I RODDI | CWBL DDIWYDRWYDD | I WNEUTHUR EU | GALWEDIGAETH A'U HETHOLEDIGAETH YN SICR. | [short tapered rule] | A GASGLWYD, YN BENAF, | Allan o Waith y Parch. JONATHAN EDWARDS, o Loegr Newydd; | SEF, EI | "DRAETHAWD AR SERCHIADAU CREFYDDOL:" | AC | *ESPONIAD Y Dr. OWEN, AR PSALM CXXX.* | [short tapered rule] | GAN JOHN ROBERTS. | [short tapered rule] | [ornament] BALA [ornament] | ARGRAFFEDIG GAN R. SAUNDERSON. | 1809. | *(Pris Tair Ceiniog.)*

16.6 x 10.3 cm.; [A]^2, B-C^6; iv, [5]-28 p.

Notes: a Welsh translation of a brief selection from *Religious Affections*, the first of nine works of Edwards published in Welsh in the nineteenth century; for the complete text in Welsh, see 174.

Contents: p. [i]: title (verso blank); p. [iii]: AT YR | EGLWYS A'R GWRANDAWYR, | ARFEROL O | *YMGYNNULL YN YR HEN GAPEL*, | LLANBRYNMAIR. [signed] LLANBRYNMAIR, | JOHN ROBERTS. | *Medi* 18, 1809.; p. [5]: *Cyfarwyddiadau*, &c.; p. 28: *Bala: argraffedig gan R. Saunderson.*

Harvard University

161 • A | TREATISE | CONCERNING | RELIGIOUS AFFECTIONS, | IN THREE PARTS. | [short tapered rule] | PART I.—CONCERNING THE NATURE OF THE AFFECTIONS, | AND THEIR IMPORTANCE IN RELIGION. | PART II.—SHEWING WHAT ARE NO CERTAIN SIGNS THAT | RELIGIOUS AFFECTIONS ARE GRACIOUS, OR THAT THEY | ARE NOT. | PART III.—SHEWING WHAT ARE DISTINGUISHING SIGNS | OF TRULY GRACIOUS AND HOLY AFFECTIONS. | [short thick-thin rule] | BY JONATHAN EDWARDS, A. M. | AND PASTOR OF THE FIRST CHURCH IN NORTHAMPTON. | [short thin-thick rule] | EDINBURGH: | PRINTED FOR J. OGLE, PARLIAMENT-SQUARE; M. OGLE, AND | J. STEVEN & CO. GLASGOW; R. OGLE, AND T. HAMILTON, | LONDON; AND T. JOHNSTON, DUBLIN. | [short rule] | 1810. | [short wavy rule | *GEORGE CAW, PRINTER.*

18.2 x 10.5 cm.; [A]^4, B-Z^6, Aa-Kk^6, Ll^2; viii, 388 p.

Contents: p. [i]: title (verso blank); p. [iii]: *INTRODUCTION*.; pp. [1]-388: text; p. 388: *GEO. CAW, Printer,* | *Libberton-wynd.* | [brace].

THJ 110 NUC NE0046852 OCLC 14050028
Drew University

162 • A | TREATISE | CONCERNING | RELIGIOUS AFFECTIONS, | IN THREE PARTS. | [short tapered rule] | PART I....CONCERNING THE NATURE OF THE AFFECTIONS, | AND THEIR IMPORTANCE IN RELIGION. | PART II....SHEWING WHAT ARE NO CERTAIN SIGNS THAT RE- | LIGIOUS AFFECTIONS ARE GRACIOUS, OR THAT THEY ARE | NOT. | PART III....SHEWING WHAT ARE DISTINGUISHING SIGNS, OR | TRULY GRACIOUS AND HOLY AFFECTIONS. | [short thick-thin rule] | BY JONATHAN EDWARDS, A. M. | AND PASTOR OF THE FIRST CHURCH IN NORTHAMPTON. | [short thin-thick rule] | EDINBURGH: | PRINTED FOR J. OGLE; M. OGLE, GLASGOW; R. OGLE, | AND T. HAMILTON, LONDON; AND | T. JOHNSTON, DUBLIN. | [short rule] | 1812. | [short wavy rule] | *GEO. CAW, PRINTER.*

17.6 x 10.3 cm.; π^4, B-Z^6, Aa-Kk^6, Ll^2; viii, 388 p.

Contents: p. [i]: title (verso blank); p. [iii]: *INTRODUCTION*.; pp. [1]-388: text; p. 388: *Geo. Caw, Printer,* | *Libberton-wynd.* | [brace].

THJ 112 NUC NE0046853

Lutheran Theological Seminary

163 • A | TREATISE | CONCERNING | RELIGIOUS AFFECTIONS, | IN THREE PARTS. | [short tapered rule] | PART I....CONCERNING THE NATURE OF THE AFFECTIONS, | AND THEIR IMPORTANCE IN RELIGION. | PART II....SHEWING WHAT ARE NO CERTAIN SIGNS THAT RE- | LIGIOUS AFFECTIONS ARE GRACIOUS, OR THAT THEY ARE | NOT. | PART III....SHEWING WHAT ARE DISTINGUISHING SIGNS, OR | TRULY GRACIOUS AND HOLY AFFECTIONS. | [short thick-thin rule] | BY JONATHAN EDWARDS, A. M. | AND PASTOR OF THE FIRST CHURCH IN NORTHAMPTON. | [short thin-thick rule] | EDINBURGH: | PRINTED FOR J. OGLE; M. OGLE, GLASGOW; R. OGLE, | AND T. HAMILTON, LONDON; AND | T. JOHNSTON, DUBLIN. | [short rule] | 1812. | [short wavy rule] | *GEO. CAW, PRINTER.*

21.7 x 13.7 cm. (uncut); π^1, A^4, B-Z^8, Aa-Gg^8; [2], viii, 464 p.

Notes: identical title page of the above but a different edition.

Contents: prp. [1]: title (verso blank); p. [i]: INTRODUCTION; pp. [1]-464: text; p. 464: *Geo. Caw, Printer,* | *Libberton-wynd.* | [brace].

THJ 111 NUC NE0046854

Newberry Library

164 • THE | TREATISE | ON | RELIGIOUS AFFECTIONS, | BY THE LATE | Rev. JONATHAN EDWARDS, A.M. | SOMEWHAT ABRIDGED, | *By the Removal of the principal Tautologies of the Original; and by an Attempt* | *to render the Language throughout more perspicuous and energetic.* | [short rule] | "It is no disparagement to any one to say that he [President | Edwards] is, without a rival, the greatest *Divine* that the present | century has produced.—His book on Religious Affections, his Essays | On the Conversions in New England, &c. discover his superior skill | in experimental Theology.——We take this opportunity of recom- | mending, with all the energy of which we are capable, the Works | of President EDWARDS." | *Evangelical Mag. Vol.* III. *p.* 36 & 37. | [short rule] | London: | PUBLISHED BY LONGMAN, HURST, REES, ORME, AND BROWN; | AND ROBINSON, SON, AND HOLDSWORTH, LEEDS. | [short rule] | 1817.

18.1 x 10.7 cm.; $[A]^{12}$, B-N^{12}; xxiii, [1], 288 p.

Contents: p. [i]: title (verso blank); p. [iii]: THE EDITOR's PREFACE. [signed] W. ELLERBY. | Albion-Street, York, July 31, 1817.; p. [viii]: blank; p. [ix]: THE | ORIGINAL PREFACE, | Abridged.; p. [xiv]: blank; p. [xv]: CONTENTS.; p. [xxiv]: blank; pp. [1]-288: text; p. 288: LEEDS: PRINTED BY B. DEWHIRST.

THJ 113 NUC NE0046855 OCLC 43639614
Princeton University

165 • A | TREATISE | CONCERNING | RELIGIOUS AFFECTIONS, | IN THREE PARTS. | I. NATURE OF THE AFFECTIONS, AND THEIR IMPORTANCE IN RELIGION. | II. SHOWING WHAT ARE NO CERTAIN SIGNS THAT RELIGIOUS AFFECTIONS ARE | GRACIOUS, OR THAT THEY ARE NOT. | III. SHOWING WHAT ARE DISTINGUISHING SIGNS OF TRULY GRACIOUS AND HOLY | AFFECTIONS. | [short rule] | BY THE LATE REVEREND | JONATHAN EDWARDS, A. M. | PRESIDENT OF PRINCETON COLLEGE. | [short rule] | TO WHICH IS PREFIXED, | *A Sketch of the Life of the Author* | [short thick-thin rule] | PHILADELPHIA: | PUBLISHED BY JAMES CRISSY, NO. 177, CHESTNUT STREET, | OPPOSITE THE STATE HOUSE. | G. GOODMAN, PRINTER. | 1821.

22.3 x 13.2 cm.; π^2, 1-3^4, A-Z^4, 2A-$2Z^4$, 3A-$3G^4$, $3H^2$; [i]-xxviii, [iii]-xi, [1], [13]-432 [i.e., 430] p.

Notes: pp. [iii]-xi repeated; lacks pp. 147-148 (pp. [i]-xi, [iii]-xi, [12]-[13], 14-146, 149-432).

Contents: p. [i]: title (verso blank); p. [iii]: ADVERTISEMENT. | [11 lines] | *Recommendation.* | [signed] JAMES P. WILSON. | J. J. JANEWAY. | WILLIAM NEILL. | T. H. SKINNER. | EZRA STILES ELY. | J. BRODHEAD. (verso blank); p. [v]: A SKETCH | OF THE | LIFE OF PRESIDENT EDWARDS, | WITH | EXTRACTS FROM HIS DIARY, AND OTHER PRIVATE | WRITINGS; | TOGETHER WITH HIS OWN | ACCOUNT OF HIS CONVERSION.; p. [iii] (repeated): INTRODUCTION.; p. [xii]: blank; p. [13]: RELIGIOUS AFFECTIONS.

THJ 114 NUC NE0046857 OCLC 2420973
Drew University

166 • THE | TREATISE | ON | RELIGIOUS AFFECTIONS, | BY THE LATE | REV. JONATHAN EDWARDS, A. M. | SOMEWHAT ABRIDGED, | *By the Removal of the principal Tautologies of the Original; and by* | *an attempt to render the Language throughout more* | *perspicuous and energetic.* | [short thick-thin rule] | TO WHICH IS NOW ADDED, | *A COPIOUS INDEX OF SUBJECTS.* | [short rule] | "It is no disparagement to any one to say that he [President | Edwards] is, without a rival, the greatest *Divine* that the present cen- | tury has produced.—His book on Religious Affections, his Essays | on the Conversions in New England, &c. discover his superior skill | in experimental Theology.——We take this opportunity of recom- | mending, with all the energy of which we are capable, the Works | of President EDWARDS." | *London Evangel. Mag. Vol.* III. *p.* 36 & 37. | [short rule] | BOSTON: | PRINTED AND PUBLISHED BY JAMES LORING, | NO. 2, CORNHILL. | [short line of stops] | 1821.

15.7 x 9.6 cm. (uncut); A^8, B-W-Z^6, Aa^6, Bb^8; xiv [i.e., xvi], [2], [13]-315, [1] p.

Notes: p. xvi misnumbered xiv; p. 314 misnumbered 134 (pp. i-xv, xiv, [13]-313, 134, 315-[316]); in some copies, these errors have been corrected and the order of the front matter altered.

Contents: p. [i]: title; p. [ii]: [affidavit] [signed] JNO. W. DAVIS, [brace] | *Clerk of the District* | *of Massachusetts*; p. [iii]: EXTRACT | FROM THE ECLECTIC REVIEW OF 1820; p. [v]: THE EDITOR'S PREFACE. [signed] W. ELLERBY; p. [ix]: THE | ORIGINAL PREFACE | ABRIDGED.; pp. [xiii-xiv]: blank; p. [xv]: CONTENTS.; p. [13]: A | TREATISE | ON | RELIGIOUS AFFECTIONS.; p. [304]: INDEX OF SUBJECTS.; p. [316]: [advertisement].

THJ 115 NUC NE0046856 OCLC 7437828
American Antiquarian Society

166A • Loring's Second Edition. | Boston: | PRINTED AND PUBLISHED BY JAMES LORING, | NO. 2 CORNHILL. | [short line of stops] | 1824.

14.4 x 8.6 cm.; A^8, B-W-Z^6, Aa^6, Bb^8; xiv [i.e., xvi], [2], [13]-315, [1] p.

Notes: p. xvi misnumbered xiv (pp. i-xv, xiv, [13]-315, [316]); in some copies, this error is corrected.

THJ 117 NUC NE0046859 OCLC 3564768
American Antiquarian Society

167 • A | TREATISE | CONCERNING | RELIGIOUS AFFECTIONS, | IN THREE PARTS. | [short tapered rule] | PART I.—CONCERNING THE NATURE OF THE AFFECTIONS, | AND THEIR IMPORTANCE IN RELIGION. | PART II.—SHEWING WHAT ARE NO CERTAIN SIGNS THAT RE- | LIGIOUS AFFECTIONS ARE GRACIOUS, OR THAT THEY ARE | NOT. | PART III.—SHEWING WHAT ARE DISTINGUISHING SIGNS OR, | TRULY GRACIOUS AND HOLY AFFECTIONS. | [short thick-thin rule] | BY JONATHAN EDWARDS, A. M. | AND PASTOR OF THE FIRST CHURCH IN NORTHAMPTON. | [short thin-thick rule] | EDINBURGH: | PRINTED FOR T. CLARK, PARLIAMENT SQUARE. | [short rule] | 1822.

22.2 x 14.4 cm. (uncut); π^1, A-Z^4, 2A-$2Z^4$, 3A-$3I^4$, $3K^5$; [2], 453 [i.e., 449] [1] p.

Notes: lacks pp. 353-356 (pp. [9]-352, 357-453, [454]).

Contents: prp. [1]: title (verso blank); p. [1]: INTRODUCTION.; pp. [9]-453: text; p. 453: W. FALCONER, PRINTER, | 3, High Street, Glasgow. | [brace]; p. [454]: blank.

THJ 116 NUC NE0046858 OCLC 4872914
Cleveland Public Library

167A • GLASGOW: | PRINTED BY W. FALCONER, 3, HIGH STREET. | [short rule] | 1822.

22.5 x 14 cm. (uncut); π^1, A-Z^4, 2A-$2Z^4$, 3A-$3I^4$, $3K^5$; [2], 453, [i.e., 449], [1] p.

Notes: lacks pp. 353-356 (pp. [9]-352, 357-453, [454]).

THJ 116A OCLC 17553039
Calvin College and Theological Seminary

168 • A | TREATISE | CONCERNING | RELIGIOUS AFFECTIONS. | BY | JONATHAN EDWARDS, A. M. | [short rule] | WITH | AN INTRODUCTORY ESSAY, | BY THE | REV. DAVID YOUNG, | PERTH. | [short tapered rule] | GLASGOW: | PRINTED FOR CHALMERS AND COLLINS; | WILLIAM WHYTE & CO. AND WILLIAM OLIPHANT, EDINBURGH; | R. M. TIMS, AND WM. CURRY, JUN. & CO. DUBLIN; | AND G. B. WHITTAKER, LONDON. | [short rule] | 1825.

12mo.; 18.3 x 11.3 cm.; $[A]^{12}$, B-Z^{12}, Aa-Dd^{12}, Ee^8; lviii, [59]-664 p.

Notes: in some copies, four leaves of advertisement (pp. [1]-8) follow p. 664.

Contents: p. [i]: SELECT | CHRISTIAN AUTHORS, | WITH | INTRODUCTORY ESSAYS. (verso blank); frontispiece: [engraving] | REV[D]. JONATHAN EDWARDS | PUBLISHED BY CHALMERS & COLLINS GLASGOW | Eng[d] on Steel by W. H. Lizars Edin[r]; p. [iii]: title; p. [iv]: Printed by W. Collins & Co. | Glasgow.; p. [v]: INTRODUCTORY ESSAY. [signed] D. Y. | *Perth, April*, 1825.; p. [lvii]: CONTENTS.; p. [59]: PREFACE.; p. [68]: blank; pp. [69]-638: text; p. [639]: APPENDIX. | [short tapered rule] | TWO LETTERS TO MR. GILLESPIE, | IN REPLY TO HIS OBJECTIONS TO SOME THINGS IN THE PRECEDING | TREATISE.; p. [639]: LETTER I. | NORTHAMPTON, SEPT. 4, 1747.; p. 65: LETTER II. | NORTHAMPTON, APRIL 2, 1750.; p. 664: Printed by W. Collins & Co. | Glasgow.

THJ 118 NUC NE0046680 OCLC 28789684
Congregational Library

169 • A | TREATISE | CONCERNING | RELIGIOUS AFFECTIONS | In Three Parts: | PART I. | CONCERNING THE NATURE OF THE AFFECTIONS, AND THEIR | IMPORTANCE IN RELIGION. | PART II. | SHEWING WHAT ARE NO CERTAIN SIGNS THAT RELIGIOUS | AFFECTIONS ARE GRACIOUS, OR THAT THEY ARE NOT. | PART III. | SHEWING WHAT ARE DISTINGUISHING SIGNS, OR TRULY GRACIOUS | AND HOLY AFFECTIONS. | BY JONATHAN EDWARDS, A. M. | PRESIDENT OF NEW JERSEY COLLEGE. | PRINTED FOR L. B. SEELEY AND SON, | FLEET STREET, LONDON. | MDCCCXXVII.

18.4 x 11.2 cm.; [A]^4, B-Z^6, 2A-2L^6; vii, [1], 396 p.

Contents: p. [i]: SELECT BRITISH DIVINES. | EDITED BY THE REV. C. BRADLEY, | VOL. XXVII. | [short rule] | JONATHAN EDWARDS. | [short rule] | PRINTED FOR L. B. SEELEY AND SON | FLEET-STREET, LONDON. | MDCCCXXVII. (verso blank); p. [iii]: title (verso blank); p. [v]: Biographical Sketch of President Edwards; p. [viii]: blank; p. [1]: Introduction.; pp. 8-396: text.

THJ 120 OCLC 19621074

Drew University

170 • A | TREATISE | ON | RELIGIOUS AFFECTIONS: | IN THREE PARTS. | [short wavy rule] | PART I. *Containing the Nature of the Affections, and their Importance in | Religion.* | PART II. *Showing what are no certain Signs that Religious Affections are | gracious, or that they are not.* | PART III. *Showing what are Distinguishing Signs of truly Gracious and | Holy Affections.* | BY THE REV. JONATHAN EDWARDS, A. M. | *President of the College of New-Jersey.* | ABRIDGED BY | THE REV. JOHN WESLEY.

Contents: p. [307]: title; p. [308]: TO THE READER [signed] JOHN WESLEY | *Bristol, Sept.* 1, 1773.; pp. [309]-376 in A | CHRISTIAN LIBRARY: | CONSISTING OF | EXTRACTS FROM AND ABRIDGMENTS OF | THE | CHOICEST PIECES | OF | Practical Divinity | WHICH HAVE BEEN PUBLISHED IN THE ENGLISH TONGUE. | [short decorative rule] | IN THIRTY VOLUMES: | FIRST PUBLISHED IN 1750, IN FIFTY VOLUMES, DUODECIMO | [short rule] | BY THE REV. JOHN WESLEY, A. M., | SOMETIME FELLOW OF LINCOLN COLLEGE, OXFORD. | [short rule] | Vol. XXX. | [short thick-thin rule] | *LONDON:* PUBLISHED AND SOLD BY J. KERSHAW. | 14, *City-Road, and* 66, *Paternoster-Row.* | [short rule] | 1827.

21.1 x 12.8 cm.; 481 p.

THJ 119 NUC NE0046862 OCLC 6969185

Boston University

171 • A | TREATISE | CONCERNING | RELIGIOUS AFFECTIONS: | IN THREE PARTS. | [short rule] | [in 2 cols., col. 1] PART I. | *Concerning the Nature of the | Affections, and their Impor- | tance in Religion.* | PART II. | *Shewing why there are no cer- | tain Signs that Religious Af-* | [short vertical rule, col. 2] *fections are gracious, or that | they are not.* | PART III. | *Shewing what are distinguish- | ing Signs of truly gracious | and holy Affections.* | [short rule] | Lev. ix. ult. and x. 1. 2.—And there came a fire out from before the Lord,—upon the | altar;—which when all the people saw, they shouted and fell on their faces. And | Nadab and Abihu—offered strange fire before the Lord, which he commanded | them not: And there went out a fire from the Lord, and devoured them, and they | died before the Lord. | Cant. ii. 12, 13.—The flowers appear on the earth, the time of the singing of birds | is come, and the voice of the turtle is heard in our land. The fig-tree putteth | forth her green figs, and the vines with the tender grape give a good smell. | Ver. 15. Take us the foxes, the little foxes, which spoil the vines: for our vines | have tender grapes. | [short rule] | NEW-YORK: | G. AND C. CARVILL, 108 BROADWAY. | [short rule] | 1828.

21.6 x 13.5 cm.; π^1, 1-43^4; [2], 344 p.

Contents: prp. [1]: title (verso blank); p. [1]: PREFACE.; p. [6] blank; p. [7]: A | TREATISE | CONCERNING | RELIGIOUS AFFECTIONS.; p. [322]: APPENDIX | TO THE TREATISE OF THE AFFECTIONS, IN TWO LETTERS.

THJ 121 NUC NE0046863 OCLC 14048324

Oberlin College

172 • A | TREATISE | CONCERNING | RELIGIOUS AFFECTIONS. | BY | JONATHAN EDWARDS, A. M. | [short rule] | WITH | AN INTRODUCTORY ESSAY, | BY THE | REV. DAVID YOUNG, | PERTH. | SECOND EDITION. | [short tapered rule] | GLASGOW: | PRINTED FOR

WILLIAM COLLINS; | OLIVER & BOYD, WM. WHYTE & CO. AND WM. OLIPHANT, EDINBURGH; | W. F. WAKEMAN, AND WM. CURRY, JUN. & CO. DUBLIN; | WHITTAKER, TREACHER, & ARNOT; HAMILTON, ADAMS, & CO. | SIMPKIN AND MARSHALL; BALDWIN & CRADOCK; | AND HURST, CHANCE, & CO. LONDON | [short rule] | MDCCCXXXI.

17.7 x 10.3 cm.; [A]^{12}, B-Z^{12}, 2A-2D^{12}; lx, [61]-648 p.

Contents: p. [i]: SELECT | CHRISTIAN AUTHORS, | WITH | INTRODUCTORY ESSAYS. (verso blank); frontispiece: [engraving] | REV^{D}. JONATHAN EDWARDS | PUBLISHED BY WILLIAM COLLINS GLASGOW | Eng^{d} on Steel by W. H. Lizars Edin^{r}; p. [iii]: title; p. [iv]: Printed by W. Collins & Co. | Glasgow.; p. [v]: INTRODUCTORY ESSAY. [signed] D. Y. | *Perth, April*, 1825.; p. [lvi]: blank; p. [lvii]: CONTENTS.; p. [61]: PREFACE.; p. [70]: blank; pp. [71]-628: text; p. [629]: APPENDIX. | [short tapered rule] | TWO LETTERS TO MR. GILLESPIE, | IN REPLY TO HIS OBJECTIONS TO SOME THINGS IN THE PRECEDING | TREATISE.; p. 648: Printed by W. Collins & Co. | Glasgow.

THJ 122 NUC NE0046865 OCLC 38118914

Princeton Theological Seminary

173 • THE | TREATISE | ON | RELIGIOUS AFFECTIONS, | BY THE LATE | REV. JONATHAN EDWARDS, A. M. | SOMEWHAT ABRIDGED. | [short decorative rule] | PUBLISHED BY THE | AMERICAN TRACT SOCIETY, | NO. 150 NASSAU-STREET, NEW-YORK. | [short line of stops] | D Fanshaw, Printer.

14.3 x 8.7 cm.; [1]^{6}, 2-23^{6}; iv, [5]-276.

Notes: published c. 1833; in some copies, D. Fanshaw; publisher's note (in all American Tract Society issues and in others based upon it): This edition of this invaluable Treatise is that of W. ELLERBY, | slightly abridged, and with some emendations suggested by | a careful collation with the original work. Mr. ELLERBY, | attributing his own confirmed hope in Christ in no small | degree to the instrumentality of this Treatise, and having | subsequently, for a considerable period, made it his con- | stant companion, was induced, in the hope of presenting it | in a more acceptable and attractive form, to transcribe the | entire work; attempting, with the most scrupulous fidelity, | to present the precise thoughts of EDWARDS, as far as prac- | ticable in his own language, but in a more modern and | perspicuous style; with no addition, and the omission only | of his tautologies, redundances, repetitions, and more ex- | tended illustrations.

Contents: frontispiece: [engraving] | PRESIDENT EDWARDS' HOUSE, NORTHAMPTON, MASS.; p. [i]: title; p. [ii]: [publisher's note]; p. [iii]: CONTENTS.; p. [5]: INTRODUCTION.; p. [9]: A | TREATISE | ON | RELIGIOUS AFFECTIONS.

THJ 123 NUC NE0046847 OCLC 7023898

Library of Congress

173A • THE | TREATISE | ON | RELIGIOUS AFFECTIONS, | BY THE LATE | REV. JONATHAN EDWARDS, A. M. | SOMEWHAT ABRIDGED. | [short decorative rule] | PUBLISHED BY THE | AMERICAN TRACT SOCIETY, | NO. 150 NASSAU-STREET, NEW-YORK. | [short line of stops] | D Fanshaw, Printer.

14.8 x 8.9 cm.; [1]^{6}, 2-23^{6}, 1-8^{6}; iv, [5]-276, iv, [5]-96 p.

Notes: in some copies, not bound with Flavel or Alleine (below), there are variations in wording and line spacings of the title page: A | TREATISE | ON | RELIGIOUS AFFECTIONS. | BY REV. JONATHAN EDWARDS, | LATE PRESIDENT OF NASSAU-HALL, PRINCETON, NEW JERSEY. | REWRITTEN AND ABRIDGED. | PUBLISHED BY THE | AMERICAN TRACT SOCIETY, | 150 NASSAU-STREET, NEW YORK.

Contents: frontispiece: [engraving] | S. S. Jocelyn Sc. | PRES^{T} EDWARDS | [facsimile autograph] Jonathan Edwards; facing frontispiece: THE | Evangelical | FAMILY LIBRARY | VOL. III. | [engraving] | Morse del. Dick sc. | PUBLISHED BY THE | *American Tract Society*.; p. [i]: title; p. [ii]: [publisher's note]; p. [iii]: CONTENTS.; p. [5]: INTRODUCTION.; p. [9]: A | TREATISE | ON | RELIGIOUS AFFECTIONS.; p. [i]: THE | TOUCHSTONE OF SINCERITY, | OR | TRIAL | OF | True and False Religion. | [short rule] | BY THE REV. JOHN FLAVEL. | [short rule] | WRITTEN ANEW FROM THE ORIGINAL. | [short thick-thin rule] | PUBLISHED BY THE | AMERICAN TRACT SOCIETY | NO. 150 NASSAU-STREET, NEW-YORK. | D. Fanshaw, Printer.; p. [ii]: This volume is reprinted from an edition which has | been extensively circulated in this country, and in which | such alterations were made, in regard to style, as it is be- | lieved the original author would have made had he lived | at the present age.; p. [iii]: CONTENTS.; p. [5]: TOUCHESTONE.

THJ 123A NUC NE0046867 OCLC 1263837
Boston Public Library

173B • THE | TREATISE | ON | RELIGIOUS AFFECTIONS, | BY THE LATE | REV. JONATHAN EDWARDS, A. M. | SOMEWHAT ABRIDGED. | [short decorative rule] | PUBLISHED BY THE | AMERICAN TRACT SOCIETY, | NO. 150 NASSAU-STREET, NEW-YORK. | [short line of stops] | D. Fanshaw, Printer.

14.8 x 9.1 cm.; $[1]^6$, $2\text{-}23^6$, $[1]^6$, $2\text{-}13^6$, 14^4; iv, [5]-276, [1]-164 p.

Contents: frontispiece: [engraving] | S. S. Jocelyn Sc. | PRES[T] EDWARDS | [facsimile autograph] Jonathan Edwards; facing frontispiece: THE | Evangelical | FAMILY LIBRARY | VOL. III. | [engraving] Morse del. Dick sc., | PUBLISHED BY THE | *American Tract Society*.; p. [i]: title; p. [ii]: [publisher's note]; p. [iii]: CONTENTS.; p. [5]: INTRODUCTION.; p. [9]: A | TREATISE | ON | RELIGIOUS AFFECTIONS.; p. [1]: AN | ALARM | TO | UNCONVERTED SINNERS; | IN | A Serious Treatise on Conversion. | [short rule] | BY JOSEPH ALLEINE. | [short rule] | PUBLISHED BY THE | AMERICAN TRACT SOCIETY. | NO. 150 NASSAU-STREET, NEW-YORK. | [short double rule] | D. Fanshaw, Printer.; p. [2]: In this Edition some obsolete words and phrases are | altered, and a few passages omitted.–The author's Six | Questions to the Unconverted, and Counsels for the Con- | verted, are added.; p. [3]: CONTENTS. (verso blank); pp. [5]-164: text.

THJ 123B NUC NE0046848 OCLC 6075296
Boston Public Library

174 • TRAETHAWD | AR Y | SERCHIADAU CREFYDDOL, | YN GYNNWYSEDIG | MEWN TAIR RHAN. | [short rule] | GAN Y | PARCH. JONATHAN EDWARDS. | WEDI EI GYFIEITHU | GAN THOMAS JONES, AMLWCH. | [short rule] | Caernarfon: | ARGRAFFWYD DROS Y CYHOEDDYDD, GAN W. POTTER & CO. | RHWYMWYR A LLYFRWERTHWYR. | [short rule] | 1833.

17.6 x 10.4 cm.; $[a]^2$, b^6, $B\text{-}S^{12}$, T^6; xvi, 419, [1] p.

Notes: a Welsh translation of *Religious Affections*; a selection was published in 1809 (see 160).

Contents: p. [i]: title (verso blank); p. [iii]: LLYTHYR Y CYFIEITHYDD | AT Y DARLLENYDD. [signed] THOMAS JONES. | Amlwch, Chwef. 18fed, 1833.; p. [vii]: RHAGYMADRODD.; p. xiv: GWALLAU.; p. [xv]: CYNNWYSIAD.; pp. [1]-419: text; p. [420]: CAERNARFON: | ARGRAFFWYD GAN WILLIAM POTTER & CO., | RHWYMWYR A LLYFRWERTHWYR.

THJ 124 NUC NE0046827 OCLC 41988991
Princeton University

175 • A | TREATISE | CONCERNING | RELIGIOUS AFFECTIONS. | BY | PRESIDENT EDWARDS | And there came a fire out from before the Lord,– upon the altar;–which when | all the people saw, they shouted, and fell on their faces. And Nadab and | Abihu–offered strange fire before the Lord, which he commanded them not. | And there went out fire from the Lord, and devoured them, and they died before | the Lord.–LEV. ix. 24, and x. 1, 2. | The flowers appear on the earth; the time of the singing of birds is come, and the | voice of the turtle is heard in our land; the fig-tree putteth forth her green figs, | and the vines with the tender grape give a good smell.–Take us the foxes, the | little foxes, that spoil the vines: for our vines have tender grapes.–CANT. ii. | 12, 13. 15. | LONDON: | THE RELIGIOUS TRACT SOCIETY; | *Instituted* 1799. | SOLD AT THE DEPOSITORY, 56, PATERNOSTER-ROW; | AND BY THE BOOKSELLERS.

15.2 x 10.5 cm.; π^2, $A\text{-}Z^6$, $2A\text{-}2T^6$, $2U^4$; xv, [1], 500 p.

Notes: Probably printed in the second quarter of the 19th century.—THJ.

Contents: p. [i]: title; p. [ii]: BUNGAY: PRINTED BY J. R [*sic*] AND C. CHILDS.; p. [iii]: CONTENTS; p. [v]: PREFACE; p. [xvi]: blank; p. [1]: A | TREATISE | CONCERNING | RELIGIOUS AFFECTIONS.; p. 500: BUNGAY: PRINTED BY J. R. AND C. CHILDS.

THJ 125 NUC NE0046830 OCLC 13097055

Drew University

176 • A | TREATISE | CONCERNING | RELIGIOUS AFFECTIONS; | A REPRINT FROM THE WORCESTER EDITION, WITHOUT | ALTERATION, MUTILATION, OR OMISSION. | BY | JONATHAN EDWARDS, D. D. | NEW-YORK: | LEAVITT, TROW & COMPANY, | 194 Broadway. | 1845.

23.1 x 14.6 cm.; π^6, 1-28^4, 29^2; xii, 228 p.

Contents: pp. [i-ii]: blank; p. [iii]: title (verso blank); p. [v]: CONTENTS. (verso blank); p. [vii]: TREATISE | CONCERNING RELIGIOUS AFFECTIONS. (verso blank); p. [ix]: INTRODUCTION.; pp. [1]-228: text.

NUC NE0046866 OCLC 5366237

Colby College

177 • A TREATISE CONCERNING THE | RELIGIOUS AFFECTIONS | BY JONATHAN EDWARDS | [ornament] | PUBLISHED BY ANDREW MELROSE | 16 PILGRIM STREET, LONDON, E.C. | MDCCCXCVIII

17 x 10.8 cm.; [a]-b^8, c^4, 1-23^8, 24^4; xl, 372, [4] p.

Contents: p. [i]: Books for the Heart | *Edited by* ALEXANDER SMELLIE, M.A. | A TREATISE CONCERNING THE | RELIGIOUS AFFECTIONS (verso blank); p. [iii]: title (verso blank); p. v: NOTE TO THE EDITOR [signed] ALEXANDER WHYTE. | EDINBURGH, | *October* 7, 1898.; p. vi: PUBLISHER'S NOTE; p. vii: CONTENTS; p. ix: INTRODUCTION; p. xxxiv: THE AUTHOR'S PREFACE; p. [1]: THE | RELIGIOUS AFFECTIONS; p. [373]: *BOOKS FOR THE HEART.*

THJ 126 NUC NE0046869 OCLC 30058305

Boston Public Library

177A • [within decorative rules] [decorative initial] A | TREATISE CON- | CERNING THE | RELIGIOUS AF- | FECTIONS [ornament] | [rule] | [4 lines within single rules] [ornament] | BY | JONATHAN EDWARDS | [ornament] | [rule] | LONDON: CHARLES H. KELLY | 2, CASTLE STREET, CITY ROAD; AND | ANDREW MELROSE, 16, PILGRIM STREET, E.C.

15.8 x 10.3 cm.; xl, 372 p.

Notes: title page (verso): *First Impression of this Edition, November 1898.* | *Reprinted June 1902.*

THJ 126A OCLC 14205209

Earlham College

178 • [on left, top, and right of an illustration of King David] THE RELIGIOUS AFFECTIONS [ornament] JONATHAN EDWARDS WORKS | SOVEREIGN GRACE PUBLISHERS | Grand Rapids, Michigan 49501 | 1971

21.5 x 14 cm.; 212 p.

Contents: p. [1]: RELIGIOUS | AFFECTIONS (verso blank); p. [3]: title (verso blank); p. [5]: CONTENTS.; p. 7: INTRODUCTION [signed] ALEXANDER SMELLIE | 1898; p. 11: THE AUTHOR'S PREFACE; pp. 15-210: text; pp. [211-212]: [advertisement].

OCLC 1116636

Gordon-Conwell Theological Seminary

179 • A | TREATISE | ON RELIGIOUS | AFFECTIONS | [rule] | JONATHAN EDWARDS | [rule]

| BAKER BOOK HOUSE | Grand Rapids, Michigan 49506

17.6 x 10.6 cm.; 359, [1] p.

Contents: prp. [1]: A | TREATISE | ON RELIGIOUS | AFFECTIONS (verso blank); prp. [3]: title; prp. [4]: Reprinted 1982 by | Baker Book House | from the edition issued by | the American Tract Society | [3 lines]; p. [1]: [publisher's note]; p. [2], frontispiece: [engraving] | PRESIDENT EDWARDS; p. [3]: CONTENTS; p. [5]: INTRODUCTION; p. [9]: A | TREATISE | ON | RELIGIOUS AFFECTIONS.; p. [360]: blank.

ISBN 0801033748 OCLC 8855520

Saint Michael's College

180 • [5 lines within decorative rules] RELIGIOUS | AFFECTIONS | HOW MAN'S WILL AFFECTS | HIS CHARACTER BEFORE GOD. | [decorative initial] CLASSICS [ornament] | OF FAITH | & DEVOTION | by | Jonathan Edwards | introduction by | Charles Colson | [publisher's device] | MULTNOMAH PRESS | PORTLAND, OREGON 97266

20.9 x 13.2 cm.; xxxiv, [2], 226 p.

Contents: p. [i]: RELIGIOUS | AFFECTIONS (verso blank); p. [iii]: title; p. [iv]: [7 lines] | All author royalties received from the sale of this book are being used to support | Prison Fellowship's ministry to prisoners, ex-prisoners, and their families. | [3 lines] | This abridged edition | © 1984 by Multnomah Press | [9 lines] | Abridged ed. of: Treatise concerning the religious affections. 1808. | [8 lines]; p. [v]: CONTENTS; p. [viii]: blank; p. ix: PREFACE TO THE CLASSICS OF | FAITH AND DEVOTION [signed] James M. Houston; p. [xii]: [pen and ink drawing of Jonathan Edwards by Sarah Chamberlain]; p. xiii: EDITOR'S NOTE ABOUT JONATHAN | EDWARDS AND THE RELEVANCE | OF THIS CLASSIC [signed] James M. Houston; p. [xxii]: blank; p. xxiii: INTRODUCTION by Charles W. Colson; pp. [xxxv-xxxvi]: blank; pp. [1]-188: text; p. 189: A GUIDE TO DEVOTIONAL | READING; p. 215: Scripture Index; p. [222]: blank; p. 223: Subject Index.

ISBN 0880700645 OCLC 10996570

Boston College

181 • [rule] | THE RELIGIOUS | AFFECTIONS | [rule] | JONATHAN EDWARDS | [rule] | THE BANNER OF TRUTH TRUST

21.3 x 13.5 cm.; 382 p.

Notes: reprint of the third volume of *Select Works of Jonathan Edwards* (1961); first published in 1986 and reissued in 1991, 1994, and 1997.

Contents: p. [1]: THE RELGIOUS | AFFECTIONS (verso blank); p. [3]: title; p. [4]: THE BANNER OF TRUTH TRUST | 3 Murrayfield Road, Edinburgh EH 12 6EL | PO Box 621, Carlisle, Pennsylvania 17013, U.S.A. | [6 lines] | Printed in Great Britain by | Billing & Sons Ltd., Worcester; p. [5]: PUBLISHERS' NOTE (verso blank); p. 7: CONTENTS; p. 9: INTRODUCTION [signed] ALEXANDER SMELLIE | 1898; p. 15: THE AUTHOR'S PREFACE; pp. 21-382: text.

ISBN 0851514855 OCLC 14187717

Boston University

182 • The experience that counts! | or | Spiritual experience, true or false? | An abridged version, re-written for today's readers, of the | classic 'A treatise concerning religious affections' by | Jonathan Edwards, A.M. (1703-58) | The full work is available with The Banner of Truth Trust, | Edinburgh, EH12 6EL. | Prepared by Dr. N. R. Needham, B.D., PhD. | Grace Publications Trust | Joint managing editors J. P. Arthur, M.A. | H. J. Appleby

19.2 x 12.3 cm.; 127, [1] p.

Contents: p. [1]: The experience that counts! (verso blank); p. [3]: title; p. [4]: © Grace Publications Trust | 139 Grosvenor Avenue | LONDON N5 2NH | England | First published 1991 | [11 lines]; p. [5]: Contents; p. [8]: blank; p. [9]: Introduction [signed] N.R.N. | Edinburgh 1991; p. [12]: blank; p. [13]: Preface [signed] Jonathan Edwards; p. [16]: blank; pp. [17]-127: text; p. [128]: blank.

ISBN 0946462232 OCLC 24846977
Reformed Theological Seminary

183 • [portrait of Edwards] | [publication data] | Zongjiao qingcao zhenwei bian

21 x 14.7 cm.; [6], 118, [2] p.

Notes: a Chinese translation of *The Experience that Counts*.

Contents: prp. [1]: title; prp. [2]: The Experience That Counts | By Jonathan Edwards | Copyright © 1994 by | Grace Publications Trust | Translated by | Theological Translation Fellowship | Publisher, Jonathan Chao, Ph. D. | Edited by Phoebe Ma | Chinese Copyright © 1994 by | Reformation Translation Fellowship | P.O. Box 17-154 | Taipei, Republic of China | [4 lines]; prp. [3]: [preface to the Chinese edition]; prp. [5]: [contents]; pp. 1-118: text; p. [119]: [publication data]; p. [120]: blank.

ISBN 9579995141 OCLC 32145314
Reformed Presbyterian Theological Seminary

184 • FROM THE WORK BY | JONATHAN EDWARDS | Religious Affections | *A Christian's | Character Before God* | EDITED BY | Dr. James M. Houston | INTRODUCTION BY | Charles Colson | [double decorative rule] | BETHANY HOUSE PUBLISHERS | MINNEAPOLIS, MINNESOTA 55438

20.3 x 13.5 cm.; xxxiv, [2], 206 p.

Notes: pp. [v-vii] misnumbered [155]-157 (pp. [i-iv], [155]-157, [viii]-[xxxvi], [1]-206).

Contents: p. [i]: title; p. [ii]: *Religious Affections* | Copyright © 1984, 1996 | James M. Houston | [1 line] | Originally published in 1984 by Multnomah Press. | [12 lines]; p. [iii]: [biography of James M. Houston]; p. [iv]: [advertisement]; p. [v]: CONTENTS; p. [viii]: blank; p. ix: PREFACE TO THE CLASSICS OF | FAITH AND DEVOTION [signed] James M. Houston; p. [xii]: blank; p. xiii: EDITOR'S NOTE ABOUT JONATHAN | EDWARDS AND THE RELEVANCE | OF THIS CLASSIC [signed] James M. Houston; p. [xxii]: blank; p. xxiii: INTRODUCTION by Charles W. Colson; pp. [xxxv-xxxvi]: blank; pp. [1]-188: text; p. 189: Scripture Index; p. 195: Subject Index; p. 199: STUDY GUIDE FOR GROUP | DISCUSSION.

ISBN 1556618298 OCLC 35839711
Boston College

185 • RELIGIOUS | AFFECTIONS | BY | JONATHAN EDWARDS | ABRIDGED AND | UPDATED BY | ELLYN SANNA | CHRISTIAN BOOK CLUB | [short rule] | *Since 1948, The Book Club You Can Trust*

20.2 x 12.3 cm.; 319, [1] p.

Notes: in some copies, BARBOUR | PUBLISHING, INC. | Uhrichsville, Ohio replaces CHRISTIAN BOOK CLUB | [short rule] | *Since 1948, The Book Club You Can Trust*

Contents: p. [1]: title (verso blank); p. [3]: RELIGIOUS | AFFECTIONS; p. [4]: © MCMXCIX by Barbour Publishing, Inc. | [11 lines]; p. [5]: CONTENTS; p. [6]: blank; p. [7]: INTRODUCTION [signed] ELLYN SANNA, EDITOR; p. [15]: AUTHOR'S PREFACE; pp. 17-319: text; p. [320]: [advertisement].

ISBN 1577485254 OCLC 43185291
Gordon College

186 • [on the left vertically] Religious Affections | [imposed on a portrait of Edwards] Xin yang de shen qing | Shangdi mian qian de Jidu tu bing xing | Dr. James M. Houston

20.4 x 13.8 cm.; [2], 6, 4, 15, 19, 254 p.

Notes: a Chinese translation of *Religious Affections*, no. 4 in Philosophical Classics of Western Mysticism, published in Beijing in 2001; title page: [on the right vertically] Zhang Xiangling [series editor]; [on the left, below title] Du Liyan [translator]; five plates of illustration follow the title page.

Contents: prp. [1]: title; prp. [2]: [publisher's note on the series]; pp. 1-6 (first count): [contents]; pp. 1-4 (second count): [mysticism]; pp. 1-15 (third count); [preface by the editor]; pp. 1-19 (fourth count): [introduction]; pp. 1-237 (fifth count): text; pp. 238-249: [appendix: philosophical foundations of Edwards's ideas]; pp. 250-254: [chronology].

ISBN 7800967662 OCLC 48614421
Queens Borough Public Library

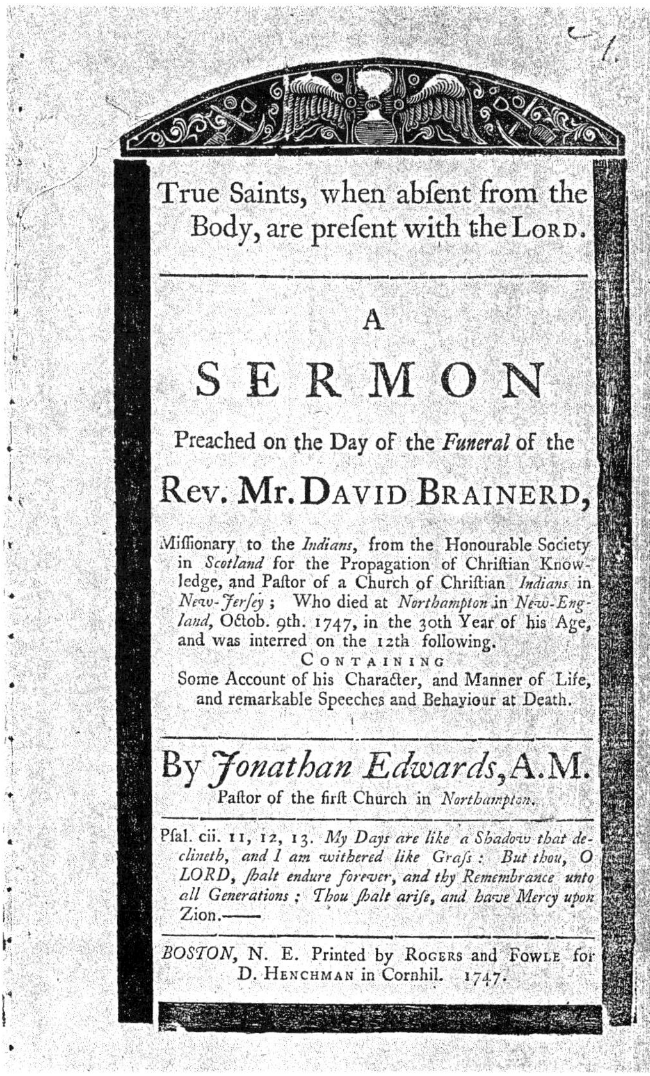

True Saints, when abſent from the Body, are preſent with the LORD.

A

SERMON

Preached on the Day of the *Funeral* of the

Rev. Mr. DAVID BRAINERD,

Miſſionary to the *Indians*, from the Honourable Society in *Scotland* for the Propagation of Chriſtian Knowledge, and Paſtor of a Church of Chriſtian *Indians* in *New-Jerſey*; Who died at *Northampton* in *New-England*, Octob. 9th. 1747, in the 30th Year of his Age, and was interred on the 12th following.

CONTAINING

Some Account of his Character, and Manner of Life, and remarkable Speeches and Behaviour at Death.

By *Jonathan Edwards*, A.M.

Paſtor of the firſt Church in *Northampton*.

Pſal. cii. 11, 12, 13. *My Days are like a Shadow that declineth, and I am withered like Graſs: But thou, O LORD, ſhalt endure forever, and thy Remembrance unto all Generations; Thou ſhalt ariſe, and have Mercy upon* Zion.——

BOSTON, N. E. Printed by ROGERS and FOWLE for D. HENCHMAN in Cornhil. 1747.

Title page, *True Saints* (1747). Permission of the Massachusetts Historical Society.

TRUE SAINTS, WHEN ABSENT FROM THE BODY, ARE PRESENT WITH THE LORD

187 • [within mourning borders surmounted by a headstone engraving] True Saints, when abſent from the | Body, are preſent with the LORD. | [rule] | A | SERMON | Preached on the Day of the *Funeral* of the | Rev. Mr. DAVID BRAINERD, | Miſſionary to the *Indians*, from the Honourable Society | in *Scotland* for the Propagation of Chriſtian Know- | ledge, and Paſtor of a Church of Chriſtian *Indians* in | *New-Jerſey*; Who died at *Northampton* in *New-Eng- | land*, Octob. 9th. 1747, in the 30th Year of his Age, | and was interred on the 12th following. | CONTAINING | Some Account of his Character, and Manner of Life, | and remarkable Speeches and Behaviour at Death. | [rule] | By *Jonathan Edwards*, A.M. | Paſtor of the firſt Church in *Northampton*. | [rule] | Pſal. cii. 11, 12, 13. *My Days are like a Shadow that de- | clineth, and I am withered like Graſs: But thou, O | LORD, ſhalt endure forever, and thy Remembrance unto | all Generations: Thou ſhalt ariſe, and have Mercy upon* | Zion.— | [rule] | *BOSTON*, N. E. Printed by ROGERS and FOWLE for | D. HENCHMAN in Cornhil. 1747.

8vo.; 18.8 x 11.5 cm.; $[A]^4$, B-E^4; 40 p.

Contents: p. [1]: [mourning rule] | Mr. *Edwards*'s | SERMON | On the *Death* of | Mr. *Brainerd*. (verso blank); p. [3]: title (verso blank); p. [5]: Abſent from the Body, | AND | Preſent with the LORD.; p. 40: ADVERTISEMENT.

THJ 127 EAI 1:5939 NUC NE0046877 OCLC 22599262

Houghton Library

AN HUMBLE ATTEMPT TO PROMOTE EXPLICIT AGREEMENT AND VISIBLE UNION OF GOD'S PEOPLE IN EXTRAORDINARY PRAYER

188 • AN | Humble Attempt | To promote | *Explicit Agreement* | AND | Viſible UNION | Of GOD'S People in | *Extraordinary Prayer* | For the REVIVAL of *Religion* and the Ad- | vancement of *Chriſt's Kingdom* on Earth, | purſuant to Scripture-Promiſes and Pro- | phecies concerning the *laſt Time*. | [rule] | By *Jonathan Edwards*, A. M. | Miniſter of the Goſpel at *Northampton*. | [rule] | With a PREFACE by ſeveral Miniſters. | [rule] | *BOSTON*, NEW-ENGLAND: | Printed for D. HENCHMAN in *Cornhil*. 1747.

8vo.; 14.7 x 9.7; cm.; $[A]^4$, A-Z^4, Aa^3; [10], 188 p.

Notes: sig. A^4 repeated; in some copies, the secondary title page is the only title page, followed by THE | *PREFACE*. and THE | CONTENTS; in some copies, the *ERRATA* is mounted on the fly-leaf (recto) facing p. 188, others on the bottom of p. 188.

Contents: prp. [1]: title (verso blank); prp. [3]: *The* | *PREFACE*. [signed] [in 2 cols., col. 1] BOSTON, N. E. | *January* 12. | 1747,8. | [col. 2] *Joſeph Sewall*, | *Thomas Prince*, | *John Webb*, | *Thomas Foxcroft*, | *Joſhua Gee*.; | prp. [7]: THE | CONTENTS.; p. [9]: *A* HUMBLE ATTEMPT *to promote an explicit* Agree- | ment *and viſible* Union *of God's People thro' the World*, | *in* extraordinary PRAYER, *for the* REVIVAL *of* | Religion *and the Advancement of* Chriſt's Kingdom *on* | *Earth, purſuant to Scripture-Promises and Prophecies* | *concerning the* laſt Time. | [rule] | OCCASION'D | By a late MEMORIAL publiſh'd by a Number of | Miniſters in *Scotland*, and ſent over to *Ameri- | ca*; giving an Account of a certain CONCERT | *for Prayer*,—which has been already come in- | to by many Miniſters and Others in *Great- | Britain* and ſome other Parts, and in which | They deſire the *general Concurrence* of their | Chriſtian Brethren every where. | CONTAINING | A Copy of ſaid *Memorial*, with a more particular | View of the *Affair* it relates to; a Variety of *Argu- | ments* and *Perſuaſives* to comply with the Motion | therein made, for *united* and *extraordinary Prayer*; | and Anſwers to ſome *Objections*. | Together with | Seaſonable Conſiderations on the *Aſpects* of *Providence* | in many late wonderful Diſpenſations, and the pre- | ſent State of Things in the Church and moral World; | pointing out the *Fulfilling* of the

Scriptures, and the | *Voice of God* to his People, in thefe Events. | [rule] | By *Jonathan Edwards*, A. M. | Minifter of the Gofpel in *Northampton*. | [rule] | *BOSTON*, NEW-ENGLAND: | Printed for D. HENCHMAN in Cornhil. 1747.(verso blank); pp. [1]-188: text.

THJ 128 EAI 1:5938 NUC NE0046670 OCLC 6133746
Massachusetts Historical Society

189 • AN | HUMBLE ATTEMPT | TO PROMOTE | EXPLICIT AGREEMENT | AND | VISIBLE UNION | OF | GOD's PEOPLE | IN | Extraordinary Prayer, | For the REVIVAL of RELIGION and the AD- | VANCEMENT of CHRIST'S KINGDOM on | Earth, purfuant to Scripture-Promifes and | Prophecies concerning the LAST TIME. | [rule] | By JONATHAN EDWARDS, A. M. | Minifter of the Gofpel at *Northampton*. | [rule] | With a PREFACE by feveral Minifters. | [double rule] | Printed at BOSTON, in *New England*, 1747. | Re-printed at NORTHAMPTON, in *Old England*, | By T. DICEY and CO.—1789. | Sold by J. Buckland, Pater-nofter Row; W. Afh, Little Tower- | Street; W. Button, Newington Caufeway; J. Lepard, N° 91, | Newgate-Street, and J. Reynolds, Crooked-Lane, London. | Alfo, by J. Smith, in Sheffield; N. Binns, Hallifax; J. Binns, | Leeds; and W. Gray, in Edinburgh. (Price NINE-PENCE.) *stet* Hallifax

12mo.; 17.3 x 10.4 cm. (uncut); a^6, B-P^6; x, [2], 168 p.

Contents: p. [i]: title (verso blank); p. [iii]: PREFACE by the EDITOR. [signed] JOHN SUTCLIFF. | OLNEY, May 4th, 1789; p. vii: *The PREFACE.* [signed] [in 2 col., col. 1] BOSTON, N. E. | *January* 12, | 1747-8. | [col. 2] *Jofeph Sewall*, | *Thomas Prince*, | *John Webb*, | *Thomas Foxcroft*, | *Jofhua Gee*.; p. [xi]: *An* HUMBLE ATTEMPT *to promote an explicit* Agree- | ment *and vifible* Union *of God's People through the* | *World*, *in* extraordinary PRAYER, *for the* RE- | VIVAL *of* Religion, *and the Advancement of* Chrift's | Kingdom *on Earth, purfuant to Scripture-Promises* | *and Prophecies* | *concerning the* laft Time. | [short tapered rule] | OCCASIONED | By a late MEMORIAL publifh'd by a Number of | Minifters in *Scotland*, and fent over to *America*; | giving an Account of a certain CONCERT *for* | *Prayer*,—which has been already come into | by many Minifters and Others in *Great-Britain* | and fome other Parts, and in which they de- | fire the *general Concurrence* of their Chriftian | Brethren every where. | CONTAINING | A Copy of faid *Memorial*, with a more particular | View of the *Affair* it relates to; a Variety of *Argu-* | *ments* and *Perfuafives* to comply with the Motion | therein made, for *united* and *extraordinary Prayer*; | and Anfwers to fome *Objections*. | TOGETHER WITH | Seafonable Confiderations on the *Afpects* of *Providence* | in many late wonderful Difpenfations, and the | prefent State of Things in the Church and moral | World; pointing out the *Fulfilling* of the *Scriptures*, | and the *Voice of God* to his People, in thefe Events. | [rule] | By JONATHAN EDWARDS, A. M. | Minifter of the Gofpel in *Northampton*, N.E.; p. [xii]: The CONTENTS.; pp. [1]-168: text; p. 168: [advertisement].

THJ 129 ESTC N31793 NUC NE0046672 OCLC 31381831
John Carter Brown Library

190 • AN | HUMBLE ATTEMPT | TO PROMOTE | EXPLICIT AGREEMENT | AND | VISIBLE UNION OF GOD'S PEOPLE | IN | *EXTRAORDINARY PRAYER*, | FOR THE | REVIVAL OF RELIGION | AND THE | ADVANCEMENT OF CHRIST'S KINGDOM | ON | EARTH, | PURSUANT TO | SCRIPTURE-PROMISES AND PROPHECIES | CONCERNING THE | LAST TIME. | [tapered rule] | BY *JONATHAN EDWARDS*, A. M. | *Minifter of the Gofpel at Northampton*. | [short tapered rule] | WITH A PREFACE BY SEVERAL MINISTERS. | [tapered rule] | *Printed at Bofton, in New-England*, 1747. *Reprinted at North-* | *ampton, in Old England*, 1789. | [short rule] | *ELIZABETHTOWN*: | Printed by SHEPARD KOLLOCK, Printer and Bookfeller. 1794.

8vo.; 20.2 x 12.1 cm.; π^8, [A]^4, B-Z^4, Aa-Zz^4, 3A-3G^4; viii, [4], [9]-426, [2] p.

Notes: frontispiece: [engraving] | JONATHAN EDWARDS | Prefident. | *Engraved by Amos Doolittle, N* [*sic*] *Haven*; p. [liii]: PREFACE | BY THE | EDITOR, IN ENGLAND. | OLNEY, May 4, 1789. [signed] JOHN SUTCLIFF.; p. [lvii]: THE | *PREFACE*. [signed] *Jofeph Sewall*, | *Thomas Prince*, | *John Webb*, | *Thomas Foxcroft*, | *Jofhua Gee*. | [brace]

| Miniſters | in Boſton. | BOSTON, N. E. *January* 12, 1747-8.

Contents: pp. [li]-lxii, [63]-321 in THE | MILLENNIUM; | OR, THE | *THOUSAND YEARS* OF *PROSPERITY*, | PROMISED TO THE | CHURCH OF GOD, | IN THE OLD TESTAMENT AND IN THE NEW | SHORTLY TO | COMMENCE, | AND TO BE CARRIED ON TO | PERFECTION, | UNDER THE AUSPICES OF *HIM*, | WHO, IN THE *VISION*, WAS PRESENTED TO ST. *JOHN* | AND I SAW, AND, BEHOLD, A WHITE HORSE; AND HE THAT | SAT ON HIM HAD A BOW; AND A CROWN WAS GIVEN UNTO | HIM: AND HE WENT FORTH CONQUERING AND TO CONQUER. | [short tapered rule] | *We are journeying unto the place, of which the Lord ſaid, I will | give it to you: come thou with us, and we will do thee good, for the | Lord hath ſpoken good concerning Iſrael.* MOSES. | [tapered rule] | *ELIZABETHTOWN*: | PRINTED BY SHEPARD KOLLOCK—1794.

THJ 130 NUC NE0046673 OCLC 4980191

Harvard Divinity School

191 • UNITED PRAYER | FOR THE | Spread of the Gospel, | *EARNESTLY RECOMMENDED;* | OR, | AN ABRIDGMENT | OF "AN HUMBLE ATTEMPT TO PROMOTE EXPLICIT AGREEMENT | AND VISIBLE UNION OF GOD'S PEOPLE IN | EXTRAORDINARY PRAYER | For the Revival of Religion, and the Advancement of Christ's | Kingdom on Earth." | [short rule] | WRITTEN BY | PRESIDENT EDWARDS, | OF NEW ENGLAND, IN THE YEAR 1748. | [short rule] | *LONDON:* | PRINTED BY R. WILLIAMS, COPPICE ROW; | SOLD BY WILLIAMS & SON, STATIONERS' COURT. | [short rule] | 1814.

17.3 x 10.5 cm.; [A]-B^6, C^5; 32, [2] p.

Contents: p. [1]: title (verso blank); p. [3]: *PREFACE.* [signed] *London, March* 24, 1814. | GEORGE BURDER.; p. [5]: UNITED PRAYER, | *&c. &c.*; p. 32: *The success which has attended the preaching of the gospel by | missionaries in the East Indies, in the West Indies, and in Africa, | in answer to prayer, affords the most ample encouragement to | continue, and abound still more and more in this duty.— | (Editor.)* | [short rule] | *Printed by R. Williams, Coppice Row, London.*; p. [33]: [advertisement] (verso blank).

THJ 131 NUC NE0046885

Boston Public Library

192 • No. 60. | UNITED AND EXTRAORDINARY | PRAYER | FOR THE | REVIVAL OF RELIGION, | AND THE | *ADVANCEMENT OF CHRIST'S KINGDOM,* | EARNESTLY RECOMMENDED.

19.6 x 11.4 cm. (uncut); 24 p.

Notes: in some copies, [No. 60.

Contents: caption title; p. [1] (also paged [109]): INTRODUCTION.; pp. [3]-24 (also paged [111]-132): text; p. 24 (also paged 132): ANDOVER: | PRINTED FOR THE NEW ENGLAND TRACT SOCIETY | BY FLAGG AND GOULD. | 1815 [First edit. 6000.

Massachusetts Historical Society

192A • No. 60. | UNITED AND EXTRAORDINARY | PRAYER | FOR THE | REVIVAL OF RELIGION, | AND THE | *ADVANCEMENT OF CHRIST'S KINGDOM,* | EARNESTLY RECOMMENDED.

Notes: identical with the above except for the colophon; p. 24 (also paged 132): ANDOVER: | PRINTED FOR THE NEW ENGLAND TRACT SOCIETY | BY FLAGG AND GOULD. | 1816 [2d Edit. 6000.

EAI 2:39142 OCLC 15440812

American Antiquarian Society

192B • No. 60. | UNITED AND EXTRAORDINARY | PRAYER | FOR THE | REVIVAL OF RELIGION, | AND THE | *ADVANCEMENT OF CHRIST'S KINGDOM,* | EARNESTLY RECOMMENDED.

Notes: identical with the above except for the colophon; p. 24 (also paged 132): ANDOVER: | PRINTED FOR THE NEW ENGLAND TRACT SOCIETY, | BY FLAGG AND GOULD. | 1820. [3d edit. 6,000.

OCLC 32963965

Harvard Divinity School

194 • L'UNION | DANS LA PRIÈRE | POUR LA | PROPAGATION DE L'ÉVANGILE, | OU | ABRÉGÉ D'UN HUMBLE ESSAI, | DONT LE BUT EST DE PROVOQUER UN ACCORD VISIBLE DU PEUPLE | DE DIEU DANS L'OFFRE DES PRIÈRES EXTRAORDINAIRES POUR | AVANCER LE RÈGNE DE CHRIST SUR LA TERRE; | PUBLIÉ EN 1748 | PAR JONATHAN EDWARDS, DD. | Président du collége de la Nouvelle-Jersey. | [short rule] | Ainsi a dit l'Eternel des armées: Il arrivera | que les peuples et les habitans de plusieurs | villes viendront; et les habitans de l'une | iront dans l'autre, et diront: Allons, allons | supplier l'Eternel et rechercher l'Eternel | des armées, je m'y en irai aussi. | (*Zacharie*, VIII. 20, 21.) | [short rule] | PARIS, | H^r^. SERVIER, LIBRAIRE, RUE DE L'ORATOIRE, N° 6. | [short wavy rule] | 1823.

12mo.; 17 x 11cm.; vi, 30, 7, [1] p.

Notes: a French translation of *Humble Attempt*, the first work of Edwards published in French; the type of the last eight pages is substantially smaller than those preceding; p. vi lettered vj.

Contents: p. [i]: title (verso blank); p. iii: *Préface*; pp. 1-30: text; p. 30: De l'imprimerie de J. Smith; p. 1: N.o 13. | Prières pour le vendredi-saint. Par J.I.S. Cellerier, ancien pasteur de Satigny.; p. [1]: A Montpellier, chez M.me V.e Picot, née Fonteny, seul imprimeur deu Roi, place Louis XVI, n.° 200.

THJ 132

British Library

195 • AN | HUMBLE ATTEMPT, | TO PROMOTE EXPLICIT | AGREEMENT AND VISIBLE UNION | OF | GOD'S PEOPLE, | IN | EXTRAORDINARY PRAYER, | FOR THE REVIVAL OF RELIGION AND THE ADVANCEMENT | OF CHRIST'S KINGDOM ON EARTH, | BY THE LATE | PRESIDENT EDWARDS, OF AMERICA; | INTRODUCED | WITH A PREFACE. | LONDON: | PUBLISHED BY JAMES NISBET, | 21 BERNERS-STREET. | 1831.

20.1 x 11.5 cm.; [a]^2, [A]^8, B-H^8, I^3; xx, 133, [1] p.

Contents: p. [i]: title; p. [ii]: IDLE: | PRINTED BY JOHN VINT, WESTGATE.; p. [iii]: CONTENTS.; p. [v]: PREFACE. [signed] R. P. | *Airedale College, Dec.* 1830.; p. [1]: AN | HUMBLE ATTEMPT, | &c. &c.; p. [134]: IDLE: | PRINTED BY JOHN VINT, WESTGATE.

THJ 133

British Library

196 • AN HUMBLE ATTEMPT | TO PROMOTE EXPLICIT AGREEMENT AND VISIBLE | UNION OF GOD'S PEOPLE, | IN EXTRAORDINARY PRAYER, | FOR THE REVIVAL OF RELIGION AND THE | ADVANCEMENT OF | CHRIST'S KINGDOM ON EARTH. | BY THE | REV. JONATHAN EDWARDS, A.M. | WITH A PREFACE TO THE AMERICAN EDITION, 1748 | AND | SUTCLIFF'S PREFACE TO THE ENGLISH EDITION | BROUGHT OUT BY HIM IN 1789. | PRINTED BY UNWIN BROTHERS, LIMITED, | AND TO BE HAD AT | THE BAPTIST MISSION HOUSE. | FURNIVAL STREET, HOLBORN, LONDON, E.C. | [short rule] | 1902.

17.4 x 11.2 cm.; [A]^8, B-O^8; 220, [2] p.

Contents: p. [1]: title (verso blank); p. [3]: INTRODUCTION | TO THE REPRINT OF 1902. [signed] *September*, 1902. | M. E. S.; p. 4: ADVERTISEMENT.; p. [5]: PREFACE | BY THE REV. JOHN SUTCLIFF, OF OLNEY [signed] JOHN SUTCLIFF. | *Olney*, *May* 4*th*, 1789.; p. 6: PREFACE | BY THE AMERICAN EDITORS. [dated] *Boston*, *New England*, *January* 12*th*, 1748. | *This preface was signed by Joseph Sewell [*sic*], Thomas Prince, | John Webb, Thomas Foxcroft, | and Joshua Gee.; p. [9]: AN HUMBLE ATTEMPT, | ETC.; pp. [221-222]: blank.

THJ 134 NUC NE0046674
Regent's Park College

A STRONG ROD BROKEN AND WITHERED

197 • [within mourning borders surmounted by a headstone engraving] *A* STRONG ROD *broken and withered.* | [rule] | A | SERMON | Preach'd at *Northampton*, on the Lord's-Day, June 26. 1748. | On the Death of | The Honourable | *John Stoddard*, Efq; | Often a Member of his Majefty's | Council, | For many Years Chief Juftice of | the Court of Common Pleas for | the County of *Hampfhire*, | Judge of the Probate of Wills, and | Chief Colonel of the Regiment, &c. | Who died at *Bofton* June 19. 1748. in the 67th Year of | his Age. | [rule] | By *Jonathan Edwards*, A.M. | Paftor of the firft Church in *Northampton.* | [rule] | Dan. iv. 35— *He doth according to his Will in the Army of* | *Heaven, and among the Inhabitants of the Earth*; *and* | *none can ftay his Hand, or fay unto Him, What doft thou?* | [rule] | BOSTON: | Printed by *Rogers* and *Fowle* for *J. Edwards* in Cornhill. | 1748.

4to.; 18.9 x 12.3 cm.; $[A]^4$, $B\text{-}C^4$, D^3; 29, [1] p.

Contents: p. [1]: [mourning rule] | Mr. *Edwards*'s | SERMON | On the Death | Of the Honourable | *John Stoddard*, Efq; | [mourning rule] (verso blank); p. [3]: title (verso blank); p. [5]: [decorative mourning rule] | GOD's awful Judgment in the | breaking and withering of the | STRONG RODS of a Community. | [mourning rule]; p. [30]: blank.

THJ 135 EAI 1:6130 NUC NE0046814 OCLC 11356166
Forbes Library

AN ACCOUNT OF THE LIFE OF THE LATE REVEREND MR. DAVID BRAINERD

198 • An | ACCOUNT of the | LIFE | Of the late Reverend | Mr. *David Brainerd*, | Minifter of the Gofpel, | *Miffionary* to the INDIANS, from the | honourable Society in *Scotland*, for | the Propagation of Chriftian Know- | ledge, and Paftor of a Church of | *Chriftian* INDIANS in *New-Jerfey.* | Who died at *Northampton* in NEW-ENGLAND, | *Octob.* 9th 1747. in the 30th Year of his Age: | Chiefly taken from his own *Diary*, and other private | Writings, written for his own Ufe; and now | publifhed, | [rule] | By JONATHAN EDWARDS, A. M. | Minifter of the Gofpel at *Northampton.* | [rule] | *BOSTON: N. E.* | Printed for and Sold by D. HENCHMAN, in Cornhill. | 1749.

8vo.; 20.3 x 11.5 cm.; $[A]^4$, aa^4, aaa^4, $aaaa^4$, $B\text{-}Z^4$, $Aa\text{-}Ss^4$; [2], xii, [18], 316 [i.e., 318], [2] p.

Notes: Extracts from Brainerd's journal were first published by William Bradford of Philadelphia in 1746 for the Scottish Society for Propagating Christian Knowledge. Though the two parts, "Mirabella Dei inter Indicos" and "Divine Grace Displayed," have separate title pages, the signature and pagination are continuous. "An Abridgment of Mr. David Brainerd's Journal . . ." was published in London in 1748. Edwards, in preparing the "Account," omitted such portions of the diary as had already been published. Though the Edinburgh 1765 edition of Edwards's "Account" incorporated the portions which Edwards had originally omitted, it was not until Dwight brought out the New Haven 1822 edition that the whole was presented in chronological sequence.—THJ; pp. 87-88 repeated (pp. [1]-88, 87-88, 89-318).

Contents: prp. [1]: title (verso blank); p. [i]: *The PREFACE.*; p. xii: Befides the Errata at the End of the Life, the Reader is defired | to correct the following. | [5 lines: errata]; p. [i]: The Names of Subfcribers to | the Rev. Mr. *Brainerd*'s Life; p. [1]: An ACCOUNT | Of the LIFE of | The Reverend | Mr. *David Brainerd.*; p. 316: *ERRATA.*; pp. [317-318]: [advertisement].

THJ 136 EAI 1:6311 NUC NB0739512 OCLC 2297584
Massachusetts Historical Society

199 • [From his Life, publiſhed by Mr. Edwards, p. 133, &c.]

Contents: caption title; pp. 415-420 in HISTORICAL COLLECTIONS | RELATING TO | REMARKABLE PERIODS | OF | THE SUCCESS | OF | THE GOSPEL, | AND | EMINENT INSTRUMENTS | EMPLOYED IN PROMOTING IT. | IN TWO VOLUMES. | MATTH. XXVIII. 19, 20. GO AND TEACH ALL NATIONS:—AND LO, | I AM WITH YOU ALWAY, EVEN TO THE END OF THE WORLD. | COMPILED BY | JOHN GILLIES, | ONE OF THE MINISTERS OF GLASGOW. | *IN MAGNIS VOLUISSE.* | VOL. II. | GLASGOW, | PRINTED BY ROBERT AND ANDREW FOULIS | MDCCLIV.

8vo.; 20.5 x 12.4 cm.; [a]-b^4, A-Z^4, AA-Zz^4, Aaa-Mmm^4, Nnn^2; 468 p.
OCLC 4800892
Harvard Divinity School

200 • HISTORIESCH VERHAAL, | VAN HET | [in red ink] GODVRUCHTIG LEVEN | EN DEN | [in red ink] ZALIGEN DOODT, | Van den Eerwaarden HEER | [in red ink] DAVID BRAINERD; | Onlangs Bedienaar des Euangeliums, gezonden van | de Eerwaarde Maatſchappye in *Schotland*, tot | voortplantinge der Chriſtelyke kenniſſe; en | Leeraar eener Gemeinte van Chriſten | *Indianen*, te *Nieuwe-Jerſey*. | Alles getrokken uit zyn Dag-regiſter, en andere | byzondere Schriften, welke tot zyn eigen gebruik | waren opgeſtelt; en nu tot algemeen nut | uitgegeven, door | [in red ink] JONATHAN EDWARDS, *A.M.* | Bedienaar des Euangeliums te *Northampton*. | Uit het Engels Vertaaldt door J. ROS. | Met een kort VOORBERIGT van | [in red ink] G. V. SCHUYLENBORGH, | *Dienaar in J. C. Kerke te THIENHOVEN* | [ornament] | *T'UTRECHT*, | By [brace] JAN JACOB VAN POOLSUM, | EN | ABRAHAM VAN PADDENBURG, | Boekverkopers, 1756.

8vo.; 22.1 x 13.7 cm. (uncut); *^{8}, **^{6}, A-Z^8, Aa-Ii^8, Kk^2; [28], 516 p.

Notes: a Dutch translation of *Life of Brainerd*, bound with [in red ink] AANMERKELYK VERHAAL | Van de opkomſt en voortgang van een zonderling werk | van Gods genade onder een groote meenigte | [in red ink] INDIANEN, | IN DE PROVINTIEN VAN | [in red ink] NIEUW-JERSEY EN PENNSYLVANIA. | DOOR | [in red ink] DAVID BRAINERD, | Bedienaar des Euangeliums, en Afgezondene | van de Eerwaaerdige Maatſchappye tot voortplan- | tinge van de Chriſtelyke Leer in Schotland. | *Waar by gevoegt is een Opdracht aan* | *gemelde Maatſchappye door* | [in red ink] P. DODDRIDGE, | Profeſſor in de Godgeleerheit, en Gereformeert | Predikant te NORTHAMPTON. | Uit het Engels Vertaaldt door J. ROS. | [ornament] | T'Utrecht, | By [brace] [in red ink] JAN JACOB VAN POOLSUM, | EN | [in red ink] ABRAHAM VAN PADDENBURG, | Boekverkoopers, 1756., separately paged and collated: *^{4}, A-F^8, G^4; [8], 104 p.

Contents: prp. [1]: title; prp. [2]: attestation [signed] DAVID MILL, *S. S. Theol.* | *Doctor en Profeſſor.* | ALBERTUS VOGE, *S. S.* | *Theol. Doct. en Profeſſor.* | WILH. VAN IRHOVEN, *S. S.* | *Theol. Doct. en Profeſſor.* | GISB. MATTH. ELSNERUS, | *S. S. Theol. Doct. en Profeſſor.* | FRANCISCUS BURMANNUS, | *Fr. Fil. Fr. Nep. S. S. Theol.* | *Doct. en Profeſſor.*; prp. [3]: VOORBERIGT. [signed] G: V: S: | Geſchreven te Thienhoven, | den 8ster October 1755.; prp. [9]: VERTAALDE | VOORREDEN. [signed] J. EDWARDS, A. M.; p. 1: VERHAAL, | VAN HET GODVRUCHTIG | LEVEN EN STERVEN | VAN DEN | EERWAARDIGEN HEER | DAVID BRAINERD.

THJ 137 NUC NB0739551 OCLC 28279689
John Carter Brown Library

201 • AN | ACCOUNT of the LIFE | Of the late REVEREND | Mr *David Brainerd*, | Miniſter of the Goſpel, | Miſſionary to the Indians, from the Honourable | Society in Scotland, for the Propagation of | Chriſtian Knowledge, and Paſtor of a Church | of *Chriſtian Indians* in New-Jerſey. | Who died at Northampton in New-England, October 9. 1747, | in the 30th Year of his Age. | Chiefly taken from his own *Diary*, and other private Wri- | tings, written for his own Uſe; and now publiſhed, | By

JONATHAN EDWARDS, A. M. | Then Minifter of the Gofpel at Northampton, afterwards | Prefident of the College of New-Jerfey. | To which is annexed, | I. Mr Brainerd's JOURNAL while among the In- | dians. | II. Mr Pemberton's Sermon at his ORDINA- | TION. With an APPENDIX relative to the | Indian Affairs. | EDINBURGH: | Printed by JOHN GRAY and GAVIN ALSTON, | For WILLIAM GRAY in the Front of the Exchange. | MDCCLXV.

8vo.; 19.5 x 11.7 cm.; $[a]^4$, b^2, A-Z^4, Aa-Zz^4, 3A-$3R^4$; xi, [1], 504 p.

Contents: p. [i]: title (verso blank); p. [iii]: THE | PREFACE.; p. [xii]: PROPOSALS; p. [1]: An ACCOUNT of the LIFE of | The late Reverend | Mr *David Brainerd.*; p. [320]: blank; p. [321]: *Mirabilia Dei inter Indicos;* | OR, The RISE and PROGRESS | OF A | REMARKABLE WORK of GRACE | Amongft a NUMBER of the INDIANS, | In the Provinces of NEW-JERSEY and PENSYLVANIA, | Juftly REPRESENTED in a | JOURNAL | Kept by order of the Honourable SOCIETY (in Scotland) for | propagating CHRISTIAN KNOWLEDGE. | With fome general REMARKS. | By DAVID BRAINERD, | Minifter of the Gofpel, and Miffionary from faid Society. | Publifhed by the Reverend and Worthy Correfpondents of | the faid Society. | With a Preface by them. | [rule] | If. lv. 13. Inftead of the thorn fhall come up the fir-tree; and inftead of the | brier fhall come up the myrtle-tree: and it fhall be to the Lord for a | name, for an everlafting fign that fhall not be cut off. | If. lxv. 1. I am fought of them that afked not for me: I am found of them | that fought me not: I faid, Behold me, behold me, unto a nation that was | not called by my name. | Pfal. cxlv. 10. 11. All thy works fhall praife thee, O Lord, and thy faints | fhall blefs thee. They fhall fpeak of the glory of thy kingdom, and talk of | thy power. | [rule] | Printed in the Year MDCCLXV. (verso blank); p. [323]: THE | PREFACE. [signed] The CORRESPONDENTS.; p. [327]: THE | RISE and PROGRESS | OF A | Remarkable WORK of GRACE, *&c.*; p. [372]: blank; p. [373]: Divine GRACE difplayed; | OR, The CONTINUANCE and PROGRESS | OF A | Remarkable WORK of GRACE | Among fome of the INDIANS | Belonging to the Provinces of NEW-JERSEY and PEN- | SYLVANIA, | Juftly REPRESENTED in a | JOURNAL | Kept by the order of the Honourable SOCIETY (in Scotland) for | propagating CHRISTIAN KNOWLEDGE. | With fome general REMARKS. | To which is fubjoined an APPENDIX, containing | fome account of fundry things, efpecially of the dif- | ficulties attending the work of a Miffionary among | the INDIANS. | By DAVID BRAINERD, | Minifter of the Gofpel, and Miffionary from the faid Society. | Publifhed by the Reverend and Worthy Correfpondents of | the ſaid Society | [rule] | Rom. ix. 25. 26. I will call them my people, that were not my people; and her, | beloved, that was not beloved. And it fhall come to pafs, that in the | place where it was faid unto them, Ye are not my people; there fhall they | be called, The children of the living God. | Eph. v. 8. Ye were fometimes darknefs, but now are ye light in the Lord. | Pfal. cxviii. 23. This is the Lord's doing, it is marvelous in our eyes. | [rule] | Printed in the Year MDCCLXV. (verso blank); pp. [375]-437: text; p. [438]: APPENDIX to the Journal.; p. [469]: The Atteftation of the Reverend Mr WILLIAM TEN- | NANT of Freehold.; p. 470: The Atteftation of the Reverend Mr MACNIGHT of | Crofwicks.; p. 471: Atteftation of the elders and deacons of the Prefbyter- | rian church in Freehold.; p. [473:] A | SERMON | PREACHED | In New-Ark, June 12. 1744. | AT THE | ORDINATION | OF | Mr *David Brainerd,* | A Miffionary among the Indians | Upon the Borders of the Provinces of New-York, New- | Jerfey, and Penfylvania. | By E. PEMBERTON, A. M. | Paftor of the Prefbyterian Church in the City of New-York. | WITH | An APPENDIX, touching the Indian Affairs. | EDINBURGH: Printed in the Year MDCCLXV. (verso blank); p. [475]: AN | Ordination SERMON.; p. [492]: An APPENDIX, | Containing a fhort Account of the Endeavours | that have been ufed by the Miffionaries of | the Society in Scotland for propagating Chri- | ftian Knowledge, to introduce the Gofpel a- | mong the Indians upon the Borders of New- | York, &c.

THJ 138 NUC NB0739518 OCLC 2293567
Boston Public Library

202 • AN | EXTRACT | OF THE | LIFE | OF THE LATE | Rev. Mr. DAVID BRAINERD, | *Miſſionary* to the *Indians.* | BY | *JOHN WESLEY,* M. A. | [ornament] | BRISTOL: | Printed by WILLIAM PINE, in WINE-STREET. | [short double rule] | M.DCC.LXVIII.

12mo.; 16.6 x 9.2 cm.; $[A]^6$, B-W-X^6, Y^5; 274 p.

Notes: title page of a variant issue: AN | EXTRACT | OF THE | LIFE | OF THE LATE | Rev. Mr. DAVID BRAINERD, | MISSIONARY TO THE INDIANS. | BY THE [*sic*] | *JOHN WESLEY,* A. M. | BRISTOL: | Printed by WILLIAM PINE, in WINE-STREET. | [short double rule] | M.DCC.LXVIII.; the following advertisement appears in all editions of the Wesley abridgment: THOSE *parts of the following* | *hiſtory that are included between* | brackets *thus* [ ], *are the words of* | *the* publifher, *Mr.* Jonathan Ed- | wards, *minifter of* Northampton *in* | New-England, *for the moft part fu-* | *mmarily reprefenting the chief things con-* | *tained in* Mr. Brainerd's *diary: the* | *reft is the account that he gives of him-* | *felf in his private writings, in his own* | *words.*

Contents: p. [1]: title (verso blank); p. [3]: ADVERTISEMENT. (verso blank); p. [5]: AN | EXTRACT | OF THE | LIFE | OF THE LATE | Rev. Mr. DAVID BRAINERD.

THJ 139 NUC NB0739538 OCLC 15061743

Drew University

202A • AN | EXTRACT | OF THE | LIFE | OF THE LATE | Rev. Mr. DAVID BRAINERD, | *Miffionary* to the *Indians.* | BY | *JOHN WESLEY,* M. A. | [ornament] | THE SECOND EDITION. | [ornament] | BRISTOL: | Printed by WILLIAM PINE, in WINE-STREET. | [short double rule] | M.DCC.LXXI.

12mo.; 16.1 x 9.7 cm.; [A]^{6}, B-W-X^{6}, Y^{5}; 274 p.

Contents: p. [1]: title (verso blank); p. [3]: ADVERTISEMENT. (verso blank); p. [5]: AN | EXTRACT | OF THE | LIFE | OF THE LATE | Rev. Mr. DAVID BRAINERD.

THJ 140 ESTC T1121 NUC NB0739540 OCLC 41975470

Drew University

203 • An EXTRACT of the LIFE | OF THE LATE | Rev. Mr. DAVID BRAINERD, | MISSIONARY to the INDIANS. | [rule] | ADVERTISEMENT.

12mo.; 16.3 x 10 cm.; [A]-O^{12}, P^{6}, I^{4}; 354, [2] p.

Notes: p. 239 misnumbered 339 (pp. 27-238, 339, 240-354).

Contents: caption title; pp. 27-354 in THE | WORKS | OF THE | Rev. JOHN WESLEY, M. A. | Late Fellow of *Lincoln-College*, OXFORD. | [rule] | VOLUME XII. | [thin-thick rule] | BRISTOL: | Printed by WILLIAM PINE, in *Wine-Street*, | MDCCLXXII.

THJ 141 NUC NB0739541 OCLC 4345136

Drew University

204 • AN | EXTRACT | OF THE | LIFE | OF THE LATE | Rev. Mr. DAVID BRAINERD, | *Miffionary* to the *Indians.* | BY | *JOHN WESLEY,* M. A. | [ornament] | THE THIRD EDITION. | [double rule] | *LONDON:* | Printed by G. PARAMORE, North-Green, Worfhip- | Street; and fold by *G. Whitfield*, at the Chapel, City- | Road; and at the Methodift Preaching-Houfes in Town | and Country. 1793.

12mo.; 16.7 x 9.8 cm.; [A]^{6}, B-W-Y^{6}; 275, [1] p.

Notes; in some copies, pp. 205-215 misnumbered 105-115 (pp. [1]-204, 105-115, 216-275).

Contents: p. [1]: title (verso blank); p. [3]: ADVERTISEMENT. (verso blank); p. [5]: AN | EXTRACT | OF THE | LIFE | OF THE LATE | Rev. Mr. DAVID BRAINERD.; p. [276]: blank.

THJ 142 ESTC N31176 NUC NB0739542 OCLC 8140596

Drew University

204A • AN | EXTRACT | OF THE | LIFE | OF THE LATE | *REV. DAVID BRAINERD,* | MISSIONARY TO THE INDIANS. | [short decorative rule] | BY THE LATE | REV. JOHN WESLEY, M. A. | [short decorative rule] | *THE FOURTH EDITION.* | [thick-thin rule] | *DUBLIN:* | PRINTED BY R. NAPPER, No. 29, CAPEL-STREET, | For the METHODIST BOOK-ROOM, 13, Whitefriar-Street. | [short tapered rule] | 1812. | [*PRICE* 3*s*. 9½*d.*]

12mo.; 17.8 x 10.5 cm.; [A]^{6}, B-W-Y^{6}; [4], [5]-275, [1] p.

Contents: p. [1]: title (verso blank); p. [3]: *ADVERTISEMENT.* (verso blank); p. [5]: AN | EXTRACT | OF THE | LIFE | OF THE LATE | REV. DAVID BRAINERD.; p. [276]: blank.

OCLC 2886569

Gordon-Conwell Theological Seminary

205 • AN ACCOUNT OF THE | LIFE | OF THE REVEREND | DAVID BRAINERD, | MINISTER OF THE GOSPEL; MISSIONARY TO THE INDIANS FROM THE | HONOURABLE SOCIETY, IN SCOTLAND, FOR THE PROPAGATION | OF CHRISTIAN KNOWLEDGE; AND PASTOR OF A CHURCH | OF CHRISTIAN INDIANS IN NEW-JERSEY. | Who died at NORTHAMPTON, in New-England, | Ooctober 9th, 1747, in the 30th year of his age. | CHIEFLY TAKEN FROM HIS OWN DIARY, AND OTHER PRIVATE | WRITINGS, WRITTEN FOR HIS OWN USE. | [short decorative rule] | BY JONATHAN EDWARDS, A. M. | LATE PRESIDENT OF THE COLLEGE IN NEW-JERSEY. | [short decorative rule] | TO WHICH ARE ADDED | EXTRACTS from MR. BRAINERD'S JOURNAL, | COMPRISING THE MOST MATERIAL THINGS IN THAT PUBLICATION. | [double rule] | PRINTED AT *WORCESTER*, MASSACHUSETTS, | BY LEONARD WORCESTER. | [short double rule] | MDCCXCIII. *stet* Ooctober

8vo.; 21.6 x 13.5 cm.; A-W-Z^8, Aa-Cc^8; 346, 84, [2] p.

Notes: p. 7 misnumbered 9; p. 246 misnumbered 226 (pp. [1]-6, [9]-245, 226, 247-346).

Contents: p. [1]: title (verso blank); p. [3]: THE EDITOR's | PREFACE. [signed] *SAMUEL AUSTIN*. | WORCESTER, May 29th, 1793.; p. [8]: [advertisement]; p. [9]: THE | LIFE | OF THE REVEREND | DAVID BRAINERD.; p. [1]: *Mirabilia Dei inter Indicos*, | OR THE | RISE AND PROGRESS | OF A REMARKABLE | *WORK* OF *GRACE* | AMONG A NUMBER OF THE | INDIANS, | IN THE PROVINCES OF NEW-JERSEY AND PENNSYLVANIA, | JUSTLY REPRESENTED IN A | JOURNAL | KEPT BY ORDER OF THE HONOURABLE SOCIETY, IN SCOTLAND, FOR PROPA- | GATING CHRISTIAN KNOWLEDGE. | WITH SOME GENERAL REMARKS. | [short decorative rule] | BY DAVID BRAINERD, | MINISTER OF THE GOSPEL, AND MISSIONARY FROM SAID SOCIETY. | [short decorative rule] | PUBLISHED, AT THE FIRST, BY THE REVEREND AND WORTHY CORRESPOND- | ENTS OF THE SAID SOCIETY. | NOW REPUBLISHED, WITH SOME DIMINUTION WHERE THE MATTER WAS LESS | INTERESTING, BY THE EDITOR. | [double rule] | Inftead of the thorn, fhall come up the fir tree; and inftead of the brier, fhall come | up the myrtle tree: And it fhall be to the Lord for a name, for an everlafting | fign that fhall not be cut off. *Ifaiah* lv. 13. | I am fought of them that afked not for me: I am found of them that fought me | not: I faid, Behold me, behold me, to a nation that was not called by my | name. *Ifaiah* lxv. 1. | All thy works fhall praife thee, O Lord, and thy faints fhall blefs thee; they fhall | fpeak of the glory of thy kingdom, and talk of thy power. *Pfalm* cxlv. 10, 11. | [double rule] | PRINTED AT *WORCESTER*, MASSACHUSETTS, | BY LEONARD WORCESTER. | [short double rule] | MDCCXCIII. (verso blank); p. [3]: THE | RISE AND PROGRESS, &c.; pp. [85-86]: blank.

THJ 143 EAI 1:25431 NUC NB0739520 OCLC 5972185

Massachusetts Historical Society

206 • AN | ACCOUNT | OF THE | LIFE | OF | *MR. DAVID BRAINERD*, | MISSIONARY | FROM THE SOCIETY FOR PROPAGATING | CHRISTIAN KNOWLEDGE, | & | PASTOR OF A CHURCH OF CHRISTIAN INDIANS | IN NEW-JERSEY. | [double rule] | *PUBLISHED BY JONATHAN EDWARDS, A. M.* | [double rule] | WITH | MR BRAINERD'S PUBLIC JOURNAL. | [short tapered rule] | TO THIS EDITION IS ADDED, | MR BEATTY's MISSION | *To the westward of the Allegheny mountains*. | [short thick-thin rule] | EDINBURGH: | PRINTED BY T. MACCLIESH AND CO. | FOR J. OGLE, PARLIAMENT SQUARE, | AND M. OGLE, GLASGOW. | 1798.

8vo.; 20.6 x 12.2 cm.; π^1, A-Z^4, Aa-Zz^4, Aaa-Zzz^4, 4A^4, [A]^4, B-G^4; [2], [1]-560, [1]-56 p.

Notes: p. 310 misnumbered 301; p. 354 misnumbered 345; p. 387 misnumbered 369; pp. 388-391 misnumbered 380-383; p. 488 misnumbered 487 (pp. [1]-309, 301, 311-353, 345, 355-386, 369, 380-383, 392-487, 487, 489-560).

Contents: prp. [1]: title (verso blank); p. [1]: PREFACE. [signed] JONATHAN EDWARDS.; p. [11]: AN | ACCOUNT | OF THE | LIFE | OF | MR. DAVID BRAINERD.; p. [356]: blank; p. [357]: *MIRABILIA DEI INTER INDICOS*. | [short double rule] | THE | RISE & PROGRESS | OF A | REMARKABLE WORK OF GRACE | AMONGST A NUMBER OF THE INDIANS | IN NEW JERSEY AND PENSYLVANIA, | REPRESENTED IN A | *JOURNAL* | KEPT BY ORDER OF THE SOCIETY (IN SCOTLAND) FOR PROPAGATA- | TING CHRISTIAN KNOWLEDGE, | BY MR DAVID BRAINERD, | MINISTER OF THE GOSPEL AND MISSIONARY FROM | THE SAID SOCIETY. | [double rule] | "Inftead of the thorn, fhall come up the fir tree; and instead of the bri- | er, fhall come up the myrtle tree: And it fhall be to the Lord for a | name, for an everlasting ſign that ſhall not be cut off." *Iſ.* lv. 13. | "I am ſought of them that aſked not for me; I am found of them that | ſought me not: I ſaid, Behold me, behold me, unto a nation that was | not called by my name." *Iſ.* lxv. 1. | [double rule] | PRINTED IN THE YEAR M.DCC.XCVIII. (verso blank); p. [359]: THE | PREFACE. [signed] THE CORRESPONDENTS.; p. [362]: blank; pp. [363]-524: text; p. [525]: A | SERMON, | PREACHED IN NEWARK, | June 12, 1744, | AT | THE ORDINATION OF MR. DAVID BRAINERD, | Miſſionary among the Indians. | [double rule] | BY | *E. PEMBERTON, M. A.* | PASTOR OF THE PRESBYTERIAN CHURCH | IN THE CITY OF NEW-YORK | [double rule] | WITH AN APPENDIX, | TOUCHING | THE INDIAN AFFAIRS. | EDINBURGH: —M.DCC.XCVIII. (verso blank); p. [527]: A | SERMON.; p. [546]: blank; p. [547]: *AN APPENDIX*; p. [1]:THE | JOURNAL | OF A | TWO-MONTHS TOUR; | [12 lines] | BY CHARLES BEATTY, M. A. | [2 lines] | Edinburgh: | PRINTED BY AND FOR T. MACCLIESH AND CO. AND FOR J. OGLE, | PARLIAMENT SQUARE | 1798. (verso blank); p. [3]: *JOURNAL, &c.*

THJ 144 ESTC T144472 NUC NB0739522 OCLC 2293585
John Carter Brown Library

206A • LONDON: | *PRINTED* | *FOR R. OGLE, BOOKSELLER.* | 1798.

20.6 x 12.2 cm.; π^1, A-Z^4, Aa-Zz^4, Aaa-Zzz^4, 4A^4, [A]^4, B-G^4; [2], [11]-560, [1]-56 p.
Notes: identical with the above except for the imprint.
THJ 144A NUC NB0739525 OCLC 23526094
Library Company of Philadelphia

207 • AN EXTRACT | OF THE | LIFE | OF THE LATE | *REV. DAVID BRAINERD,* | MISSIONARY TO THE INDIANS. | [short wavy rule] | *By JOHN WESLEY, A. M.* | Late Fellow of Lincoln-College, Oxford. | [short wavy rule] | [short wavy rule] | *THE FOURTH EDITION.* | [short wavy rule] | [short wavy rule] | *LONDON:* | Printed at the Conference-Office, North-Green, Finſbury-Square: | G. STORY, Agent. Sold by G. WHITFIELD, New-Chapel, | City-Road, and at the Methodiſt Preaching-Houſes in | Town and Country. 1800

12mo.; 17.2 x 10.1 cm.; [A]^6, B-U^6, X^4; 235 [i.e., 245], [3] p.

Notes: p. 79 misnumbered 76; pp. 103-108 misnumbered 203-208; p. 222 misnumbered 122; pp. 224-225 misnumbered 114-115; pp. 226-237 misnumbered 216-227; p. 238 misnumbered 128; pp. 239-245 misnumbered 229-235 (pp. 5-78, 76, 80-102, 203-208, 109-221, 122, 223, 114-115, 216-227, 128, 229-235).

Contents: p. [1]: title (verso blank); p. [3]: ADVERTISEMENT. (verso blank); pp. 5-235: text; p. [236]: [advertisement]; p. [238]: Conference-Office, North-Green, Finſbury-Square: | GEO. STORY, Agent. 1801.

THJ 145 ESTC N17703 NUC NB0739543 OCLC 4895934
Drew University

208 • THE | LIFE | OF | DAVID BRAINERD, | *MISSIONARY TO THE INDIANS,* | WITH | AN ABRIDGEMENT | OF HIS | DIARY AND JOURNAL. | FROM PRESIDENT EDWARDS. | [short tapered rule] | BY JOHN STYLES. | *Author of an Essay on the Stage, &c.* | [short tapered rule] | LONDON: | PRINTED FOR MESSRS. WILLIAMS AND SMITH, | STATIONER'S-COURT. | By R. TILLING, Newport, Isle of Wight. | 1808.

17.5 x 10.1 cm.; π^3, [B]^{12}, C-N^{12}, O^2; vi, 291, [1] p.

Notes: p. v: For the materials I am indebted to President Edwards, | and for the extracts in their abridged form, after I had | compared them to the original, I have to express my | obligations to Mr. Wesley.

Contents: p. [i]: title (verso blank); p. [iii]: [dedication]; p. [iv]: CONTENTS.; p. [v]: PREFACE. [signed] J. S. | *West Cowes, Isle of Wight.*; p. [1]: THE | LIFE OF BRAINERD.; p. 291: *Printed by R. Tilling, Newport, Isle of Wight.*; p. [292]: blank.

THJ 146 OCLC 13056058
Connecticut College

209 • AN ACCOUNT | OF THE | LIFE | OF THE | REV. DAVID BRAINERD, | MINISTER OF THE GOSPEL; MISSIONARY TO THE IN- | DIANS FROM THE HONOURABLE SOCIETY IN | SCOTLAND FOR THE PROPAGATION OF | CHRISTIAN KNOWLEDGE; AND PAS- | TOR OF A CHURCH OF CHRIS- | TIAN INDIANS IN NEW- | JERSEY. | WHO DIED AT NORTHAMPTON, IN NEW-ENGLAND, | OCTOBER 9th 1747, IN THE 30th YEAR OF HIS AGE. | Chiefly taken from his own Diary, and other private wri- | tings, written for his own use. | [short thick-thin rule] | BY JONATHAN EDWARDS, A. M. | *LATE PRESIDENT OF THE COLLEGE IN NEW-JERSEY.* | [short thin-thick rule] | TO WHICH ARE ADDED | EXTRACTS FROM MR. BRAINERD'S JOURNAL, | Comprising the most material things in that publication. | [short thick-thin rule] *NEWARK, N. J.* | PRINTED BY JOHN AUSTIN CRANE. | [short line of stops] | 1811.

17.3 x 10.1 cm.; [A]^4, B-Z^6, [Aa]-Ff^6, Gg^4; 284, 68 p.

Contents: p. [1]: title (verso blank); p. [3]: THE EDITOR's | PREFACE. [signed] SAMUEL AUSTIN | WORCESTER, May 29th, 1793; p. [9]: THE | LIFE | OF THE | REV. DAVID BRAINERD.; p. [1]: DIVINE GRACE DISPLAYED | AMONG A NUMBER OF THE | INDIANS, | IN | NEW-JERSEY AND PENNSYLVANIA. | REPRESENTED IN A | JOURNAL, | KEPT BY ORDER OF THE HONOURABLE SOCIETY IN | SCOTLAND FOR THE PROPAGATING CHRIS- | TIAN KNOWLEDGE. | WITH SOME GENERAL REMARKS. | [short thick-thin rule] | BY THE REV. DAVID BRAINERD, | *MISSIONARY FROM THE SAID SOCIETY.* | [short thin-thick rule] | PUBLISHED, AT THE FIRST, BY THE REVEREND AND | WORTHY CORRESPONDENTS OF THE SAID SOCIETY. | NOW REPUBLISHED, WITH SOME DIMINUTION, WHERE | THE MATTER WAS LESS INTERESTING. | [thick-thin rule] | Instead of the thorn, shall come up the fir tree; and in- | stead of the brier, shall come up the myrtle tree: And it | shall be to the Lord for a name, for an everlasting sign that | shall not be cut off. *Isaiah* lv. 13. | I am sought of them that asked not for me: I am found of | them that sought me not: I said, behold me, behold me, to a | nation that was not called by my name. *Isaiah* lxv. 1. | All thy works shall praise thee, O Lord, and thy saints | shall bless thee; they shall speak of the glory of thy king- | dom, and talk of thy power. *Psalm* cxlv. 10, 11. | [thin-thick rule] | NEWARK, N. J. | PRINTED BY JOHN AUSTIN CRANE. | [short line of stops] | 1811. (verso blank); p. [3]: DIVINE GRACE DISPLAYED, &c.

THJ 147 EAI 2:22749 NUC NB0739527 OCLC 6400916
Houghton Library

210 • THE | LIFE | OF | DAVID BRAINERD, | MISSIONARY TO THE INDIANS; | WITH | AN ABRIDGMENT | OF HIS | *DIARY AND JOURNAL.* | FROM PRESIDENT EDWARDS. | BY JOHN STYLES, | AUTHOR OF AN ESSAY ON THE STAGE, &c. | First American edition. | BOSTON: | PUBLISHED BY SAMUEL T. ARMSTRONG, | No. 50, Cornhill. | 1812.

17.8 x 10.5 cm.; [1]^4, 2-27^6; 322 [i.e., 318], [2] p.

Notes: lacks pp. [9-12] (pp. [1]-8, 13-322); in some copies, a blank leaf precedes, not follows, the title page.

Contents: p. [1]: title (verso blank); pp. [3-4]: blank; p. [5]: PREFACE. [signed] J. S. | *West Cowes, Isle of Wight*; p. [7]: CONTENTS. (verso blank); pp. [9-12]: omitted; p. [13]: THE | LIFE OF BRAINERD.; p. [323]: [advertisement] (verso blank).

THJ 148 EAI 2:26824 NS 1032812 OCLC 2886569
Library of Congress

211 • AN EXTRACT | OF THE | LIFE | OF THE LATE | *REV. DAVID BRAINERD,* | **Missionary to the Indians.** | [short thick-thin rule] | BY JOHN WESLEY, A.M. | *Late Fellow of Lincoln College, Oxford.* | [short thin-thick rule] | COCK'S EDITION. | [short thick-thin rule] | PENRYN: | PRINTED BY AND FOR W. COCK, AND SOLD BY HIS AGENTS | THROUGHOUT THE KINGDOM. | [short rule] | 1815.

19.8 x 12.3 cm.; [B]^4, C-Z^4, 2A-2P^4, 3Q^4, 3R^2; 307, [1] p.

Notes: sig. C_2 mislettered C_3; sig. $2H_2$ mislettered $3H_2$.

Contents: p. [1]: title (verso blank); p. [3]: ADVERTISEMENT. (verso blank); p. [5]: AN EXTRACT | OF THE | LIFE | OF THE LATE | *REV. DAVID BRAINERD.*; p. [308]: blank.

THJ 149 NUC NB0739545 OCLC 32165363

Northwestern University

212 • THE | LIFE | OF THE | REV. DAVID BRAINERD, | Missionary to the Indians. | FROM THE HONOURABLE SOCIETY IN SCOTLAND FOR PROPAGATING | CHRISTIAN KNOWLEDGE; | Who Died at Northampton in New England, October 9, 1747, | in the 30th Year of his Age. | [short tapered rule] | BY | JONATHAN EDWARDS, A. M. | *President of the College of New Jersey.* | [short tapered rule] | A New Edition, | CAREFULLY REVISED AND CORRECTED. | [short thick-thin rule] | LONDON: | PRINTED FOR BURTON AND SMITH, LEADENHALL STREET, | AND E. W. MORRIS, HIGH WYCOMBE; | AND SOLD BY BUTTON AND SON, PATERNOSTER ROW; AND | MARSHALL AND SIMPKIN, STATIONERS' COURT. | [short rule] | E. W. Morris, Printer, High Wycombe. | [short rule] | 1818.

20.6 x 12.1 cm.; $[A]^8$, $B\text{-}Z^8$, $Aa\text{-}Ii^8$, Kk^2; xv, [1], 500 p.

Contents: p. [i]: title (verso blank); p. [iii]: ADVERTISEMENT.; p. [iv]: CONTENTS.; p. [v]: PREFACE. [signed] JONATHAN EDWARDS.; p. [xvi]: blank; p. [1]: The Life | OF | *DAVID BRAINERD.*; p. [253]: REMAINS OF THE REV. D. BRAINERD.; p. [260]: LETTERS | *Written by Mr. Brainerd to his Friends.*; p. [276]: REFLECTIONS | ON THE PRECEDING MEMOIRS.; p. [317]: THE | *RISE AND PROGRESS* | OF A | Remarkable work of grace amongst a number of Indians in the Provinces | of New=Jersey and Pensylvania, | Justly represented in a | JOURNAL | KEPT BY THE HONOURABLE SOCIETY IN SCOTLAND FOR PROPAGATING | CHRISTIAN KNOWLEDGE; | *With some general Remarks,* | BY DAVID BRAINERD, | Minister of the Gospel, and Missionary for the said Society. | PUBLISHED BY THE REVEREND AND WORTHY CORRESPONDENTS OF THE | SAID SOCIETY WITH A PREFACE BY THEM. (verso blank); p. [319]: PREFACE. [signed] The CORRESPONDENTS.; pp. [321]-467: text; p. [468]: blank; p. [469]: A | SERMON | PREACHED | *IN NEWARK, June* 12, 1744, | AT THE ORDINATION | OF | REV. DAVID BRAINERD, | *A Missionary among the Indians.* | [short tapered rule] | BY E. PEMBERTON, A. M. | Pastor of the Presbyterian Church in the City of New-York. | [short tapered rule] | TO WHICH IS ADDED, | AN APPENDIX, | *On Indian affairs.*; p. [487]: APPENDIX; p. 500: E. W. MORRIS, PRINTER, WYCOMBE.

THJ 150 NUC NB0739572 OCLC 9130892

Princeton University

213 • THE | LIFE | OF | DAVID BRAINERD, | MISSIONARY TO THE INDIANS, | WITH | AN ABRIDGEMENT | OF HIS | Diary and Journal. | FROM PRESIDENT EDWARDS. | short decorative rule] | BY JOHN STYLES, D. D. | [short decorative rule] | Second Edition. | [short thick-thin rule] | LONDON: | *Printed by A. J. Valpy, Took's Court, Chancery Lane*; | FOR F. WESTLEY, STATIONER'S-COURT, AND AVE-MARIA-LANE. | [short rule] | 1820.

18.7 x 10.9 cm. (uncut); π^4, $A\text{-}M^{12}$; viii, 283, [5] p.

Contents: p. [i]: title (verso blank); p. [iii]: [dedication] (verso blank); p. [v]: CONTENTS.; p. [vii]: PREFACE. [signed] J. S.; p. [1]: THE | LIFE OF BRAINERD.; p. 283: A. J. Valpy, Printer, Took's Court, Chancery-Lane.; p. [284]: blank; pp. [285-288]: [advertisement].

THJ 151 NS 1032813 OCLC 7292369

Library of Congress

214 • THE | LIFE | OF | DAVID BRAINERD, | MISSIONARY TO THE INDIANS; | WITH | *AN ABRIDGMENT* | OF HIS | DIARY AND JOURNAL. | FROM PRESIDENT EDWARDS. | [short thin-thick rule] | BY JOHN STYLES, | Author of an Essay on the Stage, &c. | [short thick-thin rule] | *Second American Edition.* | BOSTON: | PUBLISHED BY SAMUEL T. ARMSTRONG, | AND CROCKER & BREWSTER, | No. 50, Cornhill. | 1821.

17.6 x 9.5 cm.; [1][6], 2-24[6]; xi, [1], [9]-280, [1], 3 p.

Notes: in some copies, p. 223 misnumbered 173 (pp. [1]-222, 173, 224-280).

Contents: p. [i]: BRAINERD'S MEMOIRS. (verso blank); p. [iii]: title (verso blank); p. [v]: PREFACE. [signed] J. S. | *West Cowes, Isle of Wight*; p. [ix]: CONTENTS.; p. [xii]: blank; p. [9]: THE | LIFE OF BRAINERD.; pp. [1]-4: [advertisement].

THJ 152 NS 1032814 OCLC 3756586

American Antiquarian Society

215 • MEMOIRS | OF THE | REV. DAVID BRAINERD; | MISSIONARY | TO THE INDIANS | *ON THE BORDERS OF NEW-YORK, NEW-JERSEY, AND* | *PENNSYLVANIA:* | CHIEFLY TAKEN FROM HIS OWN DIARY. | BY REV. JONATHAN EDWARDS, OF NORTHAMPTON. | INCLUDING HIS JOURNAL, NOW FOR THE FIRST TIME INCORPORATED WITH THE | REST OF HIS DIARY, IN A REGULAR CHRONOLOGICAL SERIES. | BY SERENO EDWARDS DWIGHT. | [short tapered rule] | NEW-HAVEN: | PRINTED AND PUBLISHED BY | S. CONVERSE. | [two short lines of stops] | 1822.

20.8 x 13.3 cm.; [1][4], 2-63[4], 64[2]; 507, [1] p.

Contents: p. [1]: title; p. [2]: [affidavit] [signed] CHA'S. A. INGERSOLL, | *Clerk of the District of Connecticut*; p. [3]: ADVERTISEMENT BY THE EDITOR [signed] SERENO EDWARDS DWIGHT | Boston, February 22, 1822.; p. [11]: A | SERMON, | PREACHED IN NEWARK, | JUNE 12, 1744, | AT THE ORDINATION OF | MR. DAVID BRAINERD, | A MISSIONARY TO THE INDIANS | ON THE BORDER OF NEW-YORK, NEW-JERSEY AND PENNSYLVANIA. | BY EBENEZER PEMBERTON, A. M. | PASTOR OF THE PRESBYTERIAN CHURCH | IN THE CITY OF NEW-YORK. (verso blank); p. [13]: AN ORDINATION SERMON, &c.; p. [29]: PREFACE [signed] JONATHAN EDWARDS.; p. [35]: MEMOIRS, &c.; p. [472]: blank; p. [473]: *Christians, when absent from the body, are present with the Lord;* | A | SERMON, | PREACHED AT THE FUNERAL OF THE | REV. DAVID BRAINERD, | *MISSIONARY TO THE INDIANS*, | FROM THE SOCIETY IN SCOTLAND FOR PROPAGATING CHRISTIAN KNOWLEDGE, | AND PASTOR OF A CHURCH OF CHRISTIAN INDIANS IN NEW- | JERSEY; WHO DIED AT NORTHAMPTON, OCT. 9, | 1747, AND WAS INTERRED ON THE 12th. | BY REV. JONATHAN EDWARDS. (verso blank); p. [475]: A SERMON.; p. [505]: CONTENTS.; p. [508]: blank.

THJ 153 NUC NB0739581 OCLC 418605

Harvard Divinity School

215A • NEW-HAVEN: | PRINTED AND PUBLISHED BY | S. CONVERSE. | [2 short lines of stops] | 1822. | Republished, 1970 | Scholarly Press, 22929 Industrial Drive East, St. Clair Shores, Michigan 48080

Notes: facsimile reprint of the above.

21.5 x 14.2 cm.; 504 p.

ISBN 0403002338 OCLC 59453

Gordon-Conwell Theological Seminary

216 • THE FOLLOWING | *EXTRACTS* | WERE TAKEN FROM THE | LIFE OF DAVID BRAINERD, | AN | *Excellent and Pious Missionary*, | WHO ENDURED MANY GREAT HARDSHIPS AND | SUFFERINGS AMONGST THE | *INDIANS* | IN | **North=America**, | With great Cheerfulness and Resignation, in order | to bring them to the saving Knowledge of | the Lord Jesus Christ. | For this Cause he devoted his Life and all that was | near and dear, till the Thirtieth Year of his Age, | when his tender Constitution gave way—and he died | in full Assurance of Faith, in the Year 1747; and | having seen the fruits of his labour in a number of | those amongst whom his Lot had been cast, it af- | forded him great Consolation at the close of his Life. | [short double rule] | MALTON: | FROM THE OFFICE OF R. SMITHSON, JUN. PRINTER, | IN YORKERSGATE. | [short tapered

rule] | 1823.

19.7 x 11.1 cm.; 8 p.

Notes: no attribution in the text; except for slight changes in language and punctuation, the brief text follows Edwards both in Brainerd's journal entries and the commentary upon them; see *The Life of David Brainerd*, ed. Norman Pettit, *The Works of Jonathan Edwards*, vol. 7 (New Haven: Yale University Press, 1985), pp. 212, 225, 232, 237, 241, 259, 271, 277, 357, and 464.

Contents: p. [1]: title; pp. 2-8: text; p. 8: *R. SMITHSON, Jun. Printer, MALTON.*

NUC NB0739549   OCLC 21421264

Detroit Public Library

217 • THE | LIFE | OF THE | REV. DAVID BRAINERD, | *Missionary to the Indians,* | FROM THE SOCIETY IN SCOTLAND FOR PROPAGATING | CHRISTIAN KNOWLEDGE; | Who died at Northampton in New-England, October 9, 1747, in the | 30th Year of his Age. | [short rule] | BY | JONATHAN EDWARDS, A. M. | *President of the College of New-Jersey.* | [short thick-thin rule] | EDINBURGH: | PRINTED FOR H. S. BAYNES AND CO. | AND | WILLIAM BAYNES & SON, LONDON. | [short rule] | 1824.

13.8 x 8.7 cm.; π^4, A-Z^6, Aa-Yy^6, Zz^4, $3A^4$; viii, xv, [1], [17]-560 p.

Notes: lacks pp. v-vi in the first count (pp. i-iv, vii-viii); lacks pp. i-ii in the second count (pp. iii-xv); some copies lack half title and frontispiece.

Contents: p. [i]: LIFE | OF THE | REV. DAVID BRAINERD. (verso blank); frontispiece: FRONTISPIECE | [engraving] | *W. H. Lizars sculpt* | I am persuaded also that the Lord touched their | consciences; or I never saw such attention raised | in them before. | *See page 144* | *Published by H. S. Baynes Edinburgh*; p. [iii]: title; p. [iv]: Printed by Anderson & Bryce, | Edinburgh, 1824.; p. [vii]: CONTENTS.; p. [iii]: ADVERTISEMENT.; p. [v]: PREFACE. [signed] JONATHAN EDWARDS.; p. [xvi]: blank; pp. [17]-524: text; p. [525]: A | SERMON | PREACHED | *IN NEWARK, June* 12, 1744, | AT THE ORDINATION | OF THE | REV. DAVID BRAINERD, | *A Missionary among the Indians.* | [short tapered rule] | BY E. PEMBERTON, A. M. | Pastor of the Presbyterian Church in the City of New-York. | [short tapered rule] | TO WHICH IS ADDED, | AN APPENDIX, | *On Indian affairs.* (verso blank); p. [527]: ORDINATION SERMON.; p. [546]: APPENDIX; p. 560: Printed by Anderson & Bryce, | Edinburgh, 1824.

THJ 154   NUC NB0739573   OCLC 35720291

Yale University

218 • AN EXTRACT | OF | The Life of | THE | LATE REV. DAVID BRAINERD, | *MISSIONARY TO THE INDIANS.* | [short rule] | BY THE REV. JOHN WESLEY, M. A. | [short rule] | LONDON: | PRINTED FOR J. KERSHAW, 14, CITY ROAD, AND | 66, PATERNOSTER ROW. | [short rule] | 1825.

14.4 x 9 cm.; $[A]^6$, B-Z^6, 2A-$2M^6$, $2N^5$; 422, [8] p.

Contents: p. [1]: title (verso blank); p. [3]: ADVERTISEMENT. (verso blank); pp. [5]-422: text; p. 422: JAMES NICHOLS, *Printer,* | 2, *Warwick Square, Newgate Street.*; pp. [423-430]: [advertisement].

THJ 155   NUC NB0739546   OCLC 8339788

Free Library of Philadelphia

219 • LIFE AND JOURNAL | OF THE | REV. DAVID BRAINERD, | MISSIONARY TO THE INDIANS. | [short rule] | BY | JONATHAN EDWARDS, A. M. | EDINBURGH: | PUBLISHED BY H. S. BAYNES, | 26, GEORGE STREET; | AND W. BAYNES & SON, LONDON. | MDCCCXXVI.

17.9 x 10.8 cm.; π^6, $[A]^{12}$, B-R^{12}, S^8, T^1; xii, 426 p.

Contents: prp. [1]: title; prp. [2]: PRINTED BY ANDERSON & BRYCE.; p. [i]: CONTENTS; p. [iii]: PREFACE. [signed] JONATHAN EDWARDS.; p. [1]: THE LIFE | OF | DAVID BRAINERD.; p. 225: REMAINS OF THE REV. D. BRAINERD.; p. 231: LETTERS.; p. 245: REFLECTIONS | ON THE PRECEDING MEMOIRS.; p. 283: THE | RISE AND PROGRESS | OF A | REMARKABLE WORK OF GRACE | AMONG THE INDIANS, | WITH | *GENERAL REMARKS.* | BY DAVID BRAINERD.; p. 327: DIVINE GRACE DISPLAYED; OR, THE CONTINUANCE

AND | PROGRESS OF A REMARKABLE WORK OF GRACE AMONG | THE INDIANS.; p. [385]: APPENDIX TO THE JOURNAL.; p. 426: Printed by Anderson & Bryce, | Edinburgh, 1826.

THJ 156   NUC NB0739558   OCLC 14956035

Grace College and Seminary

220 • LIFE | OF THE | REV. DAVID BRAINERD, | MISSIONARY TO THE AMERICAN INDIANS. | BY | JONATHAN EDWARDS, A. M. | [short rule] | REVISED AND ABRIDGED, | WITH | AN INTRODUCTORY ESSAY, | BY | JAMES MONTGOMERY, | AUTHOR OF "THE WORLD BEFORE THE FLOOD," "SONGS OF ZION," | "THE CHRISTIAN PSALMIST," "THE CHRISTIAN POET," &c. | [short rule] | "AN Indian woman inquired, whether I was not sent to preach to the Indians | by some good people a great way off. I replied, Yes, by the good people of | Scotland. She answered, that her heart loved those people so the even- | ing before, that she could scarce help praying for them all night. Her heart | *would* go to God for them!"–*Brainerd's Divine Grace Displayed, Jan.* 5, 1746. | [short rule] | GLASGOW: | PRINTED FOR WILLIAM COLLINS; | OLIVER & BOYD, WM. WHYTE & CO. AND WM. OPLIPHANT, EDINBURGH; | W. F. WAKEMAN; AND WM. CURRY, JUN. & CO. DUBLIN; | WHITTAKER, TREACHER, & ARNOT; HAMILTON, ADAMS, & CO. | SIMPKIN AND MARSHALL; BALDWIN & CRADOCK; | AND HURST, CHANCE, & CO. LONDON. | [short rule] | MDCCCXXIX.

18.1 x 10.3 cm.; π^1, A-Z^{12}, $2A^{12}$, $2B^4$; [2], lii, [53]-583, [1] p.

Notes: in some copies, pp. [i-ii]: blank; in some copies, four pages of advertisement follow the text.

Contents: p. [i]: SELECT | CHRISTIAN AUTHORS, | WITH | Introductory Essays. | No. 52. (verso blank).; frontispiece: [engraving] | REV[D]. JONATHAN EDWARDS | PUBLISHED BY WILLIAM COLLINS GLASGOW | Eng[d]. on Steel by W. H. Lizars Edinr.; p. [iii]: title: p. [iv]: Printed by W. Collins & Co. | Glasgow.; p. [v]: INTRODUCTORY ESSAY. [signed] J. M. | SHEFFIELD, *January*, 1830; p. [li]: CONTENTS.; p. [53]: PREFACE [signed] JONATHAN EDWARDS.; p. [65]: LIFE | OF | DAVID BRAINERD. (verso blank); p. [67]: LIFE | OF | DAVID BRAINERD.; p. [328]: REMAINS | OF THE | REV. DAVID BRAINERD.; p. [339]: LETTERS | WRITTEN BY | MR. BRAINERD TO HIS FRIENDS.; p. [361]: REFLECTIONS | ON THE | PRECEDING MEMOIRS.; p. [420]: blank; p. [421]: DIVINE GRACE DISPLAYED; | OR, THE | RISE AND PROGRESS | OF | A REMARKABLE WORK OF GRACE | AMONGST | A NUMBER OF INDIANS IN THE PROVINCES | OF | NEW JERSEY AND PENNSYLVANIA, | JUSTLY REPRESENTED IN | A JOURNAL, | KEPT BY THE HONOURABLE SOCIETY IN SCOTLAND | FOR PROPAGATING CHRISTIAN KNOWLEDGE: | WITH SOME GENERAL REMARKS, | BY DAVID BRAINERD, | Minister of the Gospel, and Missionary from the said Society. | PUBLISHED BY THE REVEREND AND WORTHY CORRESPONDENTS OF | THE SAID SOCIETY, | WITH A PREFACE BY THEM. (verso blank); p. [423]: PREFACE. [signed] THE CORRESPONDENTS.; p. [427]: DIVINE GRACE DISPLAYED; | OR, THE | RISE AND PROGRESS | OF A | REMARKABLE WORK OF GRACE, | *&c.*; p. 583: Printed by W. Collins & Co. | Glasgow.; p. [584]: blank.

THJ 157   NUC NB0739574   OCLC 15537779

New York Public Library

221 •THE | LIFE | OF | REV. DAVID BRAINERD, | CHIEFLY EXTRACTED FROM HIS DIARY. | BY PRESIDENT EDWARDS. | SOMEWHAT ABRIDGED. | EMBRACING, | IN THE CHRONOLOGICAL ORDER | BRAINERD'S PUBLIC JOURNAL | OF THE | MOST SUCCESSFUL YEAR | OF HIS | MISSIONARY LABORS. | PUBLISHED BY THE | AMERICAN TRACT SOCIETY, | 150 NASSAU-STREET, NEW YORK.

14.9 x 9.4 cm.; $[1]^8$, $2\text{-}22^8$, 23^4; iv, [5]-360 p.

Notes: The Society's Life of Brainerd was reprinted many times, always without date, and sometimes with slight variations of the title page.... Probably some 68,000 or 70,000 copies of this edition were distributed between 1833 (when it was first published) and 1892 (when it ceased to be listed among the Society's publications).—THJ. The text of the several editions seems to have been printed from the original plates, but in some copies, though the pagination remains the same (360 p.), the collation ($1\text{-}30^6$) and measurements (14.6 x 8.6 cm.) differ; bound with some copies is John Flavel, *A Treatise on Keeping of the Heart*; some copies include a series title page, *The Evangelical Family Library*; most copies include illustrations and the following editorial note: It is a striking characteristic of the life of BRAINERD, from | the time of his entering on the study of Theology till his | death, that he *daily* "walked with God," or mourned the | absence of the light of his countenance. President Edwards | has endeavored to exhibit the state of his mind *each day*, as | described in his diary. In this edition, many passages thus | inserted by Edwards, especially such as much resembled | those preceding or following, have been omitted.

Contents: frontispiece: [engraving] H. Page | [A.] Anderson S. | VIEW OF THE PARSONAGE IN CRANBURY, NEW JERSEY, JULY, 1833. | Occupying the ground where Brainerd preached to the Indians, 1746.; p. [i]: title; p. [ii]: editorial note; p. [iii]: CONTENTS.; p. [5]: FROM | PRESIDENT EDWARDS' PREFACE. [signed] JONATHAN EDWARDS.; p. [9]: THE LIFE | OF | REV. DAVID BRAINERD. (facing p. 132: [engraving] H. Page d. | A. A. s. | View of the Creek and Village of Crosswicks, New Jersey, July, 1833.; facing p. 337: [engraving] Page D | A. A. | PRESIDENT EDWARDS' HOUSE, NORTHAMPTON, MASSACHUSETTS.); p. 360: Perpetuated by the Donations of Messrs. George Douglass, Charles Starr, | and William A. Hallock, of New-York.

THJ 159 NUC NB0739563 OCLC 2301870
Yale Divinity School

222 • THE LIFE | OF | REV. DAVID BRAINERD, | CHIEFLY EXTRACTED FROM HIS DIARY. | BY PRESIDENT EDWARDS. | [short rule] | SOMEWHAT ABRIDGED. | [short rule] | *EMBRACING, IN THE CHRONOLOGICAL ORDER*, | BRAINERD'S PUBLIC JOURNAL | OF THE MOST SUCCESSFUL YEAR OF HIS | Missionary Labors. | [short thick-thin rule] | PUBLISHED BY THE | AMERICAN TRACT SOCIETY, | NO. 150 NASSAU-STREET, NEW- YORK. | D. Fanshaw, Printer.

14.3 x 8.8 cm.; [1]^6, 2-30^6; iv, [5]-360 p.
Notes: variant title page and collation.
OCLC 35720388
Harvard Divinity School

222A • THE LIFE | OF | REV. DAVID BRAINERD, | CHIEFLY EXTRACTED FROM HIS DIARY | BY PRESIDENT EDWARDS | [short rule] | SOMEWHAT ABRIDGED | [short rule] | *EMBRACING, IN THE CHRONOLOGICAL ORDER*, | BRAINERD'S PUBLIC JOURNAL | OF THE MOST SUCCESSFUL YEAR OF HIS | Missionary Labors | BAKER BOOK HOUSE | Grand Rapids, Michigan

17.8 x 10.8 cm.; iv, 360 p.
Notes: a facsimile reprint first issued in 1978; reprinted in 1981, 1985, and 1988.
OCLC 7344727
Gordon College

223 • THE LIFE | OF | REV. DAVID BRAINERD, | CHIEFLY EXTRACTED FROM HIS DIARY. | BY PRESIDENT EDWARDS. | [short rule] | SOMEWHAT ABRIDGED. | [short rule] | *EMBRACING, IN THE CHRONOLOGICAL ORDER*, | BRAINERD'S PUBLIC JOURNAL | OF THE MOST SUCCESSFUL YEAR OF HIS | MISSIONARY LABORS. | [short thick-thin rule] | PUBLISHED BY THE | AMERICAN TRACT SOCIETY, | NO. 150 NASSAU-STREET, NEW-YORK. | D. Fanshaw, Printer.

14.7 x 9.1 cm.; [1]^6, 2-30^6; iv, [5]-360 p.; [1]^6, 2-9^6, [1]-108 p.

Contents: frontispiece: [engraving] H. Page | [A.] Anderson S. | View of the Parsonage in Cranbury, New Jersey, July, 1833. | Occupying the ground where Brainerd preached to the Indians, 1746.; opposite frontispiece: THE | Evangelical | FAMILY LIBRARY | VOL. VII | [engraving] | Morse del. Dick Sc. | Published by the | *American Tract Society*; p. [i]: title; p. [ii]: editorial note; p. [iii]: CONTENTS; p. [5]: FROM | PRESIDENT EDWARDS' PREFACE. [signed] JONATHAN EDWARDS.; p. [9]: THE LIFE | OF | REV. DAVID BRAINERD. (facing p. 132: [engraving] H. Page d. | A. A. s. | View of the Creek and Village of Crosswicks, New Jersey, July, 1833.; facing p. 336: [engraving] Page D | A.

A. | President Edwards' House, Northampton, Massachusetts, 1747.; p. 360: Perpetuated by the Donations of Messrs. George Douglass, Charles Starr, | and William A. Hallock, of New-York.; p. [1]: A | TREATISE | ON | KEEPING THE HEART. | SELECTED FROM THE WORKS OF | THE REV. JOHN FLAVEL. | The style adapted to the present state of improvement, [*sic*] | [short decorative rule] | PUBLISHED BY THE | AMERICAN TRACT SOCIETY | NO. 150 NASSAU-STREET, NEW-YORK. | [short double rule] | D. Fanshaw, Printer. (verso blank); p. [3]: CONTENTS. (verso blank); p. [5]: ON | KEEPING THE HEART.

NUC NB0739563 OCLC 31230154
Boston Public Library

224 • THE LIFE OF | THE | REV. DAVID BRAINERD, | MISSIONARY TO THE NORTH AMERICAN INDIANS. | COMPILED FROM THE MEMOIR PUBLISHED BY PRES. EDWARDS, | BY THE REV. JOSIAH PRATT, B.D. | AND NOW RE-PUBLISHED BY HIS PERMISSION. | PUBLISHED BY R. B. SEELEY AND W. BURNSIDE; | AND SOLD BY L. B. SEELEY AND SONS, | FLEET STREET, LONDON. | MDCCCXXXIV.

16.5 x 10.2 cm.; $[A]^8$, $B\text{-}Z^8$, $2A\text{-}2B^8$, $2C^6$; xvi, 396 p.

Contents: p. [i]: THE LIFE OF | THE | REV. DAVID BRAINERD.; p. [ii]: L. B. SEELEY AND SONS, WESTON GREEN, THAMES DITTON.; p. [iii]: title (verso blank); p. [v]: CONTENTS.; p. [vii]: INTRODUCTION [signed] EDWARD BICKERSTETH. | *Watton Rectory,* | *Oct.* 20, 1834.; pp. [1]-385: text; p. [386]: REMAINS.

THJ 160 NUC NP0547936 OCLC 4951786
Library of Congress

224A • THE LIFE OF | THE | REV. DAVID BRAINERD, | MISSIONARY TO THE NORTH AMERICAN INDIANS | COMPILED FROM | THE MEMOIR PUBLISHED BY PRESIDENT EDWARDS. | BY THE REV. JOSIAH PRATT, B.D. | SEELEY, BURNSIDE, AND SEELEY, | FLEET STREET, LONDON. | MDCCCXLV.

15.7 x 9.4 cm.; π^1, a^8, $B^8\text{-}Z^8$, $2A\text{-}2B^8$, $2C^6$; xviii [i.e., xvi], [2], 396 p.

Notes: lacks pp. iii-iv (pp. i-ii, v-xviii).

Contents: p. [i]: title (verso blank); p. [v]: CONTENTS.; p. [vii]: INTRODUCTION. [signed] EDWARD BICKERSTETH. | *Watton Rectory,* | *Oct.* 20, 1834.; p. [xix]: THE LIFE OF | THE | REV. DAVID BRAINERD. (verso blank); pp. [1]-392: text; pp. [393-396]: [advertisement].

NUC NP0547935 OCLC 9332878
Yale Divinity School

225 • QUELQUES RÉFLEXIONS | SUR LA | VIE DU MISSIONNAIRE BRAINERD. | Traduit de l'Anglais. | Quoique mort, il parle encore: | Soyez mes imitateurs, comme aussi *je l'ai* | *été* de Christ. | HÉBR. XI, 4. 1 COR. XI, 1. | [short decorative rule] | LAUSANNE, | *Libraire de Marc Ducloux; et ailleurs, dans les* | *divers dépôts de la Société ci-dessus nommée.* | [short rule] | 1838.

20.4 x 12.8 cm.; 18 p.

Notes: a French translation (and abridgment) of the closing section of *Life of Brainerd.* The blue paper covers are not included in the pagination; the front cover repeats the title page, except for the following between the quotation and the imprint: SE VEND AU PROFIT DE LA SOCIÉTÉ VAUDOISE POUR LA | SANCTIFICATION DU DIMANCHE. | Prix: 15 rappes.

Contents: p. [1]: title (verso blank); pp. 3-4: [advertisement]; pp. 5-18: text.

THJ 158
Zentralbibliothek Zürich

226 • [Extracts]

Notes: first extract from *Life of Brainerd*: The closing Scenes of Brainerd's Life, the second from *True Saints.*; p. [ii]: Entered according to the Act of Congress in the year 1843, by | ALEXANDER W. MITCHELL, M. D. | In the office of the Clerk of the District Court for the | Eastern District of Pennsylvania.

Contents: pp. 112-127 and pp. 128-143 in THE | MISSIONARY IN THE WILDERNESS, | OR | GRACE DISPLAYED | AMONG THE HEATHEN. | PREPARED FOR THE PRESBYTERIAN BOARD OF PUBLICATION. | [short rule] | PHILADELPHIA: | PRESBYTERIAN BOARD OF PUBLICATION, | No. 821 CHESTNUT STREET.

THJ 161 NUC NB0739603 OCLC 2168213

Gordon-Conwell Theological Seminary

227 • LIFE, | REMAINS, AND LETTERS, | OF | DAVID BRAINERD: | WITH | HIS JOURNALS, | DETAILING | THE RISE AND PROGRESS | OF | A REMARKABLE WORK OF GRACE | AMONG THE INDIANS; | COMPLETE. | [short wavy rule] | NEW EDITION, REVISED. | [short wavy rule] | ABERDEEN: | GEORGE & ROBERT KING, 28, ST. NICHOLAS STREET; | WARD & CO., PATERNOSTER ROW, LONDON. | [short rule] | 1845.

14.9 x 9.1 cm.; π^2, $[B]^6$, $C\text{-}Z^6$, $2A\text{-}2Z^6$, $3A\text{-}3D^6$, $3E^4$; xix, [1], [21]-595, [5] p.

Notes: in some copies, half title precedes title page; some copies lack advertisement.

Contents: p. [i]: title (verso blank); p. [iii]: CONTENTS.; p. [v]: LIFE OF DAVID BRAINERD. (verso blank); p. [vii]: PREFACE. [signed] JONATHAN EDWARDS.; p. [xx]: blank; p. [21]: LIFE | OF | DAVID BRAINERD.; p. [417]: DIVINE GRACE DISPLAYED; | OR, THE | RISE AND PROGRESS | OF A REMARKABLE WORK OF GRACE | AMONGST | A NUMBER OF INDIANS IN THE PROVINCES | OF | NEW JERSEY AND PENNSYLVANIA, | JUSTLY REPRESENTED IN | A JOURNAL, | KEPT BY THE HONOURABLE SOCIETY IN SCOTLAND | FOR PROPAGATING CHRISTIAN KNOWLEDGE: | WITH SOME GENERAL REMARKS, | BY DAVID BRAINERD, | Minister of the Gospel, and Missionary from the said Society. | PUBLISHED BY THE REVEREND AND WORTHY COR- | RESPONDENTS OF THE SAID SOCIETY, | WITH A PREFACE BY THEM. (verso blank); pp. [419]-595: text; p. 595: PRINTED BY | GEORGE AND ROBERT KING, | 28, St. Nicholas Street, Aberdeen. (verso blank); pp. [1-4]: [advertisement].

THJ 162 NUC NB0739577

National Library of Scotland

227A • LONDON: | WILLIAM TEGG AND CO.; | WARD AND CO.; AND GEORGE AND ROBERT KING, ABERDEEN. | [short rule] | 1848.

Notes: identical with the above except for the imprint; following p. 595, pp. [1]-4 and [1]-18: [advertisement].

THJ 162A NUC NB0739578 OCLC 43522670

Yale University

228 • **Das Leben | des Indianermissionars | David Brainerd.** | [short rule] | **Ein Bild | aus der älteren Mission, | dem | heutigen Christenvolke vorgestellt | von | Christoph Friedrich Eppler, | Verfasser von Hakub Natscharoff's Leben.** | [short decorative rule] | **Zürich. | Verlag von Franz Hanke. | 1851.**

17.4 x 10.8 cm.; viii, 256 p.

Notes: a German translation of *Life of Brainerd*.

Contents: p. [i]: title (verso blank); p. [iii]: Vorwort.; p. [vi]: Inhalts=Verzeichnitz.; pp. [9]-256: text.

THJ 163

Zentralbibliothek Zürich

229 • [within rules] THE LIFE | OF | DAVID BRAINERD, | MISSIONARY TO THE INDIANS: | CHIEFLY TAKEN FROM HIS OWN DIARY, AND OTHER PRIVATE | WRITINGS. | BY JONATHAN EDWARDS. | WITH PREFACE, | BY THE REV. HORATIUS BONAR, | KELSO. | JOHNSTONE AND HUNTER, | EDINBURGH AND LONDON. | [short rule] | M.DCCC.LI.

16.8 x 10.3 cm.; π^2, $[a]\text{-}b^8$, $A\text{-}S^8$, T^7; xxxv, [1], 302 p.

Contents: p. [i]: The | Christian's Fireside Library. | VOL. III. (verso blank); p. [iii]: title (verso blank); p. [v]: CONTENTS. (verso blank); p. [vii]: PREFACE.; p. [xxxvi]: blank; pp. [1]-302: text; p. 302: EDINBURGH: | PRINTED

BY JOHNSTONE AND HUNTER, HIGH STREET.
THJ 165 NUC NB0739568 OCLC 3564481
Princeton University

229A EDINBURGH: | JOHNSTONE AND HUNTER. | [short rule] | M.DCCC.LIII.
Notes: identical with the above except for the imprint.
THJ 165A
British Library

230 • THE | LIFE OF DAVID BRAINERD | MISSIONARY TO THE NORTH AMERICAN INDIANS. | A.D. 1742–1747. | "In weariness and painfulness, in watchings often, in hunger and thirst, in fastings | often in cold and nakedness."–2 *Cor*. xi. 27. | SEELEY, JACKSON, AND HALLIDAY, FLEET STREET; | AND B. SWEENEY, HANOVER STREET. | LONDON. MDCCCLVI.
17.3 x 10.4 cm.; [A]^8, B-U^8; xvi, 304 p.
Contents: p. [i]: THE LIFE OF DAVID BRAINERD.; p. [ii]: *No Portrait of Brainerd is known to exist; but the present | volume contains, in lieu, more matter than the average | proposed for these volumes*.; p. [iii]: title (verso blank); p. [v]: INTRODUCTION. [signed] E. B. | *Watton Rectory*.; p. [xv]: CONTENTS.; pp. [1]-296: text; p. 297: REMAINS, | ETC.; p. 304: LONDON: | Printed by G. BARCLAY, Castle St. Leicester Sq.
NUC NP0547935 OCLC 15067802
Point Loma Nazarene University

231 • Das Leben | von | David Brainerd, | Missionar unter den Indianern. | [short rule] | Nach dem, von Jonathan Edwards herausgegebnen Tage= | buche Brainerd's beschrieben. | [short rule] | Herausgegeben von der | Amerikanischen Tractat=Gesellschaft. | Neu=York, 150 Nassau=Strasse. | Life of Brainerd
15.1 x 9.4 cm.; [1]^8, 2-19^8, 20^3; 310 p.
Notes: published by the American Tract Society in 1856.
Contents: frontispiece: [engraving] | VIEW OF THE PARSONAGE IN CRANBURY, NEW JERSEY, JULY, 1833. | Occupying the ground where Brainerd preached to the Indians, 1746.; p. [1]: title; p. [2]: Dies Buch ist ein Auszug aus dem, von de Amerikan. | Tractat=Gesellschaft herausgegebnen englischen Buche: | "The life of Rev. David Brainerd. Chiefly extracted from | his Diary. By President Edwards. Somewhat abridged." | Vielfach benutzt ist bei Anfertigung dieses Auszugs eine deut= | sche Schrift, die 1851 bei F. Hanke in Zürich erschienen ist | unter dem Titel: "Das Leben des Indianer-Missionars | David Brainerd. Ein Bild aus der ältern Mission, dem | heutigen Christenvolke vorgestellt von Christoph Friedrich | Eppler," (Lehrer am Missionshause in Basel.); p. [3]: Vorwort.; p. [7]: Inhalts=Verzeichnitz.; pp. [9]-310: text (facing p. 301: [engraving] | PRESIDENT EDWARDS' HOUSE, NORTHAMPTON, MASSACHUSETTS.).
THJ 164 NUC NB0739552 OCLC 13753956
Harvard Divinity School

233 • Indian=Missionären | David Brainerds | Lefwerne, | beskrifwet hufwudsakligen efter hans egen | Dagbok. | [short rule] | Swensk bearbetning efter det engelska originalet | af | Presidenten Jonathan Edwards. | [short decorative rule] | Utgifwet af Stockholms Missionsförening.
14.3 x 9.4 cm.; viii, 216 p., 1 leaflet (map).
Notes: a Swedish translation of *Life of Brainerd*; front matter pagination in capital roman numerals.
Contents: p. [i]: title; p. [ii]: Stockholm, truckt hos P. P. Elde & Comp. 1862.; p. [iii]: Innehåll.; p. v: Öfwersättarens Förord.; p. vii: Utdrag af Jonathan Edwards företal. [signed] Jonathan Edwards.; p. 1: Missionären David Brainerds Lefwerne.
OCLC 29056013
Sveriges Nationalbibliotek

234 • MEMOIRS OF | REV. DAVID BRAINERD, | *Missionary to the Indians of North America*. |

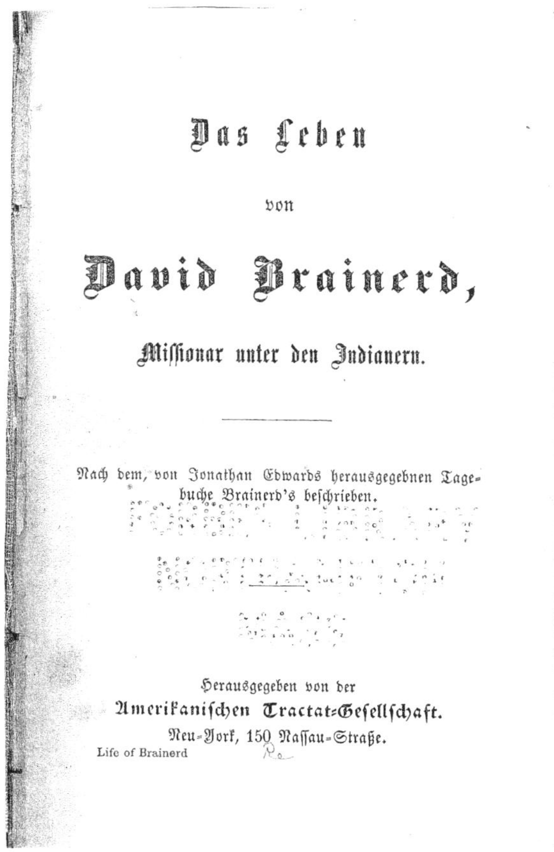

Das Leben

von

David Brainerd,

Missionar unter den Indianern.

Nach dem, von Jonathan Edwards herausgegebnen Tagebuche Brainerd's beschrieben.

Herausgegeben von der

Amerikanischen Tractat-Gesellschaft.

Neu-York, 150 Nassau-Straße.

Life of Brainerd

Title page, *Das Leben von David Brainerd* (1856). Permission of the Forbes Library, Northampton.

BASED ON THE LIFE OF BRAINERD PREPARED | BY JONATHAN EDWARDS, D.D., AND AFTERWARDS REVISED | AND ENLARGED BY SERENO E. DWIGHT, D.D. | EDITED | BY J. M. SHERWOOD | *Author of "The History of the Cross."* | WITH AN INTRODUCTION ON | THE LIFE AND CHARACTER OF DAVID BRAINERD | BY THE EDITOR. | ALSO AN ESSAY ON | GOD'S HAND IN MISSIONS, | BY ARTHUR T. PIERSON, D. D. | [short decorative rule] | FUNK & WAGNALLS. | [in 2 cols., col. 1] NEW YORK: | 10 AND 12 DEY STREET. | [col. 2] LONDON: | 44 FLEET STREET. | 1884.

4to; 18.7 x 12.2 cm.; [2], lxxx, 354, [2] p.

Notes: no signatures; in some copies, imprint: YOUNG PEOPLE'S MISSIONARY MOVEMENT | NEW YORK.

Contents: p. [i]: title; p. [ii]: Entered according to Act of Congress, in the year 1884, by | FUNK & WAGNALLS, | In the office of the Librarian of Congress at Washington, D.C. | ALL RIGHTS RESERVED.; p. [iii]: TABLE OF CONTENTS.; p. [v]: PRESIDENT EDWARD'S [*sic*] PREFACE TO THE | ORIGINAL EDITION. [signed] JONATHAN EDWARDS.; p. [xv]: PREFACE TO THE PRESENT EDITION [signed] JAMES M. SHERWOOD | BROOKLYN, *June* 1884; p. [xxi]: INTRODUCTION. | THE | LIFE AND CHARACTER | OF | DAVID BRAINERD. | BY | J. M. SHERWOOD. (verso blank); p. [xxiii]: LIFE AND CHARACTER OF BRAINERD.; p. [lii]: blank; p. [liii]: GOD'S HAND IN | MISSIONS. | BY | ARTHUR T. PIERSON, D.D. (verso blank); p. [lv]: GOD'S HAND IN MISSIONS. | BY THE REV. ARTHUR T. PIERSON, D.D.; p. [1]: MEMOIRS | OF | DAVID BRAINERD.; pp. [355-356]: [advertisement].

THJ 167 NUC NB0739586 OCLC 3564659

Gordon College

234A • FUNK & WAGNALLS. | [in 2 cols., col. 1] NEW YORK: | 10 AND 12 DEY STREET. | [col. 2] LONDON: | 44 FLEET STREET. | 1885.

Notes: identical with the above except for the imprint.

THJ 167A NUC NB0739590 OCLC 11081489

Yale Divinity School

234B • FUNK & WAGNALLS COMPANY | 1891 | TORONTO | LONDON | NEW YORK

Notes: identical with the above except for the imprint.

THJ 167B NUC NB0739592 OCLC 945719

Andover Newton Theological School

235 • CHRISTIAN BIOGRAPHY. | [short rule] THE LIFE OF THE | REV. DAVID BRAINERD. | BY THE | REV. JONATHAN EDWARDS, A.M., | *President of the College of New Jersey.* | ABRIDGED. | [short rule] | Religious Tract Society, | *Instituted* 1799; | PUBLISHED AND SOLD AT THE DEPOSITORY, 56, PATER- | NOSTER ROW; BY J. NISBET, 21, BERNERS STREET; | AND OTHER BOOKSELLERS.

14.2 x 8.9 cm.; [A]^{6}, B-M^{6}; 144 p.

Contents: p. [1]: title; p. [2]: Printed by J. Rider, Little Britain, London; pp. [3]-144: text.

THJ 168 NUC NB0739571 OCLC 43639632

Library of Congress

235A • LIFE OF | THE REV. DAVID BRAINERD.

13.8 x 8.8 cm.; [A]^{6}, B-Z^{6}, 2A-2N^{6}; 144, 144, 72, 72 p

Notes: separately paged, continuously signed; p. [2]: London. J. Rider, Printer, 14, Bartholomew Close.

Contents: caption title; pp. [3]-144 [first count] in CHRISTIAN BIOGRAPHY. | [short rule] | CONTAINING | THE LIVES OF | REV. DAVID BRAINERD, | REV. EDWARD PAYSON, | REV. VAVASOR POWELL, | ARCHBISHOP USHER. | *LONDON*: | RELIGIOUS TRACT SOCIETY, | *Instituted* 1799. | SOLD AT THE DEPOSITORY, 56, PATERNOSTER ROW; | AND BY THE BOOKSELLERS.

THJ 168A OCLC 13321292

Princeton University

236 • No. 537. | TRUE RELIGION. | FROM PRESIDENT EDWARDS' REFLECTIONS ON THE | LIFE OF DAVID BRAINERD.

18.3 x 11.1 cm.; 4 p.

Notes: reprinted, pp. [1]-4 (also paged [273]-276) in TRACTS | OF THE | AMERICAN TRACT SOCIETY. | General Series. | [engraving] | Vol. XIII. | PRINTED BY THE | AMERICAN TRACT SOCIETY, | 150 NASSAU-STREET, NEW YORK.

Contents: caption title; p. 4: PUBLISHED BY THE AMERICAN TRACT SOCIETY.

THJ 169 NUC NE0046876 OCLC 43639566

American Tract Society

237 • [within rules] David Brainerd | [double rule] | The Mighty Man of Prayer | Except a corn of wheat fall into the ground | and die, it abideth alone; but if it die it | beareth much fruit.–John xii. 24. | [ornament] | A. SIMS, PUBLISHER | 5 Simpson Ave., Toronto, Ontario, Canada

16.9 x 11.4 cm.; 75, [1] p.

Notes: published c. 1890; p. [4]: In making these selections we have used Brainerd's | Journal as it appears in Jonathan Edwards' Collected | Works. Perhaps the best modern arrangement of | Brainerd's life is that by J. M. Sherwood, published by | Funk & Wagnalls, New York.

Contents: p. [1]: title; p. [2]: DAVID BRAINERD | Missionary to the Indians; p. [3]: PREFATORY NOTE.; p. [5]: SELECTIONS | FROM | THE JOURNAL | OF | DAVID BRAINERD; p. [76]: blank.

OCLC 32725952

Pitts Theological Library

237A • EXTRACTS FROM THE | Journal | OF | DAVID BRAINERD | Missionary to the Indians | [ornament] | SELECTED BY WM. R. NEWELL | Except a corn of wheat fall into the ground and | die, it abideth alone; but if it die it beareth much fruit. | JOHN xii. 24 | [ornament] | THE MOODY BIBLE INSTITUTE, CHICAGO | 1900

15 x 9 cm.; 75, [1] p.

Notes: identical with the above except for the title page.

NUC NB0739547 OCLC 20031830

Point Loma Nazarene University

237B • HENDERSON & COMPANY | PUBLISHERS, | 8-16 Lombard St., Toronto, Canada

14.8 x 9.5 cm.; 75, [1] p.

Notes: identical with the above except for the imprint and p. [76]: [poem]; published c. 1909.

OCLC 131113766

Asbury Theological Seminary

238 • THE DIARY OF | DAVID BRAINERD | [ornament] | VOLUME I | PUBLISHED BY ANDREW MELROSE | 16 PILGRIM STREET, LONDON, E.C. | MDCCCCII

17 x 10.6 cm.; $[a]^8$, b-c ^{8}, d^4, 1-23^8, 24^4, 25^1; lvi, 377, [1] p.

Contents: p. [i]: Books for the Heart | *Edited by* ALEXANDER SMELLIE, M.A. (verso blank); p. [iii]: THE | DIARY OF DAVID BRAINERD (verso blank); p. [v]: [dedication] (verso blank); p. vii: CONTENTS (verso blank); p. ix: INTRODUCTION; p. xli: JONATHAN EDWARDS'S PREFACE [signed] JONATHAN EDWARDS; p. [lv]: blank; p. lvi: *The reader scarcely needs to be reminded that those | passages in this book which are within square | brackets are from the pen of Jonathan Edwards. | These it has been necessary to curtail somewhat. | But everything which is distinctively Brainerd's own | has been kept intact.*; p. [1]: THE DIARY OF | DAVID BRAINERD; p. 377: PRINTED BY MORRISON AND GIBB LIMITED, EDINBURGH.; p. [378]: blank.

NUC NB0739532 OCLC 2414413

Mount Holyoke College

VOLUME II | PUBLISHED BY ANDREW MELROSE | 16 PILGRIM STREET, LONDON, E.C. | MDCCCCII

17 x 10.6 cm.; [a]4, b1, 1-188, 192; x, 292 p.

Contents: p. [i]: Books for the Heart | *Edited by* ALEXANDER SMELLIE, M.A. (verso blank); p. [iii]: THE | JOURNAL OF DAVID BRAINERD (verso blank); p. [v]: [dedication] (verso blank); p. vii: CONTENTS (verso blank); p. vii: PREFACE [signed] THE CORRESPONDENTS; p. ix: INTRODUCTION; p. xli: JONATHAN EDWARDS'S PREFACE [signed] JONATHAN EDWARDS; p. [lv]: blank; p. lvi: *The reader scarcely needs to be reminded that those | passages in this book which are within square | brackets are from the pen of Jonathan Edwards. | These it has been necessary to curtail somewhat. | But everything which is distinctively Brainerd's own | has been kept intact.*; p. [1]: THE JOURNAL OF | DAVID BRAINERD; p. 377: PRINTED BY MORRISON AND GIBB LIMITED, EDINBURGH.; p. [378]: blank.

NUC NB0739532 OCLC 2414413

Mount Holyoke College

239 • The Life of David Brainerd | Missionary to the Indians | *Taken from His Diary and other Private Writings* | By | JONATHAN EDWARDS | Edited and Abridged by | REV. HOMER W. HODGE | Introduction by | DR. A. J. GORDON | The Christian Alliance Publishing Company | 260 West 44th St., New York, N.Y.

18.6 x 12.5 cm.; [1]8, 2-128, 136; 201, [3] p.

Contents: frontispiece: [photocopy] | The cut showing minister preaching to Indians is supposed to be | Brainerd preaching to his Indians at Kaunaumeek. This cut, taken | from a picture in an old volume of Brainerd, is over a hundred | years old.; p. [1]: title; p. [2]: Copyright. 1925 | CHRISTIAN ALLIANCE PUBLISHING CO.; p. 3: CONTENTS; p. 5: FOREWORD [signed] HOMER W. HODGE. | September 28, 1925.; p. [8]: blank; p. 9: INTRODUCTION | [short rule] | A MAN OF PRAYER | BY DR. A. J. GORDON; pp. 11-201: text; p. [202]: blank; p. [203]: [photograph] | THE GRAVE OF DAVID BRAINERD AT NORTHAMPTON, MASS.; p. [204]: blank.

THJ 170 NUC NB0739561 OCLC 1512794

Gordon College

240 • EXTRACTS FROM THE | Journal | OF | DAVID BRAINERD | [ornament] | SELECTED BY WM. R. NEWELL | Except a corn of wheat fall into the | ground and die, it abideth alone; but if it | die it beareth much fruit.— John xii. 24. | [ornament] | Issued by | GRACE PUBLICATIONS, INC. | 100 West Chicago Avenue | CHICAGO, ILLINOIS | U.S.A. | 1940

14 x 8.8 cm.; 95, [1] p.

Contents: p. [1]: title; p. [2]: [13 lines] | [short rule] | Not Copyrighted | [short rule] | Printed in U.S.A. | By | THE GEOGRAPHICAL PUB. CO. | Chicago, Ill.; p. 3: Note [signed] W. R. N. | January 1940; p. 4: In making these selections we have used Brainerd's | Journal as it appears in Jonathan Edwards' Collected | Works.; p. 5: [within double rules] SELECTIONS | *from the* | JOURNAL | *of* | DAVID BRAINERD; p. [96]: [poem].

NUC NB0739548 OCLC 15305952

Pittsburgh Theological Seminary

241 • DAVID BRAINERD | *THE MAN OF PRAYER* | *Compiled from his Diary as recorded in* | "THE WORKS OF JONATHAN EDWARDS" | Abridged and Edited | by | *Oswald J. Smith, LITT.D.* | *Commemorating the two hundredth* | *anniversary of his conversion.* | [publisher's device] | ZONDERVAN PUBLISHING HOUSE | GRAND RAPIDS MICHIGAN

19 x 12.8 cm.; 86 p.

Notes: published c. 1941.

Contents: p. [1]: DAVID BRAINERD | THE MAN OF PRAYER (verso blank); p. [3]: title; p. [4]: COPYRIGHT, MCMXLI, BY | ZONDERVAN PUBLISHING HOUSE | GRAND RAPIDS, MICHIGAN; p. [5]: FOREWORD | by *Dr. A. J. Gordon*; p. [7]: INTRODUCTION [signed] OSWALD J. SMITH | *The Peoples Church* | *Toronto, Canada*; p. [8]: CONTENTS.; pp. 9-86: text.

NUC NB0739531 OCLC 30482406
Yale Divinity School

241A • *DAVID BRAINERD* | THE MAN OF PRAYER | Compiled from his Diary as recorded in | *The Works of Jonathan Edwards* | Abridged and Edited by | Oswald J. Smiths, Litt.D. | COMMEMORATING THE TWO HUNDREDTH | ANNIVERSARY OF HIS CONVERSION | *Second Edition* | [publisher's device] | ZONDERVAN PUBLISHING HOUSE | Grand Rapids, Michigan *stet* Smiths

19 x 12.8 cm.; 86 p.
Notes: identical with the above except for the title page.
OCLC 20011129
Wake Forest University

241B • *DAVID BRAINERD* | THE MAN OF PRAYER | Compiled from his Diary as recorded in | *The Works of Jonathan Edwards* | Abridged and Edited by | Oswald J. Smith, Litt.D. | COMMEMORATING THE TWO HUNDREDTH | ANNIVERSARY OF HIS CONVERSION | THIRD EDITION | [publisher's device] | ZONDERVAN PUBLISHING HOUSE | Grand Rapids, Michigan

19 x 12.8 cm.; 86 p.
Notes: identical with the above except for the title page.
OCLC 4587006
Dallas Theological Seminary

242 • DAVID BRAINERD | *His Message for Today* | *Compiled and Edited by* | OSWALD J. SMITH Litt.D. | *Pastor of The Peoples Church, Toronto* | *Foreword by* | DR. A. J. GORDON | MARSHALL, MORGAN & SCOTT, LTD. | LONDON [ornament] EDINBURGH

18.5 x 12.3 cm.; 95, [1] p.

Notes: published c. 1949; pp. 11-95 in THE LIVES OF | BRAINERD AND | FLETCHER | *Compiled and Edited by* | OSWALD J. SMITH, Litt.D. | *Founder and Minister of Missions of The Peoples Church, Toronto* | *Foreword by* | DR. A. J. GORDON | [publisher's device] | *London* | MARSHALL, MORGAN & SCOTT | *Edinburgh*; pp. 7-85 in MEN OF GOD | [in 2 cols., col. 1] David Brainerd | Thomas Crosby | [col. 2] John Fletcher | George Whitefield | *Compiled and Edited by* | OSWALD J. SMITH, Litt.D. | *Founder of The Peoples Church, Toronto* | *Foreword by* | DR. A. J. GORDON | [publisher's device] | MARSHALL, MORGAN & SCOTT | *London*.

Contents: p. [i]: DAVID BRAINERD | *His Message for Today*; p. [ii]: [advertisement]; p. [iii]: title; p. [iv]: [12 lines] | *First published in England 1949* | [2 lines]; p. v: FOREWORD [signed] A. J. G.; p. vii: INTRODUCTION [signed] OSWALD J. SMITH | *The Peoples Church,* | *Toronto, Canada*; p. [ix]: CONTENTS; p. [x]: [photocopy] | "... *had raised hopes today of the heathen. O that God* | *would bring in great numbers of them to Jesus Christ* ..."; pp. 11-95: text; p. [96]: WAITING ON JESUS | Oswald J. Smith | COPYRIGHT, 1939, BY THE RODEHEAVER CO. | INTERNATIONAL COPYRIGHT SECURED | B. D. Ackley | [words and music].

NUC NB0739530 OCLC 5780835
Boston College

242A • DAVID BRAINERD | *Man of Prayer* | *Compiled and Edited by* | OSWALD J. SMITH, Litt.D. | *Founder of the Peoples Church, Toronto* | *Foreword by* | DR. A. J. GORDON | MARSHALL, MORGAN & SCOTT | *London*

18.5 x 12.3 cm.; 95, [1] p.
Notes: title page (verso): *This tenth impression (paperback) 1975.*

ISBN 055105428X OCLC 32748612
Taylor University

242B • DAVID BRAINERD | *His Message for Today* | *Compiled and Edited by* | OSWALD J. SMITH Litt.D. | *Pastor of The Peoples Church, Toronto* | *Foreword by* | DR. A.J. GORDON | Published By: | Larry Harrison | 219-365-4905 | 9066 Knickerbocker | St. John, Indiana 46373
stet A.J.

21.7 x 14.5 cm.; 104 p.

Contents: front cover (verso): Give Attendance to Reading; p. [1]: title; p. 2: FOREWORD [signed] A. J. G.; p. 4: INTRODUCTION [signed] OSWALD J. SMITH. | *The Peoples Church* | *Toronto, Canada*.; p. [6]: CONTENTS; p. [7]: [photocopy] | "... *had raised hopes today of the heathen. O that God would* | *bring in great numbers of them to Jesus Christ*..."; pp. 8-97: text; p. [98]: WAITING ON JESUS | COPYRIGHT, 1939, BY THE RODEHEAVER CO. | Oswald J. Smith INTERNATIONAL COPYRIGHT SECURED B. D. Ackley | [words and music]; p. 99: BOOKS; p. 100: RULES TO LIVE BY; back cover (recto and verso): [advertisement].

OCLC 38829717
Southeastern Baptist Theological Seminary

243 • DAVID BRAINERD | [short rule] | *His Life and Diary* | *Edited by* | JONATHAN EDWARDS | WITH A BIOGRAPHICAL SKETCH | OF PRESIDENT EDWARDS | BY | PHILIP E. HOWARD, JR. | MOODY PRESS | CHICAGO

20.2 x 12.7 cm.; 385, [1] p.

Notes: reprinted 1967 and 1980; in some copies, half title: THE WYCLIFFE SERIES | OF CHRISTIAN CLASSICS | WILBUR M. SMITH | General Editor; in some copies, title page: THE LIFE AND DIARY | OF | DAVID BRAINERD | *Edited by* | JONATHAN EDWARDS | [ornament] | NEWLY EDITED, AND WITH A | BIOGRAPHICAL SKETCH | OF | PRESIDENT EDWARDS | BY | PHILIP E. HOWARD, JR. | [publisher's device] | CHICAGO | MOODY PRESS | 1949

Contents: p. [1]: DAVID BRAINERD | [short rule] | *His Life and Diary* (verso blank); p. [3]: title; p. [4]: *Copyright, 1949, by* | *The Moody Bible Institute* | *of Chicago* | [1 line]; p. 7: PREFATORY NOTE [signed] PHILIP E. HOWARD, JR. | OCTOBER, *1948*; p. 9: CONTENTS; p. 11: A BIOGRAPHICAL SKETCH | OF THE LIFE AND WORK | OF JONATHAN EDWARDS [signed] Philip E. Howard, Jr. | October, 1948.; p. [40]: blank; p. 41: THE WORKS OF PRESIDENT EDWARDS; p. 43: PREFACE | BY JONATHAN EDWARDS; p. 53: INTRODUCTORY NOTE | BY PRESIDENT EDWARDS; p. [55]: DAVID BRAINERD'S | LIFE AND DIARY | PART I-VI (verso blank); p. [201]: BRAINERD'S | JOURNAL (verso blank); p. 203: THE RISE AND PROGRESS OF A REMARKABLE | WORK OF GRACE | BRAINERD'S JOURNAL, PART I; p. [254]: blank; p. 255: THE RISE AND PROGRESS OF A REMARKABLE | WORK OF GRACE | BRAINERD'S JOURNAL, PART II; p. [309]: DAVID BRAINERD'S | LIFE AND DIARY | PART VII-VIII (verso blank); p. 311: PART VII | FROM THE CLOSE OF HIS JOURNAL TO HIS RETURN | FROM THE SUSQUEHANNAH; p. [330]: blank; p. 331: AFTER HIS RETURN FROM HIS LAST JOURNEY TO SUSQUEHAN- | NAH, UNTIL HIS DEATH; p. [378]: blank; p. 379: APPENDIX I | WHY BRAINERD WAS EXPELLED FROM COLLEGE | *Jonathan Edwards's Explanation*; p. 383: APPENDIX II | *Jonathan Edwards* | (*page 159*).; p. 385: APPENDIX III: Inscription on the Tombstone of Jonathan Edwards at Princeton, N.J. Translated by | Paul Coleman-Norton Associate Professor of Classics at Princeton University; p. [386]: blank.

OCLC 6849338
Duke University

243A • The Life and Diary | of David Brainerd | *Edited by* | Jonathan Edwards | With a Biographical Sketch | of the Life and Work | of Jonathan Edwards | *by* | Philip E. Howard, Jr. | [publisher's device] | BAKER BOOK HOUSE | Grand Rapids, Michigan 49516

20.2 x 12.7 cm.; 385, [1] p.

Notes: identical with the above except for the title page; first published in 1989, eleventh printing, 2000.

ISBN 0801009766 OCLC 20338175
Princeton University

244 • Life and Diary | of | David Brainerd | [along short vertical rule] CORNER | [above rule] STONE Publishing Company | [below rule] P.O. Box 7953, Newark, Delaware 19711
21.2 x 13.2 cm.; x, 150 p.
Notes: published c. 1950; p. [ii]: In this edition the diary and the journal have been woven together into one narrative. . . . A great portion of the material originally included in the Reflections has been omitted in this edition.
Contents: p. [i]: title; p. [ii]: NOTE; p. [iii]: Contents; p. v: Preface [signed] Jonathan Edwards; pp. [11]-138: text; p. 139: Letters to His Friends.
OCLC 17198992
Hope International University

244A • Life | and | Diary | of | David Brainerd | SOVEREIGN GRACE PUBLISHERS | Grand Rapids, Michigan 49315 | 1971
21.5 x 14 cm.; 146 p.
Notes: identical with the above except for the title page.
OCLC 9717286
Grand Rapids Baptist College and Seminary

245 • THE LIFE AND DIARY | OF | DAVID BRAINERD | *Edited by* | JONATHAN EDWARDS | [publisher's device] | MOODY PRESS | CHICAGO
17.3 x 12 cm.; 256 p.
Notes: published c. 1957; front cover: CAREFULLY CONDENSED FROM | THE WYCLIFFE SERIES OF | CHRISTIAN CLASSICS.
Contents: p. [1]: THE LIFE AND DIARY | OF | DAVID BRAINERD (verso blank); p. [3]: title; p. [4]: THE LIFE AND DIARY | OF DAVID BRAINERD | [1 line]; p. 5: PREFACE | BY JONATHAN EDWARDS | *President of Princeton, 1758*; p. [12]: blank; p. 13: CONTENTS; p. 15: INTRODUCTORY NOTE | BY PRESIDENT EDWARDS; p. [17]: DAVID BRAINERD'S | LIFE AND DIARY | PART I-VI (verso blank); p. [126]: blank; p. [127]: BRAINERD'S | JOURNAL; p. [203]: DAVID BRAINERD'S | LIFE AND DIARY | PART VII-VIII (verso blank).
OCLC 27215397
Missouri Baptist College

AN HUMBLE INQUIRY INTO THE RULES OF GOD CONCERNING THE QUALIFICATIONS REQUISITE TO A COMPLETE STANDING AND FULL COMMUNION IN THE VISIBLE CHRISTIAN CHURCH

246 • AN | *Humble INQUIRY* | INTO | The Rules of the WORD of GOD, | CONCERNING | The QUALIFICATIONS | Requifite to a | *Compleat Standing* and *full Communion* | IN THE | Vifible Chriftian CHURCH. | [rule] | By *Jonathan Edwards*, A.M. | Paftor of the firft Church in *Northampton*. | [rule] | With an Appendix by Mr. *Foxcroft*. | [rule] | JOB xxxiii. 2, 3. *Behold now I have opened my Mouth:--- My Words* | *ſhall be of the Uprightneſs of my Heart*. | Confitebatur [*Lutherus*] dolorem fuum, quod ab ipfis reflorefcentis Evan- | gelii Primordiis, quofvis abfque Difcrimine ad Cœnam dominicum ad- | mififfet, quodque Difciplinam, Fratrum Difciplinæ fimilem, apud fuos | non conftituiffet.--- Quia objiciebatur, Fratres non habere Ecclefiam | apertam;--- Refponfum fuit, Sancta dare non Sanctis prohibuiffe | Chriftum: --- Errorem [in *Papatu*] corrigi non poffe *aliter quam ut* | *certa*

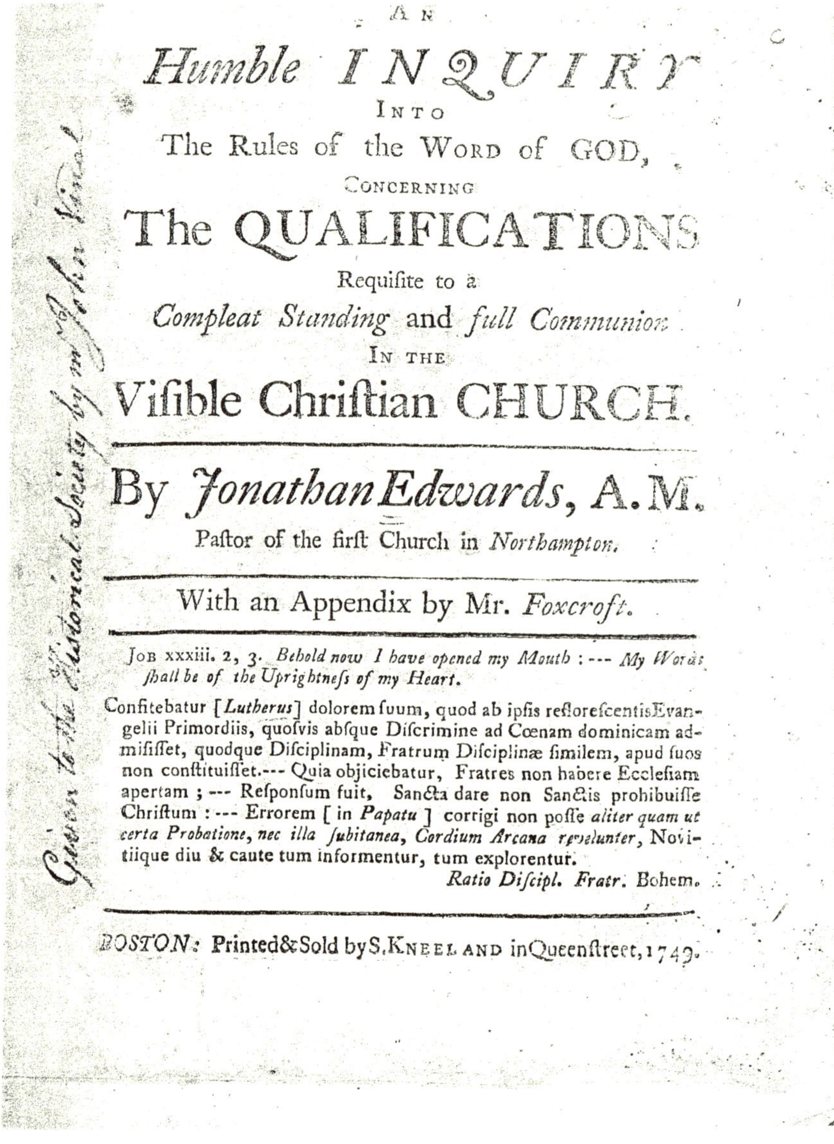

AN

Humble INQUIRY

INTO

The Rules of the WORD of GOD,

CONCERNING

The QUALIFICATIONS

Requifite to a

Compleat Standing and *full Communion*

IN THE

Vifible Chriftian CHURCH.

By *Jonathan Edwards*, A.M.

Paftor of the firft Church in *Northampton*.

With an Appendix by Mr. *Foxcroft*.

JOB xxxiii. 2, 3. *Behold now I have opened my Mouth* : --- *My Words fhall be of the Uprightnefs of my Heart.*

Confitebatur [*Lutherus*] dolorem fuum, quod ab ipfis reflorefcentis Evangelii Primordiis, quofvis abfque Difcrimine ad Cœnam dominicam admififfet, quodque Difciplinam, Fratrum Difciplinæ fimilem, apud fuos non conftituiffet.--- Quia objiciebatur, Fratres non habere Ecclefiam apertam ; --- Refponfum fuit, Sancta dare non Sanctis prohibuiffe Chriftum : --- Errorem [in *Papatu*] corrigi non poffe *aliter quam ut certa Probatione, nec illa fubitanea, Cordium Arcana revelunter*, Novitiique diu & caute tum informentur, tum explorentur.

Ratio Difcipl. Fratr. Bohem.

BOSTON: Printed & Sold by S. KNEELAND in Queenftreet, 1749.

Title page, *Humble Inquiry* (1749). Permission of the Massachusetts Historical Society.

Probatione, nec illa ſubitanea, Cordium Arcana revelunter, Novi- | tiique diu & caute tum informentur, tum explorentur. | *Ratio Diſcipl. Fratr*. Bohem. | [rule] | *BOSTON:* Printed & Sold by S. KNEELAND in Queenſtreet, 1749.

4to.; 20.2 x 14.7 cm. (uncut); [A]^4, B-V^4; [2], v, [1], 136, I, 2-16 p.

Notes: p. 1 misnumbered I in the second count; Edwards's autograph copy–bound with Solomon Williams, *The True State of the Question Concerning the Qualifications Necessary to Lawful Communion in the Christian Sacraments* (Boston, 1751)–at Presbyterian Historical Society includes his marginalia, the basis for his answer to Williams in *Misrepresentations Corrected* (Boston, 1752); see 256.

Contents: prp. [1]: title (verso blank); p. [i]: *The Author's* PREFACE. [signed] *J. E.*; p. v: *ERRATA*; p. [vi]: PREFACE. [signed] [in 2 cols., col.1] *Boſton, Auguſt* 11th | 1749. | [col. 2] Thomas Prince | John Webb | Thomas Foxcroft | M. Byles.; p. 1: An *Inquiry* into the *Qualifications* | for full Communion in the viſible | Church of CHRIST.; p. i: An APPENDIX. | BEING | A LETTER to the *Author*, in Anſwer to his Requeſt of Inform- | ation concerning the Opinion of *Proteſtant* Divines and Churches | in general, of the Preſbyterians in *Scotland* and Diſſenters in | *England* in particular, reſpecting *five* QUESTIONS that relate | to this Controverſy. [signed] *Boſton*, June 26. | 1749. | THOMAS FOXCROFT.

THJ 171 EAI 1:6312 NUC NE0046675 OCLC 11356665
Massachusetts Historical Society

247 • AN | HUMBLE INQUIRY | INTO THE | *RULES OF THE WORD OF GOD*, | CONCERNING THE | QUALIFICATIONS | REQUISITE TO A | *COMPLETE STANDING AND FULL COMMUNION* | IN THE | VISIBLE CHRISTIAN CHURCH. | By the Late JONATHAN EDWARDS, A. M. | THEN PASTOR OF THE FIRST CHURCH IN NORTHAMPTON; | AFTERWARDS PRESIDENT OF THE COLLEGE OF | NEW JERSEY. | WITH AN APPENDIX BY MR. FOXCROFT. | *EDITION SECOND*. | [double rule] | BEHOLD NOW I HAVE OPENED MY MOUTH:—MY WORDS SHALL | BE OF THE UPRIGHTNESS OF MY HEART. JOB XXXIII. 2. 3. | [double rule] | EDINBURGH: | PRINTED FOR WILLIAM COKE, LEITH. | [short rule] | *Anno* 1790.

12mo.; 16.2 x 9.8 cm.; a^6, b^2, A-S^6, T^4; xv, [1], 221, [3] p.

Contents: p. [i]: title; p. [ii]: Confitebatur [*Lutherus*] dolorem ſuum, quod ab ipſis refloreſcen- | tis Evangelii Primordiis, quoſvis abſque Diſcrimine ad Cœnam | Dominicum admiſiſſet, quodque Diſciplinam, Fratrum Diſci- | plinæ ſimilem, apud ſuos non conſtituiſſet.—Quia objiciebatur, | Fratres non habere Eccleſiam apertam;—Reſponſum fuit, | Sancta dare non Sanctis prohibuiſſe Chriſtum:—Errorem [in | *Papatu*] corrigi non poſſe *aliter quam ut certa Probatione, nec illa* | *ſubitanea, Cordium Arcana revelunter*, Novitiique diu & caute | tum informentur, tum explorentur. | *Ratio Diſcipl. Fratr*. Bohem.; p. [iii]: ADVERTISEMENT | TO THIS | EDITION. [dated] EDINBURGH, *May* 15, 1790.; p. [v]: THE | AUTHOR's PREFACE. [signed] J. E.; p. [xiii]: *PREFACE*. [signed] [in 2 cols., col. 1] BOSTON, *Auguſt* 11. | 1749. | [brace, col. 2] THOMAS PRINCE, | JOHN WEBB, | THOMAS FOXCROFT, | M. BYLES.; p. xv: *CONTENTS*. (verso blank); p. [1]: AN | HUMBLE INQUIRY | INTO THE | QUALIFICATIONS | FOR | *Full Communion in the Viſible Church of* CHRIST.; p. [198]: blank; p. [199]: APPENDIX. | *Being a LETTER to the* AUTHOR, *in anſwer to his* | *requeſt of information concerning the opinion of Pro-* | *teſtant divines and churches in general, of the Pre-* | *ſbyterians in Scotland and Diſſenters in England in* | *particular, reſpecting* FIVE QUESTIONS *that re-* | *late to this controverſy*. [signed] BOSTON, *June* 26, | 1749. | [brace] THOMAS FOXCROFT.; pp. [222-224]: blank.

THJ 172 ESTC N33393 NUC NE004677 OCLC 8881325
Congregational Library

247A • EDINBURGH: | PRINTED BY HUGH INGLIS. | SOLD BY GEORGE PEATTIE, BOOKSELLER, LEITH. | [short rule] | *Anno* 1790.

Notes: variant imprint; some copies lack the bookseller.

THJ 172A ESTC N53785 NUC NE0046678 OCLC 23645614
Yale University

CHRIST THE GREAT EXAMPLE OF GOSPEL MINISTERS

248 • *CHRIST the great EXAMPLE of Goſpel Miniſters.* | [broken rule] | A | SERMON | Preach'd at *Portſmouth,* | At the ORDINATION of the Reverend | Mr. *Job Strong,* | To the Paſtoral Office over the *South* Church in that | Place, | *June* 28. 1749, | [broken rule] | By *Jonathan Edwards,* A. M. | Paſtor of the firſt Church in *Northampton.* | [broken rule] | *BOSTON:* | Printed and ſold by *T. Fleet,* at the *Heart* and *Crown* | in Cornhill. 1750.

8vo.; 16.8 x 10.9 cm.; [A]^4, B-C^4, D^2; 28 p.

Contents: p. [1]: Mr. *Edwards*'s | SERMON | At the ORDINATION | Of the Reverend | Mr. *Job Strong,* | *June* 28. 1749. (verso blank); p. [3]: title (verso blank); p. 5: *Chriſt the Example of Miniſters.*

THJ 173 EAI 1:6492 NUC NE0046490 OCLC 26451691

Andover Newton Theological School

PREFACES

249 • *True* RELIGION *delineated;* | OR, | EXPERIMENTAL RELIGION, | As diſtinguiſhed from FORMALITY on the one Hand, and | ENTHUSIASM on the other, ſet in a Scriptural and | Rational Light. | In TWO DISCOURSES. | In which ſome of the principal Errors both of the | ARMINIANS and ANTINOMIANS are confuted, the | Foundation and Superſtructure of their different Schemes | demoliſhed, and the Truth as it is in JESUS, explained | and proved. | The whole adapted to the weakeſt Capacities, and deſigned for the | Eſtabliſhment, Comfort and Quickening of the People of GOD, | in theſe Evil Times. | [rule] | By *Joseph Bellamy,* A. M. | Miniſter of the Goſpel at *Bethlem* in *Connecticut.* | [rule] | With a Preface by the Rev. Mr. EDWARDS. | [rule] | Iſai. xxx. 21. *And thine Ears ſhall hear a Word behind thee, ſaying, This* | *is the Way, walk ye in it, when ye turn to the right Hand, and when* | *ye turn to the left.* | Matth. vii. 13, 14. *Enter ye in at the ſtrait Gate; for wide is the Gate,* | *and broad is the Way that leadeth to Deſtruction, and many there be* | *which go in thereat: Becauſe ſtrait is the Gate, and narrow is the Way* | *which leadeth unto Life, and few there be that find it.* | [rule] | *BOSTON:* | Printed and Sold by S. KNEELAND, in Queen-Street. 1750.

8vo.; 20 x 12.2 cm.; [A]^4, aa^4, B-Z^8, Aa-Dd^8, Ee-Gg^4; [2], viii, vi, 421, [19] p.

Notes: pp. [i]-vi repeated; p. 360 misnumbered 560 (pp. [i]-vi, [i]-vi, [1]-359, 560, 361-421).

Contents: prp. [1]: title (verso blank); p. [i]: *PREFACE* [signed] NORTHAMPTON, | *Auguſt* 4. 1750. | JONATHAN EDWARDS.; p. [i]: The AUTHOR's | PREFACE. [signed] BETHLEM, April | 25th 1750. | Joſeph Bellamy.; p. [1]: *True Religion delineated.*; p. [422]: THE | CONTENTS of the *firſt* Difcourse.; p. [425]: THE | CONTENTS of the *ſecond* Difcourse.; p. [427]: A Liſt of *SUBSCRIBERS,* | in an Alphabetical Order.; pp. [439-440]: blank.

THJ 174 EAI 1:6462 NUC NB0283283 OCLC 7595796

Houghton Library

250 • TRUE RELIGION DELINEATED; | OR, | EXPERIMENTAL RELIGION, | *Diſtinguiſhed from* Formality *on the one hand, and* Enthuſiasm | *on the other, ſet in a Scriptural and Rational light.* | IN TWO DISCOURSES. | In which ſome of the principal Errors both of the ARMINIANS and | ANTINOMIANS are confuted, | The Foundation and Superſtructure of their different Schemes | demoliſhed, | And the Truth, as it is in JESUS, explained and proved. | *The whole adapted to the weakeſt*

Capacities, and deſigned for the Eſtablishment, | *Comfort, and Quickening of the people of God, in theſe evil times.* | BY JOSEPH BELLAMY, A. M. | MINISTER OF THE GOSPEL AT BETHLEM IN CONNECTICUT. | WITH A PREFACE BY THE REVEREND MR. EDWARDS. | *THE SECOND EDITION.* | [double rule] | *And thine ears ſhall hear a word behind thee, ſaying, This is the way, walk ye* | *in it, when ye turn to the right hand, and when ye turn to the left.* | Iſa. xxx. 21. | *Enter ye in at the ſtrait gate; for wide is the gate, and broad is the way that* | *leadeth to deſtruction, and many there be which go in thereat: Becauſe ſtrait* | *is the gate, and narrow is the way which leadeth unto life, and few there be* | *that find it.* Matth. vii. 13, 14. | [double rule] | EDINBURGH: | PRINTED FOR M. GRAY, FRONT OF THE EXCHANGE. | *Anno* 1788.

12mo.; 17.8 x 10.5 cm.; π^2, a^6, A-Z^6, Aa-Ii^6, Kk^4; [4], xii, 390, [2] p.

Notes: in some copies, prp. [1]: TRUE RELIGION DELINEATED | AND | *Diſtinguiſhed from all Counterfeits* (verso blank); in some copies, last leaf advertisement.

Contents: prp. [1-2]:blank; prp. [3]: title (verso blank); p. [i]: *PREFACE.* [signed] NORTHAMPTON, | *Auguſt* 4. 1750. | [brace] | JONATHAN EDWARDS.; p. [v]: THE AUTHOR's | PREFACE. [signed] BETHLEM, | *April* 25. 1750. | [brace] | JOSEPH BELLAMY.; p. [xi]: CONTENTS.; p. [1]: TRUE RELIGION DELINEATED.; pp. [391]-392: blank.

THJ 175 NUC NB0283288 OCLC 9472333

Houghton Library

251 • TRUE RELIGION DELINEATED; | OR, | EXPERIMENTAL RELIGION, | AS DISTINGUISHED FROM | FORMALITY ON THE ONE HAND, AND ENTHUSIASM | ON THE OTHER. | SET IN A SCRIPTURAL AND RATIONAL LIGHT. | IN TWO DISCOURSES. | BY | JOSEPH BELLAMY, D. D. | BOSTON: | CONGREGATIONAL BOARD OF PUBLICATION. | CHAUNCEY STREET.

22.2 x 14.2 cm.; $[1]^6$, 2^6-30^6, 31^1; 361, [1] p.

Notes: published c. 1800.

Contents: p. [1]: title; p. [2]: PRINTED BY | W. F. DRAPER, ANDOVER, MASS.; p. [3]: PREFACE. [signed] JONATHAN EDWARDS. | NORTHAMPTON, *August* 4, 1750.; p. [7]: AUTHOR'S PREFACE.; p. [12]: blank; pp. [13]-361: text; p. [362]: blank.

NUC NB0283282 OCLC 27991092

Wesley Theological Seminary

251A • [within rules] True Religion | Delineated | and Distinguished From | All Counterfeits | by | Joseph Bellamy | (1719-1790) | With a Preface by | Jonathan Edwards | and | A Biographical Sketch by | John F. Thornbury | *International Outreach, Inc.* | *P. O. Box 1286, Ames, Iowa 50014*

Notes: facsimile reprint; prp. [1]: title; prp. [2]: [5 lines] | *True Religion Delineated* was first published in 1750. This reprint is taken from the | Congregational Board of Publication's 1800 edition | [2 lines] | Copyright © 1997 by International Outreach, Inc. | [1 line]; p. [i]: AN INTRODUCTION TO JOSEPH BELLAMY | By John F. Thornbury, Th.M., D.Min.

ISBN 09464180367 OCLC 36842956

Mount Holyoke College

252 • TRUE RELIGION DELINEATED; | OR, | Experimental Religion, | AS DISTINGUISHED FROM FORMALITY ON THE ONE HAND, AND | ENTHUSIASM ON THE OTHER, | SET IN A SCRIPTURAL AND RATIONAL LIGHT. | In two Discourses: | IN WHICH | SOME OF THE PRINCIPAL ERRORS BOTH OF THE ARMINIANS AND AN- | TINOMIANS ARE CONFUTED....THE FOUNDATION AND SUPER- | STRUCTURE OF THEIR DIFFERENT SCHEMES DE- | MOLISHED....AND THE TRUTH, AS IT | IS IN JESUS, EXPLAINED | AND

PROVED. | The whole adapted to the weakest capacities, and designed for | the establishment, comfort, and quickening | of the people of GOD. | [short thick-thin rule] | BY JOSEPH BELLAMY, D. D. | LATE OF BETHLEM, CONNECTICUT. | [short thin-thick rule] | WITH A PREFACE BY THE REV. MR. EDWARDS. | [short double line of stops] | ISAIAH XXX. 21....*And thine ears shall hear a word behind thee, saying, This | is the way, walk ye in it, when ye turn to the right hand, and when ye turn | to the left.* | MATTHEW VII. 13, 14....*Enter ye in at the strait gate; for wide is the | gate, and broad is the way that leadeth to destruction, and many there be | which go in thereat: Because strait is the gate, and narrow is the way which | leadeth unto life, and few there be that find it.* | [short thick-thin rule] | BOSTON, PRINTED...1750. | *MORRIS-TOWN*, | RE-PRINTED BY HENRY P. RUSSELL. | [short line of stops] |1804.

8vo.; 20.9 x 12.3 cm.; [A][4], B-W-Z[4], Aa-Ww-Zz[4], 3A-3F[4], G[6]; x, 428, [6] p.

Contents: p. [i]: title (verso blank); p. [iii]: PREFACE. [signed] JONATHAN EDWARDS. | *Northampton, August* 4, 1750.; p. [vii]: THE AUTHOR's PREFACE. [signed] JOSEPH BELLAMY | *Bethlem, April* 25, 1750.; p. [1]: True Religion delineated.; p. [429]: Contents of the First Discourse.; p. [431]: Contents of the Second Discourse.; pp. [433-434]: blank.

THJ 176 NUC NB0283289 OCLC 784578
Congregational Library

253 • [within double rules] TRUE RELIGION DELINEATED: | OR, | EXPERIMENTAL RELIGION, | DISTINGUISHED FROM FORMALITY AND ENTHUSIASM. | BY | JOSEPH BELLAMY, D.D. | MINISTER OF THE GOSPEL AT BETHLEHEM, | IN NEW ENGLAND. | [short rule] | LONDON: | THOMAS WARD AND CO. | PATERNOSTER ROW.

24.1 x 15.5 cm.; [A][8], B-K[8]; 159, [1] p.

Notes: published c. 1852; text within double rules, printed in double columns.

Contents: front cover: title (verso blank); p. [3]: PREFACE [signed] JONATHAN EDWARDS. | NORTHAMPTON, Aug. 4, 1750; p. [5]: THE AUTHOR'S PREFACE [signed] JOSEPH BELLAMY. | BETHLEHEM, April 25, 1750.; p. [7]: CONTENTS.; p. [8]: PLAN OF THE FIRST DISCOURSE.; p. 9: PLAN OF THE SECOND DISCOURSE; p. [11]: TRUE RELIGION DELINEATED.; p. 159: T. C. SAVILL, PRINTER, 107, ST. MARTIN'S LANE, CHARING CROSS.; p. [160]: blank; back cover (recto and verso): [advertisement]; back cover (verso): T. C. SAVILL, PRINTER, ST. MARTIN'S LANE.

THJ 177
British Library

A FAREWELL SERMON

254 • A | FAREWEL-SERMON | Preached at the firft Precinct in | *NORTHAMPTON*, | After the People's publick Rejection of their Minifter, and re- | nouncing their Relation to Him as Paftor of the Church there, | On *June* 22. 1750. | Occafion'd by Difference of Sentiments, | concerning the requifite Qualifications | of Members of the Church, in compleat | Standing. | [rule] | By *Jonathan Edwards*, A. M. | [rule] | Acts xx. 18. *Ye know, from the firſt Day that I came into* Afia, | *after what Manner I have* been with you, at all Seafons. | ver. 20. *And how I kept back nothing that was profitable unto you*; | *but have ſhewed you, and have taught you publickly, and from Houſe* | *to Houſe*. | ver. 26, 27. *Wherefore I take you to Record this Day, that I am pure* | *from the Blood of all Men: For I have not ſhunned to declare unto* | *you all the Counſel of God.* | Gal. iv. 15, 16. *Where is then the Bleſſedneſs ye ſpake of? For I* | *bear you Record, that if it had been poſſible, ye would have plucked* | *out your own Eyes, and have given them to me. Am I therefore be-* | *come your Enemy, becauſe I tell you the Truth?* | [rule] | *BOSTON:* | Printed and Sold by S. KNEELAND over againft the Prifon in *Queen-* |

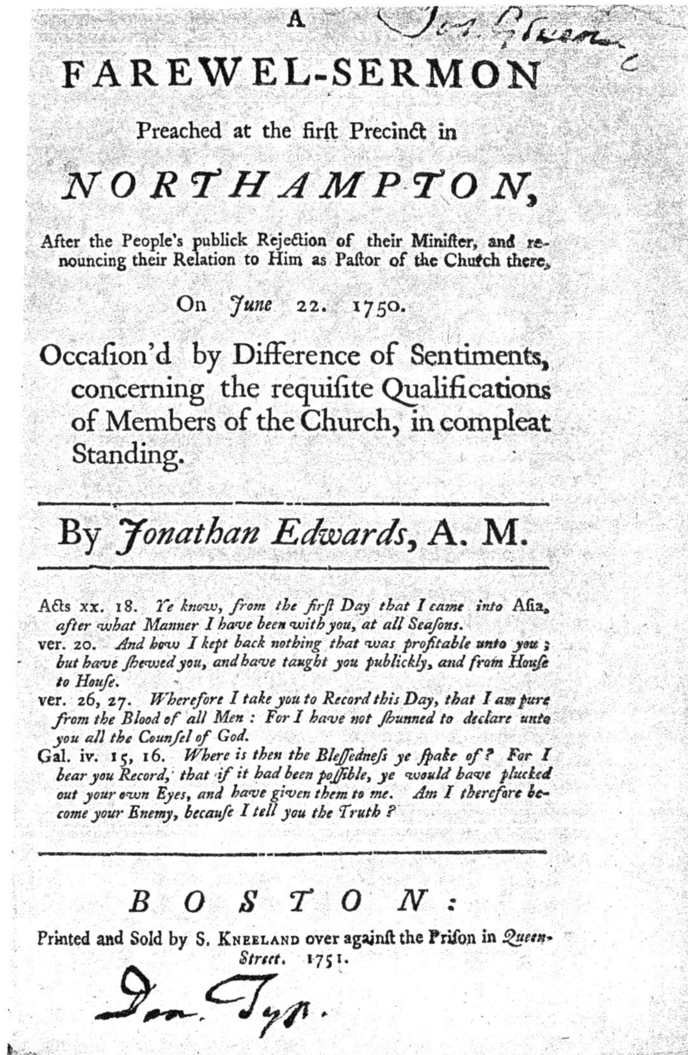

A

FAREWEL-SERMON

Preached at the first Precinct in

NORTHAMPTON,

After the People's publick Rejection of their Minister, and renouncing their Relation to Him as Pastor of the Church there,

On *June* 22. 1750.

Occasion'd by Difference of Sentiments, concerning the requisite Qualifications of Members of the Church, in compleat Standing.

By *Jonathan Edwards*, A. M.

Acts xx. 18. *Ye know, from the first Day that I came into* Asia, *after what Manner I have been with you, at all Seasons.*
ver. 20. *And how I kept back nothing that was profitable unto you; but have shewed you, and have taught you publickly, and from House to House.*
ver. 26, 27. *Wherefore I take you to Record this Day, that I am pure from the Blood of all Men: For I have not shunned to declare unto you all the Counsel of God.*
Gal. iv. 15, 16. *Where is then the Blessedness ye spake of? For I bear you Record, that if it had been possible, ye would have plucked out your own Eyes, and have given them to me. Am I therefore become your Enemy, because I tell you the Truth?*

BOSTON:

Printed and Sold by S. Kneeland over against the Prison in *Queen-Street*. 1751.

Title page, *Farewell Sermon* (1751). Permission of the Massachusetts Historical Society.

Street. 1751.

8vo.; 19 x 12 cm. (uncut); [A]^4, B-F^4; [4], vii, [1], 36 p.

Contents: prp. [1]: Mr. *Edwards*'s | Farewel-SERMON. | To his People at Northampton, | *June* 22. 1750. (verso blank); prp. [3]: title (verso blank); p. [i]: THE | PREFACE.; p. [viii]: Advertifement.; p. [1]: A | *FAREWEL-SERMON*.

THJ 178 EAI 1:6665 NUC NE0046583 OCLC 9524341

Massachusetts Historical Society

255 • A | FAREWEL-SERMON | Preached at the firft Precinct in | *NORTHAMPTON*, | On *June* 22, 1750. | [rule] | By *Jonathan Edwards*, A.M. | [rule] | Acts xx. 18. *Ye know, from the firſt day that I came into* Afia, | *after what manner I have been with you, at all ſeaſons*. | ver. 20. *And how I kept back nothing that was profitable unto* | *you: but have ſhewed you, and have taught you publickly, and* | *from houſe to houſe*. | ver. 26, 27. *Wherefore I take you to record this day, that I am* | *pure from the blood of all men: For I have not ſhunned to* | *declare unto you all the counſel of God.* | Gal. iv. 15, 16. *Where is then the bleſſedneſs ye ſpeak of?* | *For I bear you record, that if it had been poſſible, ye would have* | *plucked out your own eyes, and have given them to me. Am* | *I therefore become your enemy, becauſe I tell you the truth?* | [rule] | *HARTFORD:* | Printed by GREEN, and WATSON, | oppofite the *Court-Houſe*.

8vo.; 17.6 x 11.5 cm.; [A]^4, B-D^4, E^1; 34 p.

Notes: Thomas Green and Ebenezer Watson maintained a printing establishment in partnership at Hartford, Connecticut, between 1765 and 1767.—THJ.

Contents: p. [1]: title (verso blank); p. 3: A | FAREWEL-SERMON.

THJ 179 EAI 1:10887 NUC NE0046584 OCLC 31023404

Forbes Library

MISREPRESENTATIONS CORRECTED AND TRUTH VINDICATED

256 • MISREPRESENTATIONS | Corrected, | And *TRUTH vindicated.* | IN | A Reply to the Rev. Mr. SOLOMON WIL- | LIAMS'S Book, intitled, *The True State of* | *the* QUESTION *concerning the* QUALIFICA- | TIONS *neceſſary to lawful Communion in* | *the* CHRISTIAN SACRAMENTS. | [rule] | *By* JONATHAN EDWARDS, M. A. | Minifter of the Gofpel at *Stockbridge*. | [rule] | Prov. xii. 17. *He that ſpeaketh Truth, ſheweth forth Righteouſneſs*. | Chap. xxii. 20, 21. *Have I not written to thee excellent Things in Counſels* | *and Knowledge; That I might make thee know the Certainty of the Words* | *of Truth, that thou mightſt anſwer the Words of Truth in them that ſend* | *unto thee?* | [decorative rule] | *BOSTON: N. E.* | Printed and Sold by S. KNEELAND, oppofite the Prifon in | *Queen-Street*. 1752.

8vo.; 20.6 x 12.4 cm.; [A]^4, B-Z^4; [2], iv, 173, [5] p.

Contents: prp. [1]: title (verso blank); p. [i]: THE | *PREFACE*.; p. [1]: Mifreprefentations corrected, and | Truth vindicated.; p. 167: An *APPENDIX*. | BEING | A LETTER to the People of the firft Church | and Congregation in NORTHAMPTON. [signed] J. E.; p. 173: *ERRATA*.; p. [174]: *An* INDEX, | Or Alphabetical TABLE of the principal | Contents.; p. [178]: blank.

THJ 180 EAI 1:6839 NUC NE0046726 OCLC 6922101

Massachusetts Historical Society

TRUE GRACE DISTINGUISHED FROM THE EXPERIENCE OF DEVILS

257 • TRUE GRACE, | Diftinguifhed from the | EXPERIENCE OF DEVILS; | IN A | SERMON, | Preached before the | SYNOD OF *NEW-YORK*, | Convened at | New-Ark, in *NEW-JERSEY*, | On

September 28. *N. S.* 1752. | [rule] | By Jonathan Edwards, A. M. | *Paſtor of the Church of* CHRIST *in* Stockbridge *in* New-England. | [rule] | (Printed by the Deſire of the SYNOD.) | [rule] | 2 Cor. xi. 3. *I fear, leſt by any Means, as the Serpent beguiled Eve* | *through his Subtilty, ſo your Minds ſhould be corrupted from the Simplicity* | *that is in* CHRIST. | V. 14. *For* Satan *Himſelf, is transformed into an Angel of Light.* | [double rule] | *NEW-YORK*: | Printed by JAMES PARKER, at the *New Printing-Office* in | *Beaver-Street*, MDCCLIII.

4to.; 18.7 x 12.3 cm.; [A]^4, B-E^4, F^1; 42 p.

Notes: bound with Samuel Hopkins, *Sin Through Divine Interposition* (1759) and Jonathan Mayhew, *The Snare Broken* (1766).

Contents: p. [1]: title; p. [2]: *At a Meeting of the* SYNOD *of* NEW-YORK, *at* | NEWARK, September 28, 1752. | The SYNOD agree, to deſire the Reverend Mr. | EDWARDS, to publiſh his Sermon, preached before | them. | *A true Copy*, | RICHARD TREAT, *Syn. Clerk.*; p. [3]: TRUE GRACE, | Diſtinguiſhed from the | EXPERIENCE OF DEVILS.

THJ 181 EAI 1:6996 NUC NE0046872

Beinecke Library

257A • *NEW-YORK*: | Printed by JAMES PARKER, at the *New Printing-Office* in | *Beaver-Street*, MDCCLIII.

4to.; 19.2 x 11.2 cm.; [A]^4, B-G^4, H^3; 62 p.

Notes: sig. H_2 mislettered G_2; bound with *Sinners in the Hands of an Angry God*, separately titled but continuously paged and signed, it does not appear to have been issued separately.

Contents: p. [1]: title; p. [2]: *At a Meeting of the* SYNOD *of* NEW-YORK, *at* | NEWARK, September 28, 1752. | The SYNOD agree, to deſire the Reverend Mr. | EDWARDS, to publiſh his Sermon, preached before | them. | *A true Copy*, | RICHARD TREAT, *Syn. Clerk.*; p. [3]: TRUE GRACE, | Diſtinguiſhed from the | EXPERIENCE OF DEVILS.; p. [43]: SINNERS | In The Hands of | An angry GOD. | A | SERMON | Preached at *Enfield, July 8th* 1741. | At a Time of great Awakenings; and attended with remark- | able Impreſſions on many of the Hearers. | [rule] | By *Jonathan Edwards*, A. M. | Paſtor of the Church of CHRIST in *Northampton.* | [rule] | Amos ix. 2, 3. *Though they dig into Hell, thence ſhall mine Hand* | *take them; though they climb up to Heaven, thence will I bring them* | *down. And though they hide themſelves in the Top of Carmel, I will* | *ſearch and take them out thence*; *and though they be hid from my Sight* | *in the Bottom of the Sea, thence I will command the Serpent, and he* | *ſhall bite them.* | [rule] | *The* SECOND EDITION. | [double rule] | *BOSTON:* Printed: | NEW-YORK: Re-printed by *James Parker*, at the *New* | *Printing-Office* in *Beaver-Street*, MDCCLIII. (verso blank); p. [45]: SINNERS | In the Hands of an angry GOD.

THJ 181A EAI 1:6996 NUC NE0046873 OCLC 25492162

Princeton University

258 • A | SERMON | Preached at NEW-ARK, in *New-Jerſey*, before the Synod | of NEW-YORK and PHILADELPHIA, by the Rev. | JONATHAN EDWARDS, | Late Preſident of the College in NEW-JERSEY: | ENTITLED, | TRUE GRACE, | Diſtinguiſhed from the Experience of Devils. | [rule] | "*Thou believeſt that there is one* GOD; *thou doſt well*; *the* | *Devils alſo believe and tremble.*" JAMES 11. 19. | [rule] | STOCKBRIDGE: | PRINTED BY LORING ANDREWS: | [short double rule] | M,D,CC,XCI.

4to.; 19.2 x 12.6 cm. (uncut); [A]^4, B-F^4; 46, [2] p.

Contents: p. [1]: A | SERMON, | ENTITLED | TRUE GRACE, | Diſtinguiſhed from the | Experience of Devils. (verso blank); p. [3]: title; p. [4]: TRUE GRACE | Diſtinguiſhed from the | EXPERIENCE OF DEVILS.; pp. [47-48]: blank.

THJ 182 EAI 1:23344 NUC NE0046767

Houghton Library

259 • TRUE GRACE, | DISTINGUISHED FROM THE | EXPERIENCE OF DEVILS; | IN A | SERMON, | PREACHED BEFORE THE | *SYNOD* OF *NEW-YORK*, | CONVENED AT | *NEWARK* IN *NEW-JERSEY*, | On SEPTEMBER 28, N. S. 1752. | [short tapered rule] | [PRINTED BY THE

DESIRE OF THE SYNOD.] | [short tapered rule] | BY JONATHAN EDWARDS, A. M. | Paſtor of the Church of Chriſt in Stockbridge in New-England. | [short tapered rule] | 2 CORINTHIANS xi. 3. | *I fear, leſt by any means, as the Serpent beguiled Eve through | his ſubtilty, ſo your minds ſhould be corrupted from the ſim- | plicity that is in Chriſt.* | Verſe 14.–*For Satan himſelf is transformed into an angel of | light.* | [tapered rule] | *ELIZABETHTOWN:* | PRINTED BY SHEPARD KOLLOCK. | [short rule] | M.DCC.XCI.

12mo.; 17.8 x 10.6 cm. (uncut); $[A]^6$, B-C^6, D^4; 43, [1] p.

Notes: in some copies, bound with *Faithful Narrative* (1790).

Contents: p. [1]: title; p. [2]: *At a Meeting of the* SYNOD *of* NEW-YORK, *at* | NEWARK, September 28, 1752. | The SYNOD agree, to deſire the Reverend | Mr. EDWARDS, to publiſh his Sermon, preach- | ed before them. | *A true Copy*, | RICHARD TREAT, *Syn. Clerk*.; p. [3]: TRUE GRACE, | DISTINGUISHED FROM THE | EXPERIENCE OF DEVILS.; p. [44]: blank.

THJ 183 EAI 1:23343 NUC NE0046874 OCLC 41419450

Harvard Divinity School

A CAREFUL AND STRICT INQUIRY INTO THE MODERN PREVAILING NOTIONS OF THAT FREEDOM OF WILL

260 • A careful and ſtrict | ENQUIRY | INTO | The *modern* prevailing Notions | OF THAT | *FREEDOM of WILL*, | Which is ſuppoſed to be eſſential | TO | *Moral Agency, Vertue* and *Vice*, | *Reward* and *Puniſhment, Praiſe* | and *Blame*. | [rule] | By JONATHAN EDWARDS,A.M. | Paſtor of the Church in *Stockbridge*. | [rule] | Rom. ix. 16. *It is not of him that willeth*—— | [rule] | *BOSTON, N. E.* | Printed and Sold by S. KNEELAND, in Queen-ſtreet. | MDDCCLIV. *stet* EDWARDS,A.M.

8vo.; 19.2 x 12.3 cm.; $[A]^4$, aa^2, B^8, C-Z^4, Aa-Pp^4, Qq^2; [2], vi, [4], 294, [14] p.

Notes: in some copies, names of subscribers vary on the final page; in some copies, *ERRATA* mounted over the following advertisement: UPon a curſory Review of theſe Sheets, the *Errata* obſerv'd | in the Preſs-work appear of ſo little Importance, as not to | be worth the Formality of noting them for Correction. How- | ever, the candid Reader will allow of the uſual Excuſes for | ſuch Imperfections, almoſt unavoidable in printing Books of | any Length.

Contents: prp. [1]: title (verso blank); p. [i]: THE | *PREFACE*.; p. [vii]: A | General TABLE | Of the *CONTENTS*.; pp. [1]-294: text; p. [295]: INDEX.; p. [299]: Advertiſement.; p. [300]: A LIST of *SUBSCRIBERS*, | in Alphabetical Order.

THJ 184 EAI 1:7187 NUC NE0046457 OCLC 5718762

Forbes Library

261 • A careful and ſtrict | ENQUIRY | INTO | The *modern* prevailing Notions | OF THAT | *FREEDOM of WILL*, | Which is ſuppoſed to be eſſential | TO | *Moral Agency, Vertue* and *Vice, Re- | ward* and *Puniſhment, Praiſe* and | *Blame*. | [rule] | By JONATHAN EDWARDS, A. M. | Paſtor of the Church in *Stockbridge*. | [rule] | Rom. ix. 16. *It is not of him that willeth*—— | [double rule] | BOSTON Printed: | LONDON, Re-printed for THOMAS FIELD, | at the Wheatſheaf, the Corner of Pater- | noſter-Row, Cheapſide. | [short rule] | M.DCC.LXII.

8vo.; 20.3 x 12.2 cm.; $[A]^8$, B-Z^8, Aa-Dd^8, Ee^4; [2], ix, [5], 414, [10] p.

Contents: prp. [1]: title (verso blank); p. [i]: THE | PREFACE.; p. [x]: A | General TABLE | OF THE | CONTENTS.; pp. [1]-414: text; p. [415]: INDEX.; pp. [423-424]: [advertisement].

THJ 185 ESTC t78810 NUC NE0046459 OCLC 7889464

Congregational Library

262 • A careful and ftrict | INQUIRY | INTO | The *modern* prevailing Notions | OF THAT | *FREEDOM of WILL*, | Which is fuppofed to be effential | TO | MORAL AGENCY, VIRTUE and VICE, | REWARD and PUNISHMENT, PRAISE | and BLAME. | [rule] | By JONATHAN EDWARDS, A. M. | [rule] | Rom. ix. 16. *It is not of him that willeth*—— | [rule] | The THIRD EDITION. | [double rule] | LONDON: | Printed for J. JOHNSON, N° 8, in Pater-nofter-Row. | [short rule] | M.DCC.LXVIII.

8vo.; 20.2 x 12.5 cm.; [A]^8, B-Z^8, Aa-Ee^8, Ff^4; xi, [5], 414, [8], 18 p.

Notes: Edwards's *Remarks on the Essays on the Principles of Morality and Natural Religion*, by Henry Home, Lord Kames, included here for the first time and separately paged, was issued separately in the same year (see 218); it was first published in Edinburgh in 1758 (see 217) and often incorporated in later editions of *Freedom of the Will* as part iv, section xv, continuously paged. Addressed to John Erskine, it was followed by another letter to him on August 3 on the same subject; see *Works* (Yale), 16:705-718 and 718-724.

Contents: p. [i]: title (verso blank); p. [iii]: THE | PREFACE.; p. [xii]: A | General TABLE | OF THE | CONTENTS.; pp. [1]-414: text; p. [415]: INDEX.; p. [1]: REMARKS | ON THE | ESSAYS on the PRINCIPLES of MORA- | LITY and NATURAL RELIGION, | In a LETTER to a Minifter of the CHURCH | of SCOTLAND: | By the Reverend Mr. JONATHAN EDWARDS, | Prefident of the College of NEW JERSEY, and | Author of the late INQUIRY into the MODERN | NOTIONS of the FREEDOM of WILL. [signed] J. EDWARDS | STOCKBRIDGE, | *July* 25, 1757.

THJ 186 ESTC T133878 NUC NE0046462 OCLC 11528300

Library of Congress

263 • EEN BEPAALD EN NAUWKEURIG | ONDERZOEK | VAN DE | THANS HEERSCHENDE DENKBEELDEN | OVER DE | VRYHEID VAN DEN WIL, | WELKE ONDERSTELD WORD WEZENDLYK | TOT DE | ZEDELYKE WERKZAAMHEID, DEUGD | EN ONDEUGD, BELONING EN STRAF- | FE, LOF EN SCHANDE | TE BEHOREN. | DOOR | JONATHAN EDWARDS, A. M. | [rule] | *Rom: IX.* 16. *Het is niet des genen die Wil*-----. | [rule] | Naar den derden druk uit het Engelfch vertaald, en met het | leven van den Schryver vermeerderd. | [short double rule] | *Te UTRECHT*, | By GISBERT TIMON VAN PADDENBURG, | Boekverkoper MDCCLXXIV.

8vo.; 22.3 x 13.2 cm. (uncut); *^{8}, **^{8}, A-Z^8, Aa-Qq^8, Rr^2; [32], 628 p.

Notes: a Dutch translation of *Freedom of the Will.*

Contents: prp. [1]: title (verso blank); prp. [3]: OPDRAGT | AAN DE | EERWAARDIGE OPZIENDERS VAN | HET GENOODSCHAP | DER | REMONSTRASNSCH-HERVORMDEN | IN | NEDERLAND. [signed] *De aan UH. W. Eerw. verplichte* | CHRISTIANUS BATAVUS.; prp. [9]: VOORREDE; prp. [17]: *VOORREEDEN*.; prp. [26]: Algemeen TAFEL | VAN DEN | INHOUD; pp. [1]-594: text; p. [595]: AANMERKINGEN | OP | DE PROEVEN OVER DE GRONDBE- | GINZELEN DER ZEDEKUNDE, | EN DER NATUURLYKE | GODSDIENST, | IN EENE BRIEF AAN EENEN LEERAAR | DER SCHOTSCHE-KERKE: | *Door den Eerw. Heere* JONATHAN ED- | WARDS, *Prefident van bet Collegie te New* | *Jerfey, en Schryver van bet onlangs uitge-* | *kome* ONDERZOEK *betreffende de* HE- | DENDAAGSCHE DENKBEEL- | DEN *over de* VRYHEID | *van den* WIL. [signed] J. EDWARDS. | STOKBRIDGE [*sic*] | den 25 July | 1757.; p. 622: BLADWYZER.

THJ 187 NUC NE0046454 OCLC 43639582

Harvard Divinity School

264 • A | CAREFUL and STRICT | ENQUIRY | INTO THE | *MODERN* PREVAILING NOTIONS | OF THAT | *FREEDOM of WILL*, | WHICH IS SUPPOSED TO BE ESSENTIAL | TO | MORAL AGENCY, VIRTUE and VICE, | REWARD and PUNISHMENT, PRAISE | and BLAME. | [rule] | By JONATHAN EDWARDS, A. M. | [rule] | Rom. ix. 16. *It is not of him that willeth*— | [rule] | The FOURTH EDITION. | [thin-thick rule] | LONDON, | Printed for J. JOHNSON, No. 72, St. Paul's Church-yard. | MDCCLXXV.

8vo.; 20.1 x 12.2 cm.; [A]^8, B-Z^8, Aa-Ee^8, Ff^4; xi, [5], 414, [8], 18 p.

Contents: p. [i]: title (verso blank); p. [iii]: THE | PREFACE.; p. [xii]: A | GENERAL TABLE | OF THE | CONTENTS.; pp. [1]-414: text; p. [415]: INDEX.; p. [1]: REMARKS | ON THE | ESSAYS on the PRINCIPLES of MORA-

| LITY and NATURAL RELIGION, | In a LETTER to a Minifter of the CHURCH | of SCOTLAND: | By the Reverend Mr. JONATHAN EDWARDS, | Prefident of the College of NEW JERSEY, and | Author of the late INQUIRY into the MODERN | NOTIONS of the FREEDOM of WILL. [signed] J. EDWARDS | STOCKBRIDGE, | *July* 25, 1757.

THJ 188 ESTC N3249 NUC NE0046463 OCLC 4914793

Boston Public Library

265 • A | CAREFUL and STRICT | ENQUIRY | INTO THE | *MODERN* PREVAILING NOTIONS | OF THAT | *FREEDOM of WILL,* | WHICH IS SUPPOSED TO BE ESSENTIAL | TO | MORAL AGENCY, VIRTUE and VICE, | REWARD and PUNISHMENT, PRAISE | and BLAME. | [rule] | By JONATHAN EDWARDS, A. M. | [rule] | Rom. ix. 16. *It is not of him that willeth*— | [rule] | The FIFTH EDITION. | [thin-thick rule] | LONDON: Printed for J. MURGATROYD, No. 72, Chifwell-Street; | Sold alfo by Mr. BINNS, Leeds. | MDCCXC.

8vo.;21.3 x 12.6 cm.; [A]^8, B-Z^8, Aa-Ee^8, Ff^5; xi, [5], 415, [9], 18 p.

Contents: p. [i]: title (verso blank); p. [iii]: THE | PREFACE.; prp. [1]: A GENERAL TABLE OF THE CONTENTS.; prp. [5]: [advertisement]; pp. [1]-415: text; p. [416]: INDEX.; p. [424]: blank; p. [1]: REMARKS | ON THE | ESSAYS on the PRINCIPLES OF MORALITY | and NATURAL RELIGION. | In a LETTER to a Minifter of the CHURCH of | SCOTLAND | By the Reverend Mr. JONATHAN ED- | WARDS, Prefident of the College of NEW- | JERSEY, and Author of the late INQUIRY into | the MODERN NOTIONS of the FREEDOM of | WILL. [signed] STOCRBRIDGE [*sic*], | *July* 25, 1757. | J. EDWARDS.

THJ 189 ESTC N3251 NUC NE0046466 OCLC 8335049

Gordon-Conwell Theological Seminary

266 • A | CAREFUL AND STRICT | ENQUIRY | INTO THE | MODERN PREVAILING NOTIONS | OF THAT | *FREEDOM of WILL,* | WHICH IS SUPPOSED TO BE ESSENTIAL | TO | MORAL AGENCY, VIRTUE AND VICE, | REWARD AND PUNISHMENT, PRAISE | AND BLAME. | [rule] | By JONATHAN EDWARDS, A. M. | [rule] | Rom. ix. 16. *It is not of him that willeth*— | [short tapered rule] | LONDON: | Printed for C. DILLY in the Poultry, and the other | Bookfellers. 1790.

8vo.; 20 x 11.6 cm.; [A]^8, B-Z^8, Aa-Ee^8, Ff^4; xvi, 440 p.

Notes: This is a new edition, though the signatures and contents are identical with the London 1775 edition. There is also close line-by-line correspondence throughout. Pagination, on the other hand, is continuous, beginning with p. [1]. Spelling and capitalization have been modernized, and the catchwords omitted. It is evident that new type was set, probably using a London 1775 (or possibly 1790) edition for copy.—THJ.

Contents: p. [i]: title (verso blank); p. [iii]: THE | PREFACE.; p. [xii]: A | GENERAL TABLE | OF THE | CONTENTS.; pp. [1]-414: text; p. [415]: THE | INDEX.; p. 423: REMARKS | ON THE | ESSAYS on the PRINCIPLES of MORALITY | and NATURAL RELIGION. | In a LETTER to a Minifster of the CHURCH of | SCOTLAND: | By the Reverend Mr. JONATHAN EDWARDS, | Prefident of the College of NEW JERSEY, and | Author of the late ENQUIRY into the MODERN | NOTIONS of the FREEDOM of WILL. [signed] STOCKBRIDGE, | July 25, 1757. | J. EDWARDS.

THJ 190 ESTC N3250 NUC NE0046465 OCLC 5718749

John Carter Brown Library

266A • GLASGOW: | PRINTED BY DAVID NIVEN; | For, and Sold by, JAMES DUNCAN, Jun. Bookfeller, Saltmarket. | M,DCC,XC.

8vo.; 20.3 x 11.6 cm.; [A]^8, B-Z^8, Aa-Ee^8, Ff^4; xvi, 440 p.

Notes: identical with the above except for the imprint.

THJ 190A ESTC N26633 NUC NE0046464 OCLC 5718775

Harvard Divinity School

267 • A | *CAREFUL* and *STRICT* | INQUIRY | INTO | The *modern* prevailing Notions | OF THAT |

FREEDOM of WILL, | Which is ſuppoſed to be eſſential | TO | MORAL AGENCY, VIRTUE and VICE, | REWARD and PUNISHMENT, PRAISE | and BLAME. | [rule] | By the late Reverend and Learned | JONATHAN EDWARDS, A. M. | Preſident of the College of *New-Jerſey* | [rule] | Rom. ix. 16. *It is not of him that willeth——* | [rule] | The FOURTH EDITION. | [double rule] | *WILMINGTON*, (*Delaware*) | Printed and Sold by JAMES ADAMS, in *High-ſtreet*. | [short rule] | M.DCC.XC.

8vo.; 20.3 x 12.1 cm.; [A]^4, B-W-Z^4, Aa-Rr^4; xi, 299 [i.e., 300], [1], 13, [3] p.

Notes: p. 64 misnumbered 62; facing p. 134: blank (pp. 1-63, 62, 65-134, [1], 135-294); p. 1 in the second count misnumbered i (pp. i, 2-13); in some copies, first two errors corrected.

Contents: p. [i]: title (verso blank); p. iii: THE | PREFACE.; p. viii: A | General TABLE | OF THE | CONTENTS.; pp. 1-294: text; p. 295: INDEX; p. [300]: blank; p. i: REMARKS | ON THE | ESSAYS on the PRINCIPLES of | MORALITY and NATURAL | RELIGION, | In a LETTER to a Miniſter of the | CHURCH of | SCOTLAND: | By the Reverend Mr. JONATHAN ED- | WARDS, Preſident of the College of NEW- | JERSEY, and Author of the late INQUIRY in- | to the MODERN NOTIONS of the FREEDOM | of WILL. [signed] STOCKBRIDGE, | *July* 25, 1757. | J. EDWARDS.; pp. [14-16]: blank.

THJ 191 EAI 1:22476 NUC NE0046467 OCLC 1014987

Massachusetts Historical Society

268 • A | CAREFUL AND STRICT | INQUIRY | INTO THE | MODERN PREVAILING NOTIONS | OF THAT | *FREEDOM OF WILL*, | WHICH IS SUPPOSED TO BE ESSENTIAL | TO | MORAL AGENCY, VIRTUE AND VICE, | REWARD AND PUNISHMENT, PRAISE | AND BLAME. | [short decorative rule] | BY JONATHAN EDWARDS, A. M. | [short decorative rule] | Rom. ix. 16. *It is not of him that willeth.* | [double rule] | ALBANY: | PRINTED FOR AND SOLD BY WHITING, BACKUS & WHITING, | NO. 45, STATE-STREET: | SOLD ALSO BY THEM AT THEIR STORES IN SCHENECTADY, UTICA AND | CANANDAIGUA. | [short rule] | 1804.

8vo.; 20.8 x 12.6 cm.; π^8, C-W-Z^4, 2A-2W-2Z^4, 3A-3E^4; xiv, [2], 407, [l] p.

Contents: p. [i]: title (verso blank); p. [iii]: THE | PREFACE.; p. [x]: blank; p. [xi]: A | GENERAL TABLE | OF THE | CONTENTS.; pp. [xv-xvi]: blank; pp. [1]-383: text; p. [384]: blank; p. [385]: THE | INDEX.; p. [390]: blank; p. [391]: REMARKS | ON THE | ESSAYS on the PRINCIPLES of MORALITY | and NATURAL RELIGION, | In a LETTER to a Miniſter of the CHURCH of | SCOTLAND: | By the Rev. Mr. JONATHAN EDWARDS, Preſ- | ident of the College of NEW-JERSEY, and Author | of the late INQUIRY into the MODERN NOTIONS | of the FREEDOM of WILL. [signed] J. EDWARDS. | STOCKBRIDGE, | July 25, 1757.; p. [408]: blank.

THJ 192 EAI 2:6222 NUC NE0046470 OCLC 687394

Congregational Library

269 • A | CAREFUL AND STRICT | ENQUIRY | INTO | THE MODERN PREVAILING NOTIONS | OF THAT | FREEDOM OF THE WILL, | WHICH IS SUPPOSED TO BE ESSENTIAL | TO | Moral Agency, | *VIRTUE AND VICE, REWARD AND PUNISHMENT, PRAISE AND BLAME.* | [short tapered rule] | BY J. EDWARDS, A. M. | [short tapered rule] | "It is not of him that willeth."–Rom. ix. 16. | [thin-thick rule] | *LONDON:* | PRINTED FOR T. HAMILTON, | 33, *Paternoster Row*. | [short rule] | 1816.

22.4 x 13.7 cm. (uncut); [A]^8, B-Z^8, Aa-Ee^8, [Ff]^2; xv, [1], 414, 18, [4] p.

Contents: p. [i]: title; p. [ii]: PRINTED BY WILLIAMS AND BIRTLES, | *Vineyard Walk, Clerkenwell.*; p. [iii]: PREFACE.; p. [xii]: blank; p. [xiii]: CONTENTS.; p. [xvi]: blank; p. [1]: *ENQUIRY* | INTO THE | FREEDOM OF THE WILL, | *&c. &c.*; p. [1]: REMARKS | ON THE | *ESSAYS ON THE PRINCIPLES OF MORALITY* | AND | NATURAL RELIGION. | [short thick-thin rule] | IN A LETTER TO A MINISTER OF THE CHURCH OF SCOTLAND. | [short thin-thick rule] | *BY THE REV. MR. JONATHAN EDWARDS*, | President of the College of New Jersey | Author of the late Inquiry into the Modern Notions of the Freedom of the Will. | [short thin-thick rule]; p. [19]: INDEX; p. [22]: PRINTED BY WILLIAMS AND BIRTLES, | *Vineyard Walk, Clerkenwell.*

THJ 193
Smith College

270 • A | CAREFUL AND STRICT | *ENQUIRY* | INTO THE | MODERN PREVAILING NOTIONS | OF THAT | FREEDOM OF THE WILL, | WHICH IS SUPPOSED TO BE ESSENTIAL | TO | Moral Agency, | *VIRTUE AND VICE, REWARD AND PUNISHMENT,* | *PRAISE AND BLAME.* | [short thick-thin rule] | BY THE LATE REV. JONATHAN EDWARDS, | *PRESIDENT OF THE COLLEGE OF NEW JERSEY.* | [short thin-thick rule] | *"It is not of him that willeth"*—ROM. ix. 16. | [short tapered rule] | London: | PUBLISHED BY RICHARD BAYNES, | 25, IVY LANE, PATERNOSTERROW. | [short tapered rule] | 1818.

18.3 x 10 cm.; π^1, a^4, b^2, B-Z^6, AA-FF^6, GG^4; [2], [iii]-x, [4], 343, [1] p.
Notes: in some copies, between pp. vi -vii, two unnumbered leaves: CONTENTS.
Contents: prp. [1]: title (verso blank); p. [iii]: PREFACE.; p. [xi]: CONTENTS.; pp. [1]-343: text; p. [344]: blank.
THJ 194 NUC NE0046471 OCLC 36872097
Bryn Mawr College

270A • Edinburgh: | PRINTED BY THOMAS TURNBULL, | OLD ASSEMBLY CLOSE. | [short tapered rule] |1818.

18.3 x 10 cm.; π^1, a^4, b^2, B-Z^6, AA-FF^6, GG^4; [2], [iii]-x, [4], 343, [1] p.
Notes: identical with the above except for the imprint.
OCLC 9798137
Boston College

270B • Edinburgh: PRINTED FOR OLIVER AND BOYD. | [short tapered rule] | 1818.

18.3 x 10 cm.; π^1, a^4, b^2, B-Z^6, AA-FF^6, GG^4; [2], [iii]-x, [4], 343, [1] p.
Notes: identical with the above except for the imprint.
OCLC 26920594
Dallas Theological Seminary

271 • A | CAREFUL AND STRICT | ENQUIRY | INTO THE | MODERN PREVAILING NOTIONS | OF | THAT FREEDOM OF WILL, | WHICH IS SUPPOSED TO BE ESSENTIAL | TO | MORAL AGENCY, | VIRTUE AND VICE, REWARD AND PUNISHMENT, | PRAISE AND BLAME. | [short rule] | Rom. ix. 16.—IT IS NOT OF HIM THAT WILLETH. | [short rule] | BY REV. JONATHAN EDWARDS, A. M. | President of Nassau Hall. | [short thick-thin rule] | NEW-YORK: | G. AND C. CARVILL, 108 BROADWAY. | 1828.

21.1 x 12.7 cm.; π^1, 2-37^4, 38^2; [2], 300 [i.e., 294] p.
Notes: lacks pp. [3-8] between the title and half title (pp. [1-2], [9]-300).
Contents: prp. [1]: title (verso blank); p. [9]: A | CAREFUL AND STRICT | ENQUIRY | INTO THE | MODERN PREVAILING NOTIONS | OF | THAT FREEDOM OF WILL, | WHICH IS SUPPOSED TO BE ESSENTIAL | TO | MORAL AGENCY, | VIRTUE AND VICE, REWARD AND PUNISHMENT, | PRAISE AND BLAME. | [short rule] | ROM. IX. 16.—IT IS NOT OF HIM THAT WILLETH. (verso blank); p. [11]: PREFACE.; p. [15]: A | CAREFUL AND STRICT ENQUIRY, | &c.; p. 290: APPENDIX. | [short rule] | SECT. IV. | *Containing Remarks on "Essays on the Principles of Morali- | ty and Natural Religion," in a letter to a Minister of the | Church of Scotland.* [signed] J. EDWARDS. | STOCKBRIDGE, JULY 25th, 1757.
THJ 196 NUC NE0046472 OCLC 5542672
Harvard University

272 • A | CAREFUL AND STRICT | INQUIRY | INTO THE | MODERN PREVAILING NOTIONS

| OF THAT | FREEDOM OF THE WILL, | WHICH IS SUPPOSED TO BE ESSENTIAL TO | MORAL AGENCY, VIRTUE AND VICE, REWARD | AND PUNISHMENT, PRAISE AND BLAME. | TO WHICH IS ANNEXED, | REMARKS ON THE ESSAYS ON THE PRINCIPLES OF | MORALITY AND NATURAL RELIGION. | [short tapered rule] | BY THE LATE | REV. JONATHAN EDWARDS, | PRESIDENT OF THE COLLEGE OF NEW JERSEY. | [short rule] | "IT IS NOT OF HIM THAT WILLETH."—ROM. IX. 16. | [short rule] | EDINBURGH: | PETER BROWN AND THOMAS NELSON. | [short rule] | MDCCCXXX.

17.2 x 9.9 cm.; π^6, A-N^{12}, $[O]^3$; 330 p.

Contents: p. [1]: title; p. [2]: ANDREW JACK & CO. PRINTERS; p. [3]: PREFACE.; p. [9]: CONTENTS.; p. [13]: INQUIRY | INTO THE | FREEDOM OF THE WILL, | &c. &c.; p. [321]: REMARKS | ON THE | ESSAYS ON THE PRINCIPLES OF MORALITY | AND | NATURAL RELIGION, | IN A LETTER TO THE LATE REV. DR. ERSKINE, GREYFRIARS, | EDINBURGH, | BY THE LATE REV. JONATHAN EDWARDS. [signed] J. EDWARDS. | STOCK-BRIDGE [*sic*], | JULY 25, 1757.

NUC NE0046473 OCLC 26470322

Duke University

273 • AN | INQUIRY | INTO THE | MODERN PREVAILING NOTIONS | RESPECTING THAT | FREEDOM OF WILL | WHICH IS SUPPOSED TO BE ESSENTIAL TO | MORAL AGENCY, VIRTUE AND VICE, REWARD AND | PUNISHMENT, PRAISE AND BLAME. | [short decorative rule] | BY JONATHAN EDWARDS, A. M. | [short rule] | *A NEW EDITION:* | WITH | AN INTRODUCTORY ESSAY, | BY THE | AUTHOR OF "NATURAL HISTORY OF ENTHUSIASM." | [short rule] | LONDON: JAMES DUNCAN, 37, PATERNOSTER ROW. | [short rule] | M.DCCC.XXXI.

21.1 x 13.3 cm.; $[a]^8$, b-k^8, h^4, B-Z^8, AA-FF^8, GG^4; clxviii, 434, 20, [2] p.

Notes: sig. h_{1-4} repeated; some copies lack the introductory essay.

Contents: frontispiece: [engraving] | PAINTED BY REMBRANT PEAL [*sic*] ENGRAVED BY W C [*sic*] EDWARDS | [facsimile autograph] Jonathan Edwards | London: Published 1834 by Westley & Davis, Stationers Court; p. [i]: title; p. [ii]: LONDON: | J. MOYES, TOOK'S COURT, CHANCERY LANE.; p. [iii]: PREFACE.; p. [xiii]: CONTENTS.; p. [xvii]: INTRODUCTORY ESSAY; p. clxvi: ERRATUM.; p. [clxvii]: AN INQUIRY, | ETC. ETC. (verso blank); p. [1]: AN INQUIRY, | ETC. ETC.; p. [430]: blank; p. [431]: INDEX.; p. [1]: REMARKS | ON THE | ESSAYS ON THE PRINCIPLES OF MORALITY | AND NATURAL RELIGION: | IN A LETTER TO A MINISTER OF THE CHURCH OF SCOTLAND. | BY THE REV. MR. JONATHAN EDWARDS, | *President of the College of New Jersey, and Author of the late Inquiry* | *into the Modern Notions of the Freedom of Will.* [signed] J. EDWARDS | *Stockbridge, July* 25, 1757.; p. 20: LONDON: | J. MOYES, TOOK'S COURT, CHANCERY LANE.; pp. [21-22]: blank.

THJ 197 NUC NE0046683 OCLC 2299175

Gordon-Conwell Theological Seminary

273A • *An Inquiry into the Modern* | *Prevailing Notions Respecting that* | FREEDOM OF WILL | Jonathan Edwards | Introduction by Isaac Taylor | [publisher's device] | THOEMMES PRESS

21.2 x 13 cm.; clxviii, 434, 20 p.

Notes: facsimile reprint.

Contents: prp. [1]: 18th & 19th CENTURY | WORKS | THOEMMES; prp. [2]: Printed in Great Britain by Anthony Rowe Ltd, Chippenham, Wiltshire; prp. [3]: title; prp. [4]: © Thoemmes Press 1993 | Published in 1993 by | Thoemmes Press | 85 Park Street | Bristol BS1 5PJ | England | [1 line] | This is a reprint of the 1831 Edition | [11 lines].

ISBN 1855061899 OCLC 31676129

Boston College

274 • A | CAREFUL AND STRICT | INQUIRY | INTO THE | MODERN PREVAILING NOTIONS

| OF THAT | FREEDOM OF THE WILL | WHICH IS SUPPOSED TO BE ESSENTIAL TO | MORAL AGENCY, VIRTUE AND VICE, REWARD | AND PUNISHMENT, PRAISE AND BLAME. | BY THE LATE | REV. JONATHAN EDWARDS, A. M. | PRESIDENT OF THE COLLEGE OF NEW JERSEY. | [short rule] | "IT IS NOT OF HIM THAT WILLETH."—Rom. ix. 16. | [short rule] | EDINBURGH: | PUBLISHED BY PETER BROWN. | [short rule] | MDCCCXXXVII.

18.8 x 10.8 cm. (uncut); a^6, A-L^{12}, M^6; xii, 264, 12 p.

Contents: p. [i]: title; p. [ii]: EDINBURGH: | PRINTED BY H. & J. PILLANS, 7, JAMES'S COURT.; p. [iii]: PREFACE.; p. [ix]: CONTENTS.; pp. [1]-264: text; p. 264: H. & J. PILLANS, PRINTERS, EDINBURGH.; p. [1]: REMARKS ON | LORD KAMES' ESSAYS ON THE PRINCIPLES OF | MORALITY AND NATURAL RELIGION: | IN A LETTER TO A MINISTER OF THE CHURCH OF SCOTLAND. | BY THE REV. MR. JONATHAN EDWARDS, | *President of the College of New Jersey, and Author of the late | Inquiry into the Modern Notions of the Freedom of Will.* [signed] J. EDWARDS | *Stockbridge, July* 25, 1757.

OCLC 30847379
Princeton University

275 • AN | INQUIRY | INTO THE | MODERN PREVAILING NOTIONS | RESPECTING THAT | FREEDOM OF WILL | WHICH IS SUPPOSED TO BE ESSENTIAL TO | MORAL AGENCY, VIRTUE AND VICE, REWARDS AND | PUNISHMENT, PRAISE AND BLAME. | BY | JONATHAN EDWARDS, A. M. | With an Index. | ANDOVER: | GOULD, NEWMAN AND SAXTON. | NEW YORK: | CORNER OF FULTON AND NASSAU STS. | 1840. *stet* REWARDS

17.9 x 11.5 cm.; $[1]^6$, $2\text{-}36^6$; xii, [13]-432 p.

Contents: p. [i]: title (verso blank); p. [iii]: PREFACE.; p. [ix]: CONTENTS.; p. [13]: INQUIRY, | ETC. ETC.; p. [412]: blank; p. [413]: INDEX.; p. [416]: blank; p. [417]: REMARKS | ON THE | ESSAYS ON THE PRINCIPLES OF MORALITY | AND NATURAL RELIGION: | IN A LETTER TO A MINISTER OF THE CHURCH OF SCOTLAND. | BY THE REV. MR. JONATHAN EDWARDS, | *President of the College of New Jersey, and Author of the late Inqui- | ry into the Modern Notions of the Freedom of Will.* [signed] J. EDWARDS. | *Stockbridge, July* 25, 1757.

THJ 198 NUC NE0046585 OCLC 742527
Congregational Library

276 • AN INQUIRY | INTO | THE MODERN PREVAILING NOTIONS | OF THAT | FREEDOM OF THE WILL | WHICH IS SUPPOSED TO BE ESSENTIAL TO | MORAL AGENCY, VIRTUE AND VICE, REWARD AND | PUNISHMENT, PRAISE AND BLAME. | BY THE LATE | REV. JONATHAN EDWARDS, | PRESIDENT OF THE COLLEGE O[F] NEW JERSEY. | [short wavy rule] | "It is not of him that willeth."—*Rom.* ix. 16. | [short wavy rule] | THOMAS NELSON, LONDON, | AND EDINBURGH. | [short wavy rule] | MDCCCXLV.

16.7 x 10.6 cm.; $[A]^8$, B-D^8, D-Y^8; xvi, 348, [4] p.

Notes: sig. D^8 repeated.

Contents: p. [i]: EDWARDS | ON THE | FREEDOM OF THE WILL. (verso blank); p. [iii]: title; p. [iv]: EDINBURGH: | ANDREW JACK, PRINTER, | NIDDRY STREET.; p. [v]: PREFACE.; p. [xiii]: CONTENTS.; p. [1]: INQUIRY, | ETC. ETC.; p. 348: ANDREW JACK, PRINTER.; pp. [349-352]: blank.

THJ 199 NUC NE0046686 OCLC 20673852
Forbes Library

276A • Soli Deo Gloria Publications | *...for instruction in righteousness...*

21.4 x 13.5 cm.; xvi, 348 p.

Notes: facsimile reprint; p. [iv]: Soli Deo Gloria Publications | P.O. Box 451, Morgan, PA 15064 | [1 line] | This edition of *The Freedom of the Will* was taken | from the edition published by Thomas Nelson | in London in 1845. This Soli Deo Gloria | reprint is 1996. Printed in the USA. | [1 line].

ISBN 1573580333 OCLC 35020088
Andover Newton Theological School

277 • A | CAREFUL AND STRICT INQUIRY | INTO THE | MODERN PREVAILING NOTIONS | OF THAT | FREEDOM OF THE WILL, | WHICH IS | SUPPOSED TO BE ESSENTIAL TO MORAL AGENCY, VIRTUE AND VICE, | REWARD AND PUNISHMENT, PRAISE AND BLAME. | [short rule] | IT IS NOT OF HIM THAT WILLETH.–Rom. ix. 16. | [short rule] | NEW YORK: | LEAVITT AND COMPANY. | [short rule] | 1851.

23.1 x 14.7 cm.; π^3, 1-24^4; iv, [2], 190, [2] p.

Notes: In many copies the last leaf is missing, but it is genuine when present.—THJ; the title pages of the reprints differ slightly with different imprints.

Contents: p. [i]: title (verso blank); p. [iii]: CONTENTS OF VOLUME II.; prp. [1]: A CAREFUL AND STRICT INQUIRY | INTO THE | MODERN PREVAILING NOTIONS | OF THAT | FREEDOM OF THE WILL, | WHICH IS | SUPPOSED TO BE ESSENTIAL TO MORAL AGENCY, VIRTUE AND VICE, REWARD | AND PUNISHMENT, PRAISE AND BLAME. | [short rule] | ROM. IX. 16. IT IS NOT OF HIM THAT WILLETH. (verso blank); pp. [1]-190: text; pp. [191-192]: blank.

THJ 200 NUC NE0046474 OCLC 3281758
Brown University

277A • NEW YORK: | PUBLISHED BY LEAVITT & ALLEN, | 27 DEY STREET. | 1852.
THJ 200A NUC NE0046475 OCLC 16655484
Princeton University

277B • NEW YORK: | PUBLISHED BY LEAVITT & ALLEN, | 27 DEY STREET. | 1856.
THJ 200B NUC NE0046476 OCLC 4872635
McMaster University

277C • NEW YORK: | PUBLISHED BY LEAVITT & ALLEN, | 379 BROADWAY. | 1857.
THJ 200C NUC NE0046477 OCLC 26920610
Dallas Theological Seminary

277D • NEW YORK: | PUBLISHED BY LEAVITT & ALLEN, | 379 BROADWAY. | 1858.
THJ 200D NUC NE0046479 OCLC 26457341
Andover Newton Theological School

277E • NEW YORK: | PUBLISHED BY LEAVITT & ALLEN, | 21 & 23 MERCER ST.
THJ 200E NUC NE0046456
Presbyterian Historical Society

277F • NEW YORK: | ROBERT CARTER & BROTHERS, | 530 BROADWAY. | 1866.
Notes: The plates were taken over by Carter & Brothers in 1866.–THJ.
THJ 200F NUC NE0046480 OCLC 10890313
Forbes Library

277G • NEW YORK: | ROBERT CARTER AND BROTHERS, | 530 BROADWAY. | 1866.
THJ 200G
Harvard University

277H • NEW YORK: | ROBERT CARTER & BROTHERS, | 530 BROADWAY. | 1869.
THJ 200H NUC NE0046481 OCLC 27878871
New York Public Library

277I • NEW YORK: | ROBERT CARTER & BROTHERS, | 530 BROADWAY. | 1875.
THJ 200I NUC NE0046483 OCLC 24197832
Amherst College

277J • NEW YORK: | ROBERT CARTER & BROTHERS, | 530 BROADWAY | 1881.
THJ 200J NUC NE0046484 OCLC 3564310
Brown University

277K • NEW YORK: | ROBERT CARTER & BROTHERS, | 530 BROADWAY.
Notes: cited by THJ at Pedagogical Library, Philadelphia Board of Education; that copy is no longer available.
THJ 200K NUC NE0046455

277L • PHILADELPHIA: | THE PRESBYTERIAN BOARD OF PUBLICATION | AND SABBATH SCHOOL WORK. | 1903.
Notes: The plates were taken over by the Presbyterian Board of Publication in 1903. The title page corresponds identically with the earlier printings, except for imprint.—THJ.
THJ 200L NUC NE0046485 OCLC 16398411
Princeton University

278 • AN INQUIRY | INTO THE PREVAILING NOTIONS | OF THE | FREEDOM OF WILL, | WHICH IS SUPPOSED TO BE | ESSENTIAL TO MORAL AGENCY, VIRTUE AND VICE, REWARD | AND PUNISHMENT, PRAISE AND BLAME. | BY JONATHAN EDWARDS, A.M. | "It is not of him that willeth."–Rom. ix., 16. | NEW EDITION, CAREFULLY CORRECTED. | LIVERPOOL: | EDWARD HOWELL, CHURCH STREET. | [short rule] | MDCCCLV.
17 x 10.5 cm.; [A]^4, B-U^8, V^4; viii, 310, [2] p.
Contents: p. [i]: title (verso blank); p. [iii]: PREFACE. [signed] JONATHAN EDWARDS.; pp. [1]-303: text; p. 304: INDEX.; p. 310: Printed by Edward Howell, Church Street, Liverpool.; pp. [311-312]: [advertisement].
THJ 201 NUC NE0046688 OCLC 35444719
Princeton University

278A • LONDON: | HAMILTON, ADAMS, & CO., PATERNOSTER ROW. | [short rule] | MDCCCLV.
17 x 10.5 cm.; [A]^4, B-U^8, V^4; viii, 310, [2] p.
Notes: identical with the above except for the imprint.
THJ 201A
National Library of Scotland

278B • [decorative initial] An [decorative initial] Inquiry | INTO THE PREVAILING NOTIONS | OF THE | Freedom of Will, | WHICH IS SUPPOSED TO BE | *Essential to Moral Agency, Virtue and Vice, Reward* | *and Punishment, Praise and Blame.* | By | Jonathan Edwards, A.M. | [ornament] | "It is not of him that willeth."–Rom. ix. 16. | [ornament] | *NEW EDITION, CAREFULLY CORRECTED.* | LONDON: WARD AND LOCK, 158, FLEET STREET.
17 x 10.5 cm.; [A]^4, B-U^8, V^4; viii, 310, [2] p.

Notes: published c. 1855; identical with the above except for the title page.
NUC NE0046689 OCLC 11688328
Hamilton College

278C • FREEDOM OF THE WILL | WHICH IS SUPPOSED TO BE | ESSENTIAL TO MORAL AGENCY, | VIRTUE AND VICE, | REWARD AND PUNISHMENT, | PRAISE AND BLAME. | BY JONATHAN EDWARDS, D. D., | *President of Yale College, Connecticut.* | NEW EDITION, CAREFULLY CORRECTED. | LONDON: | HAMILTON, ADAMS & CO., PATERNOSTER ROW. | 1860.

17 x 10.5 cm.; [A]^4, B-U^8, V^4; viii, 310, [2] p.
Notes: identical with the above except for the title page.
OCLC 31246691
Harvard Divinity School

279 • [within double rules] YMCHWILIAD GOFALUS A MANWL | I'R | SYNIADAU SYDD YN DDIWEDDAR AR LED | YNGHYLCH | RHYDDID YR EWYLLYS, | FEL Y MAE YN CAEL EI YSTYRIED | YN HANFODOL I WEITHREDIANT MOESOL, | RHINWEDD A DRYGIONI, GWOBR A CHOSP, | CANMOLIAETH A BAI. | GAN JONATHAN EDWARDS, D.D. | GYDA NODIADAU, GAN DR. WILLIAMS, ROTHERHAM. | CYFIEITHEDIG GAN Y | PARCH. DANIEL ROWLANDS, A.M. LLANIDLOES. | AT YR HYN YR YCHWANEGWYD | HANES BYWYD YR AWDWR, | GAN Y PARCH. ROBERT THOMAS, BANGOR. | [short rule] | CAERNARFON: | CYHOEDDWYD GAN H. HUMPHREYS, CASTLE SQUARE.

18 x 11 cm.; [a]-b^8, c^2, A-U-V^8; xxxvi, 336 p.
Notes: a Welsh translation of *Freedom of the Will*, published c. 1865.
Contents: p. [i]: title (verso blank); p. [iii]: JONATHAN EDWARDS [signed] ROBERT THOMAS | BANGOR, GOR., 1865.; p. [xxx]: TYSTIOLAETH | Y PARCH. | LEWIS EDWARDS, M. A., BALA, | AM Y PARCH. | JONATHAN EDWARDS, AMERICA.; p. [xxxi]: RHAGYMADRODD. [signed] JONATHAN EDWARDS; pp. [1]-327: text; p. [328]: MYNEGAI; p. 336: H. HUMPHREYS, ARGRAFFYDD, CAERNARFON
THJ 202 NUC NE0046893 OCLC 43639555
Princeton University

280 • THE | MODERN PREVAILING NOTIONS | RESPECTING THAT | FREEDOM OF WILL | WHICH IS SUPPOSED TO BE ESSENTIAL TO | MORAL AGENCY, VIRTUE AND VICE, REWARD AND | PUNISHMENT, PRAISE AND BLAME | BY JONATHAN EDWARDS, A.M. | WITH | *AN INTRODUCTORY ESSAY* | BY ISAAC TAYLOR | AUTHOR OF "THE HISTORY OF THE TRANSMISSION OF ANCIENT | BOOKS," ETC. | Liverpool | EDWARD HOWELL | MDCCCLXXVII

16.8 x 10.3 cm.; [A]^8, B-Z^8, 2A-2O^8; clxiii, [3], 422, 4 p.
Notes: Though Howell brought out a new edition in 1855 (*q.v.*), he reprinted this 1827 edition in 1877–THJ [THJ 195]. Howell did not begin publishing in Liverpool until the 1840s and did not publish Edwards there until 1855; neither of the locations THJ cites, Boston Public nor Yale, holds a copy of a 1827 issue, though both hold the 1877. The Taylor essay was first published in 1831.
Contents: p. [i]: FREEDOM OF WILL. (verso blank); p. [iii]: title (verso blank); p. [v]: PREFACE.; p. [xiii]: CONTENTS.; p. [xvii]: INTRODUCTORY ESSAY.; p. [clxiv]: blank; p. [clxv]: AN INQUIRY, | ETC., ETC. (verso blank); pp. [1]-417: text; p. [418]: blank; p. [419]: INDEX.; p. 422: EDWARD HOWELL, PRINTER, LIVERPOOL.; pp. [1]-4: [advertisement].
THJ 195A NUC NE0046729 OCLC 9886360
Yale Divinity School

281 • *Jonathan Edwards* | *Freedom of the Will* | EDITED, WITH AN INTRODUCTION, | BY ARNOLD S. KAUFMAN | AND WILLIAM K. FRANKENA | *University of Michigan* | *The Library of Liberal Arts, published* | *by The Bobbs-Merrill Company, Inc.* | *Indianapolis and New York*

20.3 x 13.6 cm.; xl, 269, [5] p.

Contents: p. [I]: *Freedom* | *of the Will* | *The Library* | *of Liberal Arts* (verso blank); p. [iii]: title; p. [iv]: *Jonathan Edwards: 1703-1758* | *Copyright © 1969 by The Bobbs-Merrill Company, Inc.*; p. v: Contents; p. ix: *Introduction* [signed] ARNOLD S. KAUFMAN | WILLIAM K. FRANKENA | *Ann Arbor, Michigan* | *January 1968*; p. xxxix: *Bibliography*; p. xl: *Editors' Note* [signed] A.S.K. | W.K.F.; p. [xli]: *Freedom* | *of the Will* (verso blank); pp. 1-269: text; p. [270]: blank; pp. [271-274]: [advertisement].

OCLC 10440

Gordon-Conwell Theological Seminary

281A • [ornament] IRVINGTON PUBLISHERS, INC. | 551 FIFTH AVENUE NEW YORK, N.Y. 10017

Notes: title page (verso): First Irvington Edition 1982 | Copyright © 1969 by The Bobbs-Merrill Company, Inc. | [18 lines].

ISBN 082901263X OCLC 8928020

Smith College

281B • [within rules] FREEDOM OF | THE WILL | JONATHAN EDWARDS | [short rule] | EDITED BY ARNOLD S. KAUFMAN | AND WILLIAM K. FRANKENA | *A Limited Edition* | [short rule] | THE FRANKLIN LIBRARY | FRANKLIN CENTER, PENNSYLVANIA | *1984*

Notes: title page (verso): [2 lines] | From Jonathan Edwards, *Freedom of the Will*, | edited by Arnold S. Kaufman and William K. Frankena, | copyrighted © 1969 by the Bobbs-Merrill Co., Inc. | [3 lines].

OCLC 10963902

University of Maine

THE GREAT CHRISTIAN DOCTRINE OF ORIGINAL SIN DEFENDED

282 • THE | Great Chriſtian Doctrine | OF | *ORIGINAL SIN* | defended; | Evidences of it's *Truth* produced, | AND | Arguments to the *Contrary* anſwered. | Containing, in particular, | A Reply to the Objections and Arguings of | Dr. JOHN TAYLOR, in his Book, Intitled, | "The Scripture-Doctrine of *Original Sin* pro- | "poſed to free and candid Examination, &c. | [rule] | By the late Reverend and Learned | JONATHAN EDWARDS, A. M. | Preſident of the College of *New-Jerſey*. | [rule] | MATTH. ix. 12. *They that be whole, need not a Phyſician; but* | *they that are ſick.* | ---Et hæc non tantum ad Peccatores referenda eſt; quia in | omnibus Maledictionibus primi Hominis, omnes ejus Gene- | rationes conveniunt.--- R. SAL. JARCHI. | Propter Concupiſcentiam, innatam Cordi humano, dicitur, In | Iniquitate genitus ſum; atque Senſus eſt, quod à Nativitate | implantatum ſit Cordi humano *Jetzer harang*, Figmentum | malum.--- ABEN-EZRA. | ---- Ad Mores Natura recurrit | damnatos, fixa et mutari neſcia.--- | ---- Dociles imitandis | turpibus et pravis omnes ſumus.--- JUV. | [rule] | *BOSTON, NEW-ENGLAND:* | Printed and Sold by S. KNEELAND, oppoſite to the Probate- | Office in Queen-ſtreet. 1758. *stet* it's *stet* Examination, &c.

8vo.; 19.9 x 12.4 cm.; $[A]^4$, aa^4, $Sſ^2$, $B\text{-}K^8$, $L\text{-}Z^4$, $Aa\text{-}Sſ^4$, $[R]^1$; [2], xviii, 386, [8] p.

Notes: sig. bb mislettered Sſ; sig. C_4 mislettered D_4; pp. 145-152 misnumbered 153-160 (pp. [1]-144, 153-160,

153-386); the list of subscribers varies in different copies, extending in some to an additional leaf.

Contents: prp. [1]: title (verso blank); p. [i]: A brief ACCOUNT of the Book and it's [*sic*] | AUTHOR.; p. xi: *The Author*'s PREFACE. [dated] *Stockbridge*, May 26. 1757.; p. xiv: *ADVERTISEMENT.*; p. xv: The CONTENTS.; p. [1]: The great Chriftian Doctrine of | *ORIGINAL SIN* | defended.; p. 386: *ERRATA.*; p. [387]: A Lift of *SUBSCRIBERS*, | in Alphabetical Order.; p. [394]: blank.

THJ 203 EAI 1:8118 NUC NE0046600 OCLC 4720993

Congregational Library

283 • THE | Great Chriftian Doctrine | OF | ORIGINAL SIN | DEFENDED; | EVIDENCES of its TRUTH produced, | AND | ARGUMENTS to the contrary anfwered. | Containing, in particular, | A REPLY to the Objections and Arguings of | Dr. JOHN TAYLOR, in his Book, Intitled, | "The Scripture-Doctrine of *Original Sin* pro- | "pofed to free and candid Examination, &c." | [rule] | By the late Reverend and Learned | JONATHAN EDWARDS, A. M. | Prefident of the College of *New-Jerfey*. | [rule] | MATTH. ix. 12. *They that be whole, need not a Phyfician; but* | *they that are fick.* | —Et hæc non tantum ad Peccatores referenda eft; quia in | omnibus Maledictionibus primi Hominis, omnes ejus Gene- | rationes conveniunt.— R. SAL. JARCHI. | Propter Concupifcentiam, innatam Cordi humano, dicitur, | In Iniquitate genitus fum; atque Senfus eft, quod à Nati- | vitate implantatum fit Cordi humano *Jetzer harang*, Fig- | mentum malum.— ABEN-EZRA. | —Ad Mores Natura recurrit | Damnatos, fixa & mutari nefcia.— | —Dociles imitandis | Turpibus & pravis omnes fumus.— JUV. | [thick-thin rule] | *BOSTON* Printed, *LONDON* Re-printed, | For G. KEITH, in *Gracechurch-Street*; and J. JOHNSON and | Co. at the *Globe*, in *Paternofter-Row*. | [short rule] | M.DCC.LXVI.

8vo.;20.2 x 12.5 cm.; a^8, b^4, B-Z^8, Aa-Gg^8, Hh^4; xxiii, [1], 470, [2] p.

Notes: p. xvi: The Editor has taken the Liberty of ftriking out | a few Things from the Preface and the Account | of the Author, the better to adapt them to the | European Reader; and has altered all the Re- | ferences, fo as to fuit them to the laft London | Editions of Dr. *T—r*'s Books; whereas Mr. ED- | WARDS made ufe of the Irifh.

Contents: p. [i]: title (verso blank); p. iii: A brief ACCOUNT of the Book and its | AUTHOR; p. xiv: THE | AUTHOR'S PREFACE [dated] *Stockbridge*, May 26, 1757.; p. xvi: [editor's note] | *ADVERTISEMENT.*; p. xvii: THE | CONTENTS.; p. [xxiv]: blank; p. [1]: THE | GREAT CHRISTIAN DOCTRINE | OF | ORIGINAL SIN | DEFENDED.; pp. [471-472]: [advertisement].

THJ 204 ESTC T78820 NUC NE0046602 OCLC 1426849

New York Public Library

283A • *BOSTON* Printed, *LONDON* Re-printed, | For J. JOHNSON and Co. at the *Globe*, in *Paternofter-Row*; | and G. KEITH, in *Gracechurch-Street* | [short rule] | M.DCC.LXVI.

20.2 x 12.5 cm.; a^8, b^4, B-Z^8, Aa-Gg^8, Hh^4; xxiii, [1], 470, [2] p.

Notes: identical with the above except for the imprint; in some copies, four leaves of advertisement are added.

THJ 204A ESTC T151903

John Carter Brown Library

284 • THE | Great Chriftian Doctrine | OF | *ORIGINAL SIN* | DEFENDED; | Evidences of its *Truth* produced, | AND | Arguments to the *Contrary* anfwered. | Containing, in particular, | A Reply to the Objections and Arguings of Dr. | JOHN TAYLOR, in his Book, Intitled, "The | "Scripture-Doctrine of *Original Sin* propofed | "to free and candid Examination, *&c.* | [rule] | By the late Reverend and Learned | JONATHAN EDWARDS, A. M. | Prefident of the College of *New-Jerfey*. | [rule] | MATTH. ix. 12. *They that be whole, need not a Phyfician; but* | *they that are fick.* | — Et hæc non tantum ad

Peccatores referenda eſt; quia in omni- | bus Maledictionibus primi Hominis, omnes ejus Generationes | conveniunt.—— R. SAL. JARCHI. | Propter Concupiſcentiam, innatam Cordi humano, dicitur, In | Iniquitate genitus ſum; atque Senſus eſt, quod à Nativitate | implantatum ſit Cordi humano *Jetzer harang*, Figmentum | malum.—— ABEN-EZRA. | —— Ad Mores Natura recurrit | damnatos, fixa & mutari neſcia.— | ——Dociles imitandis | turpibus et pravis omnes ſumus.—— JUV. | [double rule] | GLASGOW: | Printed by ROBERT URIE. M DCC LXVIII. *stet* Examination, &c.

12mo.; 16.7 x 9.9 cm.; $[A]^{12}$, $B\text{-}T^{12}$, U^{6}, X^{2}; xxiv, 447, [1] p.

Contents: p. [i]: title (verso blank); p. [iii]: A brief Account of the BOOK, | and its AUTHOR.; p. xv: The | *Author*'s PREFACE. [dated] *Stockbridge*, May 26. 1757.; p. xviii: *ADVERTISEMENT.*; p. xix: THE | CONTENTS.; p. [1]: The great Chriſtian Doctrine of | *ORIGINAL SIN* | Defended.; p. [448]: blank.

THJ 205 ESTC T78821 NUC NE0046604 OCLC 45063302

Beinecke Library

284A • DUBLIN: | Printed for ROBERT JOHNSTON, Bookſeller in | *Bridge-ſtreet, Belfaſt.* MDCCLXVIII.

12mo.; 16.7 x 9.9 cm.; $[A]^{12}$, $B\text{-}T^{12}$, U^{6}, X^{2}; xxiv, 447, [1] p.

Notes: identical with the above except for the imprint.

THJ 205A ESTC T133884 NUC NE0046603 OCLC 43639585

Houghton Library

284B • GLASGOW: | Printed for JAMES MEUROS, Bookſeller in Kilmarnock. | MDCCLXXII.

12mo.; 16.7 x 9.9 cm.; $[A]^{12}$, $B\text{-}T^{12}$, U^{6}, X^{2}; xxiv, 447, [1] p.

Notes: identical with the above except for the imprint.

OCLC 33237341

Midwestern Baptist Theological Seminary

285 • THE | Great CHRISTIAN DOCTRINE | OF | ORIGINAL SIN | DEFENDED; | Evidences of its *Truth* Produced. | AND | Arguments to the *Contrary* Anſwered. | CONTAINING, IN PARTICULAR, | A REPLY to the Objections and Argu- | ings of Dr. *John Taylor*, (and others) in his Book, in- | tituled, "The Scripture-Doctrine of *Original Sin* pro- | "poſed to free and candid Examination," &c. | [rule] | By the late Reverend and Learned | JONATHAN EDWARDS, A. M. | Preſident of the College of *New-Jerſey*. | [rule] | MATT. ix. 12. *They that be whole, need not a Phyſician; but* | *they that are ſick.* | —Et hæc non tantum ad Peccatores referenda eſt; quia in | omnibus Maledictionibus primi Hominis, omnes ejus Ge- | nerationes conveniunt.--- R. SAL. JARCHI. | Propter Concupiſcentiam, innatam Cordi humano, dicitur, | In Iniquitate genitus ſum; atque Senſus eſt, quod à Na- | tivitate implantatum ſit Cordi humano *Jetzer harang*, Fig- | mentum malum.--- EBEN-EZRA. | ——Ad Mores Natura recurrit | damnatos, fixa et mutari neſcia.- | ——Dociles imitandis | turpibus et pravis omnes ſumus.--- JUV. | [double rule] | *WILMINGTON*, | Printed, and Sold by JAMES ADAMS, in Market-ſtreet. | [short rule] | M,DCC,LXXI. *stet* EBEN-EZRA

8vo.; 17.6 x 10.2 cm.; $[A]^{8}$, $B\text{-}T^{8}$, $U\text{-}Z^{4}$, $Aa\text{-}Cc^{4}$; xv, [1], 341, [3] p.

Notes: pp. 173-174 misnumbered 273-274 (pp. 1-173, 273-274, 175-335).

Contents: p. [i]: title (verso blank); p. iii: A | BRIEF ACCOUNT | OF | The BOOK and its AUTHOR.; p. xii: THE | AUTHOR'S PREFACE. [dated] *Stockbridge, May* 26. 1757.; p. xv: *Advertiſement.*; p. [xvi]: blank; p. 1: THE | Great CHRISTIAN DOCTRINE | OF | ORIGINAL SIN | DEFENDED &c.; p. [336]: blank; p. 337: CONTENTS.; pp. [342-344]: blank.

THJ 206 EAI 1:12032 NUC NE0046605 OCLC 2025625
Forbes Library

286 • THE GREAT | CHRISTIAN DOCTRINE | OF | *ORIGINAL SIN* | DEFENDED; | EVIDENCES OF ITS TRUTH PRODUCED, | AND | ARGUMENTS TO THE CONTRARY ANSWERED. | CONTAINING IN PARTICULAR, | A REPLY to the Objections and Arguings of Dr. | JOHN TAYLOR, in his Book, intitled, "The | "Scripture Doctrine of *Original Sin* propofed | "to free and candid Examination," &c. | [rule] | By the Late Reverend and Learned | JONATHAN EDWARDS, A. M. | Prefident of the College of NEW JERSEY. | [short tapered rule] | FOURTH EDITION. | RECOMMENDED BY THE REV. C. DE COETLOGON. | [short tapered rule] | *They that be whole, need not a Phyfician; but* | *they that are fick.* | Matth. ix. 12. | —Et hæc non tantum ad Peccatores referenda eft; quia in omnibus | Maledictionibus primi Hominis, omnes ejus Generationes conveniunt. | R. SAL. JARCHI. | Propter Concupifcentiam, innatam Cordi humano, dicitur, In Iniquitate | genitus fum; atque Senfus eft, quod a Nativitate | implantatum fit Cordi humano *Jetzer harang*, Figmentum malum. ABEN-EZRA. | —Ad Mores Natura recurrit | damnatos, fixa et mutari nefcia.— | —Dociles imitandis | turpibus et pravis omnes fumus.— JUV. | [thin-thick rule] | *BOSTON, NEW-ENGLAND*, PRINTED; | *LONDON*, REPRINTED BY R. NOBLE, 36, NOBLE-STREET, | For J. MURGATROYD, No. 73, *Chifwell-Street, Moorfields.* | Sold alfo by Mr. BINNS, *Leeds.* M.DCC.LXXXIX.

8vo.; 22.2 x 13.8 cm. (uncut); $[a]^8$, b^4, c^2, B-Z^8, Aa-Ee^8, Ff^2; xxviii, 436 p.

Contents: p. [i]: title (verso blank); p. [iii]: *To the Editor of* EDWARDS'S Great | Chriftian Doctrine, &c. [signed] C. E. DE COETLOGON | LOWER GROSVENOR PLACE.; p. [v]: A BRIEF | ACCOUNT | OF THE | BOOK AND ITS AUTHOR.; p. [xvi]: blank; p. [xvii]: THE AUTHOR's | PREFACE. [dated] *Stockbridge, May* 26, 1757; p. [xxii]: [advertisement]; p. [xxiii]: THE | CONTENTS.; p. [1]: THE GREAT | CHRISTIAN DOCTRINE | OF | *ORIGINAL SIN* | DEFENDED.

THJ 207 ESTC T78822 NUC NE0046606 OCLC 17828411
Library of Congress

287 • DE | *LEER* | DER | ERFZONDE | *VERDEEDIGD.* | DOOR | JONATHAN EDWARDS, | *Profesfor en Predikant, te* NORTHAMPTON, | in NOORD-AMERIKA. | [short rule] | VERTAALD EN UITGEGEEVEN DOOR | MARINUS VAN WERKHOVEN, | MET EENE AANPRIJZENDE | VOORREDE | VAN DEN | WELEERWAARDIGEN ZEERGELEERDEN HEERE | JOH. CONR. APPELIUS, | *Predikant te* ZUIDBROEK en MUNTENDAM. | [short rule] | EERSTE STUK. | [short, three-part thick-thin rule] | *Te AMSTERDAM*, | BIJ MARTINUS DE BRUYN, | In de Warmoesftraat, het zesde Huis van de | Vischfteeg, Noordzijde. | M D C C X C.

8vo.; 22.7 x 13.5 cm.; π^1, $*^8$, $**^8$, $***^2$, A-P^8, Q^2, $[R]^1$; [2], xxxvi, 244, [2] p.

Notes: a Dutch translation of the first part of *Original Sin*; two years later the same publishers issued a complete text (see 288); front matter pagination in capital roman numerals; last leaf cut below the printed text, indicating a spine label, not a colophon.

Contents: prp. [1]: title; prp. [2]: Onderzocht en goedgekeurd, door | de E. Clasfis van *Schieland*, den | 20 van *Grasmaand*, 1790.; p. [i]: VOORREDE [signed] JOH. CONR. APPELIUS. | *Pred. te Zuidbroek en* | *Muntendam.* | ZUIDBROEK | *den 27 Augustus*, | 1789.; pp. [1]-244: text; p. [245]: J. EDWARDS, | OVER DE | ERFZONDE. | I. STUK. [. . .]; p. [246]: blank.

THJ 208 NUC NE0046703
Huntington Library

288 • DE | LEER | DER | ERFZONDE | *VERDEEDIGD.* | DOOR | JONATHAN EDWARDS, |

Profesfor en Predikant, te NORTHAMPTON, | in NOORD-AMERIKA. | [short rule] | VERTAALD EN UITGEGEEVEN DOOR | MARINUS VAN WERKHOVEN, | MET EENE AANPRIJZENDE | *VOORREDE* | VAN DEN | WELEERWAARDIGEN ZEERGELEERDEN HEERE | JOH. CONR. APPELIUS, | *Predikant te* ZUIDBROEK en MUNTENDAM. | [short, three-part thick-thin rule] | *Te AMSTERDAM,* | BIJ MARTINUS DE BRUYN, | In de Warmoesftraat, het zesde Huis van de | Vischfteeg, Noordzijde. | M D C C X C I I.

8vo.; 20.3 x 12.5 cm.; π[1], *[7], **[8], ***[2], ****[4], A-P[8], Q[2], R-Z[8], Aa-Ii[8], Kk[7], Ll-Xx[8]; [2], xliv, 689, [1] p.

Notes: a Dutch translation of *Original Sin*; front matter pagination in capital roman numerals.

Contents: prp. [1]: title; prp. [2]: Onderzocht en goedgekeurd, door | de E. Clasfis van *Schieland*, den | 12 van *Slagtmaand*, 1792.; p. [i]: VOORREDE [signed] JOH. CONR. APPELIUS. | *Pred. te Zuidbroek en* | *Muntendam.* | ZUIDBROEK | *den 27 Augustus*, | 1789.; p. XXIX: VOORREDE | DES | *SCHRIJVERS.*; p. XXXVII: INHOUD.; pp. [1]-689: text; p. [670]: blank.

NUC NE0046703 OCLC 15718460
Calvin College and Theological Seminary

289 • THE GREAT | CHRISTIAN DOCTRINE | OF | *ORIGINAL SIN* | DEFENDED; | EVIDENCES OF ITS TRUTH PRODUCED, | AND | ARGUMENTS TO THE CONTRARY ANSWERED. | Containing, in particular, | A REPLY to the Objections and Arguings of Dr JOHN TAY- | LOR, in his Book, intitled, "The Scripture-Doctrine of | "*Original Sin* propofed to free and candid Examination," &c. | [rule] | By the Late Reverend and Learned | JONATHAN EDWARDS, A. M. | Prefident of the College of NEW JERSEY. | [rule] | A NEW EDITION. | [rule] | *They that be whole need not a Phyfician, but they that are fick.* Mat. ix. 12. | —Et hæc non tantum ad Peccatores referenda eft; quia in | omnibus Maledictionibus primi Hominis, omnes ejus Genera- | tiones conveniunt. R. SAL. JARCHI. | Propter Concupifcentiam, innatam Cordi humano, dicitur, | In Iniquitate genitus fum; atque Senfus eft, quod a Nativitate | implantatum fit Cordi humano *Jetzer Harang*, Figmentum ma- | lum. ABEN-EZRA. | —Ad Mores Natura recurrit | damnatos, fixa et mutari nefcia.— | —Dociles imitandis | turpibus et pravis omnes fumus.— JUV. | [short tapered rule] | *EDINBURGH:* | PRINTED and SOLD by MURRAY and COCHRANE. | [short double rule] | 1798.

12mo.; 17.2 x 10.1 cm.; [a][4], b[6], B[6], B-Z[6], Aa-Nn[6], Oo[2]; xx, 436, [2] p.

Notes: sig. B[6] repeated; pp. x and xiv repeated as pp. [x] and [xiv]; lacks pp. xii and xvi (pp. [i]-x, [x], xi, xiii-xiv, [xiv], xv, xvii-xx).

Contents: p. [i]: title (verso blank); p. [iii]: A BRIEF | ACCOUNT | OF THE | BOOK AND ITS AUTHOR.; p. [x]: THE AUTHOR's | PREFACE. [dated] *Stockbridge, May* 26. 1757.; p. [xiv]: THE | CONTENTS.; p. [1]: THE GREAT | CHRISTIAN DOCTRINE | OF | ORIGINAL SIN | DEFENDED.; pp. [437-438]: [advertisement].

THJ 209 ESTC T78823 NUC NE0046607 OCLC 6884248
Houghton Library

290 THE | *DOCTRINE* | OF | ORIGINAL SIN | DEFENDED; | EVIDENCES OF ITS TRUTH PRODUCED, | AND | ARGUMENTS TO THE CONTRARY ANSWERED. | CONTAINING IN PARTICULAR, | A REPLY TO THE OBJECTIONS AND ARGUINGS OF DR. JOHN | TAYLOR, IN HIS BOOK, INTITLED, "THE SCRIPTURE | DOCTRINE OF ORIGINAL SIN PROPOSED TO FREE | AND CANDID EXAMINATION," &C. | [short decorative rule] | By the late Reverend and Learned | JONATHAN EDWARDS, A. M. | *President of the College in Newjersey* | [short decorative rule] | Matth. ix. 12. *They that be whole, need not a Physician; but they that are sick.* | Et hæc non tantum ad Peccatores referenda est; quia in omnibus Maledic- | tionibus primi Hominis, omnes ejus

Generationes conveniunt.... | R. SAL. JARCHI. | Propter Concupiscentiam, innatam Cordi humano, dicitur, In Iniquitate geni- | tus sum; atque Sensus est, quod a Nativitate implantatum sit Cordi hu- | mano *Jetzer harang* Figmentum malum.... ABEN EZRA. | ....Ad Mores Natura recurrit | Damnatos, fixa et mutari nescia.... | ....Dociles imitandis | Turpibus et pravis omnes sumus.... JUV. | [short thick-thin rule] | PUBLISHED AT WORCESTER, | BY ISAIAH THOMAS, JUN. | [short decorative rule] | *ISAAC STURTEVANT, PRINTER.*

8vo.; 20.6 x 12.4 cm.; $[A]^4$, B-W-Z^4, 2A-2W-$2X^4$, $2Y^2$; vii, [1], [9]-370, [2] p.

Notes: pp. 137-144 misnumbered 147-154 (pp. [9]-136, 147-154, 145-370); advertisement of forthcoming first American edition of Edwards's works, [signed] SAMUEL AUSTIN | WORCESTER, (Mass.) *November* 1, 1808.

Contents: frontispiece: [engraving] | *Drawn and Engraved by Abner Reed, from an original Portrait, in the possession of J. W. Edwards, Esq. Hartf*[d]. | Rev. JONATHAN EDWARDS, | *President of Nassau-Hall College,* | *NEWJERSEY.*; p. [i]: title (verso blank); p. [iii]: PREFACE. [dated] STOCKBRIDGE, MAY 26, 1757; p. [v]: CONTENTS.; p. [viii]: blank; p. [9]: DOCTRINE | OF | ORIGINAL SIN | DEFENDED.; p. [371: *Edwards's Works*.

THJ 210 EAI 2:14919 NUC NE0046542 OCLC 7289147

Harvard Divinity School

291 • THE GREAT | CHRISTIAN DOCTRINE | OF | ORIGINAL SIN, | *DEFENDED;* | Evidences of its Truth Produced, | AND | *Arguments to the Contrary Answered.* | [short decorative rule] | BY THE LATE REV. AND LEARNED | JONATHAN EDWARDS, A. M. | *President of the College of New Jersey.* | [wavy rule] | THEY THAT BE WHOLE NEED NOT A PHYSICIAN, BUT THEY | THAT ARE SICK. MAT. ix. 12 | [wavy rule] | A NEW EDITION. | [short thick-thin rule] | GLASGOW: | *Printed in the Concord Office, Bell Street,* | FOR JOHN WYLIE & CO. | OGLE, ALLARDYCE & THOMSON, EDINBURGH; AND OGLES, | DUNCAN & CO. LONDON | [short wavy rule] | 1819.

17.8 x 10.6 cm.; $[A]^6$, B-Z^6, Aa-Mm^6, Nn^3; 426 p.

Contents: p. [1]: title (verso blank); p. [3]: A BRIEF | ACCOUNT | OF THE | BOOK AND ITS AUTHOR; p. [14]: blank; p. [15]: THE | AUTHOR'S PREFACE. [dated] *Stockbridge,* | *26th May,* 1757. | [brace]; pp. [19]-419: text; p. 419: *Printed in the Concord Office*; p. [420]: blank; p. [421]: CONTENTS.

THJ 211 OCLC 17462357

Lancaster Theological Seminary

292 • EXTRACTS | FROM | A WORK BY THE | LEARNED AND CELEBRATED | PRESIDENT EDWARDS, | ON | *ORIGINAL SIN.* | [short thin-thick rule] | PHILADELPHIA: | JOHN W. ALLEN, PRINTER, 26, STRAWBERRY-STREET. | [short line of stops] | 1825.

20.3 x 12.8 cm.; $[A]^4$, B-F^4; 47, [1] p.

Contents: p. [1]: title; p. [2]: ADVERTISEMENT.; pp. [3]-47: text; p. [48]: blank.

THJ 212 NUC NE0046561 OCLC 1400609

American Antiquarian Society

293 • VIEWS | IN | THEOLOGY. | [short rule] | NO. III. | [short rule] | PRESIDENT EDWARDS' | DOCTRINE OF ORIGINAL SIN. | THE | DOCTRINE | OF | PHYSICAL DEPRAVITY. | [short decorative rule] | *NEW-YORK:* | PUBLISHED BY F. & R. LOCKWOOD, 154 BROADWAY. | C. S. Van Winkle, Printer, No. 2 Thames-street. | [short line of stops] | 1825.

22.4 x 13 cm.; $[1]^4$, 2-13^4; 104 p.

Notes: a series of quotations from *The Works of President Edwards* (Worcester, 1808), 6:129-490, in an answer to T. R., "Edwards's Views of Original Sin," *Christian Spectator* 6 (November 1824):567-575.

Contents: p. [1]: title (verso blank); p. [3]: VIEWS | IN | THEOLOGY.

THJ 213 NUC NE0046539 OCLC 11059064

Harvard Divinity School

294 • THE | GREAT CHRISTIAN DOCTRINE | OF | ORIGINAL SIN | DEFENDED; | EVIDENCES OF ITS TRUTH PRODUCED; | AND | ARGUMENTS TO THE CONTRARY ANSWERED: | CONTAINING, IN PARTICULAR, | A REPLY TO THE OBJECTIONS | OF | DR. JOHN TAYLOR, | IN HIS BOOK, ENTITLED | "THE SCRIPTURE DOCTRINE OF ORIGINAL SIN PROPOSED TO | FREE AND CANDID EXAMINATION, &c." | [short rule] | Matt. ix. 12. They that be whole, need not a Physician; but they that are sick. | –Et hæc non tantum ad Peccatores referenda est; quia in omnibus Maledictionibus primi Hominis, | omnes ejus Generationes conveniunt.– *R. Sal. Jarchi.* | Propter Concupiscentiam, Innatam Cordi humano, dicitur, In Iniquitate genitus sum; atque Sensus | est, quod a Nativitate implantatum Cordi sit humano *Jetzer harang*, Figmentum malum. | *Aben-Ezra.* | –Ad Mores Natura recurrit | Damnatos, fixa et mutari nescia.– | –Dociles imitandis | Turpibus et pravis omnes sumus.–*Juv.* | [short rule] | BY REV. JONATHAN EDWARDS, A. M. | President of Nassau Hall. | [short thick-thin rule] | NEW-YORK: | G. AND C. CARVILL, 108 BROADWAY. | 1828. *stet* Cordi sit humano

21.7 x 13.7 cm.; π^3, 2-36^4; [2], 283, [1] p.

Notes: p. 4 misnumbered 304 (pp. [1-3], 304, 5-283).

Contents: prp. [1]: title (verso blank); p. [1]: THE | GREAT CHRISTIAN DOCTRINE | OF | ORIGINAL SIN | DEFENDED; | EVIDENCES OF ITS TRUTH | PRODUCED, | AND | ARGUMENTS TO THE CONTRARY ANSWERED. | CONTAINING, IN PARTICULAR, | *A REPLY TO THE OBJECTIONS* | OF | DR. JOHN TAYLOR, | IN HIS BOOK, ENTITLED | "THE SCRIPTURE DOCTRINE OF ORIGINAL SIN PROPOSED TO | FREE AND CANDID EXAMINATION, &c." | [short thick-thin rule] | Matt. ix. 12. They that be whole, need not a Physician; but they that are sick. | –Et hæc non tantum ad Peccatores referenda est; quia in omnibus Maledictionibus primi Hominis, | omnes ejus Generationes conveniunt.– *R. Sal. Jarchi.* | Propter Concupiscentiam, Innatam Cordi humano, dicitur, In Iniquitate genitus sum; atque Sensus | est, quod a Nativitate implantatum Cordi sit humano [*sic*] *Jetzer harang*, Figmentum malum. | *Aben-Ezra.* | –Ad Mores Natura recurrit | Damnatos, fixa et mutari neſcia.– | –Dociles imitandis | Turpibus et pravis omnes sumus.–*Juv.* (verso blank); p. [3]: ADVERTISEMENT, | CONTAINING A | BRIEF ACCOUNT OF THIS BOOK AND ITS AUTHOR, | BY THE FIRST EDITOR.; p. [7]: THE AUTHOR'S PREFACE [dated] *Stockbridge, May* 26, 1757.; p. [9]: THE | GREAT CHRISTIAN DOCTRINE | OF | ORIGINAL SIN DEFENDED.; p. [284]: blank.

THJ 214 NUC NE0046608 OCLC 7143865

Lutheran Theological Seminary

295 • THE | GREAT CHRISTIAN DOCTRINE | OF | ORIGINAL SIN | DEFENDED; | EVIDENCES OF ITS TRUTH PRODUCED, | AND | ARGUMENTS TO THE CONTRARY ANSWERED. | [short rule] | BY THE LATE REV. AND LEARNED | JONATHAN EDWARDS, A.M. | PRESIDENT OF THE COLLEGE OF NEW JERSEY. | [short rule] | They that be whole need not a physician, but they that are sick.—MATT. ix. 12. | [short rule] | A NEW EDITION. | [short rule] | EDINBURGH: | PUBLISHED BY PETER BROWN. | MDCCCXXXVII.

19.1 x 11.7 cm. (uncut); π^4, A-Z^6, 2A-2B^6; vii, [1], 300 p.

Contents: p. [i]: title; p. [ii]: EDINBURGH: | BALFOUR & JACK, Printers, Niddry Street.; p. [iii]: CONTENTS.; p. [viii]: blank; p. [1]: THE | AUTHOR'S PREFACE. [dated] STOCKBRIDGE, | *26th May* 1757. | [brace]; p. [5]: THE GREAT | CHRISTIAN DOCTRINE | OF | ORIGINAL SIN | DEFENDED.; p. 300: EDINBURGH: | BALFOUR & JACK, Printers, Niddry Street.

THJ 215 NUC NE0046609 OCLC 16835660

University of Pennsylvania

296 • [within double rules] YR | ATHRAWIAETH FAWR GRISTIONOGOL | O | BECHOD GWREIDDIOL | YN CAEL EI HAMDDIFFYN, | PROFION O'I GWIRIONEDD YN CAEL EU DWYN YN | MLAEN, A RHESYMAU YN EI HERBYN | YN CAEL EU HATEB. | GAN JONATHAN EDWARDS, D.D. | CYFIEITHEDIG GAN Y | PARCH. DAVID HUGHES, B.A., |

TREDEGAR. | MATH. IX. 13. NID RHAID I'R RHAI IACH WRTH FEDDYG; OND I'R | RHAI CLEIFION. | [short rule] | CAERNARFON: | CYHOEDDWYD GAN H. HUMPHREYS, CASTLE SQUARE.

17.4 x 10.5 cm.; π^2, A-U-V^8, [X]^4; iv, 336, [8] p.

Notes: a Welsh translation of *Original Sin*; all pages are within double rules; published c. 1900.

Contents: p. [i]: title (verso blank); p. [iii]: RHAGYMADRODD. [dated] *Stockbridge, Mai* 26, 1757.; p. [1]: YR ATHRAWIAETH FAWR GRISTIONOGOL | O | BECHOD GWREIDDIOL | YN CAEL EI HAMDDIFFYN.; p. 336: H. HUMPHREYS, ARGRAFFYDD, CAERNARFON.; pp. [337-344]: [advertisement].

THJ 216 NE 0046452 OCLC 43639619

Harvard University

REMARKS ON THE ESSAYS

297 • REMARKS | ON THE | ESSAYS, | ON THE | PRINCIPLES of MORALITY, | AND | NATURAL RELIGION. | IN A | LETTER | To a Minifter of the CHURCH of SCOTLAND. | By the Reverend Mr. JONATHAN EDWARDS, | Prefident of the College of NEW JERSEY, and Author of | the late ENQUIRY into the MODERN NOTIONS of the | FREEDOM of WILL. | EDINBURGH: | Printed in the Year, M, DCC, LVIII. | Price Four-pence.

8vo.; 20.3 x 12.7 cm.; π^1, A^4, B^5; 19, [1] p.

Notes: p. 19 misnumbered 17 (pp. [3]-18, 17); in some copies, the error is corrected.

Contents: p. [1]: title (verso blank); pp. [3]-17: text; p. 17: [signed] J. EDWARDS | STOCKBRIDGE | JULY 25, 1757.; p. [20]: blank.

THJ 217 ESTC N26261 NUC NE0046752 OCLC 43856728

Library of Congress

298 • REMARKS | ON THE | ESSAYS | ON THE | PRINCIPLES OF MORALITY, | AND | NATURAL RELIGION. | IN A | LETTER | To a Minifter of the CHURCH of SCOTLAND. | By the Reverend | Mr. JONATHAN EDWARDS, | Prefident of the College of NEW JERSEY, and | Author of the late INQUIRY into the MODERN | NOTIONS of the FREEDOM of WILL. | [rule] | THIRD EDITION. | [thick-thin rule] | LONDON: | Printed for J. JOHNSON, N° 8, in Pater-nofter-Row. | [short rule] | M.DCC.LXVIII.

8vo.; 19.6 x 12.6 cm.; [A]^6, Ff^4; 20 p.

Notes: a reprint of the final pages of the publisher's 1768 issue of *Freedom of the Will*; see 262.

Contents: p. [1]: title (verso blank); pp. [3]-20: text; p. 20: [signed] J. EDWARDS | STOCKBRIDGE, *July* 25, 1757.

THJ 218 ESTC T78834

British Library

THE LIFE AND CHARACTER OF THE LATE REVEREND MR. JONATHAN EDWARDS

299 • THE | LIFE and CHARACTER | OF THE LATE REVEREND | Mr. *JONATHAN EDWARDS*, | PRESIDENT of the COLLEGE at NEW-JERSEY. | Together with a Number of his | SERMONS | ON | Various important | SUBJECTS. | [rule] | *BOSTON:* | Printed and Sold by S. KNEELAND, oppofite to the | Probate-Office in Queen-Street. | [short rule] | M, DCC, LXV.

8vo.; 18.3 x 11.4 cm.; π^1, [A]^4, B-G^8, H^5, A-M^8, N-Z^4; [10], 98, [8], 279, [1] p.

Notes: in some copies, p. 98, first count, misnumbered 97; Samuel Hopkins's *Life of Edwards* was issued separately (see 300), but his selection of eighteen sermons (or six titles) was not.

Contents: prp. [1]: title (verso blank); prp. [3]: THE | LIFE | OF THE | LATE REVEREND, LEARNED AND PIOUS | Mr. *JONATHAN EDWARDS*, | Some Time MINISTER of the Gofpel at *Northampton*, | in *New-England*, and then MISSIONARY to the | INDIANS at *Stockbridge*, and after that PRESIDENT | of NEW-JERSEY COLLEGE. | Who departed this Life at *Princeton*, *March* 22. | 1758. in the 55th. Year of his Age. | [rule] | "The fweet Remembrance of the Juft | "Shall flourifh when he fleeps in Duft. | PSAL. 112. 6. | [rule] | *BOSTON:* | Printed and Sold by S. KNEELAND, oppofite | the Probate-Office, in *Queen-Street.* | [short rule] | M,DCC,LXV. (verso blank); prp. [5]: The PREFACE. [dated] Auguft 20. 1764.; prp. [8]: The CONTENTS.; prp. [10]: ERRATA.; p. [1]: THE | LIFE | Of the Reverend | Mr. JONATHAN EDWARDS.; p. 88: *APPENDIX*, N° I. | Containing a brief ACCOUNT of Mrs. | ESTTER [*sic*] BURR, and fome Extracts of | LETTERS wrote by her.; p. 92: *APPENDIX*, N° II. | Containing a fhort Sketch of Mrs. EDWARDS'S | LIFE and CHARACTER.; prp. [1]: SERMONS | ON | Various important | SUBJECTS. | Being fome of the Remains of the late | Reverend and Learned | Mr. *JONATHAN EDWARDS*, | PRESIDENT of the COLLEGE at NEW-JERSEY. | [rule] | *BOSTON:* | Printed and Sold by S. KNEELAND, in Queen-Street. | M,DCC,LXV. (verso blank); prp. [3]: The PREFACE. [signed] April 25. 1765. | The Editor.; prp. [7]: The CONTENTS.; prp. [8]: ERRATA.; p. [1]: JESUS CHRIST gloriouflу ex- | alted above all Evil, in the | Work of Redemption. | [LECTURE *Auguft* 1738]; p. [24]: JOSEPH'S great Temptation, | and gracious Deliverance. | —— 1738.; p. [59]: Man's natural Blindnefs in the | Things of Religion. | [*February* 1740.]; p. [104]: Men Naturally GOD'S Enemies. | *Auguft*, 1736.; p. [165]: The Wifdom of GOD, as dif- | play'd in the Way of Salvation | by JESUS CHRIST, far fuperior | to the Wifdom of the Angels. | [*March* 1733.]; p. [253]: The true Chriftian's Life, a Journey | towards Heaven. | [*Sept.* 1733.]; p. [280]: blank.

THJ 219 EAI 1:9961 NUC NE0046712 OCLC 2339886
Massachusetts Historical Society

300 • THE | LIFE | OF THE | LATE REVEREND, LEARNED AND PIOUS | Mr. *JONATHAN EDWARDS*, | Some Time MINISTER of the Gofpel at *Northampton*, | in *New-England*, and then MISSIONARY to the | INDIANS at *Stockbridge*, and after that PRESIDENT | of NEW-JERSEY COLLEGE. | Who departed this Life at *Princeton*, *March* 22. | 1758. in the 55th. Year of his Age. | [rule] | "The fweet Remembrance of the Juft | "Shall flourifh when he fleeps in Duft. | PSAL. 112. 6. | [rule] | *BOSTON:* | Printed and Sold by S. KNEELAND, oppofite | the Probate-Office, in *Queen-Street.* | [short rule] | M,DCC,LXV.

8vo.; 18.3 x 11.4 cm.; $[A]^4$, $B\text{-}G^8$, H^1; [8], 98 p.

Contents: prp. [1]: title (verso blank); prp. [3]: The PREFACE. [dated] Auguft 20. 1764.; p. [6]: The CONTENTS.; prp. [8]: ERRATA.; p. [1]: THE | LIFE | Of the Reverend | Mr. JONATHAN EDWARDS.; p. 88: [mourning rule] | *APPENDIX*, N° I. | Containing a brief ACCOUNT of Mrs. | ESTTER [*sic*] BURR, and fome Extracts of | LETTERS wrote by her.; p. 92: [rule] | *APPENDIX*, N° II. | Containing a fhort Sketch of Mrs. EDWARDS'S | LIFE and CHARACTER.

EAI 1:10008 NUC NE0046772 OCLC 7432840
Massachusetts Historical Society

301 • THE | LIFE and CHARACTER | OF THE | LATE REVEREND, LEARNED, AND PIOUS | MR. JONATHAN EDWARDS, | PRESIDENT of the COLLEGE of NEW-JERSEY: | TOGETHER WITH | EXTRACTS from his PRIVATE WRITINGS and DIARY. | AND ALSO, EIGHTEEN | SELECT SERMONS | On Various Important Subjects. | [rule] | *The righteous ſhall be in everlaſting remembrance.* PSALM cxii. 6. | [rule] | [rule] | THE SECOND EDITION. | [rule] | GLASGOW: | PRINTED BY DAVID NIVEN; | For JAMES DUNCAN, Jun. Bookfeller, & Stationer, Saltmarket; | And fold by him and JOHN BROWN, Bookfeller in Dunce. | MDCCLXXXV.

4to.; 18.8 x 12.1 cm.; $[A]^4$, $B\text{-}Z^4$, $Aa\text{-}Zz^4$, $Aaa\text{-}Ccc^4$, Ddd^2, Eee^4, Fff^2; 408 p.

Notes: p. 224 misnumbered 242 (pp. [1]-223, 242, 245-408).

Contents: p. [1]: title (verso blank); p. [3]: The PREFACE. [dated] Auguft 20th. 1764.; p. [6]: The CONTENTS.; p. [8]: blank; p. [9]: THE | LIFE | OF THE REVEREND | Mr. JONATHAN EDWARDS.; p. 108: APPENDIX, N° I. |

Containing a brief ACCOUNT of Mrs. ESTHER | BURR, and fome Extracts of LETTERS wrote | by her.; p. 113: APPENDIX, N° II. | Containing a fhort Sketch of Mrs. EDWARDS' | LIFE and CHARACTER.; p. [120]: blank; p. [121]: SERMONS | ON | VARIOUS IMPORTANT | SUBJECTS. | Being fome of the Remains of the late | Reverend and Learned | Mr. JONATHAN EDWARDS, | PRESIDENT of the COLLEGE at NEW-JERSEY. | [short tapered rule] | GLASGOW: PRINTED BY DAVID NIVEN; | For JAMES DUNCAN, Junior, Bookfeller, Saltmarket. | MDCCLXXXV. (verso blank); p. [123]: The PREFACE. [signed] *April 25th, 1765.* | *The* EDITOR.; p. 127: JESUS CHRIST glorioufly exalted above | all Evil, in the Work of Redemption; p. 149: JOSEPH'S great Temptation, and | gracious Deliverance; p. 181: Man's natural Blindnefs in the Things | of Religion; p. [224]: Men naturally GOD's Enemies; p. 284: The Wifdom of GOD, as difplayed in the | Way of Salvation by JESUS CHRIST, | far fuperior to the Wifdom of the | Angels; p. 370: The true Chriftian's Life, a Journey | towards Heaven; p. [395]: CONTENTS.; p. [397]: Lift of Subfcribers.

THJ 220 ESTC T78854 NUC NE0046709 OCLC 13486862
Brown University

301A • [short tapered rule] | LONDON: | Printed for C. DILLY, in the Poultry. | MDCCLXXXV.

4to.; 18.8 x 12.6 cm.; [A]^4, B-Z^4, Aa-Zz^4, Aaa-Ccc^4, Ddd^2; 394, [2] p.

Notes: identical with the above except omits THE SECOND EDITION. and the list of subscribers.

THJ 220A ESTC N19178 NUC NE0046708 OCLC 23896002
John Carter Brown Library

302 • HET | LEEVEN | VAN DEN | Weleerwaarden en zeer Geleerden Herr | *JONATHAN EDWARDS.* | IN DESZELFS LEEVEN PRESIDENT VAN HET | COLLEGIE VAN NEW-JERSEY; | MET UITTREKZELS UIT ZIJNE BIJZONDERE | SCHRIFTEN EN DAGBOEK. | *NAA DEN TWEEDEN DRUK* | UIT HET ENGELSCH VERTAALD DOOR | ENGELBERT NOOTEBOOM. | [ornament] | *Te UTRECHT,* | Bij WILLEM VAN YZERWORST, | Academie Drukker, 1791.

8vo.; 21.2 x 12.2 cm.; *^{8}, A-O^8; xvi, 222, [2] p.

Notes: a Dutch translation of the *Life of Edwards*, it lacks Hopkins's selection of sermons; a Dutch translation of *The Wisdom of God* was published separately the same year (see 384).

Contents: p. [i]: title; p. [ii]: Zijn naam, beroemd door zijn bedrijven, | Zal eeuig in gedagtnis blijven. | PSALM CXII: 4. | De rechtvaardige zal in eeuwige gedagtenis zijn.; p. [iii]: *VOORREEDEN* [dated] Den 20ften Auguftus 1764.; p. xi: INHOUD; p. [1]: HET | LEEVEN | VAN DEN WELEERWAARDEN | HERR | *JONATHAN EDWARDS.*; p. [218]: BIJVOEGZEL (*).; p. [223]: HET | LEEVEN | VAN DEN | HEER | JONATHAN | EDWARDS. (repeated); p. [224]: blank.

THJ 221 OCLC 43639590
John Carter Brown Library

303 • THE | LIFE AND CHARACTER | OF THE LATE REVEREND, LEARNED, AND PIOUS | MR *JONATHAN EDWARDS,* | PRESIDENT OF THE COLLEGE OF NEW JERSEY. | TOGETHER WITH | Extracts from his Private Writings and Diary. | AND ALSO EIGHTEEN | SELECT SERMONS | ON VARIOUS IMPORTANT SUBJECTS. | [rule] | *The righteous ſhall be in everlaſting remembrance,* Pſal. cxii. 6. | [rule] | [ornament] | *EDINBURGH:* | Printed for and by ALEXANDER JARDINE, Back of | Gavin Loch's Land, Forrefter's Wynd. | [short rule] | 1799.

12mo.; 17.1 x 10.1 cm.; π^4, A-Z^6, Aa-Ii^6, Kk^2; viii, 388 p.

Notes: p. 379 misnumbered 399 (pp. [1]-378, 399, 380-388).

Contents: p. [i]: title (verso blank); p. [iii]: PREFACE. [dated] *Auguſt* 20, 1764.; p. [vi]: CONTENTS.; p. [1]: THE LIFE | OF THE REVEREND | *MR JONATHAN EDWARDS.*; p. 104: APPENDIX. | N° I. | *Containing a brief* ACCOUNT *of Mrs* ESTHER BURR, *and* | *ſome Extracts of* LETTERS *wrote by her.*; p. 109: N° II. | *Containing a ſhort Sketch of Mrs* EDWARDS's LIFE and | CHARACTER.; p. [117]: SERMONS | ON | VARIOUS IMPORTANT | SUBJECTS. | [short tapered rule] | BEING SOME OF THE REMAINS OF THE LATE REVEREND | AND LEARNED | *MR JONATHAN EDWARDS.* | PRESIDENT OF THE COLLEGE OF NEW JERSEY. | [thin-thick rule] | [short tapered rule] | *EDINBURGH:* | Printed for and by ALEXANDER JARDINE, Back of | Gavin Loch's Land, Forrefter's Wynd. | [short tapered rule] | 1799. (verso blank); p. [119]:

PREFACE. [signed] *April* 25. 1765. The EDITOR.; p. 121: JESUS CHRIST glorioufly exalted above all | Evil, in the Work of Redemption. | [LECTURE Auguft 1738.]; p. 143: JOSEPH'S great Temptation, and gracious | Deliverance. | —— 1738.; p. 175: Man's natural Blindnefs in the Things of | Religion. | [*February* 1740.]; p. 218: Men Naturally GOD'S Enemies. | Auguft, 1736.; p. 278: The Wifdom of GOD, as difplayed in the | Way of Salvation by JESUS CHRIST, far fu- | perior to the Wifdom of the Angels. | [March 1733.]; p. 364: The True Chriftian's Life, a Journey towards | Heaven. | [Sept. 1733.]; p. 388: Printed and Sold by ALEXANDER JARDINE, | Forrefter's Wynd, Edinburgh.

THJ 222 ESTC T78852 NUC NE0046710 OCLC 7608348

Harvard Divinity School

304 • THE | LIFE AND CHARACTER | OF THE LATE REVEREND, LEARNED, AND PIOUS | *Mr. JONATHAN EDWARDS,* | PRESIDENT OF THE COLLEGE OF NEW-JERSEY. | TOGETHER WITH | Extracts from his Private Writings & Diary. | AND ALSO SEVENTEEN | SELECT SERMONS | ON VARIOUS IMPORTANT SUBJECTS. | [wavy rule] | *The righteous ſhall be in everlaſting remembrance*, Pfal. cxii. 6. | [wavy rule] | [short tapered rule] | *NORTHAMPTON:* | Printed by ANDREW WRIGHT, For S. & E. BUTLER, | and Sold at their Book Store. | [short rule] | 1804.

12mo.; 16.6 x 10 cm.; [A][6], B-W-Z[6], Aa-Hh[6]; xi, [1], 372 p.

Contents: p. [i]: title (verso blank); p. [iii]: PREFACE. [dated] *Auguſt* 20. 1764.; p. [viii]: CONTENTS.; p. [xii]: blank; p. [1]: THE | LIFE | OF THE REVEREND | *Mr. JONATHAN EDWARDS.*; p. 93: APPENDIX. | No. I. | *Containing a brief* ACCOUNT *of Mrs* ESTHER | BURR, *and ſome Extracts of* LETTERS *wrote* | *by her.*; p. 98: APPENDIX. | No. II. | *Containing a ſhort Sketch of Mrs* EDWARDS'S LIFE | *and* CHARACTER.; p. 105: *FAREWELL SERMON*; p. [140]: blank; p. [141]: SERMONS | ON | VARIOUS IMPORTANT | SUBJECTS. | [short wavy rule] | BEING SOME OF THE REMAINS OF THE LATE REVER- | END AND LEARNED | *Mr JONATHAN EDWARDS.* | PRESIDENT OF THE COLLEGE OF NEW-JERSEY. | [wavy rule] | [ornament] | PRINTED at *NORTHAMPTON*, Maffachufetts, | By ANDREW WRIGHT.—*For S. & E. BUTLER.* | [short rule] | 1804. (verso blank); p. [143]: *PREFACE.* [signed] The EDITOR. | *April* 25. 1765.; p. 145: JOSEPH'S great Temptation and gracious | Deliverance. | —— 1738.; p. 176: Man's natural Blindnefs in the Things of | Religion. | [February 1740.]; p. 216: Men naturally God's Enemies. | Auguft 1736.; p. 271: The Wifdom of GOD, as difplayed in the | Way of Salvation by JESUS CHRIST, far | fuperior to the Wifdom of Angels. | [March 1733.]; p. 351: The True Chriftian's Life, a Journey tow- | ards Heaven. | [Sept. 1733.].

THJ 223 EAI 2:6499 NUC NE0046711 OCLC 5738062

Boston Public Library

305 • THE | LIFE | AND | EXPERIENCE | OF THE | Rev. JONATHAN EDWARDS, | LATE | *PRESIDENT* | OF | NEW JERSEY COLLEGE, | *In AMERICA.* | [double rule] | The Righteous shall be in everlasting Remembrance. | PSALM, CXII. 6. | [double rule] | *BRISTOL:* | Printed by J. YOUNG, for | THE BRISTOL RELIGIOUS TRACT SOCIETY, | At the Depository, No. 9, Christmas-Street. | [short rule] | No. IX. | [short rule] | PRICE 1½d. or 8s. per 100.

17.4 x 10.4 cm.; 16 p.

Notes: derived from Hopkins's *Life of Edwards*.

Contents: p. [1]: title; p. [2]: THE | *LIFE and EXPERIENCE of* | JONATHAN EDWARDS.; p. 16: TRACTS | [15 lines] | [rule] | Bristol: Printed by J. YOUNG, No. 9, Christmas-Street.

OCLC 16308643

Pitts Theological Library

306 • THE | LIFE | OF | PRESIDENT EDWARDS: | [short rule] | BY S. E. DWIGHT. | [short rule] | NEW YORK: | G. & C. & H. CARVILL. | 1830.

21.7 x 13.8 cm.; [1][4], 2-96[4]; 766, [2] p.

Notes: p. 233 misnumbered 237; p. 365 misnumbered 465 (pp. [9]-232, 237, 234-364, 465, 366-625).

Contents: frontispiece: [engraving] | Engraved by S. S. Jocelyn & S. B. Munson. | REV. JONA. EDWARDS.; p. [1]: title; p. [2]: [affidavit] | [signed] CHARLES A. INGERSOLL, Clerk of the District of Connecticut.; p. [3]:

ADVERTISEMENT.; p. [5]: CONTENTS.; p. [9]: LIFE | OF | PRESIDENT EDWARDS.; p. [626]: FAREWELL SERMON. (verso blank); p. [653]: APPENDIX. | [A.-G.: notes]; p. 664: H. | "THE MIND."; p. 702: I. | NOTES ON NATURAL SCIENCE.; p. 762: K. | FAMILY AND DESCENDENTS OF PRESIDENT EDWARDS.; p. 765: L. | CATALOGUE OF PRESIDENT EDWARDS' WORKS, HERETOFORE PUBLISHED.; pp. [767-768]: blank.

THJ 224 OCLC 2624082
American Antiquarian Society

307 • CHRISTIAN BIOGRAPHY. | [short rule] | LIFE OF THE | REV. JONATHAN EDWARDS, | *President of Princetown College, New Jersey.* | [short rule] | LONDON: | RELIGIOUS TRACT SOCIETY, | *Instituted* 1799. | SOLD AT THE DEPOSITORY, 56, PATERNOSTER ROW; | AND BY THE BOOKSELLERS. *stet Princetown*

14.2 x 8.4 cm.; 72 p.
Notes: published c. 1833; p. [3]: *Selected from Dr. Hopkins and Rev. S. E. Dwight.; in some copies, p. [2]: blank.
Contents: p. [1]: title; p. [2]: Printed by J. Rider, Little Britain, London.; p. [3]: LIFE OF THE | REV. JONATHAN EDWARDS, * [*sic*].
OCLC 43646773
Pittsburgh Theological Seminary

307A • LIFE OF THE | REV. JONATHAN EDWARDS.

13.8 x 8.8 cm.; $[A]^6$, $B\text{-}Z^6$, $2A\text{-}2N^6$; 144, 144, 72, 72 p.
Notes: separately paged, continuous signatures; p. [2]: London. J. Rider, Printer, 14, Bartholomew Close.
Contents: caption title; pp. [3]-72 [fourth count] in CHRISTIAN BIOGRAPHY. | [short rule] | CONTAINING | THE LIVES OF | REV. GEORGE WHITEFIELD, | REV. JOHN WESLEY, | REV. AUGUSTUS HERMANN FRANCKE, | REV. JONATHAN EDWARDS. | LONDON: | THE RELIGIOUS TRACT SOCIETY, | *Instituted* 1799. | SOLD AT THE DEPOSITORY, 56, PATERNOSTER ROW; | AND BY THE BOOKSELLERS.
OCLC 7585662
Princeton University

RUTH'S RESOLUTION

308 • *Ruth*'s RESOLUTION: | [rule] | A | DISCOURSE, | Delivered | By the late Reverend | JONATHAN EDWARDS, | Of *Northampton.* | [rule] | [ornament] | [rule] | HARTFORD: | Re-printed by THOMAS GREEN, at the Heart and | Crown, oppofite the Court-Houfe.

8vo.; 17.4 x 11.3 cm.; 16 p.
Notes: Thomas Green conducted his printing establishment in Hartford from 1764 to 1767.—THJ.
Contents: p. [1]: title; p. [2]: *Ruth's* Refolution.
THJ 225 EAI 1:8589 NUC NE0046759 OCLC 26457367
Forbes Library

SERMONS ON VARIOUS IMPORTANT SUBJECTS

309 • SERMONS | ON VARIOUS | IMPORTANT SUBJECTS. | BY | JONATHAN EDWARDS, A. M. | Paftor of the Church of CHRIST in *Northampton.* | [short tapered rule] | BOSTON, printed. | EDINBURGH: Reprinted for M. Gray. | MDCCLXXXV.

12mo.; 17.1 x 10.1 cm.; π^3, $A\text{-}Z^6$, $Aa\text{-}Ll^6$; [6], vi, [7]-408 p.
Notes: issued with the same title as the selection appended to Hopkins's *Life of Edwards* (1765), this compilation

Ruth's RESOLUTION:

A

DISCOURSE,

Delivered

By the late Reverend

JONATHAN EDWARDS,

Of *Northampton*.

HARTFORD:

Re-printed by THOMAS GREEN, at the Heart and Crown, oppofite the Court-Houfe.

Title page, *Ruth's Resolution* (c. 1765). Permission of the Forbes Library, Northampton.

includes those sermons in *Discourses on Various Important Subjects* (1738) and three others, *God Glorified*, *Sinners in the Hands of an Angry God*, and *Farewell Sermon*.

Contents: prp. [1]: title (verso blank); prp. [3]: CONTENTS.; prp. [5]: FIVE DISCOURSES | ON | Important Subjects, nearly Concerning the | great Affair of the Soul's Eternal Salvation, | viz. | I. Juftification by Faith alone. | II. Preffing into the Kingdom of GOD. | III. Ruth's Refolution. | IV. The Juftice of GOD in the Damnation of | Sinners. | V. The Excellency of JESUS CHRIST. | Delivered at Northampton, chiefly at the time of | the late wonderful pouring out of the Spirit of | God there. | Deut. iv. 9.—*Take heed to thyfelf, and keep thy foul diligently, | left thou forget the things which thine eyes have seen, and left they | depart from thy heart all the days of thy life.* (verso blank); p. [i]: *PREFACE.*; p. [7]: DISCOURSE I. | Juftification by Faith alone.; p. [147]: DISCOURSE II. | Preffing into the Kingdom of God.; p. [192]: DISCOURSE III. | Ruth's Refolution.; p. [212]: DISCOURSE IV. | The Juftice of God in the Damnation of Sinners.; p. [267]: DISCOURSE V. | The Excellency of Chrift.; p. [313]: GOD GLORIFIED IN THE WORK OF RE- | DEMPTION, BY THE GREATNESS OF | MAN's DEPENDANCE UPON HIM | IN THE WHOLE OF IT. | A SERMON. | Preached on the Public Lecture in BOSTON, | July 8. 1731. | And publifhed at the defire of feveral Minifters and | others in Bofton, who heard it. | Judges vii. 2. *Left Ifrael vaunt themfelves againft me, | faying, Mine own hand hath faved me.* | This was the firft piece publifhed by Mr EDWARDS.(verso blank); p. [315]: TO THE READER. [signed] T. PRINCE. | W. COOPER. | Bofton, Auguft | 17. 1731. | [brace]; p. [317]: DISCOURSE VI. | God Glorified in Man's Dependance.; p. [338]: DISCOURSE VII*. | Sinners in the Hands of an angry God.; p. [359]: A | FAREWELL SERMON | Preached at the firft Precinct in | *NORTHAMPTON*, | After the People's public Rejection of their Minifter, and re- | nouncing their Relation to him as Paftor of the Church there, | On June 22. 1750. | Occafioned by Difference of Sentiments, con- | cerning the requifite Qualifications of Mem- | bers of the Church in complete Standing. | Acts xx. 18. *Ye know, from the firft Day that I came into* Afia, | *after what manner I have been with you at all feafons.* | Verf. 20. *And how I kept back nothing that was profitable unto | you, but have fhewed you, and have taught you publicly, and from houfe to houfe.* | Ver. 26. 27. *Wherefore I take you to record this day, that I am pure from the blood of all men. For I have not fhunned to declare | unto you all the counfel of God.* | Gal. iv. 15. 16. *Where is then the bleffednefs you fpake of? For I | bear you record, that if it had been poffible, ye would have pluck- | ed out your own eyes, and have given them to me. Am I there- | fore become your enemy, becaufe I tell you the truth?* (verso blank); p. [361]: *PREFACE.*; p. [367]: DISCOURSE VIII. | A Farewell Sermon.; p. [404]: The RESULT of a Council of Nine Churches, | met at Northampton, June 22. 1750; with | a PROTEST againft the fame, by a Number | of the faid Council.

THJ 226 NUC NE0046773 ESTC T78836 OCLC 13619993
Boston Public Library

310 • SERMONS | ON VARIOUS | IMPORTANT SUBJECTS. | BY | JONATHAN EDWARDS, A. M. | Paftor of the Church of CHRIST in *Northampton*. | [short tapered rule] | *LONDON:* | PRINTED for the BOOKSELLERS | M,DCC,XCV

12mo.; 17.6 x 10.2 cm.; π^3, A-Z^6, Aa-Hh^6, [ii]^3; [6], [iv], [5]-377, [1] p.

Notes: p. iv misnumbered vi (pp. [i]-iii, vi).

Contents: prp. [1]: title (verso blank); prp. [3]: CONTENTS.; prp. [5]: FIVE DISCOURSES | ON | Important Subjects, nearly Concerning the great | Affair of the Soul's Eternal Salvation, viz. | I. Juftification by Faith alone. | II. Preffing into the Kingdom of GOD. | III. Ruth's Refolution. | IV. The Juftice of GOD in the Damnation | of Sin- | ners. | V. The Excellency of JESUS CHRIST. | Delivered at Northampton, chiefly at the time of the | late wonderful pouring out of the Spirit of God there. | Deu vi. 9. [*sic*]—*Take heed to thyfelf, and keep thy foul diligently, left thou for- | get the things which thine eyes have seen, and lest they depart from thy heart | all the days of thy life.* (verso blank); p. [i]: *PREFACE.*; p. [5]: Juftification by Faith alone; p. [132]: Preffing into the Kingdom of God; p. [173]: Ruth's Refolution; p. [192]: The Juftice of God in the Damnation of finners; p. [243]: The Excellency of Chrift; p. [286]: blank; p. [287]: GOD GLORIFIED IN THE WORK OF REDEM- | PTION, BY THE GREATNESS OF MAN's DEPEN- | DANCE UPON HIM IN THE WHOLE OF IT. | A SERMON. | Preached on the Public Lecture in BOSTON | July 8. 1731. | And publifhed at the defire of feveral Minifters and others | in Bofton, who heard it. | Judges vii. 2. *Left Ifrael vaunt themfelves againft me, faying | Mine own hand hath faved me.* | This was the firft piece publifhed by Mr EDWARDS.(verso blank); p. [289]: TO THE READER. [signed] T. PRINCE. | W. COOPER. | Bofton, Auguft | 17. 1731. | [brace]; p. [291]: God Glorified in Man's Dependance; p. [310]: Sinners in the Hands of an angry God; p. [330]: blank; p. [331]: A | FAREWELL SERMON | Preached at the firft Precinct in | *NORTHAMPTON*, | After the People's publick Rejection of their Minifter, and | renouncing their Relation to

Him as Paſtor of the Church | there, | On June 22. 1750. | Occaſioned by Difference of Sentiments, concern- | ing the requiſite Qualifications of Members of | the Church in complete Standing. | Acts xx. 18. *Ye know from the firſt Day that I came into* | Aſia *after what manner I have been with you, at all ſeaſons.* | Verſe 20. *And how I kept back nothing that was profitable* | *unto you, but have ſhewed you, and have taught you pub-* | *lickly, and from houſe to houſe.* | Ver. 26, 27. *Wherefore I take you to record this day, that I* | *am pure from the blood of all men: For I have not ſhun-* | *ned to declare unto you all the council of God.* | Gal. iv. 15. 16. *Where is then the bleſſedneſs ye ſpake of?* | *For I bear you record, that if it had been poſſible, ye would* | *have plucked out your own eyes, and have given them to* | *me. Am I therefore become your enemy, becauſe I tell* | *you the Truth?* (verso blank); p. [333]: *PREFACE.*; p. [338]: blank; p. [339]: A Farewell Sermon.; p. 373: The RESULT of a Counſel [*sic*] of Nine Churches | met at Northampton, June 22. 1750; with a | PROTEST againſt the ſame, by a Number of | the ſaid Counſel.; p. [378]: blank.

THJ 227 ESTC N24250 NUC NE0046774 OCLC 10829936

Andover Newton Theological School

TWO DISSERTATIONS

311 • TWO | DISSERTATIONS, | I. Concerning the END for which GOD created | the WORLD. | II. The Nature of TRUE VIRTUE. | [rule] | By the late REVEREND, LEARNED and PIOUS | *JONATHAN EDWARDS*, A. M. | PRESIDENT of the COLLEGE in NEW-JERSEY. | [rule] | [ornament] | [rule] | *BOSTON:* | Printed and Sold by S. KNEELAND, oppoſite to the | Probate-Office in Queen-Street. | [two horizontal braces] | M,DCC,LXV.

4to.; 18.5 x 12.1 cm.; [A]^4, B-Z^4, Aa-Bb^4; [2], iii, [3], 191, [1] p.

Notes: p. 103 misnumbered 203 (pp. [1]-102, 203, 104-191); in some copies, the error is corrected.

Contents: prp. [1]: title (verso blank); p. [i]: THE | PREFACE. [signed] July 12. | 1765. | [brace] | The Editor.; p. iii: ERRATA.; p. [iv]: The CONTENTS.; p. [vi]: blank; p. [1]: Concerning the END for which | GOD created the WORLD.; p. [116]: The Nature of true Virtue.; p. [192]: blank.

THJ 228 EAI 1:9962 NUC NE0046882 OCLC 10685864

Massachusetts Historical Society

312 • TWO | DISSERTATIONS | CONCERNING THE END FOR WHICH | GOD CREATED THE WORLD; | AND THE | NATURE OF TRUE VIRTUE. | [thick-thin rule] | BY THE LATE REVEREND, LEARNED, AND PIOUS, | JONATHAN EDWARDS, A. M. | PRESIDENT OF THE COLLEGE OF NEW-JERSEY. | [thin-thick rule] | EDINBURGH: | PRINTED BY WILLIAM DARLING; | FOR W. LAING, BOOKSELLER, EDINBURGH. | [short thick-thin rule] | MDCCLXXXVIII.

12mo.; 15.8 x 9.9 cm.; [a]^4, A-R^6, S^2; viii, 208 p.

Contents: p. [i]: title (verso blank); p. [iii]: THE | PREFACE. [signed] THE EDITOR.; p. vi: THE | CONTENTS.; p. viii: CONTENTS | OF THE | SECOND DISSERTATION.; p. [1]: Concerning the End for which GOD | created the World.; p. [125]: The Nature of true Virtue.

THJ 229 ESTC T78851 NE0046883 OCLC 4185875

Boston Public Library

313 • TWO | DISSERTATIONS, | I. CONCERNING THE END FOR WHICH GOD CREATED | THE WORLD. | II. THE NATURE OF TRUE VIRTUE. | BY | *The late Reverend, Learned and Pious* | *JONATHAN EDWARDS*, A. M. | *Preſident of the College in New-Jerſey.* | [short tapered rule] | *PHILADELPHIA:* | PRINTED AND SOLD BY *R. AITKEN & SON*, | N°. 22. MARKET STREET. | [short rule] | M.DCC.XCI.

12mo.; 16.2 x 9.8 cm.; π^4, A-R^6, S^2; [8], 206, [2] p.

Contents: prp. [1-2]: blank; prp. [3]: title (verso blank); prp. [5]: THE PREFACE. [signed] THE EDITOR.; prp. [7]: THE CONTENTS.; p. [1]: *Concerning the End for which God* | *created the World.*; p. [124]: The Nature of True Virtue.;

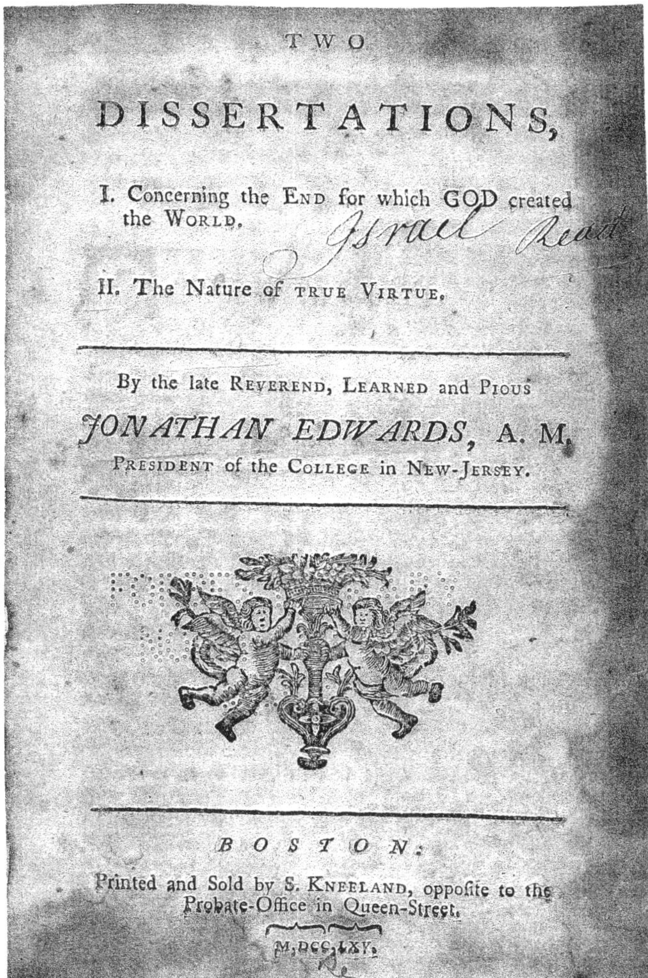

TWO

DISSERTATIONS,

I. Concerning the END for which GOD created the WORLD.

II. The Nature of TRUE VIRTUE.

By the late REVEREND, LEARNED and PIOUS

JONATHAN EDWARDS, A. M.

PRESIDENT of the COLLEGE in NEW-JERSEY.

BOSTON:

Printed and Sold by S. KNEELAND, oppoſite to the Probate-Office in Queen-Street.

M,DCC,LXV.

Title page, *Two Dissertations* (1765). Permission of the Forbes Library, Northampton.

pp. [207-208]: blank.
THJ 230 EAI 1:23345 NUC NE0046884 OCLC 4185914
Massachusetts Historical Society

THE JUSTICE OF GOD IN THE DAMNATION OF SINNERS

314 • THE JUSTICE OF GOD IN THE DAM- | NATION OF SINNERS. | [rule] | A | DISCOURSE | Delivered at Northampton, | AT THE | Time of the late wonderful Revi- | val of Religion there. | [rule] | By *Jonathan Edwards*, A.M. | Late Paſtor of the Church of CHRIST in *Northampton.* | [rule] | [double rule] | *BOSTON:* | Re-printed and Sold by J. KNEELAND, next to | the Treaſurer's Office, in Milk-Street. | MDCCLXXIII.

4to.; 19.8 x 12.3 cm. (uncut); $[A]^4$, B-H^4; 64 p.

Contents: p. [1]: Mr. *Edwards*'s | DISCOURSE, | On Romans III. 19. (verso blank); p. [3]: title (verso blank); p. [5]: The Juſtice of GOD in the | Damnation of Sinners.

THJ 236 EAI 1:12757 NUC NE0046694 OCLC 35911938
Harvard Divinity School

315 • *The Juſtice of God in the Damnation of Sinners,* | *explained, illuſtrated, and proved,* | IN A | SERMON | UPON | ROMANS III. 19. | By JONATHAN EDWARDS, A. M. | Late Preſident of NEW JERSEY College, NEW ENGLAND. | Reviſed and Corrected by C. DE COETLOGON, A. M. | Not *thus*, our infidels th' *Eternal* draw, | A God all o'er, conſummate, abſolute, | Full-orb'd, in his whole round of rays complete: | *They* ſet at odds Heav'n's jarring attributes; | And, with one excellence, another wound; | Maim Heav'n's perfection, break its equal beams, | Bid *Mercy* triumph over—God himſelf, | Undeify'd by their opprobrious praiſe: | A God *all mercy*, is a God *unjuſt*. YOUNG. | That to the height of this great argument | I may aſſert eternal Providence, | And juſtify the ways of God to man. MILTON. | BOSTON, PRINTED: LONDON, RE-PRINTED: | For J. BUCKLAND, Paternoſter-Row; VALLANCE and SIMMONS, No. 120, Cheapſide; and J. MATHEWS, Charing-Croſs. | MDCCLXXIV.

8vo.; 20.5 x 12.8 cm.; π^2, B-E^4; [4], 31, [1] p.

Contents: prp. [1]: title (verso blank); prp. [3]: ADVERTISEMENT. (verso blank); p. [1]: A | SERMON | ON ROMANS III. 19. | – THAT EVERY MOUTH MAY BE STOPPED.–; p. [32]: blank.

THJ 237 ESTC T78829 NUC NE0046695 OCLC 17557676
Boston Public Library

316 • *The Justice of God in the Damnation of Sinners,* | *explained, illustrated, and proved,* | IN A | SERMON | UPON | ROMANS III.19. | By JONATHAN EDWARDS, A. M. | Late PRESIDENT of NEW JERSEY College, NEW ENGLAND. | [rule] | A NEW EDITION. | [rule] | Revised and Corrected by C. DE COETLOGON, A. M. | Not *thus*, our Infidels th' *Eternal* draw, | A God all o'er, conſummate, abſolute, | Full-orb'd, in his whole round of rays complete: | *They* ſet at odds Heav'n's jarring attributes; | And, with one excellence, another wound; | Maim Heav'n's perfection, break its equal beams, | Bid *Mercy* triumph over—God himſelf, | Undeify'd by their opprobrious praiſe: | A God *all mercy*, is a God *unjuſt*. YOUNG. | That to the height of this great argument | I may aſſert eternal Providence, | And juſtify the ways of God to man. MILTON. | [thick-thin rule] | BOSTON, PRINTED: LONDON, RE-PRINTED: | FOR J. MATHEWS, No. 18, STRAND. | MDCCLXXXVIII. | [PRICE SIXPENCE.]

8vo.; 20.4 x 12.9 cm.; π^2, B-E^4, [F]^2; [4], 31, [5] p.

Notes: some copies lack the advertisement, pp. [33-36].

Contents: prp. [1]: title (verso blank); prp. [3]: ADVERTISEMENT. (verso blank); p. [1]: A | SERMON | ON | ROMANS III. 19. | – THAT EVERY MOUTH MAY BE STOPPED.–; p. [32]: blank.; pp. [33-36]: [advertisement].

THJ 238 ESTC N2777 NUC NE0046696 OCLC 6046324

Boston Public Library

317 • THE | JUSTICE OF GOD | IN THE | DAMNATION OF SINNERS. | A DISCOURSE | *DELIVERED AT NORTHAMPTON, AT THE TIME | OF THE REVIVAL OF RELIGION THERE, | IN THE YEAR* 1734. | [short rule] | BY JONATHAN EDWARDS, A. M. | Paſtor of the Church of Chriſt in Northampton, and afterwards | Preſident of Princeton College. | [short rule] | *HARTFORD:* | PRINTED BY JOHN BABCOCK. | [short rule] | 1799.

12mo.; 16.4 x 10.1 cm.; [A]^6, B-L^6; 132 p.

Notes: pp. 128-132 set in smaller type.

Contents: p. [1]: TWO | DISCOURSES, | PREACHED BY THE LATE | President Edwards. | [short rule] | *REPRINTED FOR THE USE OF THE TRUSTEES OF | THE MISSIONARY SOCIETY.* (verso blank); p. [3]: title (verso blank); p. [5]: THE | JUSTICE OF GOD | *IN THE* | Damnation of Sinners.; p. [78]: TRUE GRACE | *DISTINGUISHED FROM THE* | EXPERIENCE OF DEVILS.

THJ 239 EAI 1:35437 NUC NE0046698 OCLC 1314186

Massachusetts Historical Society

318 • *The JUSTICE of* GOD *in the DAMNA- | TION of SINNERS.* | ILLUSTRATED IN A | SERMON. | TO WHICH IS ADDED | A | *FAREWELL SERMON*; | BY JONATHAN EDWARDS, A. M. | Delivered at NORTHAMPTON, June 22d, 1750. | AFTRR THE PEOPLE'S PUBLIC REJECTION OF HIM | AS THEIR MINISTER, AND RENOUNCING THEIR | RELATION TO HIM AS PASTOR OF THE CHURCH. | [double rule] | PRINTED AT NORTHAMPTON, | BY DANIEL WRIGHT & Co. | *For SIMEON BUTLER. stet* AFTRR

12mo.; 13.3 x 8 cm.; [A]^{12}, B^6, C^{12}, D^6, E^{12}, F^6, G^{12}, H^6; 143, [1] p.

Notes: published c. 1800.

Contents: p. [1]: title (verso blank); p. [3]: SERMON I. | The Juſtice of God in the Damnation of | Sinners.; p. [83]: *PREFACE* | TO THE | *FAREWELL SERMON.*; p. [91]: *A* | *FAREWELL SERMON.*; p. [144]: [advertisement].

THJ 240 EAI 1:49067 NUC NE0046699 OCLC 5879353

Forbes Library

319 • THE | JUSTICE OF GOD | IN THE | *DAMNATION OF SINNERS;* | ILLUSTRATED | IN A | SERMON, | BY THE LATE | Rev. JONATHAN EDWARDS, | PRESIDENT OF THE COLLEGE OF NEW-JERSEY. | [short wavy rule] | RE-PUBLISHED | UNDER THE PATRONAGE OF THE | CENT SOCIETY, | IN NEWARK. | [short decorative rule] | NEWARK, N. J. | PRINTED BY JOHN TUTTLE & CO. | 1814.

19.8 x 11.7 cm. (uncut); [A]^6, B-D^6, E^4; 56 p.

Contents: p. [1]: title (verso blank); p. [3]: A SERMON. | THE JUSTICE OF GOD IN THE DAMNATION OF SINNERS.; p. 54: THE | SWEARER'S PRAYER, | OR, | HIS OATH EXPLAINED.

THJ 241 EAI 2:31395 NUC NE0046700 OCLC 43639586

Princeton University

320 • NO. 43. | THE JUSTICE OF GOD | DISPLAYED IN THE | ENDLESS PUNISHMENT OF THE WICKED. | BY PRESIDENT EDWARDS.

17.9 x 10.7 cm.; 10-11^6; 24 p.

Notes: front cover: DOCTRINAL TRACT. | [short rule] | NO. 43. | [short rule] | THE | JUSTICE OF GOD | DISPLAYED IN THE | ENDLESS PUNISHMENT OF THE WICKED. | BY PRESIDENT EDWARDS. | [short rule] | [short thick-thin rule] | PUBLISHED BY THE | AMERICAN DOCTRINAL TRACT SOCIETY. | PERKINS & MARVIN, AGENTS. | *Depository*, 114 *Washington Street, Boston.*

Contents: caption title; pp. [1]-24: text; p. 24: PUBLISHED BY THE AMERICAN DOCTRINAL TRACT SOCIETY.

THJ 242 NUC NE0046697 OCLC 10096589
Boston Public Library

320A • NO. 43. | THE | JUSTICE OF GOD | DISPLAYED IN THE | ENDLESS PUNISHMENT OF THE WICKED. | BY PRESIDENT EDWARDS.

17 x 11 cm.; 10-11^6; 24 p.

Notes: reprinted, *Doctrinal Tracts* (Boston: American Doctrinal Tract Society, 1837), so paged and signed, p. 10: VOL. III.

Contents: caption title; pp. [1]-24: text; p. 24: PUBLISHED BY THE AMERICAN DOCTRINAL TRACT SOCIETY.

THJ 242A OCLC 35313613
Pitts Theological Library

A HISTORY OF THE WORK OF REDEMPTION

321 • A | HISTORY | Of the WORK of | REDEMPTION. | CONTAINING, | The Outlines of a Body of Divinity, | In a Method entirely new. | By the late REVEREND | Mr JONATHAN EDWARDS, | Prefident of the College of New Jerfey. | EDINBURGH: | Printed for W. GRAY, Edinburgh, and J. BUCKLAND | and G. KEITH, London. | MDCCLXXIV.

8vo.; 20 x 12.6 cm.; [a]^4, b^2, A-Z^4, Aa-Zz^4, 3A^4, 3Bb^2; [2], xi, [1], 378, [2] p.

Notes: Jonathan Edwards, the younger (1745-1801), helped prepare the text and wrote the preface. There are two frequently reprinted advertisements variously placed. The first by John Erskine explains the nature of the text: THEY who have a relifh for the ftudy | of the fcriptures, and have accefs to | perufe the following fheets, will, I am per- | fuaded, deem themfelves much indebted to | the Reverend Mr Edwards of Newhaven | for confenting to publifh them. Though | the acute philofopher and deep divine ap- | pears in them, yet they are in the general | better calculated for the inftruction and im- | provement of ordinary Chriftians, than thofe | of Prefident Edwards's writings, where the | abftrufe nature of the fubject, or the fubtle | objections of oppofers of the truth, led him | to more abftract and metaphyfical reafon- | ings. The manufcript being intrufted to | my care, I have not prefumed to make any | change in the fentiments or compoftion. | I have, however, taken the liberty to reduce | it from the form of fermons, which it ori- | ginally bore, to that of a continued trea- | tife; and I have fo altered and diverfified | the marks of the feveral divifions and fub- | divifions, that each clafs of heads might be | eafily diftinguifhed. The second advertisement (unsigned) proposes future publication: THE late learned and ingenious Mr Ed- | wards left in MS. feveral hundred fer- | mons on doctrinal and practical fubjects, explications of above 500 texts of fcripture, | and effays on the truth and excellency of | the Chriftian religion, the harmony of the | Old and New Testament, the divinity of | Christ, the neceffity and reafonablenefs of | atonement and of the imputation of merit, | the eternity of hell-torments, the foreknow- | ledge of God, predeftination, univerfal and | particular redemption, efficacious grace, ju- | ftification, perfeverance, &c. Though he | had no defign to publifh thefe in the form | which he left them, yet, in the opinion | of good judges in America who have per- | ufed them, they contain a variety of new | and ftriking fentiments, on many import- | and difficult fubjects, which might | communicate to the Chriftian world much | ufeful inftruction. | When writers excel only in ftyle and com- | poftion, they can derive little honour, and | the public can reap fmall improvement, | from the printing their loofe unfinifhed pa- | pers; but important original thoughts, tho' | not accurately methodized, nor adorned | with the beauties of eloquence, well merit | being preferved from oblivion. If fo much | of the author's penetration and judgement | appear in the preceding fheets, written a- | bout twenty years before his death, much more may be expected from compofitions in

A

HISTORY

Of the WORK of

REDEMPTION.

CONTAINING,

The Outlines of a Body of Divinity,

In a Method entirely new.

By the late REVEREND

Mr JONATHAN EDWARDS,

President of the College of New Jersey.

EDINBURGH:

Printed for W. GRAY, Edinburgh, and J. BUCKLAND and G. KEITH, London.

MDCCLXXIV.

Title page, *A History of the Work of Redemption* (1774). Permission of the Forbes Library, Northampton.

| a period, when years, study, and expe- | reience, had greatly increafed his ftock of | knowledge. Whether the publifher fhall | favour the world with any more of thefe | valuable remains, will probably in a good | meafure depend on the encouragement this | work meets with.

Contents: p. [i]: title (verso blank); p. [iii]: PREFACE. [signed] *Newhaven, Feb.* 25. | 1773. | Jonathan Edwards.; p. [vi]: ADVERTISEMENT. | [signed] *Edinburgh, April* 29. | 1774. | JOHN ERSKINE. | [5 lines: errata]; p. [vii]: CONTENTS.; p. [xii]: blank; p. [1]: A | HISTORY | Of the WORK of | REDEMPTION.; p. [379]: ADVERTISEMENT.

THJ 243 ESTC T72105 NUC NE0046626 OCLC 5144875

Boston Public Library

322 • GESCHIEDENIS | VAN HET | WERK DER VERLOSSING: | BEHELZENDE | *De Schetszen van een ZAMENSTEL van* | GODGELEERDHEID, | *In een geheel nieuwe orde*; | DOOR | Wylen den Wel-Eerwaarden en zeer geleer- | den HEER, | JONATHAN EDWARDS, | Prefident van het College van *New-Jerfey.* | *Uit het Engelfch vertaald;* | DOOR | ENGELBERT NOOTEBOOM. | Eerfte Stuk. | [decorative rule] | *TE UTRECHT.* | By ABRAHAM van PADDENBURG, | Academie Drukker en Boekverkooper. | MDCCLXXVI.

8vo.; 19.9 x 12.3 cm.; $*^8$, A-Z^8, Aa^8, Bb^6, Cc-Vv^8; [16], 1-391, [5], 393-680 p.

Notes: a Dutch translation of *History of Redemption*, in two volumes bound as one; pp. 183, 206, 271, 282-283, 284, 285, 287, 401, and 453 misnumbered 383, 174, 272, 182-183, 294, 185, 187, 411, and 353 (pp. 1-182, 383, 184-205, 174, 207-270, 272, 272-281, 182-183, 294, 185, 286, 187, 288-400, 411, 402-452, 353, 454-680); sig. Pp_3 mislettered Oo_3.

Contents: prp. [1]: title; prp. [2]: Uytgegeeven na voorgaande Onderzoek en | met Goedkeuring van de Wel-Eerw: | Claffis van Utrecht, 't welk wy getuygen | PAULUS RUTGERS, Pred. Te Utrecht. | *Cl. Ultraj. Deputatus* | JOHANNES THIELEN, Pred. Te Vleuten. | *Cl. Ultraj. Deputatus* | CORNELIS JAN VAN SEYST, Pred. Te Wilnis. | *Cl. Ultraj. Deputatus.* | UTRECHT | 5 *Decemb.* 1776.; prp. [3]: VOORREDEN. [signed] JONATHAN EDWARDS | NEWHAVEN | 25. *February* | 1773; prp. [7]: BERICHT. [signed] JOHN ERSKINE | EDINBURGH | 29. *April* | 1774; prp. [9]: INHOUD.; p. [1]: GESCHIEDENIS | VAN HET | WERK DER | VERLOSSING.; p. [392]: DRUKFEILEN.; prp. [1]: blank; p. [2]: [advertisement]; prp. [3]: GESCHIEDENIS | VAN HET | WERK DER VERLOSSING: | BEHELZENDE | *De Schetszen van een ZAMENSTEL van* | GODGELEERDHEID, | *In een geheel nieuwe orde*; | DOOR | Wylen den Wel-Eerwaarden en zeer geleer- | den HEER, | JONATHAN EDWARDS, | Prefident van het College van *New-Jerfey.* | *Uit het Engelfch vertaald;* | DOOR | ENGELBERT NOOTEBOOM. | Tweede Stuk. | [decorative rule] | *TE UTRECHT.* | By ABRAHAM van PADDENBURG, | Academie Drukker en Boekverkooper. | MDCCLXXVII.; prp. [4]: Uytgegeeven na voorgaande Onderzoek en | met Goedkeuring van de Wel-Eerw: | Claffis van Utrecht, 't welk wy getuygen | PAULUS RUTGERS, Pred. Te Utrecht. | *Cl. Ultraj. Deputatus* | JOHANNAS THIELEN, Pred. Te Vleuten. | *Cl. Ultraj. Deputatus* | CORNELIS JAN VAN SEYST, Pred. Te Wilnis. | *Cl. Ultraj. Deputatus.* | UTRECHT | 5 *Decemb.* 1776.; p. 393: GESCHIEDENIS | VAN HET | WERK DER | VERLOSSING.

THJ 244 NUC NE0046593 OCLC 15718708

Harvard Divinity School

323 • A | HISTORY | Of the WORK of | REDEMPTION. | CONTAINING, | The Outlines of a Body of Divinity, | In a Method entirely new. | [rule] | By the late REVEREND | Mr. JONATHAN EDWARDS, | Prefident of the College of *New Jerfey* | [thick-thin rule] | EDINBURGH PRINTED: | BOSTON: Re-printed by DRAPER & FOLSOM, | near the Market. | M.DCCLXXXII.

8vo.; 21.4 x 12.3 cm.; π^6, A-Z^4, Aa-Nn^4, Oo^2; viii [i.e., ix], 6-296 [i.e., 298], [2] p.

Notes: p. [vi] repeated (pp. [i-vi, vi-viii]); pp. 151-152 repeated; p. 249 misnumbered 246; p. 292 misnumbered 262 (pp. [6]-152, 151-248, 246, 250-291, 262, 293-296).

Contents: p. [i]: title (verso blank); p. [iii]: PREFACE. [signed] *Newhaven, Feb.* 25 | 1773. | JONATHAN EDWARDS.; p. [vi]: ADVERTISEMENT. [signed] *Edinburgh, April* 29. | 1774. JOHN ERSKINE.; p. [vi] (repeated): CONTENTS.; p. [6]: A | HISTORY | Of the WORK of | REDEMPTION.; p. 296: ERRATA.; p. [297]: ADVERTISEMENT. (verso blank).

THJ 245 EAI 1:17525 NUC NE0046629 OCLC 67222388

Congregational Library

324 • A | HISTORY | OF THE WORK OF | REDEMPTION. | CONTAINING | The Outlines of a Body of Divinity, | In a Method entirely new. | [rule] | By the late REVEREND | MR. JONATHAN EDWARDS, | Prefident of the College of New-Jerfey. | [thin-thick rule] | *NEW-YORK:* | Printed by SHEPARD KOLLOCK, for ROBERT | HODGE, *No.* 38, *Maiden-Lane.* | M,DCC,LXXXVI.

8vo.; 20 x 11.6 cm.; [a]^4, b-c^4, c_5, A-Z^4, Aa-Zz^4, 3A^4, 3Bb^2; xxiv, [2], [25]-402, [2] p.

Notes: p. 315 misnumbered 215 (pp. [25]-314, 215, 316-402); some copies lack an additional leaf SUBSCRIBERS NAMES OMITTED; in others, pp. xvii-xxiv are reset, the final page containing thirty-three rather than nine subscribers.

Contents: p. [i]: title (verso blank); p. [iii]: PREFACE. [signed] JONATHAN EDWARDS. | *New-Haven, Feb.* 25, 1773.; p. [vi]: ADVERTISEMENT. [signed] JOHN ERSKINE. | *Edinburgh, April* 29, 1774.; p. [vii]: CONTENTS.; p. [xii]: blank; p. [xiii]: SUBSCRIBERS NAMES.; p. [xxv]: SUBSCRIBERS NAMES OMITTED. (verso blank); p. [25]: A | HISTORY | OF THE WORK OF | REDEMPTION.; pp. [403-404]: [advertisement].

THJ 246 EAI 1:19616 NUC NE0046630 OCLC 5839739

Houghton Library

325 • A | HISTORY | Of the WORK of | REDEMPTION. | CONTAINING, | THE | OUTLINES OF A BODY OF DIVINITY, | In a Method entirely new. | By the late REVEREND | Mr JONATHAN EDWARDS, | Prefident of the College of New Jerfey. | [short tapered rule] | EDINBURGH: | Printed for M. GRAY, Edinburgh;–and | J. BUCKLAND and T. VERNOR, London. | MDCCLXXXVIII

12mo.; 17.3 x 10.2 cm.; π^1, a^6, A-Z^6, Aa-Nn^6, Oo^2; [2], xii, 434, [2] p.

Contents: prp. [1]: title (verso blank); p. [i]: ADVERTISEMENT.; p. [iii]: PREFACE. [signed] *Newhaven, Feb* [*sic*] 25. | 1773. | JONATHAN EDWARDS.; p. [vii]: ADVERTISEMENT. [signed] *Edinburgh, April* 29. | 1774. | JOHN ERSKINE.; p. [viii]: CONTENTS.; p. [1]: A | HISTORY | of the WORK of | REDEMPTION.; pp. [435-436]: [advertisement].

THJ 247 ESTC N7916 NUC NE0046631 OCLC 6722393

Princeton University

326 • A | HISTORY | Of the WORK of | REDEMPTION. | CONTAINING, | THE | OUTLINES OF A BODY OF DIVINITY, | In a Method entirely new. | By the late REVEREND | Mr JONATHAN EDWARDS, | Prefident of the College of New Jerfey. | [short tapered rule] | EDINBURGH: | Printed for M. GRAY, Edinburgh;—and | J. BUCKLAND and T. VERNOR, London. | MDCCLXXXVIII.

8vo.; 20.7 x 12.3 cm.; a^4, b^2, A-Z^4, Aa-Zz^4, 3A-3C^4, 3D^2; xii, 395, [1] p.

Notes: although their title pages are identical but for the rule, this issue differs from that above in size, signatures, and pagination.

Contents: p. [i]: title (verso blank); p. [iii]: ADVERTISEMENT.; p. [v]: PREFACE. [signed] *Newhaven, Feb* [*sic*] 25. | 1773. | JONATHAN EDWARDS.; p. [viii]: ADVERTISEMENT. [signed] *Edinburgh, April* 29. | 1774. | JOHN ERSKINE.; p. [ix]: CONTENTS.; p. [1]: A | HISTORY | Of the WORK of | REDEMPTION.; p. [396]: [advertisement].

ESTC N66728 NUC NE0046632 OCLC 32956272

Harvard Divinity School

327 • HISTORY | OF | REDEMPTION, | ON A PLAN ENTIRELY ORIGINAL: | EXHIBITING THE | GRADUAL DISCOVERY AND ACCOMPLISHMENT OF THE | DIVINE PURPOSES | IN THE | SALVATION OF MAN; | INCLUDING A COMPREHENSIVE VIEW OF | CHURCH HISTORY, | AND THE FULFILMENT OF | SCRIPTURE PROPHECIES. | BY THE LATE REVEREND | JONATHAN EDWARDS, | PRESIDENT OF THE COLLEGE OF NEW JERSEY. | TO WHICH ARE NOW ADDED | NOTES, | HISTORICAL, CRITICAL, AND THEOLOGICAL, | WITH THE | LIFE AND EXPERIENCE | OF THE AUTHOR. | [short tapered rule] | *Whofo is wife, and will confider thefe things, even they fhall under- | ftand the loving kindnefs of the* LORD.—Pf. cvii. | [thick-thin rule] | LONDON: | Printed for T. PITCHER, No. 44, Barbican. | M.DCC.LXXXVIII.

8vo.; 20.9 x 12.8 cm.; π[1], a[2], [B][4], C-Z[4], Aa-Zz[4], 3A-3Z[4], 4A-4F[4]; [2], viii, [3]-573, [19] p.

Contents: frontispiece: [engraving] | JONATHAN EDWARDS, | President. | *Watker, sc*; prp. [1]: title (verso blank); p. [i]: recommendation [signed] THOMAS PITCHER | No. 44, BARBICAN (verso blank); p. [iii]: PREFACE | TO THE FIRST EDITION. [signed] *Newhaven, Feb.* | 25, 1773. JONATHAN EDWARDS.; p. [vi]: ADVERTISEMENT | TO THIS EDITION. [dated] LONDON, DEC. 27, 1788.; p. viii: AUTHORS cited in the following Work.; p. [3]: THE | LIFE AND EXPERIENCE | OF THE REVEREND | JONATHAN EDWARDS.; p. 35: SYLLABUS | OF THE | HISTORY OF REDEMPTION.; p. [43]: HISTORY | OF | REDEMPTION.; p. [574]: INDEX.; p. [587]: TABLE OF TEXTS | More or leſs explained in this Work.; p. [591]: ERRATA.; p. [592]: [advertisement].

THJ 248 ESTC T78825 NUC NE0046635 OCLC 3067177

Massachusetts Historical Society

327A • HISTORY | OF | REDEMPTION, | ON A PLAN ENTIRELY ORIGINAL: | EXHIBITING | The gradual diſcovery and accompliſhment of the DIVINE PURPOSES | IN THE | SALVATION OF MAN; | Including a comprehenſive View of | CHURCH HISTORY, | AND THE FULFILMENT OF | SCRIPTURE PROPHECIES. | BY THE LATE REVEREND | JONATHAN EDWARDS, | PRESIDENT OF THE COLLEGE OF NEW JERSEY. | To which are now added | NOTES, | HISTORICAL, CRITICAL, and THEOLOGICAL, | WITH THE | LIFE AND EXPERIENCE | OF THE AUTHOR. | [short tapered rule] | *Whoſo is wiſe, and will conſider theſe things, even they ſhall underſtand the* | *loving kindneſs of the* LORD.——Pſ. cvii. | [thick-thin rule] | LONDON: | Printed by S. GOSNELL, No. 13, Rolls Buildings, Fetter Lane; and | publiſhed by C. DILLY, Poultry, and J. MATTHEWS, Strand. | M.DCC.XCI. | [Entered at Stationers=Hall.]

8vo.; 21.4 x 12.8 cm.; π[1], a[2], [B][4], C-Z[4], Aa-Zz[4], 3A-3Z[4], 4A-4F[4]; [2], viii, [3]-573, [19] p.

Notes: identical with the above except for the title page.

THJ 248A ESTC T188603 NUC NE0046636

Library of Congress

328 • A | HISTORY | OF THE | WORK OF REDEMPTION. | CONTAINING THE | OUTLINES | OF A | BODY OF DIVINITY, | IN A METHOD ENTIRELY NEW. | [short decorative rule] | BY THE LATE REVEREND | MR. JONATHAN EDWARDS, | *PRESIDENT OF THE COLLEGE OF NEWJERSEY.* | [short decorative rule] | The Third American Edition. | [double rule] | PRINTED AT *WORCESTER*, MASSACHUSETTS, | BY ISAIAH THOMAS & LEONARD WORCESTER, | FOR ISAIAH THOMAS. | Sold at his Bookſtore in WORCESTER, and by him and COMPANY in BOSTON. | [short double rule] | MDCCXCII.

8vo.; 21.3 x 12.7 cm.; π[4], A-Z[4], Aa-Uu[4], Xx[2]; x, [11]-355, [1] p.

Contents: p. [i]: title (verso blank); p. iii: [advertisement]; p. iv: PREFACE. [signed] *JONATHAN EDWARDS.* | *Newhaven, Feb.* 25, 1773.; p. vii: ADVERTISEMENT. [signed] JOHN ERSKINE. | *Edinburgh, April* 29, 1774.; p. viii: CONTENTS.; p. [11]: A | HISTORY | OF THE | WORK OF REDEMPTION.; p. [356]: blank.

THJ 249 EAI 1:24288 NUC NE0046637 OCLC 3067182

Boston Public Library

329 • HISTORY | OF | REDEMPTION, | ON A PLAN ENTIRELY ORIGINAL: | EXHIBITING THE | GRADUAL DISCOVERY AND ACCOMPLISHMENT OF THE | DIVINE PURPOSES | IN THE | SALVATION OF MAN; | INCLUDING A COMPREHENSIVE VIEW OF | CHURCH HISTORY, | AND THE FULFILMENT OF | SCRIPTURE PROPHECIES. | BY THE LATE REVEREND | JONATHAN EDWARDS, | PRESIDENT OF THE COLLEGE OF NEW JERSEY. | TO WHICH ARE NOW ADDED | NOTES, | HISTORICAL, CRITICAL, AND THEOLOGICAL, | WITH THE | LIFE

AND EXPERIENCE | OF THE AUTHOR. | [short tapered rule] | *Whoſo is wiſe, and will conſider theſe things, even they ſhall underſtand* | *the loving kindneſs of the* LORD.—Pſ. cvii. | [thick-thin rule] | NEW-YORK: | Printed by T. and J. SWORDS, for the Editor, | M,DCC,XCIII.

8vo.; 20.4 x 12.2 cm.; $[A]^4$, B-Z^4, Aa-Zz^4, 3A-$3Z^4$, 4A-$4F^4$; xii, [3]-573 [i.e., 571], [18], 1 p.

Notes: lacks pp. 223-224 (pp. [43]-222, 225-573).

Contents: frontispiece: [engraving] | JONATHAN EDWARDS | Preſident. | Engraved by Amos Doolittle, N [*sic*] Haven; p. [i]: title (verso blank); p. [iii]: ADVERTISEMENT | To the *firſt* American Edition of EDWARDS's | HISTORY of REDEMPTION, with *Notes*. [signed] DAVID AUSTIN. | Elizabeth-Town, | Dec. 1, 1793. | [brace]; p. [vi]:blank; p. [vii]: PREFACE | To the FIRST EDITION. [signed] JONATHAN EDWARDS. | *New Haven, Feb.* 25, 1773.; p. [x]: ADVERTISEMENT | TO THIS EDITION.; p. xi: AUTHORS cited in the following Work.; p. [3]: THE | LIFE AND EXPERIENCE | OF THE REVEREND | JONATHAN EDWARDS.; p. 35: SYLLABUS | OF THE | HISTORY OF REDEMPTION.; p. [43]: HISTORY | OF | REDEMPTION.; p. [574]: INDEX; p. [587]: TABLE OF TEXTS; pp. [1]-2: [advertisement].

THJ 250   EAI 1:25433   NUC NE0046640   OCLC 4299321

Harvard Divinity School

330 • A | HISTORY | Of the WORK of | REDEMPTION. | CONTAINING, | THE | OUTLINES OF A BODY OF DIVINITY, | In a Method entirely new. | By the late REVEREND | Mr JONATHAN EDWARDS, | Preſident of the College of New Jerſey. | FOURTH EDITION. | EDINBURGH: | Printed for M. GRAY, Edinburgh;— | and T. VERNOR, London. | MDCCXCIII.

12mo.; 17.3 x 10.4 cm.; π^1, a^6, A-Z^6, Aa-Nn^6, Oo^2; [2], xii, 434, [2] p.

Notes: numeral on p. 3 reversed; p. 415 misnumbered 145 (pp. [1]-414, 145, 416-434).

Contents: prp. [1]: title (verso blank); p. [i]: ADVERTISEMENT.; p. [iii]: PREFACE. [signed] *Newhaven, Feb.* 25. | 1773. | JONATHAN EDWARDS.; p. [vii]: ADVERTISEMENT. [signed] *Edinburgh, April* 29. | 1774. | JOHN ERSKINE.; p. [viii]: CONTENTS.; pp. [1]-434: text; pp. [435-436]: [advertisement].

THJ 251   ESTC N7914   NUC NE0046638   OCLC 13554729

Princeton University

331 • A | HISTORY | OF THE WORK OF | REDEMPTION. | CONTAINING THE | OUTLINES OF A BODY OF DIVINITY, | *IN A METHOD ENTIRELY NEW.* | [short tapered rule] | BY THE LATE REVEREND | Mr. *JONATHAN EDWARDS,* | PRESIDENT OF THE COLLEGE OF NEW JERSEY. | [thin-thick rule] | [thick-thin rule] | SECOND EDITION. | [double rule] | *EDINBURGH:* | Printed for and by ALEXANDER JARDINE and | EDMUND WHITEHEAD. | [short tapered rule] | 1799.

12mo.; 17.4 x 10.3 cm.; $[a]^6$, A-Z^6, Aa-Nn^6; xii, 432 p.

Notes: published twenty-five years after the first Edinburgh edition (see 321), this second edition follows more nearly the collation and pagination of the fourth (see 330).

Contents: p. [1]: title (verso blank); p. [3]: *ADVERTISEMENT.*; p. [v]: PREFACE. [signed] NEWHAVEN, | *Feb.* 25. 1773 [(right) brace] | JOHNATHAN [*sic*] EDWARDS.; p. [viii]: *ADVERTISEMENT.* [signed] EDINBURGH, | *April* 29 . 1774. [(right) brace] | JOHN ERSKINE.; p. [ix]: CONTENTS.; p. [1]: A | HISTORY | OF THE WORK OF | REDEMPTION.

THJ 252   ESTC T78827   NUC NE0046643   OCLC 31776168

Houghton Library

332 • A | HISTORY | OF THE | WORK OF REDEMPTION; | CONTAINING THE | OUTLINES OF A BODY OF DIVINITY, | *IN A METHOD ENTIRELY NEW.* | BY THE LATE REVEREND | MR JONATHAN EDWARDS, | PRESIDENT OF THE COLLEGE OF NEW JERSEY. | [short thick-thin rule] | ALTERED FROM THE FORM OF SERMONS, | TO THAT OF A CONTINUED TREATISE; | BY JOHN ERSKINE, D. D. | [short thin-thick rule] | WITH | AN ACCOUNT | OF THE | **Author's Life and Writings.** | [short tapered rule] | **Edinburgh:** | PRINTED AND SOLD BY JOHN WALKER, | *Foot of Lady Stairs' Close, Lawnmarket.* | 1808.

17.7 x 10.2 cm.; [a]^4, b^6, 1-22^6, 23^2; xx, 268 p.

Contents: p. [i]: title (verso blank); p. [iii]: CONTENTS.; p. [v]: AN ACCOUNT | OF THE | *Author's Life and Writings*.; p. [xvii]: HISTORY | OF THE | WORK OF REDEMPTION.; p. [xviii]: *ADVERTISEMENT.* [signed] EDINBURGH, | *April* 29. 1774. | [brace] | JOHN ERSKINE.; p. [xix]: PREFACE. [signed] NEWHAVEN, | *Feb.* 25. 1773. | [brace] | JONATHAN EDWARDS.; p. [1]: AN | HISTORY | OF THE | WORK OF REDEMPTION.; p. 268: *J. Walker, Printer.*

THJ 253 NUC NE0046646 OCLC 38911124
Princeton University

332A • A | HISTORY | OF THE | WORK OF REDEMPTION; | CONTAINING THE | OUTLINES OF A BODY OF DIVINITY, | *IN A METHOD ENTIRELY NEW.* | [short thick-thin rule] | BY THE LATE REVEREND | MR. JONATHAN EDWARDS, | *President of the College of New Jersey.* | [short thick-thin rule] | [short thick-thin rule] | ALTERED FROM THE FORM OF SERMONS, | TO THAT OF A CONTINUED TREATISE; | *BY JOHN ERSKINE, D. D.* | [short tapered rule] | A NEW EDITION; | WITH AN ACCOUNT OF THE | *AUTHOR'S LIFE AND WRITINGS.* | [short tapered rule] | LONDON: | Printed by W. Nicholson, Warner Street, | FOR W. BAYNES, 54, PATERNOSTER ROW. | 1808.

17.7 x 10.2 cm.; [a]^4, b^6, 1-22^6, 23^2; xx, 268 p.

Notes: identical with the above except for the title page.

THJ 253A NUC NE0046647
Boston Public Library

333 • A | HISTORY | OF THE | WORK OF REDEMPTION. | CONTAINING THE | *OUTLINES* | OF A | BODY OF DIVINITY, | IN A | METHOD ENTIRELY NEW. | [short decorative rule] | BY THE LATE REVEREND | JONATHAN EDWARDS, A. M. | PRESIDENT OF THE COLLEGE OF NEWJERSEY. | [short decorative rule] | PRINTED AT WORCESTER, | FOR ISAIAH THOMAS, JUN. | Sold by him, in *Worcester;* by THOMAS & WHIPPLE, *Newburyport*, and by | THOMAS & TAPPAN, *Portsmouth*......MARCH, 1808. | [short decorative rule] | *ISAAC STURTEVANT, PRINTER.*

20.3 x 12.6 cm.; [A]^4, B-W-Z^4, 2A-2W-2Z^4, 3A^4; viii, [9]-392 p.

Contents: p. [i]: title (verso blank); p. [iii]: ADVERTISEMENT. [signed] JOHN ERSKINE. | EDINBURGH, *April* 29, 1774. (verso blank); p. [v]: PREFACE. [signed] JONATHAN EDWARDS | *Newhaven, Feb.* 25, 1773.; p. [vii]: CONTENTS.; p. [9]: WORK | OF REDEMPTION.

THJ 254 EAI 2:14921 NUC NE0046648 OCLC 3688680
Harvard Divinity School

334 • A | HISTORY | OF THE | WORK OF REDEMPTION, | CONTAINING | THE OUTLINES OF A BODY OF DIVINITY, | INCLUDING | *A VIEW OF CHURCH HISTORY,* | IN A METHOD ENTIRELY NEW. | [thick-thin rule] | BY THE LATE | *REV. JONATHAN EDWARDS,* | PRESIDENT OF THE COLLEGE OF NEW JERSEY. | [thin-thick rule] | [short decorative rule] | *LONDON:* | PRINTED FOR BAYNES, WILLIAMS AND SON, | HAMILTON AND CONDER; | BY EDWARD BAINES, LEEDS. | [short tapered rule] | 1812.

22.2 x 13.2 cm.; [A]^4, B-Z^4, Aa-Oo^4, Pp^2; 303 [i.e., 299], [1] p.

Notes: p. 6 misnumbered 8; p. 8 misnumbered 12 (pp. [1-5], [8], [7], 12, 9-303).

Contents: p. [1]: title (verso blank); p. [3]: CONTENTS.; p. [5]: *PREFACE.* [signed] JONATHAN EDWARDS. | *Newhaven, Feb.* 25, 1773. |[short thin-thick rule] | *ADVERTISEMENT.* [signed] JOHN ERSKINE. | *Edinburgh, April* 29, 1774.; p. [7]: A HISTORY | OF THE | *WORK OF REDEMPTION.*; p. 303: Edward Baines, Printer, Leeds.; p. [304]: blank.

THJ 255 OCLC 36814359
National Library of Wales

335 • A | HISTORY | OF THE | WORK OF REDEMPTION: | CONTAINING THE | OUTLINES OF

A BODY OF DIVINITY, | *IN A METHOD ENTIRELY NEW.* | [short thick-thin rule] | BY THE LATE REVEREND | MR JONATHAN EDWARDS, | PRESIDENT OF THE COLLEGE OF NEW JERSEY. | [short thin-thick rule] | ALTERED FROM THE FORM OF SERMONS, | *TO THAT OF A CONTINUED TREATISE,* | BY JOHN ERSKINE, D. D. | [short thick-thin rule] | WITH | AN ACCOUNT | OF THE | AUTHOR'S LIFE AND WRITINGS. | [short thick-thin rule] | EDINBURGH: | PRINTED FOR JOHN OGLE, JAMES ROBERTSON, AND | JAMES SOUTER, PARLIAMENT SQUARE; M. OGLE, GLASGOW; | OGLES, DUNCAN, & COCHRAN, LONDON; AND | T. JOHNSTON, DUBLIN. | [short rule] | 1816.

17.4 x 10.4 cm.; [a]^8, b^2, A-T^8, V^6; xx, 316 p.

Contents: p. [i]: title page (verso blank); p. [iii]: CONTENTS.; p. [v]: AN ACCOUNT | OF THE | AUTHOR'S LIFE AND WRITINGS.; p. [xviii]: blank; p. [xix]: PREFACE. [signed] NEWHAVEN, | *Feb.* 25. 1773. [brace] JONATHAN EDWARDS.; p. xx: *ADVERTISEMENT.* [signed] EDINBURGH, | *April* 29. 1774. [brace] JOHN ERSKINE.; p. [1]: HISTORY | OF THE | WORK OF REDEMPTION.; p. 316: G. CAW, Printer.

THJ 256

British Library

336 • A | HISTORY | OF THE | WORK OF REDEMPTION: | CONTAINING THE | OUTLINES OF A BODY OF DIVINITY, IN A METHOD ENTIRELY NEW. | [short rule] | BY THE LATE | REV. JONATHAN EDWARDS, | PRESIDENT OF THE COLLEGE OF NEW JERSEY. | [short rule] | WITH A LIFE OF THE AUTHOR. | [short thick-thin rule] | EDINBURGH: | JOHN BOYD, 37, GEORGE STREET: | WESTLEY & DAVIS, SIMPKIN & MARSHALL, JAMES DUNCAN, | JAMES NISBET, AND ANDREW PANTON, LONDON; JOHN LAWSON, | GLASGOW; AND WESTLEY & TYRRELL, DUBLIN. | [short rule] | M.DCCC.XXVIII.

17.5 x 10.2 cm.; π^1, [A]^{12}, B-O^{12}, P^{10}; xxvii, [1], 329, [1] p.

Contents: pp. [i-ii]: blank; p. [iii]: title; p. [iv]: Edinburgh: Printed by A. Balfour & Co. Merchant Court.; p. [v]: PREFACE. [signed] NEWHAVEN, | *Feb.* 25, 1773. [brace] | JONATHAN EDWARDS.; p. [viii]: ADVERTISEMENT. [signed] EDINBURGH, | *April* 29, 1774. [brace] | JOHN ERSKINE.; p. [ix]: AN ACCOUNT | OF THE | AUTHOR'S LIFE AND WRITINGS.; p. [xxiv]: blank; p. [xxv]: CONTENTS.; p. [xxviii]: blank; pp. [1]-329: text; p. 329: EDINBURGH: | PRINTED BY A. BALFOUR & CO. MERCHANT COURT.; p. [330]: blank.

OCLC 17461869

University of Alabama

337 • A HISTORY | OF | THE WORK OF REDEMPTION, | CONTAINING THE | OUTLINES OF A BODY OF DIVINITY | INCLUDING | A VIEW OF CHURCH HISTORY, | IN A | METHOD ENTIRELY NEW. | [short rule] | BY REV. JONATHAN EDWARDS, A. M. | President of Nassau Hall. | [short thick-thin rule] | NEW-YORK: | G. AND C. CARVILL, 108 BROADWAY. | [short rule] | 1828.

21.8 x 13.6 cm.; π^1, 1-34^4, 35^2, [2], 276 p.

Notes: p. 190 misnumbered 350 (pp. [1]-189, 350, 191-276).

Contents: prp. [1]: title (verso blank); p. [1]: PREFACE. [signed] JONATHAN EDWARDS. | *Newhaven, Feb.* 25, 1773.; p. [3]: ADVERTISEMENT [signed] JOHN ERSKINE. | *Edinburgh, April* 29, 1774. (verso blank); p. [5]: A HISTORY | OF THE | WORK OF REDEMPTION.

THJ 257 NUC NE0046649 OCLC 16118356

Presbyterian Historical Society

338 • HANES | GWAITH Y PRYNEDIGAETH, | AR DDULL HOLLOL NEWYDD: | YN DANGOS, | GRADDOL AMLYGRWYDD A CHYFLAWNIAD | Y | BWRIADAU DWYFOL | YN |

IACHAWDWRIAETH DYN: | YN CYNNWYS | GOLYGIADAU CYRHAEDDGAR | AR | HANESYDDIAETH EGLWYSIG, | A | CHYFLAWNIAD PROPHWYDOLIAETHAU YR YSGRYTHYRAU. | [short rule] | A GYFIEITHIWYD | O WAITH Y PARCH. JONATHAN EDWARDS, | *O'r Americ*, | *GAN THOMAS JONES, AMLWCH.* | [short rule] | At yr hyn y chwanegwyd | HANES BYWYD YR AWDWR, | A'I BROFIADAU. | [short rule] | BALA: | ARGRAPHEDIG GAN ROBERT SAUNDERSON. | 1829.

21.4 x 12.8 cm.; a-c^4, A-D^4, E-Y^8, Z^2; xxii, [2], 323, [1] p.

Notes: a Welsh translation of *History of Redemption*; a selection was published shortly after (see 339).

Contents: p. [i]: title (verso blank); p. [iii]: HANES | BYWYD Y PARCH. JONATHAN EDWARDS, | A'I BROFIADAU.; p. [xxiii]: CYNNWYSIAD.; p. [1]: HANES | *GWAITH Y PRYNEDIGAETH*.; p. [324]: HYSPYSIAD. | [short rule] | Y mae THOMAS JONES, Cyfieithydd y Gwaith hwn, yn hyspysu | i'w gydwladwyr, os bydd iddo gad estyniad oes, a mwynhau iechyd, | ei fod yn bwriadu cyfieithu llyfr arall, o waith yr un awdwr, ar | "Y SERCHIADAU CREFYDDOL," | Cynnwysir y gwaith mewn oddeutu Chwech neu Saith o Rifynau, | Swllt yr un.

THJ 258 NUC NE0046612 OCLC 37562903

Harvard University

339 • DULL | Y | FARN DDIWEDDAF; | GWEDI EI DYNU ALLAN O WAITH Y | PARCH. JONATHAN EDWARDS, D. D. | *Rhaglaw Jersey Newydd, y' Ngogledd America.* | AT BA UN YR YCHWANEGWYD, | PIGION O DDOETH-WERSI, | A dynwyd allan o waith y | PARCH. J. MASON, A. C. | [short thin-thick rule] | A Mab y dyn pan ddel yn ei ogoniant, a'r holl angylion | sanataidd gydag ef, yna eistedd ar orseddfainc ei ogoniant. | MAT. 25. 31. | A'r llyfrau a agorwyd, a barnwyd y meirw wrth y pethau | oedd wedi eu hysgrifenu yn y llyfrau, yn ol eu gweithred- | oedd..... Dat. 20. 12. | A hwy a ddeuant allan: y rhai a wnaethant dda, I adgyf- | odiad bywyd; ond y rhai a wnaethant ddrwg, I adgyfodiad | barn..... Ioan 5. 29. | [short decorative rule] | *ABERTAWY:* ARGRAFFWYD GAN E. GRIFFITHS, | DROS HOWEL POWEL. | [short rule] | *Pris Tuir Ceiniog.*

14.4 x 9 cm.; a-c^6, 36 p.

Notes: a Welsh translation of an extract of *History of Redemption*, published c. 1830; for the complete Welsh text, see 338 and 351.

Contents: p. [1]: title (verso blank); pp. [3]-24: [History of Redemption, Period III, Part IX]; pp. 24-25: [religious verse (anonymous)]; pp. [26]-32: [extracts from the work of the Rev. John Mason, 1706-1763]; pp. [33]-36: [religious verse by Evan Powell]; p. 36: E. Griffiths, Argraffydd, Heol Fawr, Abertawy.

National Library of Wales

340 • THE | HISTORY OF REDEMPTION, | COMPRISING | A SUMMARY OF THE HISTORY OF THE JEWS, | UP TO THE DESTRUCTION OF JERUSALEM. | [short rule] | BY PRESIDENT EDWARDS. | A. D. 1739. | [short rule] | LONDON: | PRINTED FOR | THE RELIGIOUS TRACT SOCIETY; | *And Sold at the Depository*, | 56, PATERNOSTER-ROW, | BY J NISBET, BERNERS STREET; AND OTHER BOOKSELLERS. | [short rule] | 1831. *stet* J NISBET

14.8 x 9.5 cm.; [A]^6, B-Z^6, 2A-2D^6; xii, 312 p.

Contents: pp. [i-ii]: blank; p. [iii]: title; p. [iv]: LONDON: | PRINTED BY W. CLOWES, | Stamford-street.; p. [v]: PREFACE.; p. [vii]: CONTENTS.; p. [1]: THE | HISTORY OF REDEMPTION.; p. 312: London: Stereotyped by W. CLOWES, Stamford-street.

THJ 259 NUC NE0046650 OCLC 4872690

Cleveland Public Library

340A • LONDON: | RELIGIOUS TRACT SOCIETY; | *Instituted* 1799. | SOLD AT THE DEPOSITORY, 56, PATERNOSTER ROW; | AND BY THE BOOKSELLERS. | 1835.

THJ 259A NUC NE0046652
Presbyterian Historical Society

340B • LONDON: | THE RELIGIOUS TRACT SOCIETY; | *Instituted* 1799. | SOLD AT THE DEPOSITORY, 56, PATERNOSTER ROW; | AND BY THE BOOKSELLERS. | 1837.
THJ 259B NUC NE0046653
Victoria University

340C • LONDON: | THE RELIGIOUS TRACT SOCIETY; | *Instituted* 1799. | DEPOSITORY, 56, PATERNOSTER ROW; AND 65, ST. | PAUL'S CHURCHYARD; AND SOLD BY THE | BOOKSELLERS. | 1838.
Notes: p. 312: London: J. Hill, Printer, Black Horse Court, Fleet Street.
OCLC 2808367
Georgia State University

340D • LONDON: | THE RELIGIOUS TRACT SOCIETY; | *Instituted* 1799. | SOLD AT THE DEPOSITORY, 56, PATERNOSTER ROW, | AND 65, ST. PAUL'S CHURCHYARD; AND | BY THE BOOKSELLERS. | 1841.
Notes: p. 312: London:. J. Hill, Printer, Black Horse Court, Fleet Street.
THJ 259C NUC NE0046660
University of Chicago

340E • LONDON: | THE RELIGIOUS TRACT SOCIETY; | *Instituted* 1799. | DEPOSITORY, 56, PATERNOSTER ROW, | 65, ST. PAUL'S CHURCHYARD, AND 164, PICCADILLY; | AND SOLD BY THE BOOKSELLERS.
Notes: p. 312: Religious Tract Society: Instituted 1799.
THJ 259D
Princeton University

340F • LONDON: | THE RELIGIOUS TRACT SOCIETY; | *Instituted* 1799. | DEPOSITORY, 56, PATERNOSTER ROW, AND 65, ST. PAUL'S | CHURCHYARD; AND SOLD BY THE BOOKSELLERS.
McMaster University

340G • LONDON: | THE RELIGIOUS TRACT SOCIETY; | *Instituted* 1799. | DEPOSITORIES, 56, PATERNOSTER ROW, | 65, ST. PAUL'S CHURCHYARD, AND 164, PICCADILLY; | AND SOLD BY THE BOOKSELLERS.
THJ 259E NUC NE0046618 OCLC 22245021
Buffalo and Erie County Public Library

340H • LONDON: | THE RELIGIOUS TRACT SOCIETY; | *Instituted* 1799. | DEPOSITORIES, 56, PATERNOSTER ROW; 65, ST. PAUL'S CHURCHYARD; | AND 164, PICCADILLY; | AND SOLD BY THE BOOKSELLERS.
Notes: published c. 1872.
THJ 259F NUC NE0046668
Wesley Theological Seminary

341 • A | HISTORY | OF THE | WORK OF REDEMPTION: | CONTAINING THE | OUTLINES OF

A BODY OF DIVINITY, | IN A METHOD ENTIRELY NEW. | BY THE LATE | REV. JONATHAN EDWARDS, | PRESIDENT OF THE COLLEGE OF NEW JERSEY. | WITH | A NEW LIFE OF THE AUTHOR, | AND NOTES, | BY JAMES BROWNLEE, ESQ. ADVOCATE. | EDINBURGH: | PRINTED FOR STIRLING AND KENNEY; | JAMES DUNCAN, LONDON; | R. M. TIMS; AND W. CURRY, JUN. & CO. DUBLIN. | [short rule] | 1832.

17.6 x 10.5 cm. (uncut); $[a]^4$, b-c^{12}, d^2, B-P^{12}, Q^{11}; lx, 357, [1] p.

Contents: p. [i]: title; p. [ii]: EDINBURGH | PRINTED BY JAMES CLARKE & CO.; p. [iii]: NOTE BY THE EDITOR. [dated] EDINBURGH, *December*, 1831.; p. [v]: PREFACE. [signed] JONATHAN EDWARDS | NEWHAVEN, *Feb.* 25, 1773.; p. [viii]: ADVERTISEMENT. [signed] JOHN ERSKINE | EDINBURGH, *April* 29, 1774.; p. [ix]: MEMOIR | OF | THE LIFE AND WRITINGS | OF | MR. JONATHAN EDWARDS.; p. [lvii]: CONTENTS.; pp. [1]-357: text; p. 357: EDINBURGH | PRINTED BY JAMES CLARKE & CO.; p. [358]: blank.

THJ 260 NUC NE0046651 OCLC 23241870

Princeton University

342 • HISTORY | OF | REDEMPTION, | ON A PLAN ENTIRELY ORIGINAL: | EXHIBITING THE | *GRADUAL DISCOVERY AND ACCOMPLISHMENT OF THE* | DIVINE PURPOSES | IN THE | SALVATION OF MAN; | INCLUDING A COMPREHENSIVE | VIEW OF CHURCH HISTORY, | AND THE FULFILMENT OF | SCRIPTURE PROPHECIES. | [rule] | BY JONATHAN EDWARDS, | PRESIDENT OF THE COLLEGE OF NEW JERSEY. | [rule] | WITH THE | LIFE AND EXPERIENCE OF THE AUTHOR. | NEW AND CORRECTED EDITION. | [short double rule] | LONDON: | PUBLISHED BY JONES AND CO. | TEMPLE OF THE MUSES (LATE LACKINGTON'S), FINSBURY SQUARE. | 1835.

20.6 x 12.8 cm.; π^1, B-D^4, B-Z^4, 2A-$2Z^4$, 3A-$3C^4$, $3D^3$; [2], [1]-24, [1]-390 p.

Notes: sigs. B-D^4 repeated; pp. [1]-24 repeated (pp. [1]-24, [1]-390).

Contents: frontispiece: [engraving] | REV[D] JON[THN] EDWARDS, A.M. | *London: Published by J. Jones, Warwick Square.*; prp. [1]: title (verso blank); p. [1]: CONTENTS.; p. [3]: THE | LIFE AND EXPERIENCE | OF | PRESIDENT EDWARDS.; p. [1]: HISTORY OF REDEMPTION.; p. 390: *J. M. Morris, Printer, Bungay*

OCLC 8892793

Dallas Theological Seminary

343 • A HISTORY | OF THE | WORK OF REDEMPTION; | COMPRISING | AN OUTLINE OF CHURCH HISTORY. | [short rule] | BY PRESIDENT EDWARDS. | [short rule] | PUBLISHED BY | THE AMERICAN TRACT SOCIETY, | 150 NASSAU-STREET, NEW-YORK. | [short rule] | D. Fanshaw, Printer.

14.8 x 9.4 cm.; $[1]^6$, 2-37^6; 444 p.

Notes: First published by the American Tract Society in 1838, 60,100 copies of the *History* were distributed up to 1875.—THJ. The following editorial note appears in American Tract Society reprints: This inestimable work was written by President | Edwards in 1739, in a series of sermons preached at | Northampton, and left by him in manuscript at his | death, which occurred in 1748 [*sic*]. In 1773, his son, the younger President Edwards, committed the manu- | script to Rev. Dr. JOHN ERSKINE, of Edinburgh, who | reduced it from the form of sermons to that of a con- | tinued treatise, and published it in 1774. | This edition is a reprint from the standard edition | of Edwards' Works now generally circulated in Great | Britain and the United States, and has been com- | pared throughout with the first American edition pub- | lished at Worcester in 1808. Slight additional im- | provements have been made in the language and form | of the subdivisions, and a new table of contents pre- | pared; with a few lines of abridgment, chiefly occa- | sioned by the lapse of time since it was written, and | wholly unessential to the integrity of the work.

Contents: frontispiece: THE | Evangelical | FAMILY LIBRARY | VOL. IX. | [engraving.] | *Morse del.* | *Dick Sc.* | PUBLISHED BY THE | *American Tract Society*; p. [1]: title (verso blank); p. [3]: [editorial note] (verso blank); p. [5]: CONTENTS.; p. [10]: blank; p. [11]: A HISTORY | OF THE | WORK OF REDEMPTION.

THJ 261 NUC NE0046654 OCLC 2806456
Princeton University

344 • A HISTORY | OF THE | WORK OF REDEMPTION; | COMPRISING | AN OUTLINE OF CHURCH HISTORY. | [short rule] | BY PRESIDENT EDWARDS. | [short rule] | PUBLISHED BY | THE AMERICAN TRACT SOCIETY, | 150 NASSAU-STREET, NEW-YORK. | [short rule] | D. Fanshaw, Printer.

15.2 x 9.4 cm.; $[1]^6$, $2\text{-}37^6$, $[38]^1$; 444, [2] p.

Notes: identical with the above except for the frontispiece and two blank pages following p. 444.

THJ 262 NUC NE0046656 OCLC 4371472
Presbyterian Historical Society

345 • A HISTORY | OF | THE WORK OF REDEMPTION; | COMPRISING | AN OUTLINE OF CHURCH HISTORY. | BY PRESIDENT EDWARDS. | REVISED AND SLIGHTLY ABRIDGED. | PUBLISHED BY THE | AMERICAN TRACT SOCIETY, | 150 NASSAU-STREET, NEW-YORK.

15.1 x 9.4 cm.; $[1]^8$, $2\text{-}33^8$; 34^4, 536 p.

Notes: closing sentence of the editorial note: Slight | language and form of the subdivisions, and a new | table of contents prepared; with the omission (in- | dicated by . . . .) of a few lines alluding to points | on which evangelical Christians differ; in some copies: Some | additional improvements have been made in the | language and form of the subdivisions, and a new | table of contents prepared; with the omission (in- | dicated by . . . .) of a few lines alluding to points | on which evangelical Christians differ.; in some copies, New York substituted for New-York.

Contents: p: [1]: title (verso blank); p. [3]: editorial note (verso blank); p. [5]: CONTENTS.; p. [11]: A HISTORY | OF THE | WORK OF REDEMPTION.

THJ 263 NUC NE0046658 OCLC 10320581
Princeton University

346 • A | HISTORY | OF THE | WORK OF REDEMPTION; | COMPRISING | AN OUTLINE OF CHURCH HISTORY. | BY PRESIDENT EDWARDS. | REVISED AND SLIGHTLY ABRIDGED. | PUBLISHED BY THE | AMERICAN TRACT SOCIETY, | 150 NASSAU-STREET, NEW YORK.

15.2 x 9.4 cm.; $[1]^8$, $2\text{-}27^8$, 28^7; 446 p.

Notes: in some copies, collation: $[1]\text{-}37^6$, 38^1; in some copies, title page: A | HISTORY | OF THE | WORK OF REDEMPTION; | COMPRISING | AN OUTLINE OF CHURCH HISTORY. | [short rule] | BY PRESIDENT EDWARDS. | [short rule] | REVISED AND SLIGHTLY ABRIDGED. | PUBLISHED BY THE | AMERICAN TRACT SOCIETY, | 150 NASSAU-STREET, NEW YORK.

OCLC 38118551
Lutheran Theological Seminary

347 • A | HISTORY | OF THE | WORK OF REDEMPTION. | BY | JONATHAN EDWARDS, A.M. | EDINBURGH: | PUBLISHED BY THOMAS NELSON. | 1839.

13.4 x 7.8 cm.; $[a]\text{-}b^8$, $A\text{-}Z^8$, $2A\text{-}2G^8$; xxxii, 477, [3] p.

Notes: a rare item; stamped on title page: Biblical Theological | Seminary Library | P.O. BOX 9 (200 N. MAIN) | HATFIELD, PA 19440.

Contents: p. [i]: title (verso blank); p. [iii]: PREFACE. [signed] NEWHAVEN, | *Feb.* 25, 1773. | [brace] JONATHAN EDWARDS.; p. [vi]: ADVERTISEMENT. [signed] EDINBURGH. | *April* 29, 1774. | [brace] | JOHN ERSKINE.; p. [vii]: AN ACCOUNT | OF THE | AUTHOR'S LIFE AND WRITINGS.; p. [xxviii]: blank; p. [xxix]: CONTENTS.; p. [1]: HISTORY | OF THE | WORK OF REDEMPTION.; pp. [478-480]: blank.

OCLC 45995979
Spirit Life Bible College

348 • A HISTORY | OF THE | WORK OF REDEMPTION, | CO[N]TAINING THE | OUTLINES OF A BODY OF DIVINITY, | IN A METHOD ENTIRELY NEW. | BY | JONATHAN EDWARDS, A.M. | EDINBURGH: | PUBLISHED BY THOMAS NELSON. | 1844.

13 x 7.8 cm.; [a]-b⁸, A-Z⁸, 2A-2G⁸; xxxii, 477, [3] p.

Notes: identical with the above except for the title page; mounted on the inside cover: A very rare item, | unique as far as | I know. | T. H. Johnson.

THJ 264 NUC NE0046661

Congregational Library

349 • A | HISTORY | OF THE | WORK OF REDEMPTION; | A REPRINT FROM THE WORCESTER EDITION, WITHOUT | ALTERATION, MUTILATION, OR OMISSION. | BY | JONATHAN EDWARDS, D. D. | NEW-YORK: LEAVITT, TROW & COMPANY, | 194 Broadway. | 1845.

23 x 14.2 cm.; $[37]^4$, $38\text{-}64^4$, 65^2; [289]-516 p.

Notes: reprint of the text in the first volume of the publisher's collected edition (1843); see 513.

Contents: p. [289]: title (verso blank); p. [291]: CONTENTS. (verso blank); p. [293]: A HISTORY | OF THE | WORK OF REDEMPTION. (verso blank); p. [295]: ADVERTISEMENT | TO THE EDINBURGH EDITION. [signed] JOHN ERSKINE. | EDINBURGH, *April* 29, 1774.; p. [296]: PREFACE. [signed] JONATHAN EDWARDS. | *New Haven, Feb.* 25, 1773.; p. [297]: WORK OF REDEMPTION.

NUC NE0046662 OCLC 40638178

University of Iowa

350 • A | HISTORY | OF THE | WORK OF REDEMPTION. | CONTAINING THE | OUTLINES OF A BODY OF DIVINITY, | IN A METHOD ENTIRELY NEW. | BY THE LATE | REV. JONATHAN EDWARDS, | PRESIDENT OF THE COLLEGE OF NEW JERSEY. | Copied accurately from the third American edition, printed at Worcester, | Massachusetts. | PHILADELPHIA: | PRESBYTERIAN BOARD OF PUBLICATION.

18.8 x 11.2 cm.; $[1]^6$, $2\text{-}30^6$; xii, 13-359, [1] p.

Notes: Described as No. 183 in the Board's first report for 1846: "Price 62½ and 75 cts. 1000 copies."—THJ.

Contents: p. [i]: title (verso blank); p. iii: PREFACE. [signed] JONATHAN EDWARDS. | *New Haven, Feb.* 25, 1773.; p. [vi]: blank; p. vii: ADVERTISEMENT. [signed] JOHN ERSKINE. | *Edinburgh, April* 29, 1774. (verso blank); p. ix: CONTENTS.; p. [13]: A | HISTORY | OF THE | WORK OF REDEMPTION.; p. [360]: blank.

THJ 265 NUC NE0046659 OCLC 3564423

Princeton Theological Seminary

350A • THE | HISTORY | OF | REDEMPTION | BY | JONATHAN EDWARDS | [publisher's device] | THE SOVEREIGN GRACE BOOK CLUB | Evansville 13, Indiana | 1959

21 x 13 cm.; xii, 13-359 p.

Notes: facsimile reprint of the above; a Puritan Classics edition.

OCLC 5191699

Gordon-Conwell Theological Seminary

350B • The | History | of | Redemption | *by* | *JONATHAN* | *EDWARDS* | [imposed on a map of the United States] The | National Foundation | for | Christian Education | MARSHALLTON, DEL. 19808

21 x 13 cm.; xii, 13-359 p.

Notes: identical with the above except for the title page; published c. 1969.

Gordon-Conwell Theological Seminary

350C • The | History | of | Redemption | *by* | *JONATHAN* | *EDWARDS* | [around publisher's device] ASSOCIATED PUBLISHERS AND AUTHORS INC. | *GRAND RAPIDS, MICH. 49315*

21 x 13 cm.; xii, [13]-359 p.

Notes: identical with the above except for the title page; published c. 1972, reissued c. 1975.

OCLC 3927487

University of Richmond

351 • HANES | GWAITH Y PRYNEDIGAETH; | YN CYNNWYS | BRASLUN O HANESYDDIAETH EGLWYSIG. | GAN Y LLYWYDD EDWARDS. | Wedi ei ddiwygio a'i dalfyru I raddau. | GYHOEDDWYD GAN Y | GYMDEITHAS DRAETHODOL AMERICANAIDD, | 150 HEOL NASSAU, CAEREFROG-NEWYDD.

18.8 x 11.2 cm.; $[1]^{12}$, $2\text{-}16^{12}$, 17^{6}; vi, [7]-395, [1] p.

Notes: a Welsh translation of *History of Redemption*, published c. 1850 by the American Tract Society.

Contents: p. [i]: title (verso blank); p. [iii]: CYNNWYSIAD.; pp. [7]-395: text; p. [396]: [advertisement].

THJ 269 NUC NE0046613 OCLC 17573505

Harvard University

352 • HISTORY | OF | REDEMPTION, | ON A PLAN ENTIRELY ORIGINAL: | EXHIBITING THE | *GRADUAL DISCOVERY AND ACCOMPLISHMENT OF THE* | DIVINE PURPOSES | IN THE | **Salvation of Man**; | INCLUDING A COMPREHENSIVE | VIEW OF CHURCH HISTORY, | AND THE FULFILMENT OF | SCRIPTURE PROPHECIES. | [rule] | BY JONATHAN EDWARDS, | PRESIDENT OF THE COLLEGE OF NEW JERSEY. | [rule] | WITH THE | LIFE AND EXPERIENCE | OF THE AUTHOR. | NEW AND CORRECTED EDITION. | [short thick-thin rule] | LONDON: | GEORGE VIRTUE, 26, IVY LANE, PATERNOSTER ROW. | BUNGAY: PRINTED BY JOHN CHILDS AND SON.

21.2 x 12.9 cm.; π^{5}, C-D^{4}, B-Z^{4}, 2A-$2Z^{4}$, 3A-$3C^{4}$, $3D^{3}$; [2], [1]-24, [1]-390 p.

Notes: Date of printing given in *The English Catalogue* as 1849.—THJ. The copy at New York Public Library, the copy THJ cites, dates it 1853 and adds advertisements (pp. [1]-16) after p. 390;sigs. C-D^{4} repeated; pp. [1]-24 repeated.

THJ 266 NUC NE0046663 OCLC 3474712

Alma College

353 • HISTOIRE | DE L'ŒUVRE | DE LA RÉDEMPTION | PAR | JONATHAN EDWARDS. | [short decorative rule] | TOULOUSE, | SOCIÉTÉ DES LIVRES RELIGIEUX. | Dépôt: rue du Lycée, 14. | [short rule] | 1854.

17.9 x 11.2 cm.; $1\text{-}18^{12}$, 19^{6}, 20^{2}; 448 p.

Notes: a French translation of *History of Redemption*; in some copies the title is within decorative rules.

Contents: p. [1]: HISTOIRE | DE | L'ŒUVRE DE LA RÉDEMPTION.; p. [2]: PUBLIÉ PAR LA SOCIÉTÉ DES LIVRES RELIGIEUX | DE TOULOUSE. | [rule] | TOULOUSE. IMP. DE CHAUVIN ET FEILLÈS, RUE MIREPOIX, 3; p. [3]: title (verso blank); p. [5]: INTRODUCTION; pp. [19]-446: text; p. [447]: TABLE DES MATIÈRES; p. 448: TOULOUSE, IMP. DE CHAUVIN ET FEILLÈS, RUE MIREPOIX, 3.

THJ 267 NUC NE0046615 OCLC 38118549

New York Public Library

354 • [within decorative rules] Kitab | ta'rikh al-fida' | [short rule] | ta'lif alfadil alra'is Yunathan Adwards | Tubia fi Bairut sanat 1868.

19.5 x 12 cm.; π^{1}, $1\text{-}33^{6}$, 34^{4}; [2], 403, [1] p.

Notes: an Arabic translation of *History of Redemption*, published in Beirut by the American Mission Press, 1868.

Contents: prp. [1]: title; prp. [2]: [translator's introduction]; pp. 1-403: text; p. [404]: blank.

THJ 268 OCLC 43639625
New York Public Library

355 • THE MILLENNIUM | *by* | JONATHAN EDWARDS | [ornament] | WESTMINSTER STANDARD | [short rule] | PRINTED BY GISBORNE HERALD CO., LTD.

17.1 x 12 cm.; 36 p.

Notes: selections from *History of Redemption*; published c. 1960.

Contents: p. [1]: title; p. 2: PREFACE [signed] ERGATEES; p. 4: [12 lines] | Psalm 72, 17-19 (Metrical version); p. 5: THE MILLENNIUM | By Jonathan Edwards | (Extracts from The History of Redemption); p. 36: A Westminster Standard Publication. For further copies write to— | Westminster Standard, 183 Rutene Road, Gisborne, New Zealand. | No. 34. Price 2/- (20c).

OCLC 17653561
Reformed Theological Seminary

AN ESSAY ON THE NATURE OF TRUE VIRTUE

356 • AN | ESSAY | ON THE | NATURE | OF | TRUE VIRTUE. | [rule] | *It does not conſiſt in the moroſity of a* Cynick, *in* | *the ſeverity of an* Aſcetick, *in the demureneſs* | *of a* Preciſian, *nor in the ſullenneſs of a* Quaker: | *it is neither in a drooping head, a mortified face,* | *or a primitive beard: but it is ſomething very* | *different from, and much more excellent than* | *all this.* NORRIS'S Eſſays. | [thick-thin rule] | LONDON: | Printed by W. OLIVER, N° 12, in Bartholomew-Cloſe: | Sold by T. PAYNE and Son, Mews Gate, Charing- | Croſs; T. CADELL, in the Strand; Meſſrs DILLY, | in the Poultry; C. PARKER, New Bond-ſtreet; | MR PRINCE, at Oxford; MR MERRIL, | at Cambridge. | MDCCLXXVIII.

8vo.; 16 x 9.2 cm.; $[A]^8$, $B\text{-}S^8$, T^3; xv, [1], 278 p.

Contents: p. [i]: title (verso blank); p. [iii]: TO THE | RIGHT REVEREND | THE LORD BISHOP OF | Litchfield and Coventry [signed] THE EDITOR.; p. xiii: CONTENTS. (verso blank); p. [1]: THE | NATURE | OF | TRUE VIRTUE.

THJ 231 ESTC T57073 NUC NE0046548 OCLC 12374604
Beinecke Library

357 • THE NATURE | OF TRUE VIRTUE | by JONATHAN EDWARDS | *With a Foreword by William K. Frankena* | ANN ARBOR PAPERBACKS | THE UNIVERSITY OF MICHIGAN PRESS

20.3 x 13.7 cm.; xv, [1], 107, [3] p.

Notes: reprinted 1966, 1981, 1982, 1983, 1984, and 1996.

Contents: p. [i]: THE NATURE OF TRUE VIRTUE (verso blank); p. [iii]:title; p. [iv]: *First edition as an Ann Arbor Paperback 1960* | *Foreword © by the University of Michigan 1960* | [4 lines]; p. v: *Foreword* | *by William K. Frankena*; p. [xiv]: blank; p. [xv]: CONTENTS (verso blank); pp. 1-107: text; pp. [108-109]: blank; p. [110]: [advertisement].

OCLC 373897
Northeastern University

AN ACCOUNT OF THE CONVERSION AND RELIGIOUS EXPERIENCE OF THE LATE REVEREND AND LEARNED MR. JONATHAN EDWARDS

358 • AN | ACCOUNT | OF THE | CONVERSION | AND | RELIGIOUS EXPERIENCE | Of the late Reverend and Learned | Mr. JONATHAN EDWARDS, | MINISTER OF THE GOSPEL. | Who

departed this Life at Princeton, | March 22, 1758, | IN THE 55th YEAR OF HIS AGE. | [thick-thin rule] | LONDON: Printed for J. MATHEWS, No. 18, *Strand.* | M.DCC.LXXX. | [Price Two Pence.] | Or 14s. per 100 to those who give them away.

8vo.; 13.3 x 8.2 cm.(uncut); [A]^6, B-C^6; 36 p.

Notes: title (and text) derived from Samuel Hopkins's *Life of Edwards* (1765); the more common title, *Personal Narrative*, derived from Sereno E. Dwight, *Life of President Edwards* (1829), *His Personal Narrative* (pp. 58-62 and 64-67).

Contents: p. [1]: title; pp. [2]-36: text.

THJ 270 ESTC N67301 NUC NE0046445

Beinecke Library

359 • [No. 144. | CONVERSION | OF | PRESIDENT EDWARDS. | WRITTEN BY HIMSELF.

17.3 x 10.6 cm.; 16 p.

Notes: published c. 1823

Contents: caption title; pp. [1]-16 (also paged [181]-196): text; p. 16: PRINTED FOR THE | AMERICAN TRACT SOCIETY | *By* FLAGG & GOULD; *and sold by them at the Society's General | Depository, Andover, (Mass.) Sold also by* S. T. ARMSTRONG, | No. 50, Cornhill, Boston; *and by Agents of the Society's Depos- | itories in the principal towns in the United States. The established price is* one cent for ten pages. *To Auxiliary and other benevolent | Societies, which send either to the General Depository, of the De- | pository in Boston,* ten percent discount | [1st edit. 6000.

NUC NE0046501

American Antiquarian Society

359A • [No. 144. | CONVERSION | OF | PRESIDENT EDWARDS. | [short tapered rule] | WRITTEN BY HIMSELF. | [engraving] | "I walked abroad alone, in a solitary place, for contemplation." | Page 5. | PRINTED FOR THE | AMERICAN TRACT SOCIETY, | *By* FLAGG & GOULD; and sold by them at the Society's General Deposito- | ry, Andover, Mass. by S. T. ARMSTRONG, No. 50, CORNHILL, | BOSTON; and by Agents of the Society in the principal towns in | the United States. The established price is *one cent for ten pages.* | To Auxiliary Societies *ten percent discount.* | [2d edit. 4000.

17.1 x 10.6 cm.; 16 p.

Contents: p. [1]: title; pp. [2]-16 (also paged [181]-196): text; p. 16: [biography].

American Antiquarian Society

359B • No. 144. | CONVERSION | OF | PRESIDENT EDWARDS. | [short thick-thin rule] | WRITTEN BY HIMSELF. | [short thin-thick rule] | [engraving] | "I walked abroad alone, in a solitary place, for contemplation." | Page 5. | [rule] | PRINTED FOR | THE AMERICAN TRACT SOCIETY, | 1825

16.8 x 10.4 cm.; 16 p.

Notes: front cover: [engraving] | [double rules] PUBLISHED BY THE | AMERICAN TRACT SOCIETY | *Instituted at Boston in* 1814. | SOLD AT THEIR GENERAL DEPOSITORY, | Stone Church, Hanover-street, Boston, | MR. AARON RUSSELL, GENERAL AGENT AND ASSISTANT TREASURER. | SOLD ALSO AT THEIR OTHER DEPOSITORIES IN VARIOUS | PARTS OF THE UNITED STATES.

Contents: p. [1]: title; pp. [2]-16 (also paged [174]-188): text; p. 16: [biography].

Mount Holyoke College

359C • NO. 144. | CONVERSION | OF | President Edwards. | [short rule] | FROM AN ACCOUNT WRITTEN BY HIMSELF. | [short rule] | [engraving] | I walked abroad alone, in some solitary place, for contemplation. | *See page* 5. | [short double rule] | PUBLISHED BY THE | AMERICAN TRACT SOCIETY, | AND SOLD AT THEIR DEPOSITORY, NO. 144 NASSAU-STREET, NEAR | THE CITY-HALL, NEW-YORK; AND BY AGENTS OF THE | SOCIETY, ITS BRANCHES, AND AUXILIARIES, IN | THE PRINCIPAL CITIES AND TOWNS | IN THE UNITED STATES.

17.2 x 10.7 cm.; 16 p.

Notes: First published in 1827. Up to 1875, 124,000 copies had been distributed.—THJ.

Contents: p. [1]: title; pp. [2]-16 (also paged [249]-264): text; p. 16: [biography]; p. 16 (repeated), back cover (verso): *Delight in God.* | [28 lines] | WATTS. | [double rule] | Orders for Tracts will receive prompt attention, if ad- | dressed to the "*The American Tract Society, No.* 144 *Nassau-* | *street, New-York.*" | No. 144 | [short rule] | Fanshaw, *Printer*.

THJ 271 NUC NE0046502 OCLC 5692974

Beinecke Library

359D • No. 144. | CONVERSION | OF | PRESIDENT EDWARDS. | FROM A NARRATIVE WRITTEN BY HIMSELF.

18.8 x 11.1 cm.; 16 p.

Notes: in some copies, also paged [181]-196.

Contents: caption title; pp. [1]-16 in TRACTS | OF THE | AMERICAN TRACT SOCIETY. | **General Series.** | [engraving] | Vol. V. | PRINTED BY THE | AMERICAN TRACT SOCIETY, | 150 NASSAU-STREET, NEW YORK.

OCLC 12795784

Harvard Divinity School

360 • DOCTRINAL TRACT. | [short rule] | NO. 48. | [short rule] | CONVERSION AND EXPERIENCE | OF | PRESIDENT EDWARDS. | [short rule] | [short thick-thin rule] | BOSTON: | CONGREGATIONAL BOARD OF PUBLICATION, | 24

18.4 x 11.3 cm.; 1-2^6; 23, [1] p.

Contents: prp. [1]: title (verso blank); p. [1]: No. 48. | CONVERSION AND EXPERIENCE | OF | PRESIDENT EDWARDS. | [short rule] | INTRODUCTION.; p. 3: CONVERSION AND EXPERIENCE OF | PRESIDENT EDWARDS. | [short rule] | WRITTEN BY HIMSELF.; p. [24]: blank.

THJ 272 NUC NE0046498 OCLC 40436447

Boston Public Library

361 • SOME | ACCOUNT | OF THE | CONVERSION AND EXPERIENCES | Of the late | *Rev. JONATHAN EDWARDS*, | Of *New-England*, PRESIDENT OF NEW- | JERSEY COLLEGE, &c.

14.7 x 8.4 cm.; 18 p.

Notes: no imprint; British Library cites it as [Boston, Mass.? 1760?], but the text, derived from Hopkins's *Life of Edwards*, was first published in Boston in 1765 and first published separately in London in 1780.

Contents: p. [1]: title (verso blank); p. [3]: SOME ACCOUNT | OF THE | CONVERSION AND EXPERIENCES | Of the late | Rev. JONATHAN EDWARDS, | Of *New-England*, PRESIDENT OF NEW-JERSEY | COLLEGE, &c.; p. 17: An extract from Mr. EDWARD's [*sic*] PRIVATE | DIARY.–written about the 20th year of his age. | *Saturday Jan.* 12, 1723.

THJ 273 ESTC W42699

British Library

362 • CONVERSION AND EXPERIENCE | OF | PRESIDENT EDWARDS. | BOSTON: | CONGREGATIONAL BOARD OF PUBLICATION.

15.9 x 9.9 cm.; $[1]^8$, 2-3^8; vi, [7]-48 p.

Contents: p. [i]: title; p. [ii]: RIVERSIDE, CAMBRIDGE: | STEREOTYPED AND PRINTED BY | H. O. HOUGHTON AND COMPANY.; p. [iii]: INTRODUCTION [signed] C.; pp. [7]-48: text.

THJ 274 NUC NE0046499

Amherst College

363 • No. 22 | **Mittheilungen** | **aus dem innern Leben** | **von** | **Jonathan Edwards,** | **Präsidenten des Collegiums von Neu=Jersey.** | [short rule] | **Herausgegeben von der** | **Amerikanischen Tractat=Gesellschaft.** | **No. 150 Nassau=Strasse, Neu=York.** | Gr. 22.

18.5 x 10 cm.; 24^4, 25^6; 20 p.

Notes: a German translation of *Personal Narrative*, published by the American Tract Society; pp. 2 and 3 repeated.

Contents: pp. 2, 3 (inner covers): Christi Herrlichkeit in den Seinen | [56 lines] | Nikol. Ludwig von Zinzendorf. | [short rule] | Uebergabe an Christus zu Seinem Dienste. | (Röm. 12, 1.) | [7 lines]; p. [1]: No. 22 | Mittheilungen | aus dem innern Leben | von | Jonathan Edwards, | Präſidenten des Collegiums von Neu=Jerſey.

NUC NE0046727

Schwenckfelder Library

364 • The "Narrative" of Jonathan | Edwards

Contents: caption title; *The Chautauquan* 49 (December 1907):124-125.

THJ 275 OCLC 1553932

Harvard University

THE EXCELLENCY OF CHRIST

365 • THE | EXCELLENCY | OF | CHRIST. | A SERMON, | PREACHED AT | NORTHAMPTON, in NEW-ENGLAND, | In the Time of the wonderful Work of | GRACE there, in the Year 1738. | [rule] | By the late Preſident EDWARDS. | [thin-thick rule] | BOSTON, Printed: | And Re-printed at NORTHAMPTON, | In OLD ENGLAND, 1780, | By THOMAS DICEY. | [Price 4d. or 3s. per Dozen to thoſe who give them away.]

8vo.; 16 x 9.7 cm.; $[A]^4$, $B\text{-}G^4$, H^1; 55, [3] p.

Notes: in some copies, p. 54 misnumbered 45 (pp. [1]-53, 45, 55-58); some copies lack ERRATA; some copies add a leaf of advertisement.

Contents: p. [1]: title (verso blank); p. [3]: PREFACE. [signed] JOHN RYLAND. | NORTHAMPTON, | December 14, 1779.; p. [7]: THE | EXCELLENCY | OF | CHRIST.; p. 55: ERRATA.; p. [56]: CONTENTS.; p. [58]: [advertisement].

THJ 276 ESTC T54785 NUC NE0046555 OCLC 4499290

Boston Public Library

365A • The SECOND EDITION. | [rule] | By the late Preſident EDWARDS. | [rule] | BOSTON, Printed: | And Re-printed at NORTHAMPTON, | In OLD ENGLAND, 1780, | By THOMAS DICEY. | [Price 4d. or 3s. per Dozen to thoſe who give them away.]

8vo.; 15.6 x 9.7 cm.; $[A]^4$, $B\text{-}G^4$, H^2; 55, [5] p.

Contents: p. [1]: title (verso blank); p. [3]: PREFACE. [signed] JOHN RYLAND. | NORTHAMPTON, | December 14, 1779.; p. [7]: THE | EXCELLENCY | OF | CHRIST.; p. [56]: CONTENTS.; p. [58-60]: [advertisement].

ESTC T56310 NUC NE0046556 OCLC 36868275

Massachusetts Historical Society

366 • *The Excellency of Christ.* | [short decorative rule] | A | SERMON, | ON | *REVELATIONS V.* 5, 6. | [short decorative rule] | BY JONATHAN EDWARDS, D.D. | LATE PRESIDENT OF THE COLLEGE IN NEW-JERSEY. | [short decorative rule] | [thick-thin rule] | BOSTON: | *PRINTED AND SOLD BY E. LINCOLN, WATER-STREET.* | [short tapered rule] | 1805.

12mo.; 19.2 x 11.9 cm.; $[A]^6$, $B\text{-}C^6$; 36 p.

Contents: p. [1]: title (verso blank); p. [3]: THE EXCELLENCY OF CHRIST.; p. 36: [Price 10 cents; 1 dollar per dozen; 6 dollars per 100.].

THJ 277 EAI 2:8376 NUC NE0046557 OCLC 5742645

Massachusetts Historical Society

367 • SELECT SERMONS. (No. 11.) | [short rule] | THE | EXCELLENCY OF CHRIST. | BY THE LATE PRESIDENT EDWARDS.

16.8 x 10.1 cm.; 20 p.

Notes: p. 20: *London: Printed for the Religious Tract Society, 56, Paternoster | Row, by Knight and Bagster, 14, Bartholomew Close.*

Contents: caption title; pp. [1]-20 in SELECT | SERMONS. | [short rule] | VOL. I. | [short rule] | CONTAINING | FIFTEEN SERMONS | ON | VARIOUS IMPORTANT SUBJECTS. | [publisher's device] | [short thick-thin rule] | LONDON: | *Printed for* | THE RELIGIOUS TRACT SOCIETY; *Instituted* 1799. | SOLD BY J. DAVIS, 56, PATERNOSTER ROW; AT THE SOCIETY'S DEPO- | SITORY, 15, PICCADILLY, MANCHESTER; BY J. NISBET, 21, BERNERS | STREET; AND OTHER BOOKSELLERS.

THJ 278 NUC NE0046553 OCLC 16853632

Oberlin College

368 • THE | EXCELLENCY | OF | CHRIST. | BY | PRESIDENT EDWARDS. | LONDON: | THE RELIGIOUS TRACT SOCIETY; | *Instituted* 1799. | SOLD AT THE DEPOSITORY, 56, PATERNOSTER ROW, | AND 65, ST. PAUL'S CHURCHYARD; AND | BY THE BOOKSELLERS.

Notes: No copy examined. Reported in the British Museum. Printed probably in the second quarter of the 19th century.—THJ. The British Library reports that this copy, published c. 1844, was destroyed during World War II.

THJ 279

369 • THE EXCELLENCY OF CHRIST.

Notes: text within rules.

Contents: caption title; pp. [91]-164 in ON | GLORYING IN THE CROSS OF CHRIST. | BY REV. JOHN MACLAURIN. | THE EXCELLENCY OF CHRIST. | BY REV. JONATHAN EDWARDS. | CHRIST IS ALL. | BY REV. WILLIAM ROMAINE. | THIRD EDITION. | Edinburgh: | JAMES TAYLOR, 21 GEORGE STREET. | LONDON: J. NISBET AND CO. W. ALLAN. | GLASGOW: D. BRYCE.

14.4 x 8.6 cm.; 176 p.

NUC NE0046554 OCLC 38910792

Yale University

370 • The Excellency of Christ | [short rule] | A Sermon | delivered by | Jonathan Edwards | at Northampton, Massachusetts

21.6 x 13.5 cm.; 47, [1] p.

Contents: front cover: The Excellency of Christ | *by* | Jonathan Edwards | Messages from God's servants | in former days | [6 lines] | [ornament] | [in 2 cols., col. 1]: The Teleios Ministry of | Camelback Bible Church | 3900 East Stanford Drive | Paradise Valley, AZ 85253 | 955-6370 | [col. 2]: June, 1996; front cover (verso): Teleios Sermon # 9 | [34 lines]; p. [1]: title; p. [48]: *Notes and Personal Application*; back cover (recto): [advertisement].

OCLC 49538165

Gordon-Conwell Theological Seminary

SERMONS ON THE FOLLOWING SUBJECTS

371 • SERMONS, | ON THE | Following SUBJECTS; | [in 2 cols., col. 1] The Manner in which | Salvation is to be ſought. | The unreaſonableneſs of | Indetermination in Re- | ligion. | Unbelievers contemn the | glory of CHRIST. | The folly of looking back | in fleeing out of So- | dom. | The Warnings of Scrip- | ture in the beſt Manner | adapted to the awaken- | [short double vertical rule, col. 2] ing and converſion of | Sinners. | Hypocrites deficient in | the Duty of Prayer. | The future Puniſhment | of the

wicked unavoid- | able and intolerable. | The *eternity* of hell-tor- | ments. | The Peace which CHRIST | gives his true Followers. | The perpetuity & change | of the Sabbath. | [rule] | BY THE LATE REVEREND | MR. JONATHAN EDWARDS, | PRESIDENT of the COLLEGE of NEW-JERSEY. | [double rule] | *HARTFORD:* | PRINTED BY HUDSON AND GOODWIN. | M.DCC.LXXX.

8vo.; 17.7 x 11.3 cm.; [A]^4, B-W-Z^4, Aa-Ii^4, Kk^5; v, [1], [7]-282, [i.e., 272], [2] p.

Notes: pp. 256-272 misnumbered 266-282 (pp. 7-255, 266-282).

Contents: p. [i]: title (verso blank); p. [iii]: PREFACE. [signed] *JONATHAN EDWARDS.* | *New Haven, Dec.* 21, 1779; p. [vi]: blank; p. [7]: The Manner in which Salvation of | the Soul is to be fought.; p. [37]: The unreafonablenefs of Indeterminati- | on in Religion.; p. [57]: Unbelievers contemn the Glory and Ex- | cellency of CHRIST.; p. [72]: blank; p. [73]: The Folly of looking back in fleeing | out of Sodom.; p. [93]: The Warnings of Scripture are in the beft | manner adapted to the awakening | and converfion of Sinners.; p. [110]: blank; p. [111]: Hypocrites deficient in the Duty of | Prayer.; p. [143]: The future Punifhment of the Wicked | unavoidable and intolerable.; p. [170]: The Eternity of Hell Torments.; p. [201]: The Peace which CHRIST gives his true | Followers.; p. [221]: The Perpetuity and Change of the | Sabbath.; p. [283]: ERRATA. (verso blank).

THJ 280 EAI 1:16767 NUC NE0046771 OCLC 12881418

Congregational Library

A DISSERTATION ON GOD'S LAST END IN THE CREATION OF THE WORLD

372 • A | DISSERTATION | ON | GOD'S LAST END | IN THE | CREATION OF THE WORLD. | BY THE LATE | PRESIDENT EDWARDS, A. M. | REVISED AND CORRECTED | BY THE REV. C. DE COETLOGON, A. M. | [rule] | Eϰ Σϰ παγτα, ιν Σοι παγτα, εις Σε παγτα | ANTONIUS. | [double rule] | LONDON: | PRINTED BY H. TRAPP, NO. I. PATER-NOSTER-ROW. | M.DCC.LXXXVIII.

8vo.; 20.4 x 12.4 cm.; [A]^4, B-R^4, S^2; 138, [2] p.

Notes: in some copies, pp. [139-140]: blank.

Contents: p. [1]: title (verso blank); p. [3]: A | DISSERTATION, &c. | CONCERNING THE END FOR WHICH GOD | CREATED THE WORLD.; pp. [139-140]: [advertisement].

THJ 232 ESTC T78812 NUC NE0046513

Boston Public Library

373 • VERHANDELING | OVER | GODS | LAATSTE EINDE | IN DE | SCHEPPING | DER | *WEERELD.* | DOOR | JONATHAN EDWARDS, | *Profesfor en Predikant, te* NORTHAMPTON, | *in* NOORD-AMERIKA. | [rule] | UIT HET ENGELSCH VERTAALD | DOOR | M. VAN WERKHOVEN, | En uitgegeeven, met eene Voorrede, en | Aanteekeningen, | DOOR | CORNELIS BREM. | [thick-thin rule] | *Te AMSTERDAM,* | BIJ MARTINUS DE BRUYN, | In de Warmoesftraat, het zesde Huis van de | Vischfteeg, Noordzijde. | M. DCC. LXXXVIII.

8vo.; 21.9 x 12.1 cm.; *^{4}, A-M^8, N^3; [8], 198 p.

Notes: a Dutch translation of Edwards's *End of Creation*, the copy is bound with his son's *Eternal Punishment in a Future Life* (1792) in Dutch.

Contents: prp. [1]: title; prp. [2]: Onderzocht en goedgekeurd door | de E. Clasfis van *Schieland*, | den 6 van *Bloeimaand* | 1788; prp. [3]: VOORREDEN | VAN DEN | UITGEVER [signed] ROTTERDAM | *den* 19 *April*, 1788 | CORN. BREM.; prp. [6]: INHOUD.; p. [1]: GODS | LAATSTE EINDE | IN DE | SCHEPPING DER WEERELD.

THJ 233 OCLC 16066219

Calvin College and Theological Seminary

374 • A DISSERTATION | CONCERNING | THE END FOR WHICH GOD CREATED THE WORLD. | BY JONATHAN EDWARDS, A.M. | PRESIDENT OF THE COLLEGE OF NEW

JERSEY.

Notes: p. 291: title (verso blank); p. [293]: PREFATORY NOTICE.; p. 409: EDINBURGH: | FULLERTON AND MACNAB, PRINTERS, LEITH WALK.; p. [410]: blank.

Contents: pp. [291]-409 in THEOLOGICAL TRACTS, | SELECTED AND ORIGINAL. | EDITED | BY JOHN BROWN, D.D. | PROFESSOR OF EXEGETICAL THEOLOGY TO THE UNITED PRESBYTERIAN CHURCH, | AND SENIOR PASTOR OF THE UNITED PRESBYTERIAN CONGREGATION, | BROUGHTON PLACE, EDINBURGH | VOL. II | A. FULLARTON & CO.: | 44 SOUTH BRIDGE, EDINBURGH; AND 106 NEWGATE | STREET, LONDON. | 1853.

17.7 x 11.4 cm. (uncut); A-Z^8, 2A^8, 2B^6, 2C^5; vi, 409 p.

THJ 234 NUC NE0046512 OCLC 10222967

Harvard Divinity School

375 • TRAETHAWD | AR Y | DYBEN | I BA UN | Y CREODD DUW Y BYD. | [short rule] | GAN JONATHAN EDWARDS, D.D. | AMERICA. | [short rule] | CYFIEITHEDIG GAN D. HUGHES, B.A., TREDEGAR. | CAERNARFON | CYHOEDDEDIG AC AR WERTH GAN H. HUMPHREYS, | *A chan y Llyfrwerthwyr yn gyffredinol.*

16.5 x 10.3 cm.; [A]^8, B-I^8; 143, [1] p.

Notes: a Welsh translation of *End of Creation* (c. 1907), it was also issued in two parts, with paper covers; some copies add seven leaves of advertisement.

Contents: frontispiece: [engraving] | CRIST A'R DDAU DDYSGYBL YN EMMAUS.; p. [1]: title; p. [2]: CAERNARFON: | ARGRAFFWYD GAN H. HUMPHREYS, | CASTLE SQUARE.; p. [3]: RHAGYMADRODD | GAN Y CYHOEDDWR CYNTAF.; p. [5]: CYNWYSIAD.; pp. [7]-143: text; p. [144]: CAERNARFON: | CYHOEDDWYD AE ARGRAFFWYD GAN H. HUMPHREYS.

THJ 235 NUC NE0046826 OCLC 43639621

Princeton University

376 • GOD'S PASSION FOR | HIS GLORY | [rule] | Living the Vision of Jonathan Edwards | With the Complete Text of | *The End for Which God Created the World* | [rule] | JOHN PIPER | CROSSWAY BOOKS • WHEATON, ILLINOIS | A DIVISION OF GOOD NEWS PUBLISHING

22.8 x 15.2 cm.; xvii, [1], [19]-266 p.

Notes: derived from the Hickman edition of *The Works of Jonathan Edwards* (1834), v. 1; see 512.

Contents: p. [i]: GOD'S PASSION FOR | HIS GLORY (verso blank); p. [iii]: title; p. [iv]: *God's Passion for His Glory* | Copyright © 1998 by John Piper | [32 lines]; p. [v]: TO | JONATHAN EDWARDS (verso blank); p. [vii]: TABLE OF CONTENTS; p. [ix]: OTHER BOOKS | BY THE AUTHOR (verso blank); p. [xi]: PREFACE; p. [xv]: ACKNOWLEDGMENTS; p. [xviii]: blank; p. [19]: PART ONE | [rule] | A PERSONAL | ENCOUNTER WITH | JONATHAN EDWARDS | [rule] | *by John Piper*; p. [114]: blank; p. [115]: PART TWO | [rule] | THE END FOR WHICH | GOD CREATED | THE WORLD | [rule] *by Jonathan Edwards* (verso blank); p. [117]: A NOTE ON HOW TO READ | *THE END FOR WHICH* | *GOD CREATED THE WORLD* | *(by John Piper)*; p. [120]: blank; p. [121]: CONCERNING THE TEXT | USED IN THIS EDITION OF | *THE END FOR WHICH* | *GOD CREATED THE WORLD* | *(by John Piper)*; p. [124]: [19 lines] | JONATHAN EDWARDS | *The End for Which God Created the World*; p. [125]: THE END FOR WHICH GOD | CREATED THE WORLD | *by Jonathan Edwards*; p. [252]: blank; p. [253]: A NOTE ON RESOURCES (verso blank); p. [255]: SCRIPTURE INDEX; p. [261]: PERSON INDEX; p. [263]: SUBJECT INDEX.

ISBN 1581340079 OCLC 39124371

Harvard Divinity School

376A • Inter-Varsity Press

Notes: identical with the above; p. [iv]: INTER-VARSITY PRESS | *38 De Montfort Street, Leicester LE1 7GP, England* | Copyright © 1998 by John Piper | [25 lines].

ISBN 0851117554 OCLC 40752545

University of Notre Dame

THE ETERNITY OF HELL TORMENTS

377 • THE | Eternity of Hell Torments, | BY THE LATE | REV. JONATHAN EDWARDS, A. M. | PRESIDENT OF NEW JERSEY COLLEGE. | [rule] | REVISED AND CORRECTED BY THE | REV. C. E. DE COETLOGON, A. M. | [rule] | Regions of Sorrow, doleful Shades; where Peace | And Reſt can never dwell; Hope never comes, | That comes at all: but Torture without End | Still urges, and a fiery Deluge fed, | With ever-burning Sulphur unconſum'd. | MILTON. | [thick-thin rule] | *LONDON:* | PRINTED BY W. JUSTINS, SHOEMAKER-ROW, BLACKFRIARS; FOR | R. THOMSON, NO. 30, LITTLE PULTENEY-STREET, SOHO. | SOLD ALSO BY MATTHEWS, STRAND; BUCKLAND, | PATERNOSTER-ROW; MURRAY, PRINCES- | STREET, SOHO; MURGATROYD, CHIS- | WELL-STREET; | ASH, TOWER-STREET; | WATTS, WINDMILL-HILL; AND | BUTTON, NEWINGTON- | CAUSEWAY. | MDCC,LXXXVIII. | [short tapered rule] | Where may be had, | The JUSTICE of GOD in the DAMNATION of SINNERS | By the ſame AUTHOR. Price 6d. I. Low, NO. 5, MAID-LANE, | BOROUGH. | M,DCC,LXXXVIII | [short tapered rule] | [PRICE SIXPENCE.]

8vo.; 21.4 x 12.8 cm. (uncut); π^1, B-E^4, F^1; [2], 32, [2] p.

Notes: in some copies, imprint: *LONDON:* | PRINTED BY W. JUSTINS, SHOEMAKER-ROW, BLACKFRIARS; FOR | R. THOMSON, NO. 30, LITTLE PULTENEY-STREET, SOHO. | SOLD ALSO BY MATTHEWS, STRAND; BUCKLAND, | PATERNOSTER-ROW; MURRAY, PRINCES- | STREET, SOHO; MURGATROYD, CHIS- | WELL-STREET; ASH, TOWER-STREET; | WATTS, WINDMILL-HILL; AND | I. LOW, NO. 5, MAID-LANE, | BOROUGH. | M,DCC,LXXXVIII | [short tapered rule] | [PRICE SIXPENCE.]; some copies lack extra leaf.

Contents: prp. [1]: title (verso blank); p. [1]: THE | Eternity of Hell Torments. | A | SERMON.; p. [33]: [advertisement] (verso blank).

THJ 281 ESTC T78815 NUC NE0046551 OCLC 22406062

John Carter Brown Library

378 • THE | Eternity of Hell Torments, | BY THE LATE | REV. JONATHAN EDWARDS, A. M. | PRESIDENT OF NEW JERSEY COLLEGE. | [rule] | REVISED AND CORRECTED BY THE | REV. C. E. DE COETLOGON, A. M. | [rule] | Regions of Sorrow, doleful Shades; where Peace | And Reſt can never dwell; Hope never comes, | That comes at all: but Torture without End | Still urges, and a fiery Deluge fed, | With ever-burning Sulphur unconſum'd. | MILTON. | [thick-thin rule] | The SECOND EDITION. | [thick-thin rule] | *LONDON:* | PRINTED BY W. JUSTINS, Blackfriars, for R. THOMSON, No. 326, Oxford- | Street; Sold also by MATHEWS, Strand; BUCKLAND, Paternoster-Row; | MURGATROYD, Chiswell-Street; RISDEN, Back Hill, Clerkenwell; | and BUTTON, Newington Cauſeway. | M,DCC,LXXX,IX. | [short rule] | [Entered at STATIONER'S HALL.]

8vo.; 19.9 x 12 cm.;π^1, B-E^4; [2], 32 p.

Contents: prp. [1]: title (verso blank); p. [1]: THE | Eternity of Hell Torments. | A | SERMON.

THJ 282 ESTC T183480 NUC NE0046552 OCLC30598233

Boston Public Library

379 • THE | PUNISHMENT OF THE WICKED | ETERNAL. | BY THE LATE | JONATHAN EDWARDS, | PRESIDENT OF THE COLLEGE OF NEW JERSEY, U. S. | *Reprinted in a slightly abridged form from the Edition published at* | *Edinburgh in* 1789. | "Where their worm dieth not, and the fire is not quenched." | BRISTOL: | I. E. CHILLCOTT, STEAM PRESS, CLARE STREET. | LONDON: W. MACINTOSH, PATERNOSTER ROW. | [short rule] | 1864.

17.2 x 9.2 cm.; [A]^6-B^6; 24 p.

Contents: p. [1]: title; p. [2]: I. E. CHILLCOTT, PRINTER, BRISTOL.; p. [3]: SERMON.; p. 24: I. E. Chillcott, Steam Press, Clare Street, Bristol.

THJ 283
British Library

PRACTICAL SERMONS NEVER BEFORE PUBLISHED

380 • PRACTICAL | SERMONS, | NEVER BEFORE PUBLISHED. | [rule] | BY THE LATE REVEREND | Mr JONATHAN EDWARDS, | Prefident of the College of New-Jerfey. | [rule] | [short tapered rule] | EDINBURGH: | Printed for M. GRAY, FRONT of the EXCHANGE. | [short rule] | M.DCC.LXXXVIII.

8vo.; 21.1 x 12.8 cm.; π^1, b^4, A-Z^4, Aa-Zz^4, 3A-$3C^4$, $3D^5$; [2], viii, 401, [1] p.

Notes: p. 374 misnumbered 347 (pp. [1]-346, 374, 348-401); in some copies, the pagination is: [2], viii, 1-224, 229-32, 225-28, 233-401, [1] p.; first advertisement (p. [i]): THESE Sermons were tranfcribed from the Author's | original manufcripts by his fon, the Reverend Dr | Jonathan Edwards of Newhaven, and never before | publifhed. By the following extract from a letter of | Dr Edwards to the Reverend Mr Ryland junior, the | public will learn, that on proper encouragement, his | Mifcellaneous Thoughts on various Doctrines, and his | Notes on various texts of Scripture, will be publifhed. | "As to manufcripts of my father, his Mifcellanies are | "the moft complete and important. They contain his | "Thoughts on the various doctrines of Theology; | "and what is written on any doctrine is kept diftinct, | "though written at different times, and interfperfed | "through one thoufand pages. Thefe diftinct effays | "may be collected under their proper heads, and | "would afford great pleafure and improvement to all | "who have a tafte for his writings. Perhaps enough | "out of thefe Mifcellanies may be collected to fill | "three fuch volumes as that on the 'Freedom of the | "Will.' Nor is any thing wanting to the publica- | "tion of them, but a profpect of their fale. Befide thefe, | "his Commentaries on Scripture may, at leaft many of | "them, be publifhed with advantage, under the title of, | "'Notes on various Texts of Scripture.' His diary | "was not written in fhort hand. A more particular | "account of my father's life may be publifhed, if it be | "judged beft."

Contents: prp. [1]: title (verso blank); p. [i]: ADVERTISEMENT.; p. [ii]: CONTENTS.; p. [1]: The Importance and Advantage of a thorough | Knowledge of Divine Truth.; p. [26]: GOD the beft Portion of the Chriftian.; p. [39]: The fole confideration that *God is God*, fufficient to | ftill all objections to his Sovereignty.; p. [54]: Great Guilt no Obftacle to the Pardon of the returning | Sinner.; p. [67]: The Moft High a Prayer-hearing God.; p. [86]: Great Care neceffary, left we live in fome way of | Sin.; p. [133]: The great Guilt of thofe who attend on the Ordinances | of Divine Worfhip, and yet allow themfelves in any | known Wickednefs.; p. [151]: The World judged righteoufly by Jefus Chrift.; p. [191]: The vain Self-flatteries of the Sinner.; p. [203]: Wicked Men ufeful in their Deftruction only.; p. [224]: The Fearfulnefs, which will hereafter furprife Sinners | in Zion, reprefented and improved.; p. [247]: When the Wicked fhall have filled up the Meafure of | their Sin, Wrath will come upon them to the utter- | moft.; p. [260]: The Torments of the Wicked in Hell, no Occafion of | Grief to the Saints in Heaven.; p. [282]: The Precioufnefs of Time.; p. [297]: The Sin and Folly of depending on future Time.; p. [321]: The Sin of Theft and of Injuftice.; p. [343]: The Duty of *Charity* to the Poor, explained and en- | forced.; p. [386]: The Nature and End of Excommunication; p. [402]: [advertisement].

THJ 284 ESTC T78832 NUC NE0046748 OCLC 3685423
Houghton Library

TWENTY SERMONS ON VARIOUS SUBJECTS

381 • TWENTY | SERMONS, | ON | VARIOUS SUBJECTS. | [rule] | BY THE LATE REVEREND | Mr JONATHAN EDWARDS, | Prefident of the College of New-Jerfey. | [rule] | [short tapered rule] | EDINBURGH: | Printed for M. GRAY, FRONT of the EXCHANGE. | [short thick rule] M.DCC.LXXXIX.

12mo.; 18.1 x 10.6 cm.; a^5, A-Z^6, Aa-Mm^6, Nn^3; x, 426 p.

Notes: p. iv misnumbered v (pp. [iii], v, v-vi); in some copies, six leaves (sig. B^6) of advertisement added at end.

Contents: p. [i]: title (verso blank); p. [iii]: CONTENTS.; p. [vii]: [thick-thin rule] | FIFTEEN | SERMONS | ON THE | FOLLOWING SUBJECTS, | [in 2 cols., col. 1] The Manner in which Salvation | is to be ſought. | The unreaſonableneſs of Indeter- | mination in Religion. | Unbelievers contemn the Glory of | Chriſt | The Folly of Looking Back in flee- | ing out of Sodom. | The Warnings of Scripture are in the | beſt Manner adapted to the Awa- | kening and Converſion of Sinners. | [short double vertical rule, col. 2] Hypocrites deficient in the Duty of Prayer. | The future Puniſhment of the | Wicked unavoidable and into- | lerable. | The Eternity of Hell Torments. | The Peace which Chriſt gives his | true Followers. | The Perpetuity and Change of the | Sabbath. | FIRST PUBLISHED AT HERTFORD [*sic*], IN CONNECTICUT, | in 1780. | [thin-thick rule] (verso blank); p. [ix]: PREFACE. [signed] JONATHAN EDWARDS. | *New-Haven, Dec.* 21. 1779. (verso blank); p. [1]: The Manner in which Salvation of the Soul | is to be ſought.; p. [28]: The Unreaſonableneſs of Indetermination in | Religion.; p. [46]: Unbelievers contemn the Glory and Excellency | of Chriſt.; p. [60]: The Folly of Looking Back in fleeing out of | Sodom.; p. [79]: The Warnings of Scripture are in the beſt man- | ner adapted to the Awakening and Conver- | ſion of Sinners.; p. [95]: Hypocrites Deficient in the Duty of Prayer.; p. [125]: The future Puniſhment of the Wicked un- | avoidable and intolerable.; p. [150]: The Eternity of Hell Torments.; p. [179]: The Peace which Chriſt gives his true Follow- | ers.; p. [198]: The Perpetuity and Change of the Sabbath.; p. [246]: blank; p. [247]: [thick-thin rule] | FIVE | SERMONS | ON | DIFFERENT OCCASIONS, | SEPARATELY PUBLISHED IN Mr EDWARDS's LIFE-TIME. | [thin-thick rule] (verso blank); p. [249]: A Divine and Supernatural Light, immediately | imparted to the Soul by the Spirit of God, | ſhown to be both a Scriptural and Rational | Doctrine.; p. [274]: The Church's Marriage to her Sons, and to her | God.; p. [315]: True Saints, when abſent from the Body, are | preſent with the Lord.; p. [360]: God's awful Judgement in the breaking and wi- | thering of the Strong Rods of Community.; p. [382]: True Grace diſtinguiſhed from the Experience of | Devils.

THJ 285 ESTC T175001 NUC NE0046879 OCLC 6240479
John Carter Brown Library

382 • TWENTY | SERMONS, | ON | VARIOUS SUBJECTS. | [rule] | BY THE LATE REVEREND | MR. JONATHAN EDWARDS, | *President of the College of New Jersey.* | [rule] | [short tapered rule] | [*From an Edinburgh Edition.*] | CARLISLE: | PRINTED BY GEORGE KLINE, | [short decorative rule] | 1803.

12mo.; 17.9 x 10.8 cm.; π^6, A-Z^6, Aa-Nn^6; [2], viii, [2], 426, [6] p.

Contents: p. [i]: TWENTY | SERMONS. (verso blank); p. [iii]: title (verso blank); p. [v]: CONTENTS.; p. [ix]: PREFACE. [signed] JONATHAN EDWARDS. | *New-Haven, Dec.* 21. 1779. (verso blank); p. [1]: The Manner in which Salvation of the Soul is to | be ſought.; p. [29]: The Unreaſonableneſs of Indetermination in Religion.; p. [47]: Unbelievers contemn the Glory and Excellency of | Chriſt.; p. 61: The Folly of Looking Back in fleeing out of Sodom.; p. [80]: The Warnings of Scripture are in the beſt manner | adapted to the awakening and converſion of Sinners.; p. [96]: Hypocrites Deficient in the Duty of Prayer.; p. [126]: The future Puniſhment of the Wicked unavoidable | and intolerable.; p. [151]: The Eternity of Hell Torments.; p. 180: The Peace which Chriſt gives his true Followers.; p. [200]: The Perpetuity and Change of the Sabbath.; p. [248]: A Divine and Supernatural Light, immediately im- | parted to the Soul by the Spirit of God, ſhown to be | both a Scriptural and Rational Doctrine.; p. 273: The Church's Marriage to her Sons, and to her God.; p. [316]: True Saints, when abſent from the Body, are preſent | with the Lord.; p. [358]: God's awful Judgement in the breaking and withering | of the Strong Rods of a Community.; p. 380: True Grace diſtinguiſhed from the Experience of | Devils.; p. [427]: *SUBSCRIBERS NAMES.*; pp. [431-432]: blank.

THJ 286 EAI 2:4138 NUC NE0046880 OCLC 3940732
Boston Public Library

383 • TWENTY | SERMONS, | ON | *VARIOUS SUBJECTS.* | [double rule] | BY THE LATE REVEREND | MR JONATHAN EDWARDS, | PRESIDENT OF THE COLLEGE OF NEW-JERSEY. | [double rule] | [short decorative rule] | *EDINBURGH:* | PRINTED BY ALEX. LAWRIE AND CO. FOR JOHN FAIRBAIRN AND OGLE & AIKMAN; | AND W. COKE, LEITH. | [short double rule] | 1804.

12mo.; 16.7 x 10.2 cm.; a^6, A-Z^6, 2A-2I^6; x, [2], 384 p.

Contents: p. [i]: title (verso blank); p. [iii]: CONTENTS.; p. [viii]: blank; p. [ix]: PREFACE. [signed] JONATHAN EDWARDS. | *New-Haven, Dec.* 21. 1779.; p. [xi]: FIFTEEN | SERMONS | ON THE | FOLLOWING SUBJECTS | . . . [*sic*] FIRST PUBLISHED AT HERTFORD [*sic*], IN CONNECTICUT, | IN 1789. (verso blank); p. [1]: THE MANNER IN WHICH SALVATION OF THE | SOUL IS TO BE SOUGHT.; p. [25]: THE UNREASONABLENESS OF INDETERMINATION IN | RELIGION.; p. [41]: UNBELIEVERS CONTEMN THE GLORY AND EXCEL- | LENCY OF CHRIST.; p. 54: THE FOLLY OF LOOKING BACK, IN FLEEING OUT OF | SODOM.; p. 72: THE WARNINGS OF SCRIPTURE ARE IN THE BEST | MANNER ADAPTED TO THE AWAKENING AND CON- | VERSION OF SINNERS.; p. 86: HYPOCRITES DEFICIENT IN THE DUTY OF PRAYER.; p. 112: THE FUTURE PUNISHMENT OF THE WICKED | UNAVOIDABLE AND INTOLERABLE.; p. 134: THE ETERNITY OF HELL TORMENTS.; p. 160: THE PEACE WHICH CHRIST GIVES HIS TRUE | FOLLOWERS.; p. 177: THE PERPETUITY AND CHANGE OF THE SABBATH.; p. [221]: FIVE | SERMONS | ON | DIFFERENT OCCASIONS, | SEPARATELY PUBLISHED | IN MR. EDWARDS'S LIFETIME. (verso blank); p. [223]: A DIVINE AND SUPERNATURAL LIGHT, IMMEDIATELY | IMPARTED TO THE SOUL BY THE SPIRIT OF GOD, | SHOWN TO BE BOTH A SCRIPTURAL AND RATIONAL | DOCTRINE.; p. 246: THE CHURCH'S MARRIAGE TO HER SONS, AND TO HER | GOD.; p. [283]: TR[UE] SAINTS, WHEN ABSENT FROM THE BODY, ARE | PRESENT WITH THE LORD.; p. 324: GOD'S AWFUL JUDGEMENT IN THE BREAKING AND | WITHERING OF THE STRONG RODS OF A COMMU- | NITY.; p. 344: TRUE GRACE DISTINGUISHED FROM THE EXPERI- | ENCE OF DEVILS.; p. 384: Alex. Lawrie & Co. Printers.

THJ 287 OCLC 21132714

Earlham College

THE WISDOM OF GOD, AS DISPLAYED IN THE WAY OF SALVATION BY JESUS CHRIST, FAR SUPERIOR TO THE WISDOM OF ANGELS

384 • DE | WIJSHEID VAN GOD | IN DEN WEG DER ZALIGHEID | DOOR | JESUS CHRISTUS | TEN TOON GESPREID, | ALS VERRE VERHEEVEN BOOVEN | DE | WIJSHEID VAN DEN ENGELEN. | In ſes LEERREEDENEN | over | EPHESEN III: 10.

8vo.; 20.8 x 12.8 cm.; $*^4$, $[A]^8$, B-K^8, L^7; viii, 174 p.

Notes: a Dutch translation of a sermon on Eph. 3:10, delivered in March 1733, and first published in *Sermons on Various Important Subjects* (nos. 11-16), the selection of sermons appended to Hopkins's *Life of Edwards* (1765); except for this translation, it was apparently never published separately; front matter pagination in capital roman numerals.

Contents: p. [i]: LEERREEDENEN | OVER | VERSCHEIDE GEWIGTIGE | ONDERWERPEN, | NAAGELAATEN DOOR DEN WELEERWAAR- | DEN EN ZEER GELEERDEN HEER | JONATHAN EDWARDS, | *In deszelfs leeven Preſident van het Collegie* | *van New-Jerſey* | NAA DEN TWEEDEN DRUK UIT HET ENGLESCH VERTAALD. | DOOR | ENGELBERT NOOTEBOOM. | [short, two-part thick-thin rule] | *Te UTRECHT*, | BIJ WILLEM VAN YZERWORST, | Academie-Drukker, 1791.; p. [ii]: Uitgegeven volgens Kerken Or- | de: na voorafgaande Viſitatie | en Approbatie de E. Claſsis | van Utrecht.; p. [iii]: VOORREEDEN | VAN DEN | UITGEEVER. [signed] DE [ENGELSCHE] UITGEEVER.; p. [1]: DE | WIJSHEID VAN GOD | IN DEN WEG DER ZALIGHEID | DOOR | JESUS CHRISTUS | TEN TOON GESPREID, | ALS VERRE VERHEEVEN BOOVEN | DE | WIJSHEID VAN DEN ENGELEN. | In ſes LEERREEDENEN | over | EPHESEN III: 10. (verso blank); p. [3]: DE WIJSHEID VAN GOD IN DEN WEG DER ZA- | LIGHEID DOOR JESUS CHRISTUS TEN TOON | GESPREID, ALS VERRE VERHEEVEN | BOOVEN DE WIJSHEID VAN DEN | ENGELEN. | [Maart 1733.]

Harvard Divinity School

MISCELLANEOUS OBSERVATIONS ON IMPORTANT THEOLOGICAL SUBJECTS

385 • MISCELLANEOUS | OBSERVATIONS | ON | IMPORTANT | THEOLOGICAL SUBJECTS,

| ORIGINAL AND COLLECTED. | [rule] | By the late REVEREND | Mr JONATHAN EDWARDS, | Prefident of the College of New Jerfey. | [rule] | EDINBURGH: | Printed for M. GRAY, EDINBURGH; | AND FOR | VERNOR & HOOD, and OGILVIE & SPEARE, | LONDON. | [short tapered rule] | M.DCC.XCIII.

12mo.; 18.2 x 10.4 cm.; π^2, A-Z^6, 2A-$2Q^6$, $2R^4$; [4], 476 p.

Notes: in some copies, six leaves of advertisement added at the end.

Contents: prp. [1]: title (verso blank); prp. [3]: PREFACE. [signed] JOHN ERSKINE. | EDIN. Sept. 30. | 1793. [brace]; p. [1]: MISCELLANEOUS OBSERVATIONS | ON | IMPORTANT THEOLOGICAL SUBJECTS, | ORIGINAL AND COLLECTED.; p. 476: ERRATUM.

THJ 288 ESTC T78830 NUC NE0046723 OCLC 5092553

Boston Public Library

REMARKS ON IMPORTANT THEOLOGICAL CONTROVERSIES

386 • REMARKS | ON | IMPORTANT THEOLOGICAL | CONTROVERSIES. | [double rule] | By the late REVEREND | Dr JONATHAN EDWARDS, | Prefident of the College of New Jerfey. | [double rule] | EDINBURGH: | Printed for J. GALBRAITH, and ARCH. CONSTABLE; | AND SOLD BY | T. LONGMAN, and VERNOR & HOOD, LONDON. | [short tapered rule] | M.DCC.XCVI.

12mo.; 17.3 x 10.6 cm.; π^2, A-Z^6, Aa-Rr^6; [4], 480 p.

Notes: prp. [3]: *THE greatest Part of thefe* REMARKS *are ORI- | ginal, and may be confidered as a Second Volume | of* President Edwards'*s Mifcellaneous Ob- | fervations; but, as they relate to Subjects entirely | different, make by themfelves a Book.*

Contents: prp. [1]: title (verso blank); prp. [3]: [editorial note]; prp. [4]: *CONTENTS*.; p. [1]: MISCELLANEOUS OBSERVATIONS | ON | IMPORTANT DOCTRINES.

THJ 289 ESTC T78833 NUC NE0046751 OCLC 9875148

Congregational Library

ADVICE TO YOUNG CONVERTS

387 • ADVICE TO YOUNG CONVERTS. | A Letter | FROM THE LATE | REV. JONATHAN EDWARDS | *OF NORTHAMPTON*, | TO A YOUNG LADY AT SUFFIELD, CONN. | TO WHICH IS ADDED, | A DISCOURSE, | RECOMMENDING RELIGIOUS CONVERSATION; | AND | *AN EXTRACT FROM A SERMON* | ON | CHRISTIAN CONVERSATION. | [short line of stops] | "Let your speech be always with grace, seasoned with salt." | [short line of stops] | [short thick-thin rule] | *NORTHAMPTON:* | PRINTED AND SOLD BY THOMAS M. POMROY. | [2 short lines of stops] | 1807.

16.6 x 10.9 cm.; π^2, a^4, B^2, b^3; 22 p.

Notes: the letter, dated June 3, 1741, was addressed to Deborah Hatheway, an eighteen-year-old convert who had sought Edwards's advice: see *Works* (Yale), 16:90-95; some editions add a selection of his *Resolutions* to the text.

Contents: p. [1]: title (verso blank); p. [3]: Advice | TO YOUNG CONVERTS | [short line of stops] | A letter from the late JONATHAN EDWARDS of North- | ampton, to a young Lady at Suffield, a young Convert. | [short line of stops] | *Northampton*, June 3, 1741. [signed] JONATHAN EDWARDS; p. [11]: Religious Conversation | RECOMMENDED. | [short line of stops] | "Let your conversation be always with grace, seaoned [*sic*] | with salt."; p. 20: *EXTRACTS from a SERMON on CHRIST- | IAN CONVERSATION from* Col. iv. 6. | [short line of stops] | "Let your speech be always with grace, seasoned with | salt."

THJ 290 EAI 2:12492 OCLC 13355761
American Antiquarian Society

388 • ADVICE | TO YOUNG CONVERTS. | *A Letter from the late Rev. Jonathan Edwards of | Northampton, to a young Lady at Suffield, a | young Convert.*

16.6 x 10.3 cm.; 8 p.

Notes: in blue covers: p. [1]: ADVICE TO YOUNG | CONVERTS. | [short decorative rule] | PUBLISHED FOR THE | HARTFORD EVANGELICAL TRACT SOCIETY. | AND TO BE HAD OF THEIR AGENT, BARZILLAI | HUDSON, JUN. IN HARTFORD, AND AT | THEIR DEPOSITORIES IN THE PRIN- | CIPAL TOWNS IN THIS STATE. | *Price,* 1 *cent; or* $1 *per* 100. | [short tapered rule] | HARTFORD, CONN. | 1821.; p. [2]: Consider well these tokens of a | State of Danger.; p. 4: HYMN.

Contents: caption title; pp. [1]-6: text; p. [7]: *Resolutions made and written at dif- | ferent times by Jonathan Edwards.*

OCLC 1925621
American Antiquarian Society

389 • No. 196. | ADVICE TO | YOUNG CONVERTS. | BY REV. JONATHAN EDWARDS. | [short decorative rule] | *Originally addressed to a Young Lady At S——, Con., | in the year* 1741.

17.6 x 10.4 cm.; $[A]_{7-8}$; 4 p.

Notes: First published by the Society in 1827, this tract was very widely distributed. By 1875 at least 328,000 copies had been issued.—THJ; some copies omit No. 196 and vary the form of the caption title.

Contents: caption title; pp. [1]-4 (also paged [13]-16) in THE | PUBLICATIONS | OF THE | AMERICAN TRACT SOCIETY. | [short rule] | Vol. VII. | [short rule] | "For we write none other things unto you, that what ye read or | acknowledge, and I trust ye shall acknowledge even to the end."– | 2 Cor. I. 13. | [short thick-thin rule] | PUBLISHED BY THE | AMERICAN TRACT SOCIETY, | AND SOLD AT THEIR DEPOSITORY, NO.144 NASSAU-STREET, NEAR | THE CITY-HALL, NEW-YORK; AND BY AGENTS OF THE | SOCIETY, ITS BRANCHES, AND AUXILIARIES, IN | THE PRINCIPAL CITIES AND TOWNS | IN THE UNITED STATES.; p. 4: PUBLISHED BY THE AMERICAN TRACT SOCIETY.

THJ 291 OCLC 36681916
American Antiquarian Society

390 • No. 196. | ADVICE TO | YOUNG CONVERTS. | BY REV. JONATHAN EDWARDS. | [short ornament rule] | Originally addressed to a Young Lady at S——, Con., | in the year 1741.

17.9 x 10.9 cm.; 4 p.

Notes: some copies vary the form of the caption title; reprinted, pp. [1]-4 (also paged [13]-16) in TRACTS | OF THE | AMERICAN TRACT SOCIETY. | General Series. | [engraving] | Vol. VI. | PRINTED BY THE | AMERICAN TRACT SOCIETY, | 150 NASSAU-STREET, NEW YORK.

Contents: caption title; p. 4: PUBLISHED BY THE AMERICAN TRACT SOCIETY.

THJ 292 NUC NE0046449
American Tract Society

391 • ADVICE TO YOUNG CONVERTS. | BY REV. JONATHAN EDWARDS. | ORIGINALLY ADDRESSED TO A YOUNG LADY AT S——, | CONN., IN THE YEAR 1741.

Contents: caption title; pp. 46-55 in A | PASTOR'S COUNSEL. | [short rule] | PUBLISHED BY THE | AMERICAN TRACT SOCIETY, | 150 NASSAU-STREET, NEW YORK.

10.8 x 6.9 cm.; $[1]^8$, $2\text{-}6^8$; 96 p.

THJ 293 OCLC 9454620
Southern Baptist Theological Seminary

392 • ADVICE TO | PROFESSING CHRISTIANS, | BY REV. JONATHAN EDWARDS. | *Originally addressed to a young Lady at S——, Con. in the year* 1741.

Contents: caption title; pp. 29-33 in A | CHURCH MANUAL | FOR THE | COMMUNICANTS | OF THE | FIFTH PRESBYTERIAN CHURCH | OF PHILADELPHIA: | CONTAINING THEIR NAMES, WITH THE NAMES OF THE OFFICERS. | ALSO THE | FORM OF ADMISSION | TO CHURCH MEMBERSHIP; | CHURCH NOTICES—QUESTIONS OF SELF-EXAMINATION FOR PRO- | FESSED CHRISTIANS—ADVICE TO THE SAME BY | PRESIDENT EDWARDS—AND A | DISCOURSE BY THEIR PASTOR, | ON THE DUTIES OF CHURCH MEMBERS. | [thick-thin rule] | COMPILED AND PRINTED AGREEABLY TO AN ORDER OF SESSION. | [thin-thick rule] | PHILADELPHIA: | PRINTED BY W. F. GEDDES, NO. 59 LOCUST STREET. | 1829.

17.1 x 10.5 cm.; π^2, A^7, $C\text{-}D^6$; [4], 47, [1] p.

THJ 294 NUC NE0046447 OCLC 32967038

American Antiquarian Society

393 • ADVICE | TO YOUNG CONVERTS. | *A Letter from the late Rev. Jonathan Edwards of | Northampton, to a young Lady at Suffield, a | young Convert.*

16.7 x 10.6 cm.; A^4; 8 p.

Contents: caption title; pp. [1]-6: text; p. [7]: *Resolutions made and written at dif- | ferent times by Jonathan Edwards.*

THJ 295 NUC NE0046448

Beinecke Library

394 • ADVICE | TO YOUNG CONVERTS. | *A Letter from the late Rev. Jonathan Edwards of North- | ampton, to a young Lady at Suffield, Con.*

17.8 x 10.8 cm.; 12 p.

Notes: Pp. [8]-9 in a group of tracts. Source unidentified.—THJ. This note is repeated as THJ 302, Resolutions | Written At Different Times | By Jonathan Edwards., found at Congregational Library.

Contents: caption title; pp. [1]-7: text; p. 7: HYMN. | THE CONVERT.–*By Cowper.*; p. [8]: RESOLUTIONS | WRITTEN AT DIFFERENT TIMES | BY JONATHAN EDWARDS.; p. 9: HYMN.; p. [10]: TOKENS OF PERDITION.; p. 12: HYMN. | PARABLE OF THE WHEAT AND TARES.—*By Newton.*

THJ 296 NUC NE0046756

Congregational Library

395 • GROWTH IN GRACE: | OR, THE YOUNG PROFESSOR DIRECTED HOW TO | ATTAIN TO EMINENT PIETY. | [short rule] | BY JONATHAN EDWARDS AND JOHN A. JAMES.

Notes: published c. 1842; p. 42 is signed J. EDWARDS.

Contents: caption title; pp. [35]-42 in A | CASKET | OF | FOUR JEWELS, | FOR | YOUNG CHRISTIANS. | [short rule] | BOSTON: | GOULD, KENDALL, & LINCOLN.

11.1 x 6.7 cm.; $[1]^8$, $2\text{-}8^8$; 128 p.

NC 0185252 OCLC 11729229

Harvard University

RESOLUTIONS

396 • *EXTRACT from the private Writings of | the Rev.* JONATHAN EDWARDS. | [short thick-thin rule] His *RESOLUTIONS.*

14.6 x 8.9 cm.; $[A]^{12}$, B^6, C^{12}, D^6, E^{12}, F^6, G^{12}, H^6; 143, [1] p.

Notes: reprints the forty "Resolutions" first published in Samuel Hopkins's *Life of Edwards* (1765); all seventy were first published in Sereno E. Dwight's *Memoir* (1829) (see 299 and 509); see *Works* (Yale), 16:750, 753-759.

Contents: caption title; pp. 139-143 in SEVEN | SERMONS: | –*VIZ.*– | I. Of the Unpardonable SIN against the HOLY | GHOST: Or, The Sin unto Death. | II. The Saint's Duty and Exercife: In two Parts: | Being an Exhortation to, and Direction for | Prayer. | III. The Accepted Time and Day of Salvation. | IV. The End of Time, and Beginning of Eternity.

| V. *Joſhua's* Reſolutions to ſerve the Lord. | VI. The Way to Heaven made Plain. | VII. The future State of Man: Or, A Treatiſe of | the Reſurrection. | [thick-thin rule] | By ROBERT RUSSEL, | At *Wadhurſt*, in SUSSEX. | [rule] | The FIFTY-SECOND Edition | [thin-thick rule] | *LONDON*, PRINTED: | *NEW-YORK*: RE-PRINTED BY HUGH GAINE, | AT THE BIBLE, IN HANOVER-SQUARE, | M,DCC,XCIII.

OCLC 9619180
Houghton Library

397 • Preſident Edwards's | RESOLUTIONS. | EXTRACTED | *From his private Writings* | And Inſerted, in Part, | BY | DR. HOPKINS, | In his Account of | MR. EDWARDS's LIFE. | *Prefixed to* | His XVIII. SERMONS.

Contents: caption title; pp. [70]-93 in CHRISTIANÆ MILITIÆ | Viaticum: | OR, A | *BRIEF DIRECTORY* | FOR | Evangelical Miniſters. | [short thick-thin rule] | *Philadelphia:* | Printed by S. C. USTICK, | No. 79, North Third St. | 1798.

7.9 x 4.6 cm.; A^{16}, B-C^{8}, E-F^{8}; 96 p.
EAI 1:33515
American Antiquarian Society

398 • ARTICLES OF FAITH, | AND | FORM OF COVENANT, | ADOPTED BY THE | THIRD CONGREGATIONAL CHURCH | IN | *BEVERLY*, | AT ITS FORMATION, NOV. 9, 1802. | WITH SCRIPTURE PROOFS AND ILLUSTRATIONS. | *To which are added*, | RESOLUTIONS OF PRESIDENT EDWARDS. | [short decorative rule] | *Published by Order of the Church for the use of the* | *Members*. | [short decorative rule] | JOSEPH EMERSON, | *Pastor of said Church*. | [thick-thin rule] | BOSTON: | PRINTED BY E. LINCOLN, WATER STREET. | 1807.

17.5 x 10.8 cm.; 12 p.

Notes: although the following editorial note was printed only in this and the next item, its provisions were incorporated in most subsequent editions: FOR the benefit of the young reader, it may be proper to ob- | serve, that in referring to Scripture under the following Articles, | a comma is used to separate verses of the same chapter; as | John 6. 44, 65, 67, refers to the forty-fourth, sixty-fifth, and sixty- | seventh | verses of the sixth chapter of John. When several contiguous verses are referred to, a blank line denotes all but the | two outer verses, as John 6. 44—65, refers not only to the forty- | fourth and sixty-fifth verses of the sixth chapter of John, but | likewise to all the intermediate verses, as 45, 46, 47, &c to 65. | When two or more chapters of the same book are referred to in | the same set of references, each chapter, except the first men- | tioned, is immediately preceded by the well known character &, | as Prov. 1. 3 & 4. 5, 6 & 6. 6—11, 15, refers tot he third verse of | the first chapter of Proverbs, the fifth and sixth verses of | the fourth chapter, and the 6, 7, 8, 9, 10, 11 and 15th verses of the | sixth chapter of Proverbs. This reference may be easily understood by the hearer, if read thus, *Proverbs* | *first, third; and fourth,* | *fifth, sixth; and sixth, sixth to the eleventh, fifteenth.*–Ps. stands | for Psalm, and Is. for Isaiah.

Contents: p. [1]: title page; p. [2]: [editorial note]; p. [3]: ARTICLES OF FAITH.; p. 8: COVENANT.; p. [9]: Resolutions | OF MR. JONATHAN EDWARDS; | *One of the greatest of men, and best Christians; author* | *of the History of Redemption, Treatise of Religious Af-* | *fections, Freedom of Will, &c. &c. who was born Oct.* | 5, 1703, *at Windsor, in Connecticut; settled in the* | *ministry at Northampton,* 1727; *dismissed,* 1750; | *made President of New Jersey College,* 1758 *and di-* | *ed of the small pox, a few weeks after.*

THJ 297 EAI 2:12115 OCLC 35986488
Massachusetts Historical Society

399 • ARTICLES OF FAITH, | AND | FORM OF COVENANT, | ADOPTED BY THE CONGREGATIONAL CHURCH | IN | [blank] | WITH SCRIPTURE PROOFS AND ILLUSTRATIONS. | TO WHICH ARE ADDED, | Resolutions of President Edwards. | [short wavy rule] | *First published for the use of a particular* | *Church in Massachusetts, and repub-* | *lished by the desire of a number of* | *Ministers in Vermont, and* | *recommended to Church-* | *es for general use.* [short wavy rule] | *BURLINGTON VT.* | PRINTED BY SAMUEL MILLS. | [short double line of stops]

| 1808.

16.5 x 10.4 cm.; 12 p.

Contents: p. [1]: title; p. [2]: [editorial note]; p. [3]: ARTICLES OF FAITH.; p. 7: COVENANT.; p. 8: RESOLUTIONS | OF | MR. JONATHAN EDWARDS; | *One of the greateſt of men, and beſt Christians; author | of the Hiſtory of Redemption, Treatiſe of Religious Af- | fections, Freedom of Will, &c. &c. who was born Oct.* | 5, 1703, *at Windſor, in Connecticut; ſettled in the | miniſtry at Northampton,* 1727; *diſmiſſed,* 1750; | *made Preſident of New Jerſey College,* 1758; *and di- | ed of the ſmall pox, a few weeks after.*

THJ 298 EAI 2:14763 OCLC 12384160

American Antiquarian Society

400 • ARTICLES OF FAITH, | AND | FORM OF COVENANT, | ADOPTED BY THE | *Congregational Church in Leicester*, | OCTOBER 3, 1805: | WITH SCRIPTURE PROOFS AND ILLUSTRATIONS. | TO WHICH ARE ADDED, | RESOLUTIONS OF PRESIDENT EDWARDS. | [short thick-thin rule] | *Published by Order of the Church for the use of the Members.* | [short thick-thin rule] | ZEPHANIAH SWIFT MOORE, PASTOR. | [short line of stops] | BOSTON: | PRINTED BY LINCOLN & EDMANDS, | No. 53 Cornhill.

17.8 x 10.4 cm.; 12 p.

Contents: p. [1]: title (verso blank); p. [3]: ARTICLES OF FAITH; p. [8]: FORM OF COVENANT; p. [9]: RESOLUTIONS | OF THE LEARNED AND EMINENTLY PIOUS | DIVINE, JONATHAN EDWARDS, MINISTER | OF THE GOSPEL IN NORTHAMPTON, MAS- | SACHUSETTS, AND AFTERWARDS PRESI- | DENT OF THE COLLEGE OF NEWJERSEY.

THJ 299 EAI 2:8770 OCLC 15137922

American Antiquarian Society

401 • ARTICLES OF FAITH, | AND | FORM OF GOVERNMENT, | ADOPTED | BY THE | CONGREGATIONAL CHURCH IN | LEICESTER, MASSACHUSETTS, | OCTOBER 3, 1805, | WHILE UNDER THE PASTORAL CARE OF REV. ZEPHANIAH SWIFT | MOORE, NEW PRESIDENT OF WILLIAMS' COLLEGE; | BY THE CHURCH OF CHRIST IN CANDIA, | NEW-HAMPSHIRE, | MAY 22, 1816; | AND ALSO, | BY THE CONGREGATIONAL CHURCH IN CHESTER, | JANUARY 13, 1818. | WITH | SCRIPTURE PROOFS AND ILLUSTRATIONS. | TO WHICH ARE ADDED, | *RESOLUTIONS OF PRESIDENT EDWARDS.* | *CONCORD*: | PRINTED BY GEORGE HOUGH. | *April*....1818.

17.6 x 10.7 cm.; 12 p.

Contents: p. [1]: title (verso blank); p. [3]: ARTICLES OF FAITH.; p. 8: *FORM OF COVENANT*; p. 9: RESOLUTIONS.

EAI 2:44557 OCLC 32512952

University of New Hampshire

402 • *ARTICLES OF FAITH*, | AND | FORM OF GOVERNMENT, | ADOPTED | BY THE CONGREGATIONAL CHURCH IN LEICES- | TER, MASS. OCTOBER 3, 1805, | While under the pastoral care of Rev. Zephaniah Swift Moore, now | President of Williams' College; | BY THE CHURCH OF CHRIST IN CANDIA, NEW-HAMPSHIRE, | MAY 22, 1816; | AND ALSO, BY THE CONGREGATIONAL CHURCH IN CHESTER, | JANUARY 13, 1818. | WITH | [reversed italics] *Scripture Proofs & Illustrations.* | TO WHICH ARE ADDED, | RESOLUTIONS OF PRESIDENT EDWARDS. | [short decorative rule] | CONCORD: | PRINTED BY JACOB B. MOORE. | 1823.

16.5 x 10.4 cm.; 12 p.

Contents: p. [1]: title (verso blank); p. [3]: [reversed italics] *ARTICLES OF FAITH*.; p. 8: [reversed italics] *FORM OF COVENANT*; p. 9: [reversed italics] *RESOLUTIONS*.

OCLC 39323434
American Antiquarian Society

403 • *CONFESSION OF FAITH* | AND | COVENANT, | OF | THE CHURCH OF CHRIST, | IN PEMBROKE, N. H. | [short rule] | Published by order of the Church. | [short rule] | ALSO, | RESOLUTIONS OF PRESIDENT EDWARDS. | [short double rule] | CONCORD: | PRINTED BY JACOB B. MOORE. | 1823.

18.2 x 11.3 cm.; 12 p.

Contents: p. [1]: title; p. [2]: NOTE.; p. [3]: CONFESSION OF FAITH.; p. [7]: [reversed italics] *COVENANT.*; p. [9]: [reversed italics] *RESOLUTIONS.*

THJ 300 NUC NE0046755 OCLC 13633334
American Antiquarian Society

404 • ARTICLES OF FAITH, | AND | FORM OF COVENANT, | DRAWN UP | BY REV. ZEPHANIAH S. MOORE, | LATE PRESIDENT OF WILLIAMS' COLLEGE; | AND | ADOPTED BY THE CONGREGATIONAL CHURCH IN LEICESTER, MAS- | SACHUSETTS; SINCE, BY CHURCHES IN CANDIA, AND | CHESTER, NEW-HAMPSHIRE; AND MARCH 31, | 1825, BY THE CONGREGATIONAL | CHURCH IN HAMPTON, N.H. | WITH | SCRIPTURE PROOFS AND ILLUSTRATIONS. | TO WHICH ARE ADDED, | *RESOLUTIONS OF PRESIDENT EDWARDS.* | [short thick-thin rule] | Worcester: | GRIFFIN AND MORRILL....PRINTERS. | 1827.

17.8 x 10.6 cm.; 12 p.

Contents: p. [1]: title (verso blank); p. [3]: ARTICLES OF FAITH.; p. 8: FORM OF COVENANT.; p. 9: RESOLUTIONS.

OCLC 2518896
American Antiquarian Society

405 • PRESIDENT | EDWARDS'S RESOLUTIONS. | *Extracted from his private Writings, | and inserted, in part, by* | DR. HOPKINS, | In his account of | MR. EDWARDS'S LIFE. | Prefixed to his | XVIII. SERMONS.

Contents: caption title; pp. [65]-85 in CHRISTIANÆ MILITIÆ | VIATICUM: | FOR | EVANGELICAL MINISTERS. | [short rule] | NEW YORK: | TAYLOR AND GOULD, | Brick Church Chapel, opposite the City Hall. | [short rule] | M DCCC XXXVI.

7.6 x 5.1 cm.; 89 p.
OCLC 26756162
Houghton Library

406 • THE SEVENTY RESOLUTIONS.

Notes: published c. 1832; the text cites a life of Phebe Bartlet "lately" published by the American Sunday School Union (p. 52), but no copy has been located.

Contents: caption title; pp. 26-42 in THE | LIFE | OF | PRESIDENT EDWARDS. | WRITTEN FOR THE AMERICAN SUNDAY SCHOOL UNION, | AND REVISED BY THE COMMITTEE OF PUBLICATION. | [short double rule] | AMERICAN SUNDAY SCHOOL UNION | *PHILADELPHIA*: | NO. 146 CHESTNUT STREET | [short rule] | 1832.

14.3 x 9.7 cm.; 143 p.
OCLC 11845525
Congregational Library

407 • RESOLUTIONS | BY | REV. JONATHAN EDWARDS.

Notes: in some copies, JAMES RUSSELL, PUBLISHING AGENT. | 1841. follows the last line on the title page;

on the verso: PRINTED BY | WILLIAM S. MARTIEN.

Contents: caption title; pp. 57-72 in THE | CHRISTIAN'S | SCRIPTURE DIRECTORY. | BY THE | REV. JOHN WILLISON, A. M. | TOGETHER WITH | RESOLUTIONS | BY THE REV. JONATHAN EDWARDS. | [short decorative rule] | PHILADELPHIA: | PRESBYTERIAN BOARD OF PUBLICATION.

11 x 7 cm.; $[1]^8$, $2\text{-}4^8$, 5^4; 72 p.

THJ 301 OCLC 11845525

Presbyterian Historical Society

408 • PRESIDENT EDWARDS' | RESOLUTIONS, | *Extracted from his private writings,* | *and inserted, in part, by* | DR. HOPKINS, | IN HIS ACCOUNT OF | MR. EDWARDS' LIFE, PREFIXED TO HIS | EIGHTEEN SERMONS.

Contents: caption title; pp. [63]-84 in DAILY PROVISION: | OR, | A BRIEF DIRECTORY | FOR | CHRISTIANS IN GENERAL, | AND MORE PARTICULARLY | MINISTERS. | [short rule] | FIRST AMERICAN, | FROM THE SIXTH EDINBURGH EDITION. | [short rule] | HARTFORD: | HENRY BENTON, PUBLISHER, | EXCHANGE BUILDINGS. | [short double line of stops] | 1832.

8.4 x 5 cm.; 96 p.

American Antiquarian Society

409 • EXTRACT | FROM THE PRIVATE WRITINGS | OF THE | REV. JONATHAN EDWARDS. | [short rule] | HIS RESOLUTIONS.

Contents: caption title; pp. [172]-176 in RUSSELL'S [*sic*] | SEVEN | SERMONS: | ON | I. THE UNPARDONABLE SIN AGAINST THE HOLY GHOST. | II. THE SAINT'S DUTY AND EXERCISE. | III. THE ACCEPTED TIME AND DAY OF SALVATION. | IV. THE END OF TIME AND BEGINNING OF ETERNITY. | V. RESOLUTION TO SERVE THE LORD. | VI. THE WAY TO HEAVEN MADE PLAIN. | VII. THE FUTURE STATE OF MAN. | [short rule] | PUBLISHED BY | JAMES STERRET. | A MAN DESTITUTE OF EYESIGHT SINCE AUGUST, 1846. | Circulated for the benefit of a generous Christian commu- | nity, as well as for the pecuniary assistance of the | sufferer, who feels desirous to become as | useful as possible in the few re- | maining days of his life. | FROM THE FIFTY-SECOND LONDON EDITION. | [short rule] | MOUNTAIN VALLEY, VA. | [NEAR HARRISONBURG:] | PRINTED AT THE OFFICE OF JOSEPH FUNK & SONS. | 1853.

14.3 x 9.7 cm.; 176 [i.e., 175] p.

OCLC 4708443

College of William and Mary

410 • RESOLUTIONS

Notes: pp. [721]-728: JONATHAN EDWARDS; running title: A WELL ORDERED LIFE.

Contents: caption title; *The American Journal of Education*, 27 (October 15, 1876):724-727.

THJ 303 OCLC 9216534

Harvard University

411 • President Edwards' | Seventy Resolutions. | Extracted From His Private Writings.

18 x 10.2 cm.; 8 p.

Notes: no title page; no publisher, no date.

Contents: caption title; pp. [1]-8: text.

NUC NE0046777

New York Public Library

412 • RESOLUTIONS | OF A | SAINTLY SCHOLAR | Jonathan Edwards | Introduction by | Robert E. Coleman | The Department of Evangelism | Asbury Theological Seminary | Wilmore, Kentucky 40340

13.9 x 8.8 cm.; 46 p.

Contents: p. [1]: title; p. [2]: Copyright © 1974 by Robert E. Coleman | [4 lines]; p. 3: Introduction; p. 11: His

Spiritual Delight; p. 19: Personal Resolutions; p. 31: Constant Review; p. 44: blank; p. 45: Footnotes.
OCLC 18829298
Cincinnati Bible College and Seminary

412A • [4 lines over double rules] Resolutions | of a | SAINTLY | Scholar | Jonathan Edwards | Introduction by | Robert E. Coleman | World Wide Publications

17.8 x 10 cm.; 47, [17] p.

Contents: p. [1]: Resolutions | of a | SAINTLY | Scholar (verso blank); p. [3]: title; p. [4]: *Resolutions of a Saintly Scholar* | © 1974 by Robert E. Coleman | Used by Permission | Published by World Wide Publications 1992 | [4 lines]; p. [5]: Contents (verso blank); p. [7]: Introduction; p. [14]: blank; pp. [15]-47: text; pp. [48-64]: Notes [blank].

ISBN 0890662290 OCLC 34539420
Gordon-Conwell Theological Seminary

413 • Jonathan Edwards' | Resolutions | And Advice to Young Converts | Introduced and edited | by Stephen J. Nichols | P&R | PUBLISHING | P.O. BOX 817 • PHILLIPSBURG • NEW JERSEY 08865-0817

21.6 x 13.4 cm.; 39, [1] p.

Contents: p. [1]: title; p. [2]: © 2001 by Stephen J. Nichols | [31 lines]; p. 3: CONTENTS; p. 4: LIST OF ILLUSTRATIONS; p. 5: INTRODUCTION; p. [16]: blank; p. 17: RESOLUTIONS; p. 27: ADVICE TO YOUNG CONVERTS; p. 37: FOR FURTHER READING; p. [38]: [biography]; p. [39]: WANT TO KNOW MORE?; p. 40: blank.

ISBN 0875521894 OCLC 4696231
The Master's College

ON FULFILLING ENGAGEMENTS AND PAYING DEBTS

414 • ON FULFILLING ENGAGEMENTS | AND | PAYING DEBTS. | [short thick-thin rule] | [*From a Sermon by the late President Edwards, on Ex- | odus* xx. 15. *Thou shalt not steal*."] | [short thin-thick rule] *stet Thou shalt not steal*."

17.5 x 9.7 cm.; xvi, 181, [1] p.

Notes: preached July 1740; first published as *The Sin of Theft and of Injustice* in *Practical Sermons Never Before Published* (1788), pp. 321-342.

Contents: caption title; pp. [179]-181 in ESSAYS TO DO GOOD, | ADDRESSED | To all Christians, | WHETHER IN | PUBLIC OR PRIVATE CAPACITIES. | [short thick-thin rule] | BY THE LATE | *COTTON MATHER, D.D.F.R.S.* | [short thin-thick rule] | To do good, and to communicate, forget not. | *Hebr.* xiii.16 | [short line of stops] | *A NEW EDITION*, | IMPROVED BY GEORGE BURDER. | [short line of stops] | [rule] | *From the latest Boston and London Editions.* | [rule] | TO WHICH ARE ADDED, | *TREATISES*, | ON | ENGAGEMENTS, RELIGIOUS EDUCATION | AND | SANCTIFYING THE SABBATH-DAY. | [thick-thin rule] | JOHNSTOWN: | *PRINTED AND SOLD BY ASA CHILD.* | [short line of stops] | 1815.

EAI 2:35227 NUC NE0046741 OCLC 20020731
Houghton Library

415 • ON FULFILLING ENGAGEMENTS | AND | PAYING DEBTS. | [short tapered rule] | [*From a Sermon by the late President Edwards,* | *on Exodus* xx. 15. *Thou shalt not steal.*] | [short tapered rule]

13.8 x 8.5 cm.; 228 [i.e., 232] p.

Notes: pp. [229]-232 misnumbered [129]-132.

Contents: caption title; pp. [229]-232 in ESSAYS TO DO GOOD, | ADDRESSED | TO ALL CHRISTIANS, | WHETHER | IN PUBLIC OR PRIVATE CAPACITIES. | [short tapered rule] | BY THE LATE | COTTON MATHER, D.D. F.R.S. | [double rule] | To do good, and to communicate, forget not. - *Heb.* xiii.16. | [double rule] | *A NEW EDITION*,|

IMPROVED BY GEORGE BURDER. | [short tapered rule] | *From the latest Boston and London Editions.* | [short tapered rule] | *NEW-YORK:* | PUBLISHED BY WHITING AND HUDSON. | Sold by Whiting & Tiffany, *New-Haven*, Con.; D. Whiting, *Troy*; | and B. B. Hopkins, *Philadelphia.* | J. SEYMOUR, PRINTER. | [short double rule] | 1815.

EAI 2:35228 OCLC 4126451

Houghton Library

ACCOUNT OF ABIGAIL HUTCHINSON

416 • [78. | ACCOUNT OF | ABIGAIL HUTCHINSON, | A YOUNG WOMAN, HOPEFULLY CONVERTED AT NORTHAMP- | TON, MASS. 1734 | [short decorative rule] | BY JONATHAN EDWARDS. | [short decorative rule]

17.5 x 10.9 cm.; 8 p.

Notes: published separately and reissued in THE | PUBLICATIONS | OF THE | N. ENG. TRACT SOCIETY. | VOL. IV. | [short thick-thin rule] | "The benefits to be derived from Education may be | greatly assisted by the dispersion of small cheap Tracts | on religious an moral duties." BISHOP OF DURHAM. | [short thin-thick rule] | ANDOVER: | PRINTED BY FLAGG AND GOULD | 1820, pp. [1]-8 (also paged [121]-128). The account first appears in *Faithful Narrative* (1737); see *The Great Awakening*, ed. C. C. Goen, *The Works of Jonathan Edwards*, vol. 4 (New Haven: Yale University Press, 1972), pp. 191-199.

Contents: caption title; pp. [1]-8 (also paged [121]-128): text; p. 8: [poem] | [thick-thin rule] | ANDOVER: | PRINTED FOR THE NEW ENGLAND TRACT SOCIETY | BY FLAGG AND GOULD. | 1816. [First edit. 6000.

THJ 304 EAI 2:37499 NUC NE0046441

American Tract Society

417 • [No. 78. | ACCOUNT OF | ABIGAIL HUTCHINSON, | A YOUNG WOMAN, HOPEFULLY CONVERTED AT NORTHAMP- | TON, MASS. 1734. | [short decorative rule] | BY JONATHAN EDWARDS. | [short decorative rule].

17.5 x 11.1 cm.; 8 p.

Contents: caption title; pp. [1]-8: text; p. 8: [poem] | ANDOVER: | PRINTED FOR THE NEW ENGLAND TRACT SOCIETY | BY FLAGG AND GOULD. | 1817. [2d Edit. 6000.

THJ 305 EAI 2:40733 NUC NE0046442

Boston Public Library

418 • ACCOUNT OF | ABIGAIL HUTCHINSON, | A YOUNG WOMAN, HOPEFULLY CONVERTED AT NORTH- | AMPTON, MASS. 1734. | *BY REV. JONATHAN EDWARDS.* | [short rule] | TO WHICH IS ADDED, | THE FISHERMAN. | [rule] | Published by "The Religious Tract Society of Philadelphia," and | sold at their Depository, No. 8 South Front-street. | JANUARY —1818. | [rule]

18.2 x 10.4 cm.; 12 p.

Contents: caption title; pp. [1]-8: text; p. 8: THE | FISHERMAN.

THJ 306 EAI 2:43919 NUC NE0046443 OCLC 7381071

Pittsburgh Theological Seminary

419 • [No. 78. | ACCOUNT OF | ABIGAIL HUTCHINSON, | A YOUNG WOMAN HOPEFULLY CONVERTED AT NORTHAMPTON, | MASS. 1734. | [short thick-thin rule] | BY JONATHAN EDWARDS. | [short thin-thick rule]

17 x 10.7 cm.; 8 p.

Contents: caption title; pp. [1]-8 (also paged [121]-128): text; p. 8: [poem] | [thick-thin rule] | ANDOVER: | PRINTED FOR THE NEW ENGLAND TRACT SOCIETY | BY FLAGG AND GOULD. | 1819. [3d edit. 6000.

EAI 2:47882
American Antiquarian Society

420 • [No. 78. | ACCOUNT OF | ABIGIAL HUTCHINSON, | A YOUNG WOMAN, HOPEFULLY CONVERTED AT NORTHAMPTON, MASS. | 1734. | [short rule] | BY JONATHAN EDWARDS. *stet* ABIGIAL

16.7 x 10.2 cm.; 8 p.

Contents: caption title; pp. [1]-8 (also paged [121]-128): text; p. 8: [poem] | [thick-thin rule] | ANDOVER: | PRINTED FOR THE NEW ENGLAND TRACT SOCIETY, | BY FLAGG AND GOULD. | 1820. [4th edit. 6,000.

THJ 307 NUC NE0046444
Boston Public Library

421 • [No. 141. | ACCOUNT | OF | ABIGAIL HUTCHINSON, | *A Young Woman hopefully Converted at Northampton* | *Massachusetts*, 1734.

17.6 x. 10.6 cm.; 8 p.

Contents: caption title; pp. [1]-8: text; p. 8: *Published by the New-York Religious Tract Society*, | And sold by D. H. Wickham, Agent for the Society, at his Theological | Book-Store, No. 59 Fulton-street. | [in 2 cols., col. 1] [short rule] | July, 1820.–3000.] | [col. 2] [short rule] | [J. SEYMOUR, printer.

American Antiquarian Society

422 • No. 78. | ACCOUNT OF | ABIGAIL HUTCHINSON, | A YOUNG WOMAN HOPEFULLY CONVERTED AT NORTHAMPTON, MASS. | 1734. | BY JONATHAN EDWARDS.

16.7 x 10.2 cm.; 8 p.

Notes: no copy of a fifth edition has been located; the only holder of the sixth edition cannot locate it.

Contents: caption title; pp. [1]-8: text; p. 8: PRINTED FOR THE AMERICAN TRACT SOCIETY, | *By* FLAGG & GOULD; *and sold by them* | *at the General Depository, Andover, Mass.* | *By* S. T. ARMSTRONG, No. 50, Cornhill, Boston, | *and by Agents of the Society in the principal towns* | *in the United States.* 6th edit. 4000.

THJ 308 NUC NE0046439

423 • [No. 29. | ACCOUNT OF | ABIGAIL HUTCHINSON. | BY JONATHAN EDWARDS. | [engraving] | "I think it pleasure to sit and see the wind blowing in the trees, | and to behold what God has made." *See p. 5.*

17.4 x 11 cm.; 8 p.

Notes: published c. 1823 for juvenile readers.

Contents: caption title; pp. [1]-8 (also paged [100]-108): text; p. 8: PHILADELPHIA: | Published by the Sunday and Adult School Union, | And for sale at their Depository, 29 North Fourth Street. | R. PIGGOT, AGENT.

OCLC 44796303
Duke University

424 • NO. 78. | ACCOUNT | OF | **Abigail Hutchinson**, | A YOUNG WOMAN HOPEFULLY CONVERTED AT | NORTHAMPTON, MASS. 1734. | [short double rule] | BY REVEREND JONATHAN EDWARDS. | [short double rule] | [engraving] | She often expressed a sense of the glory of God appearing in the | trees and the works of God's hands.–*Page* 5. | [short double rule] | PUBLISHED BY THE | AMERICAN TRACT SOCIETY, | AND SOLD AT THEIR DEPOSITORY, NO. 144 NASSAU-STREET, NEAR | THE CITY-HALL, NEW-YORK; AND BY AGENTS OF THE | SOCIETY, ITS BRANCHES, AND AUXILIARIES, IN | THE PRINCIPAL CITIES AND TOWNS | IN THE UNITED STATES. | Vol. 3 H

16.6 x 10.4 cm.; 8 p.

Notes: in some copies, fonts of the title page and addresses of imprint vary; also issued, pp. [1]-8 (also paged [165]-172), in THE | PUBLICATIONS | OF THE | AMERICAN TRACT SOCIETY. | [short rule] | VOL. III. | [short rule] | "There never was, in any age of the world, either philosophy, or sect, or religion, or law, or discipline, which did so highly exalt the | public good, as the Christian Faith." BACON | [short double rule] | PUBLISHED BY THE | AMERICAN TRACT SOCIETY, | AND SOLD AT THEIR DEPOSITORY, NO. 144 NASSAU-STREET, NEAR | THE CITY-HALL, NEW-YORK; AND BY AGENTS OF THE | SOCIETY, ITS BRANCHES, AND AUXILIARIES, IN | THE PRINCIPAL CITIES AND TOWNS | IN THE UNITED STATES.

Contents: p. [1]: title; pp. 2-8: text.

THJ 309 NUC NE0046440 OCLC 15503760

American Antiquarian Society

425 • No. 78. | CONVERSION | OF | ABIGAIL HUTCHINSON. | FROM PRESIDENT EDWARDS' NARRATIVE | OF | A SURPRISING WORK OF GOD | IN | NORTHAMPTON, MASS., 1735. | [engraving] | She often expressed a sense of the glory of God appearing in the trees and the works of | God's hands.–PAGE 5. | [short rule] | PUBLISHED BY THE | AMERICAN TRACT SOCIETY, | 150 NASSAU-STREET, NEW YORK.

17.9 x 10.8 cm.; 8 p.

Contents: front cover (recto): title; front cover (verso): IS ANY THING TOO HARD FOR THE LORD?; p. [1] (also paged [165]): title; pp. [2]-8 (also paged [166]-172): text; back cover (recto): [continued from front cover (verso)] | AN AFFECTING ANECDOTE.; back cover (verso): Loving Kindness. | [25 lines] | [double rule] | [advertisement].

THJ 310 NUC NE0046500 OCLC 31430368

Princeton University

426 • No. 78. | CONVERSION | OF | ABIGAIL HUTCHINSON. | FROM | PRESIDENT EDWARDS' NARRATIVE OF A SURPRISING | WORK OF GOD IN NORTHAMPTON, MASS., 1735

18.8 x 11.1 cm.; 8 p.

Contents: caption title; pp. [1]-8 in TRACTS | OF THE | AMERICAN TRACT SOCIETY. | General Series. | [engraving] | Vol. III. | PRINTED BY THE | AMERICAN TRACT SOCIETY, | 150 NASSAU-STREET, NEW YORK.

THJ 311 OCLC 12795784

Harvard Divinity School

THEOLOGICAL QUESTIONS

427 • THE | THEOLOGICAL QUESTIONS | OF | PRESIDENT EDWARDS, SENIOR, | AND | DR. EDWARDS, HIS SON. | [short rule] | And Isaac digged again the wells of water, which they had digged in the | days of Abraham his father; for the Philistines had stopped them after the | death of Abraham; and he called their names after the names by which his fa- | ther had called them. And Isaac's servants digged in the valley, and found | there a well of springing water. *Gen. XXVI.* 18, 19. | [short rule] | PROVIDENCE: | PRINTED BY MILLER & HUTCHENS. | June—1822.

21.3 x 12.6 cm.; $[1]^4$, 2^5; 17, [1] p.

Contents: p. [1]: title (verso blank); p. [3]:THEOLOGICAL QUESTIONS, | BY REV. JONATHAN EDWARDS, | *President of the College in New-Jersey. He died* 22d *March*, 1758, | *Aged* 54.; p. [6]: *By JONATHAN EDWARDS, D. D. President of Union College,* | *Schenectady. He died* 1*st August*, 1801.–*Aged* 56.; p. [18]: blank.

THJ 312 NUC NE0046816 OCLC 1218994

Congregational Library

428 • *Theological Questions of the Elder Edwards.*

Notes: pp. 370-381: *Theological Questions for the Younger Edwards.*

Contents: caption title; pp. 367-370 in Article VII. | THEOLOGICAL EDUCATION. | No. IX—QUESTIONS OF THE TWO EDWARDSES FOR THEIR PUPILS IN THEOLOGY, *Bibliotheca Sacra*, 39 (April 1882).

THJ 313 OCLC 6288728

Gordon-Conwell Theological Seminary

JUSTIFICATION BY FAITH ALONE

429 • EXTRACTS FROM PRESIDENT ED- | WARDS' "DISCOURSE ON JUSTIFI- | CATION BY FAITH ALONE." | *What is meant in Scripture by being | justified.*

Notes: two-part article; title of the second part: EXTRACTS FROM PRESIDENT ED- | WARDS' "DISCOURSE ON JUSTIFI- | CATION BY FAITH ALONE." | *Why we must be justified by faith | only, without any manner of good- | ness of our own.*

Contents: caption title(s); *The Christian Advocate*, 2 (August 1824):343-346; (September 1824):388-392.

THJ 314 OCLC 1554425

Gordon-Conwell Theological Seminary

430 • Justification | by | Faith Alone | "But to him that worketh not, but believeth on | Him that justifieth the ungodly, his faith | is counted for righteousness." | Romans 4:5 | by | Jonathan Edwards | Edited by Rev. Don Kistler | Soli Deo Gloria Publications | *...for instruction in righteousness...*

21.4 x 13.8 cm.; v, 154 p.

Contents: p. [i]: title; p. [ii]: Soli Deo Gloria Publications | P.O. Box 451, Morgan, PA 15064 | [2 lines] | *Justification by Faith Alone* was retypeset from the 1838 | Hickman edition of *The Works of Jonathan Edwards.* | This Soli Deo Gloria edition, in which spelling, | grammar, and formatting changes have | been made, is © 2000 by Don Kistler | and Soli Deo Gloria. | [1 line]; p. iii: Contents; p. [v]: Publisher's Preface (verso blank); pp. 1-154: text.

ISBN 1573581070 OCLC 43873667

Harvard Divinity School

JESUS CHRIST GLORIOUSLY EXALTED ABOVE ALL EVIL

431 • JESUS CHRIST | GLORIOUSLY EXALTED ABOVE ALL EVIL, | IN THE WORK | OF | [reversed italics] *REDEMPTION;* | A SERMON, | DELIVERED AT NORTHAMPTON, 1738; | BY THE LATE REV. JONATHAN EDWARDS, | *President of the College of New-Jersey.* | [short thick-thin rule] | [This sermon is not included in the eight volumes of President Edwards' | works, published at Worcester, as were many other Discourses, for the want | of room: The same was published in a volume at Glasgow, in 1785, and it is | now re-printed at the expense of an individual, for gratuitous distribution, to | serve the cause of Religion.] | [short thick-thin rule] | *PROVIDENCE*: | BROWN & DANFORTH, PRINTERS. | 1824.

21.2 x 12.8 cm.; 16 p.

Contents: p. [1]: title (verso blank); p. [3]: [reversed italics] *JESUS CHRIST gloriously exalted above | all Evil, in the Work of Redemption.*; p. 16: [This valuable Sermon, the production of an eminently pious and learned | divine, being almost out of print, is now republished with a view to promote | the cause of experimental religion. That it may be as extensively useful as | possible, the publisher requests those who possess a copy, *to loan it to others;* as, in this manner, it will be more widely circulated.]

THJ 315 NUC NE0046690 OCLC 26457356

Congregational Library

THE IMPORTANCE AND ADVANTAGE OF A THOROUGH KNOWLEDGE OF DIVINE TRUTH

432 • EXTRACTS | FROM | EDWARDS' SERMON | ON THE IMPORTANCE OF THE KNOWLEDGE OF DIVINE TRUTH.

Contents: caption title; pp. [23]-24 in THE IMPORTANCE OF DIVINE KNOWLEDGE: | A Sermon, | PREACHED AT THE | ORDINATION OF THE REV. DAVID JEWETT, | TO THE PASTORAL CARE | OF THE | FIFTH CHURCH AND SOCIETY IN GLOUCESTER, | OCTOBER 30, 1805. | [short thick-thin rule] | BY SAMUEL WORCESTER, A. M. | *PASTOR OF THE TABERNACLE CHURCH IN SALEM.* [short thick-thin rule] | SECOND EDITION, | CORRECTED BY THE AUTHOR. | [short thick-thin rule] | New=York: | PRINTED BY VANDERPOOL & COLE FOR CORNELIUS DAVIS. | [short rule] | 1827.

21 x 12.7 cm.; [3], 4-24 p.
OCLC 3919010
Winterthur Library

433 • [triple decorative rule] | The Importance and . . . | Advantage of a Thorough | Knowledge of Divine Truth | [triple decorative rule] | by Jonathan Edwards | [double decorative rule] | FROM THE INHERITANCE OF OUR FATHERS | – Series XVI, No. 8 | [double decorative rule]

13.5 x 9 cm.; 28, [3] p.
Notes: published c. 1964.
Contents: front cover, p. [1]: title; p. [2]: [publisher's note] | [1 line]; p. 3: The Importance and Advantage | of a Thorough Knowledge | of Divine Truth; pp. [29-31]: [advertisement]; back cover (verso): [advertisement] | [double decorative rule] | THE INHERITANCE PUBLISHERS | P.O. Box 334 | Grand Rapids 1, Michigan | [1 line].
NUC NE0046681 OCLC 38910880
Yale Divinity School

434 • Christian Knowledge | OR THE | IMPORTANCE AND ADVANTAGE OF A | THOROUGH KNOWLEDGE OF DIVINE TRUTH. | A Sermon | BY | JONATHAN EDWARDS

21.6 x 13.5 cm.; 24 p.
Contents: front cover: Christian knowledge | BY | JONATHAN EDWARDS | Messages from God's servants | in former days | [6 lines] | [ornament] | [in 2 cols., col. 1]: The Teleios Ministry of | Camelback Bible Church | 3900 East Stanford Drive | Paradise Valley, AZ 85253 | 955-6370 | [col. 2]: December, 1998; front cover (verso): Teleios Sermon # 39 | [40 lines]; p. [1]: title; back cover (recto): [advertisement].
OCLC 49538163
Gordon-Conwell Theological Seminary

GREAT GUILT NO OBSTACLE TO THE PARDON OF THE RETURNING SINNER

435 • GREAT GUILT NO OBSTACLE TO THE PARDON OF | THE RETURNING SINNER. | A SERMON. | [short rule] | BY THE LATE REV. JONATHAN EDWARDS, | *President of the College in New-Jersey*. | [short rule] | DELIVERED ABOUT THE YEAR 1732. | [intended for gratuitous distribution.] | PROVIDENCE: | H. H. BROWN....25 MARKET SQUARE. | 1839.

19.1 x 11.7 cm.; [1]-2^4; 15, [1] p.
Notes: first published in *Practical Sermons Never Before Published* (1788), pp. 54-66.
Contents: p. [1]: title (verso blank); p. [3]: A SERMON.; p. [16]: blank.
THJ 327 NUC NE0046611 OCLC 22863622
Houghton Library

PARDON FOR THE GREATEST SINNERS

436 • No. 514. | PARDON | FOR | THE GREATEST SINNERS. | THE | GREATNESS OF OUR SIN NO IMPEDIMENT, | IF | WE TRULY COME TO GOD FOR MERCY. | BY PRESIDENT EDWARDS. | PUBLISHED BY THE | AMERICAN TRACT SOCIETY, | 150 NASSAU-STREET, NEW YORK.

19.2 x 11.5 cm.; 16 p.

Notes: a shorter version of 435; bound in tan wrappers; back cover (recto): 3; back cover (verso): 16 pages.

Contents: front cover, prp. [1]: title (verso blank); pp. [1]-12: text.

NUC NE0046744 OCLC 20841577

Buffalo and Erie County Public Library

437 • No. 514. | PARDON | FOR | THE GREATEST SINNERS. | BY PRESIDENT EDWARDS.

18.8 x 13.1 cm.; 12 p.

Notes: reprinted, pp. [1]-12 (in some copies, also sig. 32^6) in TRACTS | OF THE | AMERICAN TRACT SOCIETY. | General Series. | [engraving] | Vol. XII. | PRINTED BY THE | AMERICAN TRACT SOCIETY, | 150 NASSAU-STREET, NEW YORK

Contents: caption title; pp. [1]-12: text.

THJ 317

American Tract Society

THE MANNER IN WHICH THE SALVATION OF THE SOUL IS TO BE SOUGHT

438 • Y DULL Y DYLID YMOFYN | IECHYDWRIAETH YR ENAID: | NEU | DRAETHAWD | AR GENESIS VI. 22. | GAN JONATHAN EDWARDS, A. M. AMERICA. | [short wavy rule] | CYFIEITHWYD GAN H. JONES. | [short rule] | LLANGOLLEN: | ARGRAFFWYD A CHYHOEDDWYD GAN H. JONES. | [short rule] | 1845.

16.7 x 9.8 cm.; $[A]^6$, B-C^6; 36 p.

Notes: a Welsh translation of a sermon on Gen. 6:22, preached September 1740; first published in *Sermons on the Following Subjects* (Hartford, 1780), pp. 7-36, and included in the collected works.

Contents: p. [1]: title (verso blank); pp. [3]-36: text; p. 36: HUGH JONES, ARGRAFFYDD, LLANGOLLEN.

THJ 328 NUC NE0046543 OCLC 23088832

Princeton University

438A • Y DULL Y DYLID YMOFYN | IECHYDWR- | IAETH YR ENAID. | [short rule] | TRAETHAWD | AR GENESIS VI. 22. | [short wavy rule] | GAN JONATHAN EDWARDS, A. M. AMERICA. | [short wavy rule] | [short rule] | CYFIEITHWYD GAN H. JONES. | [short rule] | Llangollen: | ARGRAFFWYD A CHYHOEDDWYD GAN H. JONES.

16.7 x 9.8 cm.; $[A]^6$, B-C^6; 36 p.

Notes: identical with the above except for the title page; published c. 1860.

British Library

439 • [within decorative rules] FROM THE | INHERITANCE | OF OUR FATHERS | [rule] | Series VI NO. 11 | [rule] | THE MANNER IN WHICH | THE SALVATION OF THE SOUL | IS TO BE SOUGHT | By the | REV. JONATHAN EDWARDS

15.1 x 8.6 cm.; 32 p.

Contents: front cover (recto): title; front cover (verso): advertisement | [short rule] | The Inheritance Publishing Co.

| P. O. Box 334 | Grand Rapids, Michigan; pp. 3-[32]: text.
OCLC 22894937
Reformed Theological Seminary

THE WAY TO HEAVEN

440 • No. 466. | THE | WAY TO HEAVEN. | BY PRESIDENT EDWARDS.
18.8 x 11.3 cm.; 4 p.
Notes: An adaptation from Edwards's sermon: "God the Best Portion of the Christian" or perhaps "The True Christian's Life, A Journey Towards Heaven."—THJ. It was reprinted, pp. [1]-4 (in some copies, also sig. $37_{5\text{-}6}$), in TRACTS | OF THE | AMERICAN TRACT SOCIETY. | General Series. | [engraving] | Vol. XI. | PRINTED BY THE | AMERICAN TRACT SOCIETY, | 150 NASSAU-STREET, NEW YORK.; p. 4: PUBLISHED BY THE AMERICAN TRACT SOCIETY.
Contents: caption title; p. 4: PUBLISHED BY THE AMERICAN TRACT SOCIETY, | 150 NASSAU-STREET, NEW YORK.
THJ 318
American Tract Society

LOST CONVICTIONS

441 • No. 467. | LOST CONVICTIONS. | [short rule] | BY PRESIDENT EDWARDS.
18.8 x 10.8 cm.; 4 p.
Notes: It has been impossible to identify the source of this item. It has clearly been rewritten, and may be a composite of more than one of Edwards's sermons.—THJ. It was reprinted, pp. [1]-4 (in some copies, also sig. $38_{1\text{-}2}$), in TRACTS | OF THE | AMERICAN TRACT SOCIETY. | General Series. | [engraving] | Vol. XI. | PRINTED BY THE | AMERICAN TRACT SOCIETY, | 150 NASSAU-STREET, NEW YORK.; p. 4: PUBLISHED BY THE AMERICAN TRACT SOCIETY.
Contents: caption title; p. 4: PUBLISHED BY THE AMERICAN TRACT SOCIETY.
THJ 316
American Tract Society

442 • EVANGELICAL TRACT SOCIETY, | PETERSBURG, Va. [brace] No. 101. | LOST CONVICTIONS. | BY PRESIDENT EDWARDS.
17.9 x 11.1 cm.; 4 p.
Notes: unpaged; part of the Confederate Collection.
Contents: caption title.
Boston Athenaeum

CHARITY AND ITS FRUITS

443 • [within rules] CHARITY | AND ITS FRUITS; | OR, | CHRISTIAN LOVE AS MANIFESTED IN | THE HEART AND LIFE. | BY | JONATHAN EDWARDS, | SOMETIME PASTOR OF THE CHURCH AT NORTHAMPTON, MASS., AND | PRESIDENT OF THE COLLEGE OF NEW JERSEY. | EDITED FROM THE ORIGINAL MANUSCRIPTS, | WITH AN INTRODUCTION, | BY TRYON EDWARDS. | NEW YORK: | ROBERT CARTER & BROTHERS, | 285 BROADWAY. |

[short rule] | 1852.

18.6 x 11.4 cm.; π^5, 1-33^8, 34^1; ix, [1], 530, p.

Notes: all pages within rules; in some copies, five leaves of advertisement follow p. 530.

Contents: p. [i]: title; p. [ii]: [wavy rule] Entered, according to Act of Congress, in the year 1851, by | CARTER & BROTHERS, | In the Clerk's Office of the Southern District of New York. | [wavy rule] [in 2 cols., col. 1] T. B. SMITH, STEREOTYPER, | 216 William Street, New York. | [col. 2] R. CRAIGHEAD, PRINTER, | 112 Fulton Street.; p. [iii]: INTRODUCTION. [signed] T. E. | NEW LONDON, CONN. | *November*, 1851; p. [vii]: CONTENTS.; p. [x]: blank; pp. [1]-530: text.

THJ 329 NUC NE0046487 OCLC 4421211

Andover Newton Theological School

443A • NEW YORK: | ROBERT CARTER & BROTHERS, | 285 BROADWAY. | [short rule] | 1854.

THJ 329A NUC NE0046468 OCLC 9510746

Forbes Library

443B • NEW YORK: | ROBERT CARTER & BROTHERS, | 530 BROADWAY. | [short rule] | 1856.

NUC NE0046489 OCLC 11892654

Princeton University

443C • NEW YORK: | ROBERT CARTER & BROTHERS, | 530 BROADWAY. | [short rule] | 1857.

Notes: in some copies, 285 Broadway.

THJ 329B NUC NE0046469

Harvard University

443 D • NEW YORK: | ANSON D. F. RANDOLPH & CO., | 770 BROADWAY, COR. 9th ST.

THJ 329C OCLC 45063202

New York Public Library

444 • CHARITY | AND ITS FRUITS; | OR, | CHRISTIAN LOVE AS MANIFESTED IN THE | HEART AND LIFE. | BY | JONATHAN EDWARDS, | SOMETIME PASTOR OF THE CHURCH AT NORTHAMPTON, MASSACHUSETTS, AND | PRESIDENT OF THE COLLEGE OF NEW JERSEY. | EDITED FROM THE ORIGINAL MANUSCRIPTS, | WITH AN INTRODUCTION, | BY THE | REV. TRYON EDWARDS, D.D. | LONDON: | JAMES NISBET & CO., 21 BERNERS STREET. | M.DCCC.LII.

22.4 x 14.4 cm.; π^6, A-Z^8; [2], viii, [2], 368 p.

Notes:in some copies, two leaves of advertisement follow p. 368; p. 4: Macintosh, Printer, Great New-street, London.

Contents: prp. [1]: CHARITY | AND ITS FRUITS.; prp. [2]: BALLANTYNE, PRINTER, EDINBURGH.; p. [i]: title (verso blank); p. [iii]: INTRODUCTION [signed] T. E. | NEW LONDON, CONN. | *November* 1851.; p. [vii]: CONTENTS.; pp. [1]-368: text; p. 368: BALLANTYNE, PRINTER, EDINBURGH.

THJ 330 NUC NE0046486 OCLC 44821199

Princeton Theological Seminary

444A • CHARITY | AND ITS FRUITS | *Christian love as manifested* | *in the heart and life* | Jonathan Edwards | *Edited from* | *the original manuscripts* | *with an introduction* | *by Tryon Edwards* | THE BANNER OF TRUTH TRUST

21.5 x 13.7 cm.; [2], viii, [2], 368 p.

Notes: facsimile reprint; p. [ii]: THE BANNER OF TRUTH TRUST | 3 *Murrayfield Road, Edinburgh EH*12 6*EL* | *P O Box* 621, *Carlisle, Pennsylvania* 17013, *USA*. | [7 lines]. The first Banner of Truth edition was published in 1969 and

reissued in 1978, 1982, 1986, 1991, 1996, and 1998.
ISBN 0851510094 OCLC 104774
Duke University

445 • CHRISTIAN LOVE, | AS MANIFESTED IN THE HEART AND LIFE. | BY | JONATHAN EDWARDS, | SOMETIME PASTOR OF THE CHURCH AT NORTHAMPTON, MASSACHUSETTS, | AND PRESIDENT OF THE COLLEGE OF NEW JERSEY. | EDITED FROM THE ORIGINAL MANUSCRIPT | BY THE REV. TRYON EDWARDS, D. D. | [short rule] | *SIXTH AMERICAN EDITION.* | [short rule] | PHILADELPHIA: | PRESBYTERIAN BOARD OF PUBLICATION, | 1334 CHESTNUT STREET.

17.4 x 11.2 cm.; $[1]^8$, $2\text{-}34^8$; xi, [1], 530, [2] p.

Contents: p. [i]: title; p. [ii]: Entered according to Act of Congress, in the year 1874, by | THE TRUSTEES OF THE | PRESBYTERIAN BOARD OF PUBLICATION, | In the Office of the Librarian of Congress, at Washington; p. iii: INTRODUCTION. [signed] T. E.; p. vii: PREFACE | TO THE SIXTH AMERICAN EDITION. [dated] OCTOBER, 1872; p. [ix]: CONTENTS.; p. [xii]: blank; pp. 1-530: text; pp. [531-532]: blank.

THJ 331 NUC NE0046492 OCLC 2975039
Harvard Divinity School

446 • No. 563. | AM I CHRIST'S? | BY PRESIDENT EDWARDS. | "Ye shall know them by their fruits." Matt. 7:16.

18.8 x. 10.8 cm.; 4 p.

Notes: reprinted, pp. [1]-4 (in some copies, also sig. $14_{1\text{-}2}$) in TRACTS | OF THE | AMERICAN TRACT SOCIETY. | General Series. | [engraving] | Vol. XIII. | PRINTED BY THE | AMERICAN TRACT SOCIETY, | 150 NASSAU-STREET, NEW YORK

Contents: caption title; p. 4: From President Edwards' "Charity and its Fruits." | [short rule] | PUBLISHED BY THE AMERICAN TRACT SOCIETY.

THJ 332 NUC NE0046450
American Tract Society

447 • CHRISTIAN | LOVE | *Originally published as* | *CHARITY AND ITS FRUITS* | *by* | *JONATHAN EDWARDS* | [imposed upon a map of the United States] The | National Foundation | for | Christian Education | MARSHALLTON, DEL. 19808

21.6 x 13. 5 cm.; [4], 177, [3] p.

Notes: published c. 1970.

Contents: prp. [1]: title (verso blank); prp. [3]: CONTENTS (verso blank); pp. [1]-177: text; pp. [178-179]: [advertisement]; p. [180]: blank.

OCLC 6404042
Boston College

447A • SOVEREIGN GRACE PUBLISHERS | Grand Rapids, Michigan 49315 | 1971

21.6 x 13. 5 cm.; [4], 177, [3] p.

Notes: identical with the above except for the imprint.

OCLC 10572628
Grace College and Seminary

448 • [4 lines within rules] The | Believer's | Secret of | Christian | Love | *Compiled from the writings of* | ANDREW MURRAY | JONATHAN EDWARDS | *by Louis Gifford Parkhurst, Jr.* | [decorative rule] | BETHANY HOUSE PUBLISHERS | MINNEAPOLIS, MINNESOTA 55438 | A Division of Bethany

Fellowship, Inc.

20.2 x 13.4 cm.; 141 p.

Notes: excerpts from *Charity and Its Fruits*, Banner of Truth edition.

Contents: p. [1]: [within rules] The | Believer's | Secret of | Christian | Love (verso blank); p. [3]: title; p. [4]: Copyright © 1990 | [18 lines]; p. [5]: [biographical note] (verso blank); p. [7]: [advertisement] (verso blank); p. 9: *Preface*; p. 11: *Contents*; p. [13]: blank; p. 14: [3 lines] | *1 John 3:23*; pp. 15-141: text.

OCLC 20754463

Dallas Theological Seminary

449 • Heaven: | A World | of Love | *Calvary Press | Amityville, New York*

21 x 12.7 cm.; 64 p.

Notes: excerpted from *Charity and Its Fruits*, sermon no. 15 (1738).

Contents: p. [1]: Heaven: | A World of Love (verso blank); p. [3]: title; p. [4]: *Calvary Press | P.O. Box 805 | Amityville, NY 11701* | [5 lines] | Excerpted from *Charity and Its Fruits*, currently in print through | The Banner of Truth Trust, Carlisle, PA, USA | © 1999 Calvary Press | [23 lines]; p. [5]: *Table of Contents*; p. [6]: [quotations]; p. 7: *Preface* [signed] Dr. John H. Gerstner, February 26, 1992; pp. 9-60: text; p. 61: *Endnotes*; p. [64]: [advertisement].

ISBN 1879737361   OCLC 42240546

Gordon-Conwell Theological Seminary

JONATHAN EDWARDS'S LAST WILL

450 • ARTICLE III. | JONATHAN EDWARDS' LAST WILL, AND THE INVENTORY | OF HIS ESTATE.

Contents: caption title; *Bibliotheca Sacra*, 33 (July 1876):438-443

THJ 333   OCLC 6288728

Gordon-Conwell Theological Seminary

OBSERVATIONS CONCERNING THE SCRIPTURE OECONOMY OF THE TRINITY AND COVENANT OF REDEMPTION

451 • OBSERVATIONS | CONCERNING | THE SCRIPTURE OECONOMY | OF THE | TRINITY | AND COVENANT OF REDEMPTION | BY | JONATHAN EDWARDS | *WITH AN INTRODUCTION AND APPENDIX* | BY EGBERT C. SMYTH | NEW YORK | CHARLES SCRIBNER'S SONS | 743 AND 745 BROADWAY | 1880

18.7 x 12.3 cm.; π^2, [1]-6^8, $[7]^2$; [4], 97, [3] p.

Contents: prp. [1]: OBSERVATIONS | CONCERNING THE | SCRIPTURE OECONOMY OF THE TRINITY.; prp. [2]: Πιστεύομεν | Εἰς ἕνα Θεόν, Πατέρα παντοκράτορα· | Καὶ εἰς ἕνα Κύριον Ἰησοῦν Χρωτόν, τὸν Ὑιὸν τοῦ Θεοῦ, | ὁμοούσιον τῷ Πατρί, τὸν δὶ ἡμᾶς ἐνανθρωπήσαντα· | Καὶ εἰς τὸ Ἅγιον Πνεῦμα.; prp. [3]: title; prp. [4]: *Copyright*, 1880, | BY EGBERT C. SMYTH. | UNIVERSITY PRESS: | JOHN WILSON AND SON, CAMBRIDGE.; p. [1]: INTRODUCTION. (verso blank); p. [3]: INTRODUCTION. [signed] E. C. S. | ANDOVER THEOLOGICAL SEMINARY, | August, 1880.; p. [19]: OBSERVATIONS. (verso blank); p. [21]: OBSERVATIONS | CONCERNING THE | SCRIPTURE OECONOMY OF THE TRINITY, AND | COVENANT OF REDEMPTION.; p. [58]: blank; p. [59]: APPENDIX. (verso blank); p. [61]: [notes]; p. 97: University Press: John Wilson and Son, Cambridge.; pp. [98-100]: blank.

THJ 334   NUC NE0046739   OCLC 3422223

Harvard Divinity School

THE FLYING SPIDER

452 • THE FLYING SPIDER—OBSERVATIONS BY JONA- | THAN EDWARDS WHEN A BOY. | FROM AN UNPUBLISHED MANUSCRIPT. | [With Facsimiles. See Frontispiece.]

Notes: frontispiece: [photocopy] | I. Fac-similes of a portion of the paper entitled "Of Insects". | (See the First Article).; frontispiece: [photocopy] | II. Fac-simile of a rough draft of a letter. | (See the First Article).

Contents: caption title; *The Andover Review*, 13 (January 1890):[1]-19.

THJ 335 OCLC 1481127

Gordon-Conwell Theological Seminary

453 • THE FLYING SPIDER—OBSERVATIONS BY JONA- | THAN EDWARDS WHEN A BOY. | FROM AN UNPUBLISHED MANUSCRIPT. | [With Facsimiles. See Frontispiece.]

23.8 x 14.6 cm.; 19, [1] p.

Notes: p. [1]: Copyright, 1898, by HOUGHTON, MIFFLIN & Co.

Contents: caption title; front cover: THE FLYING SPIDER | OBSERVATIONS BY JONATHAN EDWARDS WHEN | A BOY. | [REPRINTED FROM THE ANDOVER REVIEW FOR JANUARY, 1890.]; frontispiece: [photocopy] | I. Fac-similes of a portion of the paper entitled "Of Insects". | (See the First Article).; frontispiece: [photocopy] | II. Fac-simile of a rough draft of a letter. | (See the First Article).; p. [1]-19: THE FLYING SPIDER—OBSERVATIONS BY JONA- | THAN EDWARDS WHEN A BOY. | FROM AN UNPUBLISHED MANUSCRIPT. | [With Facsimiles. See Frontispiece.].; p. 19: *Egbert C. Smyth.*; p. [20]: blank.

THJ 336 NUC NE0046586 OCLC 43639623

Princeton University

454 • OF | [in red ink] INSECTS | *by* | JONATHAN EDWARDS | [publisher's device] | New Haven, 1974

25.4 x 14.6 cm.; [8], 13, [3] p.

Contents: prp. [1]: OF INSECTS | [short rule] | Jonathan Edwards (verso blank); frontispiece: [wood engraving] | *Jonathan Edwards* | *1703-1758*; prp. [3]: title; prp. [4]: © Copyright 1974 by Wallace E. Anderson. | This essay is printed from a transcript made by | Wallace E. Anderson from the original manuscript in the | Hills Library, Andover Newton Theological School. | The collaboration of the following Fellows and | students made the binding of this book possible: Polly | Lada-Mocarski, Dale Roylance, and Mary Hunter Wolf; | B. Barnes, A. Kols, K. Kuenster, K. McGoldrick, | J. Mead, G. Shakespear, M. Sidell, S. Weaver, and | L. Yang; prp. [5]: PREFACE [signed] Wallace E. Anderson | Ohio State University | January, 1974; prp. [7-8]: blank; pp. [1]-13: text; p. [14]: blank; p. [15]: THE JONATHAN EDWARDS | COLLEGE PRESS | Printed from Caslon type on Zerkall Butten paper | by George Shakespeare. Bound by students at the | Jonathan Edwards Bindery. Illustrations in wood- | engraving by Lance Hidy (frontispiece and | textual diagram) and by George | Shakespear (pp. 1 and 15). | [wood engraving] | This is copy no. XIII | of an edition of 100.; p. [16]: blank.

OCLC 1047313

Andover Newton Theological School

AN UNPUBLISHED ESSAY OF EDWARDS ON THE TRINITY

455 • AN UNPUBLISHED ESSAY OF | EDWARDS ON THE TRINITY | WITH REMARKS ON EDWARDS | AND HIS THEOLOGY | BY | GEORGE P. FISHER, D.D., LL.D. | EMERITUS PROFESSOR OF ECCLESIASTICAL HISTORY | IN YALE UNIVERSITY | NEW YORK | CHARLES SCRIBNER'S SONS | 1903.

20.3 x 13.6 cm.; xv, [3], 142 p.

Contents: p. [i]: AN UNPUBLISHED ESSAY OF | EDWARDS ON THE TRINITY (verso blank); frontispiece: [portrait] | [facsimile autograph] Jonathan Edwards.; p. [iii]: title; p. [iv]: COPYRIGHT, 1903, BY | CHARLES SCRIBNER'S

SONS | [short rule] | Published, *October*, | 1903 | TROW DIRECTORY | PRINTING AND BOOKBINDING COMPANY | NEW YORK.; p. [v]: [dedication] (verso blank); p. [vii]: PREFACE [signed] G. P. F.; p. [xvi]: blank; p. [xvii]: CONTENTS (verso blank); p. [1]: PART I | REMARKS ON EDWARDS AND HIS THEOLOGY (verso blank); p. 15: PART II | AN UNPUBLISHED ESSAY OF EDWARDS ON | THE TRINITY (verso blank); p. [134]: blank; p. [135]: APPENDIX (verso blank); p. 137: APPENDIX | I | THE DISMISSAL OF EDWARDS FROM THE CHURCH IN | NORTHAMPTON; p. 139: II | THE ACCOUNT GIVEN BY EDWARDS OF HIS METHOD | OF STUDY | [15 lines] | III | AUGUSTINE ON THE TRINITY AS IMAGED FORTH IN | THE HUMAN MIND; p. 140: IV | PRESIDENT T. D. WOOLSEY ON THE PERSONAL TRAITS | AND INFLUENCE OF EDWARDS.

THJ 337 NUC NE0046886 OCLC 2209714

Gordon-Conwell Theological Seminary

THE PERPETUITY AND CHANGE OF THE SABBATH

456 • [within rules, top and left thin, foot and right thick] THE | PERPETUITY | AND | CHANGE | OF THE | SABBATH | [ornament] | [decorative vertical rule] | BY | JONATHAN | EDWARDS | PRINTED IN U. S. A.

19.3 x 12.8 cm.; 45 p.

Notes: published c. 1930; first published in *Sermons on the Following Subjects* (1780), pp. 221-282.

Contents: p. [1]: title; p. [2]: [photocopy] | *Jonathan Edwards* | 1703-1758; p. [3]: *The* | *Perpetuity and Change* | of the | *Sabbath*; p. 45: METROPOLITAN CHURCH ASSOCIATION | - - WAUKESHA, WISCONSIN - -

OCLC 9980516

Asbury Theological Seminary

WICKED MEN USEFUL IN THEIR DESTRUCTION ONLY

457 • [within decorative rules] FROM THE | INHERITANCE | OF OUR FATHERS | [rule] | Series II NO.6 | [rule] | WICKED MEN USEFUL | IN THEIR | DESTRUCTION ONLY | By the | REV. JONATHAN EDWARDS

15.1 x 8.6 cm.; 32 p.

Notes: published c. 1932; reissued c. 1984 in a smaller format, series XXV, no. 6; first published in *Practical Sermons Never Before Published* (1788), pp. 203-222.

Contents: front cover, p. [1]: title; p. [2]: [advertisement] | [short rule] | The Inheritance Publishing Co. | P. O. Box 334 | Grand Rapids, Michigan; p. 3: THE USELESSNESS OF THE | WICKED.

OCLC 41246758

Gordon-Conwell Theological Seminary

THE SIN AND FOLLY OF PROCRASTINATION

458 • [within decorative rules] FROM THE | INHERITANCE | OF OUR FATHERS | [ornament] | Series VIII – No. 5 | The Sin and Folly | of Procrastination | By Rev. Jonathan Edwards

15.3 x 10.3 cm.; 31 p.

Notes: advertised in Series X, No. 11; no copy has been located; first published in *Practical Sermons Never Before Published* (1788), pp. 297-320, as *The Sin and Folly of Depending on Future Time*.

SINNERS IN ZION TENDERLY WARNED

459 • [within decorative rules] FROM THE | INHERITANCE | OF OUR FATHERS | [ornament] | SERIES IX – No. 6 | Sinners In Zion Tenderly | Warned | By Rev. Jonathan Edwards

15.3 x 10.3 cm.; 32 p.

Notes: first published in *Practical Sermons Never Before Published* (1788), pp. 224-246.

Contents: front cover, p. [1]: title; p. [2]: THE CHRISTIAN PROFESSOR | ADMONISHED | [short double rule] | [14 lines] | John Bunyan.; pp. [3]-31: text; p. 31: [advertisement]; back cover (verso):[decorative rule] | [advertisement] | [short rule] | THE INHERITANCE PUBLISHING CO. | P.O. Box 334 Grand Rapids, Mich. | [decorative rule].

OCLC 38910842

Yale Divinity School

THE PEACE WHICH CHRIST GIVES HIS TRUE FOLLOWERS

460 • [within decorative rules] FROM THE | INHERITANCE | OF OUR FATHERS | [ornament] | SERIES X – No. 11 | The Peace Which | Christ Gives His | True Followers | By Rev. Jonathan Edwards

15.1 x 10.1 cm.; 31 p.

Notes: published c. 1951; first published in *Sermons on the Following Subjects* (1780), pp. 201-220.

Contents: front cover, p. [1]: title (verso blank); p. 3: THE PEACE WHICH CHRIST GIVES | HIS TRUE FOLLOWERS; p. 27: CONVERSE OF A SOUL WITH JESUS; pp. [30-31]: [advertisement]; back cover (verso): [advertisement] | [short rule] | THE INHERITANCE PUBLISHING CO. | P. O. Box 334 Grand Rapids, Mich.

OCLC 47870475

Gordon-Conwell Theological Seminary

THE TRUE CHRISTIAN'S LIFE A JOURNEY

461 • [within decorative rules] FROM THE | INHERITANCE | OF OUR FATHERS | [ornament] | SERIES XI — No. 4 | The True Christian's | Life a Journey | By Rev. Jonathan Edwards

15.2 x 10.2 cm.; 31 p.

Notes: published c. 1952; first published in Hopkins's *Life* (1765), pp. 253-279.

Contents: front cover, p. [1]: title (verso blank); p. 3: THE TRUE CHRISTIAN'S LIFE | A JOURNEY; back cover (verso): [decorative rule] | THE INHERITANCE PUBLISHING COMPANY | P. O. Box 334 Grand Rapids, Mich. | [advertisement] | [ornament] | [decorative rule].

OCLC 47885677

Gordon-Conwell Theological Seminary

FLEEING OUT OF SODOM

462 • [decorative vertical rule] *Fleeing Out* | *of Sodom* | [ornament] | *By Jonathan Edwards* | [rule] | FROM THE INHERITANCE OF OUR FATHERS | – Series XIV, No. 2

15.2 x 10.3 cm.; 30 p.

Notes: published c. 1959; reissued as Series XXXIII, No. 5, adding pp. 33-35: Regarding Iniquity | in the Heart by John Witherspoon; first published in *Sermons on the Following Subjects* (1780), pp. 73-92.

Contents: front cover, p. [1]: p. [2]: [publisher's note] | [1 line]; p. 3: Fleeing out of Sodom; back cover (recto): [advertisement]; back cover (verso): [decorative rule] | [advertisement] | [decorative rule] | THE INHERITANCE

PUBLISHERS | P. O. Box 334 Grand Rapids, Mich.
OCLC 49291787
Gordon-Conwell Theological Seminary

HYPOCRITES DEFICIENT IN THE DUTY OF PRAYER

463 • WILL YOU | ALWAYS | CALL UPON | GOD | ? | Jonathan Edwards | Reprinted by | BREM, Inc. | Box 40161 | Nashville, Tennessee 37211 | Price 25¢

16.6 x 11.2 cm.; 24 p.

Notes: first published in *Sermons on the Following Subjects* (1780), pp. 111-142.

Contents: front cover (recto): title; front cover (verso): Original date: June 1740 | Reprinted: 1972 | The original title of this sermon was: "Hypocrites Deficient in | the Duty of Prayer."; pp. 1-24: text.

OCLC 40530105
University of California

THE VAIN SELF-FLATTERIES OF THE SINNER

464 • [decorative rule] | The Vain Self-Flatteries | Of The Sinner | [decorative rule] | by Jonathan Edwards | [double decorative rule] | FROM THE INHERITANCE OF OUR FATHERS | – Series XXVII, No. 6 | [decorative rule]

13.3 x 8.9 cm.; 30, [1] p.

Notes: published c. 1988; first published in *Practical Sermons Never Before Published* (1788), pp. 191-202..

Contents: front cover, p. [1]: title; p. [2]: JONATHAN EDWARDS | [biography]; p. 3: THE VAIN SELF-FLATTERIES OF THE SINNER; p. 29: [1 line] | [publisher's note] (verso blank); back cover (recto): blank; back cover (verso): [decorative rule] | [advertisement] | [decorative rule] | THE INHERITANCE PUBLISHERS | P. O. Box 1334 | Grand Rapids, Michigan 49501| [decorative rule].

OCLC 47885675
Gordon-Conwell Theological Seminary

BEAUTY OF THE WORLD

465 • *Beauty of the World.*

35 x 24.8 cm.; 1 p.

Notes: a gift to Norman Fiering from his students at Brown University; broadside, in two columns on light gray paper, 1992.

Contents: [text] | [footnote] From the transcription in Jonathan Edwards, *Scientific and Philosophical Writings*, ed. by Wallace E. Anderson (Yale | University Press: New Haven and London, 1980), pp. 305-306.

OCLC 37243520
Brown University

CHRISTIAN CHARITY, OR THE DUTY OF CHARITY TO THE POOR

466 • Christian Charity | OR, THE | DUTY OF CHARITY TO THE POOR, EXPLAINED AND ENFORCED. | A Sermon | BY | JONATHAN EDWARDS

21.6 x 13.5 cm.; 40, [1] p.

Notes: first published in *Practical Sermons Never Before Published* (1788), pp. 343-385, as *The Duty of Charity to the Poor*.

Contents: front cover: Christian Charity | by | Jonathan Edwards | Messages from God's servants | in former days | [6 lines] | [ornament] | [in 2 cols., col. 1]: The Teleios Ministry of | Camelback Bible Church | 3900 East Stanford Drive | Paradise Valley, AZ 85253 | 955-6370 | [col. 2]: February, 1999; front cover (verso): Teleios Sermon # 41 | [40 lines]; p. [1]: title; p. [41]: blank; back cover (recto): [advertisement].

OCLC 49537963

Gordon-Conwell Theological Seminary

THE MOST HIGH, A PRAYER-HEARING GOD

467 • [within decorative rules] THE MOST HIGH, | A PRAYER-HEARING | GOD | Jonathan Edwards | TREASURED MEDITATIONS | Series 2 No. 2

13.3 x 8.5 cm.; 35 p.

Notes: publshed in 1999; a sermon on Ps. 65:2, preached January 8, 1735/6, and first published in *Practical Sermons Never Before Published* (1788), pp. 67-85.

Contents: front cover, p. [1]: title; p. 2: JONATHAN EDWARDS | 1703-1758 | [biography]; pp. 3-35: text; back cover, p. [36]: [10 lines] | *Treasured Meditations* | *P.O. Box 2753* | *Grand Rapids, Michigan 49501-2753* | [4 lines].

OCLC 42611162

Reformed Presbyterian Theological Seminary

SELECTIONS

468 • TWO REMARKABLE SERMONS, | *By that great and good Man the late* | REV. JONATHAN EDWARDS, | Prefident of the College of New Jerfey in | NORTH-AMERICA.

Notes: prp. [2]: In the Evangelical Magazine, for January 1795, the Review- | ers in fpeaking of eminent Men inftructing the World by their | literary labours, has the following: "In this lift, Jonathan | Edwards, of New England, ranks among the firft. It is no dif- | paragement to any one to fay that he is without Rival, the | greateft Divine the prefent Century has produced. His Treatifes | on Original Sin, on the Freedom of the Will, and on Virtue, merit the attentive perufal of every lover of the Gofpel, and his Sermons difcover the fuperior fkill in experimental Theology. | His death in the midft of Vigour and Ufefulnefs, was an infi- | nitely greater Calamity to Mankind, than that of the greateft He- | ro, or moft enlightened Statefman. It may be faid | that the Gleanings of Mr. Edwards are better than the Vintage | of moft other Divines."

Contents: p. [197]: title (verso blank); p. [199]: SERMON I. | Sinners in the Hands of an Angry God; p. 227: SERMON II. | The Excellency of Chrift. in SERMONS, | *Selected from the Works of that* | Laborious and Faithful Servant of Chrift | THE LATE | REV. JOHN CENNICK. | TO WHICH ARE ADDED | TWO ADMIRABLE SERMONS | BY THAT | Great, Learned, and good Man, | THE LATE | REV. JONATHAN EDWARDS, | *Prefident of New Jerfey College in North America.* | At the end of the Sermons are annexed fome LETTERS, | by that Eminent, Pious, and Sincere Chriftian, the | late Mrs. A——'s, of Goodman's Fields, London; | whofe Soul was made fit for Glory, and entered into | Eternal Reft, on the 28th of July, 1789.—Thefe | Letters were written during her Illnefs, to her Hufband, | Children, &c. to be delivered after her deceafe. | [decorative rule] | [publisher's device] | Bath: | PRINTED BY S. HAZARD, FOR C. ADAMS. | 1796.

12mo.; 18.5 x 10.3 cm.; $[A]^{1}$, $B\text{-}N^{12}$, O^{10}; [2], 308 p.

OCLC 8551023

Wheaton College

469 • SELECT SERMONS | OF | PRESIDENT EDWARDS. | LONDON: | RELIGIOUS TRACT SOCIETY, | *Instituted* 1799. | SOLD AT THE DEPOSITORY, 56, PATERNOSTER ROW; | AND BY

THE BOOKSELLERS. | MDCCCXXXIV.

14.7 x 9 cm.; π[3], B-Z[6], 2A-2N[6], 2O[3]; v, [1], 426 p.

Contents: p. [i]:title; p. [ii]: [A few paragraphs, relating chiefly to local or temporary | subjects, are omitted in some of the following sermons.] | BUNGAY: PRINTED BY J. R. AND C. CHILDS.; p. [iii]: CONTENTS.; p. [vi]: blank; p. [1]: MEN IN A STATE OF NATURE GOD'S | ENEMIES.; p. [64]: THE JUSTICE OF GOD | IN THE CONDEMNATION OF SINNERS.; p. [119]: THE FUTURE PUNISHMENT OF THE WICKED | UNAVOIDABLE AND INTOLERABLE.; p. [143]: WICKED MEN USEFUL IN THEIR | DESTRUCTION ONLY.; p. [168]: DIVINE SOVEREIGNTY.; p. [186]: PARDON FOR THE GREATEST SINNERS.; p. [201]: THE MANNER IN WHICH THE SALVATION | OF THE SOUL IS TO BE SOUGHT.; p. [230]: THE UNREASONABLENESS OF INDECISION | IN RELIGION.; p. [250]: THE PRECIOUSNESS OF TIME.; p. [268]: PROCRASTINATION.; p. [297]: PRESSING INTO THE KINGDOM OF GOD.; p. [325]: TRUE GRACE DISTINGUISHED FROM THE | EXPERIENCE OF DEVILS.; p. [366]: THE PEACE WHICH CHRIST GIVES TO HIS TRUE | FOLLOWERS.; p. [387]: GOD THE BEST PORTION OF THE CHRISTIAN.; p. [402]: JESUS CHRIST TRIUMPHANT OVER ALL | ENEMIES.; p. 426: BUNGAY: PRINTED BY J. R. AND C. CHILDS.

THJ 319 NUC NE0046761 OCLC 10410247

New York Public Library

469A • SOLD AT THE DEPOSITORY, 56, PATERNOSTER ROW; | AND BY THE BOOKSELLERS. | MDCCCXXXIX.

14.7 x 9 cm.; π[3], B-Z[6], 2A-2N[6], 2O[3]; v, [1], 426 p.

Notes: identical with the above except for the imprint and the colophon: BUNGAY: PRINTED BY JOHN CHILDS AND SON.

Azusa Pacific University

470 • SELECTIONS | FROM THE | UNPUBLISHED WRITINGS | OF | JONATHAN EDWARDS, | OF AMERICA. | EDITED FROM THE ORIGINAL MSS., WITH FACSIMILES | AND AN INTRODUCTION, | BY THE | REV. ALEXANDER B. GROSART, | KINROSS. | "I consider JONATHAN EDWARDS the greatest of the sons of men. He ranks with the | brightest luminaries of the Christian Church, not excluding any country, or any age, | since the apostolic." ROBERT HALL. | "This remarkable man, *the* metaphysician of America. . . . . His power of subtile ar- | gument, PERHAPS UNMATCHED, CERTAINLY UNSURPASSED AMONG MEN, was joined, as in some | of the ancient Mystics, with a character which raised his piety to fervour." | SIR JAMES MACKINTOSH. | "Edwards comes nearer Bishop Butler as a philosophical divine than any other theo- | logian with whom we are acquainted." ROBERT MOREHEAD. | [*THREE HUNDRED COPIES.*] | PRINTED FOR PRIVATE CIRCULATION. | 1865.

25.5 x 15.5 cm.; [A][8], B-N[8], [O][2]; 209, [3] p.

Notes: *Treatise on Grace*, pp. [17]-56, was published separately the same year.

Contents: p. [1]: SELECTIONS | FROM THE | UNPUBLISHED WRITINGS | OF | JONATHAN EDWARDS, | OF AMERICA.; p. [2]: EDINBURGH: | PRINTED BY BALLANTYNE AND COMPANY, | PAUL'S WORK.; frontispiece: [photocopy] | FACSIMILE OF JONATHAN EDWARDS HAND-WRITING.; p. [3]: title (verso blank); p. [5]: CONTENTS.; p. [7]: JONATHAN EDWARDS. [chronology] (verso blank); p. [9]: [dedication] (verso blank); p. [11]: INTRODUCTION. [signed] ALEXANDER B. GROSART | 1ST MANSE, | KINROSS, *December 26th*, 1864; p. [17]: TREATISE ON GRACE.; p. [18]: NOTE.; p. [57]: ANNOTATIONS ON PASSAGES OF | HOLY SCRIPTURE; | FROM | PRESIDENT EDWARDS'S INTERLEAVED BIBLE.; p. [58]: NOTE.; p. [180]: blank; p. [181]: DIRECTIONS | FOR | JUDGING OF PERSONS' EXPERIENCES.; p. [182]: NOTE.; p. [186]: blank; p. [187]: SERMONS.; p. [188]: NOTE.; pp. [189]-209: [sermon outlines]; p. 209: Ballantyne and Company, Printers, Edinburgh; p. [210]: blank; pp. [211-212]: [advertisement].

THJ 320 NUC NE0046764 OCLC 3743244

Harvard Divinity School

470A • Soli Deo Gloria Publications | *...for instruction in righteousness...*

23.4 x 15.3 cm.; 209, [1] p.

Notes: facsimile reprint; p. [2]: Soli Deo Gloria Publications | 213 W. Vincent Street, Ligonier, PA 15658 | *Selections from the Unpublished Writings* | *of Jonathan Edwards* | was first printed for private circulation in 1865 | by Rev. Alexander B. Grosart. | This Soli Deo Gloria Reprint is 1992.; p. [3]: Introduction to the Twentieth Century Edition of | "Selections from the Unpublished Writings of Jonathan Edwards" [signed] John H. Gerstner, Ph.D. | Ligonier, PA | November 1992.

ISBN 0877611433 OCLC 27092438

Andover Newton Theological School

471 • [within rules] Eternal Damnation | AND | PUNISHMENT OF SINNERS, OLD AND YOUNG, | AND THE | REJOICINGS OF THE SAINTS THEREAT, EVEN THOUGH | THOSE SAINTS MAY IN THIS WORLD BE | THEIR NEAREST RELATIVES OR | WARMEST FRIENDS. | EXTRACTS FROM THE SERMONS PREACHED BY | JONATHAN EDWARDS, | TO WHOSE MEMORY A MONUMENT HAS BEEN ERECTED ON THE TOWN SQUARE | IN STOCKBRIDGE, MASS. | [short thick rule] | 1872.

23.7 x 14.5 cm.; 8 p.

Contents: p. [1]: EXTRACTS | FROM THE | Sermons of Jonathan Edwards, | PUBLISHED IN THE 4th VOLUME OF EDWARDS'S WORKS. | TO BE FOUND AT THE PAGES INDICATED.

THJ 321

Boston Athenaeum

472 • SOME EARLY WRITINGS OF JONATHAN EDWARDS. | A. D. 1714-1726. | BY EGBERT C. SMYTH.

Notes: facing p. 212: I. FAC-SIMILE OF A VERY EARLY WRITING BY JONATHAN EDWARDS. (See Appendix A. [THE SOUL]. (verso blank); II. FAC-SIMILE OF A PORTION OF THE PAPER ENTITLED "OF BEING." (See Appendix C.) (verso blank).

Contents: caption title; *Proceedings of the American Antiquarian Society*, n.s., pt. 2, 10 (October 1895):212-247.

THJ 322 OCLC 1479298

Massachusetts Historical Society

473 • SOME | EARLY WRITINGS OF JONATHAN EDWARDS, | A. D. 1714-1726, | BY | EGBERT C. SMYTH. | [short rule] | FROM PROCEEDINGS OF THE AMERICAN ANTIQUARIAN SOCIETY AT THE | ANNUAL MEETING, OCTOBER 23, 1895. | [short rule] | Worcester, Mass. | PRESS OF CHARLES HAMILTON. | NO. 311 MAIN STREET. | 1896.

24.4 x 14.9 cm.; [1]-2^8, 3^4; 39, [1] p.

Contents: p. [1]: title (verso blank); inserted page: [photocopy] | I. FAC-SIMILE OF A VERY EARLY WRITING BY JONATHAN EDWARDS. (See Appendix A. [THE SOUL].); inserted page: [photocopy] | II. FAC-SIMILE OF A PORTION OF THE PAPER ENTITLED "OF BEING." (See Appendix C.); p. [3]: SOME EARLY WRITINGS OF JONATHAN EDWARDS. | A. D. 1714-1726.; p. 28: blank; p. [29]: APPENDIX. | [short rule] | A. | [THE SOUL]; p. 30: [diagram]; p. 31: B. | OF THE RAINBOW; p. 33: C. | OF BEING; p. 37: D [*sic*] | [COLORS.]; p. [40]: blank.

THJ 323 OCLC 39325923

Harvard Divinity School

474 • SELECTED SERMONS | OF | JONATHAN EDWARDS | EDITED WITH INTRODUCTION AND NOTES | BY | H. NORMAN GARDINER | PROFESSOR OF PHILOSOPHY IN SMITH COLLEGE | New York | THE MACMILLAN COMPANY | LONDON: MACMILLAN & CO., LTD. | 1904 | *All rights reserved*

14.2 x 10.5 cm.; π^{15}, B-M^8, N^5; xxix, [1], 181, [5] p.

Contents: p. [i]: SELECTED SERMONS OF | JONATHAN EDWARDS; p. [ii]: [advertisement]; frontispiece: [photocopy] | [facsimile autograph] Jonathan Edwards.; p. [iii]: title; p. [iv]: COPYRIGHT, 1904, | BY THE MACMILLAN COMPANY. | [short rule] | Set up and electrotyped. Published June, 1904. | **Norwood Press** | J. S. Cushing & Co.–Berwick & Smith Co. | Norwood, Mass., U.S.A.; p. v: CONTENTS (verso blank); p. vii: INTRODUCTION [dated] NORTHAMPTON, MASS., | March, 1904; p. [xxx]: blank; p. 1: GOD GLORIFIED IN MAN'S DEPENDENCE; facing p. 21: [photocopy] | FACSIMILE OF MANUSCRIPT OF FIRST PAGE OF SERMON "A DIVINE | AND SUPERNATURAL LIGHT."; p. 21: A DIVINE AND SUPERNATURAL LIGHT, IMMEDIATELY IMPARTED | TO THE SOUL BY THE SPIRIT OF GOD, SHOWN TO BE BOTH | A SCRIPTURAL AND RATIONAL DOCTRINE; p. 45: RUTH'S RESOLUTION; p. 64: THE MANY MANSIONS; p. 78: SINNERS IN THE HANDS OF AN ANGRY GOD; facing p. 98: [photocopy of engraving] | THE MEETING-HOUSE AT NORTHAMPTON IN WHICH EDWARDS | PREACHED. ERECTED 1737.; p. 98: GOD'S AWFUL JUDGMENT IN THE BREAKING AND WITHERING | OF THE STRONG RODS OF A COMMUNITY; p. 118: A FAREWELL SERMON; p. [154]: blank; p. 155: NOTES; p. [182]: blank; pp. [183-186]: [advertisement].

THJ 324 NUC NE0046763 OCLC 3987060
Harvard Divinity School

475 • *THE MODERN STUDENT'S LIBRARY* | [short rule] | BENJAMIN FRANKLIN | AND | JONATHAN EDWARDS | *SELECTIONS FROM THEIR WRITINGS* | EDITED, WITH AN INTRODUCTION | BY | CARL VAN DOREN | CHARLES SCRIBNER'S SONS | NEW YORK CHICAGO BOSTON

16.2 x 10.2 cm.; xxxiv, [2], 202, [2], 203-368 p.

Notes: in some copies, general editor omitted from half title page, series title omitted from title page.

Contents: p. [i]: *THE MODERN STUDENT'S LIBRARY* | [short rule] | EDITED BY | WILL D. HOWE | PROFESSOR OF ENGLISH AT INDIANA UNIVERSITY | BENJAMIN FRANKLIN | AND | JONATHAN EDWARDS; p. [ii]: [advertisement]; p. [iii]: title; p. [iv]: Copyright, 1920, by | CHARLES SCRIBNER'S SONS; p. v: CONTENTS; p. [viii]: blank; p. ix: INTRODUCTION; p. [xxxv]: BENJAMIN FRANKLIN (verso blank); p. 1: BENJAMIN FRANKLIN; prp. [1]: JONATHAN EDWARDS (verso blank); p. 203: JONATHAN EDWARDS | THE FLYING SPIDER; p. 208: NOTES ON THE MIND; p. 220: NOTES ON NATURAL SCIENCE | OF THE PREJUDICES OF THE IMAGINATION; p. 222: OF BEING; p. 227: THINGS TO BE CONSIDERED, OR WRITTEN | FULLY ABOUT; p. 234: RESOLUTIONS; p. 241: DIARY; p. 274: SARAH PIERREPONT; p. 274: A FAITHFUL NARRATIVE OF THE SURPRISING | WORK OF GOD IN THE CONVERSION OF | MANY HUNDRED SOULS IN NORTHAMP- | TON, AND THE NEIGHBORING TOWNS AND | VILLAGES. . . . IN A LETTER TO THE REV. | DR. BENJAMIN COLMAN OF BOSTON.; p. 344: PERSONAL NARRATIVE; p. 358: TO LADY PEPPERELL | Stockbridge, Nov. 28, 1751.; p. 364: TO THE TRUSTEES OF NASSAU HALL | Stockbridge, Oct. 19, 1757.

THJ 325 OCLC 654167
Harvard Divinity School

476 • *Jonathan Edwards* | REPRESENTATIVE SELECTIONS, WITH | INTRODUCTION, BIBLIOGRAPHY, AND NOTES | BY | CLARENCE H. FAUST | *Instructor in English* | *University of Chicago* | AND | THOMAS H. JOHNSON | *Head of the English Department* | *Hackley School, Tarrytown, N. Y.* | [publisher's device] | [rule] | AMERICAN BOOK COMPANY | *New York • Cincinnati • Chicago* | *Boston • Atlanta*

17.8 x 10.6 cm.; cxlii, 434 p.

Notes: for letters, see *Works* (Yale), 16:36-38, 246-247, 247-250, 307-310, 318-320, 645-654, 660-666, [682]-684, 688-689, and 725-730.

Contents: p. [i]: AMERICAN WRITERS SERIES | HARRY HAYDEN CLARK | *General Editor*; p. [ii]: [advertisement]; frontispiece: [photocopy] | *Pen drawing by Kerr Eby, after* | *a portrait by Rembrandt Peale* | JONATHAN EDWARDS | AET. CA. 45; p. [iii]: title; p. [iv]: COPYRIGHT, 1935, BY | AMERICAN BOOK COMPANY | *All rights reserved* | [short rule] | FAUST AND JOHNSON'S EDWARDS | W.P.I. | MADE IN U.S.A.; p. v: *PREFACE* [signed] C.H.F | T.H.J.; p. vii: *CONTENTS*; p. [x]: blank; p. xi: *INTRODUCTION*; p. cxvi: *CHRONOLOGICAL TABLE*; p. cxviii: blank; p. cxix: *SELECTED BIBLIOGRAPHY*; p. [1]: *Selections from* | JONATHAN EDWARDS (verso blank); p. 3: *EARLY WRITINGS*

| "OF INSECTS"; p. 11: [THE SOUL]; p. 13: [OF THE RAINBOW]; p. 18: [OF BEING]; p. 24: [COLOURS]; p. 27: NOTES ON THE MIND; p. 38: RESOLUTIONS; p. 46: DIARY | [REMAINDER OF DIARY]; p. 56: SARAH PIERREPONT; p. 57: PERSONAL NARRATIVE; p. 73: NARRATIVE OF SURPRISING CONVERSIONS; p. 85: NARRATIVE OF SURPRISING CONVERSIONS | (REVISED ACCOUNT); p. 92: *THEOLOGICAL AND PHILOSOPHICAL* | *WRITINGS* | GOD GLORIFIED IN MAN'S DEPENDENCE; p. 102: A DIVINE AND SUPERNATURAL LIGHT; p. 112: THE JUSTICE OF GOD IN THE DAMNATION | OF SINNERS; p. 121: THE EXCELLENCY OF CHRIST; p. 130: THE CHRISTIAN PILGRIM; p. 137: THE PEACE WHICH CHRIST GIVES | HIS TRUE FOLLOWERS; p. 144: THE FUTURE PUNISHMENT OF THE WICKED | UNAVOIDABLE AND INTOLERABLE; p. 155: SINNERS IN THE HANDS OF AN ANGRY GOD; p. 173: FUNERAL SERMON FOR DAVID BRAINERD; p. 186: FAREWELL SERMON; p. 203: SERMON NOTES; p. 206: RELIGIOUS AFFECTIONS; p. 255: MEMOIRS OF BRAINERD; p. 263: FREEDOM OF THE WILL; p. 310: REMARKS; p. 316: DOCTRINE OF ORIGINAL SIN DEFENDED; p. 340: DISSERTATION CONCERNING THE END FOR | WHICH GOD CREATED THE WORLD; p. 349: THE NATURE OF TRUE VIRTUE; p. 372: COVENANT OF REDEMPTION: | "EXCELLENCY OF CHRIST"; p. 375: AN ESSAY ON THE TRINITY; p. 382: *LETTERS* | [TO THE REV. MR. TIMOTHY EDWARDS, | WINDSOR, CONNECTICUT] | Yale Coll: March 1st 1721; p. 384: [TO MRS. SARAH EDWARDS IN BOSTON]; p. 385: [TO THE REV. MR. JOHN ERSKINE, | KIRKINTILLOCH, SCOTLAND] | Northampton Aug. 31. 1748.; p. 387: [TO THE REV. MR. JOSEPH BELLAMY, | BETHLEHEM, CONNECTICUT] | Northampton | Decem. 6. 1749; p. 389: [TO THE REV. MR. JOSEPH BELLAMY, | BETHLEHEM, CONNECTICUT] | Northampton, Jan. 15. 1749/50.; p. 392: [TO MAJ. JOSEPH HAWLEY, | NORTHAMPTON] | Stockbridge Nov. 18. 1754.; p. 402: [TO THE REV. MR. JOHN ERSKINE, | CULROSS, SCOTLAND] | Stockbridge, April 15, 1755.; p. 406: [TO THE REV. MR. AARON BURR, | PRINCETON, NEW JERSEY] | [February 12, 1756 | Stockbridge]; p. 408: [TO THE REV. MR. JOSEPH BELLAMY, | BETHLEHEM, CONNECTICUT] | Stockbridge | [June, 1756]; p. 409: [TO THE TRUSTEES OF THE COLLEGE | OF NEW JERSEY AT PRINCETON] | Stockbridge, Oct. 19, 1757.; p. 414: [TO MRS. ESTHER BURR, PRINCETON, NEW JERSEY] | Stockbridge, Novem. 20, 1757; p. [416]: blank; p. 417: *NOTES*.

THJ 326 NUC NE0046754 OCLC 1685197

Gordon-Conwell Theological Seminary

476A • Jonathan Edwards | REPRESENTATIVE SELECTIONS, WITH | INTRODUCTION, BIBLIOGRAPHY, AND NOTES | BY | CLARENCE H. FAUST | AND | THOMAS H. JOHNSON | *Revised Edition* | *American Century Series* | [publisher's device] HILL AND WANG – NEW YORK

18.3 x 10.6 cm.; cxlii, 434 p.

Notes: identical with the above except for the title page; p. [iv]: Copyright 1935, © 1962 | by Hill and Wang, Inc. | [3 lines] | FIRST AMERICAN CENTURY SERIES EDITION FEBRUARY 1962.

ISBN 809000474 OCLC 25272834

Gordon-Conwell Theological Seminary

477 • *Images or Shadows* | *of* | *Divine Things* | *by Jonathan Edwards* | Edited by PERRY MILLER | NEW HAVEN | YALE UNIVERSITY PRESS | LONDON • GEOFFREY CUMBERLEGE • OXFORD UNIVERSITY PRESS | 1948

22.5 x 14.7 cm.; viii, [1], 151, [1] p.

Contents: p. [i]: PUBLISHED ON THE | LOUIS STERN MEMORIAL FUND (verso blank); p. [iii]: title; p. [iv]: COPYRIGHT, 1948, BY YALE UNIVERSITY PRESS | [5 lines]; p. [v]: [dedication] (verso blank); p. [vii]: FOREWORD [signed] PERRY MILLER | *Harvard University* | *August 15, 1947*; p. ix: CONTENTS (verso blank); p. [1]: INTRODUCTION; p. [42]:blank; p. [43]: *IMAGES OR SHADOWS* | *OF* | *DIVINE THINGS*; p. [138]:blank; p. [139]: *NOTES*; p. [152]: blank.

NUC NE0046679 OCLC 683592

Harvard Divinity School

477A • [publisher's device] | GREENWOOD PRESS, PUBLISHERS | WESTPORT, CONNECTICUT

22.5 x 14.7 cm.; viii, [1], 151, [1] p.

Notes: identical with the above except for the imprint; p. [iv]: [18 lines] | Reprinted in 1977 by Greenwood Press, Inc. | [6 lines].

ISBN 0837169526 OCLC 2614119
Harvard University

478 • PURITAN SAGE | COLLECTED WRITINGS OF JONATHAN EDWARDS | Edited by | VERGILIUS FERM | *Compton Professor* | *and* | *Head of the Department of Philosophy* | *in* | *The College of Wooster* | [publisher's device] | LIBRARY PUBLISHERS | New York

21.5 x 13.8 cm.; xxx, 640 p.

Contents: p. [i]: PURITAN SAGE | COLLECTED WRITINGS OF JONATHAN EDWARDS; p. [ii]: [advertisement]; frontispiece: [photocopy of memorial] | THE EDWARDS MEMORIAL IN FIRST CHURCH, NORTHAMPTON | This life-size bronze tablet, designed and sculptured by Herbert Adams, was unveiled on | June 22, 1900, exactly one hundred and fifty years after the dismissal of Jonathan Edwards | from his Northampton pulpit. (*Courtesy of Forbes Library, Northampton, Mass.*); p. [iii]: title; p. [iv]: Copyright, 1953, by | LIBRARY PUBLISHERS | 8 West 40th Street, New York 18, N. Y.; p. [v]: PUBLISHER'S NOTE (verso blank); p. viii: CONTENTS; p. ix: LIST OF ILLUSTRATIONS (verso blank); p. xi: ACKNOWLEDGMENTS; p. xiii: PURITAN SAGE | COLLECTED WRITINGS OF JONATHAN EDWARDS | EDITOR'S INTRODUCTION [signed] Wooster, Ohio | 1953 | Vergilius Ferm; p. [xxviii]: blank; p. [xxix]: PURITAN SAGE | COLLECTED WRITINGS OF JONATHAN EDWARDS (verso blank); p. 1: "Of Insects"; p. 8: OF THE RAINBOW; p. 11: THE MIND; p. 47: NOTES ON NATURAL SCIENCE | OF THE PREJUDICES OF THE IMAGINATION.; p. 93: THE INSUFFICIENCY OF REASON AS A SUBSTITUTE | FOR REVELATION | (*Miscellanies*); p. 110: RESOLUTIONS; p. 116: HIS DIARY; p. 144: GOD GLORIFIED IN MAN'S DEPENDENCE; p. 157: A DIVINE AND SUPERNATURAL LIGHT, IMMEDIATELY IMPARTED TO THE SOUL BY | THE SPIRIT OF GOD, SHOWN TO BE BOTH A SCRIPTURAL AND RATIONAL DOCTRINE; p. 164: A FAITHFUL NARRATIVE OF THE SURPRISING WORK OF GOD | IN THE CONVERSION OF MANY HUNDRED SOULS IN NORTH- | AMPTON AND THE NEIGHBORING TOWNS AND VILLAGES; p. 219: JUSTIFICATION BY FAITH ALONE.; p. 266: PRESSING INTO THE KINGDOM OF GOD.; p. 293: THE JUSTICE OF GOD IN THE DAMNATION OF SINNERS.; p. 326: THE EXCELLENCY OF CHRIST.; p. 333: CHARITY AND ITS FRUITS; OR CHRISTIAN LOVE AS | MANIFESTED IN THE HEART AND LIFE.; p. 365: SINNERS IN THE HANDS OF AN ANGRY GOD; p. 379: SOME THOUGHTS CONCERNING THE PRESENT REVIVAL OF | RELIGION IN NEW ENGLAND; p. 415: TREATISE | CONCERNING | RELIGIOUS AFFECTIONS.; p. 451: AN HUMBLE INQUIRY INTO THE RULES OF THE WORD OF | GOD CONCERNING THE QUALIFICATIONS REQUISITE TO A | COMPLEAT STANDING AND FULL COMMUNION IN THE | VISIBLE CHRISTIAN CHURCH; p. 466: FAREWELL SERMON.; p. 480: A | CAREFUL AND STRICT | INQUIRY | INTO THE | MODERN PREVAILING NOTIONS | OF THAT | FREEDOM OF WILL, | WHICH IS SUPPOSED TO BE ESSENTIAL | TO | MORAL AGENCY, | VIRTUE AND VICE, REWARD AND PUNISHMENT, | PRAISE AND BLAME.; p. 516: THE | GREAT CHRISTIAN DOCTRINE | OF | ORIGINAL SIN DEFENDED; | EVIDENCES OF ITS TRUTH PRODUCED, | AND ARGUMENTS TO THE CONTRARY ANSWERED.; p. 534: TREATISE ON GRACE; p. 574: TO THE TRUSTEES OF NASSAU HALL (Princeton); p. 578: A DISSERTATION CONCERNING THE NATURE | OF TRUE VIRTUE.; p. 595: A | DISSERTATION | CONCERNING | THE END FROM WHICH GOD CREATED | THE | WORLD.; p. 602: A HISTORY OF THE WORK OF REDEMPTION; p. [614]: blank; p. [615]: APPENDIX (verso blank); p. 617: *APPENDIX A* | To Mrs. Esther Burr, Princeton, New Jersey | Stockbridge Novem. 20, 1757 [signed] Jonathan Edwards; p. 619: [photocopy] | Page 1, Edwards to his daughter.; p. 620: [photocopy] | Page 2, Edwards to his daughter.; p. 621: *APPENDIX B* | [photocopy] | A typical page from Edwards' *Catalogue*, showing his notation of Berkeley's essays. (*Courtesy, Yale University Library.*); p. 622: [photocopy] | Front of a loose-leaf discovered between the cover and first page of Edwards' *Catalogue* | [4 lines] | (*Courtesy, Yale University Library.*); p. 623: [photocopy] | From the reverse side of the loose-leaf inserted in Edwards' *Catalogue.* The item "Vid. | Aug. 28, 1723" refers to his *Diary* entry of that date. (*Courtesy, Yale University Library.*); p. 624: *APPENDIX C* | THE SACRAMENT SERMONS (p. 625: [photocopy] | Typical page from the *Sacrament Sermons* of September 12, 1742 in the handwriting of | Jonathan Edwards. The originals are in the archives of the Presbyterian Historical Society | of Philadelphia. Hitherto unpublished in any form.; p. 636: *APPENDIX D* | [photocopy] | Jonathan Edwards to the Rev. Mr. Aaron Burr (father of the Revolutionary officer) | recommending Mrs. Burr (Edwards' daughter) to the Church of Christ in Newark as a | "member in full standing." (*Courtesy, Princeton University Library.*); p. 637: *APPENDIX E* | Letter Soliciting Funds | Sheffield, May 6, 1752 [signed] JONATHAN EDWARDS; p. 639: *APPENDIX F* | Letter to Edward Wigglesworth | Stockbridge, Feb. 11, 1757. | [signed] | JONATHAN EDWARDS.

NUC NE0046750 OCLC 1896752
Gordon-Conwell Theological Seminary

479 • The Philosophy of | JONATHAN EDWARDS | From His Private Notebooks | Edited by | HARVEY G. TOWNSEND | UNIVERSITY OF OREGON | EUGENE, OREGON. PRINTED AT | THE UNIVERSITY PRESS. 1955

25.3 x 17 cm.; xxii, 270 p.

Contents: p. [i]: title; p. [ii]: UNIVERSITY OF OREGON | MONOGRAPHS. | Studies in Philosophy, | No. 2. September 1955; p. iii: Table of Contents (verso blank); p. [v]: Introduction [signed] H.G.T.; p. 1: Of Being; p. 21: The Mind; p. 74: Miscellanies; p. 269: Numerical Index to Selections | from the *Miscellanies*.

NUC NE0046746 OCLC 1421620
Gordon College

479A • [publisher's device] | GREENWOOD PRESS, PUBLISHERS | WESTPORT, CONNECTICUT

25.3 x 17 cm.; xxii, 270 p.

Notes: identical with the above except for the imprint; p. [ii]: [17 lines] | Originally published in 1955 | by the University of Oregon, Eugene | Reprinted with the permission | of the University of Oregon | First Greenwood Reprinting 1972 | [3 lines]; reprinted 1974 and 1977

ISBN 0837165113 OCLC 416839
Andover Newton Theological School

480 • Jonathan Edwards | on Evangelism | [decorative rule] | *Edited* | *by* | CARL J. C. WOLF | WM. B. EERDMANS PUBLISHING CO. | GRAND RAPIDS, MICHIGAN

20.3 x 13 cm.; xii, 137, [1] p.

Notes: p. xi: The present digest gives the gist of each of Edwards' most important writings on evangelism, and it does this in Edwards' own words.

Contents: p. [i]: *Jonathan Edwards on Evangelism* (verso blank); p. [iii]: title; p. [iv]: © WM. B. EERDMANS PUBLISHING CO., 1958 | [short rule] | [7 lines]; p. [v]: [dedication] (verso blank); p. vii: *Preface*; p. [xiii]: *Contents* (verso blank); p. [15]: *Jonathan Edwards on Evangelism* (verso blank); p. 17: *A Faithful Narrative* | *of the* | *Surprising Work of God*; p. 35: *Thoughts on the Revival* | *of Religion*; p. 74: *A Treatise Concerning* | *Religious Affections*; p. 116: *The Treatise on Grace*; p. 121: *Judging Persons' Experiences*; p. 123: *Sinners in the Hands of an Angry God*; p. 130: *Reality of Spiritual Light*; p. [138]: blank.

OCLC 3079600
Harvard Divinity School

480A • [publisher's device] | GREENWOOD PRESS, PUBLISHERS | WESTPORT, CONNECTICUT

20.3 x 13 cm.; xii, 137, [1] p.

Notes: identical with the above except for the imprint; title page (verso): [9 lines] | © Wm. B. Eerdmans Publishing Co., 1958 | [9 lines] | Reprinted in 1981 by Greenwood Press | [4 lines].

ISBN 0837165881 OCLC 7277329
Harvard University

481 • *The Select Works of* | *Jonathan* | *Edwards* | *Volume I* | With an account of his life by | IAIN H. MURRAY, B.A. | [publisher's device] | *"The Lord our God be with us, as he was with our fathers: let* | *him not leave us nor forsake us."*—I KINGS 8.57. | [rule] | THE BANNER OF TRUTH TRUST

21.5 x 13.7 cm.; map (on lining papers), 176 p.

Notes: published in 1958; p. [5]: *"It may be worthy of consideration, whether the great alteration which has* | *been made in the state of things in our nation, and some other parts of the* | *protestant world, in this and the past age, by exploding so generally* | Calvinistic *doctrines–an alteration so often spoken of a worthy to be greatly* | *rejoiced in by the friends of truth, learning, and virtue, as an instance of the* | *great increase of light in the Christian Church–be indeed a a happy change, | owing to any such cause as an increase of true knowledge and understanding | in the things of religion; or whether there is not reason to fear, that it may be | owing to some worse cause." |* JONATHAN EDWARDS.

Contents: p. [1]: *Jonathan Edwards* (verso blank); p. [3]: title; p. [4]: Printed in England by Wm. Carling Co. Ltd., London and Hitchin; p. [5]: [quotation] (verso blank); p. [7]: [photocopy, attached, within rules] | *Jonathan Edwards* (verso blank); p. [9]: CONTENTS; p. [11]: *A Memoir of | Jonathan Edwards* (verso blank); p. 60: BIBLIOGRAPHY; pp. [63-64]: blank; p. [65]: *A | Faithful Narrative | of the | Surprising Work of God |* in the | Conversion Of Many Hundred Souls, | in Northampton, | and the | Neighbouring Towns And Villages Of New Hampshire, in | New England; | in a | Letter To The Rev. Dr. Colman, Of Boston. (verso blank); p. 67: PREFACE | BY THE FIRST EDITORS, DR. ISAAC WATTS, AND DR. JOHN GUYSE; p. 71: A NARRATIVE OF SURPRISING CONVERSIONS; p. [118]: blank; p. [119]: *Sermons* (verso blank); p. 121: NATURAL MEN IN A DREADFUL CONDITION; p. 152: CHRIST EXALTED | OR | JESUS CHRIST GLORIOUSLY EXALTED ABOVE ALL EVIL IN THE | WORK OF REDEMPTION; p. 163: GOD'S SOVEREIGNTY IN THE SALVATION OF MEN.

OCLC 4159047
Harvard Divinity School

482 • SELECT WORKS OF | JONATHAN EDWARDS | Volume I | A NARRATIVE OF SURPRISING CONVERSIONS | THE DISTINGUISHING MARKS OF A | WORK OF THE SPIRIT OF GOD | AN ACCOUNT OF THE REVIVAL OF RELIGION | IN NORTHAMPTON, 1740-42 | SERMONS | THE BANNER OF TRUTH TRUST | 78b Chiltern Street, London WI

21.5 x 13.9 cm.; viii, 244 p.

Notes: reissued without the appended three sermons in 1984 as *Jonathan Edwards on Revival* (see 491); p. [iv]: *Jonathan Edwards' Select Works*, Volume I, comprising *A Narrative of | Surprising Conversions*, *Sermons* and *A Memoir* by Iain Murray published | in 1958. | This edition, omitting the *Memoir* and including *Distinguishing Marks | of a Work of the Spirit of God* and an account of the revival at North- | ampton in 1740-42 in a letter, first published in 1965.

Contents: p. [i]: SELECT WORKS OF | JONATHAN EDWARDS (verso blank); p. [iii]: title; p. [iv]:[publisher's note] | [4 lines]; p. v: CONTENTS (verso blank); p. vii: PREFACE TO THE SECOND EDITION (verso blank); p. 1: A NARRATIVE OF SURPRISING CONVERSIONS; p. 75: THE | DISTINGUISHING MARKS | OF A | WORK OF THE SPIRIT OF GOD; p. 148: AN ACCOUNT OF THE | REVIVAL OF RELIGION IN NORTHAMPTON | IN 1740-1742, AS COMMUNICATED IN A LETTER | TO A BOSTON MINISTER; p. [161]: *Sermons* (verso blank); p. 163: NATURAL MEN IN A DREADFUL CONDITION; p. 209: CHRIST EXALTED | OR | JESUS CHRIST GLORIOUSLY EXALTED ABOVE ALL | EVIL IN THE WORK OF REDEMPTION; p. 225: GOD'S SOVEREIGNTY IN THE SALVATION OF MEN.

OCLC 24887768
Gordon-Conwell Theological Seminary

483 • SELECT WORKS OF | JONATHAN EDWARDS | Volume II | SERMONS | [publisher's device] | *"The Lord our God be with us, as he was with our fathers: let him not leave us nor | forsake us."*—I KINGS 8. 57. | [rule] | THE BANNER OF TRUTH TRUST | 1959

21.5 x 13.6 cm.; 276 p.

Notes: reissued in 1990 as *Jonathan Edwards on Knowing Christ* (see 492); p. [4]: The spelling and punctuation of this volume, | apart from a few exceptional cases, has been | left in the Eighteenth Century New England | usage. The Publishers have followed the text of | the 1839 London edition of Edwards' Works.

Contents: p. [1]: SELECT WORKS OF JONATHAN EDWARDS | Volume II (verso blank); p. [3]: title; p. [4]: [publisher's note] | *Vol. I of this new edition published March 1958 | Vol. II . . . June 1959* | PRINTED IN GREAT BRITAIN BY | BILLING AND SONS LIMITED, GUILDFORD AND LONDON; p. [5]: *Contents*; p. [7]: SELECT WORKS OF JONATHAN EDWARDS (verso blank); p. 9: CHRISTIAN KNOWLEDGE; p. 31: ADVERTISEMENT TO THE READER | RESPECTING THE FOLLOWING SERMON [signed] T. PRINCE. | W. COOPER. | *Boston, August* 17, 1731.; p. 33: GOD GLORIFIED IN MAN'S DEPENDENCE; p. 49: GOD MAKES MEN SENSIBLE OF THEIR MISERY | BEFORE HE REVEALS HIS MERCY AND LOVE; p. 79: PRESSING INTO THE KINGDOM OF GOD; p. 114: THE JUSTICE OF GOD IN THE DAMNATION | OF SINNERS; p. 156: SAFETY, FULNESS, AND SWEET

REFRESHMENT, | TO BE FOUND IN CHRIST; p. 183: SINNERS IN THE HANDS OF AN ANGRY GOD; p. 200: CHRISTIANS A CHOSEN GENERATION, A ROYAL | PRIESTHOOD, A HOLY NATION, A PECULIAR | PEOPLE; p. 245: THE END OF THE WICKED CONTEMPLATED | BY THE RIGHTEOUS; p. 266: PARDON FOR THE GREATEST SINNERS.

OCLC 41303730
Harvard University

484 • SELECT WORKS OF | JONATHAN EDWARDS | Volume III | Treatise Concerning | THE RELIGIOUS AFFECTIONS | [publisher's device] | "*Whom having not seen, ye love, in whom, though now ye see him not, yet believing, | ye rejoice with joy unspeakable and full of glory.*" I PETER I. 8. | [rule] | THE BANNER OF TRUTH TRUST | 1961

21.5 x 13.6 cm.; 382 p.

Notes: p. [5]: MANY editions of *The Religious Affections* have been published | since the first edition of 1746, and there are some variations in | punctuation between them. While this edition follows the text | of the Worcester edition, the punctuation has been examined | throughout and occasionally revised to aid the modern reader. | A few minor amendments and corrections have been made in the | text, which is unabridged.

Contents: p. [1]: SELECT WORKS OF JONATHAN EDWARDS | Volume III (verso blank); p. [3]: title; p. [4]: *Vol. I. of Edwards' Select Works published March 1958 | Vol. II. . . . June 1959 | Vol. III. . . .January 1961* | [4 lines]; p. [5]: PUBLISHERS' NOTE (verso blank); p. 7: CONTENTS; p. 9: INTRODUCTION [signed] ALEXANDER SMELLIE | 1898; p. 15: THE AUTHOR'S PREFACE; pp. 21-382: text.

OCLC 6291212
Harvard University

485 • DEVOTIONS | OF | JONATHAN EDWARDS | Compiled by | RALPH G. TURNBULL | BAKER BOOK HOUSE | Grand Rapids, Michigan | 1959

15.3 x 10.2 cm.; 110 p.

Notes: these brief selections are not indexed in the *Index of Titles* (p. 237).

Contents: p. [1]: DEVOTIONS | OF | JONATHAN EDWARDS (verso blank); p. [3]: title; p. [4]: [1 line] | *Copyright, 1959, by | Baker Book House* | [1 line]; p. [5]: PREFACE [signed] Ralph G. Turnbull; p. 7: The Peace Which Christ Gives; p. 8: The Importance of Religious Affections; p. 9: The Power of True Godliness; p. 10: The Importance and Advantage of a | Thorough Knowledge of Divine Truth; p. 11: Exhortation to Come to Christ; p. 12: When Glory Redounds to God as the | Effect of Divine Wisdom; p. 13: Wonderful Things Done, by Which | Salvation Is Procured; p. 14: The Wisdom of God, | Displayed in the Way of Salvation; p. 15: Justification by Faith Alone; p. 16: Men Naturally God's Enemies; p. 17: Man's Natural Blindness | in the Things of Religion; p. 18: The Nature of True Virtue; p. 19: The Majesty and Grace of God; p. 20: The Work of Redemption; p. 21: The Promise of the Spirit; p. 22: The True Excellency of a Gospel Minister; p. 23: When God Hears and Answers Prayers; p. 24: In the Day of Judgment; p. 25: Christian Humility; p. 26: True Saints – Absent from the Body, | Present with the Lord; p. 27: The Sorrows of the Bereaved | Spread Before Jesus; p. 28: The Good Attained by Salvation; p. 29: Ministers of the Gospel; p. 30: The Church's Marriage to Her God; p. 31: The Satisfaction of Christ; p. 32: Diligence in Service; p. 33: Self-Examination; p. 34: The Spirit of Prayer; p. 35: The Duty of Prayer; p. 36: A Prayer Hearing God; p. 37: God's Excellency; p. 38: Harden Not Your Heart; p. 39: Sovereign Grace; p. 40: God's Sovereignty; p. 41: God's Choice of Men; p. 42: God the Best Portion of the Christian; p. 44: Take Heed to Thyself; p. 45: Secret Faults; p. 46: Excellency of Christ; p. 49: Benefits of Choosing Christ; p. 51: The Final Judgment; p. 53: The Vain Self-Flatteries of the Sinner; p. 54: Warnings of Scripture Adapted to Awaken | and Convert Sinners; p. 55: The Sin and Folly of Depending on | Future Time; p. 56: Unbelievers Contemn (Slight) Christ; p. 57: The Folly of Looking Back; p. 58: The Manner in Which the Salvation of the | Soul Is to Be Sought; p. 59: Pressing into the Kingdom of God; p. 61: Ruth's Resolution; p. 62: Pardon for the Greatest Sinners; p. 63: A Divine and Supernatural Light; p. 64: True Grace Distinguished; p. 65: Fearfulness Surprising Sinners in Zion; p. 66: Union in Prayer; p. 72: Christ the Example of Ministers; p. 75: God's Judgment in the Breaking of | Strong Rods; p. 76: Joseph's Temptation and Deliverance; p. 78: The True Christian's Life; p. 81: A Warning to Professors; p. 82: The Sin of Theft and of Injustice; p. 83: The Perpetuity and Change of the Sabbath; p. 85: The Nature and End of Excommunication; p. 86: Perseverance of Saints; p. 88: Spiritual Understanding; p. 91: Religious Affections; p. 94: True Religious Affections and False; p. 97: Efficacious Grace; p. 98:

Concerning Faith; p. 108: Chosen in God; p. 109: Chosen in Christ; p. 110: Longings After God.
OCLC 3185457
Harvard Divinity School

486 • MILESTONES OF THOUGHT | [rule] | SELECTED WRITINGS | OF | JONATHAN EDWARDS | Edited, with an introduction, by | HAROLD P. SIMONSON | *University of Washington* | [publisher's device] | [rule] | FREDERICK UNGAR PUBLISHING CO. | *NEW YORK*

19.7 x 12 cm.; 188 p.

Notes: p. 23: Throughout this edition the text is from *The Works of* | *President Edwards*, 4 vols., New York, 1869.

Contents: p. [1]: SELECTED WRITINGS OF | JONATHAN EDWARDS (verso blank); p. [3]: title; p. [4]: MILESTONES | OF THOUGHT | *in the History of Ideas* | Copyright © 1970 by Frederick Ungar Publishing Co. | [4 lines]; p. [5]: [dedication] (verso blank); p. 7: INTRODUCTION; p. 25: TABLE OF CONTENTS (verso blank); p. 27: PERSONAL NARRATIVE; p. 45: GOD GLORIFIED | IN MAN'S DEPENDENCE; p. 65: A DIVINE AND | SUPERNATURAL LIGHT; p. 89: JUSTIFICATION | BY FAITH ALONE; p. 96: SINNERS IN THE HANDS | OF AN ANGRY GOD; p. 114: THE EXCELLENCY OF CHRIST; p. 126: THE PEACE WHICH CHRIST | GIVES HIS TRUE FOLLOWERS; p. 134: A FAREWELL SERMON; p. 156: RELIGIOUS AFFECTIONS; p. 166: FREEDOM OF THE WILL; p. 179: THE NATURE OF TRUE VIRTUE.

ISBN 0804461325 OCLC 92743
Northeastern University

486A • *A Frederick Ungar Book* | CONTINUUM • NEW YORK

19.7 x 12 cm.; 188, [2] p.

Notes: identical with the above except for imprint; title page (verso): MILESTONES | OF THOUGHT | *in the History of Ideas* | 1990 | The Continuum Publishing Company | 370 Lexington Avenue | New York, NY 10017 | *Twelfth Printing* | Copyright © 1959 by Frederick Ungar Publishing Co., Inc. | [8 lines]; no copy of a 1959 issue has been located.

ISBN 0804461325 OCLC 21013959
Graduate Theological Union

486B • [within rules] WAVELAND | [publisher's device] | PRESS, Inc. | Prospect Heights, Illinois

21.5 x 13.8 cm.; 194 p.

Notes: identical with the above except for the imprint; title page (verso): [5 lines] | Copyright © 1970 by Harold P. Simonson | 1992 reissued with changes by Waveland Press, Inc. | [6 lines].

ISBN 0881337188 OCLC 27903533
Smith College

487 • [series data] | Aide huazi xuan ji | [publication data]

20.8 x 14.7 cm.; 31, [1], 425, [1] p.

Notes: a Chinese translation of selected writings of Edwards.

Contents: frontispiece: [engraving] | Jonathan Edwards | 1703-1758; prp. [1]: title; prp. [2]: Christian Classics Library, and Series, No. 16 | SELECTED WRITINGS | of | JONATHAN EDWARDS, SR. | *General Director:* FRANCIS P. JONES | *Advisory Editor:* JOSEPH HAROUTUNIAN | *Translator:* PING-THE HSIEH | *Revisor:* CHRISTOPHER TANG | [2 lines] | *Published by* | THE BOARD OF FOUNDERS | *of* | NANKING THEOLOGICAL SEMINARY | *in association with* | THE COUNCIL ON CHRISTIAN LITERATURE | FOR OVERSEAS CHINESE | 1 Upper Albert Road, Hong Kong | 1960; p. [1]: [preface: editing and translating the Christian Classics Library]; p. 3: [contents]; p. 5: [preface]; p. 7: [introduction]; p. [32]: blank; p. 1: [Autobiography] | [Resolutions]; p. 10: [Diary]; p. 20: [Personal Narrative]; p. 35: [Sermons] | [God Glorified]; p. 53: [Divine and Supernatural Light]; p. 72: [Excellency of Christ]; p. 108: [Sinners in the Hands of an Angry God]; p. 124: [The Christian Pilgrim]; p. 138: [God the Best Portion]; p. 149: [The Peace which Christ Gives]; p. 165: [Treatises] | [Religious Affections]; p. 208: [Freedom of the Will]; p. 247: [Original Sin]; p. 259: [End of Creation]; p. 350: [True Virtue]; p. 406: [History of Redemption]; p. 422: [Titles from the Christian Classics Library]; p. [426]: blank.

OCLC 34464944
Chinese University of Hong Kong

488 • "THE MIND" | OF | JONATHAN EDWARDS | *A Reconstructed Text* | By Leon Howard | UNIVERSITY OF CALIFORNIA PRESS | BERKELEY AND LOS ANGELES | 1963

23.4 x 15.2 cm.; xii, [2], 151, [1] p.

Contents: p. [i]: "THE MIND" OF JONATHAN EDWARDS (verso blank); p. [iii]: UNIVERSITY OF CALIFORNIA PUBLICATIONS. | ENGLISH STUDIES: 28 | [10 lines] | © 1963 by the Regents of the University of California; p. [v]: [dedication] (verso blank); p. viii: PREFACE [signed] L. H. | *Los Angeles* | *August 23, 1962*; p. [xiii]: CONTENTS (verso blank); p. 1: I. INTRODUCTION; p. 25: II. THE RECONSTRUCTED MANUSCRIPT; p. 120: III. CONCLUSION: THE MIND | OF JONATHAN EDWARDS; p. [136]: blank; p. 137: APPENDIX | THE ESSAYS "OF BEING" AND "OF THE | PREJUDICES OF IMAGINATION"; p. 149: NOTES ON SOURCES (verso blank); p. 151: INDEX OF NOTES (verso blank).

OCLC 1262157

Congregational Library

489 • *JONATHAN EDWARDS*: | *BASIC WRITINGS* | *Selected, Edited, and with a Foreword by* | *OLA ELIZABETH WINSLOW* | [publisher's device] | A SIGNET CLASSIC | Published by The New American Library, | New York and Toronto | The New English Library Limited, London

17.8 x 10.2 cm.; xxviii, 29-255, [1], p.

Contents: p. [i]: [biography] (verso blank); p. [iii] title; p. [iv]: [3 lines] | COPYRIGHT © 1966 BY THE NEW AMERICAN | LIBRARY, INC. | [12 lines]; p. [v]: Contents (verso blank); p. vii: *FOREWORD* [signed] OLA ELIZABETH WINSLOW; p. [29]: *JONATHAN EDWARDS:* | *BASIC WRITINGS* (verso blank); p. 31: *OF INSECTS*; p. 38: *OF THE RAINBOW, COLOURS,* | *THE SOUL, OF BEING*; p. 51: *THE MIND*; p. 62: (Notes on Natural Science) | *OF THE PREJUDICES OF THE IMAGINATION*; p. 66: *SARAH PIERREPONT*; p. 68: *RESOLUTIONS*; p. 76: *DIARY*; p. 81: *PERSONAL NARRATIVE*; p. 97: *A FAITHFUL NARRATIVE OF THE* | *SURPRISING WORK OF GOD*; p. 106: *GOD GLORIFIED IN THE WORK OF REDEMPTION*; p. 123: *A DIVINE AND SUPERNATURAL LIGHT*; p. 135: *THE CHRISTIAN PILGRIM*; p. 150: *SINNERS IN THE HANDS OF AN ANGRY GOD*; p. 168: *FAREWELL SERMON*; p. 184: *A TREATISE CONCERNING* | *RELIGIOUS AFFECTIONS*; p. 196: *FREEDOM OF THE WILL*; p. 224: *CHRISTIAN DOCTRINE OF ORIGINAL* | *SIN DEFENDED*; p. 233: *CONCERNING THE END FOR WHICH GOD* | *CREATED THE WORLD*; p. 241: *THE NATURE OF TRUE VIRTUE*; p. 250: *IMAGES OR SHADOWS OF DIVINE THINGS*; p. 254: *SELECTED BIBLIOGRAPHY*; p. [256]: [advertisement].

OCLC 5292449

Gordon-Conwell Theological Seminary

489A • JONATHAN EDWARDS | [thick-thin rule] | *Basic Writings* | *Selected, Edited, and with a Foreword by* | *OLA ELIZABETH WINSLOW* | [publisher's device] | A MERIDIAN BOOK | [short rule] | NEW AMERICAN LIBRARY | [short rule] | NEW YORK AND SCARBOROUGH, ONTARIO

17.8 x 10.2 cm.; xxviii, 29-255, [1], p.

Notes: identical with the above except for the title page; published in 1978.

ISBN 0452010012 OCLC 6262946

Piedmont College

490 • TREATISE ON GRACE | *and other posthumously* | *published writings* | by | Jonathan Edwards | *Edited, with an Introduction* | *by* | PAUL HELM | JAMES CLARKE & CO. LTD. | Cambridge & London

21.6 x 13.7 cm.; x, 131, [1] p.

Contents: p. [i]: TREATISE ON GRACE (verso blank); p. [iii]: title; p. [iv]: *This edition first published in 1971* Introduction © by Paul Helm | [9 lines]; p. [vii]: CONTENTS; p. [viii]: [quotation] | EDWARDS, *Personal Narrative.*; p. ix: EDITOR'S NOTE [signed] PAUL HELM; p. 1: INTRODUCTION; p. [24]: blank; p. 25: TREATISE ON GRACE; p. [76]: blank; p. 77: OBSERVATIONS CONCERNING | THE SCRIPTURE OECONOMY OF THE TRINITY, | AND COVENANT OF REDEMPTION; p. 95: APPENDIX; p. 99: AN ESSAY ON THE TRINITY; p. [132]: blank.

ISBN 0227677390 OCLC 524932
Harvard Divinity School

490A • the Attic Press, Inc. | GREENWOOD, S. C.
21.3 x 13.3 cm.; x, 131, [1] p.
Notes: identical with the above except for the imprint; published in 1971.
OCLC 16119494
Biola University

491 • [rule] | JONATHAN EDWARDS | ON REVIVAL | [rule] | A NARRATIVE OF SURPRISING CONVERSIONS | [rule] | THE DISTINGUISHING MARKS OF A | WORK OF THE SPIRIT OF GOD | [rule] | AN ACCOUNT OF THE REVIVAL OF RELIGION | IN NORTHAMPTON 1740-1742 | [rule] | THE BANNER OF TRUTH TRUST
21.3 x 13.6 cm.; [4], 160 p.
Notes: first published in 1965; first reprinted under this title 1984; reissued 1987, 1991, 1994, 1995, 1997.
Contents: prp. [1] SELECT WORKS OF | JONATHAN EDWARDS (verso blank); prp. [3]: title; prp. [4]: THE BANNER OF TRUTH TRUST | 5 Murrayfield Road, Edinburgh EH12 6EL | PO Box 621, Carlisle, Pennsylvania 17013, U.S.A. | [11 lines]; prp. [5]: CONTENTS (verso blank); p. 1: A NARRATIVE OF SURPRISING CONVERSIONS; p. 75: THE | DISTINGUISHING MARKS | OF A | WORK OF THE SPIRIT OF GOD; p. 148: AN ACCOUNT OF THE REVIVAL IN NORTHAMPTON | IN 1740-1742, AS COMMUNICATED IN A LETTER | TO A MINISTER OF BOSTON.
ISBN 0851514316 OCLC 11582892
Gordon-Conwell Theological Seminary

492 • [rule] | JONATHAN EDWARDS | ON KNOWING CHRIST | [rule] | THE BANNER OF TRUTH TRUST.
21.4 x 13.9 cm.; 276 p.
Notes: p. [2]: First published by the Banner of Truth under the title | *Select Works of Jonathan Edwards Volume 2*, 1958 | Reprinted 1959 | Reprinted as *Jonathan Edwards on Knowing Christ*, 1990. Reissued with a slightly altered title page 1993, 1995, and 1997.
Contents: p. [1]: title; p. [2]: THE BANNER OF TRUTH TRUST | 3 Murrayfield Road, Edinburgh EH12 6EL | PO Box 621, Carlisle, Pennsylvania 17013, U.S.A. | [8 lines]; p. [3]: *Contents*; pp. [5-6]: blank; p. [7]: JONATHAN EDWARDS | ON KNOWING CHRIST (verso blank); p. 9: CHRISTIAN KNOWLEDGE; p. 31: ADVERTISEMENT TO THE READER | RESPECTING THE FOLLOWING SERMON [signed] T. PRINCE. | W. COOPER. | *Boston, August* 17, 1731.; p. 33: GOD GLORIFIED IN MAN'S DEPENDENCE; p. 49: GOD MAKES MEN SENSIBLE OF THEIR MISERY | BEFORE HE REVEALS HIS MERCY AND LOVE; p. 79: PRESSING INTO THE KINGDOM OF GOD; p. 114: THE JUSTICE OF GOD IN THE DAMNATION | OF SINNERS; p. 156: SAFETY, FULNESS, AND SWEET REFRESHMENT, | TO BE FOUND IN CHRIST; p. 183: SINNERS IN THE HANDS OF AN ANGRY GOD; p. 200: CHRISTIANS A CHOSEN GENERATION, A ROYAL | PRIESTHOOD, A HOLY NATION, A PECULIAR | PEOPLE; p. 245: THE END OF THE WICKED CONTEMPLATED | BY THE RIGHTEOUS; p. 266: PARDON FOR THE GREATEST SINNERS.
ISBN 0851515835 OCLC 23176734
Duke University

493 • Experiencing God | Jonathan Edwards | *Selected readings from his spiritual classics* | *Compiled by* | Robert Backhouse | [publisher's device] | Marshall Pickering | *An Imprint of* HarperCollins*Publishers*
19.7 x 12.5 cm.; x, 182 p.
Contents: p. [i]: Experiencing God (verso blank); p. [iii]: title; p. [iv]: [4 lines] | First published in Great Britain | in 1995 by Marshall Pickering | [22 lines]; p. [v]: Contents; p. [vi]: Introduction; p. [ix]: Experiencing God (verso blank);

p. 1: God glorified in man's dependence; p. 19: Distinguishing marks of a work of the Spirit of God; p. 87: Christian charity *or*, The duty | of charity to the poor, explained | and enforced; p. 129: A treatise concerning | religious affections; p. 165: The peace which Christ | gives to his true followers; p. 181: Books by | Jonathan Edwards.

ISBN 0551029935 OCLC 34191609

University of North Carolina

494 • GOD AT WORK? | SIGNS OF TRUE REVIVAL | An easier to read and abridged version of | 'The Distinguished Marks of a Work of the Spirit of God' | by Jonathan Edwards | The full version is available from | The Banner of Truth Trust | Edinburgh EH12 6EL | *Prepared* by Gary Benfold | Pastor of Limes Avenue Baptist Church, | AYLESBURY | *Joint Managing Editors* | J.P. Arthur M.A. | H.J. Appleby

19.7 x 13 cm.; 94 p.

Notes: Great Christian Classics no. 14.

Contents: p. [1]:GOD AT WORK ? | together with | 'Sinners in the hands of an angry God' | SIGNS OF TRUE REVIVAL (verso blank); p. [3]: title; p. [4]: © GRACE PUBLICATIONS TRUST | 139 Grosvenor Avenue | London, N5 2NH, | England | First published 1995 | [9 lines]; p. [5]: Contents; p. 7: Foreword [signed] G. B.; p. [12]: blank; p. 13: Introduction; p. [16]: blank; pp. 17-76: text; p. 77: Sinners in the hands of an angry God; p. [92]: blank; p. 93: Appendix: Some Notes on Books.

ISBN 0946462380 OCLC 33278075

Midwestern Baptist Theological Seminary

495 • A Jonathan Edwards Reader | Edited by John E. Smith, Harry S. Stout, | and Kenneth P. Minkema | New Haven and London Yale University Press

20.6 x 13.3 cm.; xlv, [1], 335, [1] p.

Contents: [i]: A Jonathan Edwards Reader (verso blank); p. [iii]: title; p. [iv]: [4 lines] | Copyright © 1995 by Yale University | [31 lines]; p. [v]: Contents; p. [vii]: Editors' Introduction; p. [xli]: Chronology of Edwards' Life; p. [xliii]: Further Reading; p. [xlv]: A Jonathan Edwards Reader (verso blank); p. [1]: The Spider Letter; p. [9]: Of Being (1721); p. [14]: Beauty of the World (1725); p. [16]: Images of Divine Things (1728); p. [22]: The Mind (1723); p. [35]: Miscellanies (1722); p. [49]: Notes on the Apocalypse (begun 1723); p. [57]: A Faithful Narrative of the | Surprising Work of God (1737); p. [88]: blank; p. [89]: Sermons | Sinners in the Hands of an Angry God (1741); p. 105: A Divine and Supernatural Light, Immediately Imparted to the Soul | by the Spirit of God, Shown to be Both a Scriptural, | and Rational Doctrine (1734); p. 124: A History of the Work of Redemption (1739); p. [137]: A Treatise Concerning Religious | Affections (1746); p. [172]: The Bad Book Case (1744); p. [179]: An Humble Inquiry into the Rules | of the Word of God, Concerning | the Qualifications Requisite to a | Complete Standing and Full | Communion in the Visible | Christian Church (1749); p. [192]: A Careful and Strict Inquiry | into the Modern Prevailing Notions | of that Freedom of the Will, Which | Is Supposed to Be Essential to | Moral Agency, Virtue and Vice, | Reward and Punishment, Praise | and Blame (1754); p. [223]: The Great Christian Doctrine of | Original Sin Defended (1758); p. [244]: The Nature of True Virtue (1765); p. [266]: Personal Writings | Diary (1722); p. 274: Resolutions (1722); p. 281: Apostrophe to Sarah Pierpont (c. 1723); p. 281: Personal Narrative (c. 1739); p. 296: Receipt for Slave Venus (1731); p. [298]: Letters | To Timothy Edwards | Yale College, March 1, 1721; p. 300: To George Whitefield | Northampton in New England, Feb. 12, 1739/40; p. 302: To Moses Lyman | Northampton, May 10, 1742; p. 304: To Joseph Bellamy | Northampton, Jan. 15, 1746/47; p. 306: To Sarah Pierpont Edwards | Northampton, June 22, 1748; p. 307: To Thomas Foxcroft | May 24, 1749; p. 311: To Esther Edwards Burr | Stockbridge, March 28, 1753; p. 314: To Thomas Prince | Stockbridge, May 10, 1754; p. 321: To the Trustees of the College of New Jersey | Stockbridge, Oct. 19, 1757; p. [325]: blank; p. [327]: Index; p. [336]: blank.

ISBN 0300062036 OCLC 31519188

Yale Divinity School

496 • The Wrath | of | Almighty God | (Jonathan Edwards on | God's Judgment against Sinners) | Edited by Rev. Don Kistler | Soli Deo Gloria Publications | *...for instruction in righteousness...*

21.5 x 14 cm.; iv, 390 p.

Contents: p. [i]: title; p. [ii]: Soli Deo Gloria Publications | P.O. Box 451, Morgan PA 15064 | [1 line] | *The Wrath of Almighty God: Jonathan Edwards on God's Judgment | against Sinners* is © 1996 by Don Kistler and Soli Deo Gloria | [2 lines]; p. iii: CONTENTS; p. iv: Publisher's Preface; p. 1: Natural Men in a | Dreadful Condition; p. 61: Sinners in the Hands of | an Angry God; p. 83: The Justice of God in the | Damnation of Sinners; p. 139: The Final Judgment | or | The World Judged Righteously by Jesus Christ; p. 186: The Portion of the Wicked; p. 232: The Wicked Useful in Their Destruction Only; p. 254: The Future Punishment of | the Wicked Unavoidable | and Intolerable; p. 277: Wrath to the Uttermost; p. 291: Concerning the Endless | Punishment of Those | Who Die Impenitent; p. 337: The Eternity of Hell Torments; p. 364: The End of the Wicked | Contemplated by the | Righteous | or | The torments of the wicked in hell no occasion | of grief to the saints in heaven.

ISBN 1573580600 OCLC 37620735

Andover Newton Theological School

497 • Altogether Lovely: | Jonathan Edwards on | the Glory and | Excellency of Jesus Christ | Collected and Edited by Don Kistler | Soli Deo Gloria Publications | *...for instruction in righteousness...*

21.5 x 13.9 cm.; vi, 231, [1] p.

Contents: p. [i]: title; p. [ii]: [3 lines] | *Altogether Lovely: Jonathan Edwards on the Glory and Excellency | of Jesus Christ* © 1997 by Don Kistler and Soli Deo Gloria | [2 lines]; p. [iii]: Contents; p. iv: Foreword [signed] R. C. Sproul Orlando | September, 1997; p. 1: God the Best Portion | of the Christian; p. 14: The Excellency of Christ; p. 59: Christ Exalted; p. 79: Safety, Fullness, and Sweet | Refreshment in Christ; p. 114: Jesus Christ the Same | Yesterday, Today, | and Forever; p. 140: The Pure in Heart Blessed; p. 176: Christ the Example | of Ministers; p. 198: Unbelievers Contemn the Glory and Excellency of Christ; p. 211: Praise One of the Chief | Employments of Heaven; p. [232]: blank.

ISBN 1573580716 OCLC 38099942

Harvard Divinity School

498 • Pressing | into the | Kingdom | Jonathan Edwards on | Seeking Salvation | Compiled and Edited by Rev. Don Kistler | Soli Deo Gloria Publications | *...for instruction in righteousness...*

22.3 x 14 cm.; iv, 345, [1] p.

Contents: p. [i]: title; p. [ii]: Soli Deo Gloria Publications | P.O. Box 451, Morgan, PA 15064 | [1 line] | *Pressing into the Kingdom* is © 1998 by Don Kistler | and Soli Deo Gloria. All rights reserved. | [1 line]; p. iii: Contents; p. 1 Pressing into the | Kingdom of God; p. 52: The Preciousness of Time; p. 70: Procrastination; p. 100: Ruth's Resolution; p. 123: The Folly of Looking Back in | Fleeing out of Sodom; p. 143: God Makes Men Sensible | of their Misery; p. 187 Sinners in Zion | Tenderly Warned; p. 218: The Manner in Which the Salvation | of the Soul Is To Be Sought; p. 248: The Vain Self-Flatteries | of the Sinner; p. 265: Christ's Agony; p. 327: The Christian Pilgrim; p. [346]: blank.

ISBN 1573580872 OCLC 39876711

Bethel College and Seminary

499 • The Sermons of | Jonathan Edwards | *A Reader* | Edited by | Wilson H. Kimnach, Kenneth P. Minkema, | and Douglas A. Sweeney. | New Haven and London Yale University Press

19.8 x 13.3 cm.; xlvii, 281, [1] p.

Contents: p. [i]: The Sermons of Jonathan Edwards (verso blank); p. [iii]: title; p. [iv]: [5 lines] | Copyright © 199[illegible] by Yale University. | [31 lines]; p. [v]: [dedication] (verso blank); p. [vii]: Contents (verso blank); p. [ix]: Editors Introduction; p. [xlviii]: blank; p. [xlix]: Chronology of Edwards' Life; p. [li]: Further Reading; p. [liii]: The Sermons of Jonathan Edwards (verso blank); p. [1]: The Way of Holiness (1722); p. [13]: The Pleasantness of Religion (1723); p. [26] The Importance and Advantage of | a Thorough Knowledge of Divine | Truth (1739); p. [49]: Sinners in the Hands of an | Angry God (1741); p. [66]: God Glorified in the Work of | Redemption, by the Greatness of | Man's Dependence upon Him in | the Whole of It (1731); p. [83]: The Reality of Conversion (1740); p. [105]: To the Mohawks at the Treaty, | August 16 1751; p. [111]: He That Believeth Shall Be Saved (1751); p. [121]: A Divine and Supernatural Light, | Immediately Imparted to the Soul | By the Spirit of God, Shown to Be | Both a Scriptural, and Rational | Doctrine (1734); p. [141]: I Know My Redeemer Lives (1740); p. [161]: The Excellency of Christ (1738); p. [197]: Much in Deeds of Charity (1741); p. [212] A Farewell Sermon | Preached at the First Precinct in | Northampton, After the People's | Public Rejection of Their Minister | . . . on June 22, 1750; p. [242]: Heaven Is a World of Love | (*Charity and Its Fruits*, Sermon | Fifteen, 1738); p. [273]

Index; p. [282]: [advertisement].

ISBN 0300077661 OCLC 39936237

Yale Divinity School

500 • [within short rules, imposed] NELSON'S | ROYAL | CLASSICS | [within short rules] SINNERS | IN THE | HANDS OF AN | ANGRY GOD | AND OTHER WRITINGS | [within short rules] [photocopy] | [ornament] | JONATHAN | EDWARDS | [publisher's device] | THOMAS NELSON PUBLISHERS | Nashville

23.2 x 14.8 cm.; xvi, [2], [1]-314 p.

Contents: pp. [i-ii]: blank; p. [iii]: SINNERS | IN THE | HANDS OF AN | ANGRY GOD | AND OTHER WRITINGS | [within short rules] [photocopy] (verso blank); p. [v]: title; p. [vi]: Copyright © 2000 by Thomas Nelson Publishers, Inc. | [13 lines]; p. vii: CONTENTS (verso blank); p. ix: PUBLISHER'S PREFACE; p. xi: INTRODUCTION; p. [xiv]: blank; p. xv: JONATHAN EDWARDS, 1703-1758; p. [xvii]: [within short rules, imposed] NELSON'S | ROYAL | CLASSICS | [within short rules] SINNERS | IN THE | HANDS OF AN | ANGRY GOD | AND OTHER WRITINGS | [within short rules] [photocopy] | [ornament] | JONATHAN | EDWARDS (verso blank); p. [1]: [within short rules] SINNERS | IN THE | HANDS OF AN | ANGRY GOD | [photocopy] (verso blank); p. [19]: [within short rules] A DIVINE | AND | SUPERNATURAL | LIGHT | [photocopy] (verso blank); p. [39]: [within short rules] GOD'S | SOVEREIGNTY | IN THE SALVATION | OF MEN | [photocopy] (verso blank); p. [60]: blank; p. [61]: [within short rules] AN ESSAY | ON THE TRINITY | [photocopy] (verso blank); p. [80]: blank; p. [81]: [within short rules] A | FAREWELL | SERMON | [photocopy] (verso blank); p. [106]: blank; p. [107]: [within short rules] FREEDOM | OF THE WILL | [photocopy] (verso blank).

ISBN 078524235 OCLC 44076037

Louisville Presbyterian Theological Seminary

501 • HIS REDEEMING LOVE | [decorative rule] | Jonathan Edwards | *Compiled by* | JUDITH COUCHMAN | and LISA MARZANO | [publisher's device] | [between short rules] | VINE | BOOKS

20.2 x 12.6 cm.; [6], 7-153, [1] p.

Notes: Life Messages of Great Christian Series; commentary and brief selections from Edwards's sermons.

Contents: p. [1]: HIS REDEEMING LOVE | [ornament] (verso blank); p. [3]: title; p. [4]: © 2001 by Servant Publications | [11 lines] | Published by Servant Publications | P.O. Box 8617 | Ann Arbor, Michigan 48107 | [12 lines]; p. [5]: [dedication]; p. [6]: [advertisement]; p. 7: CONTENTS; p. 8: ACKNOWLEDGMENTS; pp. 9-141: text; p. [142]: blank; p. 143: JONATHAN EDWARDS' RESOLUTIONS | (1722-1723); p. 152: [advertisement]

ISBN 156955112 OCLC 47623939

Gordon-Conwell Theological Seminary

502 • *The* | SALVATION | *of* | SOULS | *Nine Previously Unpublished Sermons* | *on the Call of Ministry and the Gospel* | *by* | JONATHAN EDWARDS | *Edited by* | RICHARD A. BAILEY & GREGORY A. WILLS | CROSSWAY BOOKS | A DIVISION OF | GOOD NEWS PUBLISHERS | WHEATON, ILLINOIS

21.5 x 13.8 cm.; 190 p.

Contents: p. [1]: [recommendations]; p. [3]: THE SALVATION OF SOULS (verso blank); p. [5]: title; p. [6]: [1 line] Copyright © 2002 by Richard A. Bailey and Gregory A. Wills | [27 lines]; p. [7]: [dedication] (verso blank); p. [9]: CONTENTS (verso blank); p. [11]: FOREWORD | *by* | *George M. Marsden*; p. [14]: blank; p. [15]: INTRODUCTION | *by* | *Richard A. Bailey & Gregory A. Wills*; p. [27]: EDITORS' INTRODUCTION; p. [29]: THE DEATH OF FAITHFUL | MINISTERS A SIGN OF | GOD'S DISPLEASURE; p. [40]: EDITORS' INTRODUCTION; MINISTERS NEED | THE POWER OF GOD; p. [56]: blank; p. [57]: EDITORS' INTRODUCTION; p. [59]: THE KIND OF PREACHING | PEOPLE WANT; p. [70]: blank; p. [71]: EDITORS' INTRODUCTION; p. [73]: THE MINISTER BEFORE THE | JUDGMENT SEAT OF CHRIST; p. [92]: blank; p. [93]: EDITORS' INTRODUCTION; p. [95]: DEACONS TO CARE FOR | THE BODY, MINISTERS | FOR THE SOUL; p. [110]: blank; p. [111]: EDITORS' INTRODUCTION; p. [113]: MINISTERS TO PREACH | NOT THEIR OWN WISDOM | BUT THE WORD OF GOD; p. [132]: blank; p. [133]: EDITORS' INTRODUCTION; p. [135]: PASTOR AND PEOPLE | MUST LOOK TO GOD; p. [149]: EDITORS' INTRODUCTION; p. [151]: PREACHING THE GOSPEL | BRINGS POOR SINNERS | TO CHRIST; p. [155]: EDITORS'

INTRODUCTION; p. [157]: THE WORK OF THE MINISTRY | IS SAVING SINNERS; p. [180]: blank; p. [181]: SCRIPTURE INDEX; p. [185]: GENERAL INDEX

ISBN 1581344511 OCLC 50203895

Cornerstone University

503 • Standing | in | Grace | Jonathan Edwards's | *A Treatise on Grace* | Edited by Dr. Don Kistler | Soli Deo Gloria Publications | *...for instruction in righteousness...*

21 x 12.5 cm.; iv, 66 p.

Contents: p. [i]: title; p. [ii]: [4 lines] | *Standing in Grace: Jonathan Edwards's Treatise on Grace* was | first published in Edinburgh by Alexander | Grosart, under the title *A Treatise on Grace*, and was | published as part of *Selections from the Unpublished* | *Writings of Jonathan Edwards*. This Soli Deo Gloria | reprint, in which spelling, grammar, and formatting changes have been made | is © 2002 by Soli Deo Gloria. | [14 lines]; p. [iii]: Contents (verso blank); pp. [1]-66: text.

ISBN 1573581313 OCLC 49415651

Southern Baptist Theological Seminary

504 • The | True Believer | Sermons | by | Jonathan Edwards | on | The Marks and Benefits of True Faith | Edited by Dr. Don Kistler | Soli Deo Gloria Publications | *...for instruction in righteousness...*

21.5 x 13.8 cm.; [4], 315, [1] p.

Contents: prp. [1]: title; prp. [2]: [4 lines] | *The True Believer: Jonathan Edwards on the Marks* | *and Benefits of True Faith* is © 2002 by | Don Kistler and Soli Deo Gloria. | [2 lines]; prp. [3]: Contents; prp. [4]: Publisher's Preface; p. 1: Sermon 1 | *Pardon for the Greatest Sinners*; p. 16: Sermon 2 | *True Grace Distinguished from* | *the Experience of Devils*; p. 50: Sermon 3: *Hypocrites Deficient in the Duty of Prayer*; p. 80: Sermon 4 | *A Warning To Professors of Religion*; p. 104: Sermon 5 | *Christians a Chosen Generation, a Royal Priesthood,* | *a Holy Nation, a Peculiar People*; p. 166: Sermon 6: *The Peace Which Christ Gives His True Followers*; p. 186: Sermon 7 | *True Saints, When Absent from the Body,* | *are Present With the Lord*; p. 230: Sermon 8 | *The Portion of the Righteous*; p. [316]: blank.

OCLC 47899627

Gordon-Conwell Theological Seminary

COLLECTED EDITIONS

505 • THE | WORKS | OF | PRESIDENT EDWARDS, | *IN EIGHT VOLUMES.* | [short thin-thick rule] | VOLUME I. | [short thick-thin rule] | *CONTAINING,* | [in 2 cols., col. 1] I. HOPKINS'S MEMOIRS OF MR. EDWARDS, | IMPROVED AND ENLARGED. | II. ENQUIRY INTO THE FREEDOM OF THE | WILL. [short thin-thick vertical rule, col. 2] III. A DISSERTATION CONCERNING THE | END FOR WHICH GOD CREATED THE | WORLD. | [thin-thick rule] | LEEDS: | PRINTED BY EDWARD BAINES, | FOR THE EDITORS; CONDER, BUCKLERSBURY; BUTTON, PATERNOSTER-ROW; | WILLIAMS AND SMITH, STATIONERS'-COURT; BAYNES, PATERNOSTER- | ROW; OGLE, GREAT-TURNSTILE; NUNN, QUEENS-TREET; AND JONES, | PATERNOSTER-ROW, LONDON; AND FOR BAINES, AND HEATON, | LEEDS; WILSON AND SPENCE, YORK; GUTHRIE AND TAIT, | EDINBURGH; M. OGLE, GLASGOW; CROOKES, RO- | THERHAM; ABLE, NORTHAMPTON; | AND MR. FARRAND, 185, MARKET-PLACE, PHILADELPHIA. | [short rule] | 1806. *stet* QUEENS-TREET

22.7 x 13.7 cm.; π^4, $[A]^4$, B-Z^4, Aa-Zz^4, 3A-$3U^4$, $3X^2$; viii, [5]-535, [1] p.

Notes: The first collected edition of Edwards's works was published at Leeds in 8 volumes in 1806-1811. In 1817 at London, Volumes I-IV were reprinted and Volumes V-VIII were brought out in a new edition, though the whole 8-volume set of the London printing is called "A New Edition." The complication in the details by which these volumes were presented to the public is so great that a summary of the confusions will be helpful. Almost none of the many sets examined is accurately made up. A volume of the London 1817 edition, for example, shows that the title page of the equivalent volume of the 1806-1811 Leeds edition has been substituted, and the volume included as legitimate in the Leeds edition set. In other cases the error is reversed, an 1817 title page being inserted into a volume of the Leeds set, and the whole presented as the London 1817 edition. Volume V, of the Leeds edition, published in 1809, appeared later in the same year in a variant issue: new matter is added, and the title page indicates the change. Volume VI of the same edition, first published in 1810, also appeared in a variant issue, printed in 1811. At Edinburgh in 1847, two additional volumes of Edwards material were published, styled "Supplementary To The London Eight Volume Edition [of 1817]," and labeled as Volumes IX and X. But very few sets of the London 1817 edition are reported that possess the supplementary volumes. The sheets making up the 2 volumes of the so-called "Supplementary Volumes" were issued again at Edinburgh in 1875 with a new title page, as "The Posthumous Works Of President Edwards." So few copies of any of this supplementary material seem to exist that it is possible the original issue of the 1847 edition was not large, and the number of unbound sheets left over (which probably went to make up the 1875 reprint with the new title page) was smaller still.—THJ. In some copies, the frontispiece is omitted; in some copies, OGLE, GREAT-TURNSTILE is deleted from imprint; in some copies, QUEENS-TREET is corrected.

Contents: frontispiece: [engraving] | *Freeman Sculp^t.* | *The Revd Jon ^{thn} Edwards, A.M.*; p. [i]: title (verso blank); p. [iii]: THE | *EDITORS' PREFACE.* [signed] EDWARD WILLIAMS. | EDWARD PARSONS.; p. [vii]: CONTENTS OF VOLUME I.; p. [5]: MEMOIRS | OF THE | LIFE, EXPERIENCE AND CHARACTER | OF THE LATE REV. | *JONATHAN EDWARDS, A. M.* | PRESIDENT OF THE COLLEGE, | AT PRINCE-TOWN, IN NEW-JERSEY, | BY | THE REV. SAMUEL HOPKINS, D. D. | AND NOW | REVISED, CORRECTED AND ENLARGED, | *BY THE EDITORS.* (verso blank); p. [7]: *PREFACE* | TO | HOPKINS'S LIFE OF EDWARDS. [dated] *August* 20, 1764.; p. [9]: *MEMOIRS* | OF THE LATE | REV. JONATHAN EDWARDS, A. M.; p. [91]: APPENDIX | TO | THE LIFE | OF | *PRESIDENT EDWARDS*; | CONTAINING, | I. A SKETCH OF MRS. EDWARDS'S LIFE AND CHARACTER. | II. A BRIEF ACCOUNT OF THEIR DAUGHTER, MRS. ESTHER BURR. | III. THE LIFE AND CHARACTER OF THEIR SON, | DR. JONATHAN EDWARDS. (verso blank); p. [93]: APPEND. I. | [short thin-thick rule] | *A short Sketch of Mrs. Edwards's Life and Character.*; p. 98: APPEND. II. | [short thin-thick rule] | *A brief Account of Mrs. Esther Burr, President Edwards's* | *Daughter.*; p. [103]: APPEND. III. | [short thin-thick rule] | *A Sketch of the Life and Character of Jonathan Edwards, D. D.*; p. [120]: blank; p. [121]: A | CAREFUL AND STRICT | ENQUIRY | INTO THE | MODERN PREVAILING NOTIONS | OF | *THAT FREEDOM OF WILL,* | WHICH IS SUPPOSED TO BE ESSENTIAL | TO | MORAL AGENCY, | VIRTUE AND VICE, REWARD AND PUNISHMENT, | PRAISE AND BLAME. | [short thick-thin rule] | Rom. ix. 16. IT IS NOT OF HIM THAT WILLETH. (verso blank); p. [123]: *PREFACE.*; p. [127]: A | *CAREFUL & STRICT ENQUIRY,* | &c.; p. [438]: blank; p. [439]: A | DISSERTATION | CONCERNING | THE END FOR WHICH GOD CREATED | THE | *WORLD.* (verso blank); p. [441]: *PREFACE* | BY | THE FIRST EDITOR; p. [443]: A | *DISSERTATION* | CONCERNING | GOD'S CHIEF END, | &c.; p. [536]: blank.

THJ 338 NUC NE0046378 OCLC 5639484
Drew University

VOLUME II. | [short thin-thick rule] | *CONTAINING,* | [in 2 cols., col. 1] I. A DISSERTATION CONCERNING THE | NATURE OF TRUE VIRTUE. | II. THE GREAT CHRISTIAN DOCTRINE | OF ORIGINAL SIN DEFENDED. | III. MAN'S NATURAL BLINDNESS IN | [short double vertical rule, col. 2] THE THINGS OF RELIGION. | IV. AN HUMBLE ATTEMPT TO PRO- | MOTE EXPLICIT AGREEMENT AND | VISIBLE UNION OF GOD'S PEOPLE | IN EXTRAORDINARY PRAYER. [thick-thin rule] | LEEDS: | PRINTED BY EDWARD BAINES, | FOR THE EDITORS; CONDER, BUCKLERSBURY; BUTTON, PATERNOSTER-ROW; | WILLIAMS AND SMITH, STATIONERS'-COURT; BAYNES, PATERNOSTER- | ROW; NUNN, QUEEN-STREET; AND JONES, PATERNOSTER-ROW, | LONDON; AND FOR BAINES, AND HEATON, LEEDS; WILSON | AND SPENCE, YORK; GUTHRIE AND TAIT, EDINBURGH; | M. OGLE, GLASGOW; CROOKES, ROTHERHAM; | ABLE, NORTHAMPTON; | AND MR. FARRAND, 185, MARKET-PLACE, PHILADELPHIA. [short rule] | 1807.

21.4 x 13.6 cm.; π^2, A-Z^4, Aa-Zz^4, 3A-3U^4, 3X^6; 541, [3] p.

Notes: p. 287 misnumbered 237 (pp. [1]-286, 237, 288-541); some copies omit the errata and sig. 3X$_6$.

Contents: p. [1]: title (verso blank); p. [3]: CONTENTS OF VOLUME II.; p. [5]: A | DISSERTATION | CONCERNING THE | *NATURE OF TRUE VIRTUE.* (verso blank); p. [7]: THE | *NATURE OF TRUE VIRTUE.*; p. [79]: THE | GREAT CHRISTIAN DOCTRINE | OF | ORIGINAL SIN | DEFENDED; | *EVIDENCES OF ITS TRUTH* | PRODUCED, | AND | ARGUMENTS TO THE CONTRARY ANSWERED: | Containing, in particular, | *A REPLY TO THE OBJECTIONS* | OF | DR. JOHN TAYLOR, | IN HIS BOOK, INTITLED | "THE SCRIPTURE DOCTRINE OF ORIGINAL SIN PROPOSED TO | FREE AND CANDID EXAMINATION, &c." | [short thick-thin rule] | Matt. ix. 12. They that be whole, need not a Physician; but they that are sick. | –Et hæc non tantum ad Peccatores referenda est; quia in omnibus Maledictionibus | primi Hominis, omnes ejus Generationes conveniunt.– *R. Sal. Jarchi.* | Propter Concupiscentiam, Innatam Cordi humano, dicitur, In Iniquitate genitus sum; | atque Sensus est quod à Nativitate implantatum sit Cordi humano *Jetzer harang*, | Figmentum malum. *Aben-Ezra.* | –Ad Mores Natura recurrit | Damnatos, fixa et mutari nescia.– | –Dociles imitandis | Turpibus & pravis omnes sumus. *Juv.* (verso blank); p. [81]: *ADVERTISEMENT*, | CONTAINING A | BRIEF ACCOUNT OF HIS BOOK AND ITS AUTHOR, | *BY THE FIRST EDITOR.*; p. [85]: THE | *AUTHOR'S PREFACE.* [dated] *Stockbridge, May* 26,1757.; p. [87]: THE | GREAT CHRISTIAN DOCTRINE | OF | *ORIGINAL SIN DEFENDED.*; p. [388]: blank; p. [389]: MAN'S | NATURAL BLINDNESS | IN THE THINGS OF | *RELIGION.* (verso blank); p. [391]: *MAN'S NATURAL BLINDNESS,* | *&c.*; p. [422]: blank; p. [423]: AN | HUMBLE ATTEMPT | TO PROMOTE | EXPLICIT AGREEMENT AND VISIBLE UNION | OF | *GOD'S PEOPLE,* | IN | EXTRAORDINARY PRAYER, | FOR THE REVIVAL OF RELIGION AND THE ADVANCEMENT OF CHRIST's | KINGDOM ON EARTH. (verso blank); p. [425]: *ADVERTISEMENT.* (verso blank); p. [427]: *PREFACE* | BY A FORMER ENGLISH EDITOR. [signed] JOHN SUTCLIFF. | OLNEY, May 4th, 1789.; p. [429]: *PREFACE* | BY THE AMERICAN EDITORS.; p. [431]: AN | *HUMBLE ATTEMPT,* | *&c.*; p. [542]: blank; p. [543]: ERRATA IN VOL. I.; p. [544]: blank.

Drew University

VOLUME III. | [short thin-thick rule] | *CONTAINING,* | [in 2 cols., col. 1] I. A NARRATIVE OF THE SURPRISING | WORK OF GOD, IN THE CONVERSION | OF MANY HUNDRED SOULS, IN AND | ABOUT NORTHAMPTON. | II. THE LIFE AND DIARY OF THE REV. | DAVID BRAINERD, WITH NOTES AND | REFLECTIONS. | III. MR. BRAINERD'S JOURNAL IN TWO | PARTS. | IV. FIRST APPENDIX—CONTAINING HIS | GENERAL REMARKS ON THE DOC- | TRINES PREACHED, WITH THEIR EX- | TRAORDINARY EFFECTS, &C.—SECOND | APPENDIX—CONTAINING AN AC- | [short double vertical rule, col. 2] COUNT OF HIS METHOD OF LEARNING | THE INDIAN LANGUAGE, AND OF | INSTRUCTING THE INDIANS.—THIRD | APPENDIX—CONTAINING HIS BRIEF | ACCOUNT OF THE ENDEAVOURS USED | BY THE MISSIONARIES OF THE SOCI- | ETY IN SCOTLAND, FOR PROPAGAT- | ING CHRISTIAN KNOWLEDGE. | V. MR. BRAINERD'S REMAINS, CONTAIN- | ING LETTERS AND OTHER PAPERS. | VI. A SERMON PREACHED AT THE OR- | DINATION OF MR. BRAINERD, BY | E. PEMBERTON, A. M. | VII. REFLECTIONS AND OBSERVATIONS. | [thick-thin rule] | LEEDS: | PRINTED BY EDWARD BAINES, | FOR THE EDITORS; CONDER, BUCKLERSBURY; BUTTON, PATERNOSTER-ROW; | WILLIAMS AND SMITH, STATIONERS'-COURT; BAYNES, PATERNOSTER- | ROW; NUNN, QUEEN-STREET; AND JONES, PATERNOSTER-ROW, | LONDON; AND FOR BAINES, AND HEATON, LEEDS; WILSON | AND SPENCE, YORK; GUTHRIE AND TAIT, EDINBURGH; | M. OGLE, GLASGOW; CROOKES, ROTHERHAM; | ABLE, NORTHAMPTON; | AND MR. FARRAND, 185, MARKET-PLACE, PHILADELPHIA. | [short rule] | 1807.

21.4 x 13.6 cm.; π^2, A-Z^4, Aa-Zz^4, 3A-3Z^4, 4A-4C^4; [i]-iv, [i]-vii, [1], [9]-573, [3] p.

Notes: pp. [i]-iv repeated.

Contents: p. [i]: title (verso blank); pp. [iii]-iv: CONTENTS OF VOLUME III.; p. [i]: A | FAITHFUL NARRATIVE | OF THE | *SURPRISING WORK OF GOD,* | IN THE | CONVERSION OF MANY HUNDRED SOULS, | *IN NORTHAMPTON,* | AND NEIGHBOURING TOWNS AND VILLAGES OF NEW HAMPSHIRE, | IN NEW ENGLAND; | IN A | *Letter to the Rev. Dr. Colman, of Boston.* (verso blank); p. [iii]: *PREFACE* | BY THE FIRST EDITORS, Dr. ISAAC WATTS, AND | Dr. JOHN GUYSE. [signed] [in 2 cols., col. 1] LONDON | *Oct.* 12, 1737. | [col. 2] ISAAC WATTS. | JOHN GUYSE.; p. [viii]: blank; p. [9]: A | FAITHFUL | *NARRATIVE* | &c. &c.; p. [72]: blank; p. [73]:

THE | LIFE AND DIARY | OF | *THE REV. DAVID BRAINERD:* | WITH | NOTES AND REFLECTIONS. (verso blank); p. [75]: *PREFACE.* [signed] JONATHAN EDWARDS.; p. [81]: THE | *LIFE AND DIARY,* | &c.; p. [312]: blank; p. [313]: *MR. BRAINERD'S JOURNAL,* | IN | TWO PARTS. (verso blank); p. [315]: *ADVERTISEMENT.* (verso blank); p. [317]: *PREFACE.* [signed] The CORRESPONDENTS.; p. [319]: THE | RISE AND PROGRESS | OF A REMARKABLE | *WORK OF GRACE,* | &c.; p. [412]: blank; p. [413]: FIRST | APPENDIX | TO | *MR. BRAINERD'S JOURNAL:* | CONTAINING HIS | *GENERAL REMARKS* | ON THE | DOCTRINES PREACHED, | THEIR | EXTRAORDINARY EFFECTS, | &c. (verso blank); p. [415]: *GENERAL REMARKS,* | &c.; p. [430]: blank; p. [431]: SECOND | APPENDIX | TO | *MR. BRAINERD'S JOURNAL:* | CONTAINING AN ACCOUNT OF HIS | METHOD OF LEARNING THE INDIAN LANGUAGE, AND OF INSTRUCTING | THE INDIANS; | TOGETHER | *WITH THE DIFFICULTIES* | WHICH LIE IN THE WAY OF THEIR CONVERSION. (verso blank); p. [433]: *METHOD* | OF | LEARNING THE INDIAN LANGUAGE, | &c.; p. [469]: THIRD | APPENDIX | TO | *MR. BRAINERD'S JOURNAL:* | CONTAINING HIS BRIEF ACCOUNT OF | *THE ENDEAVOURS USED BY THE MISSIONARIES OF THE SOCIETY IN* | *SCOTLAND,* | FOR | PROPAGATING CHRISTIAN KNOWLEDGE, | TO INTRODUCE THE GOSPEL AMONG THE INDIANS ON THE BORDERS | OF NEW YORK, &c. (verso blank); p. [471]: *THIRD APPENDIX,* | &c.; p. [485]: *MR. BRAINERD'S REMAINS,* | CONSISTING OF | LETTERS AND OTHER PAPERS. (verso blank); p. [487]: *MR. BRAINERD'S* | LETTERS TO HIS FRIENDS.; p. [503]: *MR. BRAINERD'S* | DETACHED PAPERS.; p. [510]: blank; p. [511]: A | SERMON | PREACHED IN NEW-ARK, *JUNE* 12, 1744 | AT THE ORDINATION | OF | *MR. DAVID BRAINERD,* | A MISSIONARY AMONG THE INDIANS | *UPON THE BORDERS OF THE PROVINCES OF NEW-YORK, NEW-JERSEY,* | *AND PENNSYLVANIA.* | BY | E. PEMBERTON, A. M. | PASTOR OF THE PRESBYTERIAN CHURCH IN THE CITY OF NEW-YORK. (verso blank); p. [514]: AN | *ORDINATION SERMON,* | &c.; p. [530]: blank; p. [531]: SOME | REFLECTIONS AND OBSERVATIONS | ON THE PRECEDING | MEMOIRS, | *&c.* | OF THE | *REV. DAVID BRAINERD.* (verso blank); p. [533]: REFLECTIONS AND OBSERVATIONS | ON THE PRECEDING | *MEMOIRS,* | *&c.*; p. [574]: blank.

Princeton University

VOLUME IV. | [short thin-thick rule] | *CONTAINING,* | [in 2 cols., col. 1] I. A TREATISE CONCERNING RELIGIOUS | AFFECTIONS, IN THREE PARTS. | II. AN APPENDIX TO THE TREATISE ON | THE AFFECTIONS, IN TWO LETTERS TO | MR. GILLESPIE. | III. CHRISTIAN CAUTIONS; OR, THE NE- | CESSITY OF SELF EXAMINATION. | IV. A WARNING TO PROFESSORS; OR THE | GREAT GUILT OF THOSE WHO ATTEND | ON THE ORDINANCES OF DIVINE WOR- | SHIP, AND YET ALLOW THEMSELVES IN | ANY KNOWN WICKEDNESS. | [short double vertical rule, col. 2] V. THE FINAL JUDGMENT; OR, THE WORLD | JUDGED RIGHTEOUSLY BY JESUS CHRIST. | VI. SINNERS IN ZION TENDERLY WARNED; | OR, THE FEARFULNESS WHICH WILL | HEREAFTER SURPRISE SINNERS IN ZION, | REPRESENTED AND IMPROVED. | VII. THE END OF THE WICKED CONTEM- | PLATED BY THE RIGHTEOUS; OR, THE | TORMENTS OF THE WICKED IN HELL, NO | OCCASION OF GRIEF TO THE SAINTS IN | HEAVEN. | [thick-thin rule] | LEEDS: | PRINTED BY EDWARD BAINES, | FOR THE EDITORS; CONDER, BUCKLERSBURY; BUTTON, PATERNOSTER-ROW; | WILLIAMS AND SMITH, STATIONERS'-COURT; BAYNES, PATERNOSTER- | ROW; OGLE, GREAT-TURNSTYLE; HAMILTON, PATERNOSTER-ROW; | AND JONES, PATERNOSTER-ROW, LONDON; AND FOR BAINES, | AND HEATON, LEEDS; WILSON | AND SPENCE, YORK; | GUTHRIE AND TAIT, EDINBURGH; M. OGLE, GLASGOW; CROOKES, ROTHERHAM; | ABLE, NORTHAMPTON; | AND MR. FARRAND, 185, MARKET-PLACE, PHILADELPHIA. | [short thick-thin rule] | 1808.

21.4 x 13.6 cm.; π^2, A-Z^4, Aa-Zz^4, 3A-$3T^4$, $3U^1$; [4], vi, [7]-522 p.

Notes: in some copies, NUNN, QUEEN-STREET substituted for OGLE, GREAT-TURNSTYLE.

Contents: prp. [1]: title (verso blank); prp. [3]: CONTENTS OF VOLUME IV.; p. [i]: A | TREATISE | CONCERNING | *RELIGIOUS AFFECTIONS:* | IN | THREE PARTS. | PART I. CONCERNING THE NATURE OF THE AFFECTIONS, | AND THEIR IMPORTANCE IN RELIGION. | PART II. SHEWING WHAT ARE NO CERTAIN SIGNS THAT | RELIGIOUS AFFECTIONS ARE GRACIOUS, OR THAT THEY | ARE NOT. | PART III. SHEWING WHAT ARE DISTINGUISHING SIGNS OF | TRULY GRACIOUS AND HOLY AFFECTIONS. | [short thick-thin rule] | Lev. ix. ult. and x.

1. 2.–And there came a fire out from before the Lord.–upon the | altar;–which when all the people saw, they shouted and fell on their faces. And | Nadab and Abihu–offered strange fire before the Lord, which he commanded | them not: and there went out a fire from the Lord, and devoured them, and they | died before the Lord. | Cant. ii. 12. 13.– The flowers appear on the earth, the time of the singing of birds | is come, and the voice of the turtle is heard in our land. The fig-tree putteth | forth her green figs, and the vines with the tender grape give a good smell.– | Ver. 15. Take us the foxes, the little foxes which spoil the vines: for our vines | have tender grapes. (verso blank); p. [iii]: *PREFACE.*; p. [7]: A | *TREATISE* | CONCERNING | RELIGIOUS AFFECTIONS: p. [377]: CHRISTIAN CAUTIONS; | OR, | THE NECESSITY | OF | *SELF-EXAMINATION.* (verso blank); p. [379]: *CHRISTIAN CAUTIONS,* | &c.; p. [421]: A | WARNING TO PROFESSORS, | OR, | THE GREAT GUILT OF THOSE WHO ATTEND | ON THE | *ORDINANCES OF DIVINE WORSHIP,* | AND YET | ALLOW THEMSELVES | IN | ANY KNOWN WICKEDNESS. (verso blank); p. [423]: A | *WARNING TO PROFESSORS,* | &c.; p. [440]: blank; p. [441]: THE | FINAL JUDGMENT: | OR, | THE WORLD JUDGED RIGHTEOUSLY | BY | *JESUS CHRIST.* (verso blank); p. [443]: *THE FINAL JUDGMENT,* | &c.; p. [479]: SINNERS IN ZION | *TENDERLY WARNED:* | OR, | THE FEARFULNESS WHICH WILL HEREAFTER SURPRISE | SINNERS IN ZION, | *REPRESENTED AND IMPROVED.* (verso blank); p. [481]: *SINNERS IN ZION,* | &c. p. [501]: THE | END OF THE WICKED | CONTEMPLATED BY | *THE RIGHTEOUS:* | OR, | THE TORMENTS OF THE WICKED IN HELL, NO OCCASION OF | GRIEF TO THE SAINTS IN HEAVEN. (verso blank); p. [503]: THE | *END OF THE WICKED,* | &c.

Drew University

VOLUME V. | [short thick-thin rule] | *CONTAINING,* | [in 2 cols., col. 1] I. A HISTORY OF THE WORK OF REDEMPTION. | II. MEN ARE NATURALLY GOD'S ENEMIES. | III. THE WISDOM OF GOD DISPLAYED IN THE | WAY OF SALVATION. | IV. CHRISTIAN KNOWLEDGE: OR, THE IMPOR- | [short thin-thick vertical rule, col. 2:] TANCE AND ADVANTAGE OF A THOROUGH | KNOWLEDGE OF DIVINE TRUTH. | V. CHRISTIAN CHARITY; OR THE DUTY OF | CHARITY TO THE POOR, EXPLAINED AND | ENFORCED. | [thin-thick rule] | LEEDS: | PRINTED BY EDWARD BAINES, | FOR THE EDITORS; CONDER, BUCKLERSBURY; BUTTON, PATERNOSTER-ROW; | WILLIAMS AND SMITH, STATIONERS'-COURT; BAYNES, PATERNOSTER- | ROW; OGLE, GREAT-TURNSTYLE; HAMILTON, PATERNOSTER-ROW; | AND JONES, PATERNOSTER-ROW, LONDON; AND FOR BAINES, | AND HEATON, LEEDS; WILSON AND SPENCE, YORK; | GUTHRIE AND TAIT, EDINBURGH; M. OGLE, | GLASGOW; CROOKES, ROTHERHAM; | ABLE, NORTHAMPTON; | AND MR. FARRAND, 185, MARKET-PLACE, PHILADELPHIA. | [short thick-thin rule] |1809.

21.4 x 13.6 cm.; π^2, A-Z^4, Aa-Zz^4, 3A-3L^4, 3M^2; 463, [1] p.

Notes: in some copies, p. [6] misnumbered 8; some copies omit colophon on p. 463.

Contents: p. [1]: title (verso blank); p. [3]: *CONTENTS OF VOLUME V.*; p. [5]: A HISTORY | OF THE | WORK OF REDEMPTION, | CONTAINING | THE OUTLINES OF A BODY OF DIVINITY, | INCLUDING | *A VIEW OF CHURCH HISTORY,* | IN A METHOD ENTIRELY NEW. (verso blank); p. [7]: *PREFACE.* [signed] JONATHAN EDWARDS. | *Newhaven, Feb.* 25, 1775.; p. [9]: *ADVERTISEMENT.* [signed] JOHN ERSKINE. | *Edinburgh, April* 29, 1775. (verso blank); p. [11]: A HISTORY | OF THE | *WORK OF REDEMPTION.*; p. [304]: blank; p. [305]: MEN NATURALLY | ARE | *GOD'S ENEMIES.* (verso blank); p. [307]: *MEN* | NATURALLY GOD's ENEMIES. p. [346]: blank; p. [347]: THE | WISDOM OF GOD, | DISPLAYED | IN THE | *WAY OF SALVATION.* (verso blank); p. [349]: *WISDOM* | DISPLAYED IN SALVATION.; p. [403]: CHRISTIAN KNOWLEDGE: | OR, THE | IMPORTANCE AND ADVANTAGE | OF A | THOROUGH KNOWLEDGE | OF | *DIVINE TRUTH.* (verso blank); p. [407]: *CHRISTIAN KNOWLEDGE,* | &c. &c.; p. [426]: blank; p. [427]: CHRISTIAN CHARITY: | OR, | *THE DUTY* | OF | CHARITY TO THE POOR | *EXPLAINED AND ENFORCED.* (verso blank); p. [430]: *CHRISTIAN CHARITY,* | *&c.*; p. 463: Edward Baines, Printer, Leeds.; p. [464]: blank.

Newberry Library

Variant issue: identical title page, except that added to *CONTENTS OF VOLUME V.*: VI. SEVEN DISCOURSES, OR TRACTS.; added to signature: 3N-3Z^4, 4A-4D^4, 4E^3; added to pagination: [465]-588 p.; p. 463: [*Continuation of the Vth Vol.*] (verso blank); p. [467]: CHRIST EXALTED: | OR, | JESUS CHRIST | GLORIOUSLY EXALTED ABOVE ALL EVIL | IN THE | *WORK OF REDEMPTION.* (verso blank); p. [483]: SELF-FLATTERIES; | OR, | THE VAIN SELF-

FLATTERIES OF THE SINNER.; p. [495]: DISHONESTY; | OR, | THE SIN OF THEFT AND OF INJUSTICE.; p. [517]: TEMPTATION AND DELIVERANCE; | OR, | JOSEPH'S GREAT TEMPTATION AND GLORIOUS DELIVERANCE.; p. [541]: THE PRECIOUSNESS OF TIME, | AND THE | *IMPORTANCE OF REDEEMING IT.*; p. [554]: PROCRASTINATION; | OR, | *THE SIN AND FOLLY OF DEPENDING ON* | *FUTURE TIME.*; p. [575]: THE CHRISTIAN PILGRIM; | OR | *THE TRUE CHRISTIAN's LIFE A JOURNEY* | *TOWARDS HEAVEN.*; p. 588: Edward Baines, Printer, Leeds.

Drew University

VOLUME VI. | [short thin-thick rule] | *CONTAINING,* | [in 2 cols., col. 1] I. SOME THOUGHTS CONCERNING THE PRESENT | REVIVAL OF RELIGION IN NEW ENGLAND. | II. FIVE DISCOURSES ON THE SOUL'S ETERNAL | SALVATION. | [short thin-thick vertical rule, col. 2] III. TWO SERMONS. | [thick-thin rule] | LEEDS: | PRINTED BY EDWARD BAINES, | FOR THE EDITORS; CONDER, BUCKLERSBURY; BUTTON, PATERNOSTER-ROW; | WILLIAMS, STATIONERS'-COURT; BAYNES, PATERNOSTER- ROW; OGLE, | GREAT-TURNSTYLE; NUNN, QUEEN STREET; AND JONES, PATER- | NOSTER-ROW, LONDON; AND FOR BAINES, AND HEATON, | LEEDS; WILSON AND SPENCE, YORK; GUTHRIE & TAIT, | EDINBURGH; M. OGLE, GLASGOW; CROOKES, RO- | THERHAM; ABLE, NORTHAMPTON; | AND MR. FARRAND, 185, MARKET-PLACE, PHILADELPHIA. | [short thick-thin rule] | 1810.

21.4 x 13.6 cm.; π^2, A-Z^4, Aa-Xx^4, Xx^4, Zz^4, 3A-$3Q^4$; viii, [9]-500 p.

Notes: sig. Xx^4 repeated; pp. 393, 395: the running title for *The Justice of God* mislabeled *Pressing into the Kingdom of God.*

Contents: p. [i]: title (verso blank); p. [iii]: *CONTENTS OF VOLUME VI.* (verso blank); p. [v]: SOME THOUGHTS | CONCERNING THE | PRESENT REVIVAL OF RELIGION | IN | *NEW-ENGLAND,* | AND THE | WAY IN WHICH IT OUGHT TO BE ACKNOWLEDGED AND PROMOTED; | HUMBLY OFFERED TO THE PUBLIC, | *IN A TREATISE* | ON THAT SUBJECT. | [short thin-thick rule] | ISA. xl. 3.–PREPARE YE THE WAY OF THE LORD, MAKE STRAIGHT IN THE | DESERT A HIGH-WAY FOR OUR GOD. (verso blank); p. [vii]: THE | *PREFACE.* p. [9]: *THOUGHTS ON THE REVIVAL,* | &c.; p. [226]: blank; p. [227]: FIVE | DISCOURSES | ON | IMPORTANT SUBJECTS, | NEARLY | CONCERNING THE GREAT AFFAIR | OF THE | *SOUL'S ETERNAL SALVATION,* | *VIZ.* | [in 2 cols., col. 1] I. JUSTIFICATION BY FAITH ALONE. | II. PRESSING INTO THE KINGDOM OF GOD. | III. RUTH'S RESOLUTION. | [short vertical rule, col. 2] IV. THE JUSTICE OF GOD IN THE DAMNA- | TION OF SINNERS. | V. THE EXCELLENCY OF JESUS CHRIST. | *DELIVERED AT NORTHAMPTON,* | Chiefly at the time of the late wonderful pouring out of he Spirit of God there. | [short tapered rule] | DEUT. iv. 9.–*Take heed to thyself, and keep thy soul diligently, lest thou forget the things* | *which thine eyes have seen, and lest they depart from thy heart all the days of thy life.* (verso blank); p. [229]: *PREFACE.*; p. [233]: JUSTIFICATION BY FAITH ALONE.; p. [343]: PRESSING INTO THE KINGDOM OF GOD.; p. [376]: RUTH'S RESOLUTION.; p. [391]:THE JUSTICE OF GOD IN THE DAMNATION OF SINNERS.; p. [431]: THE EXCELLENCY OF CHRIST.; p. [465]: TWO SERMONS: | *I.* | GOD GLORIFIED IN THE WORK OF REDEMPTION, BY THE GREATNESS | OF MAN'S DEPENDENCE UPON HIM IN THE WHOLE OF IT. | *II.* SINNERS I N THE HANDS OF AN ANGRY GOD. | [short tapered rule] | JUDGES VII. 2. | *Lest Israel vaunt themselves against me, saying, Mine own* | *hand hath saved me.* (verso blank); p. [467]: ADVERTISEMENT | *TO THE READER,* | RESPECTING THE FIRST SERMON. [signed] T. PRINCE. | W. COOPER. | *Boston, August* 17, 1731.; p. [469]: GOD GLORIFIED IN MAN'S DEPENDANCE.; p. [485]: SINNERS IN THE HANDS OF AN ANGRY GOD.

Newberry Library

Variant issue: added to *CONTENTS OF VOLUME VI.* in 1811: IV. SEVEN SERMONS ON IMPORTANT SUBJECTS.; added to signature: 3R-$3Z^4$, 4A-$4E^4$; added to pagination: [501]-594 p.; p. [501]: SEVEN SERMONS | ON | *IMPORTANT SUBJECTS.* | [short decorative rule] | VIZ. | [in 2 cols., col. 1] THE BEST PORTION. | DIVINE SOVEREIGNTY. | PARDON FOR SINNERS. | THE PRAYER-HEARING GOD. | [short thin-thick vertical rule, col. 2] EXCOMMUNICATION. | WRATH TO THE UTTERMOST. | WICKED MEN USEFUL IN THEIR | DESTRUCTION ONLY. | [short tapered rule] | CONTINUATION OF VOL. VI. (verso blank); p. [503]: GOD THE BEST PORTION OF THE CHRISTIAN.; p. [513]: THE SOLE CONSIDERATION, THAT GOD IS GOD, | SUFFICIENT TO STILL | *ALL OBJECTIONS TO HIS SOVEREIGNTY.*; p. [525]: GREAT GUILT NO OBSTACLE | TO | THE | *PARDON OF THE RETURNING SINNER.*; p. [536]: THE MOST HIGH A PRAYER-HEARING GOD.; p. [552]: THE | NATURE AND END

OF EXCOMMUNICATION.; p. [566]: WHEN THE WICKED SHALL HAVE FILLED UP | THE MEASURE OF THEIR SIN, | *WRATH WILL COME UPON THEM TO THE | UTTERMOST.*; p. [577]: WICKED MEN USEFUL IN THEIR DESTRUCTION | ONLY.; p. 594: Edward Baines, Printer, Leeds.

Drew University

VOLUME VII. | [short thick-thin rule] | *CONTAINING,* | [in 2 cols., col. 1] I. INQUIRY CONCERNING QUALIFICATIONS FOR | COMMUNION. | II. MISREPRESENTATIONS CORRECTED AND | TRUTH VINDICATED, IN REPLY TO THE | REV. SOLOMON WILLIAMS. | [short thin-thick vertical rule, col. 2] III. A FAREWELL SERMON PREACHED AT | NORTHAMPTON. | IV. RESULT OF A COUNCIL OF NINE CHURCHES | MET AT NORTHAMPTON. | V. FIFTEEN SERMONS ON VARIOUS OCCASIONS. | LEEDS: | PRINTED BY EDWARD BAINES, | FOR THE EDITORS; CONDER, BUCKLERSBURY; BUTTON, PATERNOSTER-ROW; | WILLIAMS, STATIONERS'-COURT; BAYNES, PATERNOSTER- ROW; OGLE, | GREAT-TURNSTYLE; NUNN, QUEEN STREET; AND JONES, PATER- | NOSTER-ROW, LONDON; AND FOR BAINES, AND HEATON, | LEEDS; WILSON AND SPENCE, YORK; | GUTHRIE & TAIT, | EDINBURGH; M. OGLE, GLASGOW; CROOKES, RO- | THERHAM; ABLE, NORTHAMPTON; | AND MR. FARRAND, 185, MARKET-PLACE, PHILADELPHIA. | [short thick-thin rule] | 1811.

21.4 x 13.6 cm.; π^2, A-Z^4, Aa-Zz^4, 3A-3Z^4, 4A-4B^4, 4C^2; [4], 580 p.

Contents: prp. [1]: title (verso blank); prp. [3]: CONTENTS OF VOLUME VII. (verso blank); p. [1]: AN | HUMBLE INQUIRY | INTO THE | *RULES OF THE WORD OF GOD,* | CONCERNING | THE QUALIFICATIONS | REQUISITE TO A | COMPLETE STANDING AND FULL COMMUNION | IN THE VISIBLE | *CHRISTIAN CHURCH.* | [short decorative rule] | Behold now I have opened my mouth:–My words shall be of the uprightness of | my heart.—Job. xxxiii. 2,3.; p. [2]: Confitebatur [*Lutherus*] dolorem suum, quod ab ipsis reflorescentis Evan- | gelii Primordiis, quosvis absque Discrimine ad Cœnam Dominicum | admisisset, quodque Disciplinam, Fratrum Disciplinæ similem, apud | suos non constituisset.—Quia objiciebatur, Fratres non habere Ecclesiam | apertam;—Responsum fuit, Sancta dare non Sanctis prohibuisse Chris- | tum:— Errorem [in *Papatu*] corrigi non posse *aliter quam ut certa Prob- | atione, nec illa subitanea, Cordium Arcana revelunter*, Novitiique diu | et caute tum informentur, tum explorentur. | *Ratio Discipl. Fratr.* Bohem.; p. [3]: THE | AUTHOR'S PREFACE. [signed] J. E.; p. [7]: A PREFACE | BY HIS AMERICAN FRIENDS. [signed] THOMAS PRINCE, | JOHN WEBB, | THOMAS FOXCROFT, | M. BYLES. | *Boston, August* 11, 1746.; p. [9]: *ADVERTISEMENT* | TO THE | EDINBURGH EDITION. [dated] EDINBURGH, May 15, 1790. (verso blank); p. [11]: AN | *HUMBLE INQUIRY* | INTO THE | QUALIFICATIONS FOR FULL COMMUNION IN THE | *VISIBLE CHURCH OF CHRIST.*; p. [186]: blank; p. [187]: MISREPRESENTATIONS CORRECTED, | AND | TRUTH VINDICATED. | IN | *A REPLY TO* | THE | REV. MR. SOLOMON WILLIAMS's BOOK, | INTITLED, | *THE TRUE STATE OF THE QUESTION CONCERNING THE QUALIFICA- | TIONS NECESSARY TO LAWFUL COMMUNION IN THE CHRISTIAN | SACRAMENTS.* | [short tapered rule] | Prov. xii. 17. He that speaketh Truth, sheweth forth Righteousness. | Chap. xxii. 20, 21. Have I not written to thee excellent Things in Counsels and | Knowledge; That I might make thee know the Certainty of the Words of | Truth, that thou mightest answer the Words of Truth in them that send | unto thee? (verso blank); p. [189]: THE | PREFACE.; p. [192]: blank; p. [193]: MISREPRESENTATIONS CORRECTED, | AND | *TRUTH VINDICATED.*; p. [349]: A | FAREWELL SERMON, | PREACHED AT THE FIRST PRECINCT IN | *NORTHAMPTON,* | AFTER THE PEOPLE'S PUBLIC REJECTION OF THEIR MINISTER, AND RE- | NOUNCING THEIR RELATION TO HIM AS PASTOR OF THE CHURCH THERE | ON JUNE 22, 1750. | OCCASIONED BY DIFFERENCE OF SENTIMENTS, CONCERNING THE | REQUISITE QUALIFICATIONS OF MEMBERS OF THE CHURCH IN | COMPLETE STANDING. | [short tapered rule] | Acts xx. 18. Ye know from the first day that I came into Asia, after what | manner I have been with you, at all seasons. | Ver. 20. And how I kept back nothing that was profitable unto you, but have | shewed you, and have taught you publicly, and from house to house. | Ver. 26, 27. Wherefore I take you to record this day, that I am pure from the | blood of all men: For I have not shunned to declare unto you all the | counsel of God. | Gal. iv. 15. 16. Where is then the blessedness you spake of? For I bear you | record, that if it had been possible, ye would have plucked out your own | eyes, and have given them to me. Am I therefore become your enemy, | because I tell you the truth? (verso blank); p. [351]: PREFACE.; p. [355]: A | FAREWELL SERMON.; p. [383]: THE RESULT OF A COUNCIL OF NINE CHURCHES | MET AT NORTHAMPTON, JUNE 22. 1750; WITH A | PROTEST AGAINST THE SAME, BY A NUMBER OF | THE

SAID COUNCIL.; p. 386: *THE PROTEST.*; p. [388]:blank; p. [389]: FIFTEEN | SERMONS, | ON VARIOUS SUBJECTS. (verso blank); p. [391]: PREFACE. [signed] JONATHAN EDWARDS. | *New-Haven, Dec.* 21, 1779. (verso blank); p. [393]: THE MANNER IN WHICH SALVATION OF THE SOUL IS TO | BE SOUGHT.; p. 413: THE UNREASONABLENESS OF INDETERMINATION IN RELIGION.; p. [427]: UNBELIEVERS CONTEMN THE GLORY AND EXCELLENCY OF | CHRIST.; p. [438]: THE FOLLY OF LOOKING BACK IN FLEEING OUT OF | SODOM.; p. [453]: THE WARNINGS OF SCRIPTURE ARE IN THE BEST MANNER | ADAPTED TO THE AWAKENING AND CONVERSION OF | SINNERS.; p. [465]: HYPOCRITES DEFICIENT IN THE DUTY OF PRAYER.; p. [487]: THE FUTURE PUNISHMENT OF THE WICKED UNAVOIDABLE | AND INTOLERABLE.; p. [506]: THE ETERNITY OF HELL TORMENTS.; p. [528]: THE PEACE WHICH CHRIST GIVES HIS TRUE FOLLOWERS.; p. [543]: THE PERPETUITY AND CHANGE OF THE SABBATH.; p. 580: Edward Baines, Printer, Leeds.

Drew University

VOLUME VIII. | [short thin-thick rule] | *CONTAINING,* | [in 2 cols., col. 1] I. FIVE SERMONS ON DIFFERENT OCCASIONS. | II. MISCELLANEOUS OBSERVATIONS ON IM- | PORTANT THEOLOGICAL SUBJECTS. | [short thin-thick vertical rule, col. 2] III. REMARKS ON IMPORTANT THEOLOGICAL | CONTROVERSIES. | IV. DISTINGUISHING MARKS OF A WORK OF | THE SPIRIT OF GOD. | [thick-thin rule] | LEEDS: | PRINTED BY EDWARD BAINES, | FOR THE EDITORS; CONDER, BUCKLERSBURY; BUTTON, PATERNOSTER-ROW; | WILLIAMS, STATIONERS'-COURT; BAYNES, PATERNOSTER- ROW; OGLE, | GREAT-TURNSTYLE; NUNN, QUEEN STREET; AND JONES, PATER- | NOSTER-ROW, LONDON; AND FOR BAINES, AND HEATON, | LEEDS; WILSON AND SPENCE, YORK; GUTHRIE & TAIT, | EDINBURGH; M. OGLE, GLASGOW; CROOKES, RO- | THERHAM; ABLE, NORTHAMPTON; | AND MR. FARRAND, 185, MARKET-PLACE, PHILADELPHIA. | [short thick-thin rule] | 1811.

21.4 x 13.6 cm.; π^2, A-Z^4, Aa-Zz^4, 3A-3Z^4, 4A-4N^4, 4O^2; [4], 659, [1] p.

Contents: prp. [1]: title (verso blank); prp. [3]: *CONTENTS OF VOLUME VIII.*; p. [1]: FIVE | SERMONS | ON | *DIFFERENT OCCASIONS,* | SEPARATELY PUBLISHED | IN MR. EDWARDS'S LIFE-TIME. (verso blank); p. [3]: A DIVINE AND SUPERNATURAL LIGHT, IMMEDIATELY IMPARTED | TO THE SOUL BY THE SPIRIT OF GOD, SHOWN TO BE | BOTH A SCRIPTURAL AND RATIONAL DOCTRINE.; p. [22]: blank; p. [23]: THE CHURCH'S MARRIAGE TO HER SONS, AND TO HER GOD.; p. [54]: blank; p. [55]: TRUE SAINTS, WHEN ABSENT FROM THE BODY, ARE PRESENT | WITH THE LORD.; p. [89]: GOD'S AWFUL JUDGMENT IN THE BREAKING AND WITHERING | OF THE STRONG RODS OF A COMMUNITY.; p. [106]: blank; p. [107]: TRUE GRACE DISTINGUISHED FROM THE EXPERIENCE OF | DEVILS.; p. [141]: MISCELLANEOUS | OBSERVATIONS | ON | IMPORTANT | *THEOLOGICAL SUBJECTS.* (verso blank); p. [143]: PREFACE. [signed] JOHN ERSKINE. | *Edin. Sept.* 30, 1793.; p. [145]: *ADVERTISEMENT* | TO | THIS EDITION. (verso blank); p. [147]: MISCELLANEOUS OBSERVATIONS | ON | IMPORTANT | *THEOLOGICAL SUBJECTS,* | ORIGINAL AND COLLECTED.; p. [329]: REMARKS | ON | *IMPORTANT THEOLOGICAL* | CONTROVERSIES. | [short tapered rule] | *THE greatest part of these* REMARKS *are original, and* | *may be considered as a Second Volume of* PRESIDENT EDWARDS'S | *Miscellaneous Observations; but, as they relate to Subjects* | *entirely different, make by themselves a Book.* (verso blank); p. [331]: MISCELLANEOUS REMARKS | ON | *IMPORTANT DOCTRINES.*; p. [578]: blank; p. [579]: THE | DISTINGUISHING MARKS | OF A WORK | OF THE | *SPIRIT OF GOD,* | APPLIED TO THAT UNCOMMON OPERATION THAT HAS LATELY APPEARED | ON THE MINDS OF MANY OF THE PEOPLE OF NEW ENGLAND: | WITH A | PARTICULAR CONSIDERATION | OF THE | *EXTRAORDINARY CIRCUMSTANCES WITH WHICH THIS WORK IS* | *ATTENDED.* (verso blank); p. [581]: MR. COOPER'S PREFACE | *TO THE READER.* [signed] W. COOPER. | *Boston, Nov.* 20, 1741.; p. [589]: THE | *MARKS OF A WORK* | OF THE | TRUE SPIRIT.; p. [648]: blank; p. [649]: INDEX.; p. 659: Edward Baines, Printer, Leeds.; p. [660]: blank.

Drew University

506 • THE | *WORKS* | OF | PRESIDENT EDWARDS, | *IN EIGHT VOLUMES.* | [short thick-thin rule] | VOL. I. | [short thin-thick rule] | *CONTAINING,* | [in 2 cols., col. 1] I. HOPKINS'S MEMOIRS OF

MR. ED- | WARDS, IMPROVED AND EN- | LARGED. | II. A CAREFUL AND STRICT ENQUIRY | [short wavy vertical rule, col. 2] INTO THE FREEDOM OF THE | WILL. | III. A DISSERTATION CONCERNING | THE END FOR WHICH GOD | CREATED THE WORLD. | [short thick-thin rule] | *A NEW EDITION.* | [short decorative rule] | **London:** | PRINTED FOR JAMES BLACK AND SON, | *TAVISTOCK-STREET, COVENT-GARDEN.* | [short rule] | 1817.

22.5 x 13.7 cm.; π^4, [A]^4, B-Z^4, Aa-Zz^4, 3A-3U^4, 3X^3; viii, [5]-535, [3] p.

Notes: in some copies, ERRATA IN VOL. I. follows sig. π_4.

Contents: frontispiece: [engraving] | *Freeman Sculp^t.* | *The Revd Jon ^{thn} Edwards, A.M.*; p. [i]: title p. [ii]: HUGHES AND BAYNES, PRINTERS, MAIDEN-LANE, COVENT-GARDEN.; p. [iii]: THE | *EDITORS' PREFACE.* [signed] EDWARD WILLIAMS. | EDWARD PARSONS.; p. [vii]: CONTENTS OF VOLUME I.; p. [5]: MEMOIRS | OF THE | LIFE, EXPERIENCE AND CHARACTER | OF THE LATE REV. | *JONATHAN EDWARDS, A. M.* | PRESIDENT OF THE COLLEGE, | AT PRINCE-TOWN, IN NEW-JERSEY, | BY | THE REV. SAMUEL HOPKINS, D. D. | AND NOW | REVISED, CORRECTED AND ENLARGED, | *BY THE EDITORS.* (verso blank); p. [7]: *PREFACE* | TO | HOPKINS'S LIFE OF EDWARDS. [dated] | *August* 10, 1764.; p. [9]: *MEMOIRS* | OF THE LATE | REV. JONATHAN EDWARDS, A. M.; p. [91]: APPENDIX | TO | THE LIFE | OF | *PRESIDENT EDWARDS*; | CONTAINING, | I. A SKETCH OF MRS. EDWARDS'S LIFE AND CHARACTER. | II. A BRIEF ACCOUNT OF THEIR DAUGHTER, MRS. ESTHER BURR. | III. THE LIFE AND CHARACTER OF THEIR SON, | DR. JONATHAN EDWARDS. (verso blank); p. [93]: *A Short Sketch of Mrs. Edwards's Life and Character.*; p. 98: *A Brief Account of Mrs. Esther Burr, President Edwards's | Daughter.*; p. 103: *A Sketch of the Life and Character of Jonathan Edwards, D. D.*; p. [120]: blank; p. [121]: A | CAREFUL AND STRICT | ENQUIRY | INTO THE | MODERN PREVAILING NOTIONS | OF | *THAT FREEDOM OF WILL,* | WHICH IS SUPPOSED TO BE ESSENTIAL | TO | MORAL AGENCY, | VIRTUE AND VICE, REWARD AND PUNISHMENT, | PRAISE AND BLAME. | [short thick-thin rule] | Rom. ix. 16. IT IS NOT OF HIM THAT WILLETH. (verso blank); p. [123]: *PREFACE.*; p. [127]: A | *CAREFUL AND STRICT ENQUIRY,* | &c.; p. [438]: blank; p. [439]: A | DISSERTATION | CONCERNING | THE END FOR WHICH GOD CREATED | THE | *WORLD.* (verso blank); p. [441]: *PREFACE* | BY | THE FIRST EDITOR; p. [443]: A | DISSERTATION | CONCERNING | GOD'S CHIEF END, | &c.; p. [536]: blank; p. [537]: ERRATA IN VOL. I. (verso blank).

THJ 339 NUC NE0046386 OCLC 4615995

Yale Divinity School

VOL. II. | [short thin-thick rule] | *CONTAINING,* | [in 2 cols., col. 1] I. A DISSERTATION CONCERNING THE | NATURE OF TRUE VIRTUE. | II. THE GREAT CHRISTIAN DOCTRINE | OF ORIGINAL SIN DEFENDED. | III. MAN'S NATURAL BLINDNESS IN | THE THINGS OF RELIGION. | [short wavy vertical rule, col. 2] IV. AN HUMBLE ATTEMPT TO PRO- | MOTE EXPLICIT AGREEMENT | AND VISIBLE UNION OF GOD'S | PEOPLE IN EXTRAORDINARY | PRAYER. | [short thick-thin rule] | *A NEW EDITION.* | [short decorative rule] | **London:** | PRINTED FOR JAMES BLACK AND SON, | *TAVISTOCK-STREET, COVENT-GARDEN.* | [short rule] | 1817.

22.5 x 13.7 cm.; π^2, A-Z^4, Aa-Zz^4, 3A-3U^4, 3X^6; 541, [3] p.

Notes: p. 287 misnumbered 237 (pp. [1]-286, 237, 288-541).

Contents: p. [1]: title; p. [2]: HUGHES AND BAYNES, PRINTERS, MAIDEN-LANE, COVENT-GARDEN.; p. [3]: CONTENTS OF VOLUME II.; p. [5]: A | DISSERTATION | CONCERNING THE | *NATURE OF TRUE VIRTUE.* (verso blank); p. [79]: THE | GREAT CHRISTIAN DOCTRINE | OF | ORIGINAL SIN | DEFENDED; | *EVIDENCES OF ITS TRUTH* | PRODUCED, | AND | ARGUMENTS TO THE CONTRARY ANSWERED: | Containing, in particular, | *A REPLY TO THE OBJECTIONS* | OF | DR. JOHN TAYLOR, | IN HIS BOOK, INTITLED | "THE SCRIPTURE DOCTRINE OF ORIGINAL SIN PROPOSED TO | FREE AND CANDID EXAMINATION, &c." | [short thick-thin rule] | Matt. ix. 12. They that be whole, need not a Physician; but they that are sick. | –Et hæc non tantum ad Peccatores referenda est; quia in omnibus Maledictionibus | primi Hominis, omnes ejus Generationes conveniunt.– *R. Sal. Jarchi.* | Propter Concupiscentiam, Innatam Cordi humano, dicitur, In Iniquitate genitus sum; | atque Sensus est quod a Nativitate implantatum sit Cordi humano *Jetzer harang*, | Figmentum malum. | *Aben-Ezra.* | –Ad Mores Natura recurrit | Damnatos, fixa et mutari nescia.– | –Dociles imitandis | Turpibus & pravis omnes sumus.–*Juv.* (verso blank); p. [81]: *ADVERTISEMENT,* | CONTAINING A | BRIEF ACCOUNT OF HIS BOOK AND ITS AUTHOR, | *BY THE FIRST*

EDITOR.; p. [85]: THE | *AUTHOR'S PREFACE.*; p. [87]: THE | GREAT CHRISTIAN DOCTRINE | OF | *ORIGINAL SIN DEFENDED.*; p. [388]: blank; p. MAN'S | NATURAL BLINDNESS | IN THOSE THINGS OF | *RELIGION.* (verso blank); p. [422]: blank; p. [423]: AN | HUMBLE ATTEMPT | TO PROMOTE | EXPLICIT AGREEMENT AND VISIBLE UNION | *OF GOD'S PEOPLE,* IN | EXTRAORDINARY PRAYER, | FOR THE REVIVAL OF RELIGION AND THE ADVANCEMENT OF CHRIST's | KINGDOM ON EARTH. (verso blank); p. [425]: *ADVERTISEMENT.* (verso blank); p. PREFACE | BY A FORMER ENGLISH EDITOR. [signed] JOHN SUTCLIFF. | OLNEY, May 4th, 1789.; p. [429]: PREFACE | BY THE AMERICAN EDITORS.; p. [431]: AN | *HUMBLE ATTEMPT,* | *&c.*; pp. [542-544]: blank.

Yale Divinity School

VOL. III. | [short thin-thick rule] | *CONTAINING,* | [in 2 cols., col. 1] I. A NARRATIVE OF THE SURPRISING | WORK OF GOD, IN THE CON- | VERSION OF MANY HUNDRED | SOULS, IN AND ABOUT NORTH- | AMPTON. | II. THE LIFE AND DIARY OF THE REV. | DAVID BRAINERD, WITH NOTES | AND REFLECTIONS. | III. MR. BRAINERD'S JOURNAL, IN | TWO PARTS. | IV. FIRST APPENDIX: CONTAINING HIS | GENERAL REMARKS ON THE | DOCTRINES PREACHED, WITH | THEIR EXTRAORDINARY EF- | FECTS, &c.—SECOND APPENDIX: | CONTAINING AN ACCOUNT OF | HIS METHOD OF LEARNING THE | [short wavy vertical rule, col. 2] INDIAN LANGUAGE, AND OF | INSTRUCTING THE INDIANS.— | THIRD | APPENDIX: CONTAIN- | ING HIS BRIEF ACCOUNT OF | THE ENDEAVOURS USED BY | THE MISSIONARIES OF THE SO- | CIETY IN SCOTLAND, FOR PRO- | PAGATING CHRISTIAN KNOW- | LEDGE. | V. MR. BRAINERD'S REMAINS, CON- | TAINING LETTERS AND OTHER | PAPERS. | VI. A SERMON PREACHED AT THE OR- | DINATION OF MR. BRAINERD, | BY E. PEMBERTON, A.M. | VII. REFLECTIONS AND OBSERVA- | TIONS. | [short thick-thin rule] | *A NEW EDITION.* | [short decorative rule] | London: | PRINTED FOR JAMES BLACK AND SON, | *TAVISTOCK-STREET, COVENT-GARDEN.* | [short rule] | 1817.

22.5 x 13.7 cm.; π^2, A-Z^4, Aa-Zz^4, 3A-3Z^4, 4A-4C^4; [i]-iv, [i]-vii, [1], [9]-573, [3] p.

Notes: pp. [i]-iv repeated.

Contents: p. [i]: title; p. [ii]: HUGHES AND BAYNES, PRINTERS, MAIDEN-LANE, COVENT-GARDEN.; p. [iii]: CONTENTS OF VOLUME III.; p. [i]: A | FAITHFUL NARRATIVE | OF THE | *SURPRISING WORK OF GOD,* | IN THE | CONVERSION OF MANY HUNDRED SOULS, | *IN NORTHAMPTON,* | AND NEIGHBOURING TOWNS AND VILLAGES OF NEW HAMPSHIRE, | IN NEW ENGLAND; | IN A | *Letter to the Rev. Dr. Colman, of Boston.* (verso blank); p. [iii]: *PREFACE* | BY THE FIRST EDITORS, Dr. ISAAC WATTS, AND | Dr. JOHN GUYSE. [signed] [in 2 cols., col. 1] LONDON | *Oct.* 12, 1737. | [col. 2] ISAAC WATTS. | JOHN GUYSE.; p. [viii]: blank; p. [9]: A | FAITHFUL | *NARRATIVE,* | &c. &c.; p. [72]: blank; p. [73]: THE | LIFE AND DIARY | OF | *THE REV. DAVID BRAINERD:* | WITH | NOTES AND REFLECTIONS. (verso blank); p. [75]: *PREFACE.* [signed] JONATHAN EDWARDS.; p. [81]: THE | *LIFE AND DIARY,* | &c.; p. [312]: blank; p. [313]: *MR. BRAINERD'S JOURNAL,* | IN | TWO PARTS. (verso blank); p. [315]: *ADVERTISEMENT.* (verso blank); p. [317]: *PREFACE.* [signed] THE CORRESPONDENTS.; p. [319]: THE | RISE AND PROGRESS | OF A REMARKABLE | *WORK OF GRACE,* | &c.; p. [412]: blank; p. [413]: FIRST | APPENDIX | TO | *MR. BRAINERD'S JOURNAL:* | CONTAINING HIS GENERAL REMARKS | ON THE | DOCTRINES PREACHED, | THEIR | EXTRAORDINARY EFFECTS, | &c. (verso blank); p. [415]: *GENERAL REMARKS,* | *&c.*; p. [430]: blank; p. [431]: SECOND | APPENDIX | TO | *MR. BRAINERD'S JOURNAL:* | CONTAINING AN ACCOUNT OF HIS | METHOD OF LEARNING THE INDIAN LANGUAGE, AND OF INSTRUCTING | THE INDIANS; | TOGETHER | *WITH THE DIFFICULTIES* | WHICH LIE IN THE WAY OF THEIR CONVERSION. (verso blank); p. [433]: *METHOD* | OF | LEARNING THE INDIAN LANGUAGE, | &c.; p. [469]: THIRD | APPENDIX | TO | *MR. BRAINERD'S JOURNAL:* | CONTAINING HIS BRIEF ACCOUNT OF | *THE ENDEAVOURS USED BY THE MISSIONARIES OF THE SOCIETY IN* | *SCOTLAND,* | FOR | PROPAGATING CHRISTIAN KNOWLEDGE, | TO INTRODUCE THE GOSPEL AMONG THE INDIANS ON THE BORDERS | OF NEW YORK, &c. (verso blank); p. [471]: THIRD APPENDIX, | &c.; p. [485]: *MR. BRAINERD'S REMAINS,* | CONSISTING OF | LETTERS AND OTHER PAPERS. (verso blank); p. [487]: MR. BRAINERD'S | LETTERS TO HIS FRIENDS.; p. [510]: blank; p. [511]: A | SERMON | PREACHED IN NEW-ARK, *JUNE* 12, 1744 | AT THE ORDINATION | OF | *MR. DAVID BRAINERD,* | A MISSIONARY AMONG THE INDIANS

| UPON THE BORDERS OF THE PROVINCES OF NEW-YORK, NEW-JERSEY, | AND PENNSYLVANIA. | BY | E. PEMBERTON, A. M. | PASTOR OF THE PRESBYTERIAN CHURCH IN THE CITY OF NEW-YORK. (verso blank); p. [514]: AN | *ORDINATION SERMON*, | &c.; p. [530]: blank; p. [531]: SOME | REFLECTIONS AND OBSERVATIONS | ON THE PRECEDING | MEMOIRS, | *&c.* | OF THE | REV. *DAVID BRAINERD*. (verso blank); pp. [574-576]: blank.

Yale Divinity School

VOL. IV. | [short thick-thin rule] | *CONTAINING*, | [in 2 cols., col. 1] I. A TREATISE CONCERNING RELIGIOUS | AFFECTIONS, IN THREE PARTS. | II. AN APPENDIX TO THE TREATISE ON | THE AFFECTIONS, IN TWO LETTERS TO | MR. GILLESPIE. | III. CHRISTIAN CAUTIONS; OR, THE NE- | CESSITY OF SELF EXAMINATION. | IV. A WARNING TO PROFESSORS; OR THE | GREAT GUILT OF THOSE WHO ATTEND | ON THE ORDINANCES OF DIVINE WOR- | SHIP, AND YET ALLOW THEMSELVES IN | ANY KNOWN WICKEDNESS. | V. THE FINAL JUDGEMENT; OR, THE WORLD | JUDGED RIGHTEOUSLY BY JESUS CHRIST. | VI. SINNERS IN ZION TENDERLY WARNED; | OR, THE FEARFULNESS WHICH WILL | HEREAFTER SURPRISE SINNERS IN ZION, | REPRESENTED AND IMPROVED. | VII. THE END OF THE WICKED CONTEM- | PLATED BY THE RIGHTEOUS; OR, THE | TORMENTS OF THE WICKED IN HELL, NO | OCCASION OF GRIEF TO THE SAINTS IN | HEAVEN. | [short thick-thin rule] | *A NEW EDITION*. | [short decorative rule] | London: | PRINTED FOR JAMES BLACK AND SON, | *TAVISTOCK-STREET, COVENT-GARDEN*. | [short rule] | 1817.

22.5 x 13.7 cm.; π^2, A-Z^4, Aa-Zz^4, 3A-3T^4, 3U^1; [4], vi, [7]-522 p.

Contents: prp. [1]: title; prp. [2]: HUGHES AND BAYNES, PRINTERS, MAIDEN-LANE, COVENT-GARDEN.; prp. [3]: CONTENTS OF VOLUME IV.; p. [i]: A | TREATISE | CONCERNING | *RELIGIOUS AFFECTIONS:* | IN | THREE PARTS. | PART I. CONCERNING THE NATURE OF THE AFFECTIONS, | AND THEIR IMPORTANCE IN RELIGION. | PART II. SHEWING WHAT ARE NO CERTAIN SIGNS THAT | RELIGIOUS AFFECTIONS ARE GRACIOUS, OR THAT THEY | ARE NOT. | PART *III*. *SHEWING WHAT ARE DISTINGUISHING SIGNS OF* | TRULY GRACIOUS AND HOLY AFFECTIONS. | [short thick-thin rule] | Lev. ix. ult. and x. 1. 2.–And there came a fire out from before the Lord.–upon the | altar;–which when all the people saw, they shouted and fell on their faces. And | Nadab and Abihu–offered strange fire before the Lord, which he commanded | them not: and there went out a fire from the Lord, and devoured them, and they | died before the Lord. | Cant. ii. 12. 13.– The flowers appear on the earth, the time of the singing of birds | is come, and the voice of the turtle is heard in our land. The fig-tree putteth | forth her green figs, and the vines with the tender grape give a good smell.– | Ver. 15. Take us the foxes, the little foxes which spoil the vines: for our vines | have tender grapes. (verso blank); p. [iii]: *PREFACE*.; p. [7]: A | *TREATISE* | CONCERNING | RELIGIOUS AFFECTIONS.; p. [377]: CHRISTIAN CAUTIONS; | OR, | THE NECESSITY | OF | *SELF-EXAMINATION*. (verso blank); p. [379]: *CHRISTIAN CAUTIONS*, | *&c.*; p. [421]: A | WARNING TO PROFESSORS | OR, | THE GREAT GUILT OF THOSE WHO ATTEND | ON THE | *ORDINANCES OF DIVINE WORSHIP*, | AND YET | ALLOW THEMSELVES | IN | ANY KNOWN WICKEDNESS. (verso blank); p. [423]: A | *WARNING TO PROFESSORS*, | &c.; p. [440]: blank; p. [441]: THE | FINAL JUDGMENT: | OR, | THE WORLD JUDGED RIGHTEOUSLY | BY | *JESUS CHRIST*. (verso blank); p. [443]: *THE FINAL JUDGMENT*, | *&c.*; p. [479]: SINNERS IN ZION | *TENDERLY WARNED:* | OR, | THE FEARFULNESS WHICH WILL HEREAFTER SURPRISE | SINNERS IN ZION, | *REPRESENTED AND IMPROVED*. (verso blank); p. [481]: *SINNERS IN ZION*, | *&c.*; p. [501]: THE | END OF THE WICKED | CONTEMPLATED BY | *THE RIGHTEOUS:* | OR, | THE TORMENTS OF THE WICKED IN HELL, NO OCCASION OF | GRIEF TO THE SAINTS IN HEAVEN. (verso blank); p. [503]: THE | *END OF THE WICKED*, | *&c.*

Yale Divinity School

VOL. V. | [short thick-thin rule] | *CONTAINING*, | [in 2 cols., col. 1] I. A HISTORY OF THE WORK OF RE- | DEMPTION. | II. MEN ARE NATURALLY GOD'S | ENEMIES. | III. THE WISDOM OF GOD DISPLAYED | IN THE WAY OF SALVATION. | IV. CHRISTIAN KNOWLEDGE; OR, THE | [short wavy vertical rule, col. 2] IMPORTANCE AND ADVAN- | TAGE OF A THOROUGH KNOW- | LEDGE OF DIVINE TRUTH. | V. CHRISTIAN CHARITY; OR THE | DUTY OF

CHARITY TO THE POOR, | EXPLAINED AND EN- | FORCED. | VI. SEVEN DISCOURSES | [short thick-thin rule] | *A NEW EDITION.* | [short decorative rule] | London: | PRINTED FOR JAMES BLACK AND SON, | *TAVISTOCK-STREET, COVENT-GARDEN.* | [short rule] | 1817.

22.5 x 13.7 cm.; π⁴, B-Z⁸, 2A-2L⁸, 3M³; 542 p.

Notes: This volume is not, like the preceding four, a reprint of the 1806-1809 Leeds edition, but is a new edition.—THJ; p. [6] is misnumbered 8.

Contents: pp. [1-2]: blank; p. [3]: title; p. [4]: HUGHES AND BAYNES, PRINTERS, MAIDEN-LANE, COVENT-GARDEN.; p. [5]: PREFACE. [signed] JONATHAN EDWARDS. | *Newhaven, Feb.* 25, 1775.; p. [7]: CONTENTS OF VOLUME V.; p. [9]: *ADVERTISEMENT.* [signed] JOHN ERSKINE. | *Edinburgh, April* 29, 1775. (verso blank); p. [11]: A HISTORY | OF THE | *WORK OF REDEMPTION.*; p. [283]: MEN NATURALLY | ARE | *GOD'S ENEMIES.* (verso blank); p. [285]: *MEN* | NATURALLY GOD's ENEMIES.; p. [321]: THE | WISDOM OF GOD, | DISPLAYED | IN THE | *WAY OF SALVATION.* (verso blank); p. [323]: *WISDOM* | DISPLAYED IN SALVATION.; p. [373]: CHRISTIAN KNOWLEDGE: | OR, THE | *IMPORTANCE AND ADVANTAGE* | OF A | THOROUGH KNOWLEDGE | OF | *DIVINE TRUTH.* (verso blank); p. [375]: CHRISTIAN KNOWLEDGE, | *&c. &c.*; p. [395]: CHRISTIAN CHARITY: | OR, | *THE DUTY* | OF | CHARITY TO THE POOR | *EXPLAINED AND ENFORCED.* (verso blank); p. [497]: *CHRISTIAN CHARITY,* | *&c. &c.*; p. [430]: blank; p. [431]: CHRIST EXALTED: | OR, | JESUS CHRIST | GLORIOUSLY EXALTED ABOVE ALL EVIL | IN THE | *WORK OF REDEMPTION.* (verso blank); p. [433]: SERMON I. | CHRIST EXALTED, &c.; p. [448]: SERMON II. | SELF-FLATTERIES; | OR, | THE VAIN SELF-FLATTERIES OF THE SINNER.; p. [458]: SERMON III. | DISHONESTY; | OR, | THE SIN OF THEFT AND OF INJUSTICE; p. [477]: SERMON IV. | TEMPTATION AND DELIVERANCE; | OR, | JOSEPH'S GREAT TEMPTATION AND GLORIOUS DELIVERANCE; p. [499]: SERMON V. | THE PRECIOUSNESS OF TIME, | AND | *THE IMPORTANCE OF REDEEMING IT.*; p. [511]: SERMON VI. | PROCRASTINATION; | OR, | *THE SIN AND FOLLY OF DEPENDING ON* | *FUTURE TIME.*; p. [530]: SERMON VII. | THE CHRISTIAN PILGRIM; | OR, | *THE TRUE CHRISTIAN's LIFE A JOURNEY* | *TOWARDS HEAVEN.*; p. 542: Hughes and Baynes, Printers, Maiden-Lane, Covent-Garden.

Yale Divinity School

VOL. VI. | [short thin-thick rule] | *CONTAINING,* | [in 2 cols., col. 1] I. SOME THOUGHTS CONCERNING | THE PRESENT REVIVAL OF RE- | LIGION IN NEW ENGLAND. | II. FIVE DISCOURSES ON THE SOUL'S | ETERNAL SALVATION. | [short wavy vertical rule, col. 2] | III. TWO SERMONS. | IV. SEVEN SERMONS ON IMPORTANT | SUBJECTS. | [short thick-thin rule] | *A NEW EDITION.* | [short decorative rule] | London: | PRINTED FOR JAMES BLACK AND SON, | *TAVISTOCK-STREET, COVENT-GARDEN.* | [short rule] | 1817.

22.5 x 13.7 cm.; π², B-Z⁸, 2A-2M⁸, 2N³; [4], iv, [5]-550 p.

Contents: prp. [1]: title; prp. [2]: HUGHES AND BAYNES, PRINTERS, MAIDEN-LANE, COVENT-GARDEN.; prp. [3]: CONTENTS OF VOLUME VI. (verso blank); p. [i]: SOME THOUGHTS | CONCERNING THE | PRESENT REVIVAL OF RELIGION | IN | *NEW ENGLAND,* | AND THE | WAY IN WHICH IT OUGHT TO BE ACKNOWLEDGED AND | PROMOTED; | HUMBLY OFFERED TO THE PUBLIC, | *IN A TREATISE* | ON THAT SUBJECT. | [short thick-thin rule] | ISA. xl. 3.–PREPARE YE THE WAY OF THE LORD, MAKE STRAIGHT | IN THE DESERT A HIGH-WAY FOR OUR GOD. | [thin-thick rule] (verso blank); p. [iii]: THE | PREFACE. p. [5]: *THOUGHTS ON THE REVIVAL,* | *&c. &c.*; p. [207]: FIVE DISCOURSES | ON | *IMPORTANT SUBJECTS,* | NEARLY | CONCERNING THE GREAT AFFAIR | OF THE | *SOUL'S ETERNAL SALVATION,* | *VIZ.* | [in 2 cols. col. 1] I. JUSTIFICATION BY FAITH ALONE. | II. PRESSING INTO THE KINGDOM | OF GOD. | III. RUTH'S RESOLUTION. | [short double vertical rule, col. 2] IV. THE JUSTICE OF GOD IN THE | DAMNATION OF SINNERS. | V. THE EXCELLENCY OF JESUS | CHRIST. | *DELIVERED AT NORTHAMPTON,* | Chiefly at the time of the late wonderful pouring out of he Spirit of God there. | [short thick-thin rule] | DEUT. iv. 9.–*Take heed to thyself, and keep thy soul diligently, lest thou* | *forget the things which thine eyes have seen, and lest they depart* | *from thy heart all the days of thy life.* (verso blank); p. [209]: PREFACE.; p. [213]: JUSTIFICATION BY FAITH ALONE.; p. [316]: PRESSING INTO THE KINGDOM OF GOD.; p. [347]: RUTH'S RESOLUTION.; p. [361]:THE JUSTICE OF GOD IN THE DAMNATION OF | SINNERS.; p. [399]: THE EXCELLENCY OF CHRIST.; p. [431]: TWO SERMONS: | I. | GOD GLORIFIED IN THE WORK OF REDEMPTION, BY THE | GREATNESS OF MAN'S DEPENDENCE UPON HIM | IN THE WHOLE OF IT. | II. SINNERS I N THE HANDS OF AN ANGRY GOD. | [short thick-thin rule] | JUDGES VII. 2. | *Let* [*sic*] *Israel vaunt themselves against me,* *saying, Mine own hand | hath saved me.* (verso blank); p. [433]: ADVERTISEMENT | *TO THE READER,* | RESPECTING THE FIRST SERMON. [signed] T. PRINCE. | W. COOPER. | *Boston, August* 17, 1731.; p. [435]: GOD GLORIFIED IN MAN'S DEPENDENCE.; p. [450]: SINNERS IN THE HANDS OF AN ANGRY GOD.; p. [465]: SEVEN SERMONS | ON | *IMPORTANT SUBJECTS.* | *VIZ.* | [in 2 cols., col. 1] THE BEST PORTION. | DIVINE SOVEREIGNTY. | PARDON FOR SINNERS. | THE PRAYER-HEARING GOD. | [short double vertical rule, col. 2] EXCOMMUNICATION. | WRATH TO THE UTTERMOST. | WICKED MEN USEFUL IN THEIR | DESTRUCTION ONLY. (verso blank); p. [467]: GOD THE BEST PORTION OF THE CHRISTIAN.; p. [477]: THE SOLE CONSIDERATION, THAT GOD IS GOD, | SUFFICIENT TO STILL | *ALL OBJECTIONS TO HIS SOVEREIGNTY.*; p. [488]: GREAT GUILT NO OBSTACLE | TO THE | *PARDON OF THE RETURNING SINNER.*; p. [498]: THE MOST HIGH A PRAYER-HEARING GOD.; p. [512]: THE | NATURE AND END OF EXCOMMUNICATION.; p. [525]: WHEN THE WICKED SHALL HAVE FILLED UP THE MEASURE | OF THEIR SIN, WRATH WILL COME UPON THEM TO THE | UTTERMOST.; p. [435]: WICKED MEN USEFUL IN THEIR DESTRUCTION | ONLY.; p. 550: Hughes & Baynes, Printers, Maiden Lane, Covent-Garden.

Wesleyan University

VOL. VII. | [short thin-thick rule] | *CONTAINING,* | [in 2 cols., col. 1] I. INQUIRY CONCERNING QUALIFI- | CATIONS FOR COMMUNION. | II. MISREPRESENTATIONS CORRECT- | ED AND TRUTH VINDICATED, | IN REPLY TO THE REVEREND | SOLOMON WILLIAMS. | [short wavy vertical rule, col. 2] III. A FAREWELL SERMON PREACHED | AT NORTHAMPTON. | IV. RESULT OF A COUNCIL OF NINE | CHURCHES, MET AT NORTH- | AMPTON. | V. FIFTEEN SERMONS ON VARIOUS | OCCASIONS. | [short thick-thin rule] | *A NEW EDITION.* | [short decorative rule] | London: | PRINTED FOR JAMES BLACK AND SON, | *TAVISTOCK-STREET, COVENT-GARDEN.* | [short rule] | 1817.

22.5 x 13.7 cm.; π^2, B-Z^8, 2A-2L^8, 2M^3; [4], 533, [1] p.

Contents: prp. [1]: title; prp. [2]: HUGHES AND BAYNES, PRINTERS, MAIDEN-LANE, COVENT-GARDEN.; prp. [3]: CONTENTS OF VOLUME VII.; p. [1]: AN | HUMBLE INQUIRY | INTO THE | *RULES OF THE WORD OF GOD,* | CONCERNING | THE QUALIFICATIONS | REQUISITE TO A | COMPLETE STANDING & FULL COMMUNION | IN THE | *VISIBLE CHRISTIAN CHURCH.* | [short tapered rule] | Behold now I have opened my mouth:–My words shall be of the uprightness | of my heart.—Job. xxxiii. 2, 3.; p. [2]: Confitebatur [*Lutherus*] dolorem suum, quod ab ipsis reflorescentis Evan- | gelii Primordiis, quosvis absque Discrimine ad Cœnam Dominicum | admisisset, quodque Disciplinam, Fratrum Disciplinæ similem, apud | suos non constituisset.—Quia objiciebatur, Fratres non habere | Ecclesiam apertam;—Responsum fuit, Sancta dare non Sanctis | prohibuisse Christum:— Errorem [in *Papatu*] corrigi non posse | *aliter quam ut certa Probatione, nec illa subitanea, Cordium Arcana* | *revelunter*, Novitiique diu et caute tum informentur, tum explo- | rentur. | *Ratio Discipl. Fratr.* Bohem.; p. [3]: THE | AUTHOR'S PREFACE. [signed] J. E.; p. [7]: A *PREFACE* | BY HIS AMERICAN FRIENDS. [signed] THOMAS PRINCE. | JOHN WEBB. | THOMAS FOXCROFT. | M. BYLES. | *Boston, August* 11, 1746.; p. [9]: *ADVERTISEMENT* | TO THE | EDINBURGH EDITION. [dated] EDINBURGH, May 15, 1790. (verso blank); p. [11]: AN | HUMBLE INQUIRY | INTO THE | QUALIFICATIONS FOR FULL COMMUNION IN THE | *VISIBLE CHURCH OF CHRIST.*; p. [172]: blank; p. [173]: MISREPRESENTATIONS CORRECTED, | AND | TRUTH VINDICATED. | IN | *A REPLY* | TO THE | REV. MR. SOLOMON WILLIAMS's BOOK, | INTITLED, | *THE TRUE STATE OF THE QUESTION CONCERNING THE* | *QUALIFICATIONS NECESSARY TO LAWFUL COMMU-* | *NION IN THE CHRISTIAN SACRAMENTS.* | [short tapered rule] | Prov. xii. 17. He that speaketh Truth, sheweth forth Righteousness. | Chap. xxii. 20, 21. Have I not written to thee excellent Things in Counsels | and Knowledge; That I might make thee know the Certainty of the | Words of Truth, that thou mightest answer the Words of Truth in them | that send unto thee? (verso blank); p. [175]: THE | PREFACE.; p. [178]: blank; p. [179]: MISREPRESENTATIONS CORRECTED, | AND | *TRUTH VINDICATED.*; p. [323]: A | FAREWELL SERMON, | PREACHED AT THE FIRST PRECINCT IN | *NORTHAMPTON,* | After the People's public Rejection of their Minister, and renouncing | their Relation to him as Pastor of the Church there, | *On June* 22, 1750. | OCCASIONED BY DIFFERENCE OF SENTIMENTS, CONCERNING | THE REQUISITE QUALIFICATIONS OF MEMBERS OF THE | CHURCH IN COMPLETE STANDING. | [short tapered rule] | Acts xx. 18. Ye know from the first day that I came into Asia, after what | manner I have been with you, at all seasons. | Ver. 20. And how I kept back nothing that was profitable unto you, but have | shewed you, and have taught you publicly, and from house to house. | Ver. 26, 27. Wherefore I take you to record this day, that I am pure from the | blood of all men. For I have not shunned to declare unto you all the | counsel of God. | Gal. iv. 15, 16. Where is then the blessedness you spake of? For I bear you | record, that if it had been possible, ye would have plucked out your own | eyes, and have given them to me. Am I therefore become your enemy, | because I tell you the truth? (verso blank); p. [325]: PREFACE.; p. [329]: A | FAREWELL SERMON.; p. [355]: *THE RESULT* | OF A COUNCIL OF NINE CHURCHES, MET AT NORTHAMPTON, | JUNE 22. 1750; WITH A PROTEST AGAINST THE SAME, | BY A NUMBER OF THE SAID COUNCIL.; p. 358: *THE PROTEST*.; p. [360]: blank; p. [361]: FIFTEEN | SERMONS, | ON | *VARIOUS SUBJECTS*. (verso blank); p. [363]: PREFACE. [signed] JONATHAN EDWARDS. | *New-Haven, Dec*. 21, 1779. (verso blank); p. [365]: THE MANNER IN WHICH SALVATION OF THE SOUL IS | TO BE SOUGHT.; p. [383]: THE UNREASONABLENESS OF INDETERMINATION IN | RELIGION.; p. [395]: UNBELIEVERS CONTEMN THE GLORY AND EXCELLENCY | OF CHRIST.; p. [405]: THE FOLLY OF LOOKING BACK IN FLEEING OUT OF SODOM.; p. [418]: THE WARNINGS OF SCRIPTURE ARE IN THE BEST MANNER | ADAPTED TO THE | AWAKENING AND CONVERSION | OF SINNERS.; p. [429]: HYPOCRITES DEFICIENT IN THE DUTY OF PRAYER.; p. [449]: THE FUTURE PUNISHMENT OF THE WICKED UNAVOIDABLE | AND INTOLERABLE.; p. [466]: THE ETERNITY OF HELL TORMENTS.; p. [486]: THE PEACE WHICH CHRIST GIVES HIS TRUE FOLLOWERS.; p. [499]: THE PERPETUITY AND CHANGE OF THE SABBATH.; p. 533: Hughes And Baynes, Printers, Maiden-Lane, Covent-Garden.; p. [534]: blank.

Wesleyan University

VOL. VIII. | [short thin-thick rule] | *CONTAINING*, | [in 2 cols., col. 1] I. FIVE SERMONS ON DIFFERENT OC- | CASIONS. | II. MISCELLANEOUS OBSERVATIONS | ON IMPORTANT THEOLOGICAL | SUBJECTS. | [short wavy vertical rule, col. 2] III. REMARKS ON IMPORTANT THEO- | LOGICAL CONTROVERSIES. | IV. DISTINGUISHING MARKS OF A | WORK OF THE SPIRIT OF | GOD. | [short thick-thin rule] | *A NEW EDITION*. | [short decorative rule] | London: | PRINTED FOR JAMES BLACK AND SON, | *TAVISTOCK-STREET, COVENT-GARDEN*. | [short rule] | 1817.

22.5 x 13.7 cm.; π^2, B-Z^8, 2A-2P^8, 2Q^7; [4], 605, [1] p.

Contents: prp. [1]: title; prp. [2]: HUGHES AND BAYNES, PRINTERS, MAIDEN-LANE, COVENT-GARDEN.; prp. [3]: CONTENTS OF VOLUME VIII.; p. [1]: FIVE | SERMONS | ON | *DIFFERENT OCCASIONS*, | SEPARATELY PUBLISHED | IN MR. EDWARDS'S LIFE-TIME. (verso blank); p. [3]: A DIVINE AND SUPERNATURAL LIGHT, IMMEDIATELY IM- | PARTED TO THE SOUL BY THE SPIRIT OF GOD, SHEWN TO | BE BOTH A SCRIPTURAL AND RATIONAL DOCTRINE.; p. [21]: THE CHURCH'S MARRIAGE TO HER SONS, AND TO HER GOD.; p. [50]: TRUE SAINTS, WHEN ABSENT FROM THE BODY, ARE PRESENT | WITH THE LORD.; p. [81]: GOD's AWFUL JUDGMENT IN THE BREAKING AND WITHERING | OF THE STRONG RODS OF A COMMUNITY; p. [96]: TRUE GRACE DISTINGUISHED FROM THE EXPERIENCE OF | DEVILS.; p. [127]: MISCELLANEOUS | OBSERVATIONS | ON | IMPORTANT | *THEOLOGICAL SUBJECTS*. (verso blank); p. [129]: PREFACE. [signed] JOHN ERSKINE. | *Edin. Sept*. 30, 1793.; p. [131]: *ADVERTISEMENT* | TO | THIS EDITION. (verso blank); p. [133]: MISCELLANEOUS OBSERVATIONS | ON IMPORTANT | *THEOLOGICAL SUBJECTS*, | ORIGINAL AND COLLECTED.; p. [301]: REMARKS | ON | *IMPORTANT THEOLOGICAL* | CONTROVERSIES. | [short thick-thin rule] | THE *greatest part of these* REMARKS *are original, and* | *may be considered as a Second Volume of* PRESIDENT | EDWARDS'S *Miscellaneous Observations; but, as they relate to* | *Subjects entirely different, make by themselves a Book*. (verso blank); p. [303]: MISCELLANEOUS REMARKS | ON | *IMPORTANT DOCTRINES*.; p. [530]: blank; p. [531]: THE | DISTINGUISHING MARKS | OF A WORK | OF THE | *SPIRIT OF GOD*, | APPLIED TO THAT UNCOMMON OPERATION THAT HAS LATELY APPEARED | ON THE MINDS OF MANY OF THE PEOPLE OF NEW ENGLAND: | *WITH A* | PARTICULAR CONSIDERATION | OF THE | *EXTRAORDINARY CIRCUMSTANCES WITH WHICH* | *THIS WORK IS ATTENDED*. (verso blank); p. [533]: MR. COOPER'S PREFACE | *TO THE READER*. [signed] W. COOPER. | *Boston, Nov*. 20, 1741.; p. [541]: THE | *MARKS OF A WORK* | OF THE | TRUE SPIRIT.; p. [595]: INDEX.; p. 605: Hughes and Baynes, Printers, 29, Maiden-Lane, Covent-Garden.; p. [606]: blank.

Wesleyan University

507 • THE | WORKS | OF | PRESIDENT EDWARDS. | IN TEN VOLUMES. | VOLUME IX. | [SUPPLEMENTARY TO THE LONDON EIGHT VOLUME EDITION.] | CONTAINING | I. NOTES ON THE BIBLE. | II. TYPES OF THE MESSIAH. | EDINBURGH: | ROBERT OGLE AND OLIVER

AND BOYD. | GLASGOW: M. OGLE AND SON, AND WILLIAM COLLINS. | LONDON: HAMILTON, ADAMS & CO. | MDCCCXLVII.

24 x 14.7 cm.; π^3, $[A]^8$, B-T^8, X-Z^8, 2A-$2I^8$; [2], iii, [1], 494, [2] p.

Notes: probably derived from *The Works of President Edwards* (New York: S. Converse, 1830), v. 9.

Contents: prp. [1]: title; prp. [2]: New York Printed: | Reprinted By Andrew Murray, Edinburgh; p. [i]: INDEX OF TEXTS | IN THE | NOTES ON THE BIBLE.; p. [iv]: blank; p. [1]: NOTES ON THE BIBLE.; p. [398]: blank; p. [399]: TYPES OF THE MESSIAH. (verso blank); p. [401]: TYPES OF THE MESSIAH, &c.; pp. [495-496]: blank.

THJ 340 NUC NE0046388

National Library of Scotland

VOLUME X. | [SUPPLEMENTARY TO THE LONDON EIGHT VOLUME EDITION.] | CONTAINING | I. MISCELLANEOUS OBSERVATIONS. | II. SEVENTEEN OCCASIONAL SERMONS. | EDINBURGH: | ROBERT OGLE AND OLIVER AND BOYD. | GLASGOW: M. OGLE AND SON, AND WILLIAM COLLINS. | LONDON: HAMILTON, ADAMS & CO. | MDCCCXLVII.

24 x 14.7 cm.; π^2, A^8, *B-*Z^8, *2A-*$2K^8$, *$2L^4$; [4], 536 p.

Notes: probably derived from *The Works of President Edwards* (New York: S. Converse, 1830), v. 8; the sermons are identified by number, citation, and text, at times by date; except for the last three sermons, the titles are those found in the table of contents but not in the text.

Contents: prp. [1]: title; prp. [2]: New York Printed: | Reprinted By Andrew Murray, Edinburgh.; prp. [3]: CONTENTS OF THIS VOLUME. (verso blank); p. [1]: MISCELLANEOUS OBSERVATIONS.; p. [108]: blank; p. [109]: SEVENTEEN OCCASIONAL SERMONS. (verso blank); p. [111]: SERMON I. [Natural men in a dreadful condition.]; p. 146: SERMON II. [God makes men sensible of their misery before he reveals his mercy and love.]; p. 170: SERMON III. [Hope and comfort usually follow genuine humiliation and repentance.]; p. 201: SERMON IV. [God's sovereignty in the salvation of men.]; p. 216: SERMON V. [The character of Paul an example to Christians.]; p. 248: SERMON VI. [Christ's agony.]; p. 281: SERMON VII. [The portion of the wicked.]; p. 309: SERMON VIII. [The portion of the righteous.]; p. 357: SERMON IX. [The pure in heart blessed.]; p. 379: SERMON X. | THANKSGIVING SERMON, Nov. 7, 1734. [Praise, one of the chief employments of heaven.]; p. 393: SERMON XI. [Wicked men inconsistent with themselves.]; p. 424: SERMON XII. [Safety, fulness, and sweet refreshment, to be found in Christ.]; p. 445: SERMON XIII. [Christians a chosen generation, a royal priesthood, a holy nation, a peculiar people.]; p. 480: SERMON XIV. [Jesus Christ the same yesterday, to-day, and for ever.]; p. 496: SERMON XV. | THE TRUE EXCELLENCY OF A GOSPEL MINISTER.; p. 512: SERMON XVI. | CHRIST THE EXAMPLE OF MINISTERS.; p. 526: SERMON XVII. | THE SORROWS OF THE BEREAVED | SPREAD BEFORE JESUS.; p. 536: ANDREW MURRAY, PRINTER, MILNE SQUARE, EDINBURGH.

National Library of Scotland

507A • Burt Franklin: Research and Source Work Series No. 271 | [publisher's device] | Burt Franklin | New York, N.Y.

Notes: facsimile reprint of the eight-volume 1817 edition and the two-volume 1847 addition; title page (verso): Published by | BURT FRANKLIN | 235 East 44th St. | New York, N. Y. 10017 | ORIGINALLY PUBLISHED | LONDON 1817 | Reprinted 1968 | [4 lines].

OCLC 2673

Gordon-Conwell Theological Seminary

508 • THE | POSTHUMOUS WORKS | OF | PRESIDENT EDWARDS. | IN TWO VOLUMES. | VOLUME I. | CONTAINING | I. NOTES ON THE BIBLE. | II. TYPES OF THE MESSIAH. | [short rule] | EDINBURGH: | OGLE & MURRAY, 49 SOUTH BRIDGE. | LONDON: HAMILTON, ADAMS, & CO. | [short rule] | MDCCCLXXV.

24 x 14.7 cm.; π^3, $[A]^8$, B-T^8, X-Z^8, 2A-$2I^8$; [2], iii, [1], 494, [2] p.

Contents: prp. [1]: title (verso blank); p. [i]: INDEX OF TEXTS | IN THE | NOTES ON THE BIBLE.; p. [iv]: blank; p. [1]: NOTES ON THE BIBLE.; p. [398]: blank; p. [399]: TYPES OF THE MESSIAH. (verso blank); p. [401]:

TYPES OF THE MESSIAH, &c.; pp. [495-496]: blank.
THJ 341 NUC NE0046747 OCLC 12853298
Harvard Divinity School

VOL. II. | CONTAINING | I. MISCELLANEOUS OBSERVATIONS. | II. SEVENTEEN OCCASIONAL SERMONS. | [short rule] | EDINBURGH: | OGLE & MURRAY, 49 SOUTH BRIDGE. | LONDON: HAMILTON, ADAMS, & CO. | [short rule] | MDCCCLXXV.

24 x 14.7 cm.; π^2, A-Z^8, 2A-$2K^8$, $2L^4$; [4], 536 p.

Notes: except for the last three sermons, the titles are those found in the table of contents, not in the text.

Contents: prp. [1]: title (verso blank); prp. [3]: CONTENTS OF THIS VOLUME. (verso blank); p. [1]: MISCELLANEOUS OBSERVATIONS.; p. [108]: blank; p. [109]: SEVENTEEN OCCASIONAL SERMONS. (verso blank); p. [111]: SERMON I. [Natural men in a dreadful condition.]; p. 146: SERMON II. [God makes men sensible of their misery before he reveals his mercy and | love.]; p. 170: SERMON III. [Hope and comfort usually follow genuine humiliation and repentance.]; p. 201: SERMON IV. [God's sovereignty in the salvation of men.]; p. 216: SERMON V. [The character of Paul an example to Christians.]; p. 248: SERMON VI. [Christ's agony.]; p. 281: SERMON VII. [The portion of the wicked.]; p. 309: SERMON VIII. [The portion of the righteous.]; p. 357: SERMON IX. [The pure in heart blessed.]; p. 379: SERMON X. | THANKSGIVING SERMON, Nov. 7, 1734. [Praise, one of the chief employments of heaven.]; p. 393: SERMON XI. [Wicked men inconsistent with themselves.]; p. 424: SERMON XII. [Safety, fulness, and sweet refreshment, to be found in Christ.]; p. 445: SERMON XIII. [Christians a chosen generation, a royal priesthood, a holy nation, a | peculiar people.]; p. 480: SERMON XIV. [Jesus Christ the same yesterday, to-day, and for ever.]; p. 496: SERMON XV. | THE TRUE EXCELLENCY OF A GOSPEL MINISTER.; p. 512: SERMON XVI. | CHRIST THE EXAMPLE OF MINISTERS.; p. 526: SERMON XVII. | THE SORROWS OF THE BEREAVED | SPREAD | BEFORE JESUS.; p. 536: ANDREW MURRAY, PRINTER, MILNE SQUARE, EDINBURGH.

Harvard Divinity School

509 • THE | WORKS OF | PRESIDENT EDWARDS, | IN EIGHT VOLUMES. | [short decorative rule] | VOLUME I. | [short decorative rule] | *CONTAINING* | [in 2 cols., col. 1] I. MEMOIRS OF THE LATE | REVEREND JONATHAN | EDWARDS. | II. FAREWELL SERMON. | III. RESULT OF A COUNCIL | AT NORTHAMPTON. | [short double vertical rule, col. 2] IV. HUMBLE INQUIRY CON- | CERNING THE QUALIFI- | CATIONS FOR MEMBER- | SHIP IN THE VISIBLE | CHRISTIAN CHURCH. | V. REPLY TO WILLIAMS. | [short thick-thin rule] | *FIRST AMERICAN EDITION.* | [short thick-thin rule] | PUBLISHED AT WORCESTER, | BY ISAIAH THOMAS, JUN. | [short decorative rule] | *ISAAC STURTEVANT, PRINTER.* | [short line of stops] | 1808.

20.6 x 12.2 cm.; π^1, $[A]^4$, B-W-Z^4, 2A-2W-$2Z^4$, 3A-$3Q^4$, $3R^2$; viii, [2], [9]-515, [1] p.

Contents: prp. [1]: THE | WORKS | OF THE REVEREND | JONATHAN EDWARDS, | MINISTER OF THE GOSPEL | IN | *NORTHAMPTON, MASSACHUSETTS,* | AND AFTERWARDS | PRESIDENT | OF THE | COLLEGE IN NEWJERSEY. | IN EIGHT VOLUMES. (verso blank); frontispiece: [oval engraving] | [along the lower half of the engraving] *Drawn and Engraved by Abner Reed, from an original Portrait, in the possession of J. W. Edwards, Esq. Hartfd.* | Rev. JONATHAN EDWARDS, | *President of Nassau-Hall College,* | *NEW JERSEY.*; p. [iii]: title; p. [iv]: [affidavit] [signed] WM. S. SHAW | *Clerk of the District of Massachusetts.*; p. [v]: GENERAL CONTENTS. (verso blank); p. [vii]: PREFACE. | TO THE | FIRST AMERICAN EDITION. [signed] SAMUEL AUSTIN. | WORCESTER, (Mass.) *November* 1, 1808; p. [ix]: MEMOIRS | OF THE LATE REVEREND | JONATHAN EDWARDS, A. M. (verso blank); p. [9]: MEMOIRS | OF THE LATE REVEREND | JONATHAN EDWARDS, A. M.; p. [100]: blank; p. [101]: A | FAREWELL SERMON. | *PREACHED AT THE FIRST PRECINCT IN* | *NORTHAMPTON,* | AFTER THE PEOPLE'S PUBLIC REJECTION OF THEIR MIN- | ISTER, AND RENOUNCING THEIR RELATION TO HIM | AS PASTOR OF THE CHURCH THERE | JUNE 22, 1750. (verso blank); p. [103]: PREFACE. [signed] JONATHAN EDWARDS.; p. [109]: A FAREWELL SERMON.; p. 142: THE RESULT OF A COUNCIL OF NINE CHURCHES, MET AT | NORTHAMPTON, JUNE 22, 1750.; p. [145]: AN | HUMBLE INQUIRY | INTO THE | *RULES OF THE WORD OF GOD,* | CONCERNING THE | QUALIFICATIONS | REQUISITE TO A | *COMPLETE STANDING AND FULL COMMUNION* | IN THE | VISIBLE CHRISTIAN CHURCH. (verso blank); p. [147]: PREFACE. [signed] JONATHAN EDWARDS.; p. [153]: HUMBLE INQUIRY.; p. [336]: blank;

p. [337]: MISREPRESENTATIONS CORRECTED, | AND | TRUTH VINDICATED. | IN A REPLY TO THE REV. SOLOMON WILLIAMS'S BOOK | INTITLED "THE TRUE STATE OF THE QUESTION | CONCERNING THE QUALIFICATIONS NECESSARY | TO LAWFUL COMMUNION IN THE CHRIST- | IAN SACRAMENTS." (verso blank); p. [341]: PREFACE.; p. [343]: MISREPRESENTATIONS CORRECTED, | AND | TRUTH VINDICATED.; p. [516]: blank.

THJ 342 EAI 2:14925 NUC NE0046385 OCLC 932876

Massachusetts Historical Society

VOLUME II. | [short decorative rule] | *CONTAINING* | [in 2 cols., col. 1] I. WORK OF REDEMPTION. | II. DISSERTATION ON THE | NATURE OF VIRTUE, | [short double vertical rule, col. 2] III. OBSERVATIONS CON- | CERNING THE MYSTE- | RIES OF SCRIPTURE. | [short thick-thin rule] | *FIRST AMERICAN EDITION.* | [short thick-thin rule] | PUBLISHED AT WORCESTER, | BY ISAIAH THOMAS, JUN. | [short decorative rule] | *ISAAC STURTEVANT, PRINTER* | [short line of stops] | 1808.

20.6 x 12.2 cm.; [A]^4, B-W-Z^4, 2A-2W-2Z^4, 3A-3N^4, 3O^2; viii, [9]-491, [1] p.

Contents: p. [i]: title (verso blank); p. [iii]: ADVERTISEMENT. [dated] WORCESTER, April, 1808.; p. [iv]: ADVERTISEMENT | *TO THE EDINBURGH EDITION.* [signed] JOHN ERSKINE. | EDINBURGH, *April* 29, 1775.; p. [v]: PREFACE. [signed] JONATHAN EDWARDS. | *Newhaven, Feb.* 25, 1775.; p. [vii]: CONTENTS.; p. [9]: WORK | OF | REDEMPTION.; p. [393]: A | DISSERTATION | ON THE | NATURE OF VIRTUE. (verso blank); p. [395]: THE | NATURE OF VIRTUE.; p. [472]: blank; p. [473]: OBSERVATIONS | CONCERNING THE | MYSTERIES OF SCRIPTURE. (verso blank); p. [475]: MYSTERIES OF SCRIPTURE.; p. [492]: blank.

Massachusetts Historical Society

VOLUME III. | [short decorative rule] | *CONTAINING* | [in 2 cols., col. 1] I. A NARRATIVE OF MA- | NY SURPRISING CONVER- | SIONS. | II. THOUGHTS ON THE RE- | VIVAL OF RELIGION IN | NEWENGLAND. | [short double vertical rule, col. 2] III. AN HUMBLE ATTEMPT | TO PROMOTE EXPLICIT | AGREEMENT IN PRAYER. | IV. LIFE OF REV. DAVID BRAIN- | ERD AND REFLECTIONS | UPON IT. | [short thick-thin rule] | *FIRST AMERICAN EDITION.* | [short thick-thin rule] | PUBLISHED AT WORCESTER, | BY ISAIAH THOMAS, JUN. | [short decorative rule] | *ISAAC STURTEVANT, PRINTER* | [short line of stops] | 1808.

20.6 x 12.2 cm.; [A]^2, B-W-Z^4, 2A-2W-2Z^4, 3A-3U^4, 3W^2; iv, [2], [9]-548 [i.e., 546] p.

Notes: lacks pp. [vii-viii].

Contents: p. [i]: title (verso blank); p. [iii]: CONTENTS.; p. [v]: NARRATIVE | OF | SURPRISING CONVERSIONS. (verso blank); p. [9]: NARRATIVE | OF | SURPRISING CONVERSIONS.; p. [83]: THOUGHTS | ON THE | REVIVAL OF RELIGION | IN | NEWENGLAND, 1740. (verso blank); p. [85]: ADVERTISEMENT.; p. [87]: THE AUTHOR's PREFACE.; p. [89]: REVIVAL OF RELIGION | IN | NEWENGLAND.; p. [352]: blank; p. [353]: AN | HUMBLE ATTEMPT | TO PROMOTE | EXPLICIT AGREEMENT | AND | *VISIBLE UNION* | OF | GOD's PEOPLE | IN | EXTRAORDINARY PRAYER | FOR THE REVIVAL OF RELIGION AND THE ADVANCEMENT OF | CHRIST'S KINGDOM ON EARTH, PURSUANT TO SCRIPTURE | PROMISES AND PROPHECIES CONCERNING THE | LAST TIME. (verso blank); p. [355]: UNION IN PRAYER.; p. [495]: AN | ACCOUNT | OF THE | LIFE | OF THE LATE REVEREND | DAVID BRAINERD, | MINISTER OF THE GOSPEL; MISSIONARY TO THE INDIANS | FROM THE HONOURABLE SOCIETY, IN SCOTLAND, FOR | THE PROPAGATION OF CHRISTIAN KNOWLEDGE; AND PASTOR OF A CHURCH OF CHRIST- | IAN INDIANS IN NEWJERSEY. | *Who died at* Northampton *in Newengland, October* 9*th*, | 1747, *in the* 30*th year of his age.* | CHIEFLY TAKEN FROM HIS OWN DIARY, AND OTHER PRIVATE | WRITINGS, WRITTEN FOR HIS OWN USE. (verso blank); p. [497]: *ADVERTISEMENT.* (verso blank); p. [499]: CLOSING SCENE OF THE LIFE | OF THE | REV. DAVID BRAINERD.

Massachusetts Historical Society

VOLUME IV. | [short decorative rule] | *CONTAINING* | [in 2 cols., col. 1] I. A TREATISE CONCERNING | RELIGIOUS AFFECTIONS. | II. OBSERVATIONS CONCERN- | ING FAITH. | [short double vertical rule, col. 2] III. REASONS AGAINST DR. | WATTS'S NOTION OF | THE PREEXISTENCE OF | CHRIST'S HUMAN SOUL. | [short thick-thin rule] | *FIRST AMERICAN EDITION.* | [short thick-thin rule] | PUBLISHED AT WORCESTER, | BY ISAIAH THOMAS, JUN. | [short decorative rule] | *ISAAC STURTEVANT, PRINTER* | [short line of stops] | 1808.

20.6 x 12.2 cm.; π^1, $[A]^4$, $B\text{-}W\text{-}Z^4$, $2A\text{-}2W\text{-}2Z^4$, $3A\text{-}3O^4$; viii, [2], [9]-496 p.

Contents: p. [i]: title (verso blank); p. [iii]: INTRODUCTION. | TO THE TREATISE ON THE AFFECTIONS.; p. [7]: TREATISE | CONCERNING | RELIGIOUS AFFECTIONS. (verso blank); p. [9]: RELIGIOUS AFFECTIONS.; p. [417]: OBSERVATIONS | CONCERNING FAITH. (verso blank); p. [419]: OBSERVATIONS | CONCERNING FAITH.; p. [491]: *Reasons against* DR. WATTS'S *Notion of the Pre- | existence of Christ's Human Soul.*

Massachusetts Historical Society

VOLUME V. | [short decorative rule] | *CONTAINING* | [in 2 cols., col. 1] I. INQUIRY INTO THE MOD- | ERN PREVAILING NOTIONS | OF FREEDOM OF WILL. | II. MISCELLANEOUS OBSER- | VATIONS CONCERNING THE | [short double vertical rule, col. 2] DIVINE DECREES IN GEN- | ERAL AND ELECTION IN | PARTICULAR. | III. CONCERNING EFFICA- | CIOUS GRACE. | [short thick-thin rule] | *FIRST AMERICAN EDITION.* | [short thick-thin rule] | PUBLISHED AT WORCESTER, | BY ISAIAH THOMAS, JUN. | [short decorative rule] | *ISAAC STURTEVANT, PRINTER* | [short line of stops] | 1808.

20.6 x 12.2 cm.; $[A]^4$, $B\text{-}W\text{-}Z^4$, $2A\text{-}2W\text{-}2Z^4$, $3A\text{-}3P^4$; viii, [9]-504 p.

Contents: p. [i]: title (verso blank); p. [iii]: A | CAREFUL AND STRICT | INQUIRY | INTO THE | MODERN PREVAILING NOTIONS, | OF THAT | FREEDOM OF WILL, | *WHICH IS SUPPOSED TO BE ESSENTIAL* | TO | MORAL AGENCY, VIRTUE AND VICE, REWARD | AND PUNISHMENT, PRAISE AND BLAME. (verso blank); p. [vii]: PREFACE.; p. [9]: FREEDOM OF THE WILL.; p. [335]: REMARKS | ON THE ESSAYS ON THE PRINCIPLES OF MORALITY AND NAT- | URAL RELIGION, IN A LETTER TO A MINISTER OF THE | CHURCH OF SCOTLAND.; p. [349]: MISCELLANEOUS | OBSERVATIONS | CONCERNING THE | DIVINE DECREES IN GENERAL | AND | ELECTION IN PARTICULAR. (verso blank); p. [351]: MISCELLANEOUS | OBSERVATIONS.; p. 413: CONCERNING | EFFICACIOUS GRACE.

Massachusetts Historical Society

VOLUME VI. | [short decorative rule] | *CONTAINING* | [in 2 cols., col. 1] I. DISSERTATION CON- | CERNING THE END FOR | WHICH GOD CREATED | THE WORLD. | II. DOCTRINE OF ORIGIN- | AL SIN DEFENDED. | [short double vertical rule, col. 2] III. OBSERVATIONS UPON | PARTICULAR PASSAGES | OF SCRIPTURE. | IV. THEOLOGICAL QUES- | TIONS. | [short thick-thin rule] | *FIRST AMERICAN EDITION.* | [short thick-thin rule] | PUBLISHED AT WORCESTER, | BY ISAIAH THOMAS, JUN. | [short decorative rule] | *ISAAC STURTEVANT, PRINTER* | [short line of stops] | 1809.

20.6 x 12.2 cm.; $[A]^4$, $B\text{-}W\text{-}Z^4$, $2A\text{-}2W\text{-}2Z^4$, $3A\text{-}3P^4$, $3Q^2$; v, [3], [9]-508 p.

Contents: p. [i]: title (verso blank); p. [iii]: PREFACE. [signed] EDITOR. | *July* 12, 1765.; p. [vi]: [advertisement]; p. [vii]: DISSERTATION | CONCERNING THE END | FOR WHICH | GOD CREATED THE WORLD. (verso blank); p. [9]: DISSERTATION | CONCERNING THE END FOR WHICH GOD | CREATED THE WORLD.; p. [125]: THE | *GREAT CHRISTIAN DOCTRINE* | OF | ORIGINAL SIN | DEFENDED; | EVIDENCES OF ITS TRUTH PRODUCED, | AND | ARGUMENTS TO THE CONTRARY ANSWERED. | CONTAINING IN PARTICULAR, | A REPLY TO THE OBJECTIONS AND ARGUINGS OF DR. JOHN | TAYLOR, IN HIS BOOK, INTITLED, "THE SCRIPTURE | DOCTRINE OF ORIGINAL SIN PROPOSED TO FREE | AND CANDID EXAMINATION," &C. | [short decorative rule] | Matth. ix. 12. "They that be whole, need not a Physician; but | they that are sick." | Et hæc non tantum ad Peccatores referenda est; quia in omnibus Maledic- | tionibus primi Hominis, omnes ejus Generationes conveniunt.... | R. SAL. JARCHI. | Propter Concupiscentiam, innatam Cordi humano, dicitur, In Iniquitate geni- | tus sum; atque Sensus est, quod a Nativitate implantatum sit Cordi hu- | mano *Jetzer harang* Figmentum malum.... ABEN EZRA. | ....Ad Mores Natura recurrit | Damnatos, fixa et mutari nescia.... | ....Dociles imitandis | Turpibus et pravis omnes sumus.... JUV. (verso blank); p. [127]: AUTHOR'S PREFACE. [dated] STOCKBRIDGE, MAY 26, 1757.; p. [129]: DOCTRINE | OF | ORIGINAL SIN | DEFENDED.; p. [491]:

OBSERVATIONS | UPON | PARTICULAR PASSAGES | OF | SCRIPTURE. (verso blank); p. [493]: OBSERVATIONS | UPON PARTICULAR PASSAGES OF | SCRIPTURE.; p. [505]: THEOLOGICAL QUESTIONS.

Massachusetts Historical Society

VOLUME VII. | [short decorative rule] | *CONTAINING* | [in 2 cols., col. 1] FIFTEEN SERMONS ON VARI- | OUS IMPORTANT | [short double vertical rule, col. 2] SUBJECTS, DOCTRINAL AND | PRACTICAL. | [short thick-thin rule] | *FIRST AMERICAN EDITION.* | [short thick-thin rule] | PUBLISHED AT WORCESTER, | BY ISAIAH THOMAS, JUN. | [short decorative rule] | *ISAAC STURTEVANT, PRINTER* | [short line of stops] | 1809.

20.6 x 12.2 cm.; [A]^4, B-W-Z^4, 2A-2W-2Z^4, 3A-3P^4; v, [3], [9]-502, [2] p.

Contents: p. [i]: title (verso blank); p. [iii]: PREFACE OF THE EDITOR [dated] WORCESTER, MARCH, 1809. (verso blank); p. [vii]: SERMONS | ON | VARIOUS | IMPORTANT SUBJECTS. (verso blank); p. [9]: SERMONS | ON VARIOUS | IMPORTANT SUBJECTS. [short decorative rule] | SERMON I. | *Justification by Faith alone*; p. [131]: SERMON II. | *Joseph's great Temptation and gracious Deliv- | erance.*; p. [159]: SERMON III. | *Men naturally God's Enemies*; p. [208]: SERMON IV. | *The true Christian's Life, a Journey towards | Heaven.*; p. [228]: SERMON V. | *True Grace distinguished from the Experience of | Devils.*; p. [267]: SERMON VI. | *The Excellency of Christ.*; p. [308]: SERMON VII. | *Ruth's Revelation.*; p. [326]: SERMON VIII. | *The Justice of God in the Damnation of Sinners.*; p. [375]: SERMON XI. | *The future Punishment of the Wicked unavoidable | and intolerable.*; p. [396]: SERMON X. | *The Eternity of Hell Torments.*; p. [422]: SERMON XI. | *The Unreasonableness of Indetermination in Re- | ligion.*; p. [438]: SERMON XII. | *Unbelievers contemn the Glory and Excellency of | Christ.*; p. [451]: SERMON XIII. | *The Folly of Looking Back in fleeing out of Sodom.*; p. [467]: SERMON XIV. | *God Glorified in Man's Dependance.*; p. [486]: SERMON XV. | *Sinners in the Hands of an Angry God.*; pp. [503-504]: blank.

Massachusetts Historical Society

VOLUME VIII. | [short decorative rule] | *CONTAINING* | [in 2 cols., col. 1] A CONTINUATION OF | SERMONS ON VA- | [short double vertical rule, col. 2] RIOUS AND IMPORT- | ANT SUBJECTS. | [short thick-thin rule] | *FIRST AMERICAN EDITION.* | [short thick-thin rule] | PUBLISHED AT WORCESTER, | BY ISAIAH THOMAS, JUN. | [short decorative rule] | *ISAAC STURTEVANT, PRINTER* | [short line of stops] | 1809.

20.6 x 12.2 cm.; [A]^4, B-W-Z^4, 2A-2W-2Y^4, 2Y-2Z^4, 3A-3Q^4, 3R^2; 514, [10] p.

Notes: sig. 2Y repeated.

Contents: p. [1]: title (verso blank); p. [3]: SERMONS | ON VARIOUS | IMPORTANT SUBJECTS. [short decorative rule] | SERMON XVI. | *The Importance and Advantage of a thorough | Knowledge of Divine Truth.*; p. [29]: SERMON XVII. | *God the best portion of the Christian.*; p. [44]: SERMON XVIII. | *The Most High a Prayer hearing God.*; p. [66]: SERMON XIX. | *Great Care necessary, lest we live in some way | of Sin.*; p. [115]: SERMON XX. | *The vain Self Flatteries of the Sinner.*; p. [129]: SERMON XXI. | *Wicked Men useful in their Destruction only.*; p. [153]: SERMON XXII. | *The Fearfulness, which will hereafter surprise Sin- | ners in Zion, represented and improved.*; p. [178]: SERMON XXIII. | *The Sin and Folly of depending on Future Time.*; p. [204]: SERMON XXIV. | *Hypocrites Deficient in the Duty of Prayer.*; p. [230]: SERMON XXV. | *The Peace which Christ gives his true Followers.*; p. [248]: SERMON XXVI. | *The Perpetuity and Change of the Sabbath.*; p. [290]: SERMON XXVII. | *A Divine and Supernatural Light, immediately | imparted to the Soul by the Spirit of God, | shown to be both a Scriptural and Rational | Doctrine.*; p. [313]: SERMON XXVIII. | *The Church's Marriage to her Sons, and to her | God.*; p. [351]: SERMON XXIX. | *The True Excellency of a Gospel Minister.*; p. [375]: SERMON XXX. | *Christ the Example of Ministers.*; p. [396]: SERMON XXXI. | *The Sorrows of the Bereaved spread before Jesus.*; p. [412]: SERMON XXXII. | *True Saints, when absent from the Body, are pres- | ent with the Lord.*; p. [441]: SERMON XXXIII. | *God's awful Judgment in the breaking and wither- | ing of the Strong Rods of Community.*; p. [461]: SERMON XXXIV. | *The Nature and End of Excommunication.*; p. [481]: SERMON XXXV. | *The Sin of Theft and Injustice.*; p. [507]: GENERAL INDEX; p. [515]: SUBSCRIBERS TO THIS WORK.

Massachusetts Historical Society

510 • THE | WORKS | OF | PRESIDENT EDWARDS: | WITH A | MEMOIR OF HIS LIFE. | IN TEN

VOLUMES. | VOL. I. | [short double rule] | NEW-YORK. | PUBLISHED BY S. CONVERSE. | 1829.

22.2 x 13.8 cm.; [1][4], 2-95[4], 96[3]; 766 p.

Notes: title pages of vols. 2-7 and 10 omit mention of Sereno E. Dwight's *Memoir*.

Contents: frontispiece: [engraving] | Engraved by S. S. Jocelyn & S. B. Munson. | REV. JONA. EDWARDS.; p. [1]: title; p. [2]: [affidavit] [signed] CHARLES A. INGERSOLL, *Clerk of the District of Connecticut*. | [short rule] | NEW-HAVEN, | PRINTED BY BALDWIN AND TREADWAY. | [short rule]; p. [3]: ADVERTISEMENT.; p. [5]: CONTENTS.; p. [9]: LIFE | OF | PRESIDENT EDWARDS.; p. [626]: FAREWELL SERMON.; p. [652]: blank; p. [653]: APPENDIX. | [A.-G.: notes]; p. 664: H. | "THE MIND."; p. 702: I. | NOTES ON NATURAL SCIENCE.; p. 762: K. | FAMILY AND DESCENDENTS OF PRESIDENT EDWARDS.; p. 765: L. | CATALOGUE OF PRESIDENT EDWARDS' WORKS, HERETOFORE PUBLISHED.

THJ 343 NUC NE0046389 OCLC 5637524

Harvard Divinity School

VOL. II. | CONTAINING, | I. INQUIRY INTO THE FREEDOM OF THE WILL. | II. THE GREAT CHRISTIAN DOCTRINE OF ORIGINAL SIN DEFENDED. | [short thick-thin rule] | NEW-YORK: | PUBLISHED BY S. CONVERSE. | 1829.

22.2 x 13.8 cm.; [1][2], 2-73[4]; iv, [3], 12-583 [i.e., 579], [1] p.

Notes: lacks pp. 5-8.

Contents: p. [i] title (verso blank); p. [iii]: CONTENTS OF VOLUME II.; p. [9]: A | CAREFUL AND STRICT | ENQUIRY | INTO THE | MODERN PREVAILING NOTIONS | OF | THAT FREEDOM OF WILL, | WHICH IS SUPPOSED TO BE ESSENTIAL | TO | MORAL AGENCY, | VIRTUE AND VICE, REWARD AND PUNISHMENT, | PRAISE AND BLAME. | [short rule] | ROM. IX. 16–IT IS NOT OF HIM THAT WILLETH. (verso blank); p. [11]: PREFACE.; p. [15]: A | CAREFUL AND STRICT ENQUIRY, | *&c.*; p. 290: APPENDIX. | [short rule] | SECT. XV. | *Containing Remarks of "Essays on the Principles of Morali- | ty and Natural Religion," in a letter to a Minister of the | Church of Scotland.*; p. [301]: THE | GREAT CHRISTIAN DOCTRINE | OF | ORIGINAL SIN | DEFENDED; | EVIDENCES OF ITS TRUTH | PRODUCED, | AND | ARGUMENTS TO THE CONTRARY ANSWERED. | CONTAINING, IN PARTICULAR, | *A REPLY TO THE OBJECTIONS* | OF | DR. JOHN TAYLOR, | IN HIS BOOK, ENTITLED | "THE SCRIPTURE-DOCTRINE OF ORIGINAL SIN PROPOSED TO | FREE AND CANDID EXAMINATION, &c." | [short thick-thin rule] | Matt. ix. 12. They that be whole, need not a Physician; but they that are sick. | –Et hæc non tantum ad Peccatores referenda est; quia in omnibus Maledictionibus primi Hominis, | omnes ejus Generationes conveniunt.– *R. Sal. Jarchi.* | Propter Concupiscentiam, innatam Cordi humano, dicitur, In Iniquitate genitus sum; atque Sensus | est quod a Nativitate implantatum sit Cordi humano *Jetzer harang*, Figmentum malum. | *Aben-Ezra.* | –Ad Mores Natura recurrit | Damnatos, fixa et mutari nescia.– | –Dociles imitandis | Turpibus et pravis omnes sumus.–*Juv.* (verso blank); p. *[303]: ADVERTISEMENT, | CONTAINING A | BRIEF ACCOUNT OF THIS BOOK AND ITS* AUTHOR | BY THE FIRST EDITOR.; p. [307]: THE AUTHOR'S PREFACE. [dated] *Stockbridge, May* 26, 1757.; p. [309]: THE | GREAT CHRISTIAN DOCTRINE | OF | ORIGINAL SIN DEFENDED.; p. [584]: blank.

Harvard Divinity School

VOL. III. | CONTAINING, | I. DISSERTATION ON THE END FOR WHICH GOD CREATED THE WORLD. | II. DISSERTATION ON THE NATURE OF TRUE VIRTUE. | III. HISTORY OF THE WORK OF REDEMPTION. | IV. AN ATTEMPT TO PROMOTE EXPLICIT AGREEMENT AND VISIBLE UNION | OF GOD'S PEOPLE IN EXTRAORDINARY PRAYER. | V. DISTINGUISHING MARKS OF A WORK OF THE SPIRIT OF GOD. | [short thick-thin rule] | NEW-YORK, | PUBLISHED BY S. CONVERSE. | 1829.

22.2 x 13.8 cm.; π^2, [1]-76[4], 77[2]; iv, iv, [1], 6-612 p.

Notes: pp. i-iv repeated.

Contents: p. [i]:title (verso blank); p. [iii]: CONTENTS OF VOLUME III.; p. [i]: A | DISSERTATION | CONCERNING | THE END FOR WHICH GOD CREATED | THE | WORLD. (verso blank); p. [iii]: PREFACE BY THE FIRST EDITOR.; p. [5]: A | DISSERTATION | CONCERNING | GOD'S CHIEF END, &c.; p. [90]: blank; p. [91]: A | DISSERTATION | CONCERNING THE | NATURE OF TRUE VIRTUE. (verso blank); p. [93]: THE | NATURE OF TRUE VIRTUE.; p. [158]: blank; p. [159]: A HISTORY | OF | THE WORK OF REDEMPTION, | CONTAINING THE

| OUTLINES OF A BODY OF DIVINITY, | INCLUDING | A VIEW OF CHURCH HISTORY, | IN A METHOD ENTIRELY NEW. (verso blank); p. [161]: PREFACE. [signed] JONATHAN EDWARDS | *Newhaven, Feb.* 25, 1775.; p. [163]: ADVERTISEMENT. [signed] JOHN ERSKINE. | *Edinburgh, April* 29, 1775. (verso blank); p. [161]: A HISTORY | OF THE | WORK OF REDEMPTION.; p. [437]: AN | HUMBLE ATTEMPT | TO PROMOTE | EXPLICIT AGREEMENT AND VISIBLE UNION | OF | GOD'S PEOPLE, | IN | EXTRAORDINARY PRAYER, | FOR THE | REVIVAL OF RELIGION AND THE ADVANCEMENT OF CHRIST'S | KINGDOM ON EARTH. (verso blank); p. [439]: ADVERTISEMENT. (verso blank); p. [441]: PREFACE BY A FORMER ENGLISH EDITOR. [signed] JOHN SUTCLIFF | OLNEY, May 4th, 1789.; p. [443]: PREFACE BY THE AMERICAN EDITORS. [dated] *Boston, New-England, January* 12, 1784.; p. [445]: AN | HUMBLE ATTEMPT, &c.; p. [548]: blank; p. [549]: THE | DISTINGUISHING MARKS | OF A WORK OF | THE SPIRIT OF GOD, | APPLIED TO THAT | UNCOMMON OPERATION THAT HAS LATELY APPEARED ON THE | MINDS OF MANY OF THE PEOPLE OF NEW-ENGLAND: | WITH A | PARTICULAR CONSIDERATION | OF THE | *EXTRAORDINARY CIRCUMSTANCES WITH WHICH | THIS WORK IS ATTENDED.*; p. [550]: MR. COOPER'S PREFACE | TO THE READER. [signed] W. COOPER. | *Boston, Nov.* 20, 1741.; p. [559]: THE | MARKS OF A WORK OF THE TRUE SPIRIT.

Harvard Divinity School

VOL. IV. | CONTAINING, | I. NARRATIVE OF SURPRISING CONVERSIONS. | II. THOUGHTS ON THE REVIVAL IN 1740. | III. QUALIFICATIONS FOR COMMUNION. | IV. REPLY TO WILLIAMS. | [short thick-thin rule] | NEW YORK: | PUBLISHED BY S. CONVERSE. | 1830.

22.1 x 13.8 cm.; $[1]^2$, $2\text{-}75^4$, 76^1; iv, [3], xii-xvi, [1], 18-602 [i.e., 598] p.

Notes: lacks pp. 5-8.

Contents: p. [i]: title (verso blank); p. [iii]: CONTENTS OF VOLUME IV.; p. [v]: A FAITHFUL | NARRATIVE | OF THE | SURPRISING WORK OF GOD, | IN THE | CONVERSION OF MANY HUNDRED SOULS, | *IN NORTHAMPTON*, | AND THE NEIGHBOURING TOWNS AND VILLAGES OF NEW- | HAMPSHIRE, IN NEW-ENGLAND; | IN A | *Letter to the Rev. Dr. Colman of Boston.* (verso blank); p. [ix]: PREFACE BY THE FIRST EDITORS, DR. ISAAC WATTS, AND DR. JOHN GUYSE. [signed] LONDON, | *Oct.* 12, 1737. | ISAAC WATTS. | JOHN GUYSE.; p. [17]: A | FAITHFUL NARRATIVE.; p. [75]: SOME THOUGHTS | CONCERNING THE | PRESENT REVIVAL OF RELIGION | IN | NEW ENGLAND, | AND THE | WAY IN WHICH IT OUGHT TO BE ACKNOWLEDGED AND | PROMOTED; | HUMBLY OFFERED TO THE PUBLIC, IN A | TREATISE ON THE SUBJECT. | [short thin-thick rule] | ISA. xl. 3.–PREPARE YE THE WAY OF THE LORD, MAKE STRAIGHT | IN THE DESERT A HIGH-WAY FOR OUR GOD. (verso blank); p. [77]: THE PREFACE.; p. [79]: THOUGHTS ON THE REVIVAL, | &c. &c.; p. [281]: AN | HUMBLE INQUIRY | INTO THE | RULES OF THE WORD OF GOD, | CONCERNING | THE QUALIFICATIONS | REQUISITE TO A | COMPLETE STANDING AND FULL COMMUNION | IN THE | *VISIBLE CHRISTIAN CHURCH.* | [short thick-thin rule] | Behold now I have opened my mouth:–My words shall be of the uprightness | of my heart.—Job xxxiii. 2, 3.; p. [282]: Confitebatur [*Lutherus*] dolorem suum, quod ab ipsis reflorescentis | Evangelii Primordiis, quosvis absque Discrimine ad Cœnam Do- | minicum admisisset, quodque Disciplinam, Fratrum Disciplinæ | similem, apud suos non constituisset.—Quia objiciebatur, Fra- | tres non habere Ecclesiam apertam;—Responsum fuit, Sancta | dare non Sanctis prohibuisse Christum:— Errorem [in *Papatu*] | corrigi non posse *aliter quam ut certa Probatione, nec illa subi- | tanea, Cordium Arcana revelunter*, Novitiique diu & caute tum | informentur, tum explorentur. | *Ratio Discipl. Fratr.* Bohem.; p. [283]: THE | AUTHOR'S PREFACE.; p. [287]: A PREFACE | BY HIS AMERICAN FRIENDS. [signed] THOMAS PRINCE. | JOHN WEBB. | THOMAS FOXCROFT. | M. BYLES. | *Boston, August* 11, 1746.; p. [289]: ADVERTISEMENT | TO THE | EDINBURGH EDITION. [dated] EDINBURGH, May 15, 1790. (verso blank); p. [291]: AN | HUMBLE INQUIRY | INTO THE | QUALIFICATIONS FOR FULL COMMUNION IN THE | *VISIBLE CHURCH OF CHRIST*.; p. [452]: blank; p. [453]: MISREPRESENTATIONS CORRECTED, | AND | TRUTH VINDICATED, | IN | A REPLY | TO THE | REV. MR. SOLOMON WILLIAMS'S BOOK, | ENTITLED, | THE TRUE STATE OF THE QUESTION CONCERNING THE QUALIFI- | CATIONS NECESSARY TO LAWFUL COMMUNION | IN THE CHRISTIAN SACRAMENTS. | [short tapered rule] | Prov. xii. 17. He that speaketh Truth, sheweth forth Righteousness. | Chap. xxii. 20, 21. Have I not written to thee excellent things in Counsels | and Knowledge; That I might make thee know the Certainty of the Words of | Truth, that thou mightest answer the Words of Truth in them that send unto | thee? (verso blank); p. [455]: THE PREFACE.; p. [458]: blank; p. [459]: MISREPRESENTATIONS CORRECTED | AND | TRUTH VINDICATED.; p. [596]: blank; p. [597]: AN APPENDIX. | BEING A LETTER TO THE PEOPLE OF THE FIRST CHURCH AND | CONGREGATION

IN NORTHAMPTON.

Harvard Divinity School

VOL. V. | [short rule] | CONTAINING, | I. A TREATISE CONCERNING RELIGIOUS AFFECTIONS, | IN THREE PARTS. | II. FIVE DISCOURSES ON IMPORTANT SUBJECTS. | I. JUSTIFICATION BY FAITH ALONE. | II. PRESSING INTO THE KINGDOM OF GOD. | III. RUTH'S RESOLUTION. | IV. JUSTICE OF GOD IN THE DAMNATION OF SINNERS. | V. THE EXCELLENCY OF JESUS CHRIST. | [short thick-thin rule] | New=York: | PRINTED FOR S. CONVERSE. | [short rule] | 1829.

22.2 x 13.8 cm.; π^2, 1-71^4; vi [i.e., iv], [2], 566 p.

Notes: p. iv misnumbered vi.

Contents: p. [i]: title (verso blank); p. [iii]: CONTENTS OF VOLUME V.; p. [v]: A | TREATISE | CONCERNING | RELIGIOUS AFFECTIONS: | IN | IN [*sic*] THREE PARTS. | [in 2 cols., col. 1] PART I. | *Concerning the Nature of the | Affections, and their Impor- | tance in Religion.* | PART II. | *Showing why there are no cer- | tain Signs that Religious Af- |* [short vertical rule, col. 2] *fections are gracious, or that | they are not.* | PART III. | *Showing what are distinguish- | ing Signs of truly gracious | and holy Affections.* | [short rule] | Lev. ix. ult. and x. 1, 2.—And there came a fire out from before the Lord,—upon the | altar;—which when all the people saw, they shouted and fell on their faces. And | Nadab and Abihu—offered strange fire before the Lord, which he commanded | them not: and there went out a fire from the Lord, and devoured them, and they | died before the Lord. | Cant. ii. 12, 13.—The flowers appear on the earth, the time of the singing of birds | is come, and the voice of the turtle is heard in our land. The fig-tree putteth | forth her green figs, and the vines with the tender grape give a good smell. | Ver. 15. Take us the foxes, the little foxes which spoil the vines: for our vines | have tender grapes. (verso blank); p. [1]: PREFACE.; p. [6] blank; p. [7]: A | TREATISE | CONCERNING | RELIGIOUS AFFECTIONS.; p. [322]: APPENDIX | TO THE TREATISE OF THE AFFECTIONS, IN TWO LETTERS.; p. [345]: FIVE DISCOURSES | ON | IMPORTANT SUBJECTS, | NEARLY CONCERNING THE GREAT AFFAIR | OF THE | SOUL'S ETERNAL SALVATION, | VIZ. | [in 2 cols., col. 1] I. *Justification by Faith alone.* | II. *Pressing into the Kingdom of | God.* | III. *Ruth's Resolution.* | [short vertical rule, col. 2] IV. *The Justice of God in the | Damnation of Sinners.* | V. *The Excellency of Jesus | Christ.* | DELIVERED AT NORTHAMPTON, | *Chiefly at the time of the late wonderful pouring out of the Spirit of God there.* | [short rule] | DEUT. IV. 9. | Take heed to thyself, and keep they soul diligently, lest thou forget the things which | thine eyes have seen, and lest they depart from thy heart all the days of thy | life. (verso blank); p. 347]: PREFACE.; p. [351]: JUSTIFICATION BY FAITH ALONE.; p. [453]: PRESSING INTO THE KINGDOM OF GOD.; p. [484]: RUTH'S RESOLUTION.; p. [498]: THE JUSTICE OF GOD IN THE DAMNATION | OF SINNERS.; p. [535]: THE EXCELLENCY OF CHRIST.

Harvard Divinity School

VOL. VI. | CONTAINING, | I. TWENTY SERMONS. II. PRACTICAL SERMONS. | [short thick-thin rule] | NEW YORK: | PUBLISHED BY S. CONVERSE. | 1829.

22.2 x 13.8 cm.; π^2, 1-72^4, 73^2; iv, 580 [i.e., 582] p.

Notes: pp. 466-467 repeated; title page and the table of contents differ: title page has *Twenty Sermons* and *Practical Sermons*; table of contents adds *Remarks on Important Theological Controversies*, which appears in v. 7.

Contents: p. [i]: title; p. [ii]: Vanderpool & Cole, Printers.; p. [iii]: CONTENTS.; p. [1]: TWENTY SERMONS | ON | VARIOUS SUBJECTS. (verso blank); p. [3]: PREFACE. [signed] JONATHAN EDWARDS. | *New-Haven, December* 21, 1779. (verso blank); p. [5]: THE MANNER IN WHICH THE SALVATION OF THE SOUL | IS TO BE SOUGHT.; p. [23]: THE UNREASONABLENESS OF INDETERMINATION IN | RELIGION.; p. [35]: UNBELIEVERS CONTEMN THE GLORY AND EXCELLENCY | OF CHRIST.; p. [45]: THE FOLLY OF LOOKING BACK IN FLEEING OUT OF | SODOM.; p. [58]: THE WARNINGS OF SCRIPTURE ARE IN THE BEST MAN- | NER ADAPTED TO THE AWAKENING AND | CONVERSION OF SINNERS.; p. [69]: HYPOCRITES DEFICIENT IN THE DUTY OF PRAYER.; p. [89]: THE FUTURE PUNISHMENT OF THE WICKED UNAVOID- | ABLE AND INTOLERABLE.; p. [106]: THE ETERNITY OF HELL TORMENTS.; p. [125]: THE PEACE WHICH CHRIST GIVES HIS TRUE FOLLOWERS.; p. [138]: THE PERPETUITY AND CHANGE OF THE SABBATH.; p. [171]: A DIVINE AND SUPERNATURAL LIGHT, IMMEDIATELY IM- | PARTED TO THE SOUL BY THE SPIRIT OF GOD, SHOWN | TO BE BOTH A SCRIPTURAL AND RATIONAL DOCTRINE.; p. [189]: THE CHURCH'S MARRIAGE TO HER SONS

AND TO HER GOD.; p. [217]: GOD'S AWFUL JUDGMENT IN THE BREAKING AND WITH- | ERING OF THE STRONG RODS OF A COMMUNITY.; p. [232]: TRUE GRACE DISTINGUISHED FROM THE EXPERIENCE | OF DEVILS.; p. [262]: blank; p. [263]: PRACTICAL SERMONS, | FIRST PUBLISHED IN EDINBURGH. | BY THE REV. DR. ERSKINE, IN 1778. (verso blank); p. [265]: CHRISTIAN KNOWLEDGE, &c. &c.; p. [284]: GOD THE BEST PORTION OF THE CHRISTIAN.; p. [293]: THE SOLE CONSIDERATION, THAT GOD IS GOD, SUF- | FICIENT TO STILL ALL OBJECTIONS | TO HIS SOVEREIGNTY.; p. [304]: GREAT GUILT NO OBSTACLE TO THE PARDON | OF THE RETURNING SINNER.; p. [314]: THE MOST HIGH A PRAYER-HEARING GOD.; p. [328]: CHRISTIAN CAUTIONS, OR THE NECESSITY OF | SELF-EXAMINATION.; p. [365]: A WARNING TO PROFESSORS OF RELIGION: OR THE GREAT GUILT OF THOSE WHO ATTEND ON THE ORDI- | NANCES OF DIVINE WORSHIP, AND YET ALLOW THEM- | SELVES IN ANY KNOWN WICKEDNESS.; p. [381]: THE FINAL JUDGMENT, OR THE WORLD JUDGED | RIGHTEOUSLY &c. BY JESUS CHRIST.; p. [414]: SELF-FLATTERIES;—OR, THE VAIN SELF-FLATTERIES | OF THE SINNER.; p. [424]: WICKED MEN USEFUL IN THEIR DESTRUCTION ONLY.; p. [440]: SINNERS IN ZION TENDERLY WARNED; OR THE FEAR- | FULNESS WHICH SHALL HEREAFTER SURPRISE SIN- | NERS IN ZION, REPRESENTED AND IMPROVED.; p. [458]: WHEN THE WICKED SHALL HAVE FILLED UP THE | MEASURE OF THEIR SIN, WRATH WILL COME | UPON THEM TO THE UTTERMOST.; p. [468]: THE END OF THE WICKED CONTEMPLATED BY THE RIGHT- | EOUS; OR THE TORMENTS OF THE WICKED IN HELL | NO OCCASION OF GRIEF TO THE SAINTS IN HEAVEN.; p. [486]: THE PRECIOUSNESS OF TIME, AND THE IMPORTANCE OF | REDEEMING IT.; p. [498]: PROCRASTINATION; OR THE SIN AND FOLLY OF DEPEND- | ING ON FUTURE TIME.; p. [517]: DISHONESTY; OR THE SIN OF THEFT AND OF INJUSTICE.; p. [536]: CHRISTIAN CHARITY, &c. &c.; p. [569]: THE NATURE AND END OF EXCOMMUNICATION.

Harvard Divinity School

VOL. VII. | CONTAINING, | [in 2 cols., col. 1] I.—EIGHT SERMONS. | II.—MISCELLANEOUS THE- | OLOGICAL OBSERVATIONS. | [short vertical rule, col. 2] III.—MISCELLANEOUS RE- | MARKS ON IMPORTANT | THEOLOGICAL SUBJECTS. | [short thick-thin rule] | NEW YORK: | PUBLISHED BY S. CONVERSE. | 1829.

22.2 x 13.8 cm.; π^2, 1-71^4, 72^2; iv, 572 p.

Notes: title page and table of contents differ: title page has *Eight Sermons*, *Miscellaneous Theological Observations*, and *Miscellaneous Remarks on Important Theological Subjects*, all of which appear in the volume; table of contents has the first and third items and adds eleven titles of *Practical Sermons*, which appear in v. 6.

Contents: p. [i]: title; p. [ii]: Vanderpool & Cole, Printers.; p. [iii]: CONTENTS.; p. [1]: EIGHT SERMONS | ON | VARIOUS OCCASIONS. (verso blank); p. [3]: MAN'S NATURAL BLINDNESS | IN THE | THINGS OF RELIGION.; p. [31]: MEN | NATURALLY GOD'S ENEMIES.; p. [66]: WISDOM DISPLAYED IN SALVATION.; p. [115]: JOSEPH'S GREAT TEMPTATION, | AND | GRACIOUS DELIVERANCE.; p. [135]: THE CHRISTIAN PILGRIM, | OR | THE CHRISTIANS [*sic*] LIFE A JOURNEY TOWARDS HEAVEN.; p. [147]: ADVERTISEMENT | TO | THE READER RESPECTING THE FIRST SERMON. [signed] T. PRINCE. | W. COOPER. | *Boston, August* 17, 1731.; p. [149]: GOD GLORIFIED IN MAN'S DEPENDENCE.; p. [163]: SINNERS IN THE HANDS OF AN ANGRY GOD.; p. [178]: THE | WATCHMAN'S DUTY AND ACCOUNT.; p. [197]: MISCELLANEOUS | OBSERVATIONS | ON IMPORTANT | THEOLOGICAL SUBJECTS.; p. [198]: ADVERTISEMENT TO THIS EDITION.; p. [199]: PREFACE. [signed] JOHN ERSKINE. | *Edinburgh, Sept.* 30, 1793.; p. [201]: MISCELLANEOUS OBSERVATIONS | ON IMPORTANT | THEOLOGICAL SUBJECTS. | ORIGINAL AND COLLECTED.; p. [360]: MISCELLANEOUS REMARKS | ON | IMPORTANT DOCTRINES.

Harvard Divinity School

VOL. VIII. | CONTAINING, | I. SEVENTEEN OCCASIONAL SERMONS. | II. MISCELLANEOUS OBSERVATIONS. | [short thick-thin rule] | NEW YORK: | PUBLISHED BY S. CONVERSE. | 1830.

22.2 x 13.8 cm.; π^2, 2-76^4; iii, [1], 5-603, [1] p.

Notes: except for the last three sermons, the titles are noted in the table of contents, not in the text.

Contents: p. [i]: title; p. [ii]: [affidavit] [signed] CHAS. A. INGERSOLL, Clerk of the District of Connecticut.; p. [iii]: CONTENTS OF VOL. VIII. (verso blank); p. [5]: SERMON I. | [Natural men in a dreadful condition.]; p. [44]: SERMON II. | [God makes men sensible of their misery before he reveals | his mercy and love.]; p. [70]: SERMON III. |

[Hope and comfort usually follow genuine humiliation and re- | pentance.]; p. [105]: SERMON IV. | [God's sovereignty in the salvation of men.]; p. [123]: SERMON V. | [The character of Paul an example to Christians.]; p. [159]: SERMON VI. | [Christ's agony.]; p. [195]: SERMON VII. | [The portion of the wicked.]; p. [227]: SERMON VIII. | [The portion of the righteous.]; p. [280]: SERMON IX. | [The pure in heart blessed.]; p. [305]: SERMON X. | [Praise, one of the chief employments of heaven.]; p. [320]: SERMON XI. | [Wicked men inconsistent with themselves.]; p. [355]: SERMON XII. | [Safety, fullness and sweet refreshment to be found in | Christ.]; p. [379]: SERMON XIII. | [Christians a chosen generation, a royal priesthood, a holy | nation, a peculiar people.]; p. [418]: SERMON XIV. | [Jesus Christ the same yesterday, to-day, and for ever.]; p. [437]: SERMON XV. | THE TRUE EXCELLENCY OF A GOSPEL MINISTER.; p. [455]: SERMON XVI. | CHRIST THE EXAMPLE OF MINISTERS.; p. [471]: SERMON XVII. | THE SORROWS OF THE BEREAVED SPREAD BEFORE | JESUS.; p. [483]: MISCELLANEOUS OBSERVATIONS. (verso blank); p. [485]: MISCELLANEOUS OBSERVATIONS.; p. [604]: blank.

Harvard Divinity School

VOL. IX. | CONTAINING, | I. TYPES OF THE MESSIAH. | II. NOTES ON THE BIBLE. | [short thick-thin rule] | NEW YORK: | PUBLISHED BY S. CONVERSE. | 1830.

22.2 x. 13.8 cm.; π^2, 2-70^4, 71^2; iii, [2], 10-563 [i.e., 559], [1] p.

Notes: lacks pp. 5-8.

Contents: p. [i]: title; p. [ii]: [affidavit] [signed] CHAS. A. INGERSOLL, Clerk of the District of Connecticut.; p. [iii]: CONTENTS OF VOL. IX. (verso blank); p. [9]: TYPES OF THE MESSIAH, | *&c.*; p. [112]: blank; p. [113]: NOTES ON THE BIBLE. (verso blank); p. [115]: NOTES ON THE BIBLE.; p. [564]: blank.

Harvard Divinity School

VOL. X. | CONTAINING, | MEMOIRS OF THE REV. DAVID BRAINERD. | [short thick-thin rule] | NEW YORK: | PUBLISHED BY S. CONVERSE. | 1829.

22.2 x 13.8 cm.; π^4, 2-60^4, 61^2; viii, [3], 12-483, [1] p.

Contents: p. [i]: title; p. [ii]:Vanderpool & Cole, Printers.; p. [iii]: CONTENTS OF VOL. X.; p. [v]: ADVERTISEMENT BY THE EDITOR.; p. [9]: A | SERMON, | PREACHED IN NEWARK, JUNE 12, 1744, | AT THE | ORDINATION OF MR. DAVID BRAINERD, | A MISSIONARY TO THE INDIANS | ON THE | BORDERS OF NEW YORK, NEW JERSEY AND PENNSYLVANIA, | BY EBENEZER PEMBERTON, A. M. | PASTOR OF THE PRESBYTERIAN CHURCH | IN THE CITY OF NEW YORK. (verso blank); p. [11]: ORDINATION SERMON.; p. [26]: blank; p. [27]: PREFACE. [signed] JONATHAN EDWARDS.; p. [33]: MEMOIRS, &c.; p. [452]: blank; p. [453]: *Christians, when absent from the body, are present with the Lord.* | A | SERMON, | PREACHED AT THE FUNERAL OF THE | REV. DAVID BRAINERD, | *MISSIONARY TO THE INDIANS*, | FROM THE SOCIETY IN SCOTLAND FOR PROPAGATING CHRISTIAN KNOWLEDGE, | AND PASTOR OF A CHURCH OF CHRISTIAN INDIANS IN NEW- | JERSEY; WHO DIED AT NORTHAMPTON, OCT. 9, | 1747, AND WAS INTERRED ON THE 12TH. | BY REV. JONATHAN EDWARDS. (verso blank) p. [455]: A SERMON.; p. [484]: blank.

Harvard Divinity School

511 • THE | WORKS | OF | PRESIDENT EDWARDS: | WITH A | MEMOIR OF HIS LIFE. | [short rule] | IN TEN VOLUMES. | [short rule] | VOL. I. | [short double rule] | NEW YORK: | G. & C. & H. CARVILL. | 1830.

21.6 x 13.4 cm.

Notes: reprint of the Converse edition, with identical title page (except for the imprint) and slight variations in the front matter.

THJ 344 NUC NE0046391 OCLC 894859

Andover Newton Theological School

512 • THE WORKS | OF | JONATHAN EDWARDS, A. M. | WITH AN ESSAY ON HIS GENIUS AND WRITINGS, | BY HENRY ROGERS: | AND A MEMOIR BY SERENO E. DWIGHT, | REVISED AND CORRECTED BY | EDWARD HICKMAN, | PASTOR OF THE

CONGREGATIONAL CHURCH, DENTON, NORFOLK. | IN TWO VOLUMES. | VOL. I. | LONDON: | F. WESTLEY, AND A. H. DAVIS, STATIONERS' COURT. | PRINTED BY J. R. AND C. CHILDS, BUNGAY. | MDCCCXXXIV.

25.4 x 16.5 cm.; π^6, b-s^8, B-Z^8, 2A-2X^8, 2Y^2; [4], iv, cclxxvi, 691, [1] p.

Notes: Reprinted many times. In some reprints the essay by Rogers is omitted, with consequent deletion of 2 lines from the title page, and of material from the text. Reprints also show slight variations in the preliminary matter of Vol. I. This item was first issued in New York in 1835. In this (Appleton) reprint, pages 511-814 are omitted: the section containing "Remarks on important theological controversies," "Miscellaneous observations," "Types of the Messiah," and "Notes on the Bible." This edition of Edwards' *Works* was perhaps reprinted 9 times in London previous to 1865, for in that year Bohn reprinted it as the "Tenth Edition," and kept it in print at least until 1871.—THJ. Some issues lack the Dwight biography, still others the frontispiece; some show slight variations in the colophon, others in the front matter; all issues printed in two columns, one title following immediately upon the other.

Contents: frontispiece: [engraving] | PAINTED BY REMBRANT PEAL [*sic*] | ENGRAVED BY W C [*sic*] EDWARDS | [facsimile autograph] Jonathan Edwards | London, Published 1834 by Westley & Davis, Stationers Court.; prp. [1]: title (verso blank); prp. [3]: ADVERTISEMENT.(verso blank); p. [i]: CONTENTS.; p. [i]: AN ESSAY | ON | THE GENIUS AND WRITINGS | OF | JONATHAN EDWARDS.; p. [liii]: MEMOIRS | OF | JONATHAN EDWARDS, A. M.; p. [ccxl]: A FAREWELL SERMON.; p. [ccl]: APPENDIX, No. I.: [letters]; p. ccliii: APPENDIX No. II. [biography of Richard Edwards, JE's grandfather]; p. cclvi: APPENDIX, No. III. [JE's siblings]; p. cclvi: APPENDIX, No. IV. | [The Mind]; p. [cclxxiv]: APPENDIX No. V. | [genealogy]; p. ccxlxxvi: APPENDIX No. VI. | [published works]; p. [1]: A | CAREFUL AND STRICT INQUIRY | INTO THE | MODERN PREVAILING NOTIONS | OF THAT | FREEDOM OF WILL, | WHICH IS SUPPOSED TO BE ESSENTIAL TO MORAL AGENCY, VIRTUE AND VICE, | REWARD AND PUNISHMENT, PRAISE AND BLAME. | [short rule] | Rom. ix. 16. IT IS NOT OF HIM THAT WILLETH. (verso blank); p. [94]: A | DISSERTATION | CONCERNING | THE END FOR WHICH GOD CREATED THE WORLD.; p. [122]: A | DISSERTATION | CONCERNING | THE NATURE OF TRUE VIRTUE; p. [143]: THE | GREAT CHRISTIAN DOCTRINE | OF | ORIGINAL SIN DEFENDED; | EVIDENCES OF ITS TRUTH PRODUCED, | AND ARGUMENTS TO THE CONTRARY ANSWERED; p. [234]: A | TREATISE | CONCERNING | RELIGIOUS AFFECTIONS.; p. [344]: A | FAITHFUL NARRATIVE | OF THE | SURPRISING WORK OF GOD; p. [365]: SOME THOUGHTS | CONCERNING | THE PRESENT REVIVAL OF RELIGION | IN NEW ENGLAND; p. [431]: AN HUMBLE INQUIRY | INTO THE | RULES OF THE WORD OF GOD, | CONCERNING | THE QUALIFICATIONS | REQUISITE | TO A COMPLETE STANDING AND FULL COMMUNION | IN THE VISIBLE | CHRISTIAN CHURCH; p. [485]: MISREPRESENTATIONS CORRECTED, | AND | TRUTH VINDICATED; p. [532]: A HISTORY | OF THE | WORK OF REDEMPTION; p. [620]: FIVE DISCOURSES | ON | IMPORTANT SUBJECTS, | NEARLY CONCERNING THE GREAT AFFAIR | OF THE | SOUL'S ETERNAL SALVATION, | VIZ. | [in 2 cols., col. 1] I. JUSTIFICATION BY FAITH ALONE. | II. PRESSING INTO THE KINGDOM OF GOD. | III. RUTH'S RESOLUTION. | [short vertical rule, col. 2] IV. THE JUSTICE OF GOD IN THE DAMNATION OF | SINNERS. | V. THE EXCELLENCY OF JESUS | CHRIST. | DELIVERED AT NORTHAMPTON, | CHIEFLY AT THE TIME OF THE LATE WONDERFUL POURING OUT OF THE SPIRIT OF GOD THERE.; p. [690]: THEOLOGICAL QUESTIONS: p. 691: BUNGAY: PRINTED BY J. R. AND C. CHILDS.; p. [692]: blank.

THJ 345 NUC NE0046392 OCLC 3991870
University of Arkansas

VOL. II. | LONDON | F. WESTLEY, AND A. H. DAVIS, STATIONERS' COURT. | PRINTED BY J. R. AND C. CHILDS, BUNGAY. | MDCCCXXXIV.

25.4 x 16.5 cm.; [A]^2, B-Z^8, 2A-2Z^8, 3A-3P^8, 3Q^6; [2], iii, [1], 969, [1] p.

Notes: only the last three sermons of *Seventeen Sermons* are titled; other titles provided here are those of the Converse edition, v. 8, the source of all seventeen.

Contents: prp. [1]: title (verso blank); p. [i]: CONTENTS.; p. [iv]: blank; p. [1]: SERMONS.; p. [2]: TWO SERMONS: | [6 lines] | [short rule] | ADVERTISEMENT TO THE READER [signed] T. PRINCE. | W. COOPER. | *Boston, August* 17, 1731.; p. [3]: SERMON I. | GOD GLORIFIED IN MAN'S DEPENDENCE.; p. 7: SERMON II. | SINNERS IN THE HANDS OF AN ANGRY GOD.; p. 12: FIVE SERMONS | ON | DIFFERENT OCCASIONS, | SEPARATELY PUBLISHED IN MR. EDWARDS'S LIFE-TIME. | [short rule] | SERMON I. | A DIVINE AND SUPERNATURAL LIGHT, IMMEDIATELY IMPARTED TO THE SOUL BY THE SPIRIT OF GOD, SHOWN TO BE | BOTH A

SCRIPTURAL AND RATIONAL DOCTRINE.; p. 17: SERMON II. | THE CHURCH'S MARRIAGE TO HER SONS, AND HER GOD.; p. 26: SERMON III. | TRUE SAINTS, WHEN ABSENT FROM THE BODY, ARE PRESENT WITH THE LORD.; p. 36: SERMON IV. | GOD'S AWFUL JUDGMENT IN THE BREAKING AND WITHERING OF THE | STRONG RODS OF A COMMUNITY; p. 41: SERMON V. | TRUE GRACE DISTINGUISHED FROM THE EXPERIENCE OF DEVILS.; p. [51]: FIFTEEN SERMONS | ON | VARIOUS SUBJECTS. | [short rule] | PREFACE. [signed] JONATHAN EDWARDS. | *New-Haven, Dec.* 21, 1779. | [short rule] | SERMON I. | THE MANNER IN WHICH SALVATION OF THE SOUL IS TO BE SOUGHT.; p. 57: SERMON II. | THE UNREASONABLENESS OF INDETERMINATION IN RELIGION.; p. 61: SERMON III. | UNBELIEVERS CONTEMN THE GLORY AND EXCELLENCY OF CHRIST.; p. 64: SERMON IV. [and V.] | THE FOLLY OF LOOKING BACK IN FLEEING OUT OF SODOM.; p. 68: SERMON VI. | THE WARNINGS OF SCRIPTURE ARE IN THE BEST MANNER ADAPTED TO THE | AWAKENING AND CONVERSION OF SINNERS.; p. 71: SERMON VII. [and VIII.] | HYPOCRITES DEFICIENT IN THE DUTY OF PRAYER.; p. [78]: SERMON IX. [and X.] | THE FUTURE PUNISHMENT OF THE WICKED UNAVOIDABLE AND INTOLERABLE.; p. 83: SERMON XI. | THE ETERNITY OF HELL TORMENTS.; p. 89: SERMON XII. | THE PEACE WHICH CHRIST GIVES HIS TRUE FOLLOWERS.; p. 93: SERMON XIII. [and XIV., XV.] | THE PERPETUITY AND CHANGE OF THE SABBATH.; p. [104]: SEVEN SERMONS | ON | IMPORTANT SUBJECTS. | [5 lines] | SERMON I. | GOD THE BEST PORTION OF THE CHRISTIAN.; p. 107: SERMON II. | THE SOLE CONSIDERATION, THAT GOD IS GOD, SUFFICIENT TO STILL ALL OBJECTIONS | TO HIS SOVEREIGNTY.; p. 110: SERMON III. | GREAT GUILT NO OBSTACLE TO THE PARDON OF THE RETURNING SINNER.; p. 113: SERMON IV. | THE MOST HIGH A PRAYER-HEARING GOD.; p. 118: SERMON V. | THE NATURE AND END OF EXCOMMUNICATION.; p. 122: SERMON VI. | WHEN THE WICKED SHALL HAVE FILLED UP THE MEASURE OF THEIR SIN, WRATH | WILL COME UPON THEM TO THE UTTERMOST.; p. 125: SERMON VII. | WICKED MEN USEFUL IN THEIR DESTRUCTION ONLY.; p. [130]: MISCELLANEOUS DISCOURSES | [short rule] | MEN NATURALLY GOD'S ENEMIES.; p. 141: THE WISDOM OF GOD, | DISPLAYED IN THE WAY OF SALVATION.; p. [157]: CHRISTIAN KNOWLEDGE: | OR, THE | IMPORTANCE AND ADVANTAGE OF A THOROUGH KNOWLEDGE OF DIVINE TRUTH.; p. 163: CHRISTIAN CHARITY: | OR, THE | DUTY OF CHARITY TO THE POOR, EXPLAINED AND ENFORCED.; p. 173: CHRISTIAN CAUTIONS; | OR, | THE NECESSITY OF SELF-EXAMINATION.; p. 185: A WARNING TO PROFESSORS: | OR, THE | GREAT GUILT OF THOSE WHO ATTEND ON THE ORDINANCES OF DIVINE WORSHIP, | AND YET ALLOW THEMSELVES IN ANY KNOWN WICKEDNESS.; p. 190: THE FINAL JUDGMENT: | OR, | THE WORLD JUDGED RIGHTEOUSLY BY JESUS CHRIST.; p. 201: SINNERS IN ZION TENDERLY WARNED: | OR, | THE FEARFULNESS WHICH SHALL HEREAFTER SURPRISE SINNERS IN ZION, | REPRESENTED AND IMPROVED.; p. [207]: THE END OF THE WICKED | CONTEMPLATED | BY THE RIGHTEOUS: | OR, | THE TORMENTS OF THE WICKED IN HELL, NO OCCASION OF GRIEF TO THE SAINTS | IN HEAVEN.; p. [213]: CHRIST EXALTED: | OR, | JESUS CHRIST GLORIOUSLY EXALTED ABOVE ALL EVIL IN THE WORK OF | REDEMPTION.; p. 217: SELF-FLATTERIES: | OR, | THE VAIN SELF-FLATTERIES OF THE SINNER.; p. 220: DISHONESTY; | OR, | THE SIN OF THEFT AND OF INJUSTICE.; p. 226: TEMPTATION AND DELIVERANCE; | OR, | JOSEPH'S GREAT TEMPTATION AND GRACIOUS DELIVERANCE.; p. 233: THE PRECIOUSNESS OF TIME, | AND THE | IMPORTANCE OF REDEEMING IT.; p. [237]: PROCRASTINATION, | OR, | THE SIN AND FOLLY OF DEPENDING ON FUTURE TIME.; p. [243]: THE CHRISTIAN PILGRIM; | OR | THE TRUE CHRISTIAN'S LIFE A JOURNEY TOWARDS HEAVEN.; p. [247]: MAN'S NATURAL BLINDNESS | IN THE | THINGS OF RELIGION.; p. [257]: THE | DISTINGUISHING MARKS | OF A | WORK OF THE SPIRIT OF GOD | [5 lines] | [short rule] | MR. COOPER'S PREFACE TO THE READER.; p. 260: THE | MARKS OF A WORK OF THE TRUE SPIRIT.; p. [278]: AN | HUMBLE ATTEMPT | [5 lines] | [short rule] | ADVERTISEMENT. | [17 lines]; p. [278]: PREFACE BY A FORMER ENGLISH EDITOR.; p. 279: PREFACE BY THE AMERICAN EDITORS.; p. [280]: AN | HUMBLE ATTEMPT, &c.; p. [313]: THE | LIFE AND DIARY | OF | THE REV. DAVID BRAINERD: | WITH | NOTES AND REFLECTIONS. | [short rule] | PREFACE.; p. [316]: THE | LIFE AND DIARY OF DAVID BRAINERD.; p. [442]: A SERMON | PREACHED IN NEWARK, JUNE 12, 1744, | AT | THE ORDINATION OF MR. DAVID BRAINERD, | [4 lines]; p. [459]: MISCELLANEOUS OBSERVATIONS | ON | IMPORTANT THEOLOGICAL SUBJECTS. | ORIGINAL AND COLLECTED. | [short rule] | PREFACE; p. [460]: ADVERTISEMENT TO THIS EDITION.; pp. [460]-510: text; p. [511]: REMARKS | ON | IMPORTANT THEOLOGICAL CONTROVERSIES.; p. [604]: MISCELLANEOUS OBSERVATIONS.; p. [642]: TYPES OF THE MESSIAH, &c.; p. [676]: NOTES ON THE BIBLE.; p. [817]: SEVENTEEN OCCASIONAL SERMONS. | SERMON I. | [NATURAL MEN IN A DREADFUL CONDITION.]; p. 830: SERMON II. | [GOD MAKES MEN SENSIBLE OF THEIR MISERY BEFORE HE REVEALS HIS MERCY AND LOVE.]; p. 838: SERMON III. | [HOPE AND COMFORT

USUALLY FOLLOW GENUINE HUMILIATION AND REPENTANCE.]; p. 849: SERMON IV. | [GOD'S SOVEREIGNTY IN THE SALVATION OF MEN.]; p. 855: SERMON V. | [THE CHARACTER OF PAUL AN EXAMPLE TO CHRISTIANS.]; p. 866: SERMON VI. | [CHRIST'S AGONY.]; p. 878: SERMON VII. | [THE PORTION OF THE WICKED.]; p. 888: SERMON VIII. | [THE PORTION OF THE RIGHTEOUS.]; p. 905: SERMON IX. | [THE PURE IN HEART BLESSED.]; p. 913: SERMON X. | [PRAISE, ONE OF THE CHIEF EMPLOYMENTS OF HEAVEN.]; p. 918: SERMON XI. | [WICKED MEN INCONSISTENT WITH THEMSELVES.]; p. 929: SERMON XII. | [SAFETY, FULLNESS AND SWEET REFRESHMENT TO BE FOUND IN CHRIST.]; p. 936: SERMON XIII. | [CHRISTIANS A CHOSEN GENERATION, A ROYAL PRIESTHOOD, A HOLY NATION, A PECULIAR PEOPLE.]; p. 949: SERMON XIV. | [JESUS CHRIST THE SAME YESTERDAY, TO-DAY, AND FOREVER.]; p. 955: SERMON XV. | THE TRUE EXCELLENCY OF A GOSPEL MINISTER.; p. 960: SERMON XVI. | CHRIST THE EXAMPLE OF MINISTERS.; p. 965: SERMON XVII. | THE SORROWS OF THE BEREAVED SPREAD BEFORE JESUS.; p. 969: BUNGAY: PRINTED BY J. R. AND C. CHILDS. p. [970]: blank.

University of Arkansas

512A • LONDON: | F. WESTLEY AND A. H. DAVIS, STATIONERS' COURT. | MDCCCXXXV.

THJ [1835]   NUC NE0046393   OCLC 6741188

Andover Newton Theological School

512B • THE WORKS | OF | JONATHAN EDWARDS, A. M. | WITH | AN ESSAY ON HIS GENIUS AND WRITINGS, | BY HENRY ROGERS. | IN TWO VOLUMES. | . . . | LONDON: | F. WESTLEY AND A. H. DAVIS, STATIONERS' COURT. | NEW YORK: | DANIEL APPLETON AND CO., 200, BROADWAY. | PRINTED BY J. R. AND C. CHILDS, BUNGAY. | MDCCCXXXV.

25.8 x 16.2 cm.; v. 1: A^4, b-d^8, B-Z^8, 2A-$2X^8$, $2Y^2$; [4], lii, 691, [1] p.; v. 2: A^2, B-Z^8, 2A-$2K^8$, 3G-$3P^8$, $3Q^5$; [2], I, [1], 510, 815-969, [1] p.

Notes: usually bound as one volume, this issue lacks Dwight's *Memoir* of the original first volume (pp. liii- cclxxvi) and *Remarks on Important Theological Controversies*, *Miscellaneous Observations*, *Types of the Messiah*, and *Notes on the Bible* (pp. 511-814) of the second.

THJ [1835]   NUC NE0046393   OCLC 6741188

Southwestern Baptist Theological Seminary

512C • LONDON: | WILLIAM BALL, 34, PATERNOSTER-ROW. | PRINTED BY JOHN CHILDS AND SON, BUNGAY. | MDCCCXXXIX.

THJ [1839]   NUC NE0046396   OCLC 4577834

Point Loma Nazarene University

512D • [publisher's device] | LONDON: | JAMES WEBB SOUTHGATE, 22, FLEET STREET. | [short rule] | MDCCCXXXIX

NUC NE0046397   OCLC 26457374

Duke University

512E • LONDON: | BALL, ARNOLD, AND CO., 34, PATERNOSTER ROW. | MDCCCXL.

THJ [1840]   NUC NE0046398   OCLC 1291503

Boston University

512F • Tenth Edition. | LONDON: | HENRY G. BOHN, 4 & 5, YORK STREET, COVENT GARDEN. | MDCCCLXV.

THJ [1865]   NUC NE0046424   OCLC 15669021

Harvard University

512G • Tenth Edition. | LONDON: | HENRY G. BOHN, 4 & 5, YORK STREET, COVENT GARDEN. | MDCCCLXXI.

THJ [1871] NUC NE0046431 OCLC 1362831
Earlham College

512H • Twelfth Edition. | LONDON: | WILLIAM TEGG & CO., PANCRAS LANE, CHEAPSIDE. | [short rule] | 1879.

OCLC 12034332
Rice University

512I • The Works of | Jonathan Edwards | with a memoir by | SERENO E. DWIGHT | revised and corrected by | EDWARD HICKMAN | VOLUME ONE | The Banner of Truth Trust

Notes: facsimile reprint; title page (verso): THE BANNER OF TRUTH TRUST | 3 *Murrayfield Road, Edinburgh* EH12 6EL | *PO Box* 621, *Carlisle, Pennsylvania* 17013, USA | *First published* 1834 | *This edition published* 1974 *Edinburgh*; *Carlisle, Pa.*: BANNER OF TRUTH TRUST, 1974 | [3 lines]. Reprinted 1976, 1979, 1984, 1987, and 1990.

ISBN 0851571848 OCLC 1417944
Gordon-Conwell Theological Seminary

512J • [rule] | THE WORKS OF | [rule] | JONATHAN | [rule] | EDWARDS | [rule] | [ornament] | VOLUME 1 | [publisher's device] HENDRICKSON | PUBLISHERS

Notes: facsimile reprint; title page (verso): THE WORKS OF JONATHAN EDWARDS | 2 VOLUME SET | Hendrickson Publishers, Inc. | P. O. Box 3473 | Peabody, Massachusetts 01961-3473 | 1 line] | Reprinted from an 1834 edition originally published in Great Britain. | [1 line] | *First Printing — October 1998* | [1 line].

ISBN 1565630858 OCLC 41079071
Boston College

513 • THE | WORKS | OF | PRESIDENT EDWARDS, | IN FOUR VOLUMES. | A REPRINT OF THE WORCESTER EDITION, | WITH | VALUABLE ADDITIONS AND A COPIOUS GENERAL INDEX. | [short rule] | VOL. I. | CONTAINING | [in 2 cols., col. 1] I. MEMOIRS OF PRESIDENT EDWARDS. | II. FAREWELL SERMON. | III. INQUIRY CONCERNING QUALIFICATIONS | FOR COMMUNION. | IV. REPLY TO REV. SOLOMON WILLIAMS. | V. HISTORY OF THE WORK OF REDEMP- | TION. | [short vertical rule, col. 2] VI. DISTINGUISHING MARKS OF A WORK | OF THE SPIRIT OF GOD. | VII. MISCELLANEOUS OBSERVATIONS ON | IMPORTANT DOCTRINES. | VIII. ACCOUNT OF THE LIFE OF DAVID | BRAINERD. | NEW-YORK: | JONATHAN LEAVITT AND JOHN F. TROW, | 194 BROADWAY. | BOSTON: | CROCKER AND BREWSTER. | MDCCCXLIII.

23.1 x 14.3; π^2, $1\text{-}5^6$, 6^4, $10\text{-}34^4$, 33^4, $36\text{-}38^4$, 38^4, $40\text{-}84^4$; iv, [5]-672 p.

Notes: The reprints of this edition are numerous, and the imprints will be found listed below. The signatures and pagination of the reprints of Volumes II, III and IV are identical in all reprints. For Volume I they are identical beginning with p. 65, where the signatures run as follows in the first edition of 1843: 6^4, $10\text{-}34^4$, 33^4, $35\text{-}38^4$, 38^4, $40\text{-}84^4$. In all subsequent reprints, the error of misprinting signatures 35 and 39 was corrected, and the signatures run (beginning at p. 65): 6^4, $10\text{-}84^4$. In the first printing of Volume I (1843), the signatures of all matter up to p. 65, run as follows: π^2 (title page and contents leaf), $1\text{-}5^6$ (including the "Memoirs," pp. [5]-56, and the first 8 pp. of "A Farewell Sermon," pp. [57]-64). Pagination therefore is iv, [5]-64. This arrangement of material up to p. 65 is also to be found in the 1844 reprint. In the reprint of 1843, however, the signatures up to p. 65; run thus: π^3 (title page, advertisement, and contents leaf), $1\text{-}3^8$, 4^6; with pagination [2], iv, [5]-64. ("Memoirs," pp. [5]-56; "A Farewell Sermon," pp. [57]-64.) The printing has been done from the same plates as in the first edition, though the signatures through sig. 6_1 have been changed. The title page also records the fact that a complete index is added, a circumstance that holds in most of the subsequent reprintings. After 1844, almost all reprints follow the arrangement of the 1843 reprint. The reprint of 1848 may be taken as representative, and the description is thus: π^4, 1-4^8, 6^4, 10-84^4 (first leaf genuine but blank); [4], iv, 672 p. The material from the beginning through p. 64 is reset, though the text remains the same. Later reprints are set in the manner of the reprint of 1848.—THJ. The troublesome signatures would appear to read 33^4, 36-38^4, 38^4, not 33^4, 35-38^4, 38^4; the reprint of 1843 includes a publisher's note between the title page and the contents.

Contents: p. [i]: title (verso blank); p. [iii]: CONTENTS OF VOLUME I.; p. [5]: MEMOIRS | OF THE LATE | REV. JONATHAN EDWARDS, A. M.; p. [57]: A | FAREWELL SERMON, | PREACHED AT THE FIRST PRECINCT IN NORTHAMPTON | AFTER THE PEOPLE'S PUBLIC REJECTION OF THEIR MINISTER, AND RENOUNCING | THEIR RELATION TO HIM AS PASTOR OF THE CHURCH THERE, | JUNE 22, 1750. (verso blank); p. [59]: PREFACE. [signed] JONATHAN EDWARDS.; p. [62]: blank; p. [63]: A FAREWELL SERMON.; p. [83]: AN | HUMBLE INQUIRY | INTO THE | RULES OF THE WORD OF GOD, | CONCERNING | THE QUALIFICATIONS | REQUISITE TO A | COMPLETE STANDING AND FULL COMMUNION | IN THE | VISIBLE CHRISTIAN CHURCH. (verso blank); p. [85]: PREFACE. [signed] JONATHAN EDWARDS.; p. [88]: blank; p. [89]: HUMBLE INQUIRY.; p. [193]: MISREPRESENTATIONS CORRECTED, AND | TRUTH VINDICATED: | IN A REPLY TO THE REV. SOLOMON WILLIAMS'S BOOK, ENTITLED "THE TRUE | STATE OF THE QUESTION CONCERNING THE QUALIFICATION NECESSARY *TO | LAWFUL COMMUNION IN THE CHRISTIAN SACRAMENTS*." (verso blank); p. [195]: PREFACE.; p. [197]: MISREPRESENTATIONS CORRECTED, | AND | TRUTH VINDICATED.; p. [293]: A HISTORY | OF THE | WORK OF REDEMPTION. (verso blank); p. [295]: ADVERTISEMENT | TO THE EDINBURGH EDITION. [signed] JOHN ERSKINE. | EDINBURGH, *April* 29, 1775.; p. [296]: PREFACE. [signed] JONATHAN EDWARDS. | *New Haven, Feb.* 25, 1775.; p. [297]: WORK OF REDEMPTION.; p. [517]: THE | DISTINGUISHING MARKS | OF A | WORK OF THE SPIRIT OF GOD. (verso blank); p. [519]: MR. COOPER'S PREFACE TO THE READER. [signed] W. COOPER | *Boston, Nov.* 20, 1741.; p. [525]: THE | MARKS OF A WORK OF THE TRUE SPIRIT.; p. [563]: MISCELLANEOUS OBSERVATIONS | ON | IMPORTANT DOCTRINES. (verso blank); p. [565]: MISCELLANEOUS OBSERVATIONS | ON | IMPORTANT DOCTRINES.; p. [643]: AN ACCOUNT OF THE LIFE | OF THE | REV. DAVID BRAINERD, | MINISTER OF THE GOSPEL; MISSIONARY TO THE INDIANS FROM THE HONORABLE | SOCIETY, IN SCOTLAND, FOR THE PROPAGATION OF CHRISTIAN KNOWLEDGE; | WHO DIED AT NORTHAMPTON, IN NEW ENGLAND, OCTOBER 9TH, 1747, IN THE 30TH YEAR | OF HIS AGE: | CHIEFLY TAKEN FROM HIS OWN DIARY, AND OTHER PRIVATE WRITINGS, WRITTEN | FOR HIS OWN USE.; p. [644]: ADVERTISEMENT TO THE WORCESTER EDITION.; p. [645]: CLOSING SCENE OF THE LIFE | OF THE | REV. DAVID BRAINERD.

THJ 346 NUC NE0046399 OCLC 1948333

Gordon-Conwell Theological Seminary

VOL. II. | CONTAINING | [in 2 cols., col. 1] I. INQUIRY INTO THE FREEDOM OF THE | WILL. | II. DISSERTATION CONCERNING THE END | FOR WHICH GOD CREATED THE | WORLD. | III. DISSERTATION ON THE NATURE OF | TRUE VIRTUE. | [short vertical rule, col. 2] IV. DOCTRINE OF ORIGINAL SIN DEFENDED. | V. MISCELLANEOUS OBSERVATIONS CON- | CERNING THE DIVINE DECREES IN | GENERAL AND ELECTION IN PAR- | TICULAR. | VI. REMARKS ON EFFICACIOUS GRACE. | VII. OBSERVATIONS CONCERNING FAITH. | NEW-YORK: | JONATHAN LEAVITT AND JOHN F. TROW, | 194 BROADWAY. | BOSTON: | CROCKER AND BREWSTER. | MDCCCXLIII

23.1 x 14.3; π^4, 1-48^4, 29^4, 50-80^4, 81^1; v, [3], 641, [1] p.

Notes: The misprint of the signature mark on p. 385 is corrected to read "49" in the reprint of 1856 and subsequent reprints.—THJ.

Contents: p. [i]: title (verso blank); p. [iii]: CONTENTS OF VOLUME II.; p. [vi]: blank; p. [vii]: A CAREFUL AND STRICT INQUIRY | INTO THE | MODERN PREVAILING NOTIONS | OF THAT | FREEDOM OF THE WILL, | WHICH IS | SUPPOSED TO BE ESSENTIAL TO MORAL AGENCY, VIRTUE AND VICE, REWARD | AND PUNISHMENT, PRAISE AND BLAME. | [short rule] | ROM. IX. 16. IT IS NOT OF HIM THAT WILLETH.(verso blank); p. [1]: FREEDOM OF THE WILL.; p. [183]: REMARKS | ON THE ESSAYS ON THE PRINCIPLES OF MORALITY AND NATURAL RELIGION, IN A LETTER | TO A MINISTER OF THE CHURCH IN SCOTLAND. [signed] JONATHAN EDWARDS. | STOCKBRIDGE, *July* 25, 1757.; p. [191]: DISSERTATION | CONCERNING | THE END FOR WHICH GOD CREATED THE WORLD. (verso blank); p. [193]: DISSERTATION | CONCERNING THE END FOR WHICH GOD CREATED THE | WORLD.; p. [258]: blank; p. [259]: DISSERTATION | ON THE | NATURE OF TRUE VIRTUE. (verso blank); p. [261]: THE | NATURE OF TRUE VIRTUE.; p. [305]: THE GREAT DOCTRINE | OF | ORIGINAL SIN |

DEFENDED; | EVIDENCES OF ITS TRUTH PRODUCED, | AND | ARGUMENTS TO THE CONTRARY ANSWERED. | CONTAINING IN PARTICULAR, | A REPLY TO THE OBJECTIONS AND ARGUINGS OF DR. JOHN TAYLOR, IN HIS BOOK, | ENTITLED, "THE SCRIPTURE DOCTRINE OF ORIGINAL SIN PROPOSED | TO FREE AND CANDID EXAMINATION, ETC." | [short rule] | Matth. ix. 12. "They that be whole, need not a Physician; but they that are sick." | Et hæc non tantum ad Peccatores referenda est; quia in omnibus Maledictionibus primi Hominis, | omnes ejus Generationes conveniunt.... | R. SAL. JARCHI. | Propter Concupiscentiam, innatam Cordi humano, dicitur, In Iniquitate genitus sum; atque Sensus est, | quod a Nativitate implantatum sit Cordi humano *Jetzer harang* Figmentum malum.... | ABEN EZRA. | ....Ad Mores Natura recurrit | Damnatos, fixa et mutari nescia.... | ....Dociles imitandis | Turpibus et pravis omnes sumus.... JUV.; p. [306]: [advertisement]; p. [307]: AUTHOR'S PREFACE.; p. [309]: DOCTRINE | OF | ORIGINAL SIN | DEFENDED.; p. [511]: MISCELLANEOUS OBSERVATIONS | CONCERNING | THE DIVINE DECREES IN GENERAL, | AND | ELECTION IN PARTICULAR. (verso blank); p. 513: MISCELLANEOUS OBSERVATIONS.; p. [598]: blank; p. [599]: OBSERVATIONS CONCERNING FAITH. (verso blank); p. [601]: OBSERVATIONS CONCERNING FAITH.; p. [642]: blank.

Gordon-Conwell Theological Seminary

VOL. III. | CONTAINING | [in 2 cols., col. 1] I. A TREATISE CONCERNING RELIGIOUS | AFFECTIONS. | II. NARRATIVE OF SURPRISING CONVER- | SIONS. | III. THOUGHTS ON THE REVIVAL IN NEW | ENGLAND. | IV. AN ATTEMPT TO PROMOTE EXPLICIT | AGREEMENT IN EXTRAORDINARY | PRAYER. | [short vertical rule, col. 2] V. CONCERNING THE PERSEVERANCE OF | SAINTS. | VI. ON THE NOTION OF THE PRE-EXIST- | ENCE OF CHRIST'S HUMAN SOUL. | VII. MYSTERIES OF SCRIPTURE. | VIII. OBSERVATIONS UPON PARTICULAR | PASSAGES OF SCRIPTURE. | IX. THEOLOGICAL QUESTIONS. | X. SIX OCCASIONAL SERMONS. | NEW-YORK: | JONATHAN LEAVITT AND JOHN F. TROW, | 194 BROADWAY. | BOSTON: | CROCKER AND BREWSTER. | MDCCCXLIII.

23.1 x 14.3; π^6, 1-80^4; xii, 639, [1] p.

Contents: pp. [i-ii]: blank; p. [iii]: title (verso blank); p. [v]: CONTENTS OF VOLUME III. (verso blank); p. [vii]: TREATISE | CONCERNING RELIGIOUS AFFECTIONS. (verso blank); p. [ix]: INTRODUCTION.; p. [1]: RELIGIOUS AFFECTIONS.; p. [229]: NARRATIVE | OF | SURPRISING CONVERSIONS. (verso blank); p. [231]: NARRATIVE | OF | SURPRISING CONVERSIONS.; p. [273]: THOUGHTS | ON THE | REVIVAL OF RELIGION IN NEW ENGLAND, | 1740.; p. [274]: ADVERTISEMENT.; p. [275]: THE AUTHOR'S PREFACE.; p. [277]: REVIVAL OF RELIGION | IN | NEW ENGLAND.; p. [426]: blank; p. [427]: A | HUMBLE ATTEMPT TO PROMOTE | EXPLICIT AGREEMENT AND VISIBLE UNION | OF | GOD'S PEOPLE | IN | EXTRAORDINARY PRAYER, | FOR THE REVIVAL OF RELIGION AND THE ADVANCEMENT OF CHRIST'S KINGDOM ON | EARTH, PURSUANT TO SCRIPTURE PROMISES AND PROPHECIES | CONCERNING THE LAST TIME. (verso blank); p. [429]: UNION IN PRAYER.; p. [509]: CONCERNING THE | PERSEVERANCE OF SAINTS.; p. [533]: REASONS AGAINST DR. WATTS'S NOTION | OF THE | PRE-EXISTENCE OF CHRIST'S HUMAN SOUL.; p. [537]: MYSTERIES OF SCRIPTURE.; p. [547]: OBSERVATIONS | UPON | PARTICULAR PASSAGES OF SCRIPTURE.; p. [554]: THEOLOGICAL QUESTIONS; p. [557]: SIX OCCASIONAL SERMONS. (verso blank); p. [559]: THE CHURCH'S MARRIAGE TO HER SONS, AND TO HER GOD.; p. [580]: THE TRUE EXCELLENCY OF A GOSPEL MINISTER.; p. [604]: GOD'S AWFUL JUDGMENT IN THE BREAKING AND WITHERING OF THE STRONG RODS | OF A COMMUNITY.; p. [615]: THE SORROWS OF THE BEREAVED SPREAD BEFORE JESUS.; p. [624]: TRUE SAINTS, WHEN ABSENT FROM THE BODY, ARE PRESENT WITH THE LORD.; p. [640]: blank.

Gordon-Conwell Theological Seminary

VOL. IV. | CONTAINING | FORTY SERMONS ON VARIOUS SUBJECTS. | NEW-YORK: | JONATHAN LEAVITT AND JOHN F. TROW, | 194 BROADWAY. | BOSTON: | CROCKER AND BREWSTER. | MDCCCXLIII

23.1 x 14.3; π^4, 1-85^4, 86^2; [2], iv, [2], 684 p.

Notes: In all subsequent issues, in which the index is added, the signature reads: π^4, 1-89^4 (last leaf either blank or advertisement); [2], iv, [2], 710, [2] p.—THJ.

Contents: prp. [1-2]: blank; p. [i]: title; p. [ii]: ENTERED according to Act of Congress, in the year 1843, by |

JONATHAN LEAVITT& JOHN F. TROW | in the Clerk's Office of the District Court of the Southern District of New-York.; p. [iii]: CONTENTS OF VOLUME IV.; p. [v]: SERMONS | ON VARIOUS IMPORTANT SUBJECTS. (verso blank); p. [1]: THE IMPORTANCE AND ADVANTAGE OF A THOROUGH KNOWLEDGE OF DIVINE TRUTH.; p. [16]: MAN'S NATURAL BLINDNESS IN THE THINGS OF RELIGION.; p. [36]: MEN NATURALLY GOD'S ENEMIES.; p. [64]: JUSTIFICATION BY FAITH ALONE.; p. [133]: THE WISDOM OF GOD, DISPLAYED IN THE WAY OF SALVATION.; p. [169]: GOD GLORIFIED IN MAN'S DEPENDENCE.; p. [179]: THE EXCELLENCY OF CHRIST.; p. [202]: THE FINAL JUDGMENT: OR THE WORLD JUDGED RIGHTEOUSLY BY JESUS CHRIST.; p. [226]:THE JUSTICE OF GOD IN THE DAMNATION OF SINNERS.; p. [254]: THE FUTURE PUNISHMENT OF THE WICKED UNAVOIDABLE AND INTOLERABLE.; p. [266]: THE ETERNITY OF HELL TORMENTS.; p. [280]: WHEN THE WICKED SHALL HAVE FILLED UP THE MEASURE OF THEIR SIN, WRATH WILL | COME UPON THEM TO THE UTTERMOST.; p. [287]: THE END OF THE WICKED CONTEMPLATED BY THE RIGHTEOUS: OR THE TORMENTS OF | THE WICKED IN HELL, NO OCCASION OF GRIEF TO THE SAINTS IN HEAVEN.; p. [300]: WICKED MEN USEFUL IN THEIR DESTRUCTION ONLY.; p. [313]: SINNERS IN THE HANDS OF AN ANGRY GOD.; p. [322]: THE VAIN SELF-FLATTERIES OF THE SINNER.; p. [330]: THE WARNINGS OF SCRIPTURE ARE IN THE BEST MANNER ADAPTED TO THE AWAKENING | AND CONVERSION OF SINNERS.; p. [338]: THE UNREASONABLENESS OF INDETERMINATION IN RELIGION.; p. [347]: THE SIN AND FOLLY OF DEPENDING ON FUTURE TIME.; p. [361]: UNBELIEVERS CONTEMN THE GLORY AND EXCELLENCY OF CHRIST.; p. [368]: THE MANNER IN WHICH THE SALVATION OF THE SOUL IS TO BE SOUGHT.; p. [381]: PRESSING INTO THE KINGDOM OF GOD.; p. [403]: THE FOLLY OF LOOKING BACK IN FLEEING OUT OF SODOM.; p. [412]: RUTH'S RESOLUTION.; p. [422]: GREAT GUILT NO OBSTACLE TO THE PARDON OF THE RETURNING SINNER.; p. [429]: THE PEACE WHICH CHRIST GIVES HIS TRUE FOLLOWERS.; p. [438]: A DIVINE AND SUPERNATURAL LIGHT, IMMEDIATELY IMPARTED TO THE SOUL BY THE | SPIRIT OF GOD, SHOWN TO BE BOTH A SCRIPTURAL AND RATIONAL DOCTRINE.; p. [451]: TRUE GRACE DISTINGUISHED FROM THE EXPERIENCE OF DEVILS.; p. [474]: HYPOCRITES DEFICIENT IN THE DUTY OF PRAYER.; p. [488]: THE FEARFULNESS WHICH WILL HEREAFTER SURPRISE SINNERS IN ZION, REPRESENTED | AND IMPROVED.; p. [502]: GREAT CARE NECESSARY, LEST WE LIVE IN SOME WAY OF SIN.; p. [529]: A WARNING TO PROFESSORS: | OR, | THE GREAT GUILT OF THOSE WHO ATTEND ON ORDINANCES OF DIVINE WORSHIP, | AND YET ALLOW THEMSELVES IN ANY KNOWN WICKEDNESS.; p. [540]: GOD THE BEST PORTION OF THE CHRISTIAN.; p. [548]: GOD'S SOVEREIGNTY.; p. [561]: THE MOST HIGH A PRAYER HEARING GOD.; p. [573]: THE TRUE CHRISTIAN'S LIFE, A JOURNEY TO HEAVEN.; p. [585]: JOSEPH'S GREAT TEMPTATION AND GRACIOUS DELIVERANCE.; p. [601]: THE SIN OF THEFT AND OF INJUSTICE.; p. [615]: THE PERPETUITY AND CHANGE OF THE SABBATH.; p. [638]: THE NATURE AND END OF EXCOMMUNICATION.; p. [649]: GENERAL INDEX.

Gordon-Conwell Theological Seminary

513A • BOSTON: | CROCKER AND BREWSTER. | PHILADELPHIA: | GEO. S. APPLETON, 148 CHESTNUT-STREET. | MDCCCXLIII.

THJ [1843]
Presbyterian Historical Society

513B • NEW-YORK: JONATHAN LEAVITT AND JOHN F. TROW, | 194 BROADWAY. | BOSTON: | CROCKER AND BREWSTER. | PHILADELPHIA: | GEO. S. APPLETON, 148 CHESTNUT-STREET. | MDCCCXLIII.

THJ [1843] OCLC 194833
Wesley Theological Seminary

513C • NEW-YORK: | LEAVITT, TROW & CO., 194 BROADWAY. | LONDON: | WILEY & PUTNAM. | MDCCCXLIV.

THJ [1844] NUC NE0046402 OCLC 877263
Harvard Divinity School

513D • . . . | TO WHICH, FOR THE FIRST TIME, HAS BEEN ADDED, AT GREAT EXPENSE, | A COMPLETE INDEX OF SCRIPTURE TEXTS | EIGHTH EDITION IN FOUR VOLUMES. | NEW-YORK: | LEAVITT, TROW & CO., 191 BROADWAY. | LONDON | WILEY & PUTNAM. | MDCCCXLVIII.
THJ [1848] NUC NE0046406
Congregational Library

513E • NEW-YORK: | LEAVITT, TROW & CO., 191 BROADWAY. | LONDON: | WILEY & PUTNAM. | MDCCCXLIX.
THJ [1849] NUC NE0046407 OCLC 1948347
Gordon College

513F • NEW YORK: | LEAVITT AND COMPANY, | No. 191 Broadway | 1849.
THJ [1849] NUC NE0046409
Smith College

513G • NEW YORK: | LEAVITT AND COMPANY, | No. 191 Broadway | 1851.
3HJ [1851] NUC NE0046410 OCLC 39856487
Ohio Wesleyan University

513H • NEW-YORK: | PUBLISHED BY LEAVITT & ALLEN, | 27 DEY STREET | [short rule] |1852.
THJ [1852] NUC NE0046413 OCLC 12979673
Wesley Theological Seminary

513I • NEW-YORK: | PUBLISHED BY LEAVITT & ALLEN | 27 DEY STREET | [short rule] | 1854.
OCLC 30754519
Wesley Theological Seminary

513J • NEW-YORK: | PUBLISHED BY LEAVITT & ALLEN, | 27 DEY STREET | [short rule] | 1855.
THJ [1855] NUC NE0046414 OCLC 35127332
Cornell University

513K • NEW-YORK: | PUBLISHED BY LEAVITT & ALLEN. | 379 BROADWAY. | [short rule] | 1856.
THJ [1856] NUC NE0046420 OCLC 30754513
Harvard Divinity School

513L • NEW-YORK: | PUBLISHED BY LEAVITT & ALLEN, | 379 BROADWAY. | [short rule] | 1857.
THJ [1857] NUC NE0046421 OCLC 10707112
Mercer University

513M • NEW-YORK: | PUBLISHED BY LEAVITT & ALLEN, | 379 BROADWAY. | [short rule] | 1858.
THJ [1858] NUC NE0046423 OCLC 3165884
Cornell University

513N • NEW-YORK: | PUBLISHED BY LEAVITT & ALLEN, | 379 BROADWAY.
Brown University

513O • NEW YORK: ROBERT CARTER AND BROTHERS, | 530 BROADWAY. | 1864.
THJ [1864] OCLC 11581117
Boston University

513P • NEW YORK. | ROBERT CARTER AND BROTHERS, | 530 BROADWAY. | 1868.
THJ [1868] NUC NE0046425 OCLC 2545836
Union Theological Seminary

513Q • NEW YORK. | ROBERT CARTER AND BROTHERS, | 530 BROADWAY. | 1869.
THJ [1869] NUC NE0046430 OCLC 22137024
Tennessee State Library

513R • NEW YORK. | ROBERT CARTER AND BROTHERS, | 530 BROADWAY. | 1879.
THJ [1879] NUC NE0046433 OCLC 1498788
Yale University

513S • NEW YORK: | ROBERT CARTER AND BROTHERS, | 530 BROADWAY. | 1881.
THJ [1881] NUC NE0046438 OCLC 9601145
Boston University

514 • THE | WORKS | OF | PRESIDENT EDWARDS. | IN SIX VOLUMES. | [short rule] | VOL. V. | [short rule] | [SUPPLEMENTARY TO THE NEW YORK FOUR VOLUME EDITION.] | CONTAINING | I. NOTES ON THE BIBLE. | II. TYPES OF THE MESSIAH. | EDINBURGH: | ROBERT OGLE AND OLIVER AND BOYD. | GLASGOW: M. OGLE AND SON, AND WILLIAM COLLINS. | LONDON: HAMILTON, ADAMS & CO. | MDCCCXLVII.
23.1 x 14.3; π^3, [A]^8, B-T^8, X-Z^8, 2A-2I^8; [2], iii, [1], 494, [2] p.
Notes: A reprint of the two "Supplementary Volumes," originally added to the London, 1817, reprint of the Leeds edition (with Edinburgh imprint, dated 1847), was again issued with a new title page.—THJ.
THJ 346A NUC NE0046405 OCLC 38911087
Yale Divinity School

VOL. VI. | [short rule] | [SUPPLEMENTARY TO THE NEW YORK FOUR VOLUME EDITION.] | CONTAINING | I. MISCELLANEOUS OBSERVATIONS. | II. SEVENTEEN OCCASIONAL SERMONS | EDINBURGH: | ROBERT OGLE AND OLIVER AND BOYD. | GLASGOW: M. OGLE AND SON, AND WILLIAM COLLINS. | LONDON: HAMILTON, ADAMS & CO. | MDCCCXLVII.
23.1 x 14.3; π^2, A^8, *B-*Z^8, *2A-*2K^8, *2L^4; [4], 536 p.
Yale Divinity School

515 • [within rules] JONATHAN EDWARDS | Freedom of the Will | EDITED BY PAUL RAMSEY | PROFESSOR OF RELIGION, PRINCETON UNIVERSITY | New Haven | YALE UNIVERSITY PRESS, 1957 | LONDON: OXFORD UNIVERSITY PRESS
23.4 x 15.5 cm.; xii, 494 p.
Notes: The first two volumes of the Yale edition were reprinted in facsimile, but in smaller format (20 x 13.5 cm.). There is no indication in either text of a publisher or distributor other than Yale University Press; however, according to the

minutes of the Editorial Committee of the Works meeting for October 4, 1957, "The Evangelical Book Club, Great Neck, L.I., had agreed to print 10,000 copies of [Freedom of the Will]" and Religious Affections. See Stephen D. Crocco, "Perry Miller and the Early Years of the Yale Edition of 'The Works of Jonathan Edwards'" (unpublished manuscript, p. 19, n. 62). The minutes are at The Works of Jonathan Edwards Office, Yale Divinity School.

Contents: p. [i]: THE WORKS OF JONATHAN EDWARDS | VOLUME 1 | *Perry Miller, General Editor*.; p. [ii], frontispiece: [within rules] [photocopy] | *Portrait of Jonathan Edwards by Joseph Badger.* | *Yale University Art Gallery*; p. [iii]: title; p. [iv]: © *1957 by Yale University Press, Inc.* | [2 lines]; p. [v]: [within rules] [photocopy: title page, *Freedom of the Will* (Boston, 1754)]; p. [vi]: EDITORIAL COMMITTEE FOR | THE WORKS OF JONATHAN EDWARDS; p. vii: GENERAL EDITOR'S NOTE; p. ix: CONTENTS; p. 1: EDITOR'S INTRODUCTION; p. 129: AUTHOR'S PREFACE; p. [134]: blank; p. [136]: PART ONE (verso blank); p. [168]: blank; p. [169]: PART TWO (verso blank); p. [274]: blank; p. [275]: PART THREE (verso blank); p. [334]: blank; p. [335]: PART FOUR (verso blank); p. 430: THE CONCLUSION; p. [440]: blank; p. [441]: RELATED CORRESPONDENCE (verso blank); p. 443: INTRODUCTION; p. 453: REMARKS ON THE *Essays on the Principles of Morality* | *and Natural Religion*, IN A LETTER TO A MINISTER OF | THE CHURCH OF SCOTLAND: BY THE REVEREND MR. | JONATHAN EDWARDS, PRESIDENT OF THE COLLEGE OF | NEW JERSEY, AND AUTHOR OF THE LATE *Inquiry into* | *the Modern Notions of the Freedom of the Will* [signed] J. EDWARDS | *Stockbridge,* | *July 25, 1757*.; p. 465: TO MR. ERSKINE | Stockbridge, August 3, 1757 [signed] JONATHAN EDWARDS; p. 471: GENERAL INDEX; p. 491: INDEX OF BIBLICAL PASSAGES.

OCLC 393136
Yale Divinity School

516 • [within rules] JONATHAN EDWARDS | Religious Affections | EDITED BY JOHN E. SMITH | PROFESSOR OF PHILOSOPHY, YALE UNIVERSITY | New Haven | YALE UNIVERSITY PRESS, 1959

23.4 x 15.5 cm.; vii, [1], 526 p.

Contents: p. [i]: THE WORKS OF JONATHAN EDWARDS | VOLUME 2 | *Perry Miller, General Editor*; p. [ii]: PREVIOUSLY PUBLISHED; p. [iii]: title; p. [iv]: © *1959 by Yale University Press, Inc.* | [8 lines]; p. [v]: [within rules] [photocopy: title page, *Religious Affections* (Boston, 1746)]; p. [vi]: EDITORIAL COMMITTEE FOR | THE WORKS OF JONATHAN EDWARDS; p. [vii]: CONTENTS (verso blank); p. 1: EDITOR'S INTRODUCTION; p. 84: AUTHOR'S PREFACE; p. [90]: blank; p. [91] PART ONE (verso blank); p. [125]: PART TWO (verso blank); p. [191]: PART THREE (verso blank); p. [462]: blank; p. [463]: RELATED CORRESPONDENCE (verso blank); p. 465: *Introduction*; p. 470: Letter 1. Gillespie to Edwards | Carnock, Nov. 24, 1746; p. 478: Letter 2: Edwards to Gillespie | Northampton, Sept. 4, 1747 [signed] JONATHAN EDWARDS; p. 490: Letter 3. Gillespie to Edwards | Sept. 19, 1748; p. 501: Letter 4. Edwards to Gillespie | Northampton, April 2, 1750 [signed] JONATHAN EDWARDS; p. [514]: blank; p. 515: INDEX.

OCLC 243068
Yale Divinity School

517 • [within rules] JONATHAN EDWARDS | Original Sin | EDITED BY CLYDE A. HOLBROOK | PROFESSOR OF RELIGION, OBERLIN COLLEGE | New Haven and London | YALE UNIVERSITY PRESS, 1970

23.4 x. 15.5 cm.; xi, [1], 448 p.

Contents: p. [i]: THE WORKS OF JONATHAN EDWARDS | VOLUME 3 | *John E. Smith, General Editor*; p. [ii]: PREVIOUSLY PUBLISHED; p. [iii]: title; p. [iv]: *Copyright © 1970 by Yale University.* | [15 lines]; p. [v]: [photocopy: title page, *Original Sin* (Boston, 1758)]; p. [vi]: EDITORIAL COMMITTEE FOR | THE WORKS OF JONATHAN EDWARDS; p. vii: CONTENTS; p. [xii]: blank; p. 1: EDITOR'S INTRODUCTION; p. 102: THE AUTHOR'S PREFACE; p. [105]: THE GREAT CHRISTIAN DOCTRINE | OF ORIGINAL SIN DEFENDED | *PART ONE* (verso blank); p. [220]: blank; p. [221]: *PART TWO.* (verso blank); p. [350]: blank; p. [351]: *PART THREE.* (verso blank); p. [372]: blank; p. [373]: *PART FOUR.* (verso blank); p. 434: CONCLUSION; p. [438]: blank; p. 439: INDEX.

ISBN 0300011989 OCLC 231607
Yale Divinity School

518 • [within rules] JONATHAN EDWARDS | The Great Awakening | *A FAITHFUL NARRATIVE* |

THE DISTINGUISHING MARKS | *SOME THOUGHTS CONCERNING THE REVIVAL* | LETTERS RELATING TO THE REVIVAL | PREFACE TO *TRUE RELIGION* BY JOSEPH BELLAMY | EDITED BY C. C. GOEN | PROFESSOR OF CHURCH HISTORY | WESLEY THEOLOGICAL SEMINARY | New Haven and London | YALE UNIVERSITY PRESS, 1972

23.4 x 15.5 cm.; xii, 595, [1] p.

Contents: p. [I]: THE WORKS OF JONATHAN EDWARDS | VOLUME 4 | *John E. Smith, General Editor*; p. [ii]: PREVIOUSLY PUBLISHED; p. [iii]: title; p. [iv]: *Copyright © 1972 by Yale University* | [17 lines]; p. [v]: EDITORIAL COMMITTEE FOR | THE WORKS OF JONATHAN EDWARDS (verso blank); p. vii: CONTENTS; p. [x]: blank; p. [xi]: LIST OF ILLUSTRATIONS; p. [xii]: ABBREVIATIONS; p. 1: EDITOR'S INTRODUCTION (p. [24]: [photocopy of a map: (inserted) *Connecticut River Valley Towns* | *Having Revivals in 1734-35*]; p. [96]: blank; p. [97]: A FAITHFUL NARRATIVE (verso blank); p. 99: UNPUBLISHED LETTER OF MAY 30, 1735 [signed] J. E. (p. [111]: [photocopy: title page, William Williams, *The Duty and Interest of a People* (Boston, 1736)]); p. 112: BENJAMIN COLMAN'S ABRIDGMENT, NOVEMBER 1736 (p. [128]: [photocopy: title page, *Faithful Narrative* (London, 1737)]; p. [129]: [photocopy: title page, *Faithful Narrative* (Boston, 1738)]); p. 130: PREFACE TO THE FIRST EDITION (LONDON, 1737) [signed] Isaac Watts | John Guyse | London Oct. 12, 1737; p. 138: PREFACE TO THE THIRD EDITION (BOSTON, 1738) [signed] Joseph Sewall | Thomas Prince | John Webb | William Cooper | Boston, Nov. 4th, 1738; p. 143: ATTESTATION FROM SIX HAMPSHIRE MINISTERS [signed] William Williams, pastor of Hatfield | Ebenezer Devotion, of Suffield | Stephen Williams, of Longmeadow | Peter Reynolds, of Enfield | Nehemiah Bull, of Westfield | Samuel Hopkins, of W. Springfield; p. 144: TEXT OF *A FAITHFUL NARRATIVE* [signed] Jonathan Edwards. | Northampton | Nov. 6, 1736; p. [212]: blank; p. [213]: *THE DISTINGUISHING MARKS* (p. [214]: [photocopy: title page, *Distinguishing Marks* (Boston, 1741)]); p. 215: PREFACE BY WILLIAM COOPER [signed] W. Cooper | Boston | Nov. 20, 1741; p. 226: TEXT OF *THE DISTINGUISHING MARKS*; p. [289]: *SOME THOUGHTS CONCERNING* | *THE REVIVAL* (p. [290]: [photocopy: title page, *Some Thoughts* (Boston, 1742)]); p. 291: AUTHOR'S PREFACE; p. 293: PART I; p. 348: PART II; p. 384: PART III; p. 409: PART IV; p. 496: PART V; p. [531]: *SOME LETTERS RELATING TO* | *THE REVIVAL* (verso blank); p. 533: TO DEACON LYMAN OF GOSHEN, CONNECTICUT [dated] Northampton, Aug. 31, 1741; p. 535: TO THE REV. JAMES ROBE OF | KILSYTH, SCOTLAND [dated] Northampton, May 12, 1743; p. 539: TO THE REV. WILLIAM McCULLOCH OF | CAMBUSLANG, SCOTLAND [dated] Northampton, May 12, 1743; p. 542: TO THE CONVOCATION ON EVANGELICAL PASTORS [dated] County of Hampshire, June 20, 1743; p. 544 TO THE REV. THOMAS PRINCE OF BOSTON [dated] Northampton, Dec. 12, 1743; p. 558: TO WILLIAM McCULLOCH [dated] Northampton, March 5, 1743/4; p. 561: TO THE REV. THOMAS GILLESPIE OF | CARNOCK, SCOTLAND [dated] Stockbridge, July 1, 1751; p. [567]: *THE PREFACE* TO TRUE RELIGION | *BY JOSEPH BELLAMY* (p. [568]: [photocopy: title page, Joseph Bellamy, *True Religion* (Boston, 1750)]); p. 569: TEXT OF THE PREFACE TO *TRUE RELIGION*; p. 573: GENERAL INDEX; p. 588: INDEX OF SCRIPTURES; p. [596]: blank.

ISBN 0300014376 OCLC 315230

Yale Divinity School

519 • [within rules] JONATHAN EDWARDS | Apocalyptic Writings | "NOTES ON THE APOCALYPSE" | *AN HUMBLE ATTEMPT* | EDITED BY STEPHEN J. STEIN | ASSOCIATE PROFESSOR OF RELIGIOUS STUDIES | INDIANA UNIVERSITY | New Haven and London | YALE UNIVERSITY PRESS, 1977

23.4 x 15.5 cm.; x, 501, [1] p.

Contents: p. [I]: THE WORKS OF JONATHAN EDWARDS | VOLUME 5 | *John E. Smith, General Editor*; p. [ii]: PREVIOUSLY PUBLISHED; p. [iii]: title; p. [iv]: *Copyright © 1977 by Yale University.* | [26 lines]; p. [v]: EDITORIAL COMMITTEE FOR | THE WORKS OF JONATHAN EDWARDS (verso blank); p. vii: CONTENTS; p. ix: LIST OF ILLUSTRATIONS; p. x: FOREWORD; p. 1: EDITOR'S INTRODUCTION (p. [14]: [diagram: Edwards' early view of the Apocalypse]; p. [58]: [diagram: seven periods of the Apocalypse according to Moses Lowman]; p. [72]: [photocopy] | Photograph of manuscript page 7 in the "Notes on the Apocalypse"; p. [73]: [photocopy] | Photograph of manuscript page 185 in the "Notes on the Apocalypse"); p. [94]: blank; p. [95]: "NOTES ON THE APOCALYPSE" (verso blank); p. [306]: blank; p. [307]: AN HUMBLE ATTEMPT (p. [308]: [photocopy: title page, *Humble Attempt* (Boston, 1747)]); p. 309: THE PREFACE [signed in 2 cols., col. 1] *Boston, N.E.* | *January 12, 1747/8* | [col. 2.] Joseph Sewall | Thomas Prince | John Webb | Thomas Foxcroft | Joshua Gee; p. 312: PART I; p. 329: PART II; p. 368: PART III; p. 432:

THE CONCLUSION; p. [437]: APPENDIXES (verso blank); p. 439: APPENDIX A | AN OUTLINE OF THE BOOK OF REVELATION; p. 440: APPENDIX B | SERMONS ON THE APOCALYPSE; p. 444: APPENDIX C | EDWARDS' LETTER TO A CORRESPONDENT IN SCOTLAND [dated] Northampton, Nov. 20, 1745; p. 461: APPENDIX D | APOCALYPTIC THEMES IN OTHER NOTEBOOKS; p. 465: GENERAL INDEX; p. 492: INDEX OF BIBLICAL PASSAGES; p. [502]: blank.

ISBN 0300019459 OCLC 2680833

Yale Divinity School

520 • [within rules] JONATHAN EDWARDS | Scientific and Philosophical | Writings | THE "SPIDER" PAPERS | "NATURAL PHILOSOPHY" | "THE MIND" | SHORT SCIENTIFIC AND PHILOSOPHICAL PAPERS | EDITED BY WALLACE E. ANDERSON | ASSOCIATE PROFESSOR OF PHILOSOPHY | OHIO STATE UNIVERSITY | New Haven and London | YALE UNIVERSITY PRESS, 1980

23.4 x 15.5 cm.; viii, 433, [1] p.

Contents: p. [i]: THE WORKS OF JONATHAN EDWARDS | VOLUME 6 | *John E. Smith, General Editor*; p. [ii], frontispiece: [photocopy] | "That which is most astonishing is that very often there ap- | pears at the ends of these webs, spiders sailing in the air | with them, doubtless with an abundance of pleasure, though not so much as I have beheld them and shewed | them to others. And since I have seen these things I have | been very conversant with spiders." (From Edwards' letter | of October 31, 1723. Courtesy of The New-York Historical | Society, New York City.); p. [iii]: title; p. [iv]: *Copyright © 1980 by Yale University.* | [27 lines]; p. [v]: EDITORIAL COMMITTEE FOR | THE WORKS OF JONATHAN EDWARDS; p. [vi]: PREVIOUSLY PUBLISHED; p. vii: CONTENTS; p. 1: EDITOR'S INTRODUCTION; p. [144]: blank; p. [145]: PART ONE | *The "Spider" Papers* (verso blank); p. 147: NOTE ON THE "SPIDER" PAPERS; p. 154: "OF INSECTS"; p. 163: THE "SPIDER" LETTER [dated] Windsor, Oct. 31, 1723; p. [170]: blank; p. [171]: PART TWO | *"Natural Philosophy" and Related Papers* (verso blank); p. 173: NOTE ON "NATURAL PHILOSOPHY"; p. 192: "NATURAL PHILOSOPHY" | COVER-LEAF MEMORANDA; p. 196: "OF THE PREJUDICES OF THE IMAGINATION" | LEMMA TO THE WHOLE; p. 202: "OF BEING"; p. 208: ["OF ATOMS"]; p. 219: "THINGS TO BE CONSIDERED AN[D] WRITTEN FULLY ABOUT"; p. 296: NOTE ON PAPERS ON NATURE AND NATURAL | PHENOMENA; p. 302: ["OF LIGHT RAYS"]; p. 305: "BEAUTY OF THE WORLD"; p. 307: "WISDOM IN THE CONTRIVANCE OF THE | WORLD"; p. [311]: PART THREE | *"The Mind" and Related Papers* (verso blank); p. 313: NOTE ON "THE MIND"; p. 332: "*The Mind*"; p. 394: NOTE ON SHORT PHILOSOPHICAL PAPERS; p. 396: OUTLINE OF "A RATIONAL ACCOUNT"; p. 398: ["NOTES ON KNOWLEDGE AND EXISTENCE"]; p. [399]: *Appendixes* (verso blank); p. 401: APPENDIX A: "THE SOUL" | NOTE ON "THE SOUL"; p. 405: ["THE SOUL"]; p. 407: APPENDIX B: THE "SPIDER" LETTER-DRAFT | NOTE ON THE "SPIDER" LETTER-DRAFT; p. 409: "SPIDER" LETTER OF OCTOBER 31, 1723—DRAFT; p. [416]: blank; p. 417: INDEX; p. [434]: blank.

ISBN 0300022824 OCLC 4492792

Yale Divinity School

521 • [within rules] JONATHAN EDWARDS | The Life of | David Brainerd | EDITED BY NORMAN PETTIT | PROFESSOR OF ENGLISH | BOSTON UNIVERSITY | New Haven and London | YALE UNIVERSITY PRESS, 1985

23.4 x 15.5 cm.; x, 620 p.

Contents: end papers: [map] | [inserted] DAVID | BRAINERD'S | TRAVELS | 1742-1747 | 19 (B. PETIT) 61; p. [i]: THE WORKS OF JONATHAN EDWARDS | VOLUME 7 | *John E. Smith, General Editor*; p. [ii], frontispiece: [photocopy] | The first manuscript leaf of David Brainerd's diary.; p. [iii]: title; p. [iv]: [1 line] | *Copyright © 1985 by Yale University* | [25 lines]; p. [v]: EDITORIAL COMMITTEE FOR | THE WORKS OF JONATHAN EDWARDS; p. [vi]: PREVIOUSLY PUBLISHED; p. [vii]: [photocopy: title page, *Life of Brainerd* (Boston, 1749)] (verso blank; p. ix: CONTENTS; p. 1: *EDITOR'S INTRODUCTION* (p. [72]: [photocopy] : [photograph] | The slab marking David Brainerd's grave in Northampton cemetery.; p. [73]: [photocopy]: [photograph] | Headstone of Jerusha Edwards' grave, next to Brainerd's grave.); p. [86]: blank; p. [87]: *AN ACCOUNT OF THE LIFE OF | THE REVEREND MR. DAVID BRAINERD* (verso blank); p. 89: AUTHOR'S PREFACE; p. 99: An Account of the Life of | the Reverend | Mr. David Brainerd; p. [542]: blank; p. [543]: A SERMON PREACHED ON THE DAY OF THE FUNERAL OF | THE REV. MR. DAVID BRAINERD;

p. [555]: *RELATED CORRESPONDENCE* (verso blank); p. 557: INTRODUCTION; p. 568: *Brainerd to an Unidentified Correspondent* | New Haven, May 21, 1743 [signed] D. Brainerd; p. 570: *Brainerd to Ebenezer Pemberton* [signed] From the Forks of | Delaware in Pennsylvania, David Brainerd. | Nov. 5, 1744; p. 581: *Brainerd to John Sergeant* | Woodbury, March 15, 1745 [signed] David Brainerd.; p. 583: *Brainerd to Eleazar Wheelock* | Crossweeksung in N. Jersey | Dec. 30, 1745 [signed] David Brainerd; p. 585: *Brainerd to William Bradford* | Princeton N. Jersey Sept. 20, 1746 [signed] David Brainerd; p. 586: *John Brainerd to Ebenezer Pemberton* [signed] John Brainerd | From Bethel, the Indian Town | in New Jersey, June 23, 1747; p. 587: *Edwards to John Brainerd* | Northampton, Decem. 14, 1747 [signed] Jonath. Edwards; p. 591: GENERAL INDEX; p. 613: INDEX OF SCRIPTURE.

ISBN 0300030045 OCLC 10183535

Yale Divinity School

522 • JONATHAN EDWARDS | Ethical | Writings | EDITED BY PAUL RAMSEY | PROFESSOR OF RELIGION EMERITUS | PRINCETON UNIVERSITY | New Haven and London | YALE UNIVERSITY PRESS, 1989

23.4 x 15.5 cm.; ix, [1], 791, [1] p.

Contents: p. [i]: THE WORKS OF JONATHAN EDWARDS | VOLUME 8 | *John E. Smith, General Editor*; p. [ii], frontispiece: [photocopy] | "View of the Third Church, Built in Northampton, 1735-7," attributed to William F. Pratt, 1874. | Reproduced by permission of the Forbes Library, Northampton, Mass.; p. [iii]: title; p. [iv]: *Copyright © 1989 by Yale University* [31 lines]; p. [v]: EDITORIAL COMMITTEE FOR | THE WORKS OF JONATHAN EDWARDS; p. [vi]: PREVIOUSLY PUBLISHED; p. vii: CONTENTS; p. [x]: blank; p. 1: EDITOR'S INTRODUCTION; p. [122]: blank; p. [123]: *CHARITY AND ITS FRUITS* (verso blank); p. 125: TRYON EDWARDS' INTRODUCTION [signed] T. E. | *New London, Conn.* | *November, 1851*; p. [127]: blank; p. [128]: [photocopy] | Opening page from "Charity and Its Fruits" in the Andover copyist's hand. Courtesy of the | Andover Collection, Franklin Trask Library, Andover Newton Theological School, Newton | Centre, Mass.; p. [398]: blank; p. [399]: *TWO DISSERTATIONS*; p. [400]: [photocopy] | Title page from Jonathan Edwards, *Two Dissertations* (Boston, S. Kneeland, 1765). Courtesy of the | Beinecke Rare Book and Manuscript Library, Yale University, New Haven, Conn.; p. 401: [HOPKINS' PREFACE] [signed] THE EDITOR | *July 12, 1765*.; p. [403]: DISSERTATION I | *Concerning the End for which God Created the World* (verso blank); p. [537]: DISSERTATION II | *The Nature of True Virtue* (verso blank); p. [628]: blank; p. [629]: *RELATED CORRESPONDENCE* (verso blank); p. 631: INTRODUCTION by George S. Claghorn; p. 636: UNPUBLISHED LETTER ON ASSURANCE AND PARTICIPATION IN THE | DIVINE NATURE; p. [641]: *APPENDIXES* (verso blank); p. 643: APPENDIX ONE | JOSEPH BELLAMY'S COPY OF THE CHARITY SERMONS; p. [651]: blank; pp. [652-653]: [photocopy] | Opening pages from "Charity and Its Fruits," Bellamy MS. 81466. Courtesy of the Hartford | Seminary Library, Hartford, Conn.; p. [654]: blank; p. 655: Fragment One | *BEGINNING OF SERMON ONE* | SERMON I | Love the Sum of all Value | [i Cor. 13: 1-3 quoted]; p. 658: Fragment Two | *END OF SERMON ONE*; p. 661: Fragment Three | *END OF SERMON TWO AND* | *BEGINNING OF SERMON THREE*; p. 663: *SERMON III* | Nothing can make up | for the want of Sincerity | [i Cor. 13:3 quoted]; p. 665: EXAMPLE ONE; p. [668]: blank; p. 669: EXAMPLE TWO; p. [672]: blank; p. 673: EXAMPLE THREE; p. [678]: blank; p. 679: EXAMPLE FOUR; p. [688]: blank; p. 689: APPENDIX II | JONATHAN EDWARDS ON MORAL SENSE, AND THE SENTIMENTALISTS; p. 706: APPENDIX III | HEAVEN IS A PROGRESSIVE STATE; p. 739: APPENDIX IV | INFUSED VIRTUES IN EDWARDSEAN AND CALVINISTIC CONTEXT; p. 751: APPENDIX V | DEFYING AND ASSISTING THE SPIRIT; p. [760]: blank; p. 761: GENERAL INDEX; p. 779: INDEX OF BIBLICAL PASSAGES; p. [792]: blank.

ISBN 0300040202 OCLC 16951334

Yale Divinity School

523 • JONATHAN EDWARDS | A History of the | Work of Redemption | TRANSCRIBED AND EDITED BY | JOHN F. WILSON | PROFESSOR OF RELIGION | PRINCETON UNIVERSITY | New Haven and London | YALE UNIVERSITY PRESS, 1989

23.4 x 15.5 cm.; ix, [1], 594 p.

Contents: p. [i]: THE WORKS OF JONATHAN EDWARDS | VOLUME 9 | *John E. Smith, General Editor*; p. [ii], frontispiece: [photocopy] | *A North-West Prospect of Nassau-Hall, with a Front View of the Presidents House in New Jersey*, W. Tennent. | Engraving by Henry Dawkins, 1764. Princeton University Archives.; p. [iii]: title; p. [iv]: *Copyright*

© *1989 by Yale University* | 25 lines]; p. [v]: EDITORIAL COMMITTEE FOR | THE WORKS OF JONATHAN EDWARDS; p. [vi]: PREVIOUSLY PUBLISHED; p. vii: CONTENTS; p. ix: LIST OF ILLUSTRATIONS (verso blank; p. 1: EDITOR'S INTRODUCTION (p. [64]: [photocopy] | "Notebook 10," pages 89-90. Beinecke Rare Book and Manuscript Library, Yale University.; p. [65]: [photocopy] | "Notebook 10," pages 101-02. Beinecke Rare Book and Manuscript Library, Yale University.; p. [104]: [2 illus., illus. 1] [photocopy] | Sermon booklets, manuscript leaf 6.1r. Beinecke Rare Book and Manu- | script Library, Yale University. | [illus. 2] [photocopy] | Sermon booklets, leaf 11.28v. Beinecke Rare Book and | Manuscript Library, Yale University.; p. [105]: [2 illus., illus. 1] [photocopy] | Sermon booklets, manuscript leaf 2.12r. Beinecke Rare Book and Manu- | script Library, Yale University. | [illus. 2] [photocopy] | Sermon booklets, manuscript leaf 2.13v. Beinecke Rare Book and Manu- | script Library, Yale University.); p. [110]: blank; p. [111]: A HISTORY OF | THE WORK OF REDEMPTION (verso blank); p. [529]: *APPENDIXES* (verso blank); p. [531]: APPENDIX A | OUTLINE OF THE REDEMPTION DISCOURSE; p. 543: APPENDIX B | JONATHAN EDWARDS' NOTEBOOKS FOR *A HISTORY OF | THE WORK OF REDEMPTION*; p. 557: GENERAL INDEX; p. 579: INDEX OF BIBLICAL PASSAGES.

ISBN 0300041551 OCLC 17953968
Yale Divinity School

524 • JONATHAN EDWARDS | **Sermons and | Discourses | 1720–1723** | EDITED BY | WILSON H. KIMNACH | PROFESSOR OF ENGLISH | UNIVERSITY OF BRIDGEPORT | **New Haven and London** | YALE UNIVERSITY PRESS, 1992

23.4 x 15.5 cm.; xv, [1], 670 p.

Contents: p. [i]: THE WORKS OF JONATHAN EDWARDS | VOLUME 10 | *Harry S. Stout, General Editor*; p. [ii], frontispiece: [photocopy] | A duodecimo sermon manuscript. Beinecke Rare Book and Manuscript Library, | Yale University.; p. [iii]: title; p. [iv]: [7 lines] | *Copyright © 1992 by Yale University* | [31 lines]; p. [v]: EDITORIAL COMMITTEE FOR | THE WORKS OF JONATHAN EDWARDS; p. [vi]: PREVIOUSLY PUBLISHED; p. vii: CONTENTS; p. ix: LIST OF ILLUSTRATIONS (verso blank); p. xi: NOTE TO THE READER; p. [xvi]: blank; p. [1]: *GENERAL INTRODUCTION TO THE SERMONS: | JONATHAN EDWARDS' ART OF PROPHESYING* (verso blank); p. 3: CHAPTER I | EDWARDS' LITERARY MILIEU; p. 42: CHAPTER II | THE MAKING OF SERMONS (p. 49: [photocopy] | Interleaved Bible. Beinecke Rare Book and Manuscript Library, Yale University.; p. 60: [photocopy] | Sermon Notebook 14. Beinecke Rare Book and Manuscript Library, Yale University.; p. 95: [photocopy] | Sermon Booklets. Beinecke Rare Book and Manuscript Library, Yale University.); p. 130: CHAPTER III | THE SERMON CANON (p. 141: [photocopy] | Sermon Revisions. Beinecke Rare Book and Manuscript Library, Yale University.); p. 180: CHAPTER IV | LITERARY THEORY AND PRACTICE; p. [259]: *SERMONS AND DISCOURSES, 1720-1723* (verso blank); p. 261: PREFACE TO THE | NEW YORK PERIOD; p. 294: CHRISTIAN HAPPINESS; p. 308: THE VALUE OF SALVATION; p. 337: WICKED MEN'S SLAVERY TO SIN; p. 354: THE IMPORTANCE OF A FUTURE STATE; p. 377: FRAGMENT: FROM AN APPLICATION ON SEEKING GOD; p. 388: GLORIOUS GRACE; p. 400: THE NAKEDNESS OF JOB; p. 413: GOD'S EXCELLENCIES; p. 436: THE DUTY OF HEARKENING TO GOD'S VOICE; p. 451: CHRISTIAN SAFETY; p. 465: THE WAY OF HOLINESS; p. 480: THE DUTY OF SELF-EXAMINATION; p. 493: POVERTY OF SPIRIT; p. 506: TRUE REPENTANCE REQUIRED; p. 519: LIFE THROUGH CHRIST ALONE; p. 533: CHRIST, THE LIGHT OF THE WORLD; p. 547: DEDICATION TO GOD; p. 563: LIVING TO CHRIST and DYING TO GAIN; p. 566: LIVING TO CHRIST; p. [578]: blank; p. 579: DYING TO GAIN; p. 592: CHRIST'S SACRIFICE; p. 605: FRAGMENT: APPLICATION ON LOVE TO CHRIST; p. 618: CHRISTIAN LIBERTY; p. 632: TRUE LOVE TO GOD; p. [644]: blank; p. 645: APPENDIX: DATED BATCHES OF SERMONS | DATING BY THOMAS A. SCHAFER (verso blank): p. 647: GENERAL INDEX; p. 665: INDEX OF BIBLICAL PASSAGES.

ISBN 0300051360 OCLC 24626329
Yale Divinity School

525 • JONATHAN EDWARDS | **Typological Writings**, "*IMAGES OF DIVINE THINGS*" | "*TYPES*" | EDITED BY | WALLACE E. ANDERSON | LATE ASSOCIATE PROFESSOR OF PHILOSOPHY | OHIO STATE UNIVERSITY | "*TYPES OF THE MESSIAH*" | EDITED BY | MASON I. LOWANCE, JR. | PROFESSOR OF ENGLISH | UNIVERSITY OF MASSACHUSETTS | WITH | DAVID H. WATTERS | PROFESSOR OF ENGLISH | UNIVERSITY OF NEW HAMPSHIRE | **New Haven and**

London | YALE UNIVERSITY PRESS, 1993

23.4 x 15.5 cm.; xvi, 349, [1] p.

Contents: p. [i]: THE WORKS OF JONATHAN EDWARDS | VOLUME 11 | *Harry S. Stout, General Editor*; p. [ii], frontispiece: [photocopy] | Plate XIV (Ps. 84:1) by William Marshall from Francis Quarles, *Emblemes* (1693). Beinecke Rare Book and Manuscript Library, Yale University.; p. [iii]: title; p. [iv]: [2 lines] | *Copyright © 1993 by Yale University* | [37 lines]; p. [v]: Dedicated to Wallace E. Anderson (verso blank); p. [vii]: EDITORIAL COMMITTEE FOR | THE WORKS OF JONATHAN EDWARDS; p. [vii]: PREVIOUSLY PUBLISHED; p. [ix]: CONTENTS (verso blank); p. xi: ILLUSTRATIONS (verso blank); p. xiii: FOREWORD; p. [1]: *PART ONE* | *"IMAGES OF DIVINE THINGS"* | *"TYPES"* | *Edited by* | *Wallace E. Anderson* (verso blank); p. 3: *EDITOR'S INTRODUCTION TO "IMAGES* | *OF DIVINE THINGS" AND "TYPES"*; p. 34: NOTE ON THE MANUSCRIPT OF | "IMAGES OF DIVINE THINGS" (p. [36]: [diagram] | Fig. 1. "Images of Divine Things": Structure of the Manuscript. | [8 lines]); p. [49]: *"IMAGES OF DIVINE THINGS"*; p. [50]: *IMAGES OF DIVINE THINGS* | *The Book of Nature and Common Providence* | *The Language and Lessons of Nature* | See Spencer's *Similes and Sentences*; | see Mr. Mason's *Remains*, p. 49, etc.; (p. [117]: [photocopy] | Manuscript page 32 of "Images of Divine Things," containing entries 176-181. Beinecke Rare Book and Manuscript Library, Yale University.); p. 131: SCRIPTURES: p. 136: EDWARDS' TABLES TO "IMAGES OF DIVINE THINGS"; p. [143]: *"TYPES"* (verso blank); p. 145: NOTE ON THE MANUSCRIPT OF "TYPES"; p. 146: *TYPES*; p. [154]: blank; p. [155]: *PART TWO* | *"TYPES OF THE MESSIAH"* | *Edited by* | *Mason I. Lowance, Jr. with* | *David H. Watters* (verso blank); p. 157: *EDITOR'S INTRODUCTION TO* | *"TYPES OF THE MESSIAH"*; p. 183: NOTE ON THE MANUSCRIPT OF "TYPES OF THE | MESSIAH"; p. [187]: *"TYPES OF THE MESSIAH"* (verso blank); p. [189]: [photocopy] | Manuscript page 1 of "Types of the Messiah," No. 1069 in Book 7 of the "Miscellanies." | Beinecke Rare Book and Manuscript Library, Yale University. (verso blank); p. 325: EDWARDS' TABLE TO "TYPES OF THE MESSIAH"; p. 329: GENERAL INDEX; p. [338]: blank; p. 339: INDEX OF BIBLICAL PASSAGES; p. [350]: blank.

ISBN 0300053525 OCLC 27727962

Yale Divinity School

526 • JONATHAN EDWARDS | Ecclesiastical Writings | A LETTER | AN HUMBLE INQUIRY | MISREPRESENTATIONS CORRECTED | "NARRATIVE OF COMMUNION | CONTROVERSY" | EDITED BY | DAVID D. HALL | PROFESSOR OF AMERICAN RELIGIOUS HISTORY | BARTLETT LECTURER ON NEW ENGLAND CHURCH HISTORY | HARVARD UNIVERSITY | New Haven and London | YALE UNIVERSITY PRESS, 1994

23.4 x 15.5 cm.; x, 644 p.

Contents: p. [i]: THE WORKS OF JONATHAN EDWARDS | VOLUME 12 | *Harry S. Stout, General Editor*; p. [ii], frontispiece: [photocopy] | *Artist's Conception of Main Street, Northampton, 1786* (Commissioned in 1936 for the 150th | Anniversary of the *Daily Hampshire Gazette*), by Maitland de Gorgorza, Courtesy of Forbes | Library, Northampton, Massachusetts.; p. [iii]: title; p. [iv]: [2 lines] | *Copyright © 1994 by Yale University* | [36 lines]; p. [v]: EDITORIAL COMMITTEE FOR | THE WORKS OF JONATHAN EDWARDS; p. [vi]: PREVIOUSLY PUBLISHED; p. vii: CONTENTS; p. viii: LIST OF ILLUSTRATIONS; p. ix: EDITORIAL STATEMENT; p. 1: EDITOR'S INTRODUCTION; p. [91]: A LETTER TO THE AUTHOR OF THE | PAMPHLET CALLED AN ANSWER TO THE | HAMPSHIRE NARRATIVE; p. [92]: [photocopy] | Title page of *A Letter to the Author of the Pamphlet Called An Answer to the Hampshire Narrative*.; p. 93: THE PREFACE; p. [164]: blank; p. [165]: AN HUMBLE INQUIRY INTO THE RULES OF | THE WORD OF GOD, CONCERNING THE | QUALIFICATIONS REQUISITE TO A COMPLETE | STANDING AND FULL COMMUNION IN THE | VISIBLE CHRISTIAN CHURCH; p. [166]: [photocopy] | Title page of *An Humble Inquiry into the Rules of the Word of God, Concerning the Qualifications* | *Requisite to a Complete Standing and Full Communion in the Visible Christian Church*.; p. 167: AUTHOR'S PREFACE [signed] Jonathan Edwards; p. 172: PREFACE [signed] Thomas Prince | John Webb | Thomas Foxcroft | Mather Byles | Boston, August 12, 1749.; p. 326: AN APPENDIX [signed] Thomas Foxcroft | Boston, June 26, 1749.; p. [349]: MISREPRESENTATIONS CORRECTED, | AND TRUTH VINDICATED; p. [350]: [photocopy] | Title page of *Misrepresentations Corrected, and Truth Vindicated*.; p. 351: PREFACE; p. [504]: blank; p. [505]: "NARRATIVE OF COMMUNION CONTROVERSY" (verso blank); p. [620]: blank; p. 621: GENERAL INDEX; p. 639: INDEX OF BIBLICAL PASSAGES.

ISBN 0300058977 OCLC 29315531

Yale Divinity School

527 • JONATHAN EDWARDS | The "Miscellanies" | (Entry Nos. a-z, aa-zz, 1-500) | EDITED BY | THOMAS A. SCHAFER | PROFESSOR EMERITUS OF CHURCH HISTORY | McCORMICK THEOLOGICAL SEMINARY | New Haven and London | YALE UNIVERSITY PRESS, 1994

23.4 x 15.5 cm.; xvi, 596 p.

Contents: p. [i]: THE WORKS OF JONATHAN EDWARDS | VOLUME 13 | *Harry S. Stout, General Editor*; p. [ii], frontispiece: [photocopy | Jonathan Edwards' writing desk ("scrutore"), with matching cabinets supporting box | shelves. Courtesy of Jonathan Edwards College, Yale University. Photograph by William K. | Sacco.; p. [iii]: title; p. [iv]: [6 lines] | *Copyright © 1994 by Yale University* | [36 lines]; p. [v]: EDITORIAL COMMITTEE FOR | THE WORKS OF JONATHAN EDWARDS; p. [vi]: PREVIOUSLY PUBLISHED; p. vii: CONTENTS; p. viii: ILLUSTRATIONS; p. ix: TABLES (verso blank); p. xi: GENERAL EDITOR'S PREFACE; p. xiii: NOTE TO THE READER; p. 1: EDITOR'S INTRODUCTION (p. [64]: [photocopy] | Fig. 1. Details of the first sheet of English GR^{WT} paper in the "Miscellanies," center portions | showing the watermark (above) and countermark (below), along with the deckle edges and | pattern of chain lines.; p. 71: Table 1. Watermarks in the Early "Miscellanies" | and Sermons through 1732); p. [91]: Table 2. The "Miscellanies" and Chronological Parallels: May 1719–August 1731; p. [110]: blank; p. [111]: TABLE TO THE "MISCELLANIES" (verso blank); p. 113: NOTE ON THE TABLE; p. [124]: [photocopy] | Fig.2. Photograph of the first page of the Table to the "Miscellanies," showing Edwards' | headnotes, his alphabetic scheme, and the marks left by later transcribers and editors. | Courtesy of the Beinecke Rare Book and Manuscript Library, Yale University.; p. 125: TABLE; p. [151]: THE "MISCELLANIES," | ENTRY NOS. a–z, aa–zz, 1–500 (verso blank); p. 153: NOTE ON THE TEXT OF THE "MISCELLANIES" (p. 153: Table 3. "Miscellanies" Entries By Books; p. 156: Table 4. Chronological Order of "Miscellanies" *a*–500); p. [161]: blank; p. [162]: [photocopy] | Fig.3. Photograph of the first page of the "Miscellanies" text, showing entry nos. a–l. | Courtesy of the Beinecke Rare Book and Manuscript Library, Yale University.; p. 163: THE "MISCELLANIES," ENTRY NOS. a-z, aa-zz, | 1-500; p. [542]: blank; p. [543]: APPENDIXES (verso blank); p. 545: APPENDIX A | PREVIOUS PUBLICATIONS OF THE "MISCELLANIES"; p. 558: APPENDIX B | WATERMARKS IN EDWARDS' EARLY MANUSCRIPTS (pp. [560-561]: Figs. 4-11); p. 562: APPENDIX C | THE EVOLUTION OF EDWARDS' | EARLY HANDWRITING (pp. [563-565]: Figs. 12-23); p. 566: APPENDIX D | VARIETIES OF INK TEXTURES IN EDWARDS' | EARLY MANUSCRIPTS; p. [568]: Figs. 24-29; p. 569: GENERAL INDEX; p. [580]: blank; p. 581: INDEX OF BIBLICAL PASSAGES; p. 589: INDEX OF "MISCELLANIES" NUMBERS.

ISBN 0300060599 OCLC 31751876

Yale Divinity School

528 • JONATHAN EDWARDS | Sermons and | Discourses | 1723-1729 | EDITED BY | KENNETH P. MINKEMA | EXECUTIVE EDITOR, *The Works of Jonathan Edwards* | YALE UNIVERSITY | New Haven and London | YALE UNIVERSITY PRESS, 1997

23.4 x 15.5 cm.; xiv, 575, [1] p.

Contents: p. [i]: THE WORKS OF JONATHAN EDWARDS | VOLUME 14 | *Harry S. Stout, General Editor*; p. [ii], frontispiece: [photocopy] | Prospect of Yale College, engraving by T. Johnston, | 1745, showing the original building of 1718. | Courtesy of Manuscripts and Archives, Sterling | Memorial Library, Yale University. | [photocopy] | The grave of Solomon Stoddard, Northampton, | Massachusetts. Photograph by Stan Shearer.; p. [iii]: title; p. [iv]: [6 lines] | *Copyright © 1997 by Yale University.* | [31 lines]; p. [v]: EDITORIAL COMMITTEE FOR | THE WORKS OF JONATHAN EDWARDS; p. [vi]: PREVIOUSLY PUBLISHED; p. vii: CONTENTS; p. ix: LIST OF ILLUSTRATIONS (verso blank); p. xi: NOTE TO THE READER; p. [1]: *SERMONS AND DISCOURSES, 1723–1729* (verso blank); p. 3: PREFACE TO THE PERIOD; p. 47: QUÆSTIO: PECCATOR NON IUSTIFICATUR | CORAM DEO NISI PER IUSTITIAM CHRISTI | FIDE APPREHENSAM | *Introduced by George G. Levesque*; p. [54]: [photocopy] | Page one of M.A. *Quæstio*, 1723. Courtesy of the Beinecke Rare Book and Manuscript | Library, Yale University.; p. 55: QUÆSTIO: PECCATOR NON IUSTIFICATUR | CORAM DEO NISI PER IUSTITIAM CHRISTI | FIDE APPREHENSAM; p. 67: A SPIRITUAL UNDERSTANDING OF DIVINE | THINGS DENIED TO THE UNREGENERATE; p. 97: THE PLEASANTNESS OF RELIGION (p. [100]: [photocopy] | Page one of sermon on Prov. 24:13-14, 1723, showing revision in darker ink and | multiple repreaching symbols at the top. Courtesy of the Beinecke Rare Book and | Manuscript Library, Yale University.); p. 116: LIVING PEACEABLY ONE WITH ANOTHER; p. 134: NOTHING UPON EARTH CAN REPRESENT | THE GLORIES OF HEAVEN; p. 161: ALL GOD'S METHODS ARE MOST REASONABLE; p. 198: WARNINGS OF FUTURE PUNISHMENT DON'T | SEEM REAL TO THE WICKED; p. 213: IMPENDING JUDGMENTS AVERTED

ONLY BY | REFORMATION; p. 228: TRUE NOBLENESS OF MIND; p. 243: PROFITABLE HEARERS OF THE WORD; p. 278: THE SPIRITUAL BLESSINGS OF THE GOSPEL | REPRESENTED BY A FEAST; p. 297: THE TORMENTS OF HELL ARE EXCEEDING | GREAT; p. 329: NONE ARE SAVED BY THEIR OWN | RIGHTEOUSNESS; p. 357: LIVING UNCONVERTED UNDER AN EMINENT MEANS OF GRACE; p. 371: THE THREEFOLD WORK OF THE HOLY GHOST (p. [376]: [photocopy] | Page one of sermon on John 16:8, 1729. Courtesy of the Beinecke Rare Book and | Manuscript Library, Yale University.); p. 337: THE SACRIFICE OF CHRIST ACCEPTABLE; p. 458: GLORYING IN THE SAVIOR; p. 471: GOD'S ALL-SUFFICIENCY FOR THE SUPPLY OF | OUR WANTS; p. 484: SIN AND WICKEDNESS BRING CALAMITY AND | MISERY ON A PEOPLE; p. 506: THE DAY OF JUDGMENT; p. [542]: blank; p. 543: APPENDIX: DATED BATCHES OF SERMONS | 1723-1729 | DATING BY THOMAS A. SCHAFER; p. 551: GENERAL INDEX; p. [566]: blank; p. 567: INDEX OF BIBLICAL PASSAGES; p. [576]: blank.

ISBN 0300068417 OCLC 35033600

Yale Divinity School

529 • JONATHAN EDWARDS | Notes on Scripture | EDITED BY | STEPHEN J. STEIN | CHANCELLORS' PROFESSOR OF RELIGIOUS STUDIES | INDIANA UNIVERSITY | New Haven and London | YALE UNIVERSITY PRESS, 1998

23.4 x 15.5 cm.; xiv, 674 p.

Contents: p. [i]: THE WORKS OF JONATHAN EDWARDS | VOLUME 15 | *Harry S. Stout, General Editor*; p. [ii], frontispiece: [photocopy] | "A Map Shewing the General Dispersion and Settling of the Nations," from Arthur | Bedford, *The Scripture Chronology Demonstrated by Astronomical Calculations* (London, 1730), | Appendix; p. [iii]: title; p. [iv]: [5 lines] | *Copyright © 1998 by Yale University* | [31 lines]; p. [v]: EDITORIAL COMMITTEE FOR | THE WORKS OF JONATHAN EDWARDS; p. [vi]: PREVIOUSLY PUBLISHED; p. vii: CONTENTS; p. viii: ILLUSTRATIONS; p. ix: TABLES (verso blank); p. xi: NOTE TO THE READER; p. 1: EDITOR'S INTRODUCTION (pp. [16-17]: [photocopy] | Fig. 1. Pages 2-3 in No. 416, with heading "The Pentateuch written by Moses." Courtesy | of Beinecke Rare Book and Manuscript Library, Yale University.; p. [37]: [photocopy] | Fig. 2. The oilcloth cover of Book 1, showing the coat of arms, lion, scroll, etc. Courtesy | of Beinecke Rare Book and Manuscript Library, Yale University.; p. 39: [photocopy] | Fig. 3. The first page of "Notes on Scripture," Book 1, showing entry Nos. 1-11. | Courtesy of Beinecke Rare Book and Manuscript Library, Yale University.); p. [47]: *NOTES ON SCRIPTURE* (verso blank); p. [614]: blank; p. 615: GENERAL INDEX; p. [638]: blank; p. 639: INDEX OF BIBLICAL PASSAGES; p. [668]: blank; p. 669: INDEX OF "NOTES ON SCRIPTURE" ENTRIES.

ISBN 0300071981 OCLC 37155911

Yale Divinity School

530 • JONATHAN EDWARDS | Letters and Personal | Writings | EDITED BY | GEORGE S. CLAGHORN | PROFESSOR OF PHILOSOPHY | WEST CHESTER UNIVERSITY | New Haven and London | YALE UNIVERSITY PRESS, 1998

23.4 x 15.5 cm.; xxiv, 854 p.

Contents: p. [i]: THE WORKS OF JONATHAN EDWARDS | VOLUME 16 | *Harry S. Stout, General Editor*; p. [ii], frontispiece: [photocopy] | Jonathan Edwards' letter to Joseph Bellamy, April 4, 1748 (Letter No. 84), Beinecke Rare | Book and Manuscript Library, Yale University. A typical though brief example of | Edwards' correspondence, this letter discusses a business matter, the death of one of | Edwards' daughters, the Concert of Prayer, and his effort to write a biography of David | Brainerd.; p. [iii]: title; p. [iv]: [6 lines] | *Copyright © 1998 by Yale University* | [34 lines]; p. [v]: EDITORIAL COMMITTEE FOR | THE WORKS OF JONATHAN EDWARDS; p. [vi]: PREVIOUSLY PUBLISHED; p. vii: CONTENTS; p. xv: ILLUSTRATIONS; p. xvi: ABBREVIATIONS; p. [xx]: blank; p. xxi: NOTE TO THE READER; p. [1]: LETTERS (verso blank); p. 3: INTRODUCTION; p. [28]: blank; (p. 69: [photocopy] | [to the right] *Isaac Watts*, anonymous | undated, Dr. Williams' | Library, London; p. 74: [photocopy] | [to the right] *Samuel Hopkins* | anonymous, undated, | Massachusetts Historical | Society; p. 104: [photocopy] | [to the right] *Mrs. Jonathan Edwards* | (Sarah Pierpont | Edwards), by Joseph | Badger, undated, Yale | University Art Gallery, | bequest of Eugene | Phelps Edwards; p. 214: [photocopy] | [to the right] *Mrs. Aaron Burr* (Esther | Edwards Burr), | anonymous, undated, | Yale University Art | Gallery, bequest of | Oliver Burr Jennings; p. 248: [photocopy] | [to the right] *John Erskine*, by Henry |

Raeburn, undated, | National Portrait Gallery | of Scotland; p. 268: [photocopy] | [to the right] *Thomas Foxcroft* | anonymous, undated, | Harvard University | Portrait Collection, | bequest of Henry H. | Edes to the University, | 1935; p. 277: [photocopy] | [to the right] *Samuel Davies*, by James | Massalon, 1874, the Art | Museum, Princeton | University; p. 391: [photocopy] | [to the right] *William Hogg*, by Alan | Ramsay, undated, | private collection of Mr. | J. G. B. Gibson, Duns, | Berwickshire, Scotland; p. 395: [photocopy] | [to the right] *Thomas Hubbard*, by John | Singleton Copley, c. | 1767, Harvard | University Portrait | Collection, gift of Mrs. | Sarah Appleton to | Harvard College; p. 396: [photocopy] | [to the right] *Etaw Oh Koam* (Nicholas) | by John Verelst, 1710, | Archives Nationale du | Canada, Ottawa; p. 397: [photocopy] | [to the right]: *Hendrick* (Tee Yee Neen | Ho Ga Row), anonymous | engraving, 1755, John | Carter Brown Library, | Brown University; p. 401: [photocopy] | [to the right] *Sir William Johnson*, by | John Wollaston, c. 1750, | Albany Institute of | History & Art, gift of | Laura Munsell | Tremaine; p. 450: [photocopy] | [to the right] *Jasper Mauduit*, by | Samuel Webster, 1758, | Dr. Williams' Library | London; p. 478: [photocopy] | [to the right] *Aaron Burr Sr.*, by | Edward Ludlow | Mooney, undated, the | Art Museum, Princeton | University; p. 611: [photocopy] | [to the right] *Jonathan Belcher*, | anonymous mezzotint | undated, Department of | Rare Books and Special | Collections, Princeton | University Libraries; p. 727: [photocopy] | [to the right] *Richard Stockton, "The | Signer,"* attributed to | John Wollaston, | undated, the Art | Museum, Princeton | University, bequest of | Mrs. Alexander T. | McGill); p. [739]: PERSONAL WRITINGS (verso blank); p. 741: INTRODUCTION; p. 753: RESOLUTIONS; p. 759: DIARY; p. 789: ON SARAH PIERPONT; p. 790: PERSONAL NARRATIVE; p. [805]: APPENDIXES (verso blank); p. 807: APPENDIX A | BIOGRAPHICAL GLOSSARY; p. 831: APPENDIX B | FRAGMENTARY LETTERS BY JONATHAN EDWARDS; p. 832: APPENDIX C | LETTERS RECEIVED BY JONATHAN EDWARDS; p. 837: GENERAL INDEX; p. 851: INDEX OF BIBLICAL PASSAGES.

ISBN 0300072953 OCLC 37254389

Yale Divinity School

531 • JONATHAN EDWARDS | Sermons and | Discourses | 1730–1733 | EDITED BY | MARK VALERI | ERNEST TRICE THOMPSON PROFESSOR OF CHURCH HISTORY | UNION THEOLOGICAL SEMINARY IN VIRGINIA | New Haven and London | YALE UNIVERSITY PRESS, 1999

23.4 x 15.5 cm.; xii, 480 p.

Contents: p. [i]: THE WORKS OF JONATHAN EDWARDS | VOLUME 17 | *Harry S. Stout, General Editor*; p. [ii], frontispiece: [photocopy] | A sketch of the Edwards parsonage in Northampton, Massachusetts, from Edwin M. Bacon, | *Literary Pilgrimages in New England to the Homes of Famous Makers of American Literature* (1902); p. [iii]: title; p. [iv]: [5 lines] | *Copyright © 1999 by Yale University* | [30 lines]; p. [v]: EDITORIAL COMMITTEE FOR | THE WORKS OF JONATHAN EDWARDS; p. [vi]: PREVIOUSLY PUBLISHED; p. vii: CONTENTS; p. [viii]: ILLUSTRATIONS; p. ix: NOTE TO THE READER; p. [1]: *SERMONS AND DISCOURSES, 1730–1733* (verso blank); p. 3: PREFACE TO THE PERIOD (p. [30]: [photocopy: interior of the Hingham, Massachusetts, "Old Ship" church (1661) | [photocopy: sketch of the first meetinghouse in West Springfield, Massachusetts (1704)]; p. [33]: [photocopy] | Page one from the *Boston Gazette* of February 22, 1731. The left column prints the list of | delegates to the Massachusetts assembly for that year (with the name of Northampton's | deputy, Ebenezer Wright, appearing near the upper right) and the right column the text of | a speech by Gov. Jonathan Belcher berating the assembly for its uncooperativeness.; p. 45: PRACTICAL ATHEISM; p. 57: THE PURE IN HEART BLESSED; p. 87: THE DANGERS OF DECLINE; p. 101: ENVIOUS MEN; p. 121: HONEY FROM THE ROCK; p. 139: GOD MAKES MEN SENSIBLE OF THEIR MISERY | BEFORE HE REVEALS HIS MERCY AND LOVE; p. 173: STUPID AS STONES; p. 184: BORN AGAIN; p. 196: GOD GLORIFIED IN MAN'S DEPENDENCE (p. 197: [photocopy] | First page of the manuscript of *God Glorified in Man's Dependence*. Courtesy of the Beinecke Rare | Book and Manuscript Library, Yale University.; p. [198]: [photocopy] | Title page of *A Divine and Supernatural Light* (see pp. 405-26); p. 217: THE PERPETUITY AND CHANGE | OF THE SABBATH; p. 251: SERVING GOD IN HEAVEN; p. 273: CHRISTIANS A CHOSEN GENERATION; p. 329: EAST OF EDEN; p. 349: THE STATE OF PUBLIC AFFAIRS; p. 369: THE DUTY OF CHARITY TO THE POOR; p. 405: A DIVINE AND SUPERNATURAL LIGHT; p. 427: THE TRUE CHRISTIAN'S LIFE A JOURNEY | TOWARDS HEAVEN; p. 447: APPENDIX: DATED BATCHES OF SERMONS, | 1730–1732, AND DATED SERMONS, | JANUARY–DECEMBER 1733 | DATING BY THOMAS A. SCHAFER; p. 459: GENERAL INDEX; p. 471: INDEX OF BIBLICAL PASSAGES.

ISBN 0300078404 OCLC 40403638

Yale Divinity School

532 • JONATHAN EDWARDS | The "Miscellanies" | (Entry Nos. 501-832) | EDITED BY | AVA CHAMBERLAIN | WRIGHT STATE UNIVERSITY | New Haven and London | YALE UNIVERSITY PRESS, 2000

23.4 x 15.5 cm.; xi, [1], 578 p.

Contents: p. [i]: THE WORKS OF JONATHAN EDWARDS | VOLUME 18 | *Harry S. Stout, General Editor*; p. [ii], frontispiece: [photocopy] | Plate from Francis Quarles, *Emblemes* (London, 1635). Courtesy Beinecke Rare | Book and Manuscript Library, Yale University.; p. [iii]: title; p. [iv]: [5 lines] | *Copyright © 2000 by Yale University.* | [26 lines]; p. [v]: EDITORIAL COMMITTEE FOR | THE WORKS OF JONATHAN EDWARDS; p. [vi]: PREVIOUSLY PUBLISHED; p. vii: CONTENTS; p. [viii]: ILLUSTRATIONS; p. ix: NOTE TO THE READER; p. [xii]: blank; p. 1: EDITOR'S INTRODUCTION (p. [15]: [photocopy] | A page from "Miscellanies," Book 1, featuring entry No. 669, "Justification." Courtesy | Beinecke Rare Book and Manuscript Library, Yale University.; p. [22]: [photocopy] | The first two pages of entry No. 729, "Perseverance," from "Miscellanies," Book 2. Courtesy Beinecke Rare Book and Manuscript Library, Yale University.); p. [49]: THE "MISCELLANIES" | ENTRY NOS. 501–832 (verso blank); (p. [475]: [photocopy] | The beginning of entry No. 790, "Signs of Godliness," in "Miscellanies," Book 3. Courtesy | Beinecke Rare Book and Manuscript Library, Yale University.); p. [548]: blank; p. 549: GENERAL INDEX; p. 565: INDEX OF BIBLICAL PASSAGES.

ISBN 0300083300 OCLC 42888110

Yale Divinity School

533 • JONATHAN EDWARDS | Sermons and | Discourses, 1734-1738 | EDITED BY | M. X. LESSER | PROFESSOR EMERITUS OF ENGLISH | NORTHEASTERN UNIVERSITY | New Haven and London | YALE UNIVERSITY PRESS, 2001

23.4 x 15.5 cm.; xvi, 849, [1] p.

Contents: p. [i]: THE WORKS OF JONATHAN EDWARDS | VOLUME 19 | *Harry S. Stout, General Editor*; p. [ii], frontispiece: [photocopy] | The title page of *Discourses on Various Important Subjects* (1738), from the copy presented by | Jonathan Edwards to the Yale College Library. The handwritten numbers in the upper right- | hand corner indicate the shelf location in the Yale Library cataloging system of 1742. Courtesy | of the Beinecke Rare Book and Manuscript Library, Yale University.; p. [iii]: title; p. [iv]: [5 lines] | *Copyright © 2001 by Yale University.* | [28 lines]; p. [v]: EDITORIAL COMMITTEE FOR | THE WORKS OF JONATHAN EDWARDS; p. [vi]: PREVIOUSLY PUBLISHED; p. vii: CONTENTS; p. ix: ILLUSTRATIONS (verso blank); p. xi: NOTE TO THE READER; p. [1]: *SERMONS AND DISCOURSES, 1734 – 1738* (verso blank); p. 3: PREFACE TO THE PERIOD (p. [31]: [photocopy] | Seating diagram (main floor) for the new meetinghouse in Northampton, Massachusetts, 1737, with the parishioners arranged according | to social status. Courtesy of the Forbes Library, Northampton.); p. 37: HEEDING THE WORD, AND LOSING IT; p. 58: FAST DAYS IN DEAD TIMES; p. 78: YOUTH AND THE PLEASURES OF PIETY (p. 79: [photocopy] | First page of the manuscript of *Youth and the Pleasures of Piety*, with Edwards' shorthand (top | line) and longhand notations (upper right) about repreachings in Canaan and Scantic, Connecticut; Hadley, Stockbridge, and Westfield, Massachusetts; and York, Maine. Courtesy | of the Beinecke Rare Book and Manuscript Library, Yale University.); p. 91: THE UNREASONABLENESS OF | INDETERMINATION IN RELIGION; p. 106: THE DREADFUL SILENCE OF THE LORD; p. 120: FALSE LIGHT AND TRUE; p. 143: JUSTIFICATION BY FAITH ALONE (p. [146]: [photocopy] | Page 104 (leaf 52 verso) of the manuscript of *Justification by Faith Alone*, with Edwards' | markings (vertical lines and letters in margin) for revision in the printed edition of 1738. | Courtesy of the Beinecke Rare Book and Manuscript Library, Yale University.); p. 243: THE PRECIOUSNESS OF TIME; p. 261: CONVICTION AND THE USES OF ORDER; p. 272: PRESSING INTO THE KINGDOM OF GOD; p. 305: RUTH'S RESOLUTION; p. 321: THE FOLLY OF LOOKING BACK | IN FLEEING OUT OF SODOM; p. 336: THE JUSTICE OF GOD IN THE | DAMNATION OF SINNERS; p. 377: OUR WEAKNESS, CHRIST'S STRENGTH; p. 390: CONTINUING GOD'S PRESENCE; p. 418: BLESSED STRUGGLE; p. 435: THE SWEET HARMONY OF CHRIST; p. 451: GOD AMONGST HIS PEOPLE; p. 473: THE EVERLASTING LOVE OF GOD; p. 491: THE FREE AND VOLUNTARY SUFFERING | AND DEATH OF CHRIST (p. 492: [photocopy] | First page of the manuscript of *The Free and Voluntary Suffering and Death of Christ*, with repeated | symbol on top line that may represent a "decibel rating" or measure of the sermon's | imprecatory value. Courtesy of the Beinecke Rare Book and Manuscript Library, Yale | University.); p. 515: ALL THAT NATURAL MEN DO IS WRONG; p. 537: A CITY ON A HILL; p. 560: THE EXCELLENCY OF CHRIST; p. 595: PERSEVERING FAITH; p. 609:

DEGREES OF GLORY; p. 628: UNDESERVED MERCY; p. 656: PEACEABLE AND FAITHFUL AMID | DIVISION AND STRIFE; p. 680: STRIVING AFTER PERFECTION; p. 704: LIGHT IN A DARK WORLD, A DARK HEART; p. 734: THE MANY MANSIONS; p. 747: INDICTING GOD; p. 768: THE TERMS OF PRAYER; p. [792]: blank; p. 793: APPENDIX A | PREFACE TO *DISCOURSES | ON VARIOUS IMPORTANT SUBJECTS*; p. 799: APPENDIX B | DATED SERMONS, JANUARY 1734 – DECEMBER 1738; p. [812]: blank; p. 813: GENERAL INDEX; p. 835: INDEX OF BIBLICAL PASSAGES; p. [850]: blank.

ISBN 0300087144 OCLC 45446381

Yale Divinity School

534 • JONATHAN EDWARDS | The "Miscellanies" | (Entry Nos. 833-1152) | EDITED BY | AMY PLANTINGA PAUW | HENRY MOBLEY, JR. PROFESSOR OF DOCTRINAL THEOLOGY | LOUISVILLE PRESBYTERIAN SEMINARY | New Haven and London | YALE UNIVERSITY PRESS, 2002

23.4 x 15.5 cm.; xvi, 569, [1] p.

Contents: p. [i]: THE WORKS OF JONATHAN EDWARDS | VOLUME 20 | *Harry S. Stout, General Editor*; p. [ii], frontispiece: [photocopy] | Plate from Francis Quarles' *Emblemes* (1635), illustrating Ps. 137:4. Courtesy of Beinecke Rare | Book and Manuscript Library, Yale University.; p. [iii]: title; p. [iv]: [5 lines] | *Copyright © 2002 by Yale University.* | [38 lines]; p. [v]: EDITORIAL COMMITTEE FOR | THE WORKS OF JONATHAN EDWARDS; p. [vi]: PREVIOUSLY PUBLISHED; p. vii: CONTENTS; p. viii: ILLUSTRATIONS; p. ix: NOTE TO THE READER; p. [xii]: blank; p. 1: EDITOR'S INTRODUCTION; p. [40]: blank; p. [41]: THE "MISCELLANIES," | ENTRY NOS. 833-1152 (verso blank) (p. [223]: [photocopy] | The first page of "Miscellanies" No. 953, in Book 4, quoting Theophilus Gale's *Court of the | Gentiles*. Courtesy of Beinecke Rare Book and Manuscript Library, Yale University.; p. [429]: [photocopy] | The first page of "Miscellanies" No. 1062, in Book 5, "Economy of the Trinity and Covenant of | Redemption." Courtesy of Beinecke Rare Book and Manuscript Library, Yale University.); p. [526]: blank; p. 527: GENERAL INDEX; p. [552]: blank; p. 553: INDEX OF BIBLICAL PASSAGES; p. [570]: blank.

ISBN 0300091745 OCLC 50347945

Yale Divinity School

535 • JONATHAN EDWARDS | Writings on the | Trinity, Grace, | and Faith | EDITED BY | SANG HYUN LEE | KYUNG-CHIK HAN PROFESSOR OF SYSTEMATIC THEOLOGY | PRINCETON THEOLOGICAL SEMINARY | New Haven and London | YALE UNIVERSITY PRESS, 2003

23.4 x 15.5 cm.; xii, 566 p.

Contents: p. [i]: THE WORKS OF JONATHAN EDWARDS | VOLUME 21 | *Harry S. Stout, General Editor*; p. [ii], frontispiece: [photocopy] | John F. Weir, *Rev. Jonathan Edwards*, n.d., an early twentieth-century conceptualization of | Edwards in his study. Courtesy of Yale University Art Gallery.; p. [iii]: title; p. [iv]: [3 lines] | Copyright © 2003 by Yale University. | [29 lines]; p. [v]: EDITORIAL COMMITTEE FOR | THE WORKS OF JONATHAN EDWARDS; p. [vi]: PREVIOUSLY PUBLISHED; p. vii: CONTENTS; p. viii: ILLUSTRATIONS; p. ix: NOTE TO THE READER; p. 1: EDITOR'S INTRODUCTION; p. [107]:WRITINGS ON THE TRINITY, | GRACE, AND FAITH (verso blank); p. 109: DISCOURSE ON THE TRINITY (p. [112]: [photocopy] | First page of the manuscript of "Discourse on the Trinity." Courtesy of Beinecke Rare Book | and Manuscript Library, Yale University.); p. 145: ON THE EQUALITY OF THE PERSONS | OF THE TRINITY;. p. 149: TREATISE ON GRACE; p. 198: EFFICACIOUS GRACE, BOOK I; p. 223: EFFICACIOUS GRACE, BOOK II; p. 239: EFFICACIOUS GRACE, BOOK III (p. 241: [photocopy] | First two pages of "Efficacious Grace," Book III, showing the unusual semi-circular shape of | the manuscript. Courtesy of Beinecke Rare Book and Manuscript Library, Yale University.); p. 291: "CONTROVERSIES" NOTEBOOK: | EFFICACIOUS GRACE; p. 312: "CONTROVERSIES" NOTEBOOK: THE | NATURE OF TRUE VIRTUE; p. 328: "CONTROVERSIES" NOTEBOOK: JUSTIFICATION (p. [355]: [photocopy] | Page 202 of the "Controversies" notebook, which marks the beginning of the essay within the | section on "Justification" entitled, "Question: Wherein Do the Two Covenants Agree as to the | Method of Justification, and the Appointed Qualification for It?" Courtesy of Beinecke Rare | Book and Manuscript Library, Yale University.); p. 414: FAITH (p. [418]: [photocopy] | First page of the manuscript of "Faith," showing emendations by Edwards, Sr., and Edwards, Jr. | Courtesy of Beinecke Rare Book and Manuscript Library, Yale University.); p. 469: SIGNS OF GODLINESS; p. 511: CHRIST'S EXAMPLE; p. 520: DIRECTIONS FOR JUDGING |

OF PERSONS' EXPERIENCES; p. 525: GENERAL INDEX; p. [544]: blank; p. 545: INDEX OF BIBLICAL PASSAGES.

ISBN 0300095058 OCLC 49355920

Yale Divinity School

536 • JONATHAN EDWARDS | Sermons and | Discourses | 1739-1742 | EDITED BY | HARRY S. STOUT | JONATHAN EDWARDS PROFESSOR OF AMERICAN CHRISTIANITY | YALE UNIVERSITY | AND | NATHAN O. HATCH | ANDREW V. TACKES PROFESSOR OF HISTORY | UNIVERSITY OF NOTRE DAME | WITH | KYLE P. FARLEY | UNIVERSITY OF PENNSYLVANIA | New Haven and London | YALE UNIVERSITY PRESS, 2003

23.4 x 15.5 cm.; xiv, 582 p.

Contents: p. [i]: THE WORKS OF JONATHAN EDWARDS | VOLUME 22 | *Harry S. Stout, General Editor*; p. [ii], frontispiece: [photocopy] | *George Whitefield*, artist unknown, n.d. Courtesy of the Billy Graham Center Museum, Wheaton | College, Wheaton, Illinois.; p. [iii]: title; p. [iv]: [3 lines] | *Copyright © 2003 by Yale University*. | [31 lines]; p. [v]: EDITORIAL COMMITTEE FOR | THE WORKS OF JONATHAN EDWARDS; p. [vi]: PREVIOUSLY PUBLISHED; p. vii: CONTENTS; p. ix: ILLUSTRATIONS (verso blank); p. xi: NOTE TO THE READER; p. [xv]: *SERMONS AND DISCOURSES, 1739-1742* (verso blank); p. 3: PREFACE TO THE PERIOD (p/ [36]: [photocopy] | Pages 2 and 3 of Edwards' later four-page outline for *Sinners in the Hands of an Angry God*, 1741. Courtesy of the Beinecke Rare Book and Manuscript | Library, Yale University); p. 48: CHRIST THE SPIRITUAL SUN; p. 64: THE MEANS AND ENDS OF EXCOMMUNICATION; p. 80: THE IMPORTANCE AND ADVANTAGE | OF A THOROUGH KNOWLEDGE | OF DIVINE TRUTH; p. 103: GOD'S GRACE CARRIED ON IN OTHER PLACES; p. 111: MERCY AND NOT SACRIFICE; p. 136: ZEAL AN ESSENTIAL VIRTUE OF A CHRISTIAN; p. 156: THE DANGER OF CORRUPT COMMUNICATION | AMONG YOUNG PEOPLE; p. 167: CHILDREN OUGHT TO LOVE THE LORD JESUS | CHRIST ABOVE ALL; p. 181: THE SUBJECTS OF A FIRST WORK OF GRACE | MAY NEED A NEW CONVERSION; p. 203: GOSPEL MINISTERS A SAVOR | OF LIFE OR OF DEATH; p. 211: PRAYING FOR THE SPIRIT; p. 224: THEY SING A NEW SONG; p. 245: BRINGING THE ARK TO ZION A SECOND TIME; p. 262: SINNERS IN ZION (p. 266: [photocopy] | First page of the manuscript of *Sinners in Zion*, 1740. Courtesy of the Beinecke Rare Book and | Manuscript Library, Yale University.); p. 285: SEEKING AFTER CHRIST; p. 298: LIKE RAIN UPON MOWN GRASS; p. 319: YOUTH IS LIKE A FLOWER THAT IS CUT DOWN (p. 323: [photocopy] | First page of the manuscript of *Youth Is Like a Flower That Is Cut Down*, 1741, showing Edwards' | later notations for the funeral of his daughter Jerusha. Courtesy of the Beinecke Rare Book | and Manuscript Library, Yale University.); p. 339: GOD'S CARE FOR HIS SERVANTS | IN TIME OF PUBLIC COMMOTIONS; p. 365: IMPORTUNATE PRAYER FOR | MILLENNIAL GLORY; p. 378: MARY'S REMARKABLE ACT; p. 400: SINNERS IN THE HANDS OF AN ANGRY GOD (p. 419: [photocopy] | First page of the manuscript sermon on Deut. 32:35 (c), 1741, later published as *Sinners in the* | *Hands of an Angry God*. Courtesy of the Beinecke Rare Book and Manuscript Library, Yale | University.); p. 436: THE BLOWING OF THE GREAT TRUMPET; p. 448: THE IMPORTANCE OF REVIVAL | AMONG HEADS OF FAMILIES; p. 155: AGED MEN AND WOMEN | JOYFULLY RECEIVING CHRIST; p. 461: THE SORROWS OF THE BEREAVED | SPREAD BEFORE JESUS; p. 476: SEASONS OF INGATHERING; p. 490: THE CURSE OF MEROZ; p. 509: RENEWING OUR COVENANT WITH GOD; p. 519: KEEPING THE PRESENCE OF GOD; p. [536]: blank; p. 537: APPENDIX: | DATED SERMONS, | JANUARY 1739-DECEMBER 1742; p. 553: GENERAL INDEX; p. 573: INDEX OF BIBLICAL PASSAGES.

ISBN 0300095724 OCLC 49853232

Yale Divinity School

INDEX of TITLES

Numerals refer to numbered items, those in parentheses to volumes in collected editions.

Abstract from a Celebrated Sermon 116
Account of Abigail Hutchinson 416-426
Account of the Conversion of Jonathan Edwards, An *see* Personal Narrative
Account of the Life of the Late Reverend Mr. David Brainerd, An *see* Life of Brainerd
Account of the Life of the Rev. David Brainerd *see* Life of Brainerd
Advice to Young Converts 387-395, 413
Aged Men and Women Joyfully Receiving Christ 536
Aide huazi xuan ji 487
All God's Methods Are Most Reasonable 528
All That Natural Men Do Is Wrong 533
Altogether Lovely 497
Am I Christ's 446
Apocalyptic Writings 519
Apostrophe to Sarah Pierpont *see* On Sarah Pierpont
Articles of Faith and Form of Covenant *see* Resolutions

Basic Writings 489
Beauty of the World 465, 495, 520
Believer's Secret of Christian Love, The 448
Benjamin Franklin and Jonathan Edwards: Selections from Their Writings 475
Blessed Struggle 533
Blowing of the Great Trumpet, The 536
Born Again 530
Bringing the Ark to Zion a Second Time 536

Caracterististicas de un autentico avivamiento 86
Careful and Strict Inquiry into the Modern Prevailing Notion of that Freedom of the Will, A *see* Freedom of the Will
Character of Paul an Example to Christians, The 507(10), 508(2), 510(8), 512(2)
Charity and Its Fruits 443-449, 478, 499, 501
Children Ought to Love the Lord Jesus Christ above All 536
Chinnohan Hananim ui son e puttullin choeindul 126
Christian Cautions 505(4), 506(4), 510(6), 512(2)
Christian Charity *see* Duty of Charity, The
Christian Happiness 524
Christian Knowledge *see* Importance and Advantage
Christian Liberty 524
Christian Love *see* Charity and Its Fruits
Christian Pilgrim, The *see* True Christian's Life, The
Christian Safety 524
Christians a Chosen Generation, a Royal Priesthood, a Holy Nation, a Peculiar People 483, 492, 504, 507(10), 508(2), 510(8)
Christ's Agony 498, 507(10), 508(2), 510(8), 512(2)
Christ's Example 535
Christ's Sacrifice 524
Christ the Great Example of Gospel Ministers 248, 487, 497, 507(10), 508(2), 509(8), 510(8), 512(2)
Christ, the Light of the World 524
Christ the Spiritual Sun 536
Church's Marriage to Her Sons and to Her God, The 142, 381-383, 505(8), 506(8), 509(8), 510(6), 512(2), 513(3)
City on a Hill, A 210
Concerning Efficacious Grace *see* Efficacious Grace
Concerning the End for which God Created the World *see* End of Creation
Continuing God's Presence 533
"Controversies" Notebook 535
Conversion and Experience of President Edwards *see* Personal Narrative
Conversion of Abigail Hutchinson *see* Account of Abigail Hutchinson
Conviction and the Uses of Order 533
Copies of the Two Letters 49
Curse of Meroz, The 536
Cyfarwyddiadau ac annogaethau I gredinwyr 160

Danger of Corrupt Communication among Young People, The 536
Dangers of Decline, The 530
Das leben des indianermissionars 228
David Brainerd, His Message for Today 242
Day of Judgment, The 528
Dedication to God 524
Degrees of Glory 533
De leer der erfzonde verdeedigd 287, 288
Devotions of Jonathan Edwards 485
De wijsheid van God 384
Die sünder in den händen eines zornigen Gottes 117
Directions for Judging of Persons' Experiences 470, 535
Discourse on the Trinity 535
Discourses on Various Important Subjects 65, 309, 310, 507(6), 508(6), 509(6), 510(5), 512(1), 533
Dishonesty *see* Sin of Theft and of Injustice, The
Dissertation concerning the End for which God Created the World *see* End of Creation

Dissertation on God's Last End in Creation *see* End of Creation
Distinguishing Marks of a Work of the Spirit of God 42, 66-86, 482, 491, 493, 505(8), 506(8), 510(3), 512(2), 513(1), 518
Divine and Supernatural Light, A 4-6, 381-383, 474, 476, 478, 480, 486, 487, 489, 495, 499, 505(8), 506(8), 509(8), 510(6), 512(2), 513(4), 530
Divine Sovereignty *see* God's Sovereignty in the Salvation of Men
Doctrine of Original Sin *see* Original Sin
Dreadful Silence of the Lord, The 533
Dull y farn ddiweddaf 339
Duty and Interest of a People *see* Faithful Narrative
Duty of Charity to the Poor, The 380, 466, 494, 505(5), 506(5), 512(2), 530
Duty of Hearkening to God's Voice, The 524
Duty of Self-Examination, The 524
Dying to Gain 524

East of Eden 530
Ecclesiastical Writings 526
Edwards on Revivals 36, 37
Een bepaald en nauwkeurig onderzoek 263
Efficacious Grace 509(5), 513(2), 535
End of Creation 311-313, 372-376, 476, 478, 489, 505(1), 506(1), 509(6), 510(3), 512(1), 513(2), 522
End of the Wicked Contemplated by the Righteous, The 483, 492, 496, 505(4), 506(4), 510(6), 513(4)
Envious Men 530
Essay on the Nature of True Virtue *see* True Virtue
Eternal Damnation and Punishment of Sinners 471
Eternity of Hell Torments, The 5, 371, 377-379, 381-383, 496, 505(7), 505(7), 509(7), 510(6), 512(2), 513(4)
Ethical Writings 522
Everlasting Love of God, The 533
Excellency of Christ, The 65, 309, 310, 365-370, 382, 468, 476, 478, 486, 487, 497, 499, 505(6), 506(6), 509(7), 510(5), 512(1), 513(4), 533
Excellency of Jesus Christ, The *see* Excellency of Christ, The
Experience That Counts!, The 182, 183
Experiencing God 493
Expostulatory Letter, An 50
Extract from Mr. Edwards's Narrative *see* Faithful Narrative
Extract from the Private Writings *see* Resolutions
Extract of a Part of the Reverend Mr. Jonathan Edwards's Letter 53
Extract of the Life, An *see* Life of Brainerd

Faithful Narrative of the Surprising Work of God, A 7-45, 138, 475, 476, 478, 480, 481, 489, 491, 495, 502, 505(3), 506(3), 509(3), 510(4), 512(1), 513(3), 518
False Light and True 533
Farewell Sermon, A 254, 255, 304, 306, 309, 310, 318, 474, 476, 486, 489, 499, 500, 505(7), 506(7), 509(1), 510(1), 512(1), 513(1)
Fast Days in Dead Times 533
Fearfulness Which Will Hereafter Surprise Sinners in Zion, The *see* Sinners in Zion
Final Judgment, The 496, 505(4), 506(4), 510(6), 512(2), 513(4)
Five Discourses *see* Discourses on Various Important Subjects
Fleeing out of Sodom *see* Folly of Looking Back, The
Flying Spider, The 452-454, 475, 476, 478, 489, 520
Folly of Looking Back in Fleeing out of Sodom, The 371, 381-383, 462, 498, 505(7), 506(7), 509(7), 510(6), 512(2)613(4), 533
Free and Voluntary Suffering and Death of Christ, The 533
Freedom of the Will 260-281, 476, 478, 486, 487, 489, 496, 500, 505(1), 506(1), 509(5), 510(2), 512(1), 513(2), 515
From Seven Reverend Pastors 47
Funeral Sermon for David Brainerd *see* True Saints
Future Punishment of the Wicked, The 126, 371, 381-383, 469, 496, 505(7), 506(7), 509(7), 510(6), 512(2), 513(4), 528

Geloofwaardig historisch bericht 14
Geschiedenis van het werk der verlossing 322
Glaubwüridge Nachricht 13
Glorious Grace 524
Glorying in the Savior 528
God Amongst His People 533
God at Work? 494
God Glorified in the Work of Redemption 1-3, 309, 310, 474, 476, 478, 483, 486, 487, 489, 492, 493, 499, 505(6), 506(6), 509(7), 510(7), 512(2), 513(4), 530
God Makes Men Sensible of Their Misery 483, 492, 498, 507(10), 508(2), 510(8), 512(2), 530
God's All-Sufficiency for the Supply of Our Wants 428
God's Awful Judgment *see* Strong Rod Broken and Withered, A
God's Care for His Servants in Time of Public Commotions 536
God's Excellencies 524
God's Grace Carried on in Other Places 536
God's Passion for His Glory 376
God's Sovereignty in the Salvation of Men 469, 481,

482, 500, 505(6), 506(6), 507(10), 508(2), 510(8), 512(2)
God the Best Portion of the Christian 469, 487, 497, 505(6), 506(6), 509(8), 510(6), 512(2), 513(4)
Gospel Ministers a Savor of Life or of Death 536
Great Awakening, The 518
Great Care Necessary, Lest We Live in Some Way of Sin 380, 509(8), 513(4)
Great Christian Doctrine of Original Sin Defended, The *see* Original Sin
Great Concern of a Watchman for Souls, The 140, 510(7)
Great Guilt No Obstacle to the Pardon of the Returning Sinner 380, 435, 436, 437, 469, 483, 504, 505(6), 506(6), 510(6), 512(2), 513(4)
Great Guilt of Those Who Attend on the Ordinances of Divine Worship, yet Allow Themselves in Any Known Wickedness, The 380, 505(4), 506(4), 510(6), 512(2), 513(4)
Growth in Grace 395

Hanes gwaith y prynedigaeth 338, 351
Hatak yoshuba uhleha hut chihowa 104
Heaven Is a World of Love 499
Heeding the Word, and Losing It 533
Het leeven van den weleerwaarden 302
His Redeeming Love 501
Histoire de l'œuvre de la rédemption 353
Historiesch verhaal van het godvruchtig leven 200
History of Redemption 321-355, 478, 495, 505(5), 506(5), 510(3), 513(1), 523
History of the Work of Redemption, A *see* History of Redemption
Honey from the Rock 209
Hope and Comfort Usually Follow Genuine Humiliation and Repentance 507(10), 508(2), 510(8), 512(2)
Hopkins's Memoirs *see* Life of Edwards
Humble Attempt to Promote God's Explicit Agreement, An 188-196, 505(2), 506(2), 509(3), 510(3), 512(2), 513(3), 519
Humble Inquiry into the Rules of God, An 246, 247, 478, 495, 505(7), 506(7), 509(1), 510(4), 512(1), 513(1), 526
Hypocrites Deficient in the Duty of Prayer 371, 381-383, 463, 504, 505(7), 506(7), 509(8), 510(6), 512(2), 513(4)

Images and Shadows of Divine Things 477
Impending Judgments Averted Only by Reformation 528
Importance and Advantage of a Thorough Knowledge of Divine Truth, The 380, 432-434, 483, 492, 505(5), 506(5), 509(8), 512(2), 513(4), 536
Importance of a Future State, The 524
Importance of Revival among Heads of Families, The 536
Importunate Prayer for Millennial Glory 536
Indian-missionären David Brainerds lefwerne 233
Indicting God 533
Inquiry into the Modern Prevailing Notions *see* Freedom of the Will
Inquiry into the Prevailing Notions *see* Freedom of the Will

Jesus Christ Gloriously Exalted 301, 303, 431, 481, 482, 505(5), 506(5), 512(2)
Jesus Christ the Same Yesterday, To-day, and Forever 497, 507(10), 508(2), 510(8), 512(2)
Jonathan Edwards 120
Jonathan Edwards at Portsmouth, New Hampshire 62
Jonathan Edwards on Evangelism 480
Jonathan Edwards on Knowing Christ 492
Jonathan Edwards on Revival 491
Jonathan Edwards Reader, A 495
Jonathan Edwards's Last Will 450
Joseph's Great Temptation and Gracious Deliverance 299, 301, 303, 304, 485, 505(5), 506(5), 509(6), 510(7), 512(2), 513(4)
Justice of God Displayed in the Endless Punishment of the Wicked, The *see* Justice of God in the Damnation of Sinners, The
Justice of God in the Damnation of Sinners, The 65, 309, 310, 314-320, 469, 476, 478, 483, 492, 496, 505(6), 506(6), 509(7), 510(5), 512(1), 513(4), 533
Justification by Faith Alone 65, 309, 310, 429, 430, 478, 486, 505(6), 506(6), 509(7), 510(5), 512(1), 513(4), 533

Keeping the Presence of God 536
Kitab ta'rikh al-fida' 354

Letter from President Edwards 55
Letter from Rev. Jonathan Edwards 54
Letter of Jonathan Edwards 60
Letters and Personal Writings 530
Letters Written by the Celebrated President Edwards 59
Letter to the Author of the Pamphlet, A 46
Life and Character of the Late Reverend Mr. Jonathan Edwards, The *see* Life of Edwards
Life and Experience of the Rev. Jonathan Edwards, The *see* Life of Edwards
Life and Journal of the Rev. David Brainerd *see* Life of Brainerd
Life, Experience and Character of the Late Reverend Mr. Jonathan Edwards, The *see* Life of Edwards
Life of Brainerd 25, 30, 198-245,476, 505(3), 506(3),

509(3), 510(10), 512(2), 513(1), 521
Life of David Brainerd, The *see* Life of Brainerd
Life of Edwards 299-307, 505(1), 506(1)
Life of President Edwards, The *see* Life of Edwards
Life of the Late Reverend, Learned and Pious Mr. Jonathan Edwards, The *see* Life of Edwards
Life, Remains, and Letters *see* Life of Brainerd
Life Through Christ Alone 524
Light in a Dark World, a Dark Heart 533
Like Rain upon Mown Grass 536
Living Peaceably One with Another 528
Living to Christ 524
Living Unconverted under an Eminent Means of Grace 528
Lost Convictions 441, 442
L'union dans la prière 194

Manner in which the Salvation of the Soul Is to Be Sought, The 371, 381-383, 438, 439, 469, 498, 505(7), 506(7), 510(6), 512(2), 513(4)
Man's Natural Blindness 299, 300, 303, 304, 505(2), 506(2), 510(7), 512(2), 513(4)
Manuscripts of Jonathan Edwards, The 61
Many Mansions, The 474, 533
Marks of a Work of the True Spirit, The *see* Distinguishing Marks
Mary's Remarkable Act 536
Maw'izah fi ghadab Allah ala alkhutah 106
Means and Ends of Excommunication, The *see* Nature and End of Excommunication, The
Means of Revival *see* Some Thoughts
Memoirs of the Rev. David Brainerd *see* Life of Brainerd
Memoirs of the Late Rev. Jonathan Edwards *see* Life of Edwards, The
Men in a State of Nature God's Enemies *see* Men Naturally God's Enemies
Men Naturally God's Enemies 299, 300, 303, 304, 469, 505(5), 506(5), 509(7), 510(7), 512(2), 513(4)
Mercy and Not Sacrifice 536
Millennium, The 355
Miscellaneous Observations 507(10), 508(2), 509(5), 510(8), 512(2), 513(2), 514(6)
Miscellaneous Observations concerning the Divine Decrees 509(5), 513(2)
Miscellaneous Observations on Important Theological Subjects 385, 505(8), 506(8), 510(7), 512(2), 513(1), 514(6)
Miscellaneous Observations on Important Doctrines *see* Remarks on Important Theological Controversies
Miscellaneous Remarks on Important Doctrines *see* Remarks on Important Theological Controversies
Miscellaneous Theological Observations *see* Miscellaneous Observations on Important Theological Subjects
"Miscellanies," The a-500, The 527
"Miscellanies," The 501-832, The 532
"Miscellanies," The 833-1152, The 534
Misrepresentations Corrected 256, 505(7), 506(7), 509(1), 510(4), 512(1), 513(1), 526
Mittheilungen aus dem innern leben 363
Mr. Edwards's Letter to his Scots Correspondent 52
Most High, a Prayer-Hearing God, The 380, 467, 505(6), 506(6), 509(8), 510(6), 512(2), 513(4)

Nakedness of Job, The 524
Narrative, The *see* Faithful Narrative
"Narrative" of Jonathan Edwards see Personal Narrative
Narrative of Many Surprising Conversions, A *see* Faithful Narrative
Narrative of the Late Work of God, A *see* Faithful Narrative
Narrative of the Revival, A *see* Faithful Narrative
Natural Men in a Dreadful Condition 481, 482, 496, 507(10), 508(2), 510(8), 512(2)
Natural Philosophy 520
Nature and End of Excommunication, The 380, 505(6), 506(6), 509(8), 510(6), 512(2), 536
Nature of True Virtue, The *see* True Virtue
Necessity of Self-Examination, The *see* Christian Cautions
New-England. Continuation of the State of Religion 48
Nollaun hoesim iyagi 45
None Are Saved by Their Own Righteousness 528
Notes on Natural Science 306, 475, 478, 489, 510(1)
Notes on Scripture 529
Notes on the Apocalypse 495, 519
Notes on "The Mind" *see* "The Mind"
Nothing upon Earth Can Represent the Glories of Heaven 528

Observations concerning Faith 509(4), 513(2)
Observations concerning the Mysteries of Scripture 509(2), 513(3)
Observations concerning the Scripture Oeconomy of the Trinity 451, 490
Observations upon Particular Passages of Scripture 509(6), 513(3)
On Fulfilling Engagements and Paying Debts *see* Sin of Theft and of Injustice, The
Of Insects *see* Flying Spider, The
On Love to Christ 524
On Sarah Pierpont 495, 530
On Seeking God 524

On the Danger of the Unconverted *see* Sinners in the Hands of an Angry God
On the Equality of the Persons of the Trinity 535
Original Letter of President Edwards 57
Original Sin 292-296, 476, 478, 487, 495, 505(2), 506(2), 509(6), 510(2), 512(1), 513(2), 517
Our Weakness, Christ's Strength 533

Pardon for the Greatest Sinners *see* Great Guilt No Obstacle to the Pardon of the Returning Sinner
Peaceable and Faithful amid Division and Strife 533
Peacaich ann an lamhaibh dhe 'n a fheirg 105, 108
Peace which Christ Gives His True Followers, The 371, 381-383, 460, 469, 476, 486, 487, 493, 504, 505(7), 506(7), 509(8), 510(6), 512(2), 513(4)
Pecadores en manos de un Dios airado 127
Perpetuity and Change of the Sabbath, The 371, 381-383, 456, 505(7), 506(7), 509(8), 510(6), 512(2), 513(4), 530
Persevering Faith 533
Personal Narrative 34, 35, 86, 358-364, 475, 476, 487, 489, 490, 495, 505(1), 506(1), 509(1), 510(1), 512(1), 513(1), 530
Philosophy of Jonathan Edwards, The 479
Pleasantness of Religion, The 528
Portion of the Righteous, The 504, 507(10), 508(2), 510(8), 512(2)
Portion of the Wicked, The 496, 507(10), 508(2), 510(8), 512(2)
Posthumous Works of President Edwards, in Two Volumes, The 508
Poverty of Spirit 524
Practical Atheism 531
Practical Sermons Never before Published 380, 510(6)
Praise, One of the Chief Employments of Heaven 497, 507(10), 508(2), 510(8), 512(2)
Praying for the Spirit 536
Preciousness of Time and the Importance of Redeeming It, The 469, 498, 505(5), 506(5), 510(6), 512(2), 533
Pressing into the Kingdom of God 65, 309, 310, 469, 478, 483, 492, 498, 505(6), 506(6), 510(5), 512(1), 513(3), 533
Procrastination *see* Sin and Folly of Depending on Future Time, The
Profitable Hearers of the Word 528
Punishment of the Wicked Eternal, The *see* Eternity of Hell Torments, The
Pure in Heart Blessed, The 497, 507(10), 508(2), 510(8), 512(2), 530
Puritan Sage: Collected Writings 478

Quæstio: Peccator Non Iustificatur Coram Deo 528
Quelques réflexions 225

Reality of Spiritual Light, The *see* Divine and Supernatural Light, A
Religious Affections 80, 81, 83, 143-186, 476, 478, 480, 484, 486, 487, 489, 493, 495, 505(4), 506(4), 509(4), 510(5), 512(1), 513(3), 516
Remarkable Narratives *see* Faithful Narrative
Remarks on Efficacious Grace *see* Efficacious Grace
Remarks on Important Theological Controversies 386, 505(8), 506(8), 510(7), 512(2), 513(1)
Remarks on the Essays 297, 298 *see* Freedom of the Will
Renewing Our Covenant with God 536
Representative Selections 476
Resolutions 35, 388, 393, 394, 396-413, 475, 476, 478, 487, 489, 495, 501, 531
Resolutions of a Saintly Scholar *see* Resolutions
Result of a Council of Nine Churches, The 56, 309, 310, 505(7), 506(7), 509(1)
Resort and Remedy of Those That Are Bereaved by the Death of an Eminent Minister 87, 507(10), 508(2), 509(8), 510(8), 512(2), 513(3), 536
Revival of Religion in Northampton *see* Faithful Narrative
Revivals of Religion: Their Nature, Defence, and Management 38
Rev. Mr. Edwards to the Rev. Mr. Erskine, The 17
Ruth's Resolution 65, 308-310, 474, 486, 498, 505(6), 506(6), 509(7), 510(5), 512(1), 513(4), 533

Sacrifice of Christ Acceptable, The 528
Safety, Fullness and Sweet Refreshment to Be Found in Christ 483, 492, 497, 507(10), 508(2), 510(8), 512(2)
Salvation of Souls, The 502
Scientific and Philosophical Writings 520
Seasons of Ingathering 536
Seeking After Christ 536
Segni caratteristici di un'opera dello spirito 84
Selected Sermons of Jonathan Edwards 474
Selected Writings of Jonathan Edwards 487
Selections from the Unpublished Writings 470
Select Sermons of President Edwards 469
Select Works of Jonathan Edwards 481-484
Self-Flatteries *see* Vain Self-Flatteries of the Sinner, The
Sermon Preached at Enfield, A *see* Sinners in the Hands of an Angry God
Sermon Preached at Newark *see* True Grace
Sermons and Discourses, 1720-1723 524
Sermons and Discourses, 1723-1729 528
Sermons and Discourses, 1730-1733 531
Sermons and Discourses, 1734-1738 533

Sermons and Discourses, 1739-1742 536
Sermons of Jonathan Edwards, The 166, 499
Sermons on the Following Subjects 371, 381, 383, 505(7), 506(7), 512(2)
Sermons on Various Important Subjects (1765) 299, 301, 303, 304
Sermons on Various Important Subjects (1785) 309, 310
Serving God in Heaven 530
Seventy Resolutions, The *see* Resolutions
Short Sketches of the Life and Service of Jonathan Edwards 111
Signs of Godliness 535
Sin and Folly of Depending on Future Time, The 380, 458, 469, 498, 505(5), 506(5), 509(8), 518(6), 512(2), 513(4)
Sin and Folly of Procrastination *see* Sin and Folly of Depending on Future Time, The
Sin and Wickedness Bring Calamity and Misery on a People 528
Sinners in the Hands of an Angry God 45, 88-128, 257A, 309, 310, 468, 474, 476, 478, 480, 483, 486, 487, 489, 492, 494-496, 499, 500, 505(6), 506(6), 509(7), 510(7), 512(2), 513(4), 536
Sinners in the Hnads of an Angry God and Other Wrtings 500
Sinners in Zion 380, 459, 498, 505(4), 506(4), 509(8), 510(6), 512(2), 513(4), 536
Sin of Theft and of Injustice, The 380, 459, 505(5), 506(5), 509(8), 510(6), 512(2), 513(4)
Six Letters of Jonathan Edwards 63
Sole Consideration That God Is God, The 380, 505(6), 506(6), 510(6), 512(2)
Some Account of the Conversion and Experience *see* Personal Narrative
Some Early Writings 471, 472
Some Remarkable Narratives *see* Faithful Narrative
Some Thoughts concerning the Present Revival 33, 35-38, 129-139, 478, 480, 505(6), 506(6), 509(3), 510(4), 512(1), 513(3), 518
Sondaars in de Hand van 'n toornige God 128
Sorrows of the Bereaved Spread before Jesus *see* Resort and Remedy
Spider letter(s) *see* Flying Spider, The
Spirit of Revival, The *see* Distinguishing Marks
Spiritual Blessings of the Gospel Represented by a Feast, The 528
Spiritual Pride, Its Deceitful Nature 139
Spiritual Understanding of Divine Things Denied to the Unregenerate, A 528
Standing in Grace *see* Treatise on Grace
State of Public Affairs, The 530
Striving After Perfection 538
Strong Rod Broken and Withered, A 197, 381-383, 474, 505(8), 506(8), 509(8), 510(6), 512(2), 513(4)
Stupid as Stones 530
Subjects of a First Work of Grace May Need a New Conversion, The 536
Surprising Work of God, The *see* Faithful Narrative
Sweet Harmony of Christ, The 533

Terms of Prayer, The 533
"The Mind" 306, 475, 476, 478, 479, 488, 489, 495, 510(1), 512(1), 520
Theological Questions of President Edwards 427, 428, 509(6), 512(1), 513(3)
They Sing a New Song 536
Threefold Work of the Holy Ghost, The 528
Thoughts concerning the Present Revival *see* Some Thoughts
Thoughts on the Revival *see* Some Thoughts
Torments of Hell Are Exceeding Great, The 528
Torments of the Wicked in Hell *see* End of the Wicked Contemplated by the Righteous, The
To the Rev. Mr. James Robe 51
Traethawd ar y dyben 375
Traethawd ar y serchiadau crefyddol 174
Treatise concerning Religious Affections, A *see* Religious Affections
Treatise on Grace 470, 478, 480, 490, 503, 535
True Believer, The 504
True Christian's Life a Journey towards Heaven, The 299, 300, 302-304, 461, 505(5), 506(5), 509(7), 510(7), 512(2), 513(4), 530
True Excellency of a Gospel Minister, The *see* True Excellency of a Minister of the Gospel, The
True Excellency of a Minister of the Gospel, The 141, 507(10), 508(2), 509(8), 510(8), 512(2), 513(3)
True Grace Distinguished from the Experience of Devils 24, 257-259, 317, 381-383, 469, 504, 505(8), 506(8), 509(7), 510(6), 512(2), 513(4)
True Love to God 524
True Nobleness of Mind 528
True Religion *see* Life of Brainerd
True Religion Delineated 249-253
True Repentance Required 524
True Saints 187, 226, 381-383, 475, 504, 505(8), 506(8), 509(8), 510(6), 512(2), 513(3)
True Virtue 311-313, 356, 357, 476, 478, 486, 487, 489, 495, 505(2), 506(2), 510(3), 512(1), 513(2), 522
Twenty Sermons on Various Subjects 381-383, 510(6)
Two Dissertations 311-313, 522
Two Remarkable Sermons 468
Typological Writings 525

Unbelievers Contemn the Glory and Excellency of Christ

371, 381-383, 497, 505(7), 506(7), 509(7), 510(6), 512(2), 513(4)
Undeserved Mercy 533
Une œuvre du saint-esprit 82
United and Extraordinary Prayer *see* Humble Attempt
United Prayer for the Spread of the Gospel *see* Humble Attempt
Unpublished Essay of Edwards on the Trinity, An 455, 475, 490, 500, 535
Unpublished Letter by Jonathan Edwards, An 64
Unreasonableness of Indetermination in Religion, The 383, 469, 505(7), 506(7), 509(7), 510(6), 512(2), 513(4), 533

Vain Self-Flatteries of the Sinner, The 380, 464, 498, 505(5), 506(5), 510(6), 512(2), 513(4)
Value of Salvation, The 524
Van den eerwaardigen heere J. Edwards 20
Verhandeling over de godsdienstige 152
Verhandeling over Gods laatste einde 378
Views in Theology 293

Warnings of Future Punishment 528
Warnings of Scripture, The 371, 381-383, 505(7), 506(7), 510(6), 512(2), 513(4)
Warning to Professors, A *see* Great Guilt of Those Who Attend on the Ordinances of Divine Worship

Watchman's Duty and Account, The *see* Great Concern of a Watchman for Souls, The
Way of Holiness, The 524
Way to Heaven, The 440
When the Wicked Shall Have Filled up the Measure of Their Sin 126, 177, 190, 193, 198, 380, 505(6), 506(6), 510(6), 512(2), 513(4)
Wicked Men Inconsistent with Themselves 507(10), 508(2), 510(8), 512(2)
Wicked Men's Slavery to Sin 524
Wicked Men Useful in Their Destruction Only 457, 469, 496, 505(6), 506(6), 509(8), 510(6), 512(2) 513(4)
Wisdom of God Displayed in the Way of Salvation, The 384, 505(5), 506(5), 510(7), 512(2), 513(4)
Work of the Holy Spirit in the Human Heart, The 80, 81, 83
Works of Jonathan Edwards, The (1957-) 515-
Works of President Edwards, in Four Volumes, The (1843) 513
Works of President Edwards, in Eight Volumes, The (1806-1811) 505
Works of President Edwards, in Eight Volumes, The (1808-1809) 509
Works of President Edwards, in Eight Volumes, The (1817) 506
Works of President Edwards, in Six Volumes, The (1847) 514
Works of President Edwards in Ten Volumes, The (1829-1830) 510
Works of President Edwards, in Ten Volumes, The (1847) 507
Works of President Edwards, in Two Volumes, The (1834) 512
World Judged Righteously by Jesus Christ, The *see* Final Judgement, The
Wrath of Almighty God, The 496
Writings on the Trinity, Grace, and Faith 535

Xin yang de shen qing 186

Y dull y dylid ymofyn iechydwriaeth 438
Ymchwiliad gofalus a manwl 279
Youth and the Pleasures of Piety 533
Youth Is Like a Flower that Is Cut Down 536
Yr athrawlaeth fawr gristionogol 296

Zeal an Essential Virtue of a Christian 536
Zongjiao qingcao zhenwei bian 183

INDEX of TRANSLATIONS

Afrikaans

Sondaars in de Hand van 'n toornige God 128
Sinners in the Hands of an Angry God

Arabic

Kitab ta'rikh al-fida' 354
History of Redemption

Maw'izah fi ghadab Allah ala alkhutah 106
Sinners in the Hands of an Angry God

Chinese

Aide huazi xuan ji 487
Selected Writings

Xin yang de shen qing 186
Religious Affections

Zongjiao qingcao zhenwei bian 183
The Experience that Counts

Choctaw

Hatak yoshuba uhleha hut chihowa 104
Sinners in the Hands of an Angry God

Dutch

De leer der erfzonde verdeedigd 287
Original Sin, Part I

De leer der erfzonde verdeedigd 288
Original Sin

De wijsheid van God 384
The Wisdom of God

Een bepaald en nauwkeurig onderzoek 263
Freedom of the Will

Geloofwaardig historisch bericht 14
Faithful Narrative

Geschiedenis van het werk der verlossing 322
History of Redemption

Het leeven van den weleerwaarden 302
Life of Edwards

Historiesch verhaal van het godvruchtig leven 200
Life of Brainerd

Van den eerwaardigen heere J. Edwards 20
[an extract of a revival account]

Verhandeling over de godsdienstige 152
Religious Affections

Verhandeling over Gods laatste einde 378
End of Creation

French

Histoire de l'œuvre de la rédemption 353
History of Redemption

L'union dans la prière 194
Humble Attempt

Quelques réflexions 225
Life of Brainerd (an extract)

Une œuvre du saint-esprit 82
Distinguishing Marks

Gaelic

Peacaich ann an lamhaibh dhe 'n a fheirg 105, 108
Sinners in the Hands of an Angry God

German

Das leben des indianermissionars 228
Life of Brainerd

Die sünder in den händen eines zornigen Gottes 177
Sinners in the Hands of an Angry God

Glaubwüridge Nachricht 13
Faithful Narrative

Mittheilungen aus dem innern leben 363
Personal Narrative

Italian

Segni caratteristici di un'opera dello spirito 84
Distinguishing Marks

Korean

Chinnohan Hananim ui son e puttullin choeindul 126
Sinners in the Hands of an Angry God

Nollaun hoesim iyagi 45
Faithful Narrative

Spanish

Caracterististicas de un autentico avivamiento 86
Distinguishing Marks

Pecadores en manos de un Dios airado 127
Sinners in the Hands of an Angry God

Swedish

Indian-missionären David Brainerds lefwerne 233
Life of Brainerd

Welsh

Cyfarwyddiadau ac annogaethau I gredinwyr 160
an extract of *Religious Affections*

Dull y farn ddiweddaf 339
History of Redemption (a selection)

Hanes gwaith y prynedigaeth 338, 351
History of Redemption

Traethawd ar y dyben 375
End of Creation

Traethawd ar y serchiadau crefyddol 174
Religious Affections

Y dull y dylid ymofyn iechydwriaeth 438
The Manner in which the Salvation of the Soul Is to be Sought

Ymchwiliad gofalus a manwl 279
Freedom of the Will

Yr athrawlaeth fawr gristionogol 296
Original Sin

PRINTERS and PUBLISHERS

CANADA

Toronto
- Henderson and Co
- A. Sims

ENGLAND

Bath
- S. Hazard

Bristol
- Bristol Religious Tract Society
- I. E. Chillcott
- Felix Farley
- William Pine
- Thoemmes Press
- J. Young

Bungay
- J. R. and C. Childs
- John Childs and Son
- J. M. Morris

Cambridge
- James Clarke
- Merril

Carlisle
- George Kline
- J. F. Whitridge

Chippenham
- Anthony Rowe

Halifax
- Holden and Dowson

Huddersfield
- J. Brook

Kelso
- John Rutherfurd

Leeds
- Edward Baines
- Baines and Heaton
- B. Dewhirst
- Robinson, Son, and Holdsworth

Liverpool
- Edward Howell

London
- Adams
- W. Allan
- Baldwin and Craddock
- William Ball
- Ball, Arnold, and Co.
- G. Barclay
- Edward Baynes
- Billing and Sons
- James Black and Son
- Henry G. Bohn
- J. Buckland and T. Vernor
- Henry Butler
- Button
- Button and Son
- T. Cadell
- William Carling
- W. Clowes
- Henry Cock
- Conder
- E. and C. Dilly
- H. Fisher, Son, and P. Jackson
- S. Gosnell
- R. Groombridge
- T. Hamilton
- Hamilton, Adams
- Hamilton and Conder
- J. Hill
- Hughes and Baynes
- Hurst, Chance
- Jones and Co.
- W. Justins
- Charles H. Kelly
- J. Kershaw
- Knight and Bagster
- John Lawson
- J. Lewis
- T. Longman
- Longman, Hurst, Rees, Orme, and Brown
- Marshall, Morgan, and Scott
- Marshall, Baldwin, and Craddock
- John Mason
- S. Mason
- J. Matthews
- Andrew Melrose
- E. W. Morris
- J. Murgatroyd
- T. Nelson and Sons
- James Nichols
- W. Nicholson
- James Nisbet
- R. Noble
- Nunn
- Ogilvie and Speare
- Ogles, Duncan
- Ogles, Duncan, and Cochran
- W. Oliver
- John Oswald

Oxford University Press
Andrew Panton
G. Paramore
J. Paramore
C. Parker
T. Payne
Marshall Pickering
Religious Tract Society
J. Rider
Scatcherd and Whitaker
L. B. Seeley and Son
R. B. Seeley and W. Burnside
Seeley, Burnside, and Seeley
Seeley, Jackson, and Halliday
Simpkin and Marshall
A. Simpson
John Snow
George Story
W. Strahan
B. Sweeney
William Tegg
H. Trapp
T. Trye
A. J. Valpy
Vernor and Hood
John Vint
Unwin Brothers
Thomas Ward
Ward and Lock
James Webb
G. B. Whittaker
Whittaker, Treacher, and Arnot
F. Westley
F. Westley and A. H. Davis
G. Whitfield
C. Whittingham
R. Williams
Williams and Birtles
Williams and Son
Williams and Smith

Newport, Isle of Wight
R. Tilling

Northampton
Able
Thomas Dicey

Oxford
Prince

Penryn
W. Cock

Rotherham
Crookes

York
Wilson and Spence

FRANCE

Chalon-sur-Saône
Europresse

Lausanne
Marc Ducloux

Paris
H. Servier

Toulouse
Chauvin and Sons
Société des Livres Religieux

GERMANY

Magdeburg
Christ. Leberecht

Magdeburg and Leipzig
C. S. Wittwe and G. E. Scheidhaures

IRELAND

Belfast
Robert Johnston

Dublin
Chalmers and Curry
William Curry
B. Dugdale
T. Johnston
R. Napper
W. F. Wakeman
Westley and Tyrrell

ITALY

Rome
Sentieri Antichi

KOREA

Seoul
Kidokkyo Munso Son'gyohoe
Saengmyong ui Malssumsa

LEBANON

Beirut
American Mission Press

NETHERLANDS

Amsterdam
Martinus de Bruyn
Hendrik van Bos

Leeuwarden
R. J. Noordbeek

Utrecht
Abraham van Paddenburg
Gisbert Timon van Paddenburg
Jan Jacob van Poolsum
Willem van Yzerworst

NEW ZEALAND

Gisborne
- Westminster Standard

PEOPLE'S REPUBLIC OF CHINA

Beijing
- Zhongguo zhi gong chu ban she

Hong Kong
- Jinling shen xue yuan tuo shi bu

PERU

Lima
- Grafitec y Cia

REPUBLIC OF CHINA

Taipei
- Jonathan Choa

SCOTLAND

Aberdeen
- George and Robert King

Edinburgh
- Anderson and Bryce
- A. Balfour
- Balfour and Jack
- Ballantyne
- Banner of Truth
- John Boyd
- Peter Brown
- Peter Brown and Thomas Nelson
- George Caw
- James Clarke
- D. R. Collie and Sons
- William Darling
- J. Davidson
- A. Duning
- John Fairbairn
- John Gray
- John Gray and Gavin Alston
- M. Gray
- William Gray
- Guthrie and Tait
- G. Hamilton
- Hugh Inglis
- Alexander Jardine and Edmund Whitehead
- John Johnstone
- Johnstone and Hunter
- W. P. Kennedy
- Alexander Lawrie
- Thomas Lumisden and John Robertson
- T. Maccliesh
- MacLachlan and Stewart
- Morrison and Gibb
- Andrew Murray
- Murray and Cochrane
- Thomas Nelson
- J. Ogle
- Robert Ogle
- Ogle, Allardyce, and Thomson
- Ogle and Aikman
- Ogle and Murray
- William Oliphant
- William Oliphant and Sons
- Oliver and Boyd
- J. Oswald
- J. Paton
- H. and J. Pillans
- James Robertson
- James Souter
- J. Traill
- Thomas Turnbull
- John Walker
- William Whyte
- John Wylie
- Charles Ziegler

Exeter
- B. Thorne and E. Score

Glasgow
- Barrie
- J. Barrie
- Bell and Bain
- D. Bryce
- Chalmers and Collins
- William Collins
- James Duncan
- A. Duning
- W. Falconer
- Adam Ferguson
- Robert and Andrew Foulis
- Duncan Macvean
- David Niven
- R. Ogle
- Robert Urie

Leith
- W. Coke

SOUTH AFRICA

Sonlandpark
- Woordverspreiding

SPAIN

Léon
- Universidad de Léon

SWEDEN

Stockholm

P. P. Elde
Stockholms Missionsförening

SWITZERLAND

Langenthal
Pflug-Verlag
Zurich
Franz Hanke

UNITED STATES

Arizona

Paradise Valley
Teleios Ministry

Cherokee Nation

Park Hill
John Candy and John F. Wheeler
Mission Press

Connecticut

Hartford
John Babcock
Baldwin and Treadway
Henry Benton
Green and Watson
Hudson and Goodwin
Knight Sexton
New Haven
Baldwin and Treadway
Jonathan Edwards College Press
George Shakespeare
Whiting and Tiffany
Yale University Press
Westport
Greenwood Press

Delaware

Marshallton
National Foundation for Christian Education

Illinois

Chicago
Moody Bible Institute
Moody Press
Prospect Heights,
Waveland Press
Wheaton
Crossway

Indiana

Indianapolis
Bobbs-Merrill
St. John
Larry Harrison

Kentucky

Hickory
Faith Publishers
Lexington
Joseph Charless
Louisville
Baptist Book Concern
Pentecostal Publishing
Paducah
Baptist Tabernacle

Massachusetts

Amherst
Carter and Adams
Andover
W. F. Draper
Flagg and Gould
Boston
American Doctrinal Tract Society
Loring Andrews
Samuel T. Armstrong
Congregational Board of Publication
Crocker and Brewster
Draper and Folsom
T. Fleet
Gould, Kendall, & Lincoln
Green, Bushell, and Allen
D. Henchman
S. Kneeland and T. Green
S. Kneeland, T. Green, and D. Henchman
E. Lincoln
Lincoln and Edmands
James Loring
Manning and Loring
W. McAlpine
G. Rogers
Rogers and Fowle
Charlestown
Samuel Etheridge
Northampton
Simeon Butler
S. and E. Butler
J. Metcalf
Thomas M. Pomroy
Andrew Wright
Daniel Wright
Peabody
Hendrickson Publishers
Salem
G. Roulstone

Worcester
- Griffin and Morrill
- Moses W. Grout
- Charles Hamilton
- Isaiah Thomas
- Isaiah Thomas and Leonard Worcester
- Isaac Sturtevant

Michigan

Ann Arbor
- Servant Publications
- University of Michigan Press

Grand Rapids
- Associated Publishers
- Baker Book House
- William B. Eerdmans
- Inheritance Publishers
- Sovereign Grace Publishers
- Treasured Meditations
- Zondervan Publishing House

St. Clair Shores
- Scholarly Press

Minnesota

Minneapolis
- Bethany House
- World Wide

Missouri

St. Louis
- Faith Words

New Hampshire

Concord
- Jacob B. Moore

Exeter
- Henry Ranlet

New Jersey

Elizabethtown
- Shepard Kollock

Phillipsburg
- P&R Publishing

New York

Albany
- Whiting, Backus, and Whiting

Johnstown
- Asa Child

New York
- Allen
- American Book Co.
- American Tract Society
- Carlton and Phillips
- Robert Carter and Brothers
- C. and G. Carvill
- C. and G. and H. Carvill
- Christian Alliance
- Continuum
- S. Converse
- Cornelius Davis
- M. W. Dodd
- Dunning and Spalding
- D. Fanshaw
- G. Forman
- Burt Franklin
- Funk and Wagnalls
- Hugh Gaine
- Gould, Newman, and Saxton
- Hill and Wang
- John Holt
- Irvington Publishers
- Lane and Scott
- Leavitt and Allen
- Jonathan Leavitt and John F. Trow
- Library Publishers
- F. and R. Lockwood
- Joseph Longking
- New American Library
- New-York Religious Tract
- Garrat Noel
- James Oram
- James Parker
- Charles Scribner's Sons
- Sleight and Robinson
- J. Seymour
- T. and J. Swords
- Taylor and Gould
- Frederick Ungar
- Vanderpool and Cole
- Whiting and Hudson

Schenectady
- Riggs and Stevens

Troy
- D. Whiting

Utica
- Ariel Works
- B. B. Drake

Ohio

Cincinnati
- Swormstedt and Poe
- R. P. Thompson

Salem
- Schmul Publishing

Urichsville

Barbour Publishing

Oregon

Eugene
University of Oregon Press
Portland
Multinomah Press

Pennsylvania

Franklin Center
Franklin Library
Morgan
Soli Deo Gloria Publications
New Kensington
Whitaker House
Philadelphia
Aitken
John W. Allen
American Sunday School Union
Matthew Carey
James Crissy
John Dickins
Farrand
Benjamin Franklin
W. F. Geddes
G. Goodman
Parry Hall
B. B. Hopkins
William S. Martien
Presbyterian Board of Publication
S. C. Ustick
Swengel
Reiner Publications

Rhode Island

Providence
Miller and Hutchens

South Carolina

Greenwood
Attic Press

Tennessee

Murfreesboro
Sword of the Lord Publishers
Nashville
BREM
Thomas Nelson
E. Stevenson and F. A. Owen
A. A. Stitt

Texas

San Antonio
Candlestick Publishing

Vermont

Burlington
Samuel Mills

Virginia

Mountain Valley
Joseph Funk and Sons
James Sterret

Wisconsin

Waukesha
Metropolitan Church Association

WALES

Abertawy
E. Griffiths
Bala
Robert Saunderson
Caernarfon
H. Humphreys
William Potter
Llangollen
Hugh Jones

LIBRARIES

Alma College, Alma, Mich.
American Antiquarian Society, Worcester, Mass.
American Tract Society, Garland, Texas
Amherst College, Amherst, Mass.
Andover Newton Theological School, Newton, Mass.
Asbury Theological Seminary, Wilmore, Ky.
Azusa Pacific University, Azusa, Calif.
Beinecke Library, Yale University, New Haven, Conn.
Bethel College and Seminary, St. Paul, Minn.
Biblioteca Nazionale Centrale, Rome
Bibliotheque Nationale, Paris
Biola University, La Mirada, Calif.
Boston Athenaeum, Boston, Mass.
Boston College, Boston, Mass.
Boston Public Library, Boston, Mass.
Boston University, Boston, Mass.
British Library, London
Brown University, Providence, R.I.
Bryn Mawr College, Bryn Mawr, Pa.
Buffalo and Erie County Public Library, Buffalo, N.Y.
Calvin College, Grand Rapids, Mich.
Centenary College of Louisiana, Shreveport, La.
Chinese University of Hong Kong, Hong Kong
Cincinnati Bible College, Cincinnati, Ohio
Cleveland Public Library, Cleveland, Ohio
Colby College, Waterville, Me.
College of William and Mary, Williamsburg, Va.
Congregational Library, Boston, Mass.
Connecticut College, New London, Conn.
Cornell University, Ithaca, N.Y.
Cornerstone University, Grand rapids, Mich.
Dallas Theological Seminary, Dallas, Texas
Detroit Public Library, Detroit, Mich.
Drew University, Madison, N.J.
Duke University, Durham, N.C.
Earlham College, Richmond, Ind.
Emmanuel School of Religion, Johnson City, Tenn.
Forbes Library, Northampton, Mass.
Free Library of Philadelphia, Philadelphia, Pa.
Georgia State University, Atlanta, Ga.
Gordon College, Wenham, Mass.
Gordon-Conwell TheologicalSeminary, Hamilton,Mass.
Grace College and Seminary, Winona Lake, Ind.
Graduate Theological Union, Berkeley, Calif.
Grand Rapids Baptist College, Grand Rapids, Mich.
Hamilton College, Clinton, N.Y.
Harvard Divinity School, Cambridge, Mass.
Harvard University, Cambridge, Mass.
Historical Society of Pennsylvania, Philadelphia, Pa.
Hope International University, Fullerton, Calif.
Houghton Library, HarvardUniversity,Cambridge, Mass.
Huntington Library, San Marino, Calif.
John Carter Brown Library, Providence, R.I.
Lancaster Theological Seminary, Lancaster, Pa.
Library of Congress, Washington, D.C.
Library Company of Philadelphia, Philadelphia, Pa.
Louisville Presbyterian Seminary, Louisville, Ky.
Lutheran Theological Seminary, Philadelphia, Pa.
Manchester College, North Manchester, Ind.
Mary Washington College, Fredericksburg, Va.
Massachusetts Historical Society, Boston, Mass.
McMaster University, Hamilton, Ontario
Mercer University, Macon, Ga.
Midwestern Baptist Seminary, Kansas City, Mo.
Missouri Baptist College, St. Louis, Mo.
Mount Holyoke College, Mount Holyoke, Mass.
National Library of Scotland, Edinburgh
National Library of Wales, Aberyswyth
Nazarene Theological Seminary, Kansas City, Mo.
New York Public Library, New York, N.Y.
Newberry Library, Chicago, Ill.
North American Baptist Seminary, Sioux Falls, S.D.
Northeastern University, Boston, Mass.
Northwestern University, Evanston, Ill.
Oberlin College, Oberlin, Ohio
Ohio Wesleyan University, Delaware, Ohio
Pensacola Christian College, Pensacola, Fla.
Piedmont College, Demorest, Ga.
Pittsburgh Theological Seminary, Pittsburgh, Pa.
Pitts Theological Library, Atlanta, Ga.
Point Loma Nazarene University, San Diego, Calif.
Presbyterian Historical Society, Philadelphia, Pa.
Princeton University, Princeton, N.J.
Princeton Theological Seminary, Princeton, N.J.
Redwood Library and Athenaeum, Newport, R.I.
Reformed Presbyterian Seminary, Pittsburgh, Pa.
Reformed Theological Seminary, Jackson, Miss.
Regent's Park College, Oxford
Rice University, Houston, Texas
Saint Michael's College, Toronto, Ontario
Schweizerische Landesbibliothek, Bern
Schwenckfelder Library, Pennsburg, Pa.
Smith College, Northampton, Mass.
Southeastern Baptist Seminary, Wake Forest, N.C.
Southern Baptist Theological Seminary, Louisville, Ky.
Southern Methodist University, Dallas, Texas

Southwestern Baptist Seminary, Fort Worth, Texas
Spirit Life Bible College, Irvine, Calif.
State Library of South Africa, Pretoria
Sveriges Nationalbibliotek, Stockholm
Taylor University, Upland, Ind.
Tennessee State Library, Nashville, Tenn.
The Master's College, Santa Clarita, Calif.
Towson University, Towson, Md.
Union Theological Seminary, New York, N.Y.
University of Alabama, Tuscaloosa, Ala.
University of Arkansas, Fayetteville, Ark.
University of California, Santa Barbara, Calif.
University of Chicago, Chicago, Ill.
University of Iowa, Iowa City, Iowa
University of Léon, Léon
University of Maine, Orono, Me.
University of Michigan, Ann Arbor, Mich.
University of Mississippi, Oxford, Miss.
University of New Hampshire, Durham, N.H.
University of North Carolina, Chapel Hill, N.C.
University of Notre Dame, Notre Dame, Ind.
University of Pennsylvania, Philadelphia, Pa.
University of Richmond, Richmond, Va.
Utica Public Library, Utica, N.Y.
Victoria University, Toronto, Ontario
Wake Forest University, Winston-Salem, N.C.
Wesley Theological Seminary, Washington, D.C.
Wesleyan University, Middletown, Conn.
Wheaton College, Wheaton, Ill.
Winterthur Library, Winterthur, Del.
Yale Divinity School, New Haven, Conn.
Yale University, New Haven, Conn.
Zentralbibliothek Zürich, Zürich

ERRATA

A gap in enumeration follows nos. 144, 192B, and 231, but there is no loss in data.